Advances in Spatial Science

The Regional Science Series

More information about this series at http://www.springer.com/series/3302

Roberto Patuelli • Giuseppe Arbia
Editors

Spatial Econometric Interaction Modelling

Springer

Editors
Roberto Patuelli
Department of Economics
Rimini Campus
University of Bologna
Rimini, Italy

Giuseppe Arbia
Università Cattolica del Sacro Cuore
Rome, Italy

ISSN 1430-9602 ISSN 2197-9375 (electronic)
Advances in Spatial Science
ISBN 978-3-319-30194-5 ISBN 978-3-319-30196-9 (eBook)
DOI 10.1007/978-3-319-30196-9

Library of Congress Control Number: 2016947082

Printed on acid-free paper

This Springer imprint is published by Springer Nature
The registered company is Springer International Publishing AG Switzerland

Preface

Is a new book on spatial interaction modelling needed in 2016? Do we need to update our theoretical and methodological frameworks, about 20 and 30 years away from landmark books like *Gravity Models of Spatial Interaction Behavior* (Sen and Smith 1995) and *Gravity and Spatial Interaction Models* (Haynes and Fotheringham 1994)? Our answer to this question is 'yes'!

This book aims to provide a number of convincing reasons—and tools—for extending the way scientists and practitioners in regional and international economics, geography, planning and regional science have been implementing, estimating and interpreting spatial interaction models. It does so by collecting a number of invited contributions by renowned scholars in the field, who propose innovative interpretative and estimation approaches mostly relying on recent developments in spatial statistics and econometrics.

The book originates from an International Exploratory Workshop on *Advances in the Statistical Modelling of Spatial Interaction Data* held at the University of Lugano (Switzerland) in September 2011. The papers presented at the workshop have been published in a special issue of the *Journal of Geographical Systems* (15:3, 2013). This book collects such articles, as well as additional invited contributions, in order to provide a broader view on spatial econometric approaches to spatial interaction modelling.

Thanks are due to many people who made this book happen. We would first like to express our gratitude to Rico Maggi for supporting our initial idea, to the Swiss National Science Foundation (SNSF) for funding the International Exploratory Workshop and to the University of Lugano for kindly hosting it. We would also like to thank the Editors of the *Journal of Geographical Systems* for helping us organize the preceding special issue, as well as Manfred Fischer and the Editorial Board of the Advances in Spatial Science series and Springer for supporting this book project. Finally, we are grateful to all contributing authors and to the referees of both the special issue and the book.

Last but not least, we would like to thank you, the readers. The success of this project is in your hands. We sincerely hope you will enjoy this collection.

Rimini, Italy
Rome, Italy
January 2016

Roberto Patuelli
Giuseppe Arbia

Contents

Contributors

Giuseppe Arbia Department of Statistical Sciences, Università Cattolica del Sacro Cuore, Roma, Italy

François Bavaud Department of Language and Information Sciences, Institute of Geography and Sustainability, University of Lausanne, Lausanne, Switzerland

Michael Beenstock Faculty of Social Sciences, The Hebrew University of Jerusalem, Jerusalem, Israel

Guido Candela Department of Economics, University of Bologna, Bologna, Italy

Yongwan Chun School of Economic, Political and Policy Sciences, University of Texas at Dallas, Richardson, TX, USA

Tamara de la Mata Departamento de Análisis Económico: Teoría e Historia Económic, Universidad Autónoma de Madrid, Madrid, Spain

CEPREDE, Madrid, Spain

Minfeng Deng Department of Psychological Sciences and Statistics, Faculty of Health, Arts and Design, Swinburne University of Technology, Melbourne, VIC, Australia

Jorge Díaz-Lanchas Departamento de Análisis Económico: Teoría Económica e Historia Económica, Facultad de Ciencias Económicas y Empresariales, Universidad Autónoma de Madrid, Madrid, Spain

CEPREDE, Madrid, Spain

Daniel Felsenstein Department of Geography, Faculty of Social Sciences, The Hebrew University of Jerusalem, Jerusalem, Israel

Manfred M. Fischer Institute for Economic Geography and GIScience, Vienna University of Economics and Business, Vienna, Austria

Nuria Gallego Departamento de Análisis Económico: Teoría Económica e Historia Económica, Facultad de Ciencias Económicas y Empresariales, Universidad Autónoma de Madrid, Madrid, Spain

CEPREDE, Madrid, Spain

Daniel A. Griffith School of Economic, Political and Policy Sciences, University of Texas at Dallas, Richardson, TX, USA

Monghyeon Lee School of Economic, Political and Policy Sciences, University of Texas at Dallas, Richardson, TX, USA

James P. LeSage Department of Finance and Economics, McCoy College of Business Administration, Texas State University – San Marcos, San Marcos, TX, USA

Gert-Jan M. Linders Ministry of Social Affairs and Employment, The Hague, The Netherlands

Carlos Llano Departamento de Análisis Económico: Teoría Económica e Historia Económica, Facultad de Ciencias Económicas y Empresariales, Universidad Autónoma de Madrid, Madrid, Spain

CEPREDE, Madrid, Spain

Camilla Mastromarco Department of Economics and Quantitative Methods, Università del Salento, Lecce, Italy

Rodolfo Metulini IMT Institute for Advanced Studies Lucca, Lucca, Italy

Timo Mitze Department of Border Region Studies, University of Southern Denmark, Odense, Denmark

Rheinisch-Westfälisches Institut für Wirtschaftsforschung, Essen, Germany

The Rimini Centre for Economic Analysis, Rimini, Italy

Maurizio Mussoni Department of Economics, University of Bologna, Bologna, Italy

The Rimini Centre for Economic Analysis (RCEA), Rimini, Italy

Roberto Patuelli Department of Economics, University of Bologna, Bologna, Italy

The Rimini Centre for Economic Analysis (RCEA), Rimini, Italy

Francesca Petrarca Department of Methods and Models for Economics, Territory and Finance, Sapienza University of Rome, Rome, Italy

Esra Satici Productivity Analysis, Transportation Costs and Productivity, Turkish Highways, Ankara, Turkey

Laura Serlenga Department of Economics and Mathematical Methods, University of Bari Aldo Moro, Bari, Italy

Yongcheol Shin Department of Economics and Related Studies, University of York, York, UK

Kazuki Tamesue College of Policy and Planning Sciences, University of Tsukuba, Tsukuba, Japan

Morito Tsutsumi Faculty of Engineering, Information and Systems, University of Tsukuba, Tsukuba, Japan

Chapter 1
Spatial Econometric Interaction Modelling: Where Spatial Econometrics and Spatial Interaction Modelling Meet

Roberto Patuelli and Giuseppe Arbia

Keywords Gravity • Spatial econometrics • Spatial interaction

JEL Classifications: C18, C51, R11

1.1 The Spatial Interaction Model: An Established Regional Economics Workhorse

The present book is concerned with spatial interaction modelling. In particular, it aims to illustrate, through a collection of methodological and empirical studies, how estimation approaches in this field recently developed, by including the tools typical of spatial statistics and spatial econometrics (Anselin 1988; Cressie 1993; Arbia 2006, 2014), into what LeSage and Pace (2009) deemed as '*spatial econometric interaction models*'.

It is no surprise to scientists and practitioners in regional science, planning, demography or economics that spatial interaction models (or *gravity models*, following the traditional Newtonian denomination, still popular in fields like international trade) are, after a long time, some of the most widely used analytical tools in studying interactions between social and economic agents observed in space. Spatial interaction indeed underlies most processes involving individual choices in regional economics, and can apply to all economic agents (firms, workers or households, public entities, etc.).

R. Patuelli (✉)
Department of Economics, University of Bologna, Bologna, Italy

The Rimini Centre for Economic Analysis (RCEA), Rimini, Italy
e-mail: roberto.patuelli@unibo.it

G. Arbia
Department of Statistics, Università Cattolica del Sacro Cuore, Rome, Italy
e-mail: giuseppe.arbia@rm.unicatt.it

R. Patuelli, G. Arbia (eds.), *Spatial Econometric Interaction Modelling*, Advances in Spatial Science, DOI 10.1007/978-3-319-30196-9_1

Although spatial interaction models originated at the end of the nineteenth century following the Newtonian paradigm relating two masses and the distance between them (for a more detailed review, see Sen and Smith 1995), they now have solid theoretical economic foundations grounded on probabilistic theory, discrete choice modelling and entropy maximization. The works of, among others, Stewart (1941), Isard (1960) and Wilson (1970) during the twentieth century provided such foundations, allowed to see spatial interaction models not just as mechanical tools for empirical analysis, but also as a framework for theoretical and structural analyses (see, e.g., Baltagi and Egger 2016; Egger and Tarlea 2015).

A spatial interaction model describes the movement of people, items or information (the list of possible applications is long) between generic spatial units. We can loosely write it as a multiplicative model of the type:

$$T_{ij} = kO_i^{\alpha} D_j^{\beta} f\left(d_{ij}\right), \tag{1.1}$$

where T_{ij} is the flow (physical or not) moving from unit i to unit j, k is a proportionality constant, O_i and D_j are sets of potentially different variables (e.g., population, income, jobs) measured at the origin and the destination, respectively, and d_{ij} is the distance (possibly measured according to different metrics) between units i and j. The latter is solely an example of different types of deterrence variables accounting for factors which impede or favour pairwise interaction. Different functional forms—most frequently power or exponential—have been tested over the years to model the effect of distance on spatial interaction. The parameters α, β and those involved by the deterrence functions need to be properly estimated.

Such a simple specification is described as an *unconstrained model*, because it does not fix the total number of outgoing or incoming flows (the marginal sums of the origin–destination matrix). Singly- or doubly-constrained model specifications impose such limitations by including sets of balancing factors, which are nonlinear constraints requiring iterative calibration (Wilson 1970). Constrained approaches, which are often seen as the correct way of estimating the model, are, however, only seldom used in applied work, mostly because of the computational complexity involved.

Although spatial interaction models have been used for decades by researchers and practitioners in many fields, several authors have shown a renewed interest in them over the last 10–15 years, both with regard to their theoretical foundations and to the estimation approaches, the latter being greatly facilitated by the wider computing power availability. The contributions by Anderson and van Wincoop (2003, 2004) pushed the envelope in trade-related research by proposing a theory-consistent interpretation of the balancing factors, relabelled as *multilateral resistance terms*. Santos Silva and Tenreyro (2006) provided a stepping stone in the discussion on the estimation of spatial interaction (and in general multiplicative) models. They suggested that, because of Jensen's inequality and of overdispersion, these models should not be estimated in their loglinear transformation, but rather using the count data (such as the Poisson) regressions framework. The pseudo-maximum likelihood estimator proposed by the authors is now one of the most commonly used estimation approaches. Some recent studies focus on issues in complementing the above groundbreaking studies. Burger et al. (2009) reviewed alternative estimation approaches focusing on the cases of excess zeros. Krisztin and Fischer (2015) suggested spatial filtering variants of the Poisson gravity model (e.g., with zero-inflation) along with pseudo-ML estimation. Baltagi and Egger (2016) proposed a quantile regression approach; Egger (2005), Baier and Bergstrand (2009), and Egger and Staub (2016) proposed estimators for the cross-sectional model, while Egger and Pfaffermayr (2003) discussed panel estimation issues. Many more studies of recent publication could be cited in what appears to be—once more—a very active and developing field.

1.2 Spatial Interaction and Flow Dependence

One of the dimensions along which the literature on spatial interaction modelling recently developed is the explicit consideration of flow data correlation due to the spatial configuration of the units involved. Explicitly incorporating spatial structure (and its consequences) in spatial interaction is not a novel research question. It had actually emerged among regional scientists much earlier. One of the first examples in the literature is the lively debate appeared in the 1970s, generated by a paper by Leslie Curry (1972), and then involving a series of quick-reply papers, by Cliff et al. (1974, 1976), Curry et al. (1975), Sheppard et al. (1976), and Griffith and Jones (1980). This discussion layed the ground for what was actively picked up only 30 years later.

In particular, this initial debate was centred on the misspecification of spatial interaction models when it comes to the interpretation of the estimated distance deterrence parameter. As Curry et al. (1975, p. 294) pointed out, problems of interpretation of the distance parameter occur when in the model specified as a ratio the numerator (the origin- and destination-specific variables) and the denominator (the distance, when a power function is considered) are not independent. The authors went as far as to state that 'it will not be possible to determine how much of the often observed variations in the distance exponent is due to aggregate spatial pattern as opposed to that explainable by differences in spatial interaction'. The authors refer in particular to the case in which origin or destination characteristics (examples being population or income) can be seen as functions of distance (i.e., they are spatially autocorrelated). In other words, the spatial structure of the units matters, so much that Sheppard et al. (1976, p. 337) state that 'in the spatial context misspecification will almost always occur'. This type of issue will later be formalized more generally, giving birth to spatial econometrics. In a more recent contribution, Tiefelsdorf (2003) picked up the topic of spatial autocorrelation and spatial interaction, providing evidence in favour of the above statements. Similarly, Fotheringham and Webber (1980) used a simultaneous equations model to show how spatial structure and spatial interaction are 'inextricably and mutually linked' (Roy and Thill 2003, p. 353). Furthermore, Getis (1991) demonstrated mathematically how spatial autocorrelation measures are confounded in spatial interaction models, while Andersson and Gråsjö (2009) suggested how accessibility (closely tied to spatial interaction) is a prime determinant of spatial autocorrelation in areal data as well.

These contributions prompted new interest in the issue of spatial autocorrelation and spatial autocorrelation (see, e.g., Griffith 2007, 2011). Although still not a wide field of research, the general question of how to measure and treat spatial dependence in flow (dyadic) data (the so-called network autocorrelation) is now discussed in several papers. Black (1992) was an early contributor in this field, relying on graph theory to define network autocorrelation providing empirical evidence of it in real cases. Moran's I statistic was used for this purpose. More studies followed, for instance in Black and Thomas (1998), which focuses on highway accidents. More recently, Peeters and Thomas (2009) provided a review on network autocorrelation. In the context of political science, Neumayer and Plümper (2010) discuss the problem of quantifying the correlation between flow (dyadic) data and how public policies set contagion forces to work.

When it comes to indicators of network autocorrelation (or, so to say, spatial autocorrelation on networks), an extension of the Getis-Ord G_i statistic for measuring local spatial autocorrelation was proposed by Berglund and Karlström (1999), and Fischer et al. (2010). Further attempts of measuring spatial/network autocorrelation in flow data could be based on some recently developed spatial autocorrelation indices implemented for generalized linear models and primarily for count data (see, e.g., Jacqmin-Gadda et al. 1997; Lin and Zhang 2007; Griffith 2010).

1.3 Towards a New Class of Spatial Interaction Models

The renewed interest in spatial autocorrelation and spatial interaction modelling documented above is manifest in the recent econometric contributions that collectively form a new class of augmented spatial interaction models that are now often referred to as *spatial econometric interaction models*. Such models are based on the spatial statistics and econometrics techniques typically employed with areal (and sometimes point) data, and aim to 'cure' spatial/network autocorrelation and reinterpret the model parameters accordingly. A few initial attempts (see Bolduc et al. 1992; Porojan 2001; Neumayer and Plümper 2010) were made to include spatial relations in flow modelling. Bolduc et al. (1992), dealing with travel flow data, proposed spatially structured error terms, which emerged as the sum of an origin-level and a destination-level components, in addition to a non-spatial error. Porojan (2001) used both spatial lag and spatial error models (and generalized spatial models, with both terms), although without fully outlining how the row-standardized spatial weights matrix used could be adapted for the task. Neumayer and Plümper (2010) presented a similar approach, discussing contagion phenomena between countries and their influence on the signing of bilateral investment treaties.

They estimated spatial lag models where the weights matrix was alternatively constrained to model only origin- or destination-level dependence (contagion), or both.

Further and critical contributions to the above debate, providing a more in-depth view on the estimation of spatial econometric interaction models, were published between the years 2008 and 2012 (most notably by Fischer and Griffith 2008; LeSage and Pace 2008; Behrens et al. 2012) and gained immediate recognition in the scientific community. Methodologically, we can distinguish between three strains of the literature, proposing:

- spatial interaction model estimated in their log-linearized form;
- spatial interaction models estimated using Poisson-type regressions;
- spatial interaction models augmented with spatial filters (estimated as Poisson as well).

The most common spatial econometric-aware applications of the spatial interaction model belong to the first of the above categories. Estimating multiplicative models in their loglinear form has long been a widely employed approach (e.g., in economics), although the publication of Santos Silva and Tenreyro (2006), advocating Poisson-type regressions and the pseudo-Poisson maximum likelihood estimator (PPML), has greatly reduced the diffusion of this approach, in particular in the trade literature.

Fischer and Griffith (2008) proposed two competing models. The first was based on a spatial error autoregressive model specification estimated within a maximum likelihood (ML) framework. Along the same line, LeSage and Pace (2008) presented a further ML-based spatial econometric model, encompassing several alternative specifications, and providing additional economic motivations for its use. Their model included simultaneously potential origin, destination and network dependence elements, resulting in an equation of the type:

$$y = \rho_o W_o y + \rho_d W_d y + \rho_w W_w y + Z\delta + \varepsilon, \tag{1.2}$$

where y is an $n^2 \times 1$ vector containing all T_{ij} flows, ε are IID errors, and W_o, W_d and W_w are (row-normalized) spatial weights matrices obtained by means of Kronecker products of the regular $n \times n$ spatial weights matrix W with an identity matrix I_n or itself (in the case of W_w) (LeSage and Fischer 2010). An alternative to this specification, encompassing the above-mentioned one in Fischer and Griffith (2008), is a model employing the same three spatial dependence terms of Eq. (1.2) in a spatial error framework of the type:

$$\begin{aligned} y &= Z\delta + u; \\ u &= \rho_o W_o u + \rho_d W_d u + \rho_w W_w u + \varepsilon. \end{aligned} \tag{1.3}$$

LeSage and Fischer (2010) also suggest a simpler approach, consisting in employing one spatial weights matrix only in u, as the row-normalized sum of W_o and W_d. Finally, Behrens et al. (2012) presented a formal theoretical justification for the use of spatial econometrics in trade modelling, within a framework controlling for multilateral resistance terms and heterogeneity. They eventually estimated an empirical spatial error model similarly to the one specified by Fischer and Griffith (2008). Recent papers provide further extensions of these approaches (Egger and Pfaffermayr 2016; Koch and LeSage 2015), and more heterodox approaches to estimation, for example based on entropy maximization like in Bernardini Papalia (2010). Finally, a development that is worth mentioning is the recent application of the impact measures popularized by LeSage and Pace (2009) to spatial interaction models, provided by Thomas-Agnan and LeSage (2014), and LeSage and Thomas-Agnan (2015). The authors demonstrate that, similarly to the standard case of areal data, the model's estimated parameters cannot be directly interpreted as marginal effects or elasticities, and that the bidimensionality of spatial interaction models, where both origin- and destination-level effects are often estimated for a variable, introduces further complications.

Although the path of research described above is the one that is most often followed in the current literature (perhaps due to the simplicity of linear approaches), two more heterodox strategies deserve consideration: the first based on Poisson-type regression and the second on spatial filtering. Poisson-type regression models incorporating spatial dependence or heterogeneity followed the wake traced by Flowerdew and Aitkin (1982). However, while in statistics and in some applied fields (like ecology or epidemiology) researchers have proposed various spatial extensions of count models (see, e.g., Congdon 2010), mostly based on point data and spatially correlated random effects, the explicit (parametric) inclusion of spatial dependence into the models still represented a major obstacle until recent years. In fact, it wasn't until very recently that some contributions have emerged, tackling this problem. For example, outside the spatial interaction modelling paradigm, Lambert et al. (2010) proposed a two-step spatial lag model for count data providing adaptations of the direct and indirect effects (LeSage and Pace 2009), while LeSage et al. (2007) presented a first Poisson-based model grounded on Bayesian estimation and Markov chain Monte Carlo (MCMC) methods. In this last contribution, origin- and destination-level random effects with an autoregressive structure were estimated in a hierarchical Poisson specification. A similar approach was recently followed by Sellner et al. (2013), who developed a Poisson SAR estimator, based on two-stage nonlinear least squares. In their model, the flow variable y is assumed to be determined by a spatially random component y^*, and by a residual spatial component $\tilde{y}$, where only the latter is assumed to be Poisson distributed. Consistently with most of the literature cited above, the spatial component y^* is expressed as a linear combination of the origin- and destination-level spatial lags expressed by the products $W_o y$ and $W_d y$, respectively. Therefore, the dependent variable is defined as:

$$y = \tilde{y} + y^* = \rho_o W_o y + \rho_d W_d y + y^*. \tag{1.4}$$

A second alternative approach to modelling spatial and network autocorrelation in flow data employs eigenvector spatial filtering within Poisson-type regression models. This technique was first introduced by Griffith (2000, 2003, 2006) for analysing areal and grid/raster data and it is based on the mathematical relationship between Moran's I (Moran 1948) and spatial weights matrices. In synthesis, having defined M as the projection matrix $I_n - \mathbf{11}'/n$ and $\mathbf{1}$ as an $n \times 1$ vector of ones, the eigenvectors of matrix MWM represent all possible independent and orthogonal spatial patterns implied by W. Using (parsimoniously) such eigenvectors as additional covariates in regression models allows to filter spatial autocorrelation similarly to SAR models (Griffith 2000). Fischer and Griffith (2008) presented an application of spatial filtering to the spatial interaction model, where separate origin- and destination-level spatial filters (again, similarly to what has been mentioned above for fixed effects or spatially correlated random effects) were obtained by means of $n^2 \times 1$ eigenvectors piled by means of Kronecker products. Chun (2008) extended this approach to network autocorrelation, by using the eigenvectors of MW_wM, while Griffith and Chun (2015) recently showed that both origin/destination and network dependence are relevant and stressed the need to incorporate both of them in spatial interaction models. Finally, Krisztin and Fischer (2015) applied this approach within the framework of a PPML estimation (as in Santos Silva and Tenreyro 2006), directly addressing the trade modelling literature.

As it is evident from the work reported in this section, the last 10 years have shown a resurgence of the gravity/spatial interaction modelling literature, and the emergence of innovative estimation approaches making use of spatial statistics and econometrics. Due to the extreme relevance of these new contributions, this book aims at providing the state-of-the-art of such developments, and collects methodological and empirical contributions authored by some of the main contributors to the field.

1.4 The Structure of the Book

The book is divided into three parts. Part I (*General Methodological Issues*) contains general contributions on spatial econometric interaction modelling, pertaining to coefficient interpretation, constrained specifications, scale effects and spatial weights matrix specification. Part II (*Specific Methodological Issues*) concerns in particular the phase of estimation and focuses on innovative estimators and approaches, such as the treatment of intraregional flows, Bayesian PPML or VAR estimation, and Pesaran-type cross-sectional dependence. Finally, Part III (*Applications*) contains a number of empirical studies ranging from interregional tourism competition, domestic trade, to space-time migration modelling and residential relocation. In what follows, we will describe in detail the content of the various papers to orientate the reader.

Part I is composed of four chapters. In Chap. 2, James LeSage and Manfred Fischer provide an extension of the recent article by LeSage and Thomas-Agnan (2015) discussing impact measures for the case of spatial interaction modelling. The authors focus on the distinction between endogenous and exogenous spatial interactions, drawing an analytical framework consistent with the one differentiating conventional spatial models and models including only spatial lags of the independent variables (ultimately similar to spatial error models, as suggested in LeSage and Pace 2009). As a consequence, this chapter provides the reader with further guidance in correctly interpreting the parameters of spatial interaction models. In Chap. 3, Daniel Griffith and Manfred Fischer compare the (main) different approaches to estimating spatial interaction models, that is specifications including balancing factors, fixed effects (by means of sets of indicator variables), or random effects. An empirical example of the equivalence between them is provided, also employing spatially structured random effects obtained through eigenvector spatial filtering. Chapter 4 is written by François Bavaud, who develops a new approach to spatial autocorrelation testing for weighted networks by means of Moran's *I*. He provides an example based on Swiss migratory flows, showcasing a modes autocorrelation test based on the transformation of spatial weights matrices into exchange matrices. In Chap. 5, Giuseppe Arbia and Francesca Petrarca analyse the implications of the modifiable areal unit problem (MAUP, see Arbia 1989) for spatial interaction models. They focus on the 'scale' dimension of the MAUP, which pertains to the different (hierarchical) levels of geographical aggregation of flows. They illustrate their theoretical analysis with a set of simulations, and show in particular how negative spatial autocorrelation in the origin and destination variables affects mean interaction flows.

Part II of the book deals in particular with estimation issues and consists of seven chapters. In Chap. 6, Kazuki Tamesue and Morito Tsutsumi focus on how to define internal distances and to estimate models in the case of missing intraregional flows. They propose approaches based on an expectation-maximization (EM) algorithm and Heckman's two-step estimator, evaluating the sample-selection bias caused by missing intraregional flows data. Chapter 7, by James LeSage and Esra Satici describes a spatial econometric extension of the abovementioned PPML estimator by Santos Silva and Tenreyro (2006), though based on a Bayesian approach. The authors deal with intraregional flows as well, by including a separate set of parameters to be estimated for the diagonal of the origin–destination matrix. In Chap. 8, Roberto Patuelli, Gert-Jan Linders, Rodolfo Metulini and Daniel Griffith focus on the gravity model of trade, and discuss the links between the multilateral trade resistance terms popularized by Anderson and van Wincoop (2003), and the spatial filtering approach already suggested in Fischer and Griffith (2008). Moreover, they provide an empirical comparison with the approaches of Feenstra (2004) and Baier and Bergstrand (2009) within a negative binomial estimation framework. Chapter 9 is by James LeSage and Carlos Llano. They propose a spatial interaction model augmented with origin and destination spatially structured latent factors. The model is estimated in a Bayesian hierarchical framework, with spatially autoregressive random effects which incorporate the latent effects. Also Chap. 10, by Minfeng Deng, makes use of Bayesian estimation. In particular, the author develops a spatial vector autoregressive (VAR) model to predict traffic flows within a simulated system. He uses temporally and spatially lagged traffic flows as predictors, and sets up a Bayesian variable selection procedure to deal with the large VAR at hand. In Chap. 11, Michael Beenstock and Daniel Felsenstein build on the definition of spatial dependence in flow (trade) data. They first consider the case of spatial interaction models where the spatial units (regions, countries) are not simultaneously repulsing and attracting, but exert their effect only in one direction, so that bilateral relationships are one-way. Then, they propose a Lagrange multiplier spatial autocorrelation test, and a further test for spatial autoregressive conditional heteroscedasticity (SpARCH), that is, the case of spatially autocorrelated variances. Finally, in Chap. 12, Camilla Mastromarco, Laura Serlenga and Yongsheol Shin provide an empirical comparison between a trade model estimated following Behrens et al. (2012) and an alternative specification using a common factor-based approach. They stress that strong cross-sectional dependence is better accounted for by factor models. In addition, they augment their factor model by instrumental variables, in order to evaluate the effect of possibly endogenous trade determinants, such as trade barriers. They provide an application looking at the trade effects of the Euro area.

Part III of the book contains a number of applied contributions, showcasing the potential of the new class of spatial interaction models discussed in Sect. 1.3. In Chap. 13, Roberto Patuelli, Maurizio Mussoni and Guido Candela set up a model for analysing domestic tourism flows in Italy and the effect of the inclusion of landmark sites in UNESCO's World Heritage List. They model intervening opportunities in the tourists' travelling choices, and demonstrate the emergence of spatial competition between regions on the basis of their cultural amenities using spatially lagged evaluations of origin/destination characteristics. Chapter 14 is written by Jorge Díaz-Lanchas, Nuria Gallego, Carlos Llano and Tamara de la Mata. The authors focus on domestic trade in Spain, and in particular on the phenomenon of 'ambushed flows', that is, recorded flows of goods that emerge solely as a result of the multimodal operations in logistic/transport hubs. They develop a spatial interaction model for studying this issue that accounts for the related artificially generated cross-sectional dependence. In Chap. 15, Carlo Llano and Tamara de la Mata once again study domestic trade flows in Spain, but from a different perspective focusing on services. They investigate the role of social networks in influencing such flows and they proxy social linkages by means of a set of differentiated measures (such as past migration, second homes, past tourism patterns), so as to provide a sensitivity analysis. In their models, they account for social linkages by modelling spatial and network autocorrelation, and find that the resulting deterrence effect of distance is diminished, while the relevance of borders is increased. In Chap. 16, Timo Mitze estimates a spatial interaction model for domestic migration by means of a dynamic panel spatial Durbin specification. His results are consistent with a traditional neoclassical migration model, while pointing at the need to separate temporal and spatial dynamics. In addition, he computes cumulative multipliers up to 10 years ahead, in order to evaluate labour market response over a longer run. Finally, in Chap. 17, Monghyeon Lee and Yongwan Chun study residential relocation in the Seoul metropolitan area. They estimate a spatial filtering-augmented spatial interaction model, and show that accounting for network autocorrelation, even in a limited spatial domain like a metropolitan area, is needed and leads to a reduction in the estimated overdispersion.

References

Anderson JE, van Wincoop E (2003) Gravity with gravitas: a solution to the border puzzle. Am Econ Rev 93(1):170–192
Anderson JE, van Wincoop E (2004) Trade costs. J Econ Lit 42(3):691–751
Andersson M, Gråsjö U (2009) Spatial dependence and the representation of space in empirical models. Ann Reg Sci 43(1):159–180
Anselin L (1988) Spatial econometrics: methods and models. Kluwer Academic Publishers, Dordrecht/Boston
Arbia G (1989) Spatial data configuration in statistical analysis of regional economic and related problems. Kluwer, Dordrecht/Boston
Arbia G (2006) Spatial econometrics: statistical foundations and applications to regional convergence. Springer, Heidelberg
Arbia G (2014) A primer for spatial econometrics: with applications in R. Palgrave Macmillan, New York
Baier SL, Bergstrand JH (2009) Bonus vetus OLS: a simple method for approximating international trade-cost effects using the gravity equation. J Int Econ 77(1):77–85
Baltagi BH, Egger P (2016) Estimation of structural gravity quantile regression models. Empir Econ 50(1):5–15
Behrens K, Ertur C, Koch W (2012) 'Dual' gravity: using spatial econometrics to control for multilateral resistance. J Appl Econ 25(2):773–794
Berglund S, Karlström A (1999) Identifying local spatial association in flow data. J Geogr Syst 1(3):219–236
Bernardini Papalia R (2010) Generalized maximum entropy estimation of spatial panel interaction models. WSEAS Trans Bus Econ 4(7):322–331
Black WR (1992) Network autocorrelation in transport network and flow systems. Geogr Anal 24(3):207–222
Black WR, Thomas I (1998) Accidents on Belgium's motorways: a network autocorrelation analysis. J Transp Geogr 6(1):23–31
Bolduc D, Laferrière R, Santarossa G (1992) Spatial autoregressive error components in travel flow models. Reg Sci Urban Econ 22(3):371–385
Burger M, van Oort F, Linders G-J (2009) On the specification of the gravity model of trade: zeros, excess zeros and zero-inflated estimation. Spat Econ Anal 4(2):167–190
Chun Y (2008) Modeling network autocorrelation within migration flows by eigenvector spatial filtering. J Geogr Syst 10(4):317–344
Cliff AD, Martin RL, Ord JK (1974) Evaluating the friction of distance parameter in gravity models. Reg Stud 8(3–4):281–286
Cliff AD, Martin RL, Ord JK (1976) A reply to the final comment. Reg Stud 10(3):341–342
Congdon P (2010) Random-effects models for migration attractivity and retentivity: a Bayesian methodology. J R Stat Soc A Stat Soc 173(4):755–774
Cressie NAC (1993) Statistics for spatial data. Wiley, New York
Curry L (1972) A spatial analysis of gravity flows. Reg Stud 6(2):131–147
Curry L, Griffith DA, Sheppard ES (1975) Those gravity parameters again. Reg Stud 9(3):289–296
Egger P (2005) Alternative techniques for estimation of cross-section gravity models. Rev Int Econ 13(5):881–891
Egger P, Pfaffermayr M (2003) The proper panel econometric specification of the gravity equation: a three-way model with bilateral interaction effects. Empir Econ 28(3):571–580
Egger P, Pfaffermayr M (2016) A generalized spatial error components model for gravity equations. Empir Econ 50(1):177–195
Egger P, Tarlea F (2015) Multi-way clustering estimation of standard errors in gravity models. Econ Lett 134:144–147
Egger PH, Staub KE (2016) GLM estimation of trade gravity models with fixed effects. Empir Econ 50(1):137–175

Feenstra RC (2004) Advanced international trade: theory and evidence. Princeton University Press, Princeton
Fischer MM, Griffith DA (2008) Modeling spatial autocorrelation in spatial interaction data: an application to patent citation data in the european union. J Reg Sci 48(5):969–989
Fischer MM, Reismann M, Scherngell T (2010) Spatial interaction and spatial autocorrelation. In: Anselin L, Rey SJ (eds) Perspectives on spatial data analysis. Advances in spatial science. Springer, Berlin/Heidelberg, pp 61–79
Flowerdew R, Aitkin M (1982) A method of fitting the gravity model based on the Poisson distribution. J Reg Sci 22(2):191–202
Fotheringham AS, Webber MJ (1980) Spatial structure and the parameters of spatial interaction models. Geogr Anal 12(1):33–46
Getis A (1991) Spatial interaction and spatial autocorrelation: a cross-product approach. Environ Plan A 23(9):1269–1277
Griffith DA (2000) A linear regression solution to the spatial autocorrelation problem. J Geogr Syst 2(2):141–156
Griffith DA (2003) Spatial autocorrelation and spatial filtering: gaining understanding through theory and scientific visualization. Springer, Berlin/Heidelberg/New York
Griffith DA (2006) Assessing spatial dependence in count data: winsorized and spatial filter specification alternatives to the auto-poisson model. Geogr Anal 38(2):160–179
Griffith DA (2007) Spatial structure and spatial interaction: 25 years later. Rev Reg Stud 37(1):28–38
Griffith DA (2010) The Moran coefficient for non-normal data. J Stat Plan Inference 140(11):2980–2990
Griffith DA (2011) Visualizing analytical spatial autocorrelation components latent in spatial interaction data: an eigenvector spatial filter approach. Comput Environ Urban Syst 35(2):140–149
Griffith DA, Chun Y (2015) Spatial autocorrelation in spatial interactions models: geographic scale and resolution implications for network resilience and vulnerability. Netw Spat Econ 15(2):337–365
Griffith DA, Jones KG (1980) Explorations into the relationship between spatial structure and spatial interaction. Environ Plan A 12(2):187–201
Isard W (1960) Methods of regional analysis. MIT Press, Cambridge
Jacqmin-Gadda H, Commenges D, Nejjari C, Dartigues J-F (1997) Tests of geographical correlation with adjustment for explanatory variables: an application to dyspnoea in the elderly. Stat Med 16(11):1283–1297
Koch W, LeSage JP (2015) Latent multilateral trade resistance indices: theory and evidence. Scott J Polit Econ 62(3):264–290
Krisztin T, Fischer MM (2015) The gravity model for international trade: specification and estimation issues. Spat Econ Anal 10(4):451–470
Lambert DM, Brown JP, Florax RJGM (2010) A Two-step estimator for a spatial lag model of counts: theory, small sample performance and an application. Reg Sci Urban Econ 40(4):241–252
LeSage JP, Fischer MM (2010) Spatial econometric methods for modeling origin–destination flows. In: Fischer MM, Getis A (eds) Handbook of applied spatial analysis. Springer, Berlin/Heidelberg, pp 409–433
LeSage JP, Fischer MM, Scherngell T (2007) Knowledge spillovers across Europe: evidence from a Poisson spatial interaction model with spatial effects. Pap Reg Sci 86(3):393–421
LeSage JP, Pace RK (2008) Spatial econometric modeling of origin–destination flows. J Reg Sci 48(5):941–967
LeSage JP, Pace RK (2009) Introduction to spatial econometrics. CRC Press, Boca Raton
LeSage JP, Thomas-Agnan C (2015) Interpreting spatial econometric origin–destination flows models. J Reg Sci 55(2):188–208
Lin G, Zhang T (2007) Loglinear residual tests of Moran's *I* autocorrelation and their applications to Kentucky breast cancer data. Geogr Anal 39(3):293–310

Moran P (1948) The interpretation of statistical maps. J R Stat Soc B 10:243–251
Neumayer E, Plümper T (2010) Spatial effects in dyadic data. Int Organ 64(1):145–166
Peeters D, Thomas I (2009) Network autocorrelation. Geogr Anal 41(4):436–443
Porojan A (2001) Trade flows and spatial effects: the gravity model revisited. Open Econ Rev 12(3):265–280
Roy JR, Thill J-C (2003) Spatial interaction modelling. Pap Reg Sci 83(1):339–361
Santos Silva JMC, Tenreyro S (2006) The log of gravity. Rev Econ Stat 88(4):641–658
Sellner R, Fischer MM, Koch M (2013) A spatial autoregressive Poisson gravity model. Geogr Anal 45(2):180–201
Sen A, Smith TE (1995) Gravity models of spatial interaction behavior. Advances in spatial and network economics series. Springer, Heidelberg/New York
Sheppard ES, Griffith DA, Curry L (1976) A final comment on mis-specification and autocorrelation in those gravity parameters. Reg Stud 10(3):337–339
Stewart JQ (1941) On inverse distance variation for certain social influences. Science 93(2404):89–90
Thomas-Agnan C, LeSage JP (2014) Spatial econometric OD-flow models. In: Fischer MM, Nijkamp P (eds) Handbook of regional science. Springer, Berlin/Heidelberg, pp 1653–1673
Tiefelsdorf M (2003) Misspecifications in interaction model distance decay relations: a spatial structure effect. J Geogr Syst 5(1):25–50
Wilson AG (1970) Entropy in urban and regional modelling. Pion, London

Part I
General Methodological Issues

Chapter 2
Spatial Regression-Based Model Specifications for Exogenous and Endogenous Spatial Interaction

James P. LeSage and Manfred M. Fischer

Keywords Log-normal specification • Origin-destination flows

JEL: C18, C51, R11

2.1 Introduction

Spatial interaction models represent a class of models that are used for modeling origin-destination flow data. The interest in such models is motivated by the need to understand and explain the flows of tangible entities such as persons or commodities or intangible ones such as capital, information or knowledge between regions. These models attempt to explain interaction between origin and destination regions using (i) origin-specific attributes characterizing the ability of the origins to generate flows, (ii) destination-specific characteristics representing the attractiveness of destinations, and (iii) variables that characterize the way spatial separation of origins from destinations constrains or impedes the interaction. They implicitly assume that using spatial separation variables such as distance between origin and destination regions will eradicate the spatial dependence among the sample of spatial flows.

However, research dating back to the 1970s noted that spatial dependence or autocorrelation might be intermingled in spatial interaction model specifications. The idea was first put forth in a theoretical context by Curry (1972), with some subsequent debate in Curry et al. (1975). Griffith and Jones (1980) documented the presence of spatial dependence in conventional spatial interaction models. Despite

J.P. LeSage (✉)
Department of Finance and Economics, McCoy College of Business Administration, Texas State University, San Marcos, TX, USA
e-mail: james.lesage@txstate.edu

M.M. Fischer
Institute for Economic Geography and GIScience, Vienna University of Economics and Business, Vienna, Austria

R. Patuelli, G. Arbia (eds.), *Spatial Econometric Interaction Modelling*, Advances in Spatial Science, DOI 10.1007/978-3-319-30196-9_2

this, most practitioners assume independence among observations and few have used spatial lags of the dependent variable or disturbances in spatial interaction models. Exceptions are Bolduc et al. (1992), and Fischer and Griffith (2008) who rely on spatial lags of the disturbances, and LeSage and Pace (2008) who use spatial lags of the dependent variable.

The focus of this chapter is on the log-normal version of the model. In this context, we consider spatial econometric specifications that can be used to accommodate two types of dependence scenarios, one involving endogenous interaction and the other exogenous interaction. These model specifications replace the conventional assumption of independence between origin-destination-flows with formal approaches that allow for two different types of spatial dependence in flow magnitudes.

Endogenous interaction reflects situations where there is reaction to feedback regarding flow magnitudes from regions neighboring origin and destination regions. This type of interaction can be modeled using specifications proposed by LeSage and Pace (2008) who use spatial lags of the dependent variable to quantify the magnitude and extent of feedback effects, hence the term *endogenous interaction*. For example, commuters might react to congestion in regions near the origin or destination of their commute to work by adjusting future location decisions. This would of course produce changes in observed flows over time that need to be considered in light of the steady state equilibria that would characterize future period flows across the commuting network. Another example would be for the case of international trade flows, where a tariff or other impediment to flows might evoke a long-run response that changes the structure of flows across the network of trading countries. Since we typically model flows using a cross-section of observed flow magnitudes that have occurred during some type period (say the past 5 years) to estimate our model parameters that describe responsiveness of flows to characteristics of the regions and distance between regions, time is not explicit in these cross-sectional models. However, interpretation of the model estimates can take place with respect to comparative statics reflecting changes from one equilibrium steady state to another.

Exogenous interaction represents a situation where spillovers arise from nearby (or perhaps even distant) regions, and these need to be taken into account when modeling observed variation in flows across the network of regions. In contrast to endogenous interaction, these *contextual effects* do not generate reaction to the spillovers, leading to a model specification that can be interpreted without considering changes in the long-run equilibrium state of the system of flows. Spillovers arising from spatial dependence on the context in which commuters operate impact observed variation in flows between regions and we can quantify these types of impacts without reference to long-run equilibrium impacts on flows across the network. As in the case of social networks (where the term contextual effects has its origins), contextual effects are modeled using spatial lags of the explanatory variables that represent characteristics of neighboring (or more generally connected) regions, but not spatial lags of the dependent variable, hence the term *exogenous interaction*.

2.2 The Log-Normal (Independent) Spatial Interaction Model

Spatial interaction models essentially assert a multiplicative relationship between observed flows (reflecting the magnitude of interaction) and characteristics of origin and destination regions, as well as measures of separation between the regions (typically distance). As is typical of statistical model relationships, observations on the dependent variable (observed flows between origin and destination dyads, labeled i and j) are assumed independent of observed flows between other dyads, say k and l (see, for example Sen and Smith 1995, and Fischer and Wang 2011). Such a relationship is shown in (2.1).

$$Y(i,j) = CX(i)X(j)S(i,j), \quad i,j = 1, \ldots, n \tag{2.1}$$

where $Y(i,j)$ denotes flows from region i to region j, and C is a constant of proportionality. $X(i)$ and $X(j)$ represent origin-specific and destination specific characteristics, with $S(i,j)$ reflecting resistance or deterrence to flows between the origin and destination, typically modeled using some form of deterrence function reflecting spatial separation between locations i and j. At relatively large scales of geographical inquiry this might be the great circle distance between regions, measured in terms of the distance between their respective centroids. In other cases, it might be transportation or travel time, cost of transportation, perceived travel time or any other sensible measure such as political distance, language or cultural distance measured in terms of nominal or categorical attributes.

The exact functional form of the three terms $X(i)$, $X(j)$ and $S(i,j)$ on the right hand side of (2.1) is subject to varying degrees of conjecture. There is wide agreement that the origin and destination factors are best given by power functions $X(i)^{\beta_o}$ and $X(j)^{\beta_d}$ where $X(i)$ represents some appropriate variable measuring the propulsiveness of origins and $X(j)$ attractiveness of destinations in a specific spatial interaction context. The term gravity model is sometimes used in place of spatial interaction because the relationship posits that the magnitude of flows (reflecting interaction) between dyads i and j is directly proportional to size of the regions, when X is a measure of size and the coefficients β_o, β_d take values of unity. In a statistical modeling context, these coefficients are parameters to be estimated.

The deterrence function $S(i,j)$ also has a gravity interpretation such that interaction is inversely proportional to distance between dyads i and j. A number of alternative more flexible specifications have been proposed in the literature (see Fischer and Wang 2011), one being the power function:

$$S(i,j) = [G(i,j)]^{\gamma} \tag{2.2}$$

for an scalar (generalized) distance measure, $G(i,j)$, and negative parameter γ (reflecting the inverse relationship), with γ treated as a parameter to be estimated. The deterrence function reflects the way in which spatial separation or distance constrains or impedes movement across space. In general, we will refer to this as distance between an origin i and destination j, using $G(i,j)$.

LeSage and Pace (2008) use a matrix/vector representation of the log-transformed expression in (2.1) yielding the log-normal spatial interaction model, shown in (2.3)

$$y = \alpha \iota_{n^2} + X_o\beta_o + X_d\beta_d + g\gamma + \varepsilon \tag{2.3}$$

which more closely resembles a conventional regression relationship. In (2.3), y is an $n^2 \times 1$ vector of (logged) flows constructed by stacking columns of the observed $n \times n$ flow matrix Y, where we assume *destination-centric organization* throughout this chapter. This means that the i,jth element of the flow matrix represents a flow from region i to j. Similarly, applying the log transformation to the $n \times n$ matrix of distances G between the n destination and origin regions and stacking the columns results in an $n^2 \times 1$ vector g of (logged) distances, with associated coefficient γ. The term ε represents an $n^2 \times 1$ vector of constant variance, independent identically distributed normal disturbances. LeSage and Pace (2008) show that

$$X_o = \iota_n \otimes X \tag{2.4}$$

$$X_d = X \otimes \iota_n \tag{2.5}$$

for the case of a *destination-centric organization*, where X is an $n \times R$ matrix of characteristics for the n regions, $\otimes$ denotes the Kronecker product and ι_n is an $n \times 1$ vector of ones. We note that this represents a general case where the same set of R explanatory variables is used for both origins and destinations. Thomas-Agnan and LeSage (2014) point out this may be preferred to a specification where different (subsets of the R) explanatory variables are used for origin and destinations, since exclusion of important explanatory variables may result in omitted variable bias. The scalar parameter γ reflects the effect of the vector of logged (generalized) distances g on flows which is—given the power function specification in (2.2)—thought to be negative. The parameter α denotes the intercept term.

The Kronecker product repeats the same values of the n regions in a strategic way to create a matrix of characteristics associated with each origin (destination) region, hence the use of the notation $X_o = \iota_n \otimes X, X_d = X \otimes \iota_n$ to represent these explanatory variables. Recognizing this has important implications for how we interpret estimates of the parameter vectors β_o, β_d from these models. The literature has interpreted β_o as reflecting a typical regression partial derivative $\partial y/\partial X_o$, showing how changes in origin region characteristics impact flows (on average across the sample of n^2 dyads as is typical of regression estimates). Of course, this suggests we can change characteristics of origin regions while holding those of destination regions constant, since partial derivatives reflect a ceteris paribus change in X_o. It should be clear that a change in the rth characteristic of a single region i, X_i^r, will produce changes in both X_o, X_d, since by definition $\Delta X_o^r = \iota_n \otimes (X^r + \Delta X_i^r)$, and $\Delta X_d^r = (X^r + \Delta X_i^r) \otimes \iota_n$.

Intuitively, changes to the rth characteristic of a single region i will impact both inflows and outflows to all other regions engaged or connected with region i as either an origin or destination. For example, a (ceteris paribus) increase in employment in region i would lead to inflows of commuters to this region (when viewed as a destination) from (potentially) all other (origin) regions and a decrease in outflows of commuters (when viewed as an origin) to (potentially) all other (destination) regions. We will have more to say about this later.

There are some limitations to treating the spatial interaction relationship as a regression relationship between the vector of $n^2 \times 1$ logged flows and log-transformed explanatory variables. Regression relationships require the assumption of constant variance independent normally distributed disturbances in order to rely on conventional t-statistics for statistical inference regarding significance of the explanatory variables. Normal disturbances imply normally distributed flows, which is often not the case. Some flows reflect counts of migrants moving between regions, and many flow matrices contain a large proportion of dyads reflecting zero flows. These raise issues regarding the appropriate method for estimating regression-based specifications of spatial interaction model relationships, but do not have an impact on issues we will discuss pertaining to endogenous versus exogenous interaction specifications, or interpretation of estimates from these relationships.

2.3 Exogenous Versus Endogenous Spatial Interaction Specifications

We set forth spatial regression-based specifications for exogenous and endogenous spatial interaction models, with a focus on interpretative considerations pertaining to estimates from these two types of models.

2.3.1 An Endogenous Spatial Interaction Specification

As noted, this type of specification allows for flows from regions neighboring the origin region i or destination region j as well as flows between regions neighboring the origin and neighboring the destination, to exert an impact on the magnitude of observed flows between dyad (i,j). LeSage and Pace (2008) label dependence of flows on regions neighboring the origin i as origin-based dependence, that on flows neighboring the destination j as destination-based dependence, and that arising from flows between regions neighboring the origin and neighboring the destination as origin-destination based dependence.

The basic notion is that larger observed flows from an origin to a destination region are accompanied by (i) larger flows from regions nearby the origin to the destination region (origin-based dependence); (ii) larger flows from the origin region to regions neighboring the destination region (destination-based dependence), and (iii) larger flows from neighbors to the origin to regions that are neighbors of the destination (origin-to-destination-based dependence). This is accomplished using the specification in (2.6).

$$Ay = \alpha\iota_{n^2} + X_o\beta_o + X_d\beta_d + g\gamma + \varepsilon \tag{2.6}$$

$$A = (I_{n^2} - \rho_o W_o)(I_{n^2} - \rho_d W_d) \tag{2.7}$$

$$= (I_{n^2} - \rho_o W_o - \rho_d W_d + \rho_o\rho_d W_d W_o) \tag{2.8}$$

$$y = \rho_o W_o y + \rho_d W_d y + \rho_w W_w y + \alpha\iota_{n^2} + X_o\beta_o + X_d\beta_d + g\gamma + \varepsilon. \tag{2.9}$$

Some things to note regarding this specification. The matrix product $W_w = W_d W_o$ can be written as $W \otimes W$, where W is an $n \times n$ spatial weight matrix. While matrix multiplication produces the term $\rho_w = -\rho_o\rho_d$, there is no need to impose the implied restriction during estimation of the model. The resulting model statement in (2.9) captures origin-based dependence with the spatial lag term $W_o y$, destination-based dependence with $W_d y$, and origin-destination-based dependence using $W_w y$. The associated parameters ρ_o, ρ_d, ρ_w reflect the relative strength of these three different dependencies.

This specification posits a simultaneous or endogenous response relationship between the variation in the dependent variable reflecting flows between all dyads (y) and flows between other regions (specifically $W_o y, W_d y, W_w y$) within the observed network of interregional and intraregional flows.[1] This has implications for how we interpret the coefficient estimates from this type of specification, with details set forth in LeSage and Thomas-Agnan (2014). It also has implications for how we must estimate the parameters $\beta_o, \beta_d, \gamma, \rho_o, \rho_d, \rho_w$, with details provided in LeSage and Pace (2008, 2009, Chapter 8). We will discuss interpretation issues in a later section. This discussion takes the parameter estimates as given, and presumes these reflect valid estimates produced using appropriate methods (either maximum likelihood or Bayesian Markov Chain Monte Carlo procedures).

2.3.1.1 A Theoretical Motivation for Endogenous Interaction

A criticism that might be leveled at the endogenous interaction specification in (2.9) is that this appears to arise from mere matrix algebra manipulations, rather than economic theory. We present a theoretical motivation taken from LeSage and Thomas-Agnan (2014) based on the notion that location decisions of commuters are influenced by behavior of other commuters in previous periods.

They argue that commuting residents might be influenced by nearby flows (congestion) resulting from past location decisions of other residents in neighboring

[1] Intraregional flows are recorded on the main diagonal of the flow matrix.

regions. It might also be the case that firms are influenced by congestion arising from location decisions of nearby firms in the past.

They formally express this type of dyadic O-D flow dependence of y_t at time t on past flows y_{t-1} as:

$$
\begin{aligned}
y_t &= My_{t-1} + Z\delta + \varepsilon_t \\
M &= (\rho_d W_d + \rho_o W_o + \rho_w W_w) \\
Z &= \left(X_d \; X_o \; g\right) \\
\delta &= \left(\beta_d \; \beta_o \; \gamma\right)' \\
\varepsilon_t &\sim N(0, \sigma^2 I_n)
\end{aligned} \tag{2.10}
$$

where underlying characteristics of the regions X remain relatively fixed over time, allowing us to write Z without a time subscript. Since the characteristics of regions in flow models often represent *size of regions*, this assumption seems (approximately) valid.

Expression (2.10) indicates that (commuting-to-work) flows between O-D dyads at time t depend on past period flows observed by residents and firms in regions neighboring their origin ($W_o y_{t-1}$) and destination regions ($W_d y_{t-1}$), as well as flows between regions neighboring the origin to regions neighboring the destination ($W_w y_{t-1}$). This is close to the endogenous interaction specification from (2.9), but relies on a time lag or past period flows, not current period as we have in our cross-sectional model.

LeSage and Thomas-Agnan (2014) show that we can interpret the endogenous spatial interaction model as the outcome or expectation of a long-run equilibrium or steady state relationship as time $q \to \infty$, which is shown in (2.11).

$$
\begin{aligned}
\lim_{q\to\infty} E(y_{t+q}) &= (I_{n^2} - M)^{-1} Z\delta \\
&= (I_{n^2} - \rho_d W_d - \rho_o W_o - \rho_w W_w)^{-1} Z\delta.
\end{aligned} \tag{2.11}
$$

Of course, this is the expectation for the data generating process of the spatial autoregressive interaction model given in (2.9).

From a theoretical perspective, changes in transportation infrastructure (improvements in the road network) that connects commuters between regions would be expected to result in endogenous interaction of the type captured by this model specification. We would expect to see diffusion of changes in commuting flows taking place over space, that impact flows in neighboring regions with faster commuting times, regions that neighbor these regions, and so on. These *global* spillover impacts are what characterize endogenous interaction, and they presumably lead to a new long-run steady state equilibrium in residents' choices regarding routes used and firms' choices about location.

In general *shared resources* are often thought to be the basis for global spillover impacts and the associated diffusion of these impacts to neighbors, neighbors to neighbors, and so on. The highway network that passes through many regions would represent one type of resource shared by many regions. Changes taking place on one segment of the highway would have (potentially) far reaching *global* spillover impacts.

2.3.2 An Exogenous Spatial Interaction Specification

There are other modeling situations where endogenous interaction is not a likely phenomenon, but spatial spillover impacts such as congestion in neighboring regions is of interest when modeling variation in flows across the network of regions. Theoretical aspects of the modeling circumstance would provide one approach to distinguishing which type of specification is most appropriate for any given application.

Exogenous interaction specifications are characterized by spatial lags of the exogenous variables X_o, X_d, leading to a model

$$y = \alpha\iota_{n^2} + X_o\beta_o + X_d\beta_d + g\gamma + W_oX_o\theta_o + W_dX_d\theta_d + \varepsilon. \quad (2.12)$$

It should be clear that no endogenous relationship between flows (y) and flows from neighboring regions exists in this specification. Instead, we have a situation where changes in characteristics of regions neighboring the origin (W_oX_o) and regions neighboring the destination (W_dX_d) help explain variation in flows across dyads.

A change in characteristics of neighboring regions, for example, an increase in the number of retired persons (non-commuters) locating in regions that neighbor commuting residents located at origin i (W_oX_o) might influence the magnitude of flows between dyads (i,j). Similarly, retirees locating in regions that neighbor commuters' destination regions j (W_dX_d) might influence the magnitude of flows between dyads (i,j).

A distinction between this specification and the endogenous specification is that the focus here is on the *local* spillover impacts on flows arising from changes in characteristics of regions neighboring the origin or destination region. There is no implication that flows respond to feedback impacts associated with the increased number of retirees locating in regions neighboring the origin or destination, just spatial spillover impacts on the pattern of flows between origin and destination dyads due to changes in the characteristics of (say immediately) neighboring regions. Global spillovers imply diffusion over space, whereas local spillovers do not imply diffusion over space that impacts neighbors, neighbors to neighbors, and so on. Reduced congestion arising from retired persons (non-commuters) locating in a specific region would likely impact commuters from neighboring regions, but the impact would not extend to more distant neighboring regions. The number of non-commuters located in any one region does not reflect a shared resource, and would be expected to have only *local* spillover impacts.

Another consideration useful in distinguishing between these two types of specifications would be permanent and predictable events versus temporary or unpredictable events. For example, unpredictable events such as traffic delays due to construction or accidents in neighboring regions would not be expected to produce endogenous interaction effects because of the unpredictability of such events. It should be noted that congestion effects arising from unpredictable events such as these may create *local spillover congestion* that spans many regions, so we should not think of local spillovers as impacting only nearby/neighboring regions. We still label these local spillover effects because they are not associated with endogenous interaction or feedback effects whereby commuters adjust their travel routes. However, consistently higher accident rates in a group of regions might allow commuters to predict traffic delays resulting in endogenous reactions such that commuters change their routes to avoid such regions. Observed adjustments in travel routes by many commuters with widely varying origins and destinations would of course appear as a global spillover effect having impacts on regions neighboring the construction or accident zone, neighbors to these regions, neighbors to the neighbors of these regions, and so on. This of course would be reflected in the new long-run steady state equilibrium commuting flows.

2.4 Interpreting Estimates From Spatial Interaction Specifications

In Sect. 2.4.1 we consider how changes in the characteristics of regions impact flows in the case of the conventional (non-spatial) interaction model from (2.3). This discussion draws heavily on ideas set forth by LeSage and Thomas-Agnan (2014). They point out that changes in the rth characteristic of region i, ΔX_i^r, will produce changes in flows into region i from (potentially) $(n-1)$ other regions, as well as flows out of region i to (potentially) $(n-1)$ other regions. This can be seen by noting that the matrices $X_d = \iota_n \otimes X$ and $X_o = X \otimes \iota_n$ repeat X_i^r n times. Unlike the situation in conventional regression models where a change ΔX_i^r leads to changes in only observation i of the dependent variable, y_i, we cannot change single elements of X_d^r, X_o^r, nor should we interpret the coefficient estimate $\hat{\beta}_o, \hat{\beta}_d$ as reflecting the impact of this change (averaged over all observations) on a single element of the dependent variable vector y.

The fact that changes in characteristics of a single region give rise to numerous responses in the flow matrix rather than changes in a single observation (dyad) of the dependent variable (as in traditional regression) creates a challenge for drawing inferences about the partial derivative impacts of changing regional characteristics on flows. To address this challenge, Sect. 2.4.2 proposes scalar summary measures for the impact of changing regional characteristics on flows, that collapse the many changes in flows to a single number. These scalars average over the many changes that arise in the flow matrix from changing characteristics of the regions, as is typical of the way in which we interpret regression models.

In Sect. 2.4.2 we describe how LeSage and Thomas-Agnan (2014) extend the scalar summary approach to the case of an endogenous spatial interaction specification from (2.9). In this model specification, changes in the characteristics of a single region i can impact flows into and out of region i to its $2(n-1)$ dyad (i,j) partners (as described above), but also flows into and out of regions that neighbor the origin i and destination j regions that are not part of the dyad (i,j). This arises from the spatial dependence part of the spatial autoregressive interaction model. An implication is that we should not interpret the coefficient estimates β_d, β_o as if they were regression estimates that reflect *partial derivative changes* in the dependent variable associated with changes in the explanatory variables.

Section 2.4.3 adopts the scalar summary approach to the case of the exogenous spatial interaction specification introduced here, which reflects new ideas not previously considered in the literature. However, we show that interpretation of estimates from these models reflects a special case of the scalar summary approach set forth by LeSage and Thomas-Agnan (2014).

2.4.1 *Interpreting Estimates from Non-Spatial Interaction Specifications*

Before proceeding to interpretation of the model estimates, we adopt an approach suggested by LeSage and Pace (2009, p. 223) that introduces a separate model for within region (intraregional) flows, which tend to have large values relative to between region flows. This is done by creating an intercept for flows associated with the main diagonal of the flow matrix (intraregional flows) that we label $\tilde{\alpha}$, as well as a set of explanatory variables for these flows that we label X_i. The explanatory variables X_d, X_o are adjusted to have zero values for main diagonal elements of the flow matrix and the new variables matrix X_i has associated coefficients that we label β_i. This set of explanatory variables will capture variation in intraregional flows. An adjusted version of (2.3) is shown in (2.13) reflecting these modifications to the model, where vec is the operator that converts a matrix to a vector by stacking its columns.

$$y = \alpha\tilde{\iota}_{n^2} + \tilde{\alpha}\text{vec}(I_n) + \tilde{X}_o\beta_o + \tilde{X}_d\beta_d + X_i\beta_i + g\gamma + \varepsilon \tag{2.13}$$

We use $\tilde{\iota}_{n^2} = \iota_{n^2} - \text{vec}(I_n), \tilde{X}_o = X_o - X_i, \tilde{X}_d = X_d - X_i$ to reflect the adjustment made to the original intercept and explanatory variables matrices by setting these elements to zero. The matrix X_i contains non-zero values only for dyads where the origin equals the destination (i.e., intraregional flows).

We also consider the simplest possible spatial configuration of the regions, which positions these in a straight line, with a single neighbor to the left and right.[2] For simplicity, we work with a single vector of explanatory variables in the following to avoid having to designate working with a specific explanatory variable. A scalar change in the characteristics of the third region (ΔX_3) will produce an $n \times n$ matrix of changes in flows (ΔY), shown in (2.14).

$$\Delta Y / \Delta X_3 = \begin{pmatrix} 0.0 & 0.0 & \beta_o & 0.0 & 0.0 & 0.0 & 0.0 & 0.0 \\ 0.0 & 0.0 & \beta_o & 0.0 & 0.0 & 0.0 & 0.0 & 0.0 \\ \beta_d & \beta_d & \beta_i & \beta_d & \beta_d & \beta_d & \beta_d & \beta_d \\ 0.0 & 0.0 & \beta_o & 0.0 & 0.0 & 0.0 & 0.0 & 0.0 \\ 0.0 & 0.0 & \beta_o & 0.0 & 0.0 & 0.0 & 0.0 & 0.0 \\ 0.0 & 0.0 & \beta_o & 0.0 & 0.0 & 0.0 & 0.0 & 0.0 \\ 0.0 & 0.0 & \beta_o & 0.0 & 0.0 & 0.0 & 0.0 & 0.0 \\ 0.0 & 0.0 & \beta_o & 0.0 & 0.0 & 0.0 & 0.0 & 0.0 \end{pmatrix} \tag{2.14}$$

The role of the independence assumption is clear in (2.14), where we see from column 3 that the change of outflows from region 3 to all other regions equals β_o, and similarly, row 3 exhibits changes in inflows to region 3, taking the value of the coefficient β_d. The diagonal (3,3) element reflects a response equal to β_i, which reflects the change in intraregional flows arising from the change in X_3. We have only $2(n-1)$ non-zero changes in flows by virtue of the independence assumption. All changes involving flows in- and out-of regions other than those in the dyads involving region 3 are zero.

This result suggests that for the conventional gravity model, interpreting β_o as the partial derivative impact on flows arising from changes in origin-specific characteristics (X_o) is not too bad, since the only exception is the coefficient β_i in the (3,3) element. The partial derivative for changes in the ith observation ($i \neq 3$) would of course look similar to the matrix in (2.14), so averaging over changes to all observations would produce an approximately correct result when interpreting β_o, β_d *as if* they were simply regression coefficients. However, we will see that this reasoning does not apply to the spatial variants of the interaction model specification, a point made by Thomas-Agnan and LeSage (2014).

The approach taken by LeSage and Thomas-Agnan (2014) to producing scalar summary measures of the impacts arising from changes in characteristics of the regions involves averaging over the *cumulative flow impacts* associated with changes in all regions, $i = 1, \ldots, n$. Scalar summaries are consistent with how coefficient estimates for the parameters in a conventional regression model are interpreted, and cumulating the impacts makes intuitive sense in our flow setting.

[2]The west most region at the beginning of the line of regions has a single neighbor to the right, and the east most region at the end of the line has a single neighbor to the left.

They calculate scalar summaries by expressing the partial derivatives as shown in (2.15), where the $n \times n$ matrices of changes in (logged) flows arising from changing the rth explanatory variable X_i^r are stored in the $n \times n$ matrices Y_i.[3]

$$TE = \begin{pmatrix} \partial Y_1/\partial X_1^r \\ \partial Y_2/\partial X_2^r \\ \vdots \\ \partial Y_n/\partial X_n^r \end{pmatrix} = \begin{pmatrix} \tilde{J}d_1\beta_d^r + \tilde{J}o_1\beta_o^r + J\iota_1\beta_i^r \\ \tilde{J}d_2\beta_d^r + \tilde{J}o_2\beta_o^r + J\iota_2\beta_i^r \\ \vdots \\ \tilde{J}d_n\beta_d^r + \tilde{J}o_n\beta_o^r + J\iota_n\beta_i^r \end{pmatrix} \quad (2.15)$$

In (2.15), Jd_i is an $n \times n$ matrix of zeros with the ith row equal to $\iota_n'\beta_d$, and Jo_i is an $n \times n$ matrix of zeros with the ith column equal to $\iota_n\beta_o$. The matrix $J\iota_i$ is an $n \times n$ matrix of zeros with a one in the i, i row and column position. We could express $\tilde{J}d_i = Jd_i - J\iota_i$, and also $\tilde{J}o_i = Jo_i - J\iota_i$. We have n sets of $n \times n$ outcomes, (one for each change in $X_i^r, i = 1, \dots, n$) resulting in an $n^2 \times n$ matrix of partial derivatives reflecting the total effect on flows from changing the rth characteristic of all n regions, hence the label TE.

The TE consists of origin effects $OE = \left(\tilde{J}o_1\beta_o^r, \dots, \tilde{J}o_n\beta_o^r\right)'$, destination effects $DE = \left(\tilde{J}d_1\beta_d^r, \dots, \tilde{J}d_n\beta_d^r\right)'$, and intraregional effects $IE = \left(J\iota_1\beta_i^r, \dots, J\iota_n\beta_i^r\right)'$.

The total effects on flows can be cumulated and then averaged to produce a scalar summary measure of the total impact of changes in the *typical* region's rth characteristic. This takes the form: $te = (1/n^2)\iota_{n^2}' \cdot TE \cdot \iota_n$, where we follow LeSage and Thomas-Agnan (2014) and use lower case te to represent the scalar summary measure of the $n^2 \times n$ matrix TE. This scalar summary is consistent with the way that regression coefficient estimates are interpreted as averaging over changes in all observations of an explanatory variable. We can also produce scalar summary estimates of the origin effects ($oe = (1/n^2)\iota_{n^2}' \cdot OE \cdot \iota_n$), destination effects ($de = (1/n^2)\iota_{n^2}' \cdot DE \cdot \iota_n$), and intraregional effects ($ie = (1/n^2)\iota_{n^2}' \cdot IE \cdot \iota_n$).

To illustrate use of these formulas, we provide a numerical illustration based on values of $\beta_o = -0.5, \beta_d = 1, \beta_i = 0.5$ in Table 2.1. The scalar summaries sum to the scalar summary total effect. In addition to the scalar summary effects estimates, we present the parameters β_o, β_d whose estimates are typically interpreted as origin and destination effects, and whose sum is considered the total effect arising from a change in the rth explanatory variable (Table 2.1).

As Thomas-Agnan and LeSage (2014) point out, the results differ slightly from the conventional interpretation of non-spatial gravity models where the coefficient β_o is interpreted as a partial derivative reflecting the impact of changes in origin characteristics and β_d that associated with changing destination characteristics. Although the conventional approach that uses the coefficient sum $\beta_o + \beta_d$ as a measure of the total effect on flows arising from changes in origin and destination

[3]Our expressions differ slightly from those of LeSage and Thomas-Agnan (2014) because of our modification of the model specification to incorporate X_i variables to model intraregional variation in flows.

Table 2.1 Scalar summary measures of effects for the non-spatial model from a change in the (single) rth characteristic X^r averaged over all regions

Scalar summary	Correct	Conventional interpretation
Origin effects	−0.4375	$\beta_o = -0.5$
Destination effects	0.8750	$\beta_d = 1.0$
Intraregional effects	0.0625	
Total effects	0.5000	$\beta_o + \beta_d = 0.5$

Table 2.2 Scalar summary measures of effects for the exogenous spatial interaction model from a change in the (single) rth characteristic X^r averaged over all regions

Scalar summary	Correct	Conventional interpretation
Origin effects	−0.4375	$\beta_o = -0.5$
Destination effects	0.8750	$\beta_d = 1.0$
Intraregional effects	0.0625	
Network origin effects	−0.2188	$\theta_o = -0.25$
Network destination effects	0.4375	$\theta_d = 0.5$
Total effects	0.7188	$\beta_o + \beta_d + \theta_o + \theta_d = 0.75$

characteristics would produce a correct inference, the appropriate decomposition into origin, destination and intraregional effects has been wrong in the historical literature.

2.4.2 Interpreting Estimates from Exogenous Interaction Specifications

The exogenous interaction specification extended to include an intraregional specific intercept and set of explanatory variables is shown in (2.16), where we have added origin and destination specific spatial lags of the (adjusted) explanatory variables matrices.

$$y = \alpha \tilde{\iota}_{n^2} + \tilde{\alpha}\text{vec}(I_n) + \tilde{X}_o\beta_o + \tilde{X}_d\beta_d + X_i\beta_i + W_o\tilde{X}_o\theta_o + W_d\tilde{X}_d\theta_d + g\gamma + \varepsilon. \quad (2.16)$$

Changes in the rth explanatory variable now result in two additional terms in the partial derivatives expressions shown in (2.17). The new terms associated with the spatial lags of the explanatory variables reflect (local) spatial spillovers arising from neighbors to the origin and neighbors to the destination regions.

$$TE = \begin{pmatrix} \partial Y_1/\partial X_1^r \\ \partial Y_2/\partial X_2^r \\ \vdots \\ \partial Y_n/\partial X_n^r \end{pmatrix} = \begin{pmatrix} \tilde{J}d_1\beta_d^r + \tilde{J}o_1\beta_o^r + J\iota_1\beta_i^r + \tilde{J}d_1\theta_d^r + \tilde{J}o_1\theta_o^r \\ \tilde{J}d_2\beta_d^r + \tilde{J}o_2\beta_o^r + J\iota_2\beta_i^r + \tilde{J}d_2\theta_d^r + \tilde{J}o_2\theta_o^r \\ \vdots \\ \tilde{J}d_n\beta_d^r + \tilde{J}o_n\beta_o^r + J\iota_n\beta_i^r + \tilde{J}d_n\theta_d^r + \tilde{J}o_n\theta_o^r \end{pmatrix} \quad (2.17)$$

A similar approach to decomposing the total effects can be used along with conversion of these to scalar summary estimates. In this case we have: $te = oe + de + ie + noe + nde$, where the new terms: *noe* and *nde* are labeled *network origin effects* and *network destination effects*. These are calculated using: ($noe = (1/n^2)\iota'_{n^2} \cdot NOE \cdot \iota_n$), destination effects ($nde = (1/n^2)\iota'_{n^2} \cdot NDE \cdot \iota_n$), where: $NOE = \left(\tilde{J}o_1\theta_o^r, \ldots, \tilde{J}o_n\theta_o^r\right)'$, and $NDE = \left(\tilde{J}d_1\theta_d^r, \ldots, \tilde{J}d_n\theta_d^r\right)'$.

Intuitively, these new scalar summary measures of the origin- and destination-specific spatial spillover effects reflect the impact of changes in characteristics of regions neighboring the origin and destination on flows between the typical dyad. We extend our previous example, using $\theta_o = -0.25, \theta_d = 0.5$ in Table 2.2 to illustrate the difference between using $\beta_o, \beta_d, \theta_o, \theta_d$ *as if* these were partial derivatives.

In contrast to the Table 2.1 non-spatial case, the total effects calculated in Table 2.2 by summing up coefficients $\beta_o + \beta_d + \theta_o + \theta_d = 0.75$ are not equal to the true total effects. We also see discrepancies between the true origin, destination, network origin and network destination effects (based on actual partial derivatives) and those from simply interpreting the coefficient estimates *as if* they were partial derivatives.

2.4.3 Interpreting Estimates from Endogenous Interaction Specifications

The endogenous interaction specification extended to include an intraregional specific intercept and set of explanatory variables is shown in (2.18), where we have added origin and destination specific spatial lags of the dependent variable to capture origin, destination and origin-destination dependence of the type proposed by LeSage and Pace (2008).

$$\begin{aligned} y = \rho_o W_o y + \rho_d W_d y + \rho_w W_w y + \alpha\tilde{\iota}_{n^2} + \tilde{\alpha}\mathrm{vec}(I_n) + \tilde{X}_o\beta_o + \tilde{X}_d\beta_d \\ + X_i\beta_i + g\gamma + \varepsilon. \end{aligned} \quad (2.18)$$

Working with the expression for the data generating process of this model, LeSage and Thomas-Agnan (2014) show that the partial derivatives $\partial y/\partial X^{r'}$, take the form shown in (2.19).

$$\begin{aligned} TE &= \begin{pmatrix} \partial Y_1/\partial X_1^r \\ \partial Y_2/\partial X_2^r \\ \vdots \\ \partial Y_n/\partial X_n^r \end{pmatrix} \\ &= (I_{n^2} - \rho_o W_o - \rho_d W_d - \rho_w W_w)^{-1} \begin{pmatrix} \tilde{J}d_1\beta_d^r + \tilde{J}o_1\beta_o^r + J\iota_1\beta_i^r \\ \tilde{J}d_2\beta_d^r + \tilde{J}o_2\beta_o^r + J\iota_2\beta_i^r \\ \vdots \\ \tilde{J}d_n\beta_d^r + \tilde{J}o_n\beta_o^r + J\iota_n\beta_i^r \end{pmatrix}. \end{aligned} \quad (2.19)$$

These represent an extension of the partial derivatives from the non-spatial model, where in this endogenous spatial interaction specification, the $n^2 \times n^2$ matrix inverse: $A^{-1} = (I_{n^2} - \rho_o W_o - \rho_d W_d - \rho_w W_w)^{-1}$, pre-multiplies the non-spatial effects. (Of course, in the non-spatial case $\rho_o = \rho_d = \rho_w = 0$.) A similar decomposition of the total effects can be applied to produce origin effects (OE), destination effects (DE), intraregional effects (IE) and network effects (NE). The network effects reflect spatial spillovers from: neighbors to the origin, neighbors to the destination and neighbors to the origin to neighbors of the destination.

As an illustration of the nature of these partial derivatives, consider the example shown in (2.20), where we consider a change to the single observation X_3, based on the same numerical values set forth in the previous section for $\beta_o = -0.5, \beta_d = 1.0, \beta_i = 0.5$, while setting $\rho_o = 0.5, \rho_d = 0.4$ and $\rho_w = -\rho_o\rho_d = -0.2$.[4]

$$\Delta Y/\Delta X_3 = \begin{pmatrix} 0.052 & -0.086 & -0.777 & -0.069 & 0.121 & 0.171 & 0.185 & 0.187 \\ 0.337 & 0.199 & -0.492 & 0.216 & 0.406 & 0.457 & 0.470 & 0.473 \\ 2.048 & 1.910 & 1.219 & 1.927 & 2.117 & 2.168 & 2.181 & 2.184 \\ 0.318 & 0.180 & -0.511 & 0.197 & 0.387 & 0.438 & 0.451 & 0.454 \\ -0.043 & -0.181 & -0.872 & -0.164 & 0.026 & 0.077 & 0.090 & 0.093 \\ -0.118 & -0.256 & -0.947 & -0.239 & -0.050 & 0.001 & 0.015 & 0.017 \\ -0.134 & -0.272 & -0.963 & -0.255 & -0.065 & -0.014 & -0.001 & 0.002 \\ -0.136 & -0.275 & -0.965 & -0.257 & -0.068 & -0.017 & -0.004 & -0.001 \end{pmatrix}. \tag{2.20}$$

As LeSage and Thomas-Agnan (2014) point out, the spatial autoregressive specification results in the presence of *network spillover effects*, shown by the non-zero elements in rows and columns other than 3. This means that a change in say the attractiveness of region 3 impacts flows throughout the network. This arises because the spatial autoregressive model specification allows for *global spillovers* which can be viewed as diffusion throughout the network of the increased attractiveness of region 3.

Of course, the largest network spillover impacts still tend to reside in the third row and column, since the change in attractiveness of region 3 has the largest impact on flows involving region 3 in the O-D dyads. The magnitude of impact decreases as we move further from the (3,3) element, with the non-linear nature of this decay of influence determined by a number of factors. Specifically, the matrix W plays a role, as well as the spatial dependence parameters ρ_o, ρ_d, ρ_w. For this simple example, where regions are configured to lie in a line, moving to row and column elements further from the (3,3) position should reflect more distant neighbors. An implication of the increase in paths through which the flows must pass to reach the (8,8) and (1,1) dyads in the network is that smaller network effects arise in the flow matrix for these dyads.

[4]This example is identical to Thomas-Agnan and LeSage (2014).

Table 2.3 Scalar summary measures of effects for the endogenous spatial interaction model from a change in the (single) rth characteristic X^r averaged over all regions

Scalar summary	Correct	Conventional interpretation
Origin effects	−0.1817	$\beta_o = -0.5$
Destination effects	0.3725	$\beta_d = 1.0$
Intraregional effects	0.0267	
Network effects	−0.1450	
Total effects	0.0725	$\beta_o + \beta_d = 0.5$

One point is that we follow LeSage and Thomas-Agnan (2014) who calculate only a single scalar summary measure of the network effects, rather than attempt to make distinctions between origin- and destination-specific network effects. Because of the non-linearity and diffusion of effects evident in the matrix shown in (2.20), it seems prudent to focus on a single measure of spatial spillovers falling on all regions in the network. This is of course in contrast to the exogenous spatial interaction specification where it is a simple matter to produce a decomposition that separates network origin and network destination effects.

We extend our previous example, using the same values: $\beta_o = -0.5, \beta_d = 1$, $\beta_i = 0.5, \rho_o = 0.5, \rho_d = 0.4, \rho_w = -0.2$ to produce correct partial derivatives. These are contrasted with the typical interpretation of β_o, β_d *as if* these were partial derivatives in Table 2.3.

For the case of an endogenous spatial interaction specification, we see little relationship between the coefficients β_o, β_d and the true origin and destination effects. This is similar to the case of conventional spatial regression models where practitioners have historically misinterpreted these coefficient estimates *as if* they represented partial derivatives (see LeSage and Pace 2008). For an application involving commuting flows between regions in Toulouse, France see LeSage and Thomas-Agnan (2014), who provide an interpretative discussion of the various effects estimates and inferences associated with the endogenous spatial interaction model. In the next section we provide an illustration of estimates and inferences for the case of the exogenous spatial interaction model that we have proposed here.

2.5 An Applied Illustration Involving Movement of Teachers Between School Districts

We use flows of teachers between 67 county-level school district, in Florida over the period 1995 to 2004. The flows were constructed by tracing the location of 102,327 teachers in the system during 1995, who were still in the system during 2004. We ignore teachers that left the system and those that entered during this time period. The impact of this is an issue to be addressed in future work.

One way to motivate dependence is to view the county-level school districts as representing a network system. Changes by a single school district that affect working conditions, salary or employment requirements of teachers will have an impact on the own-district as well as other nearby districts that can be viewed as nodes in the statewide network. The movement of teachers may be to and from other schools within the own-county or district or they may be between districts.[5]

In the empirical trade literature, Poisson pseudo-maximum likelihood estimation methods have become popular as a way of dealing with several econometric issues that arise when modeling origin-destination flows [e.g., Santos Silva and Tenreyro 2006, 2010, 2011 and Gourieroux et al. 1984]. We rely on our exogenous spatial interaction specification that allows for spatial dependence between flows from nearby regions/school districts.

One econometric issue that arises when modeling inter-district flows of teachers is that these reflect 'count data', or observations taking discrete values or zero magnitudes in the case where no flows between dyads reflecting districts i and j occur. This suggests a Poisson spatial interaction model is most appropriate. There are several econometric advantages to this model specification along with Poisson pseudo-maximum likelihood (PPML) estimation procedures over log-normal specifications that either delete zero flows or modify the dependent variable using $ln(y + 1)$ to accommodate the log transformation of the multiplicative gravity model. One is that the coefficients on logged explanatory variables (X) in the (exponential) relationship involving non-logged flow magnitudes as the dependent variable (y) can be interpreted as the elasticity of the conditional expectation of y_i with respect to X_l. Since Jensen's inequality implies that $E(\ln y) \neq \ln E(y)$, heteroscedasticity in log-linear regression gravity models can lead to inconsistent elasticity estimates, which is not a problem with PPML estimates.[6]

In addition to dealing with heteroscedasticity, the Poisson gravity model along with PPML estimation procedures does not require taking logs of the flows, to avoid the problem of (logs) in the presence of zero flows. With regard to the zero problem, our sample of flows between 67 counties/school districts contains 1,266 non-zero flow magnitudes out of a possible $67 \times 67 = 4{,}489$ flows between the 67 districts. This reflects 28.2 % non-zeros and 71.8 % zeros. Although the prevalence of zero values has an adverse impact on the PPML estimates, Santos Silva and Tenreyro (2011) point out that the PPML model works better than alternative approaches even in the face of a large proportion of zero flow values.

This allows us to make a point that interpretative considerations discussed are based on coefficient estimates for the parameters $\beta_o, \beta_d, \theta_o, \theta_d$ which should be produced using a valid estimation approach. Our derivations hold true for any valid estimates of these parameters.

Characteristics used are shown in Table 2.4, where values for these variables are for the year 1995 in an attempt to avoid a simultaneity problem. Use of the (log) number of *teachers* (in the origin and destination districts) as explanatory variables captures the basic notion behind gravity models where the magnitude of district

[5]Florida has county-level districts so that districts and counties coincide in our analysis.

[6]Santos Silva and Tenreyro (2006) note there is strong evidence that disturbances from log-linear gravity models are heteroscedastic.

Table 2.4 District-level variables used in the model

Variable name	Description
y	Within and between district teacher flows 1995–2003
Teachers	Log (count of teachers in each district in 1995)
Salary	Log (average teacher salary in 1995)
Poverty	Percentage of students receiving free lunches in 1995
Distance	Log (distance between origin and destination district centroids)

interaction (in our case teacher movement) is directly proportional to the product of district size measures (in our case the (log) of the number of teachers in origin and destination school districts).[7] Direct proportionality would result in an elasticity coefficient for these two variables equal to one.

In addition to the origin and destination size variables, two other explanatory variables were used, one reflecting a teacher characteristic, *Salary*, and the other a student characteristic, *Poverty*. The decision to use only two other explanatory variables was for the sake of simplicity in our illustrative example.

The traditional gravity model posits that flows are inversely proportional to distance, so we would expect a coefficient of minus one on the logged distance variable. Use of the conventional log transformation of the number of teachers, salary, percentage of students in poverty and distance variables allows us to interpret these estimates as elasticities. We adopt the approach that introduces a separate model for within district flows of teachers, which tend to have large values relative to between district flows.

As argued in the previous section, the coefficients in Table 2.5 *should not* be interpreted as if they represent the true effects associated with changes in the explanatory variables of the model. Table 2.6 shows the effects estimates that represent actual partial derivatives showing how flows respond (in elasticity terms on average over the sample) to changes in the number of teachers, salary of teachers and poverty status of students in origin and destination districts, the own-district and neighboring districts.

We can use the estimates in Table 2.5 to make the point that a non-spatial interaction specification would suffer from omitted variables bias due to its exclusion of the spatial lags W_oX_o, W_dX_d variables, since all but one of these variables (W_o teachers_o) are significantly different from zero at the 99 % level.

From Table 2.6, we see that larger origin and destination districts (measured by the number of teachers in these districts) leads to an increase in flows. Given that the

[7] In the case of interregional commodity flows, the measure of regional size is typically gross regional product or regional income. The model predicts more interaction in the form of commodity flows between regions of similar (economic) size than regions dissimilar in size. For the case of migration flows, population would be a logical measure of regional size, and in other contexts such as ours involving teacher flows between school districts, use of the number of teachers in each district seems a reasonable measure of district size.

Table 2.5 Coefficient estimates from the PPML model

Variable	Coefficient	t-Statistic (p-level)
Constant	−1.2738	−0.429 (0.6678)
ι_i	0.1476	0.231 (0.8170)
Teachers_d	0.6508	41.880 (0.0000)
Salary_d	0.0596	0.267 (0.7895)
Poverty_d	−0.5153	−7.576 (0.0000)
Teachers_o	0.7397	48.581 (0.0000)
Salary_o	−0.2552	−1.154 (0.2482)
Poverty_o	0.6659	8.648 (0.0000)
Teachers_i	0.9994	185.511 (0.0000)
Salary_i	0.4653	7.432 (0.0000)
Poverty_i	−0.1638	−7.025 (0.0000)
W_d teachers_d	0.0568	2.584 (0.0098)
W_d salary_d	−0.2056	−6.598 (0.0000)
W_d poverty_d	0.3304	3.618 (0.0003)
W_o teachers_o	−0.0341	−1.550 (0.1210)
W_o salary_o	−0.3711	−12.236 (0.0000)
W_o poverty_o	−0.2656	−2.928 (0.0034)
Distance	−0.6220	−26.177 (0.0000)

effects estimates reflect elasticity responses of flows, they point to flows as having a slightly less than proportional relationship with size.

The intradistrict effects of size are positive and small, but statistically significant, suggesting more intradistrict flows for larger districts, which makes intuitive sense. Spatial spillovers from larger districts neighboring the origin district (network origin effects in the table) are negative, but not significant (using the 0.10 level), while larger districts neighboring the destination district are positive and significant. This suggests a competition effect associated with larger neighboring districts, that produces more inflows to destination regions from these larger neighboring districts. The response of teacher flows to district size overall (the total effect) is such that a 10 % increase in the size of the typical district would produce 14 % more flows across the entire network. This includes a small (0.15 %) significant increase in within district flows, a 0.562 % increase of inflows to destination districts districts from neighbors, as well as a 7.28 % increase in outflows from origins and a 6.41 % increase of inflows to destinations.

Teacher salaries (logged) exhibit insignificant origin and destination effects, suggesting these do not impact teacher decisions to move from one school district to another. Higher salaries have a small but significant effect on within district movement of teachers. This is not surprising given that higher salaries are positively correlated with years of experience. The seniority system gives teachers with more years of service preference in filling vacant jobs in other schools within the same district. The origin spillover effects of teacher salary are positive, suggesting a competitive effect where higher salaries in neighboring districts increase outflows

Table 2.6 Effects estimates from the exogenous spatial interaction model

Variable	Coefficient	t-Statistic (p-level)
Origin effects		
Teachers	0.7286	48.1762 (0.0000)
Salary	−0.2529	−1.1592 (0.2464)
Poverty	0.6572	8.6807 (0.0000)
Destination effects		
Teachers	0.6410	42.8701 (0.0000)
Salary	0.0617	0.2789 (0.7803)
Poverty	−0.5106	−7.2483 (0.0000)
Intradistrict effects		
Teachers	0.0149	188.6622 (0.0000)
Salary	0.0069	7.3095 (0.0000)
Poverty	−0.0024	−7.4486 (0.0000)
Network origin effects		
Teachers	−0.0326	−1.4976 (0.1074)
Salary	0.3659	12.1361 (0.0000)
Poverty	−0.2590	−2.8766 (0.0040)
Network destination effects		
Teachers	0.0562	2.6508 (0.0073)
Salary	−0.2036	−6.6438 (0.0000)
Poverty	0.3275	3.7598 (0.0002)
Total effects		
Teachers	1.4081	36.8098 (0.0000)
Salary	0.6611	2.4396 (0.0147)
Poverty	0.2126	1.3473 (0.1779)

from origin districts. Destination spillover effects of salary are negative, suggesting a competitive effect of districts with higher salaries that neighbor the destination decreasing inflows. Given that these effects estimates are elasticities, we can say that the positive impact of origin spillover effects are more important than the negative impact of destination spillover effects.

For the poverty variable, an increase in the (logged) proportion of students in poverty would increase outflows from the origin district, and decrease inflows to a destination district, which makes intuitive sense. The effect of poverty on within district teacher flows is small and negative, but significant. The effect of more poverty in districts neighboring the origin is negative and significant, meaning that inflows from neighboring districts would be smaller in this case. This suggests a teacher retention effect for districts surrounded by those with more students in poverty. The effect of more poverty in districts neighboring the destination is positive and significant, suggesting more inflows to destination districts having neighbors with more students in poverty. This suggests that teachers are more likely to move to a neighboring district from surrounding districts with more students in poverty, a competition effect. The retention and competition effects of poverty in neighboring school districts are reasonably large in magnitude, taking values nearly half the magnitude of origin and destination effects for the poverty variable. It is interesting that the total effect of students in poverty is not significantly different from zero. This suggests that the retention and competition effects are offsetting. One way to view this would be that teachers are needed to fill posts in all schools including those with high proportions of students in poverty.

2.6 Conclusion

We reiterate the point made by LeSage and Thomas-Agnan (2014) and Thomas-Agnan and LeSage (2014) that the structure of explanatory variables used in non-spatial and spatial interaction models is such that we cannot interpret coefficients associated with origin explanatory variables (that we label X_o here) and coefficients from destination explanatory variables (that we label X_d here) as reflecting typical regression partial derivatives $\partial y/\partial X_o$ and $\partial y/\partial X_d$, showing how changes in origin (destination) region characteristics impact flows (on average across the sample of n^2 dyads as is typical of regression estimates). This is because we cannot change characteristics of origin (destination) regions while holding those of destination (origin) regions constant, which is typical of how partial derivatives are viewed. It should be clear that a change in the rth characteristic of a single region i, X_i^r, will produce changes in both X_o, X_d, since by definition $\Delta X_o^r = \iota_n \otimes (X^r + \Delta X_i^r)$, and $\Delta X_d^r = (X^r + \Delta X_i^r) \otimes \iota_n$.

We provide a discussion of exogenous and endogenous spatial interaction model specifications that are each suited to differing applied situations. The argument advanced is that an exogenous specification is most appropriate when characteristics of neighboring regions exert an influence on variation in flows between dyads, but do not produce feedback effects producing changes in the long-run steady state equilibrium of the network of flows. Examples include situations involving temporary or unpredictable events that do not evoke endogenous interaction because of the unpredictability of changes taking place in neighboring regions. In contrast, endogenous interaction specifications are more appropriate for situations where predictable or permanent changes take place in the network structure such that economic agents react to these changes by changing decisions regarding routes of movement for people, commodities, etc.

In addition to setting forth expressions for the true partial derivatives of non-spatial and endogenous spatial interaction models and associated scalar summary measures from LeSage and Thomas-Agnan (2014), we propose new scalar summary measures for the exogenous spatial interaction specification introduced here. An illustration applies the exogenous spatial interaction model to a flow matrix of teacher movements between 67 school districts in the state of Florida.

References

Bolduc D, Laferriere R, Santarossa G (1992) Spatial autoregressive error components in travel flow models. Reg Sci Urban Econ 22(3):371–385
Curry L (1972) A spatial analysis of gravity flows. Reg Stud 6(2):131–147
Curry L, Griffith DA, Sheppard ES (1975) Those gravity parameters again. Reg Stud 9(3):289–296
Fischer MM, Griffith DA (2008) Modeling spatial autocorrelation in spatial interaction data: an application to patent citation data in the European Union. J Reg Sci 48(5):969–989
Fischer MM, Wang J (2011) Spatial data analysis: models, methods and techniques. Springer, Heidelberg
Gourieroux C, Monfort A, Trognon A (1984) Pseudo maximum likelihood methods: applications to Poisson models. Econometrica 52(3):701–720
Griffith DA, Jones KG (1980) Explorations into the relationship between spatial structure and spatial interaction. Environ Plan A 12:187–201
LeSage JP, Pace RK (2008) Spatial econometric modeling of origin-destination flows. J Reg Sci 48(5):941–967
LeSage JP, Pace RK (2009) Introduction to spatial econometrics. Taylor & Francis/CRC Press, Boca Raton, FL
LeSage JP, Thomas-Agnan C (2014) Interpreting spatial econometric origin-destination flow models. J Reg Sci 55(2):188–208
Santos Silva JMC, Tenreyro S (2006) The log of gravity. Rev Econ Stat 88(4):641–658
Santos Silva JMC, Tenreyro S (2010) On the existence of the maximum likelihood estimates for Poisson regression. Econ Lett 107(2):310–312
Santos Silva JMC, Tenreyro S (2011) Further simulation evidence on the performance of the Poisson-PML estimator. Econ Lett 112(2):220–222
Sen AK, Smith TE (1995) Gravity models of spatial interaction behavior. Springer, Heidelberg
Thomas-Agnan C, LeSage JP (2014) Spatial econometric OD-flow models. In: Fischer MM, Nijkamp P (eds) Handbook of regional science. Springer, Berlin, pp 1653–1673

Chapter 3
Constrained Variants of the Gravity Model and Spatial Dependence: Model Specification and Estimation Issues

Daniel A. Griffith and Manfred M. Fischer

Keywords Constrained gravity models • Count data • Patent citation flows • Poisson • Spatial dependence in origin-destination flows • Spatial econometrics • Spatial filtering

JEL Classifications: C13, C31, R15

3.1 Introduction

Traditionally, models that use origin-destination flow data to explain variation in the level of flows between origin and destination locations of interaction across some relevant geographic space are called gravity models,[1] in analogy with Newton's concept of gravity. Locations may be either regions or point units, and spatial interactions relate to movements of various kinds. Examples include not only migration, journey-to-work, traffic, commodity or trade flows, but also flows of less tangible entities such as capital, information and knowledge. By adopting a spatial

This paper has been previously published in the *Journal of Geographical Systems*. Special Issue on "Advances in the Statistical Modelling of Spatial Interaction Data", Vol. 15, Number 3/July 2013, ©Springer-Verlag Berlin Heidelberg, pp. 291–317.

[1]The terms gravity model and spatial interaction model are often used interchangeably. But they are not the same. Spatial interaction models not only include gravity models, but also similar models that have been derived using powerful methods of entropy maximisation from statistical mechanics (Wilson 1967), or utility maximization from economic theory (Niedercorn and Bechdolt 1969), and those based on intervening opportunities which can be derived heuristically.

D.A. Griffith (✉)
University of Texas at Dallas, Richardson, TX, USA
e-mail: dagriffith@utdallas.edu

M.M. Fischer
Vienna University of Economics and Business, Vienna, Austria
e-mail: manfred.fischer@wu.ac.at

R. Patuelli, G. Arbia (eds.), *Spatial Econometric Interaction Modelling*, Advances in Spatial Science, DOI 10.1007/978-3-319-30196-9_3

interaction perspective, attention is focused on interaction patterns at the aggregate rather than the individual level.

Gravity models[2] typically rely on three types of factors to explain mean interaction frequencies: Origin specific variables that characterise the ability of origin locations to produce or generate flows; destination specific variables that attempt to capture the attractiveness of destination locations; and, a separation function that reflects the way spatial separation of origins from destinations constrains or impedes the interaction (Fischer and Wang 2011). At larger scales of geographical inquiry spatial separation might be simply measured in terms of the great circle distance separating an origin from a destination location. In other cases, it might be transportation cost, perceived travel time or any other sensible measure such as political distance, language distance and cultural distance measured in terms of nominal or categorical attributes. One popular example of a separation or deterrence function is the exponential function that leads to gravity models known as exponential gravity models.

Alternative forms of the gravity model can be specified by imposing (exogenous) constraints on the mean interaction frequencies. These model variants include origin and/or destination specific balancing (normalising) factors that act as constraints to ensure that the origin and destination totals for spatial interactions are exactly predicted (see Wilson 1971). The model is said to be doubly constrained if both origin and destination constraints hold for each location. If either the origin or the destination constraints hold the model is singly constrained; otherwise it is unconstrained. It is worth noting that the doubly constrained gravity model has also become known as the trip distribution stage in the four-step transport planning approach.[3] One more recently recognized role of these constraints is their accounting for spatial autocorrelation effects in the geographic distribution attributes across origins and destinations.

The focus in this paper is on singly and doubly constrained exponential gravity model variants for situations involving flows taking the form of counts; for example, counts of persons commuting from home to work locations, or as in the example

[2]For a discussion of problems that plague empirical implementation of regression-based gravity models, and econometric extensions that have recently appeared in the literature, see LeSage and Fischer (2010). These new models replace the conventional assumption of independence among origin-destination flows with formal approaches that allow for spatial dependence in flow magnitudes. The econometric extensions are based on the assumption of a linear relation between the dependent and the independent variables, and this assumes the dependent variable to be normally distributed.

[3]Trip making is viewed as consisting of four components (see, for example, Fischer 2000): trip generation and attraction (the decision to make a trip and how often); trip distribution in a system of traffic zones; modal split (choice of mode of transport); and, trip assignment (choice of route through network). The gravity model is used for trip distribution, but is preceded by trip generation and attraction models that provide independent estimates of locational (zonal) trip origins and attractions that subsequently become the "mass" terms of the gravity model. Thus, the definition of the row and column sums of the predicted trip matrix coincides exactly with the definitions of the respective mass terms.

considered in this paper, the number of patent citations from one region to another. In such cases, current practice is to model origin-destination flow data with Poisson gravity model specifications. Under the assumption that the flows are independently distributed Poisson variables the constrained gravity model variants can be treated as particular cases of a generalised linear model (GLM) with fixed (or random) effects, employing a logarithmic link function and a Poisson mean flow. Maximum likelihood estimates of the model parameters can be achieved using an iterative re-weighted least squares algorithm, as implemented in statistical software packages such as GLIM (Generalised Linear Iterative Modelling).

Flows, however, are not strictly independent. Spatial (or network) dependence[4] is more likely than spatial independence when considering origin-destination flows. Spatial dependence in a flow setting refers to a situation where flows from nearby locations (either origins or destinations) are similar in magnitude. A failure to incorporate spatial dependence in model specifications leads to biased parameter estimates and incorrect conclusions. Eigenvector spatial filtering—described in Griffith (2003) for conventional regression models—offers an approach to dealing with spatial dependence in constrained gravity model variants. This approach relies on the decomposition of a spatial weight matrix into eigenvalues and eigenvectors and then uses a subset of the eigenvectors as additional explanatory variables in the singly and doubly constrained gravity model specifications to reduce potential bias in parameter estimates. A virtue of this approach is that existing software can be applied for the case of spatial dependence in constrained model variants involving flows taking the form of counts.

The purpose of this paper is twofold: first, to establish theoretical connections between the constrained gravity model versions with balancing factors, fixed effects represented by binary location specific indicator variables, and random effects; and second, to illustrate these connections with an empirical example while accounting for spatial dependence among flows during estimation. Fulfilling these goals reveals that fixed and random effects are identical and equal to the logarithm of the entropy maximisation derived factors, except for slight rounding/algorithm-convergence errors. This finding is the outcome of an equivalency between assigning a single fixed effects indicator variable to each origin/destination on the one hand, and estimating a single random effects value for an origin/destination while treating the corresponding destinations/origins as repeated measures, on the other. As with the unconstrained gravity model variant, adjusting for spatial dependence in origin-destination flows reduces bias in parameter estimates and improves model performance.

The rest of the paper is organised as follows. Section 3.2 describes unconstrained and constrained classes of the gravity model with a focus on doubly and singly constrained model variants that rely on a multiplicative adjustment scheme to

[4]Spatial dependence is also known as network autocorrelation (see Black 1992; Chun 2008; Griffith 2009; Chun and Griffith 2011) even though there are similar differences between both as between spatial dependence and spatial autocorrelation in general.

enforce satisfactorily the conservation rule. Section 3.3 presents the counterpart Poisson specifications that interpret/predict the level of flows as dependent on not only the explanatory variables (and the associated coefficient estimates), but also origin and destination specific effects coefficients. Section 3.4 describes spatial filtering as a way of filtering the sample origin-destination data for spatial dependence (i.e., transferring spatial autocorrelation effects from residuals to the mean/intercept parameter) in an effort to mimic independent data amenable to standard Poisson regression estimation procedures. Section 3.5 continues to establish theoretical connections between balancing factors, fixed effects and random effects (spatially filtered) model specifications. The results are illustrated in Sect. 3.6 with an empirical example involving knowledge flows between 257 European regions resulting in $257^2 = 66{,}049$ flow dyads. Section 3.7 concludes the paper.

3.2 Unconstrained and Constrained Classes of Gravity Models: The Classical View

Gravity models that describe mean interaction frequencies in a system of n locations can be written[5] as

$$E\left(Y_{ij}\right) = K_{ij}\, U_i\, V_j f\left(d_{ij}\right) \tag{3.1}$$

where Y_{ij} $(i, j = 1, \ldots, n)$ is a random variable denoting the level of flows from origin location i $(i = 1, \ldots, n)$ to destination location j $(j = 1, \ldots, n)$, U_i and V_j are appropriate origin and destination specific factors or functions reflecting locational propensities to emit or attract interactions, $f(d_{ij})$ is a separation function of some inter-location measure d that separates origin i from destination j, and K_{ij} is an origin-destination specific constant of proportionality, or scaling factor, which reduces to a constant scaling factor K for the unconstrained gravity model specification (which then is accompanied by attaching exponents of other than one to U_i and V_j). The role of this origin-destination specific constant of proportionality in the gravity model equation depends on how extensively the conservation rule (Ledent 1985) is enforced in the system of locations. Four alternative cases may be distinguished, giving rise to equally many classes of gravity models.

A gravity model is called unconstrained if the conservation principle is ignored altogether so that

$$K_{ij} = K \tag{3.2}$$

[5]An alternative formulation to that given in Eq. (3.1) is $Y_{ij} = K_{ij}\, U_i\, V_j f\left(d_{ij}\right) \eta_{ij} + \varepsilon_{ij}$ where ε_{ij} reflects the sample error and η_{ij} the specification error. In this case, the stochastic nature of Y_{ij} derives from assumptions made about the stochastic nature of ε_{ij} and η_{ij}.

where K is a constant scaling factor independent of all origins and destinations. If $Y_{\bullet\bullet}$ denotes the total number of flows in the spatial system, then

$$K = Y_{\bullet\bullet}\left[\sum_{\substack{i=1\\ i\neq j}}^{n}\sum_{j=1}^{n}U_iV_jf\left(d_{ij}\right)\right]^{-1} \tag{3.3}$$

where the summation is over the range $i = 1,\ldots,n$ and $j = 1,\ldots,n$. Although Eq. (3.1) has been developed by analogy with Newton's gravity equation, Isard (1960), and Sen and Smith (1995) developed versions of the unconstrained model using a probabilistic approach.

At the other extreme of the spectrum is the doubly constrained case of spatial interaction that refers to a situation in which the conservation principle is enforced from both the viewpoint of origin and destination locations. The origin-destination specific constant of proportionality, K_{ij}, now depends on both origins and destinations. For simplicity, it is generally assumed[6] that

$$K_{ij} = A_i\, B_j \tag{3.4}$$

where the origin and destination specific constants, A_i and B_j, called balancing factors, are solutions of the equation system (Wilson 1967)

$$A_i = Y_{i\bullet}\left[U_i\sum_{\substack{j=1\\ j\neq i}}^{n}B_j\,V_jf\left(d_{ij}\right)\right]^{-1} \tag{3.5}$$

$$B_j = Y_{\bullet j}\left[V_j\sum_{\substack{i=1\\ i\neq j}}^{n}A_i\,U_if\left(d_{ij}\right)\right]^{-1}. \tag{3.6}$$

These balancing factors act as constraints to ensure that the estimated inflows $\hat{Y}_{\bullet j}$ for $j = 1,\ldots,n$ and outflows $\hat{Y}_{i\bullet}$ for $i = 1,\ldots,n$ equal the observed inflow and outflow totals, respectively. Such doubly (or attraction-production) constrained models have

[6]The multiplicative form of the balancing factors A_i and B_j (Wilson 1967) ensures mathematical tractability in searching for an adequate estimation procedure. Alternatively, Tobler (1983) suggests an additive adjustment scheme, $K_{ij} = A_i + B_j$, to enforce satisfactorily the conservation rule. Ledent (1985) introduces a general functional form that subsumes both the multiplicative (Wilson) and the additive (Tobler) variants.

been extensively used as trip distribution models in transport modelling, and many variants of this model form exist for describing journey-to-work interactions.

Between these two extreme cases of unconstrained and doubly constrained spatial interaction lie many models that are subject to some constraints but not to others. Two important classes can be identified: the origin (or alternatively called production) constrained gravity model, and the destination (or alternatively called attraction) constrained gravity model. In the production constrained case the conservation principle is enforced from the viewpoint of origin locations[7] only. Hence

$$K_{ij} = A_i. \tag{3.7}$$

A_i is a factor dependent on the location of an origin, and is called an origin specific balancing factor. If $Y_{i\bullet}$ denotes the total number of outflows from location i,

$$A_i = Y_{i\bullet}\left[U_i \sum_{\substack{j=1 \\ j\neq i}}^{n} V_j f\left(d_{ij}\right)\right]^{-1}. \tag{3.8}$$

The origin constrained gravity model is useful in situations where the outflow totals are known or can be exogenously predicted for each origin location in the system. For an instructive example see Haynes and Fotheringham (1984, pp. 60–62).

The attraction constrained case of spatial interaction enforces the conservation principle from the viewpoint of destination locations. Thus

$$K_{ij} = B_j \tag{3.9}$$

where B_j is a factor dependent on the destination location. If $Y_{\bullet j}$ denotes the total number of inflows into location j,

$$B_j = Y_{\bullet j}\left[V_i \sum_{\substack{i=1 \\ i\neq j}}^{n} U_i f\left(d_{ij}\right)\right]^{-1}. \tag{3.10}$$

This model variant can be used to forecast total outflows from origin locations. Such a situation might arise, for example, in forecasting the effects of locating a new industrial park within a metropolitan area. The number of people to be

[7]In the origin constrained and the destination constrained models presented here, the constraints to which these models are subject refer to the full set of n origin or n destination locations. But it is possible to develop models that are only constrained over certain subsets of locations. Such models, which are not considered in this paper, may be found in Wilson (1970).

employed in the new development area is known, and the destination constrained gravity model can be used to forecast the demand for housing in particular locations of the metropolitan area that will result from the new employment (Haynes and Fotheringham 1984).

The models presented in Eqs. (3.1)–(3.10) are in a generalised form and no mention has yet been made to the particular set of parameters characterising such gravity models. Although the balancing factors are sometimes referred to as parameters, in this paper the term parameter is restricted to those constants that must be estimated statistically, rather than to those constants that imply the accounting constraints placed on the model.

Many different model formulations can be obtained from Eq. (3.1), despite its structural simplicity (see Baxter 1983). U_i and V_j can be treated as completely known, as parameters to be estimated (see Cesario 1973), or as simple power functions of some known variables (see Fotheringham and O'Kelly 1989). The separation function constitutes the very core of gravity models.[8] In this study we use the multivariate exponential deterrence function

$$f\left(d_{ij}\right) = \exp\left(-\theta\, d_{ij}\right) \tag{3.11}$$

in which d denotes a multivariate separation measure with an associated sensitivity parameter θ. This specification of the spatial separation function leads to the following three variants of the gravity model: the doubly constrained variant

$$E\left(Y_{ij}\right) = A_i\, B_j\, U_i\, V_j\, \exp\left(-\theta\, d_{ij}\right) \tag{3.12}$$

$$A_i = Y_{i\bullet}\left[U_i \sum_{\substack{j=1 \\ j\neq i}}^{n} B_j\, V_j \exp\left(-\theta d_{ij}\right)\right]^{-1} \tag{3.13}$$

$$B_j = Y_{\bullet j}\left[V_j \sum_{\substack{i=1 \\ i\neq j}}^{n} A_i\, U_i \exp\left(-\theta d_{ij}\right)\right]^{-1} \tag{3.14}$$

the origin constrained variant

$$E\left(Y_{ij}\right) = A_i\, U_i\, V_j\, \exp\left(-\theta\, d_{ij}\right) \tag{3.15}$$

[8]The notion that separation functions in conventional gravity models work to effectively capture spatial dependence in origin-destination flows has long been challenged. Griffith (2007) provides an historical review of the regional science literature about this topic in which he credits Curry (1972) as the first to conceptualise the problem of spatial dependence in flows.

$$A_i = Y_{i\bullet}\left[U_i\sum_{\substack{j=1\\ j\neq i}}^{n} V_j \exp\left(-\theta d_{ij}\right)\right]^{-1} \tag{3.16}$$

and, the destination constrained variant

$$E\left(Y_{ij}\right) = B_j\ U_i\ V_j\ \exp\left(-\theta\ d_{ij}\right) \tag{3.17}$$

$$B_j = Y_{\bullet j}\left[V_j\sum_{\substack{i=1\\ i\neq j}}^{n} U_i \exp\left(-\theta d_{ij}\right)\right]^{-1}. \tag{3.18}$$

The central concern in this paper is with the problem of estimating the model parameter θ rather than with the problem of determining appropriate values for the balancing factors.[9] A solution to this latter problem, for example in the case of Eqs. (3.12)–(3.14), involves using an iterative biproportional adjustment technique, known as the Deming-Stephan-Furness procedure[10] (see Sen and Smith 1995, p. 374). As Evans (1970) shows, convergence to a unique set of values for A_i and B_j is guaranteed for any non-trivial set of starting values.

3.3 Poisson Versions of the Constrained Gravity Models

Flows often take the form of counts such as numbers of migrants moving from one location to another. In such situations a common assumption is that the Y_{ij} $(i, j = 1, \ldots, n)$ follow independent[11] Poisson distributions,[12] $Y_{ij} \sim \mathcal{P}(\mu_{ij})$, where μ_{ij} is equated with the right hand side of Eq. (3.1). The mean and the variance of the distribution are equal to μ_{ij}. The Poisson specifications of the gravity model

[9]The constrained gravity model variants are intrinsically non-linear in their parameters, and thus the application of linear methods leads to biased estimates of these parameters.

[10]In the economics literature it is often called the RAS procedure.

[11]Independence means that the individual flows from origin i to destination j are independent from each other, and that origin-destination flows between any pair of locations are independent from flows between any other pair of locations.

[12]Closely related to this assumption are the assumptions that the set of observations for each origin location has a multinomial distribution, say $\mathcal{MN}(Y_{i1}, Y_{i2}, \ldots, Y_{in}; Y_{i\bullet})$, or that the set of all observations has a multinomial distribution $\mathcal{MN}(Y_{i1}, Y_{i2}, \ldots, Y_{nn}; Y_{\bullet\bullet})$, where $Y_{i\bullet}$ is the total flow from origin location i, $Y_{\bullet\bullet}$ is the overall flow, and n is the number of origin and destination locations. These multinomial distributions can be generated by assuming that the Y_{ij} $(i, j = 1, \ldots, n)$ are independent Poisson random variables sampled subject to the origin totals $Y_{i\bullet}$, or the overall total $Y_{\bullet\bullet}$, being fixed (Bishop et al. 1975).

variants interpret/predict the level of flows as dependent on not only the explanatory variables (and their associated coefficient estimates), but also origin and destination specific effects coefficients. The fixed effects version of the three constrained model variants of the gravity model can be described as in Eqs. (3.19)–(3.21), respectively.

$$E\left(Y_{ij}\right) = \mu_{ij} = U_i\ V_j \exp\left[\alpha + \sum_{h=1}^{n-1} I_{iho}\ \beta_{ho} + \sum_{k=1}^{n-1} I_{jkd}\ \beta_{kd} - \theta\ d_{ij}\right] \tag{3.19}$$

$$E\left(Y_{ij}\right) = \mu_{ij} = U_i\ \exp\left[\alpha + \sum_{h=1}^{n-1} I_{iho}\ \beta_{ho} - \theta\ d_{ij}\right] \tag{3.20}$$

$$E\left(Y_{ij}\right) = \mu_{ij} = V_j\ \exp\left[\alpha + \sum_{k=1}^{n-1} I_{jkd}\ \beta_{kd} - \theta\ d_{ij}\right] \tag{3.21}$$

with origin h and destination k specific effects coefficients $\exp(\beta_{ho})$ and $\exp(\beta_{kd})$, and corresponding binary indicator variables[13] I_{iho} and I_{jkd} for origins i and destinations j respectively,

$$I_{iho} = \begin{cases} 1 & \text{if } i = h \\ 0 & \text{otherwise} \end{cases} \tag{3.22}$$

$$I_{jkd} = \begin{cases} 1 & \text{if } j = k \\ 0 & \text{otherwise.} \end{cases} \tag{3.23}$$

The fixed effects parameters inflate or deflate the level of flows, depending on whether they are positive or negative. Of note is that one of the origin and one of the destination specific effects coefficients, β_{no} and β_{nd}, have to be set to zero to avoid perfect collinearity in the specifications, and these values are absorbed in the intercept term α.

The most direct approach to estimating the models is with maximum likelihood techniques. The likelihood function to be maximised is proportional to

$$\mathcal{L} = \prod_{i,j} \mu_{ij}^{y_{ij}} \exp\left(-\mu_{ij}\right) \tag{3.24}$$

[13]One advantage of the use of origin/destination indicator variables in a Poisson regression specification is that they yield individual rather than a single aggregate standard error, and null hypothesis probability estimates for each of the individual values in the two sets of balancing factors. One disadvantage is the amount of time necessary to estimate a GLM containing $2n - 2$ indicator variables.

where y_{ij} is the realisation of the random variable Y_{ij}. The Poisson distribution is a member of the exponential family of distributions. Hence parameter estimation can be achieved via GLMs (see McCullagh and Nelder 1983) so that the constrained gravity model variants (3.19)–(3.21) can be treated simply as particular cases of a GLM with a logarithmic link function[14] and a Poisson mean. Then for the doubly constrained case, for example, we get

$$\log\left[E\left(Y_{ij}\right)\right] = \log \mu_{ij} = \log U_i + \log V_j + \alpha + \sum_{h=1}^{n-1} I_{iho}\,\beta_{ko} + \sum_{k=1}^{n-1} I_{jkd}\,\beta_{kd} - \theta\, d_{ij} \tag{3.25}$$

where the term $\left(\log U_i + \log V_j\right)$ is included in the estimation procedure as an offset variable (that is, its coefficient is fixed to equal one).

The maximum likelihood estimates can be derived by means of an iterative re-weighted least squares procedure[15] that is implemented in many statistical software packages such as GLIM. A convenient property of the Poisson assumption along with the log-linear functional form assumed for μ_{ij} is that the resulting maximum likelihood estimates guarantee that the fitted flows $\hat{Y}_{ij}$ satisfy relationships that are consistent with the desirable origin and/or destination constraints of spatial interaction[16] (see Kirby 1974; Davies and Guy 1987, and Bailey and Gatrell 1995, pp. 353–354 for details). Hence, there is no need to modify standard maximum likelihood parameter estimation to incorporate explicit constraints on predicted flows. The goodness-of-fit of GLMs is assessed on the basis of the log-likelihood ratio statistic, known as the deviance.

Fixed effects model specifications allow the unobserved location specific effects to be correlated with the explanatory variables. If the individual effects are strictly uncorrelated with the regressors, then it might be appropriate to model the location specific constant terms as randomly distributed across the locations. The role of random effects terms in this context may be twofold: first, supporting inferences beyond the specific fixed values of covariates employed in an analysis, and, second, accounting for correlation in a non-random sample of data being analysed, in part due to missing variables, for which they function as a surrogate. Random effects may be used if the values of independent variables—which were not deliberately selected

[14]The logarithmic link function is best thought of as being an exponential conditional mean function.

[15]McCullagh and Nelder (1983) prove that the procedure converges to the maximum likelihood solution. Note that zero observed flows do not require any special treatment.

[16]The equivalence of maximum likelihood estimation with the Poisson assumption and the entropy maximisation solution for a doubly constrained gravity model with origin and destination specific balancing factors is well known (see Wilson and Kirkby 1980, p. 310). In the latter case, parameter estimation of a model such as Eq. (3.1) is obtained by maximising an objective function subject to sets of constraints on the origin and destination totals in combination with some constraint on a general measure of spatial separation in the system of locations (Baxter 1982).

by an experimenter—are thought to be a small subset of all possible values to which inferences are to be made, to account for heterogeneity/overdispersion/inter-observation correlation, or to handle observations that are not obtained by simple random sampling but come from a cluster or multi-level sampling design.

The random effects counterparts[17] of the fixed effects model specifications (3.19)–(3.21) may be formulated as in Eqs. (3.26)–(3.28).

$$E\left(Y_{ij}\right) = \mu_{ij} = U_i\, V_j \exp\left[\alpha + \xi_{io} + \xi_{jd} - \theta\, d_{ij}\right] \tag{3.26}$$

$$E\left(Y_{ij}\right) = \mu_{ij} = U_i\, \exp\left[\alpha + \xi_{io} - \theta\, d_{ij}\right] \tag{3.27}$$

$$E\left(Y_{ij}\right) = \mu_{ij} = V_j \exp\left[\alpha + \xi_{jd} - \theta\, d_{ij}\right] \tag{3.28}$$

with zero mean normally distributed origin and destination specific random effects[18] ξ_{io} and ξ_{jd}.

Finally, note that there is a constant of proportionality term, α, in the preceding Poisson gravity model specifications. This term is made explicit because the balancing factors that can be calibrated—as already mentioned – with the Deming-Stephan-Furness procedure, have a constant factored from them. This factorisation is achieved by: (i) setting the maximum A_i and/or the maximum B_j values to one at each iteration step in the procedure; (ii) arbitrarily removing one of the origin and/or destination indicator variables in the fixed effects specifications; and, (iii) imposing a mean of zero on the random effects prior distribution. This is equivalent to rewriting Eq. (3.12) as $E(Y_{ij}) = K\, A_i\, B_j\, U_i\, V_j\, \exp(-\theta\ d_{ij})$, where K is a constant.

3.4 Accounting for Spatial Dependence in the Model Specifications

origin-destination flows are not independent (Bolduc et al. 1995; Tiefelsdorf 2003), because flows are fundamentally spatial in nature (LeSage and Pace 2009). Spatial dependence in flows relates to correlations among flows between locations that are neighbouring a given origin-destination pair of locations.[19] Hence, a failure

---

[17]Whether the random effects model variants are appropriate model specifications in spatial research remains controversial. When the random effects gravity models are implemented, the spatial units of observation should be representative of a larger population, and n should potentially be able to get to infinity (see Elhorst 2010 for more details on this issue).

[18]Origin/destination specific spatial dependence in the random effects estimates motivated the gravity model set forth in LeSage et al. (2007) that formally incorporates spatially structured random effects in place of the zero mean, normally distributed independent random effects.

[19]This correlation differs from that latent in the geographic distributions of the origin and destination variables that are reflected in the balancing factors. Pace et al. (2011) show that spatial

to account for spatial dependence in model specifications may lead to biased parameter estimates and incorrect conclusions. One way to overcome this problem is by incorporating spatial dependence into the Poisson versions of the constrained gravity model variants.[20] Another way to address spatial dependence in origin-destination flows involves eigenvector spatial filtering[21] (see Chun 2008; Fischer and Griffith 2008; Griffith 2009; Chun and Griffith 2011). Eigenvector spatial filtering relies on a spectral decomposition[22] of an N-by-N spatial weight matrix W into eigenvalues and eigenvectors, and then uses a subset of these eigenvectors as additional explanatory variables in the model specifications.

Spatial filtering used here in this paper relies on a spectral decomposition of a transformed spatial weight matrix MWM, where W is an N-by-N spatial weight matrix[23]

$$W = W_n \otimes W_n \tag{3.29}$$

that captures spatial dependence between flows from locations neighbouring both the origins and destinations, labelled origin-to-destination dependence by LeSage and Pace (2008). W_n is a row-stochastic n-by-n spatial weight matrix that describes spatial neighbourhood relationships between the n locations. This matrix has—by convention—zeros in the main diagonal, and non-negative elements in the off-diagonal cells. Specifically the (i,j)th element of W_n is greater than zero if i and j are neighbouring[24] locations. $\otimes$ denotes the Kronecker product. M is the N-by-N

dependence in the explanatory variables decreases the ability of filtering to produce unbiased regression parameter estimates.

[20]In the fixed effects case of the doubly constrained gravity model, for example, this takes the form

$$E\left(Y_{ij}\right) = \mu_{ij} = U_i\, V_j \exp\left[\alpha + \sum_{h=1}^{n-1} I_{iho}\, \beta_{ho} + \sum_{k=1}^{n-1} I_{jkd}\, \beta_{kd} - \theta\, d_{ij}\right] \prod_{j \neq i}^{n} E\left(Y_{ij}\right)^{\rho W_{ij}}$$

where W_{ij} is the (i,j)th element of an N-by-N spatial weight matrix W and ρ is a scalar parameter that governs the degree of spatial dependence in origin-destination flows. Lambert et al. (2010) set forth a two-step maximum likelihood estimation approach for a spatial autoregressive Poisson model for count data which would need to be extended to the case of flows involving N observations.

[21]This is an especially valuable approach in situations where the flows are count data, because conventional spatial regression models and software tools are less developed for this data type.

[22]We assume that W is similar to a symmetric matrix so that it has real eigenvalues. If W is not symmetric, then $\frac{1}{2}\,(W + W')$, which is symmetric by construction, may be used.

[23]If intralocational flows are excluded from an analysis, the N-by-N spatial weight matrix reduces to an $n(n–1)$-by-$n(n–1)$ one, only marginally impacting upon these eigenvectors when $n > 100$.

[24]Neighbours may be defined using contiguity or measures of spatial proximity such as cardinal distance (for example, in terms of transportation costs) or ordinal distance (for example, the six nearest neighbours). In the illustrative example in Sect. 3.6, we use a binary contiguity matrix W_n to define W.

projection matrix

$$M = I - \iota\, \iota' \frac{1}{N} \tag{3.30}$$

where I is the N-by-N identity matrix, and ι the N-by-1 vector of ones.

The approach focuses on capturing correlations among flows with a spatial filter that is constructed as a linear combination of eigenvectors extracted from the matrix MWM. The eigenvalues scaled by $N/(\iota'\, W_n\, \iota)$ directly indicate Moran's I coefficient values of map patterns that are represented by the corresponding eigenvectors (Tiefelsdorf and Boots 1995). The first eigenvector, say E_1, is the set of real numbers that has the largest Moran's I value achievable by any set of real numbers for the spatial dependence structure defined by the spatial weight matrix W. The second eigenvector, E_2, is the set of real numbers that has the largest achievable Moran's I value by any set that is orthogonal to and uncorrelated with E_1. The third eigenvector is the third such set of values, and so on through E_N, the set of real numbers that has the largest negative Moran's I value achievable by any set that is orthogonal to and uncorrelated with the preceding $(N - 1)$ eigenvectors. As such, these eigenvectors furnish distinct map pattern descriptions of latent spatial dependence in the origin-destination flow variable because they are both orthogonal and uncorrelated. Their Moran's Is corresponding eigenvalues index the nature and degree of spatial dependence portrayed by each eigenvector (Tiefelsdorf and Boots 1995), which can be standardised by the largest Moran's I value, I_{max}.

The construction of a spatial filter involves a stepwise selection process. Griffith (2003) suggests identifying a set of candidate eigenvectors first, based on a critical value for the corresponding eigenvalues, a value that indicates a specific minimum spatial autocorrelation level[25] such as 0.5 measured in terms of the statistic I/I_{max}. From these candidate eigenvectors, a subset of Q eigenvectors then can be selected with standard model selection criteria such as the Akaike information criterion. In the doubly constrained case of spatial interaction, for example, this yields the following spatial filter versions of the model specifications (3.12), (3.19) and (3.26), respectively:

$$E\left(Y_{ij}\right) = A_i\, B_j\, U_i\, V_j \exp\left(\alpha - \theta\, d_{ij} + \sum_{q=1}^{Q} E_q\, \phi_q\right) \tag{3.31}$$

$$E\left(Y_{ij}\right) = \mu_{ij} = U_i\, V_j \exp\left[\alpha + \sum_{h=1}^{n-1} I_{iho}\, \beta_{ho} + \sum_{k=1}^{n-1} I_{jkd}\, \beta_{kd} - \theta\, d_{ij} + \sum_{q=1}^{Q} E_q\, \phi_q\right] \tag{3.32}$$

[25]The criterion $I/I_{max} = 0.5$ suggests a restriction of the search over eigenvectors with moderate to high spatial autocorrelation.

$$E\left(Y_{ij}\right) = \mu_{ij} = U_i\, V_j \exp\left[\alpha + \xi_{io} + \xi_{jd} - \theta\, d_{ij} + \sum_{q=1}^{Q} E_q\, \phi_q\right] \tag{3.33}$$

where E_q denotes the qth eigenvector and ϕ_q its associated coefficient. The term $\exp\left(\sum_q E_q\, \phi_q\right)$ is called a spatial filter.

The approach provides a simple way of filtering the sample flow data for spatial dependence in an effort to mimic independent data amenable to standard estimation procedures, and hence to reduce potential bias in the estimation of coefficients associated with the explanatory variables. Spatial filtering, however, also faces computational challenges in situations involving a large sample of observations.[26]

3.5 Equivalency Relationships Between the Balancing Factors, Fixed Effects, and Random Effects

This section compares the three different model variants of constrained spatial interaction with each other. First, attention is shifted toward comparisons between model specifications with balancing factors and with fixed effects, and then between model specifications with balancing factors and with random effects, for both the doubly and singly constrained cases of spatial interaction.

3.5.1 Comparisons Between Balancing Factors and Fixed Effects

The first comparison is between the doubly constrained model with balancing factors and its corresponding fixed effects model specification, and hence focuses on the relationship between Eqs. (3.31) and (3.32).

Theorem 1 *If $Y_{ij} \sim$ Poisson with mean $\mu_{ij} = \exp(\log U_i + \log V_j + \alpha + \alpha_{io} + \alpha_{jd} - \theta\, d_{ij} + + \sum_q E_q\, \phi_q)$, where α denotes the global Poisson regression intercept term, α_{io} the Poisson regression origin location intercept term, and α_{jd} the Poisson regression destination location specific intercept term, then the balancing factors for the doubly constrained gravity model are given by $A_i = \exp(\alpha_{io})$ and $B_j = \exp(\alpha_{jd})$.*

[26] Pace et al. (2011) demonstrate how using iterative eigenvalue routines on sparse matrices such as W can make filtering feasible for data sets involving a million or more observations, and empirically estimate an operation count on the order of $N^{1.1}$.

Proof Because Eqs. (3.31) and (3.32) posit the expectation for the same random variable, Y_{ij}, for $i,j = 1, \ldots, n$

$$A_i\, B_j\, U_i\, V_j \exp\left(\alpha - \theta\, d_{ij} + \sum_{q=1}^{Q} E_q\, \phi_q\right)$$

$$= U_i\, V_j \exp\left(\alpha + \beta_{io} + \beta_{jd} - \theta\, d_{ij} + \sum_{q=1}^{Q} E_q\, \phi_q\right) \tag{3.34}$$

$$A_i\, B_j = \exp\,\left(\beta_{io} + \beta_{jd}\right) = \exp\,\left(\beta_{io}\right)\, \exp\,\left(\beta_{jd}\right) \tag{3.35}$$

$$\therefore A_i = \exp\,\left(\beta_{io}\right) = \exp\left(\alpha_{io}\right)\ \text{ for all } i = 1, \ldots, n \tag{3.36}$$

$$B_j = \exp\left(\beta_{jd}\right) = \exp\left(\alpha_{jd}\right)\ \text{ for all } j = 1, \ldots, n\ \square \tag{3.37}$$

Remarks The equivalencies $\alpha_{io} = \beta_{io}$ and $\alpha_{jd} = \beta_{jd}$ relate these results not only to the doubly, but also to the singly constrained cases. Furthermore, exp(α) is the constant of proportionality, which frequently is set to one (i.e., $\alpha = 0$) for the traditional entropy maximising solution, and other than one for the conventional gravity model solution. Allowing α to deviate from one in the Deming-Stephan-Furness procedure helps to stabilise convergence for large flow matrices, and may be achieved by setting the largest A_i and the largest B_j values to one during each iteration. This adjustment is equivalent to setting one of the $\alpha_{io} = \beta_{io}$ and one of the $\alpha_{jd} = \beta_{jd}$ to zero in the fixed effects specification in order to avoid perfect multicollinearity between the location specific indicator variables and the global mean (which is a coefficient times an n-by-1 vector of ones). Estimates of β_{io} and β_{jd} are obtained with Poisson regression.

This result relates the log-balancing factors, log(A_i) and log(B_j), for the doubly constrained gravity model to their counterpart origin and destination fixed effects, α_{io} and α_{jd}. Hence fixed effects take on a particular meaning because they can be interpreted as balancing factors. Cesario (1977) characterises the meaning of the origin and destination balancing factors as follows: $1/A_i$ indexes the accessibility of all destination locations vis-à-vis origin i, and $1/B_j$ indexes the accessibility of all origin locations vis-à-vis destination j.

The next comparisons are between the model specifications with balancing factors and fixed effects in the singly constrained cases of spatial interaction. To this end, **Theorem 1** suggests the following two corollaries pertaining to the singly constrained spatial filter model specifications.

Corollary 1 *If* $Y_{ij} \sim$ *Poisson with mean* $\mu_{ij} = \exp(\log U_i + \alpha + \alpha_{io} - \theta\ d_{ij} + \sum_q E_q\, \phi_q)$, *where* α *denotes the global Poisson regression intercept term, and* α_{io} *the Poisson regression origin location specific intercept term, then the balancing* *factors for the origin constrained gravity model are given by* $A_i = \exp(\alpha_{io})$ *for* $i = 1, \ldots, n$.

Corollary 2 *If* $Y_{ij} \sim$ *Poisson with mean* $\mu_{ij} = \exp(\log V_j + \alpha + \alpha_{jd} - \theta\ d_{ij} + \sum_q E_q\ \phi_q)$, *where* α *denotes the global Poisson regression intercept term, and* α_{jd} *the Poisson regression destination location specific intercept term, then the balancing factors for the destination constrained gravity model are given by* $B_j = \exp(\alpha_{jd})$ *for* $j = 1, \ldots, n$.

These two corollaries relate the log-balancing factors for the singly constrained gravity models to their counterpart origin or destination fixed effect model specifications.

3.5.2 Comparisons Between Balancing Factors and Random Effects

Finally, comparisons can be made between the preceding results and the random effects model specifications. In this context, a specification includes ξ_{io} and/or ξ_{jd}, normal random variables, which respectively denote the random effects for origin *i* and/or destination *j*, whose stochastic quantities are added to the global intercept term. The next theorem relates to the relationship between a doubly constrained model with balancing factors and its corresponding random effects model specification, and hence focuses on the relationship between Eqs. (3.31) and (3.33).

Theorem 2 *If* $Y_{ij} \sim$ *Poisson with mean* $\mu_{ij} = \exp(\log U_i + \log V_j + \alpha + \xi_{io} + \xi_{jd} - \theta\ d_{ij} + \sum_q E_q\ \phi_q)$, *where* α *denotes the global Poisson regression intercept term,* ξ_{io} *the Poisson regression origin location random effect, and* ξ_{jd} *the Poisson regression destination location random effect, such that* $\xi_{io} \sim \mathcal{N}(0, \sigma^2_{\xi_o})$ *and* $\xi_{jd} \sim \mathcal{N}(0, \sigma^2_{\xi_d})$, *where* $\sigma^2_{\xi_o}$ *and* $\sigma^2_{\xi_d}$ *denote the origin and the destination location random effects variances respectively, then the balancing factors for the doubly constrained gravity model are given by* $A_i = \exp(\xi_{io})$ *for* $i = 1, \ldots, n$, *and* $B_j = \exp(\xi_{jd})$ *for* $j = 1, \ldots, n$.

Proof Equation (3.33) implies

$$\log\left[E\left(Y_{ij}\right)\right] = \log \mu_{ij} = \log U_i + \log V_j + \alpha + \xi_{io} + \xi_{jd} - \theta\ d_{ij} + \sum_{q=1}^{Q} E_q\ \phi_q. \tag{3.38}$$

Because Eqs. (3.31) and (3.38) posit the expectation for the same random variable, Y_{ij}, for $i, j = 1, \ldots, n$

$$A_i\, B_j\, U_i\, V_j \exp\left(\alpha - \theta\, d_{ij} + \sum_{q=1}^{Q} E_q\, \phi_q\right)$$

$$= U_i\, V_j \exp\left(\alpha + \xi_{io} + \xi_{jd} - \theta\, d_{ij} + \sum_{q=1}^{Q} E_q\, \phi_q\right) \tag{3.39}$$

$$A_i B_j = \exp(\xi_{io} + \xi_{jd}) = \exp(\xi_{io})\, \exp(\xi_{jd}) \tag{3.40}$$

$\therefore A_i = \exp(\xi_{io})$ for all $i = 1, \ldots, n$ and $B_j = \exp(\xi_{jd})$ for all $j = 1, \ldots, n$ ■

Remarks Both ξ_{io} and ξ_{jd} have a mean of zero, which is achieved by having the global mean, α, in the model specification. In other words, the individual origin and destination location means deviate from the global mean by random quantities. **Theorems 1** and **2** together imply: $A_i = \exp(\xi_{io}) = \exp(\beta_{io}) = \exp(\alpha_{io})$ for all $i = 1, \ldots, n$, and $B_j = \exp(\xi_{jd}) = \exp(\beta_{jd}) = \exp(\alpha_{jd})$ for all $j = 1, \ldots, n$. Estimates of ξ_{io} and ξ_{jd} are obtained by integrating them out of the likelihood function.

Singly constrained models are obtained by setting $\xi_{jd} = 0$ for all j, yielding the origin constrained specification, or $\xi_{io} = 0$ for all i, yielding the destination constrained specification. Accordingly, **Theorem 2** suggests the following two corollaries pertaining to the singly constrained model specifications.

Corollary 3 *If* $Y_{ij} \sim$ *Poisson with mean* $\mu_{ij} = \exp(\log U_i + \alpha + \xi_{io} - \theta\, d_{ij} + \sum_q E_q\, \phi_q)$, *where* α *denotes the global Poisson regression intercept term, and* ξ_{io} *the Poisson regression origin location random effect, such that* $\xi_{io} \sim \mathcal{N}(0, \sigma^2_{\xi_o})$, *where* $\sigma^2_{\xi_o}$ *denotes the origin location finite random effects variance, then the balancing factors for the origin constrained gravity model are given by* $A_i = \exp(\xi_{io})$ *for* $i = 1, \ldots, n$.

Corollary 4 *If* $Y_{ij} \sim$ *Poisson with mean* $\mu_{ij} = \exp(\log V_j + \alpha + \xi_{jd} - \theta\, d_{ij} + \sum_q E_q\, \phi_q)$, *where* α *denotes the global Poisson regression intercept term, and* ξ_{jd} *the Poisson regression destination location random effect, such that* $\xi_{id} \sim \mathcal{N}(0, \sigma^2_{\xi_d})$, *where* $\sigma^2_{\xi_d}$ *denotes the destination location finite random effects variance, then the balancing factors for the destination constrained gravity model are given by* $B_j = \exp(\xi_{jd})$ *for* $j = 1, \ldots, n$.

3.6 An Illustrative Example

In this section we use knowledge flows as captured by patent citation data to numerically illustrate the relationships between the aforementioned balancing factors, fixed effects and random effects in the cases of singly and doubly constrained variants of the gravity model. The origin-destination data relate to citations between European high-technology patents. By European patents we mean patent applications at the European Patent Office assigned to high-technology firms located in Europe. High-technology is defined to include the International Standard Industrial Classification (ISIC) sectors of aerospace (ISIC 3845), electronics-telecommunication (ISIC 3832), computers and office equipment (ISIC 3825), and pharmaceuticals (ISIC 3522). Self-citations (that is, citations from patents assigned to the same firm) have been excluded, given our interest in pure externalities as evidenced by interfirm knowledge spillovers.

Experts acknowledge that observations of patent citations are subject to a truncation bias, because we observe citations for only a portion of the life of an invention. To avoid this bias in the analysis, we have established a 5-year window (that is, 1985–1989, 1986–1990, ..., 1993–1997) to count citations to a patent.[27] The observation period is 1985–1997 with respect to cited patents, and 1990–2002 with respect to citing patents. The sample used in this section is restricted to inventors located in $n = 257$ European NUTS-2 regions, covering the EU-27 member states (excluding Cyprus and Malta) plus Norway and Switzerland. In case of cross-regional inventor teams, we have used the procedure of multiple full counting that—unlike fractional counting—does justice to the true integer nature of patent citations, but gives interregional cooperative inventions greater weight.

Subject to caveats relative to the relationship between patent citations and knowledge spillovers, the sample data allow us to identify and measure spatial separation effects for interregional knowledge spillovers in the spatial system of 257 regions. We use a binary 257-by-257 contiguity matrix to specify the 66,049-by-66,049 spatial weight matrix W that captures spatial dependence between patent citation flows from locations neighbouring both the origins and the destinations. Our interest is focused on the following three measures of separation: geographical distance, measured in terms of the great circle distance (in km), technological proximity, measured in terms of an index (for details see Fischer et al. 2006), and a dummy variable that represents border effects measured in terms of the presence of country borders between the regions. The product $U_i V_j$ may be interpreted simply as the number of distinct (i, j) interactions that are possible. Thus, a reasonable way to measure the origin factor U_i is in terms of the number of patents in knowledge producing region i in the time period 1985–1997, and the destination factor V_j in terms of the number of patents in knowledge absorbing region j in the time period

[27] For details about the data construction, see Fischer et al. (2006).

1990–2002 (Fischer and Griffith 2008). Accordingly, we have 66,049 observations, five (four) covariates and an intercept term in the doubly (singly) constrained cases of spatial interaction.

3.6.1 *Model Specifications Ignoring Spatial Dependence in origin-destination Flows*

Empirical experiments were conducted to numerically illustrate relationships between the aforementioned balancing factors, fixed effects, and random effects. The preceding theorems and corollaries indicate that these should be perfectly straight trend line relationships (using the log-balancing factors) with a slope of one, but not necessarily an intercept of zero. The intercept term represents an arbitrary multiplicative factor (i.e., a constant of proportionality).

Theorem 1 together with **Corollaries 1** and **2** indicate that the scatterplots of the log-balancing factors versus their concatenated Poisson regression indicator variable coefficients (augmented by zero for the arbitrarily removed indicator variables) form a perfect straight line [see Fig. 3.1]. The accompanying linear regression equations[28] relating these two pairings of values are as follows[29]: for the origin constrained case of spatial interaction: $\log(A_i) = 0.00051 + 0.99997\ \alpha_{io}$ ($R^2 = 1.0000$), the destination constrained case of spatial interaction: $\log(B_j) = 0.00001 + 0.99999\ \alpha_{jd}$ ($R^2 = 1.0000$), and the doubly constrained case of spatial interaction: $\log(A_i) = 0.00018 + 1.00114\ \alpha_{io}$ ($R^2 = 1.0000$) and $\log(B_j) = 0.00099 + 1.00110\ \alpha_{jd}$ ($R^2 = 1.0000$). Furthermore, these log-balancing factors strongly covary [see Fig. 3.2(a) and (b)], and all deviate somewhat from a normal frequency distribution as indicated by Fig. 3.2(c)–(f).

Model comparison results for the fixed effects versions of the constrained models are presented in Table 3.1. Inclusion of the origin and/or destination balancing factors as fixed effects covariates reduces overdispersion as indicated by the deviance statistic,[30] noticeably changes the three separation function component parameter estimates (especially that for the geographical distance decay), and remarkably increases the pseudo-R^2 value (measured in terms of a linear relationship between the predicted and observed counts). The last column in Table 3.1 presents estimation results for the doubly constrained spatially filtered gravity model specification, for

[28] A_{257} and B_{257} are the arbitrarily selected balancing factors set to one in each case, to avoid perfect multicollinearity with the intercept term, resulting in an expected intercept of zero and an expected slope of one.

[29] The regression equations describe each set of log-balancing factors as a function of the corresponding fixed effects indicator variables. Error terms are not included here.

[30] A deviance statistic exceeding one indicates that overdispersion is present; that is, the Poisson variance is greater than its mean. Although the existence of overdispersion does not affect the unbiased character of the parameter estimates, their standard errors are underestimated, and hence their significance is unrealistically increased.

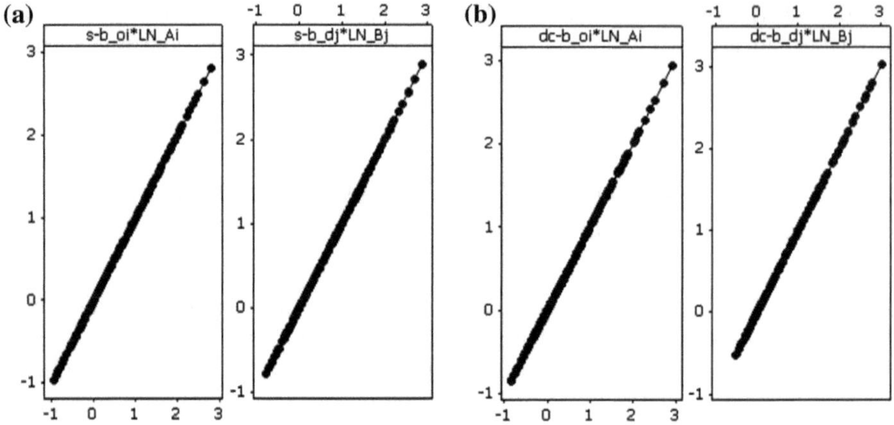

Fig. 3.1 Scatterplots of the log-balancing factors [log(A_i) and log(B_j)] versus the vector of the Poisson regression indicator variable coefficients: (**a**) the singly-constrained cases: origin and destination balancing factor plots; and (**b**) the doubly constrained case: the origin and the destination balancing factor plots

comparative purposes. The elimination of spatial dependence in the flows triggers a change of estimated parameter values and generates a decrease in the estimated overdispersion, compared with the standard doubly constrained model specification. That is, a part of the overdispersion, caused by spatial dependence, is eliminated by including eigenvectors, which are the proxy variables of the spatial dependence embedded in the standard model.

Theorem 2 together with **Corollaries 3** and **4** address the random effects model specifications for the three constrained variants of the gravity model. Treated as particular cases of a GLM with a logarithmic link function and a Poisson mean, these specifications yield the following expected values: $\log\left[E(Y_{ij})\right] = \log(\mu_{ij}) = \log(U_i) + \log(V_j) + \alpha + \xi_{io} + \xi_{jd} - \theta\ d_{ij}$ in the doubly constrained case of spatial interaction, $\log\left[E(Y_{ij})\right] = \log(\mu_{ij}) = \log(U_i) + \alpha + \xi_{io} - \theta\ d_{ij}$ in the origin constrained case, and $\log\left[E(Y_{ij})\right] = \log(\mu_{ij}) = \log(V_j) + \alpha + \xi_{jd} - \theta\ d_{ij}$ in the destination constrained case. The log terms on the right-hand side of the equations are the offset variables. Bolduc et al. (1995) argue that estimating origin and destination specific random effects in the gravity model specification is very difficult. But the implication from **Theorem 2** for the doubly constrained specification supports a numerical demonstration for it, too.

Descriptive statistics for the random effects estimates are given in Table 3.2. A frequentist approach requires integration of these effects out of the likelihood function under study. As n increases, the multidimensional integration involved becomes increasingly difficult. Here, with $n = 257$, the SAS procedure, called SAS PROC NLMIXED, fails to correctly calculate about 10 % of the random effects (see the Appendix). This complication resulted in the design of an indirect demonstration of **Theorem 2** as follows. Each balancing factor was introduced into the model

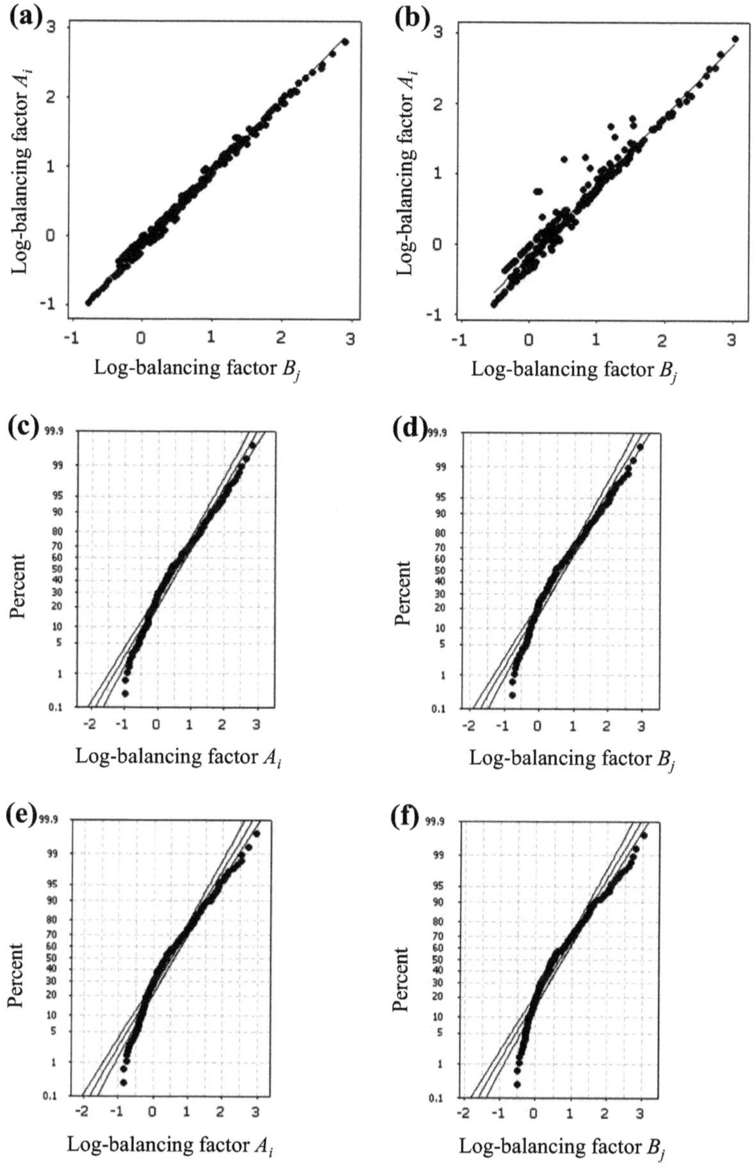

Fig. 3.2 Log-balancing factors for the constrained model variants: (**a**) scatterplot of the singly constrained origin and destination log-balancing factor pairs; (**b**) scatterplot of the doubly constrained origin and destination log-balancing factor pairs; (**c**) normal quantile plot of log(A_i) values in the origin-constrained case, with its 95 % confidence interval (CI); (**d**) normal quantile plot of log(B_j) values in the destination-constrained case, with its 95 % CI; (**e**) normal quantile plot of log(A_i) values in the doubly-constrained case, with its 95 % CI; and (**f**) normal quantile plot of log(B_j) values in the doubly-constrained case, with its 95 % CI

Table 3.1 Summary statistics for estimation of the fixed effects constrained variants of the gravity model (standard deviations in parentheses)

Statistics	Model specifications ignoring spatial dependence				Spatially filtered model specification
	Unconstrained[a]	Origin-constrained	Destination-constrained	Doubly-constrained	Doubly-constrained
Separation					
Geog. distance	−0.4750(0.0070)	−0.8317(0.0080)	−0.7539(0.0079)	−0.9092(0.0080)	−1.4992(0.0263)
Technology	−2.3407(0.0098)	−2.6041(0.0117)	−2.6845(0.0118)	−2.9788(0.0118)	−2.4919(0.0210)
Border	−1.1386(0.0049)	−1.3029(0.0058)	−1.2585(0.0057)	−1.2628(0.0057)	−0.9091(0.0136)
Deviance	4.0261	3.0574	3.2158	2.5924	1.8135
Residual mean	−0.0000	−0.0000	−0.0000	−0.0000	0.0000
Residual P(K-S)[b]	<0.01	<0.01	<0.01	<0.01	<0.01
Pseudo-R^2	0.5828	0.7221	0.7152	0.7323	0.8914

[a]The row and column totals were included with a power exponent of one
[b]K-S denotes the Kolmogorov–Smirnov statistic, a diagnostic test for normality here

Table 3.2 Summary statistics for random effects estimations: the origin-constrained, the destination-constrained and the doubly-constrained cases

	Model specifications given by Eqs. (3.14)–(3.16)			
			Doubly-constrained	
Statistics	Origin-constrained	Destination-constrained	Origin	Destination
Minimum	$-17.2 \cdot 10^{-13}$	$-15.5 \cdot 10^{-13}$	$-10.2 \cdot 10^{-13}$	$-10.5 \cdot 10^{-13}$
Mean	$-2.5 \cdot 10^{-13}$	$-2.7 \cdot 10^{-13}$	$-83.6 \cdot 10^{-13}$	$-2.3 \cdot 10^{-13}$
Median	$-2.9 \cdot 10^{-13}$	$-3.0 \cdot 10^{-13}$	$-0.1 \cdot 10^{-13}$	$-3.1 \cdot 10^{-13}$
Maximum	$10.9 \cdot 10^{-13}$	$9.8 \cdot 10^{-13}$	$11.0 \cdot 10^{-13}$	$10.4 \cdot 10^{-13}$
Standard deviation	$4.1 \cdot 10^{-13}$	$4.1 \cdot 10^{-13}$	$4.5 \cdot 10^{-13}$	$4.2 \cdot 10^{-13}$
P(Shapiro–Wilk)	<0.0001	0.0274	0.0077	<0.0001

GLMM estimation utilized a Newton–Raphson optimization procedure. The Shapiro–Wilk statistic furnishes a diagnostic statistic for normality

specification, and then a random effects term was estimated. If a balancing factor is equivalent to a random effects term, then all of the estimated random effects are approximately zero. This expectation characterises the findings summarised in Table 3.2. In other words, the estimated fixed and random effects display no consequential differences. The generalised linear mixed model (GLMM) random effects estimates are nearly identical to their balancing factor fixed effects counterparts.

Spatial filter descriptions of these variates are nearly identical,[31] as shown in Table 3.3, and comprise 17–20 of the 42 candidate eigenvectors depicting at least weak positive spatial autocorrelation map patterns. These filters allow the balancing factors to be deconstructed into spatially structured (SSRE) and spatially unstructured (SURE) random effects: the linear combination of eigenvectors constitutes the SSRE, and the (remaining) residuals constitute the SURE. The SSREs account for roughly two-thirds of the variance displayed by the total random effects terms. This spatial structuring represents moderate-to-strong positive spatial autocorrelation, and is one reason the individual terms deviate from a normal frequency distribution [all P(S-W) statistics increase, but still indicate marked deviation from a normal distribution]. These linear spatial filters account for virtually all of the spatial autocorrelation latent in the spatial distribution of these balancing factor variates, which differ from the spatial dependence latent in the flows between the regions.

[31]Because balancing factors are autoregressive specifications [see Eqs. (3.13)–(3.14)], they contain marked spatial dependence by construction. The spatial filter descriptions of these balancing factors rely on eigenvectors of the transformed spatial weight matrix $M_n W_n M_n$ where W_n is the n-by-n binary contiguity matrix and M_n is the n-by-n projection matrix defined by $M_n = I_n - \iota_n \iota_n' n^{-1}$. Forty-two candidate eigenvectors (for which $I/I_{\max} > 0.25$) are available for constructing spatial filters portraying positive spatial autocorrelation across the European regions. Of these, subsets have been selected with a stepwise regression procedure for constructing spatial filters describing the two sets of balancing factors. The criteria used for selection were statistically significant coefficients at the 10 % level associated with minimisation of the log-likelihood function, which is standard practice.

Table 3.3 Summary statistics for the balancing factors and the decomposition

	Log-balancing factor		Spatially structured random effects			Spatially unstructured random effects	
Constraint	I^{a}	P(S-W)[b]	I^{a}	# vectors	R^2	z_I[c]	P(S-W)[b]
Singly-constrained origin	0.65	0.0002	0.93	18	70	0.36	0.0009
Singly-constrained destination	0.61	<0.0001	0.93	17	67	0.13	0.0007
Doubly-constrained origin	0.63	<0.0001	0.93	20	69	−0.29	0.0006
Doubly-constrained destination	0.61	<0.0001	0.93	20	67	−0.29	0.0032

[a]*I* denotes the Moran's coefficient
[b]S-W denotes the Shapiro–Wilk statistic
[c]The asymptotic standard error for the Moran's *I* was used to compute the *z*-scores

Consequently, these particular singly constrained gravity model results confirm **Corollaries 3** and **4**, and as such indirectly demonstrate **Theorem 2**. They also illustrate that $A_i = \exp(\xi_{io}) = \exp(\beta_{io}) = \exp(\alpha_{io})$ for $i = 1, \ldots, n$, and $B_j = \exp(\xi_{jd}) = \exp(\beta_{jd}) = \exp(\alpha_{jd})$ for $j = 1, \ldots, n$. In other words, the model specifications with balancing factors, fixed effects and random effects, respectively, yield identical estimation results for the production constrained and the attraction constrained cases of spatial interaction. These findings imply that the same results hold for the doubly constrained case (Fig. 3.3).

3.6.2 Spatial Filter Model Specifications Accounting for Spatial Dependence in Flows

Estimating the balancing factors for singly and doubly constrained model specifications accounts for spatial dependence in the origin and destination factors of the gravity model, but not for spatial dependence in flows. Because only one set of indicator variables is involved in singly constrained model specifications, the intercept term can be added to each factor, forcing α to zero in the origin constrained model specification, and in the destination constrained model specification, respectively. This simple adjustment is not possible for the doubly constrained model, for which the intercept term includes the sum of the two arbitrarily selected indicator variable coefficients set to zero. Estimating random effects in the doubly constrained case also overlooks spatial dependence in flows, and treats the *n* origin flow recipients as repeated measures for each destination, and the *n* destination

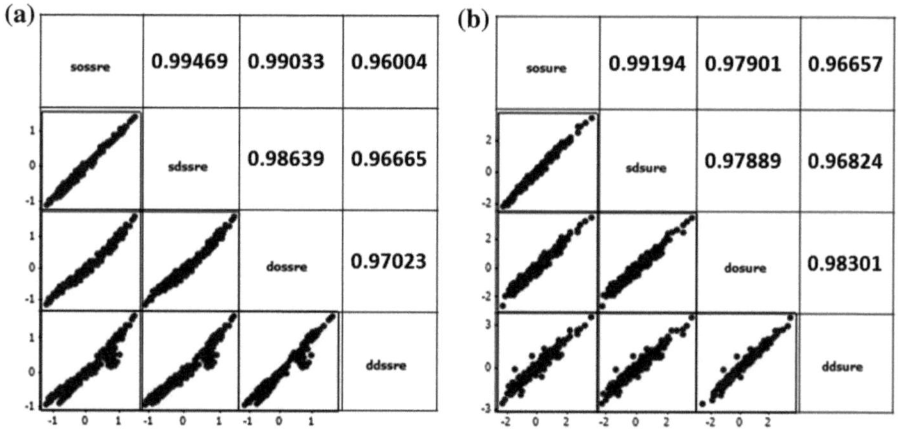

Fig. 3.3 Matrix *lower triangular* scatterplots, and *upper triangular* correlations: (**a**) spatially structured random effects (SSREs): sossre—singly-constrained origin, sdssre—singly-constrained destination, dossre—doubly-constrained origin, and ddssre—doubly-constrained destination; and (**b**) spatially unstructured random effects (SUREs): sossre—singly-constrained origin, sdssre—singly-constrained destination, dossre—doubly-constrained origin, and ddssre—doubly-constrained destination

flow sources as repeated measures for each origin, respectively. All of these specifications posit a unique value for each origin/destination for the $N = n^2$ flow data.

Origin and destination balancing factors must be estimated simultaneously (not sequentially) with the spatial filters, in order to preserve the row and column constraining totals. For the current case study, the spatial filters represent moderate-to-strong positive spatial autocorrelation ($I \approx 0.70$), decrease overdispersion by a third or more beyond the reduction attributable to the balancing factors (Table 3.1), produce a modest increase in the pseudo-R^2 value, induce a marked decrease in the distance decay parameter (for example, the confidence interval does not overlap with those for the other specifications), and comprise $Q = 221$ of the 576 candidate eigenvectors[32] of matrix *W*.

Figure 3.4 reports the scatterplots of observed versus predicted flows for the unconstrained gravity model specification, and the doubly constrained gravity model specification with and without accounting for origin-to-destination depen-

[32]Of note is that for *n* larger than about 100, current computer resources do not allow direct calculation of the eigenvectors of *W*. In order to reduce computational intensity we, followed Griffith (2009) to construct the spatial filter with a linear combination of Kronecker products of pairs of origin and destination eigenvectors. The result of this adjustment is $24^2 = 576$ candidate eigenvectors identified as Kronecker products of the 24 eigenvectors with an $I > 0.5$ extracted from matrix $(I - \iota\, \iota'\, n^{-1})\ W_n\ (I - \iota\, \iota'\, n^{-1})$. With 66,049 observations, five covariates and an intercept term, and 576 candidate eigenvectors, the numerical intensity of the problem solution becomes feasible but is still high.

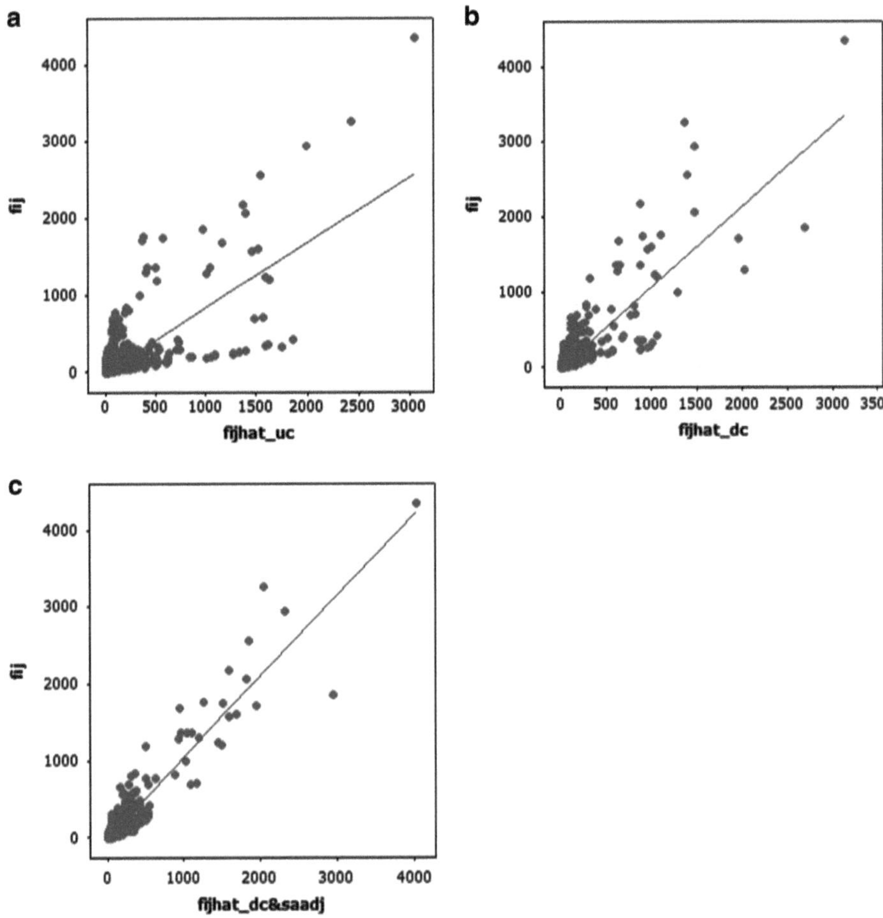

Fig. 3.4 Scatterplots of observed (vertical axis) versus predicted (horizontal axis) flows; *grey lines* denotes the line of perfect prediction. (**a**) Unconstrained model specification; (**b**) doubly constrained model specification; and (**c**) doubly constrained model specification adjusting for spatial dependence

dence in the flows. The scatterplots display a standard Poisson random variable plot of increasing variance with increasing amount of flow, and indicate a sequentially improved alignment of predicted with observed values. Imposing flow data matrix row and/or column total constraints coupled with inclusion of a spatial filter capturing spatial dependence between flows from locations neighbouring both the origins and destinations during estimation, shrinks especially the larger predicted flow values toward the perfectly straight trend line.

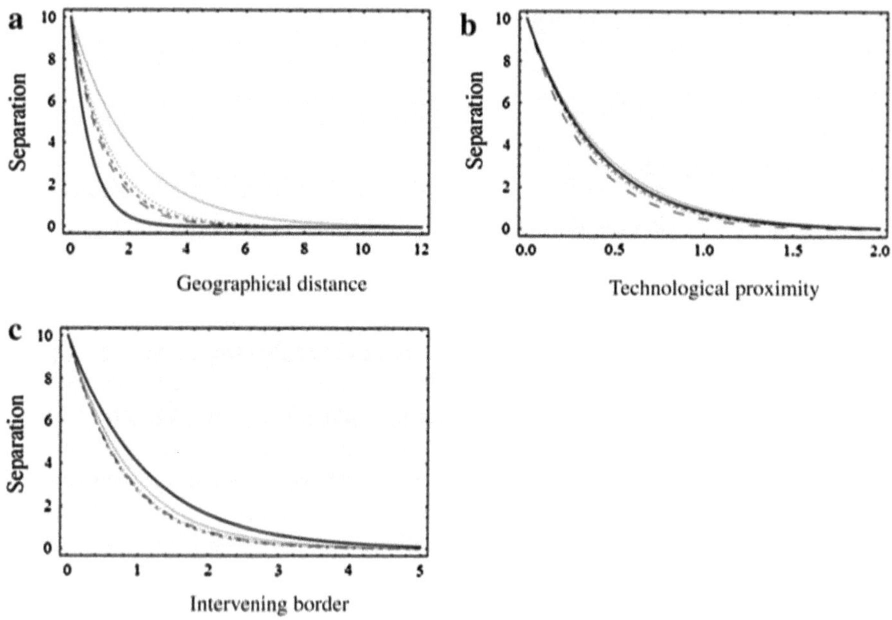

Fig. 3.5 Separation decay effects for the various model specifications: unconstrained (*thin line*), destination-constrained (*dotted line*), origin-constrained (*short dash line*), doubly-constrained (*long dash line*), doubly-constrained adjusted for network spatial autocorrelation (*thick line*). (**a**) geographical distance; (**b**) technological distance; and (**c**) intervening border

Figure 3.5 portrays the three individual separation effects. An expected finding is that the geographical distance decay parameter estimate adjusted for spatial dependence is less than in the model specifications that ignore spatial dependence in flows. And, it differs substantially from its unadjusted counterparts [see Fig. 3.5a]. The pairs of values do not have overlapping confidence intervals (CIs), in part because of the large sample size. The CI for the unconstrained case of spatial interaction is (−0.4887, −0.4613), the origin constrained case (−0.8473, −0.8161), the destination constrained case (−0.7695, −0.7384), the doubly constrained case (−0.9249, −0.8934), and the spatially filtered doubly constrained case (−1.5507, −1.4476). The technological separation decay parameter estimate exhibits little difference across the specifications [see Fig. 3.5b]. And, ignoring spatial dependence appears to exaggerate border separation effects [see Fig. 3.5c]. Of note is that the geographical distance parameter estimate has the largest spread across the model specifications.

3.7 Concluding Remarks

This paper suggests a number of interesting conclusions and implications for the statistical analysis of origin-destination data. Foremost, and quite counterintuitive, fixed effects and random effects are identical and equal the logarithm of the entropy maximisation derived balancing factors, except for slight rounding/algorithm-convergence errors. This finding is the outcome of an equivalency between assigning a single fixed effects indicator variable to each origin/destination, on the one hand, and estimating a single random effects (which is a mean) value for an origin/destination while treating the corresponding n destinations/origins as repeated measures, on the other hand. This finding also indicates that the number of degrees of freedom associated with the random effects term in this context may well be closer to $n - 1$ than to two (i.e., for estimating the mean and the variance of a random effects term) for the origins as well as the destination stochastic variable.

As with the unconstrained gravity model, adjusting for spatial dependence in flows improves the performance of the constrained variants of the gravity model in terms of both the pseudo-R^2 and the deviance statistic, and has a substantial impact on the separation parameter estimates that is in line with Curry (1972). The cost in degrees of freedom is modest. On average, at least 90 degrees of freedom are available for each parameter estimated in this case study. The eigenvectors successfully capture origin-to-destination dependence in flows. Hence, eigenvector spatial filtering provides a useful way of filtering spatial dependence in the sample origin-destination data. A virtue of this approach is that standard model specifications of the constrained gravity models and existing software can be applied to origin-destination data samples. This proves especially useful when dealing with flows taking the form of counts. However, the difficulty of computing eigenvalues and eigenvectors when dealing with a large number of locations limits the ability of filtering to capitalise on these advantages.

Appendix: Results for the Estimation of Singly Constrained Random Effects Specifications

Because of the large dimensionality of the calculus problem, multivariate integration struggles to properly estimate the random effects terms. Largest values appear to introduce the greatest difficulties. Figure 3.6 A reveals that integration is completely successful between the minimum and roughly 0.5 in our case study. Integration is only partially successful beyond 0.5. Incorrectly calculated random effects constitute about 10 % of the total number of random effects in this case study.

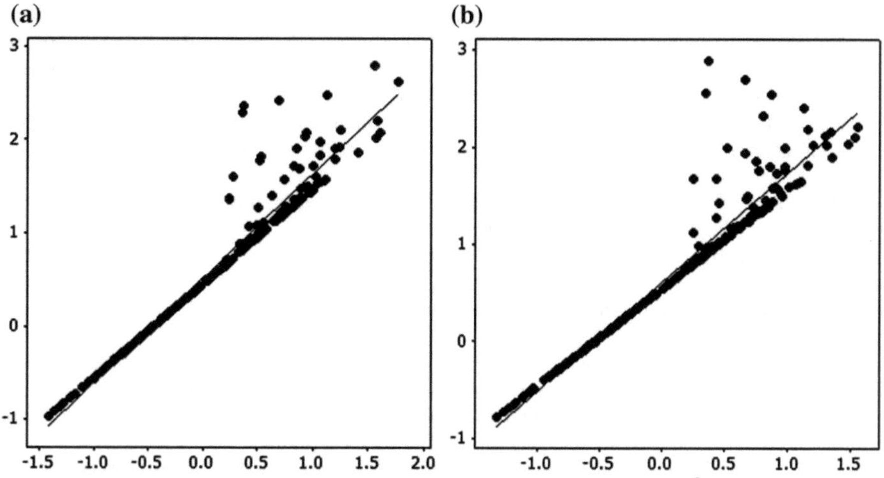

Fig. 3.6 Scatterplot of (**a**) the origin log-balancing factor (*vertical axis*) versus the Poisson regression origin location random effects (*horizontal axis*); (**b**) the destination log-balancing factor (*vertical axis*) versus the Poisson regression destination location random effects (*horizontal axis*)

References

Bailey TC, Gatrell AC (1995) Interactive spatial data analysis. Longman, Harlow

Baxter M (1982) Similarities in methods of estimating spatial interaction models. Geogr Anal 14(3):267–272

Baxter M (1983) Estimation and inference in spatial interaction models. Prog Hum Geogr 7:40–59

Bishop YMM, Fienberg SE, Holland PW (1975) Discrete multivariate analysis. MIT Press, Cambridge

Black WR (1992) Network autocorrelation in transport network and flow systems. Geogr Anal 24(3):207–222

Bolduc D, Laferrière R, Santarossa G (1995) Spatial autoregressive error components in travel flow models: an application to aggregate mode choice. In: Anselin L, Florax R (eds) New directions in spatial econometrics. Springer, Berlin/Heidelberg/New York, pp 96–108

Cesario FJ (1973) A generalized trip distribution model. J Reg Sci 13(2):233–248

Cesario FJ (1977) A new interpretation of the "normalizing" or "balancing factors" of gravity type spatial models. J Socio Econ Plan Sci 11(3):131–136

Chun Y (2008) Modeling network autocorrelation within migration flows by eigenvector spatial filtering. J Geogr Syst 10(4):317–344

Chun Y, Griffith DA (2011) Modeling network autocorrelation in space-time migration flow data: an eigenvector spatial filtering approach. Ann Assoc Am Geogr 101(3):523–536

Curry L (1972) A spatial analysis of gravity flows. Reg Stud 6(2):131–137

Davies RB, Guy CM (1987) The statistical modelling of flow data when the Poisson assumption is violated. Geogr Anal 19(4):300–314

Elhorst JP (2010) Spatial panel data models. In: Fischer MM, Getis A (eds) Handbook of applied spatial analysis. Springer, Berlin/Heidelberg/New York, pp 377–407

Evans AW (1970) Some properties of trip distribution models. Transp Res 4(1):19–36

Fischer MM (2000) Travel demand – theory. In: Polak JB, Heertje A (eds) Analytical transport economics. Edward Elgar, Cheltenham, pp 51–78

Fischer MM, Griffith DA (2008) Modeling spatial autocorrelation in spatial interaction data: a comparison of spatial econometric and spatial filtering specifications. J Reg Sci 48(5):969–989
Fischer MM, Wang J (2011) Spatial data analysis: models, methods and techniques [Springer briefs in regional science]. Springer, Berlin/Heidelberg/New York
Fischer MM, Scherngell T, Jansenberger E (2006) The geography of knowledge spillovers between high-technology firms in Europe: evidence from a spatial interaction modeling perspective. Geogr Anal 38(3):288–309
Fotheringham AS, O'Kelly ME (1989) Spatial interaction models: formulations and applications. Kluwer Academic Publishers, Dordrecht
Griffith DA (2003) Spatial autocorrelation and spatial filtering. Springer, Berlin/Heidelberg/New York
Griffith DA (2007) Spatial structure and spatial interaction: 25 years later. Rev Reg Stud 37(1):28–38
Griffith DA (2009) Modeling spatial autocorrelation in spatial interaction data: empirical evidence from 2002 Germany journey-to-work flows. J Geogr Syst 11(2):117–140
Haynes KE, Fotheringham AS (1984) Gravity and spatial interaction models. Sage, Bevery Hills
Isard W (1960) Methods of regional analysis. MIT Press, Cambridge
Kirby HR (1974) Theoretical requirements for calibrating gravity models. Transp Res 8(1):97–104
Lambert DM, Brown JP, Florax RJGM (2010) A two-step estimator for a spatial lag model of counts: theory, small sample performance and an application. Reg Sci Urban Econ 40(4):241–252
Ledent J (1985) The doubly constrained model of spatial interaction: a more general formulation. Environ Plan A 17(2):253–262
LeSage JP, Fischer MM (2010) Spatial econometric methods for modeling origin-destination flows. In: Fischer MM, Getis A (eds) Handbook of applied spatial analysis. Springer, Berlin/Heidelberg/New York, pp 409–433
LeSage JP, Pace RK (2008) Spatial econometric modeling of origin-destination flows. J Reg Sci 48(5):941–968
LeSage JP, Pace RK (2009) Introduction to spatial econometrics. CRC Press, Boca Raton
LeSage JP, Fischer MM, Scherngell T (2007) Knowledge spillovers across Europe. Evidence from a Poisson spatial interaction model with spatial effects. Pap Reg Sci 86(3):393–421
McCullagh P, Nelder JA (1983) Generalized linear models. Chapman and Hall, London
Niedercorn J, Bechdolt B (1969) An economic derivation of the "gravity law" of spatial interaction. J Reg Sci 9(2):273–282
Pace RK, LeSage JP, Zhu S (2011) Interpretation and computation of estimates from regression models using spatial filtering. Paper presented at the Fifth World Conference of the Spatial Econometrics Association, Toulouse, July 6–8, 2011
Sen A, Smith T (1995) Gravity models of spatial interaction behavior. Springer, Berlin/Heidelberg/New York
Tiefelsdorf M (2003) Misspecification in interaction model distance decay relations: a spatial structure effect. J Geogr Syst 5(1):25–50
Tiefelsdorf M, Boots B (1995) The exact distribution of Moran's I. Environ Plan A 27(6):985–999
Tobler W (1983) An alternative formulation for spatial interaction modeling. Environ Plan A 15(5):693–703
Wilson AG (1967) A statistical theory of spatial distribution models. Transp Res 1(3):253–269
Wilson AG (1970) Entropy in urban and regional modelling. Pion, London
Wilson AG (1971) A family of spatial interaction models and associated developments. Environ Plan 3(1):1–32
Wilson AG, Kirkby MJ (1980) Mathematics for geographers and planners, 2nd edn. Clarendon, Oxford

Chapter 4
Testing Spatial Autocorrelation in Weighted Networks: The Modes Permutation Test

François Bavaud

Keywords Bootstrap • Local variance • Markov and semi-Markov processes • Moran's I • Permutation test • Spatial autocorrelation • Spatial filtering • Weighted networks

JEL Classification: C12, C15, C31

4.1 Introduction

Permutation tests of spatial autocorrelation are justified under *exchangeability*, that is the premise that the observed scores follow a permutation-invariant joint distribution. Yet, in the frequently encountered case of geographical data collected on regions differing in importance, the variance of a regional score is expected to *decrease* with the size of the region, in the same way that the variance of an average is inversely proportional to the size of the sample in elementary statistics: heteroscedasticity holds in effect, already under spatial independence, thus weakening the rationale of the celebrated spatial autocorrelation permutation test (e.g. Cliff and Ord 1973; Besag and Diggle 1977) in the case of a weighted network.

This paper presents an alternative permutation test for spatial autocorrelation, whose validity extends to the weighted case. The procedure relies upon *spatial modes*, that is linear orthogonal combinations of spatial values, originally based upon the eigenvectors of the standardized connectivity or adjacency matrix (Tiefels-

*This paper has been previously published in the Journal of Geographical Systems. Special Issue on "Advances in the Statistical Modelling of Spatial Interaction Data", Vol. 15, Number 3/July 2013, ©Springer-Verlag Berlin Heidelberg, pp. 233–247.

F. Bavaud (✉)
Department of Language and Information Sciences, Institute of Geography and Sustainability, University of Lausanne, Lausanne, Switzerland
e-mail: fbavaud@unil.ch

R. Patuelli, G. Arbia (eds.), *Spatial Econometric Interaction Modelling*, Advances in Spatial Science, DOI 10.1007/978-3-319-30196-9_4

dorf and Boots 1995; Griffith 2000). In contrast to regional scores, the variance of the spatial modes turn out to be constant under spatial independence, thereby justifying the *modes permutation test* for spatial autocorrelation.

Section 4.2.1 presents the definition of the local variance and Moran's I in the arguably most general setup for spatial autocorrelation, based upon the normalised, symmetrical *exchange matrix*, whose margins define regional weights (Bavaud 2008a). Section 4.2.2 presents, in the spirit of spatial filtering (Griffith 2000), the spectral decomposition of the exchange matrix, or rather of a standardised version of it, currently used in spectral graph theory (Chung 1997; von Luxburg 2007; Bavaud 2010), supplying the orthogonal components defining in turn the spatial modes. Section 4.2.3 presents the mode permutation test, and its bootstrap variant, illustrated in Sect. 4.2.4 on Swiss migratory and linguistic data.

Section 4.3 addresses the familiar case of binary or weighted adjacency matrices, which have to be first converted into exchange matrices with a priori fixed margins. Two proposals, namely a simple rescaling with diagonal adjustment (Sect. 4.3.1) and the construction of time-embeddable exchange matrices (Sect. 4.3.2) are presented, and illustrated on the popular "distribution of Blood group A in Eire" dataset (Sect. 4.3.3).

4.2 Spatial Autocorrelation in Weighted Networks

4.2.1 Local Covariance and the Exchange Matrix

Consider a set of n regions with associated weights $f_i > 0$, normalized to $\sum_{i=1}^n f_i = 1$. Weights measure the importance of the regions, and define weighted regional averages and variances as

$$\bar{x} := \sum_{i=1}^n f_i x_i \qquad \text{var}(x) := \sum_{i=1}^n f_i (x_i - \bar{x})^2 = \frac{1}{2} \sum_{ij} f_i f_j (x_i - x_j)^2 \ . \tag{4.1}$$

Here $x = (x_i)$ represents a *density variable* or a *spatial field*, that is a numerical quantity attached to region i, transforming under aggregation $i,j \to [i \cup j]$ as $x_{[i\cup j]} = (f_i x_i + f_j x_j)/(f_i + f_j)$, as for instance " cars per inhabitants", " average income" or " proportion of foreigners".

The last identity in (4.1) is straightforward to check (Lebart 1969), and shows the variance to measure the average squared dissimilarity between pairs (i,j) of regions, selected independently with probability $f_i f_j$. A more general sampling scheme consists in selecting the regional pair (i,j) with probability e_{ij}, such that

$$e_{ij} \geq 0 \qquad e_{ij} = e_{ji} \qquad e_{i\bullet} := \sum_j e_{ij} = f_i \qquad e_{\bullet\bullet} = 1 \tag{4.2}$$

where "•" denotes the summation over the replaced index. A $n \times n$ matrix $E = (e_{ij})$ obeying (4.2) is called an *exchange matrix* (Berger and Snell 1957; Bavaud 2008a), compatible with the regional weights f. The exchange matrix defines an undirected weighted network, with edges weights e_{ij} and regional weights $f_i = e_{i\bullet}$. It contains loops in general ($e_{ii} \geq 0$), denoting regional self-interaction or autarachy (Bavaud 1998).

By construction, the exchange matrix generates a reversible Markov transition matrix $W = (w_{ij})$ (Bavaud 1998) with stationary distribution f:

$$w_{ij} := \frac{e_{ij}}{f_i} \geq 0 \qquad \sum_j w_{ij} = 1 \qquad \sum_i f_i w_{ij} = f_j \qquad f_i w_{ij} = f_j w_{ji} = e_{ij} \ . \tag{4.3}$$

W constitutes a row-normalized matrix of spatial weights, entering in the autoregressive models of spatial econometrics (see e.g. Anselin 1988; Cressie 1993; Leenders 2002; Haining 2003; Arbia 2006; LeSage and Pace 2009).

In spatial applications, the components of the exchange matrix are large for nearby regions and small for regions far apart. The quantity

$$\mathrm{var}_{\mathrm{loc}}(x) := \frac{1}{2} \sum_{ij} e_{ij} (x_i - x_j)^2 \tag{4.4}$$

defines the *local variance*, that is the average squared dissimilarity between neighbours. Comparing the local and the ordinary (weighted) variance defines *Geary's c* and *Moran's I*, measuring spatial autocorrelation (e.g. Geary 1954; Moran 1950; Cliff and Ord 1973; Tiefelsdorf and Boots 1995; Anselin 1995). Namely, $c(x) := \mathrm{var}_{\mathrm{loc}}(x)/\mathrm{var}(x)$ (differing from its usual variant by a factor $n/(n-1)$) and

$$I(x) := 1 - c(x) = \frac{\mathrm{var}(x) - \mathrm{var}_{\mathrm{loc}}(x)}{\mathrm{var}(x)} = \frac{\sum_{ij} e_{ij}(x_i - \bar{x})(x_j - \bar{x})}{\sum_i f_i (x_i - \bar{x})^2} \ .$$

4.2.2 Spatial Filtering and Spatial Modes

Spatial filtering primarily aims at visualizing and extracting the latent factors involved in spatial autocorrelation (Tiefelsdorf and Boots 1995; Griffith 2000, 2003; Griffith and Peres-Neto 2006; Chun 2008; Dray 2011; and references therein).

Its first step consists in spectrally decomposing a matrix expressing inter-regional connectivity in some way or another, such as the adjacency matrix or the exchange matrix. Various choices are often equivalent under uniform weighting of the regions, but the general weighted case calls for more precision. Arguably, the most fruitful decomposition considers the so-called *standardized exchange matrix*

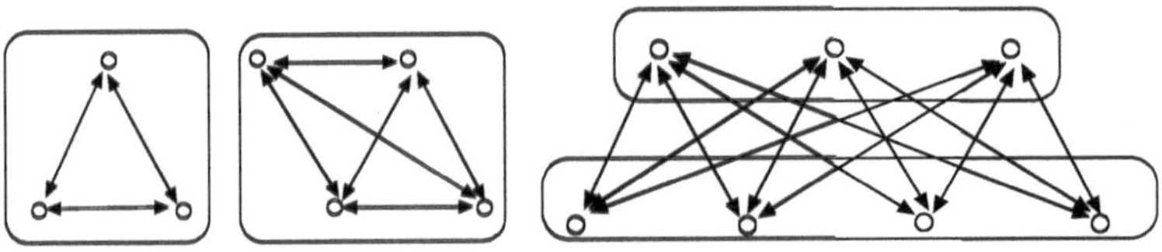

Fig. 4.1 Reducible network, with $\lambda_1 = 1$ (*left*) and bipartite network, with $\lambda_{n-1} = -1$ (*right*)

E^s, with components (Chung 1997; von Luxburg 2007; Bavaud 2010)

$$e^s_{ij} = \frac{e_{ij} - f_i f_j}{\sqrt{f_i f_j}} \quad \text{i.e.} \quad E^s = \Pi^{-\frac{1}{2}}(E - ff')\Pi^{-\frac{1}{2}} \quad \text{with} \quad \Pi = \text{diag}(f) \ . \qquad (4.5)$$

Its spectral decomposition

$$E^s = U\Lambda U' \qquad \text{with} \quad U = (u_{i\alpha}) \text{ orthogonal and } \Lambda = \text{diag}(\lambda) \text{ diagonal}$$

generates a *trivial* eigenvalue $\lambda_0 = 0$ associated with the trivial eigenvector $u_{i0} = \sqrt{f_i}$. The remaining *non-trivial* decreasingly ordered eigenvalues λ_α (for $\alpha = 1, \ldots, n-1$) lie in the interval $[-1, 1]$, as a consequence of the Perron-Froebenius theorem and the symmetry of E^s.

Also, $\lambda_1 = 1$ iff E is *reducible*, that is consisting of two or more disconnected components (Fig. 4.1), and $\lambda_{n-1} = -1$ iff E is *bipartite*, i.e. partitionable into two sets without within connections (e.g. Kijima 1997; Aldous and Fill 2002).

The exchange matrix itself expresses as

$$e_{ij} = f_i f_j + \sqrt{f_i f_j} \sum_{\alpha=1}^{n-1} \lambda_\alpha u_{i\alpha} u_{j\alpha} = f_i f_j [1 + \sum_{\alpha \geq 1} \lambda_\alpha c_{i\alpha} c_{j\alpha}] \qquad (4.6)$$

where the *raw coordinates*

$$c_{i\alpha} := \frac{u_{i\alpha}}{u_{i0}} = \frac{u_{i\alpha}}{\pm\sqrt{f_i}}$$

can be used at visualizing distinct levels of spatial autocorrelation (Griffith 2003), or at specifying the positions of the n regions in a factor space (Bavaud 2010).

Raw coordinates are orthogonal and standardized, in the sense

$$\sum_i f_i c_{i\alpha} = \delta_{\alpha 0} \qquad \sum_i f_i c_{i\alpha} c_{i\beta} = \delta_{\alpha\beta} \ . \qquad (4.7)$$

As a consequence, the n regional values x can be converted into n *modal values* $\hat{x}$, and vice-versa, as

$$\hat{x}_\alpha := \sum_i f_i c_{i\alpha} x_i \qquad\qquad x_i = \sum_{\alpha \geq 0} c_{i\alpha} \hat{x}_\alpha = \bar{x} + \sum_{\alpha \geq 1} c_{i\alpha} \hat{x}_\alpha \ . \tag{4.8}$$

Equations (4.8) express orthogonal, Fourier-like correspondence between regional values and modes. The latter depict global patterns, integrating the contributions from all regions. In particular, the trivial mode yields the field average: $\hat{x}_0 = \bar{x}$.

Borrowing an analogy from solid-state Physics, the spatial field x can describe the individual displacements of each of the n atoms of a crystal. The modes $\hat{x}$ then provide global parameters describing the *collective motion* of atoms, consisting of a superposition of sound waves or *harmonics*, whose specific eigen-frequencies are determined by the nature of the crystal, and whose knowledge permit to reconstruct the individual atomic displacements.

4.2.3 *The Modes Permutation Test*

4.2.3.1 Heterodasticity of the Spatial Field

The hypothesis H_0 of spatial independence requires the covariance matrix of the spatial field $X = (X_1, \ldots, X_n)$ to be diagonal with components *inversely proportional to the spatial weights*, that is of the form (see the Appendix)

$$\sigma_{ij} = \mathrm{Cov}(X_i, X_j) = \delta_{ij} \frac{\sigma^2}{f_i} \qquad\qquad \text{where} \quad \sigma^2 = \mathrm{Var}(\bar{X}) \ . \tag{4.9}$$

In its usual form, the *direct* or *regional permutation test* compares the observed value of Moran's $I(x)$ to a set of values $I(\pi(x))$, where $\pi(x)$ denotes a permutation (that is a sampling without replacement) of the n *regional values* x (e.g. Cliff and Ord 1973; Thioulouse et al. 1995; Li and al. 2007; Bivand et al. 2009a). Sampling with replacement, generating *bootstrap resamples* can also be carried out.

Both procedures are justified by the fact that the spatial variables X_i are identically distributed under H_0. Yet, (4.9) shows the latter assertion to be *wrong whenever the regional weights differ*, thus jeopardizing the rationale of the direct approach, based upon the permutation or the bootstrap of regional values.

The possible heteroscedasticity of regional values has been addressed by quite a few researchers, in particular in epidemiology, and various proposals (transformations of variables or weights, reformulations in terms of residuals, Bayesian approaches) have been investigated (see e.g. Waldhör 1996; Assunção and Reis 1999 or Haining 2003).

4.2.3.2 Homoscedaticity of the Spatial Modes

As announced in the introduction, this paper proposes a presumably new *modal test*, identical in spirit to the direct test but based upon *modes permutation*, together with a variant based upon *modes bootstrap*. Its existence results from two fortunate circumstances (see the Appendix), namely i) the homoscedasticity of the modes under H_0

$$\hat{\sigma}_{\alpha\beta} := \mathrm{Cov}(\hat{X}_\alpha, \hat{X}_\beta) = \delta_{\alpha\beta}\,\sigma^2 \qquad \text{with} \qquad \hat{X}_\alpha = \sum_i f_i\, c_{i\alpha}\, X_i \tag{4.10}$$

and ii) the simplicity of Moran's I expression in terms of spatial modes, which reads

$$I(x) \equiv I(\hat{x}) = \frac{\sum_{\alpha\geq 1} \lambda_\alpha \hat{x}_\alpha^2}{\sum_{\alpha\geq 1} \hat{x}_\alpha^2} . \tag{4.11}$$

As expected, the trivial mode $\hat{x}_0 = \bar{x}$ does not contribute to Moran's I. Under H_0, its expectation and variance under all remaining $(n-1)!$ non-trivial modes permutations read (see the Appendix)

$$E_\pi(I \mid \hat{x}) = \frac{1}{n-1}\sum_{\alpha\geq 1} \lambda_\alpha = \frac{\mathrm{trace}(W) - 1}{n-1} \geq \frac{-1}{n-1} \tag{4.12}$$

$$\mathrm{Var}_\pi(I \mid \hat{x}) = \frac{s(\hat{x}) - 1}{(n-1)(n-2)}\Big[\sum_{\alpha\geq 1} \lambda_\alpha^2 - \frac{1}{n-1}\Big(\sum_{\alpha\geq 1} \lambda_\alpha\Big)^2\Big] \tag{4.13}$$

where

$$s(\hat{x}) := (n-1)\frac{\sum_{\alpha\geq 1} \hat{x}_\alpha^4}{(\sum_{\alpha\geq 1} \hat{x}_\alpha^2)^2} \geq 1$$

is a measure of modes dispersion.

4.2.3.3 The Test

The *modes autocorrelation test* consists in refuting H_0, which denies spatial dependence, if the value (4.11) of $I(\hat{x})$ is extreme w.r.t. the sample $\{I(\pi(\hat{x}))\}$ of B permuted or bootstrapped mode values, that is if its quantile is near 1 (evidence of positive autocorrelation) or near 0 (negative autocorrelation).

As expected, the trivial mode $\hat{x}_0 = \bar{x}$ does not contribute to Moran's I. Also, $I(x)$ together with its permuted or bootstrapped values lie in an interval comprised in $[\lambda_{n-1}, \lambda_1] \subseteq [-1, 1]$. The interval reduces to a single point $I(\pi(\hat{x})) \equiv I_0$, invariant

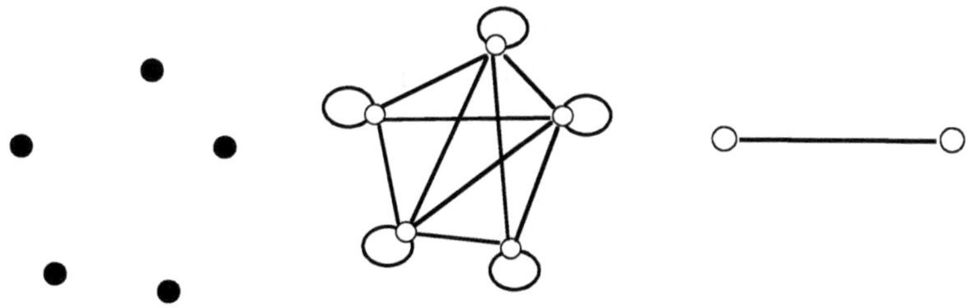

Fig. 4.2 Moran's $I(x)$ is constant, independent of the value of the field x for the disconnected or frozen network (*left*), for the fully connected or perfectly mobile network (*middle*), and their linear combinations. Its minimum $I(x) \equiv -1$ occurs for the loopless network with $n = 2$ (*right*)

under permutations or bootstrapping, with a corresponding variance (4.13) of zero, thus ruining the autocorrelation test, if (see (4.11), (4.13)):

(a) $s(\hat{x}) = 1$, that is $\hat{x}_\alpha^2 \equiv \hat{x}^2$ or equivalently $\hat{x}_\alpha \equiv \epsilon_\alpha \hat{x}$, where $\hat{x} \in \mathbb{R}$ and $\epsilon_\alpha = \pm 1$ for all $\alpha \geq 1$. Following (4.8), this occurs for "untestable" spatial fields of the form $x_i = \bar{x} + \hat{x} z_i$ where $z_i = \sum_{\alpha \geq 1} \epsilon_\alpha u_{i\alpha}/u_{i0}$ actually defines a set of 2^{n-1} configurations depending on the choice of the ϵ_α, whose sign is arbitrary, as is the sign of the eigenvectors u_α.

   Noticeably, the constant field $x_i \equiv \bar{x}$ is untestable, with a value $I(x) = 0/0$ not even defined. However intriguing, the empirical relevance of those "untestable" spatial fields is debatable, in view of the vanishing probability to encounter *exactly* such a spatial pattern.

(b) $\lambda_\alpha \equiv \lambda$ for all $\alpha \geq 1$, as with the :

   (i) *frozen networks* $E := E^{(0)}$, where $e_{ij}^{(0)} := f_i \delta_{ij}$ is the disconnected graph,[1] associated to the immobile Markov chain with $\lambda_\alpha \equiv 1$ and $I(x) \equiv 1$ (Fig. 4.2, left)

   (ii) or as with the *perfectly mobile networks* $E := E^{(\infty)}$, where $e_{ij}^{(\infty)} := f_i f_j$ is the complete weighted graph, free of distance-deterrence effects, associated to the memoryless Markov chain with $\lambda_\alpha \equiv 0$ and $I(x) \equiv 0$ (Fig. 4.2, middle)

   as well as with their linear combinations $E := aE^{(0)} + (1-a)E^{(\infty)}$. Also, networks made of $n = 2$ regions are untestable: they automatically satisfy b) and a) above (Fig. 4.2, right).

[1]Here the notations match the *higher-order discrete time extensions* of the exchange matrix, resulting (under weak regularity conditions) from the iteration of the Markov transition matrix as

$$E^{(r)} := \Pi W^r \qquad E^{(0)} = \Pi \qquad E^{(2)} = E\Pi^{-1}E \qquad E^{(\infty)} = ff' \ .$$

Under the additional normal assumption $\hat{X}_\alpha \sim N(0, \sigma^2)$ for $\alpha \geq 1$, one can show $E(s(\hat{x})) = 3(n-1)/(n+1)$ by the Pitman-Koopmans theorem (Cliff and Ord 1981, p. 43) and hence

$$E(\mathrm{Var}_\pi(I \mid \hat{x})) = \frac{2}{n^2-1}[\sum_{\alpha\geq 1} \lambda_\alpha^2 - \frac{1}{n-1}(\sum_{\alpha\geq 1} \lambda_\alpha)^2]$$
$$= \frac{2}{n^2-1}[\mathrm{tr}(W^2) - 1 - \frac{(\mathrm{tr}(W)-1)^2}{n-1}] \ . \quad (4.14)$$

4.2.4 *Illustration: Swiss Migratory and Linguistic Data*

Flows constitute a major source of exchange matrices (e.g. Goodchild and Smith 1980; Willekens J 1983; Fotheringham and O'Kelly 1989; Sen and Smith 1995; Bavaud 1998, 2002). Let $n_{ij}(T)$ denote the number of units (people, goods, matter, etc.) initially in region i and located in region j after a time T. *Quasi-symmetric* flows are of the form $n_{ij} = a_i b_j c_{ij}$ with $c_{ij} = c_{ji}$, as predicted by Gravity modelling. They generate *reversible* spatial weights $w_{ij} := n_{ij}/n_{i\bullet}$, with stationary distribution f_i, whose product $f_i w_{ij}$ defines the exchange matrix e_{ij} (Bavaud 2002).

Consider the inter-regional migrations data $n_{ij}(T)$ between the $n = 26$ Swiss cantons for $T = 5$ years (1985–1990), together with the spatial fields x = " proportion of germanophones" or x = " proportion of anglophones", for each canton. After determining the quasi-symmetric ML estimates $\hat{n}_{ij}$ (Bavaud 2002), the exchange matrix is computed, and so are the spatial modes $\hat{x}_\alpha$ from (4.8) and Moran's index $I(\hat{x})$ from (4.11). Figure 4.3 depicts the distribution of 10000 permutation and bootstrap resamples of $I(\pi(\hat{x}))$, from which the bilateral p-values of Table 4.1 can be computed (see Sect. 4.3.2 for the details).

Most people do not migrate towards other cantons in 5 years, thus making the exchange matrix "cold" (that is close to the frozen $E^{(0)}$), with a dominating diagonal, accounting for the high values of I and $E_\pi(I)$ in Table 4.1.

Swiss native linguistic regions divide into German, French and Italian. Migrants tend to avoid to cross the linguistic barriers, thus accounting for the spatial autocorrelation of "germanophones" (Table 4.1, right). Detecting spatial patterns in the anglophones repartition is, as expected from the above migratory scheme, less evident.

Bootstrap tests (modal or regional) appear here less powerful than permutation tests—a possibly true conjecture in general (Corcoran and Mehta 2002; Janssen and Pauls 2005).

Modal autocorrelation tests of "anglophones" seem more sensitive than their regional counterparts, while the opposite holds for "germanophones": the usual test of autocorrelation underestimates the dispersion of the resampled values of $I(\pi(\text{germanophones}))$ (Fig. 4.3, left), thus inflating the risk of type I errors for

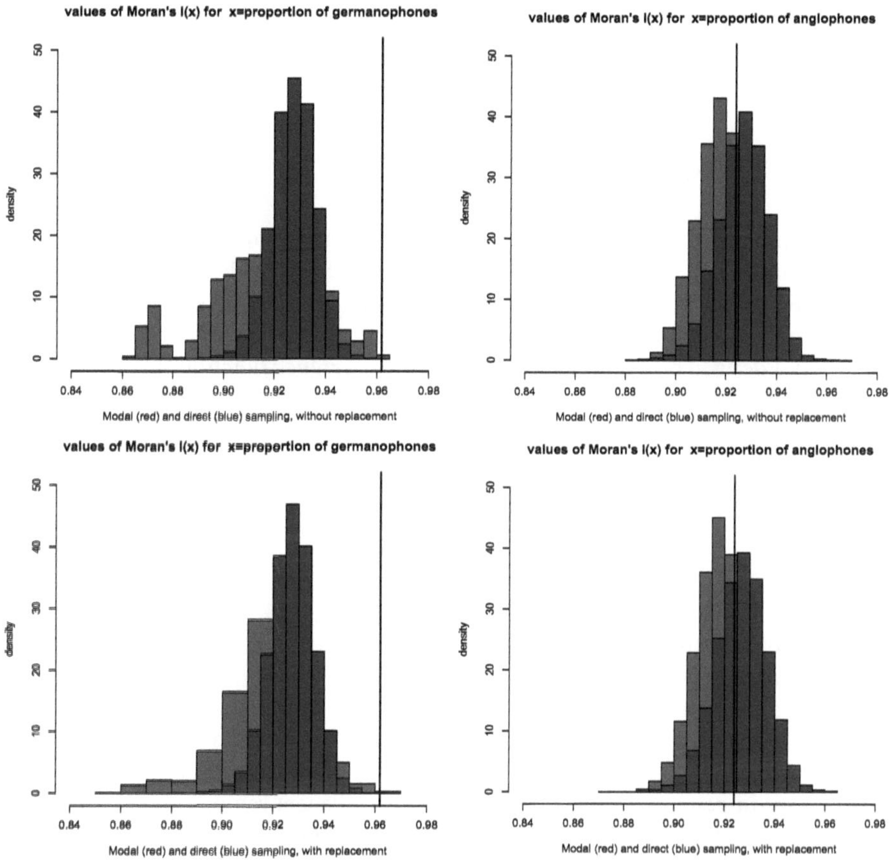

Fig. 4.3 Permutation (*above*) and bootstrap (*below*), modal (*red*) and regional (*blue*) testing of the "migation-driven" spatial autocorrelation among germanophones (*left*) and anglophones (*right*). $B = 10000$ samples are generated each time, and compared with the observed I, marked vertically (color figure online)

Table 4.1 Left: observed I, its *modal permutation* expectation (4.12) and variance (4.13) together with the z-value $z := (I - E_\pi(I))/\sqrt{\text{Var}_\pi(I|\hat{x})}$ and $s(\hat{x})$ in (4.13). Right: p-values associated to the modal and direct autocorrelation test, in their permutation and bootstrap variants

	Germanophones	Anglophones
I	0.962	0.924
$E_\pi(I)$	0.917	0.917
$\text{Var}_\pi(I\|\hat{x})$	0.00044	0.000082
z	2.13	0.74
$s(\hat{x})$	11.29	2.90

	Germanophones	Anglophones
Modal permutation	0.0006	0.048
Regional permutation	0.0002	0.075
Modal bootstrap	0.0036	0.46
Regional bootstrap	0.0004	0.76

size-unadjusted Moran's I, in accordance with the simulation results of Assunção and Reis (1999).

4.3 Adjacency Graphs and Accessibilities

Very commonly, space is defined by a binary, off-diagonal and symmetric *connectivity* or *adjacency* matrix $n \times n$ matrix $A = (a_{ij})$, specifying whether distinct regions i and j are direct neighbours ($a_{ij} = 1$) or not ($a_{ij} = 0$). This scheme can also, as in gravity modelling, be extended to "weighted adjacencies" or *accessibilities* $a_{ij} = f(d_{ij})$ defined by a non-negative *distance deterrence function* $f(d_{ij})$ decreasing with the distance d_{ij} between distinct regions i and j.

In the sequel, we consider accessibility matrices with $a_{ij} \geq 0$, $a_{ij} = a_{ji}$ and $a_{ii} = 0$, with the interpretation that distinct regions i and j are direct neighbours iff $a_{ij} > 0$. By construction, the three quantities

$$\varepsilon_{ij} = \frac{a_{ij}}{a_{\bullet\bullet}} \qquad \kappa_{ij} = \frac{a_{ij}}{a_{i\bullet}} \qquad \sigma_i = \frac{a_{i\bullet}}{a_{\bullet\bullet}} = \varepsilon_{i\bullet} \tag{4.15}$$

respectively constitute an *exchange matrix*, its associated *transition matrix* and the *stationary distribution*, proportional to the (possibly weighted) number of neighbours or *degree*.

Although the series of steps of Sect. 4.2 can be wholly carried out by adopting $\mathcal{E} := (\varepsilon_{ij})$ as the reference exchange matrix, this procedure reveals itself far form satisfactory in general: exchanges between non-adjacent regions are precluded, as are the diagonal exchanges, thus mechanically generating negative eigenvalues in view of $0 = \text{trace}(\mathcal{E}^s) = 1 + \sum_{\alpha \geq 1} \lambda_\alpha$. Even worse, the normalized degree σ in (4.15), reflecting the regions centrality, strongly differs in general from the regions weights f, reflecting their importance: a densely populated region can be weakly connected to the rest of the territory, and inversely.

Proposals A and B below aim at converting an accessibility matrix A into an exchange matrix E with given margins f, while keeping the neighborhood structure expressed by A as intact as possible.

4.3.1 Proposal A: Simple Rescaling with Diagonal Adjustment

Define the symmetric exchange matrix

$$e_{ij} := \begin{cases} Cb_i b_j a_{ij} & \text{if } i \neq j \\ h_i & \text{otherwise.} \end{cases} \tag{4.16}$$

where C, b and h are non-negative quantities obeying the normalisation condition (recall $a_{ii} = 0$)

$$Cb_i \sum_j a_{ij} b_j + h_i = f_i \qquad \text{for all } i. \tag{4.17}$$

By construction, $e_{i\bullet} = f_i$ and, for $i \neq j$, $e_{ij} = 0$ whenever $a_{ij} = 0$.

An obvious choice, among many possibilities, consists in defining b as the first normalised eigenvector of the accessibility matrix A, that is obeying $Ab = \mu b$, where $\mu > 0$ is the largest eigenvalue of A, and b (normalised to $\sum_i b_i^2 = 1$) is non-negative by the Perron-Froebenius theorem on non-negative matrices. b_i (or b_i^2) is a measure of relative centrality of region i, sometimes referred to as *eigenvector centrality* in the social networks literature.

Condition (4.17) becomes $C\mu b_i^2 + h_i = f_i$, implying $C = (1-\eta)/\mu$, where the quantity $\eta := \sum_i h_i$ fixes the diagonal parameters to $h_i = f_i - (1-\eta)b_i^2$, and ranges in $\eta \in [H, 1]$ to insure the non-negativity of C and h, where $H := 1 - \min_i(f_i/b_i^2) \geq 0$.

The free parameter η controls the "autarchy of the network": in the limit $\eta \to 1$, one recovers the frozen network of Sect. 4.2.3.3, while $\eta \to H$ yields at least one region with $e_{ii} = 0$. Note that $e_{ii} = 0$ cannot hold for all regions, unless $b \equiv \sqrt{f}$ precisely, in which case $H = 0$.

4.3.2 *Proposal B: Time-Embeddable Exchange Matrices*

The second proposal is based upon the observation that κ_{ij} in (4.15) constitutes a *jump transition matrix*, defining the probability that j will be the next, *distinct* region to be visited after having been in region i (recall $\kappa_{ii} = 0$). Suppose in addition that, once arrived in j, the state remains in j for a certain random time t_j with cumulative distribution function $F_j(t)$, with average waiting time or *sojurn time* $\tau_j = \int t\, dF_j(t)$. This set-up precisely defines a so-called *semi-Markov process* (e.g. Çinlar 1975; Barbu and Limnios 2008).

Together, the stationary distribution σ_j (4.15) of the jump transition matrix κ_{ij} and the sojurn times τ_j determine the fraction of time spend in region j, that is the regional weight f_j, as (see e.g. Bavaud 2008b)

$$f_j = \frac{\sigma_j \tau_j}{\tau} \quad \text{where} \quad \tau := \sum_j \sigma_j \tau_j \quad \text{or equivalently} \quad \frac{1}{\tau} = \sum_j \frac{f_j}{\tau_j}\ . \tag{4.18}$$

Furthermore, requiring exponentially distributed random times t_j ensures the semi-Markov process to be *continuous* or *time-embeddable*, that is of the form $W(t) = \exp(t\,R)$ (matrix exponential) where $R = (r_{ij})$ is the $n \times n$ *rate transition matrix*, with components $r_{ij} = (\kappa_{ij} - \delta_{ij})/\tau_i$. In particular,

$$\sum_j r_{ij} = 0 \qquad\qquad \sum_i f_i\, r_{ij} = 0 \quad . \tag{4.19}$$

The existence of transition matrices $W(t) = (w_{ij}(t))$ defined for *any continuous time* $t \geq 0$, rather than limited to integer values $t = 0, 1, 2, \ldots$, characterises time-embeddable Markov chains. The symmetry of the associated exchange matrices $e_{ij}(t) := f_i\, w_{ij}(t)$ follows from the reversibility of $W(t)$, itself insured by the reversibility of the jump matrix.

In summary, proposal B considers the adjacency matrix A as an *infinitesimal generator* of the exchange matrix E; tuning the freely adjustable sojurn times τ_j in (4.18) permits to transform any degree distribution σ into any given regional weights f, as required.

To achieve the practical, numerical construction of the time-embeddable exchange matrix $E(t)$, consider the "standardised rate matrix" $Q = (q_{ij})$ with components

$$q_{ij} := f_i^{\frac{1}{2}} f_j^{-\frac{1}{2}} r_{ij} = \frac{\varepsilon_{ij} - \delta_{ij}\sigma_j}{\tau\sqrt{f_i f_j}} \quad . \tag{4.20}$$

Q is semi-negative definite (see the Appendix). Its eigenvalues μ_α and associated normalised eigenvectors $u_{i\alpha}$ satisfy $\mu_0 = 0$ with $u_{i0} = \sqrt{f_i}$, together with $\mu_\alpha \leq 0$ for the non-trivial eigenvalues $\alpha = 1, \ldots, n-1$. Now the eigenvectors of the standardized exchange matrix $E^s(t) = (e^s_{ij}(t))$ (4.5) turn out to be *identical* to those of Q, irrespectively of value of t, (see the Appendix), while the non-trivial eigenvalues of $E^s(t)$ are related to those of Q by $\lambda_\alpha(t) = \exp(\mu_\alpha t)$ for $\alpha = 1, \ldots, n-1$. Substituting back in (4.6) finally yields the exchange matrix as

$$e_{ij}(t) = f_i f_j [1 + \sum_{\alpha \geq 1} \lambda_\alpha(t) c_{i\alpha} c_{j\alpha}] \quad \text{where } c_{i\alpha} = \frac{u_{i\alpha}}{\sqrt{f_i}} \text{ and } \lambda_\alpha(t) = \exp(\mu_\alpha t). \tag{4.21}$$

The eigenvalues $\lambda_\alpha(t)$ of the standardized exchange matrix $E^s(t)$ (4.5) are *non-negative*. This characterizes continuous-time Markov chain and *diffusive processes*, by contrast to *oscillatory processes* associated to negative eigenvalues, as in the bipartite network of Fig. 4.1, or as in the direct accessibility-based approach (4.15).

As a matter of fact, temporal dependence enters through the quantity t/τ only: defining Q^* as (4.20) with $\tau = 1$ and μ^* as the corresponding non-trivial eigenvalues, one gets $\lambda_\alpha(t) = (\exp(\mu^*_\alpha))^{\frac{t}{\tau}}$, which can be directly substituted into (4.11) to compute Moran's I. Note the modes $\hat{x}_\alpha = \sum_i \sqrt{f_i} u_{i\alpha} x_i$, where the $u_{i\alpha}$ are the eigenvectors of Q^*, to be time-independent.

The free parameter t (or t/τ) represents the (relative) "age of the network". $E(t)$ tends to the frozen network for $t \to 0$, and to the perfectly mobile network for $t \to \infty$ (Sect. 4.2.3.3). One expects spatial autocorrelation to be more easily detected for small values of t, that is for networks able to sustain strong contrasts between local and global variances.

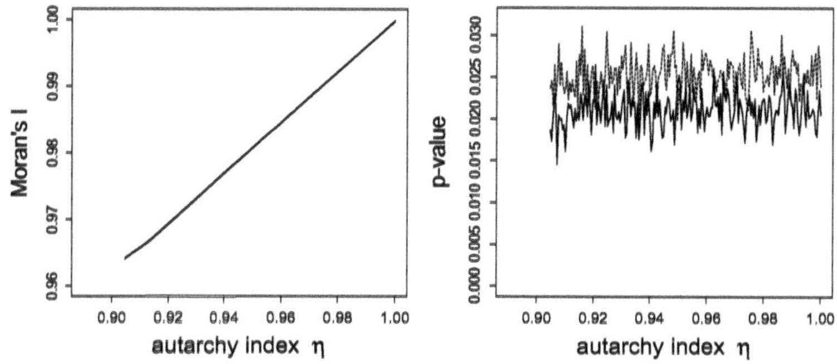

Fig. 4.4 "Blood group A in Eire" dataset: proposal A. *Left*: Moran's I as a function of $\eta \in [H, 1]$. *Right*: two-tailed p-values of the modes autocorrelation test, based upon $B = 10000$ permutation (*bold line*) or bootstrap (*dashed line*) resamples

4.3.3 *Illustration: The Distribution of Blood Group a in Eire*

Let us revisit the popular "distribution of Blood group A in Eire" dataset (Cliff and Ord 1973; Upton and Fingleton 1985; Griffith 2003; Tiefelsdorf and Griffith 2007), recording the percentage x of the 1958 adult population with of Blood group A in each of the $n = 26$ Eire counties, as well as the relative population size f, and the inter-regional adjacency matrix A (data from the R package spdep Bivand 2009b).

Following the "proposal A" procedure of Sect. 4.3.1 yields $\mu = 5.11$ and $H = 0.904$, echoing the existence of a region whose weight f_i is about ten times smaller than its "eigenvector centrality" b_i^2. Both permutation and bootstrap modes autocorrelation tests reveal statistically significant spatial autocorrelation, without obvious dependence upon the autarchy index η (Fig. 4.4).

"Proposal B" procedure of Sect. 4.3.2 yields p-values depicted in Fig. 4.5, left. As expected, they reveal statistically significant spatial autocorrelation for small values of t/τ, and increase with t/τ. Starting the procedure with one among the many possible permutations of the field produces p-values as in Fig. 4.5 (right) and indicates no spatial autocorrelation, as it must.

4.4 Conclusion

Real spatial networks are irregular and subject to aggregation. They are bound to exhibit regions differing in sizes or weights. This paper proposes a weighted analysis of Moran's I, in the possibly most general set-up provided by the exchange matrix formalism, rooted in the theory of reversible Markov chains and gravity flows of geographers.

Besides providing a rationale for overcoming the heteroscedasticity problem in the direct application of permutation or bootstrap autocorrelation tests, the concept

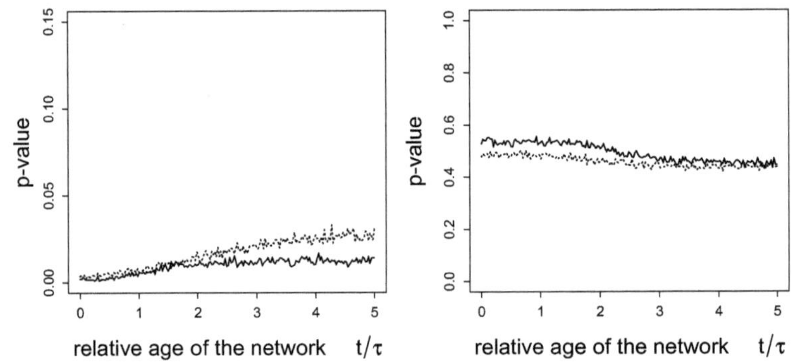

Fig. 4.5 "Blood group A in Eire" dataset: proposal B. *Left*: two-tailed p-values of the modes autocorrelation test, based upon $B = 10000$ permutation (*bold line*) or bootstrap (*dashed line*) resamples. *Right*: the same procedure, applied to an arbitrarily selected permutation $\pi(x)$ of the original spatial field x

of spatial modes we have elaborated upon arguably generalises the concept of spectrally-based spatial filtering (e.g. Griffith 2003) to a weighted setting, and helps integrating other network-related issues in a unified setting: typically, the first non-trivial raw coordinate c_1 of Sect. 4.2.2 has been known for some time to provide the optimal solution to the spectral clustering problem, partitioning a weighted graph into two balanced components (e.g. Chung 1997; von Luxburg 2007; Bavaud 2010).

Finally, local variance (4.4) can be generalised to local inertias $\frac{1}{2}\sum_{ij} e_{ij}D_{ij}$ (where D represents a squared Euclidean distance between regions) and to local covariances $\frac{1}{2}\sum_{ij} e_{ij}(x_i-x_j)(y_i-y_j)$, whose future study may hopefully enrich formal issues and applications in spatial autocorrelation.

Appendix

Proof of (4.7) U being orthogonal, $\sum_i f_i c_{i\alpha} c_{i\beta} = \sum_i u_{i\alpha} u_{i\beta} = \delta_{\alpha\beta}$ and $\sum_i f_i c_{i\alpha} = \sum_i \sqrt{f_i} u_{i\alpha} = \sum_i u_{i0} u_{i\alpha} = \delta_{\alpha 0}$.

Proof of (4.9) independence implies the functional form $\sigma_{ij} = \delta_{ij}\, g(f_i)$ where $g(f)$ expresses a possible size dependence. Consider the aggregation of regions j into super-region J, with aggregated field $X_J = \sum_{j\in J} f_j X_j / f_J$, where $f_J := \sum_{j\in J} f_j$. By construction,

$$g(f_J) = \mathrm{Var}(X_J) = \frac{1}{f_J^2} \sum_{i,j\in J} f_i f_j \sigma_{ij} = \frac{1}{f_J^2} \sum_{j\in J} f_j^2 g(f_j)$$

that is $f_J^2\, g(f_J) = \sum_{j\in J} f_j^2 g(f_j)$, with unique solution $g(f_j) = \sigma^2/f_j$ (and $g(f_J) = \sigma^2/f_J$), where $\sigma^2 = \mathrm{Var}(X)$.

Proof of (4.10) $\hat{\sigma}_{\alpha\beta} := \mathrm{Cov}(\hat{X}_\alpha, \hat{X}_\beta) = \sum_{ij} f_i f_j c_{i\alpha} c_{j\beta} \mathrm{Cov}(X_i, X_j) = \sigma^2 \sum_i f_i c_{i\alpha} c_{i\beta} = \sigma^2 \sum_i u_{i\alpha} u_{i\beta} = \sigma^2 \delta_{\alpha\beta}$.

Proof of (4.11) $\sum_{\alpha\geq 1} \hat{x}_\alpha^2 = \sum_{ij} \sqrt{f_i f_j} x_i x_j \sum_{\alpha\geq 0} u_{i\alpha} u_{j\alpha} - \hat{x}_0^2 = \sum_i f_i x_i^2 - \bar{x}^2 = \mathrm{var}(x)$. Also, $\mathrm{var}_{\mathrm{loc}}(x) = \frac{1}{2} \sum_{ij} e_{ij}(x_i - x_j)^2 = \sum_i f_i x_i^2 - \sum_{ij} e_{ij} x_i x_j = \sum_i f_i x_i^2 - \bar{x}^2 - \sum_{\alpha\geq 1} \lambda_\alpha \sum_i c_{i\alpha} x_i \sum_j c_{j\alpha} x_j = \mathrm{var}(x) - \sum_{\alpha\geq 1} \lambda_\alpha \hat{x}_\alpha^2$.

Proof of (4.12) and (4.13) define

$$a_\alpha := \frac{\hat{x}_\alpha^2}{\sum_{\beta\geq 1} \hat{x}_\beta^2} \qquad \text{with} \qquad \sum_{\alpha\geq 1} a_\alpha = 1 \qquad \text{and} \qquad I(\hat{x}) = \sum_{\alpha\geq 1} \lambda_\alpha a_\alpha \ .$$

Under H_0, the distribution of the non-trivial modes is exchangeable, i.e. $f(a) = f(\pi(a))$. By symmetry, $E_\pi(a_\alpha) = 1/(n-1)$, $E_\pi(a_\alpha^2) = s(x)/(n-1)^2$ where $s(x) = \sum_{\beta\geq 1} a_\beta^2/(n-1)$ and $E_\pi(a_\alpha a_\beta) = (1 - s(x)/(n-1))/[(n-1)(n-2)]$ for $\alpha \neq \beta$. Further substitution proves the result.

Proof of the Semi-Negative Definiteness of Q in (4.20) for any vector h,

$$0 \leq \frac{1}{2} \sum_{ij} \varepsilon_{ij}(h_i - h_j)^2 = \sum_i \sigma_i h_i^2 - \sum_{ij} \epsilon_{ij} h_i h_j = -\sum_{ij} (\epsilon_{ij} - \delta_{ij}\sigma_j) h_i h_j \ .$$

Relation Between the Eigen-Decompositions of $E^s(t)$ and Q in (4.20) in matrix notation, $Q = \Pi^{\frac{1}{2}} R \Pi^{-\frac{1}{2}}$, and hence $Q\sqrt{f} = 0$ by (4.19), showing $u_0 = \sqrt{f}$ with $\mu_0 = 0$. Consider another, non-trivial eigenvector u_α of Q, with eigenvalue μ_α, orthogonal to $\sqrt{f}$ by construction. Identity $E(t) = \Pi \exp(tR)$ together with (4.5) yield

$$E^s(t) = \sum_{k\geq 0} \frac{t^k}{k!} Q^k - \sqrt{f}\sqrt{f}' \qquad\qquad E^s(t) u_\alpha = \sum_{k\geq 0} \frac{t^k \mu_\alpha^k}{k!} u_\alpha = \exp(\mu_\alpha t) u_\alpha \ .$$

References

Aldous D, Fill J (2002) Reversible Markov Chains and Random Walks on Graphs. Draft chapters, online version available at http://www.stat.berkeley.edu/users/aldous/RWG/book.html

Anselin L (1988) Spatial econometrics: methods and models. Kluwer, Boston

Anselin L (1995) Local indicators of spatial association - LISA. Geogr Anal 27:93–115

Arbia G (2006) Spatial econometrics: statistical foundations and applications to regional convergence. Springer, Berlin

Assunção RM, Reis EA (1999) A new proposal to adjust Moran's I for population density. Stat Med 18:2147–2162

Barbu VS, Limnios N (2008) Semi-Markov chains and hidden semi-Markov models toward applications: their use in reliability and DNA analysis. Springer, New York

Bavaud F (1998) Models for spatial weights: a systematic look. Geogr Anal 30:153–171

Bavaud F (2002) The quasisymmetric side of gravity modelling. Environ Plan A 34:61–79

Bavaud F (2008a) Local concentrations. Pap Reg Sci 87:357–370

Bavaud F (2008b) The endogenous analysis of flows, with applications to migrations, social mobility and opinion shifts. J Math Sociol 32:239–266

Bavaud F (2010) Multiple soft clustering, spectral clustering and distances on weighted graphs. Proceedings of the ECML PKDD'10. Lecture notes in computer science, vol 6321. Springer, Heidelberg , pp 103–118

Berger J, Snell JL (1957) On the concept of equal exchange. Behav Sci 2:111–118

Besag J, Diggle PJ (1977) Simple Monte Carlo tests for spatial pattern. J R Stat Soc C Appl Stat 26:327–333

Bivand RS, Müller W, Reder M (2009a) Power calculations for global and local Moran's I. Comput Stat Data Anal 53:2859–2872

Bivand R (2009b) Applying measures of spatial autocorrelation: computation and simulation. Geogr Anal 41:375–384

Chun Y (2008) Modeling network autocorrelation within migration flows by eigenvector spatial filtering. J Geogr Syst 10:317–344

Chung FRK (1997) Spectral graph theory. CBMS regional conference series in mathematics, vol 92. American Mathematical Society, Washington

Çinlar E (1975) Introduction to stochastic processes. Prentice Hall, New York

Cliff AD, Ord JK (1973) Spatial autocorrelation. Pion, London

Cliff AD, Ord JK (1981) Spatial processes: models & applications. Pion, London

Corcoran CD, Mehta CR (2002) Exact level and power of permutation, bootstrap, and asymptotic tests of trend. J Mod Appl Stat Methods 1:42–51

Cressie NAC (1993) Statistics for spatial data. Wiley, New York

Dray S (2011) A new perspective about Moran's coefficient: spatial autocorrelation as a linear regression problem. Geogr Anal 43:127–141

Fotheringham AS, O'Kelly ME (1989) Spatial interaction models: formulations and applications. Kluwer, Dordrecht

Geary R (1954) The contiguity ratio and statistical mapping. Inc Stat 5:115–145

Goodchild MF, Smith TR (1980) Intransitivity, the spatial interaction model, and US migration streams. Environ Plan A 12:1131–1144

Griffith DA (2000) Eigenfunction properties and approximations of selected incidence matrices employed in spatial analyses. Linear Algebra Appl 321:95–112

Griffith DA (2003) Spatial autocorrelation and spatial filtering: gaining understanding through theory and scientific visualization. Springer, Berlin

Griffith DA, Peres-Neto PR (2006) Spatial modeling in ecology: the flexibility of eigenfunction spatial analyses. Ecology 87:2603–2613

Haining RP (2003) Spatial data analysis: theory and practice. Cambridge University Press, Cambridge

Janssen A, Pauls T (2005) A Monte Carlo comparison of studentized bootstrap and permutation tests for heteroscedastic two-sample problems. Comput Stat 20:369–383

Kijima M (1997) Markov processes for stochastic modeling. Chapman & Hall, London

Lebart L (1969) Analyse statistique de la contiguïté. Publ Inst Stat Univ Paris 18:81–112

Leenders RTAJ (2002) Modeling social influence through network autocorrelation: constructing the weight matrix. Soc Networks 24:21–47

LeSage JP, Pace RK (2009) Introduction to spatial econometrics. Chapman & Hall, Boca Raton

Li H, Calder CA, Cressie N (2007) Beyond Moran's I: testing for spatial dependence based on the spatial autoregressive model. Geogr Anal 39:357–375

Moran PAP (1950) Notes on continuous stochastic phenomena. Biometrika 37:17–23

Sen A, Smith T (1995) Gravity models of spatial interaction behavior. Springer, Berlin

Thioulouse J, Chessel D, Champely S (1995) Multivariate analysis of spatial patterns: a unified approach to local and global structures. Environ Ecol Stat 2:1–14

Tiefelsdorf M, Boots B (1995) The exact distribution of Moran's I. Environ Plan A 27:985–999

Tiefelsdorf M, Griffith DA (2007) Semiparametric filtering of spatial autocorrelation: the eigenvector approach. Environ Plan A 39:1193–221

Upton G, Fingleton B (1985) Spatial data analysis by example. Wiley, New York

von Luxburg U (2007) A tutorial on spectral clustering. Stat Comput 17:395–416

Waldhör T (1996) The spatial autocorrelation coefficient Moran's I under heteroscedasticity. Stat Med 15:887–892

Willekens FJ (1983) Specification and calibration of spatial interaction models: a contingency-table perspective and an application to intra-urban migration in Rotterdam. Tijdschr Econ Soc Geografie 74:239–252

Chapter 5
Effects of Scale in Spatial Interaction Models

Giuseppe Arbia and Francesca Petrarca

Keywords Gravity models • Modifiable areal unit problem • Spatial autoregressive random fields • Spatial interaction models

JEL Classification: C21, R19

5.1 Introduction

The MAUP (Modifiable Areal Unit Problem) is a particular form of the more general Modifiable Unit Problem (MUP) that has a long tradition in statistics, see Yule and Kendall (1950), whose spatial manifestation has been treated at length by Openshaw and Taylor (1979); Arbia (1989) among others. The MAUP presents two facets. The first is known as the "scale problem" and refers to the indeterminacy of any statistical measure with respect to changes in the level of data aggregation (e.g. from NUTS-3 to NUTS-2 in the EUROSTAT 2012). The second is referred to as the "aggregation (or zoning) problem" and concerns the indeterminacy of any statistical measure with respect to changes in the aggregation criterion at a given spatial scale (e.g. two alternative partitions of the same area at a given spatial scale). In this paper we explicitly aim to study the effects of scale on non linear spatial interaction

*This paper has been previously published in the Journal of Geographical Systems. Special Issue on "Advances in the Statistical Modelling of Spatial Interaction Data", Vol. 15, Number 3/July 2013, © Springer-Verlag Berlin Heidelberg, pp. 249–264.

G. Arbia (✉)
Department of Statistics, Catholic University of the Sacred Heart, Largo Francesco Vito, 1, 00168, Rome, Italy
e-mail: giuseppe.arbia@rm.unicatt.it

F. Petrarca
Department of Economics "Federico Caffè", Roma Tre University, Via Silvio D'Amico, 77, 00145 Roma, Italy

R. Patuelli, G. Arbia (eds.), *Spatial Econometric Interaction Modelling*, Advances in Spatial Science, DOI 10.1007/978-3-319-30196-9_5

models. A full understanding of the effects of MAUP on spatial interaction models is relevant in many practical circumstances like, e.g., in the choice of the appropriated spatial scale of analysis and of the spatial partition to be considered in geographical studies, in the identification of possible ecological fallacies, in the inference of individual (or disaggregated level) relationships from spatially aggregated data, in the correct interpretation of the parameters' estimates, and in the identification of worst case scenarios when changing the level of aggregation. Furthermore, in general a full understanding of the effects of MAUP is important to suggest grouping criteria that preserve some properties when choosing between alternative zoning systems at a given scale, in spatial interpolation and in small area estimation. Finally it is relevant to suggest how to approximate the value of parameters when we are interested at a fine level of aggregation (e.g. in EU NUTS-3), but we only avail data at a coarser level of aggregation (e.g. in EU NUTS-2). It should be noted that there is a close analogy between the problem of disaggregating information and a parametric sampling problem. In both instances we start from a limited set of information (the sample data in one case and the aggregated data in the other) and we make use of them in order to acquire knowledge about some unknown features of a wider set of data (a population parameter in one case and a parameter at the disaggregated level in the other). The parametric inferential problem based on sample data is traditionally solved by imposing some working hypotheses on the unknown population and on the sampling criterion used to derive useful indications in point and interval estimation and in hypothesis testing. BY analogy in the disaggregation problem we can impose some working hypotheses on the generating unknown disaggregated process and on the grouping criterion in order to deduce the parameters value at the aggregated level and use it to derive useful indications in the disaggregation process. This is the approach we used in the present paper.

The setup of the paper is the following. In Sect. 5.2 we present a brief literature review of the subject. In Sect. 5.3 we present a formalization of the effects of MAUP in spatial interaction models by extending the approach employed in Arbia and Petrarca (2011). In particular, we consider four different hypotheses for the origin and the destination variables assuming that they are (*a*) non-stochastic; (*b*) stochastic but without a spatial structure; (*c*) stochastic, spatially autocorrelated and mutually independent and (*d*) stochastic, spatially autocorrelated and linearly dependent. Section 5.4 reports the results of some simulations based on the theory developed in Sect. 5.3, by referring in particular to the case of perfect aggregation, (Theil 1954). The aim is to identify the worst case scenarios and to test the effects on the aggregated flows of the introduction of spatial dependence in the origin and in the destination variables. Some final remarks are reported in the concluding Sect. 5.5.

5.2 Literature Review

The effects of MUP on econometric models without reference to the peculiarity of spatial data are well known dating back to the early contributions of Prais and Aitchinson (1954); Theil (1954); Zellner (1962); Cramer (1964); Haitovsky (1973); Orcutt et al. (1968); Pesaran et al. (1989) to name only a few. The main results found in the literature are that the generalized least squares (GLS) estimators of the regression parameters based on aggregated data are still best linear unbiased (BLUE), even though they present a sampling variance greater than the one obtained when using GLS on the original data. Such an underestimation of the variance of the parameters in turn implies biases in the hypothesis testing on the parameters leading to wrong inferential conclusions. A consequence is that the null hypothesis is rejected more frequently than it should when we use aggregated data. The magnitude of this efficiency loss of the estimators depends on the grouping criterion and it is reduced to a minimum when groups are created to maximize the within-group variability with respect to the between-group variability. Furthermore the coefficient of determination is emphasized by aggregation. The general conclusion is that micro-data can better discriminate between alternative specifications of the models with respect to aggregate data. Referring specifically to spatial data Arbia (1989) derived the formal relationship between the simple Pearsons' correlation coefficient at the original process level (or level-1) and the same at the aggregate process level (level-2) when data are spatially correlated. In Arbia and Petrarca (2011) this results were extended to the effects of aggregation on a general spatial autoregressive linear econometric model. Focusing on the effects of scale this paper shows that the obvious efficiency loss of the GLS estimators (connatural to the process of aggregation) is, generally speaking, mitigated by the presence of a positive spatial correlation and conversely exacerbated by the presence of a negative spatial correlation both in the error component and in the dependent variable of the model. This result is coherent with the theoretical expectations. Positive spatial correlation implies that the aggregation between similar values preserves variability. Conversely negative spatial correlation implies a more pronounced reduction of variability and, hence, a greater efficiency loss.

5.3 A Formalization of MAUP in Spatial Gravity Models

We start considering the classical origin-destination simple gravitational model (see LeSage and Fisher 2010):

$$F_{ij} = kO_iD_jd_{ij}^{-2} \tag{5.1}$$

with F_{ij} the flow between location i and location j, k a dimensionality parameter, O_i the origin variable of the flow in location i, D_j the destination variable of the flow in location j and d_{ij} the distance (however measured) between location i and location j. Furthermore $i = 1, 2, \ldots, n, j = 1, 2, \ldots, n$ and n is the number of locations. Let us express the model in a matrix notation by setting:

$$F_{ij} \in \underset{n \cdot n}{F}; \qquad O_i \in \underset{n \cdot n}{\hat{O}}; \qquad D_j \in \underset{n \cdot n}{\hat{D}}; \qquad d_{ij}^{-2} \in \underset{n \cdot n}{\Delta} = \begin{bmatrix} 0 & d_{12}^{-2} \ldots d_{1n}^{-2} \\ d_{21}^{-2} & 0 \quad \ldots \ldots \\ \ldots \ldots & 0 \quad \ldots \\ d_{n1}^{-2} & \ldots \ldots \quad 0 \end{bmatrix}$$

the symbol ^ denoting the diagonal matrices. In the paper, we will consistently assume that d can be measured without error so that the matrix $\underset{n \cdot n}{\Delta}$ is non-stochastic.

Following this notation, we can rewrite Eq. (5.1) in matrix symbols as:

$$\underset{n \cdot n}{F} = k \underset{n \cdot n}{\hat{O}} \underset{n \cdot n}{\Delta} \underset{n \cdot n}{\hat{D}} \tag{5.2}$$

The whole system of interaction can be characterized by the *mean flow* given by:

$$\mu = \frac{1}{n^2} i^T \underset{n \cdot n}{F} i = \frac{1}{n^2} k \, i^T \underset{n \cdot n n \cdot n n \cdot n}{\hat{O} \Delta \hat{D}} i \tag{5.3}$$

where i is a unitary vector: $\underset{1 \cdot n}{i^T} = [1 \ 1 \ \ldots 1]$.

Let us now consider the case where we aggregate the original dataset, observed on n locations, into a more aggregated partition of, say, $m < n$ locations. In the present paper, we restrict to the case of perfect aggregation (Theil 1954) that is the case when the number of disaggregated units in each group is constant and it is equal to $r = n/m$. Thus defined the parameter r quantifies the idea of the *level of aggregation*. When $r = 1$ aggregation is minimal and we refer to the maximally disaggregated level. Conversely, when $r = n$ aggregation is at its maximum and all information is concentrated in one single aggregated value. In particular, we will consider 4 cases of increasing complexity:

(a) $\underset{n \cdot n}{\hat{O}}$ and $\underset{n \cdot n}{\hat{D}}$ are non stochastic;
(b) $\underset{n \cdot n}{\hat{O}}$ and $\underset{n \cdot n}{\hat{D}}$ are stochastic and with no spatial structure;
(c) $\underset{n \cdot n}{\hat{O}}$ and $\underset{n \cdot n}{\hat{D}}$ are stochastic, spatially autocorrelated and independent on one another;
(d) $\underset{n \cdot n}{\hat{O}}$ and $\underset{n \cdot n}{\hat{D}}$ are stochastic, spatially autocorrelated and mutually dependent.

These case will be discussed in turn in the following sections.

5.3.1 Case a: $\hat{O}$ and $\hat{D}$ Are Non Stochastic

Let us introduce the aggregation matrix G defined as:

$$\underset{m\cdot n}{G} = \begin{bmatrix} \overbrace{1 \; \ldots \; 1}^{r\ times} \; 0 \ldots\ldots\ldots & & 0 \\ 0 \; \ldots \; 0 \; 1 \ldots \; 1 & 0 & \ldots 0 \\ \ldots \quad \ldots & & \ldots \\ 0 \; \ldots \; 0 \; 0 \ldots \; 0 & 1 & \ldots 1 \end{bmatrix}$$

with a cell size r (an integer) given by $r = \frac{n}{m}$.

As a consequence, the aggregated origin and destination variables are given by:

$$\underset{m\cdot m}{\hat{O}^*} = \underset{m\cdot n}{G}\;\underset{n\cdot n}{\hat{O}}\;\underset{n\cdot m}{G^T}; \quad \underset{m\cdot m}{\hat{D}^*} = \underset{m\cdot n}{G}\;\underset{n\cdot n}{\hat{D}}\;\underset{n\cdot m}{G^T}$$

Thus the aggregated flows $\underset{m\cdot m}{F^*}$ are given by:

$$\underset{m\cdot m}{F^*} = h\underset{m\cdot m}{\hat{O}^*}\;\underset{m\cdot m}{\Delta^*}\;\underset{m\cdot m}{\hat{D}^*} = h\underset{m\cdot n}{G}\;\underset{n\cdot n}{\hat{O}}\;\underset{n\cdot m}{G^T}\;\underset{m\cdot m}{\Delta^*}\;\underset{m\cdot n}{G}\;\underset{n\cdot n}{\hat{D}}\;\underset{n\cdot m}{G^T} \tag{5.4}$$

where $\underset{m\cdot m}{\Delta^*}$ is a non stochastic and exogenously given matrix and h a constant term.

The whole system of interaction can again be characterized by the mean flow which can now be expressed as:

$$\begin{aligned} \mu^* &= \frac{1}{m^2} i^{*^T} \underset{m\cdot m}{F^*} i^* = \frac{1}{m^2} h i^{*^T} \underset{m\cdot m}{\hat{O}^*}\;\underset{m\cdot m}{\Delta^*}\;\underset{m\cdot m}{\hat{D}^*} i^* \\ &= \frac{1}{m^2} h i^{*^T} \underset{m\cdot n}{G}\;\underset{n\cdot n}{\hat{O}}\;\underset{n\cdot m}{G^T}\;\underset{m\cdot m}{\Delta^*}\;\underset{m\cdot n}{G}\;\underset{n\cdot n}{\hat{D}}\;\underset{n\cdot m}{G^T} i^* \end{aligned} \tag{5.5}$$

with i^* represents the unitary vector of dimension m $\underset{1\cdot m}{i^{*^T}} = [1\ 1\ \ldots 1]$.

The *relative change of mean flow* from one aggregation level to the higher can thus be measured by:

$$RC(r) = \frac{\mu^*}{\mu} = \frac{hn^2}{km^2} \frac{i^{*^T} G\,\hat{O}\,G^T\,\Delta^*\,G\,\hat{D}\,G^T i^*}{i^T\,\hat{O}\Delta\hat{D}\,i} \tag{5.6}$$

The RC(r) function represents the aggregation bias in that it describes how the mean flows are affected by the level of aggregation that (in this case of perfect aggregation that we are considering here) can be expressed by the number of units in each group given by $r = n/m$. By definition $RC(r) \geq 1$ in that aggregation, other things being constant, produces a reduction of the variability of the origin and the destination variables, that in turn generates an increase in the observed flows. However, the introduction of a more realistic dependence structure of the origin and the destination variables produces the effect of moderating or (conversely) exacerbating this effect as we will show in the next sections.

5.3.2 Case b: $\hat{O}$ and $\hat{D}$ Are Stochastic and Independent

When both the origin and the destination are stochastic, due to the presence of measurement error, we can specify O and D as follows:

$$\underset{n\cdot n}{\hat{O}} = \underset{n\cdot n}{\hat{\mu}_O} + \underset{n\cdot n}{\hat{\varepsilon}} \tag{5.7}$$

$$\underset{n\cdot n}{\hat{D}} = \underset{n\cdot n}{\hat{\mu}_D} + \underset{n\cdot n}{\hat{\eta}} \tag{5.8}$$

where $\underset{n\cdot n}{\hat{\mu}_O} = \mu_O \underset{n\cdot n}{I}$ and similarly $\underset{n\cdot n}{\hat{\mu}_D} = \mu_D \underset{n\cdot n}{I}$, with $\hat{\mu}_O$ and $\hat{\mu}_D$ constants, $\underset{n\cdot n}{I}$ the identity matrix and $\varepsilon_i \in \underset{n\cdot n}{\hat{\varepsilon}}$, $\eta_i \in \underset{n\cdot n}{\hat{\eta}}$ where $\underset{n\cdot 1}{\varepsilon}$ *iid* $N(0, \sigma_\varepsilon^2 I)$ and $\underset{n\cdot 1}{\eta}$ *iid* $N(0, \sigma_\eta^2 I)$.

Consequently the disaggregated flow reported in Eq. (5.2) now becomes:

$$\underset{n\cdot n}{F} = k\left(\underset{n\cdot n}{\hat{\mu}_O} + \underset{n\cdot n}{\hat{\varepsilon}}\right) \underset{n\cdot n}{\Delta} \left(\underset{n\cdot n}{\hat{\mu}_D} + \underset{n\cdot n}{\hat{\eta}}\right) \tag{5.9}$$

The aggregated flow Eq. (5.4), instead, becomes:

$$\underset{m\cdot m}{F^*} = h\left(\underset{m\cdot m}{\hat{\mu}_O^*} + \underset{m\cdot m}{\hat{\varepsilon}^*}\right) \underset{m\cdot m}{\Delta^*} \left(\underset{m\cdot m}{\hat{\mu}_D^*} + \underset{m\cdot m}{\hat{\eta}^*}\right) \tag{5.10}$$

where

$$\underset{m\cdot m}{\hat{\mu}_O^*} = \underset{m\cdot n}{G}\ \underset{n\cdot n}{\hat{\mu}_O}\ \underset{n\cdot m}{G^T}; \quad \underset{m\cdot m}{\hat{\varepsilon}^*} = \underset{m\cdot n}{G}\ \underset{n\cdot n}{\hat{\varepsilon}}\ \underset{n\cdot m}{G^T}; \quad \underset{m\cdot m}{\hat{\mu}_D^*} = \underset{m\cdot n}{G}\ \underset{n\cdot n}{\hat{\mu}_D}\ \underset{n\cdot m}{G^T}; \quad \underset{m\cdot m}{\hat{\eta}^*} = \underset{m\cdot n}{G}\ \underset{n\cdot n}{\hat{\eta}}\ \underset{n\cdot m}{G^T}.$$

Finally, the *relative change of mean flow* due to aggregation is now equal to:

$$RC(r, \sigma_\varepsilon^2, \sigma_\eta^2) = \frac{\mu^*}{\mu} = \frac{hn^2}{km^2} \frac{i^{*^T}\ (\hat{\mu}_O^* + \hat{\varepsilon}^*)\ \Delta^*\ (\hat{\mu}_D^* + \hat{\eta}^*)\ i^*}{i^T\ (\hat{\mu}_O + \hat{\varepsilon})\ \Delta\ (\hat{\mu}_D + \hat{\eta})\ i} \tag{5.11}$$

and can be seen as a function of the aggregation level r and of the two variances of the error terms, σ_ε^2 and σ_η^ε.

5.3.3 Case c: $\hat{O}$ and $\hat{D}$ Are Stochastic, Spatially Autocorrelated and Mutually Independent

As third case, let us assume that both the origin and the destination are stochastic and generated by a spatial autoregressive random field (for a different treatment of spatial dependence in spatial interaction models see Griffith 2009). In this case we can specify O and D as follows:

$$\underset{n\cdot n}{\hat{O}} = \rho \underset{n\cdot n}{W} \underset{n\cdot n}{\hat{O}} + \underset{n\cdot n}{\hat{\varepsilon}} + \underset{n\cdot n}{\hat{\mu}_O} \tag{5.12}$$

$$\underset{n\cdot n}{\hat{D}} = \lambda \underset{n\cdot n}{W} \underset{n\cdot n}{\hat{D}} + \underset{n\cdot n}{\hat{\eta}} + \underset{n\cdot n}{\hat{\mu}_D} \tag{5.13}$$

with W a weight matrix. It is the row-standardized n by n matrix defined according to the rook's case definition. The spatial correlation parameters λ and ρ can be specified such that $\overline{w}_{min} \le \rho \le \overline{w}_{max}$ and similarly $\overline{w}_{min} \le \lambda \le \overline{w}_{max}$, with $\overline{w}_{min}$, *and* $\overline{w}_{max}$ respectively the lower and the higher eigenvalues of W. Finally $\underset{n\cdot n}{\mu_O} = \mu_O \underset{n\cdot n}{I}$, $\underset{n\cdot n}{\hat{\mu}_D} = \mu_D \underset{n\cdot n}{I}$, with $\hat{\mu}_O$ and $\hat{\mu}_D$ constants as before. $\underset{n\cdot n}{I}$ is the identity matrix and $\varepsilon_i \in \underset{n\cdot n}{\hat{\varepsilon}}$, $\eta_i \in \underset{n\cdot n}{\hat{\eta}}$. As a consequence of Eqs. (5.12)–(5.13) we have that:

$$\underset{n\cdot n}{\hat{O}} = \left(\underset{n\cdot n}{I} - \rho \underset{n\cdot n}{W}\right)^{-1} \underset{n\cdot n}{\hat{\varepsilon}} + \left(\underset{n\cdot n}{I} - \rho \underset{n\cdot n}{W}\right)^{-1} \underset{n\cdot n}{\hat{\mu}_O} \tag{5.14}$$

$$\underset{n\cdot n}{\hat{D}} = \left(\underset{n\cdot n}{I} - \lambda \underset{n\cdot n}{W}\right)^{-1} \underset{n\cdot n}{\hat{\eta}} + \left(\underset{n\cdot n}{I} - \lambda \underset{n\cdot n}{W}\right)^{-1} \underset{n\cdot n}{\hat{\mu}_D} \tag{5.15}$$

Consequently the flow Eq. (5.2) now becomes:

$$\underset{n\cdot n}{F} = k\left[\underset{n\cdot n}{(I-\rho W)^{-1}} \underset{n\cdot n}{\hat{\varepsilon}} + \underset{n\cdot n}{(I-\rho W)^{-1}} \underset{n\cdot n}{\hat{\mu}_O}\right] \underset{n\cdot n}{\Delta} \left[\underset{n\cdot n}{(I-\lambda W)^{-1}} \underset{n\cdot n}{\hat{\eta}} + \underset{n\cdot n}{(I-\lambda W)^{-1}} \underset{n\cdot n}{\hat{\mu}_D}\right] \tag{5.16}$$

The aggregated origin and destinations are now given by:

$$\underset{m\cdot m}{\hat{O}^*} = \rho \underset{m\cdot m}{W^*} \underset{m\cdot m}{\hat{O}^*} + \underset{m\cdot m}{\hat{\varepsilon}^*} + \underset{m\cdot m}{\hat{\mu}_O^*} \tag{5.17}$$

$$\underset{m\cdot m}{\hat{D}^*} = \lambda \underset{m\cdot m}{W^*} \underset{m\cdot m}{\hat{D}^*} + \underset{m\cdot m}{\hat{\eta}^*} + \underset{m\cdot m}{\hat{\mu}_D^*} \tag{5.18}$$

and, finally, from Eqs (5.14)–(5.15), we have:

$$\underset{m\cdot m}{\hat{O}^*} = \left(\underset{m\cdot m}{I} - \rho \underset{m\cdot m}{W^*}\right)^{-1} \underset{m\cdot m}{\hat{\varepsilon}^*} + \left(\underset{m\cdot m}{I} - \rho \underset{m\cdot m}{W^*}\right)^{-1} \underset{m\cdot m}{\hat{\mu}_O^*} \tag{5.19}$$

$$\underset{m\cdot m}{\hat{D}^*} = \Big(\underset{m\cdot m}{I} - \lambda \underset{m\cdot m}{W^*}\Big)^{-1} \underset{m\cdot m}{\hat{\eta}^*} + \Big(\underset{m\cdot m}{I} - \lambda \underset{m\cdot m}{W^*}\Big)^{-1} \underset{m\cdot m}{\hat{\mu}_D^*} \tag{5.20}$$

Therefore using Eqs (5.19)–(5.20) aggregated flow Eq. (5.4) now becomes:

$$\begin{aligned}\underset{m\cdot m}{F^*} &= h\left[\underset{m\cdot m}{\left(I-\rho W^*\right)^{-1}}\underset{m\cdot m}{\hat{\varepsilon}^*} + \underset{m\cdot m}{\left(I-\rho W^*\right)^{-1}}\underset{m\cdot m}{\hat{\mu}_O^*}\right] \\ &\underset{m\cdot m}{\Delta^*}\left[\underset{m\cdot m}{\left(I-\lambda W^*\right)^{-1}}\underset{m\cdot m}{\hat{\eta}^*} + \underset{m\cdot m}{\left(I-\lambda W^*\right)^{-1}}\underset{m\cdot m}{\hat{\mu}_D^*}\right]\end{aligned} \tag{5.21}$$

and the *relative change of mean flow* due to the aggregation can be measured by:

$$\begin{aligned}RC(r,\sigma_\varepsilon^2,\sigma_\eta^2,\rho,\lambda) &= \frac{\mu^*}{\mu} = \\ &= \frac{hn^2}{km^2}\frac{i^{*T}\left[(I-\rho W^*)^{-1}\hat{\varepsilon}^* + (I-\rho W^*)^{-1}\hat{\mu}_O^*\right] \times \Delta^*\left[(I-\lambda W^*)^{-1}\hat{\eta}^* + (I-\lambda W^*)^{-1}\mu_D^*\right] i^*}{i^T\left[(I-\rho W)^{-1}\hat{\varepsilon} + (I-\rho W)^{-1}\hat{\mu}_O\right] \times \Delta\left[(I-\lambda W)^{-1}\hat{\eta} + (I-\lambda W)^{-1}\hat{\mu}_D\right] i}\end{aligned} \tag{5.22}$$

which is now a function of the aggregation level r, of the two variances of the error terms (σ_ε^2 and σ_η^2) and of the two spatial correlation parameters (λ and ρ).

5.3.4 Case d: $\hat{O}$ and $\hat{D}$ Are Stochastic, Spatially Autocorrelated and Mutually Dependent

Finally let us assume (as we already did in the case discussed in Sect. 5.3.3) that both the origin and the destination variables are stochastic and generated by spatial autoregressive random field, but that, in addition, they are also mutually dependent. In particular, without loss in generality, let us assume that the origin variable can be expressed as a linear function of the destination variable and of an additional spatial autoregressive term. We specify the relationship between O and D as follows:

$$\underset{n\cdot n}{\hat{O}} = \beta \underset{n\cdot n}{\hat{D}} + \rho \underset{n\cdot n}{W} \underset{n\cdot n}{\hat{O}} + \underset{n\cdot n}{\hat{\varepsilon}} + \underset{n\cdot n}{\hat{\mu}_O} \tag{5.23}$$

$$\underset{n\cdot n}{\hat{D}} = \lambda \underset{n\cdot n}{W} \underset{n\cdot n}{\hat{D}} + \underset{n\cdot n}{\hat{\eta}} + \underset{n\cdot n}{\hat{\mu}_D} \tag{5.24}$$

where β is a regression parameter. As a consequence of Eqs (5.23)–(5.24) we have that:

$$\underset{n\cdot n}{\hat{O}} = \underset{n\cdot n}{(I-\rho W)^{-1}}\beta \underset{n\cdot n}{\hat{D}} + \underset{n\cdot n}{(I-\rho W)^{-1}}\underset{n\cdot n}{\hat{\varepsilon}} + \underset{n\cdot n}{(I-\rho W)^{-1}}\underset{n\cdot n}{\hat{\mu}_O} \tag{5.25}$$

$$\underset{n\cdot n}{\hat{D}} = \underset{n\cdot n}{(I-\lambda W)^{-1}}\underset{n\cdot n}{\hat{\eta}} + \underset{n\cdot n}{(I-\lambda W)^{-1}}\underset{n\cdot n}{\hat{\mu}_D} \tag{5.26}$$

and, considering Eq. (5.2), we now have the disaggregated flows expressed as:

$$\underset{n\cdot n}{F} = k\left[\underset{n\cdot n}{(I-\rho W)^{-1}}\beta \underset{n\cdot n}{\hat{D}} + \underset{n\cdot n}{(I-\rho W)^{-1}}\underset{n\cdot n}{\hat{\varepsilon}} + \underset{n\cdot n}{(I-\rho W)^{-1}}\underset{n\cdot n}{\hat{\mu}_O}\right]$$
$$\underset{n\cdot n}{\Delta}\left[\underset{n\cdot n}{(I-\lambda W)^{-1}}\underset{n\cdot n}{\hat{\eta}} + \underset{n\cdot n}{(I-\lambda W)^{-1}}\underset{n\cdot n}{\hat{\mu}_D}\right] \tag{5.27}$$

The aggregated origin and destination variables are then given by:

$$\underset{m\cdot m}{\hat{O}^*} = \beta \underset{m\cdot m}{\hat{D}^*} + \rho \underset{m\cdot m}{W^*}\underset{m\cdot m}{\hat{O}^*} + \underset{m\cdot m}{\varepsilon^*} + \underset{m\cdot m}{\mu_O^*} \tag{5.28}$$

$$\underset{m\cdot m}{\hat{D}^*} = \lambda \underset{m\cdot m}{W^*}\underset{m\cdot m}{\hat{D}^*} + \underset{m\cdot m}{\eta^*} + \underset{m\cdot m}{\mu_D^*} \tag{5.29}$$

with $\hat{O}^* = G\hat{O}G^T$ and $\hat{D}^* = G\hat{D}G^T$ as usual. Using Eqs. (5.25)–(5.26) we have:

$$\underset{m\cdot m}{\hat{O}^*} = \underset{m\cdot m}{\left(I-\rho W^*\right)^{-1}}\beta \underset{m\cdot m}{\hat{D}^*} + \underset{m\cdot m}{\left(I-\rho W^*\right)^{-1}}\underset{m\cdot m}{\hat{\varepsilon}^*} + \underset{m\cdot m}{\left(I-\rho W^*\right)^{-1}}\underset{m\cdot m}{\hat{\mu}_O^*} \tag{5.30}$$

$$\underset{m\cdot m}{\hat{D}^*} = \underset{m\cdot m}{\left(I-\lambda W^*\right)^{-1}}\underset{m\cdot m}{\hat{\eta}^*} + \underset{m\cdot m}{\left(I-\lambda W^*\right)^{-1}}\underset{m\cdot m}{\hat{\mu}_D^*} \tag{5.31}$$

and the aggregated flow Eq. (5.4) now becomes:

$$\underset{m\cdot m}{F^*} = h\left[\underset{m\cdot m}{\left(I-\rho W^*\right)^{-1}}\beta \underset{m\cdot m}{\hat{D}^*} + \underset{m\cdot m}{\left(I-\rho W^*\right)^{-1}}\underset{m\cdot m}{\hat{\varepsilon}^*} + \underset{m\cdot m}{\left(I-\rho W^*\right)^{-1}}\underset{m\cdot m}{\hat{\mu}_O^*}\right]$$
$$\underset{m\cdot m}{\Delta^*}\left[\underset{m\cdot m}{\left(I-\lambda W^*\right)^{-1}}\underset{m\cdot m}{\hat{\eta}^*} + \underset{m\cdot m}{\left(I-\lambda W^*\right)^{-1}}\underset{m\cdot m}{\hat{\mu}_D^*}\right] \tag{5.32}$$

so that the *relative change of mean flow* due to the aggregation can now be expressed as:

$$RC(r,\sigma_\varepsilon^2,\sigma_\eta^2,\rho,\lambda,\beta) = \frac{\mu^*}{\mu} = \frac{hn^2}{km^2}\cdot \frac{\underset{m\cdot m}{i^{*T}} \left[(I-\rho W^*)^{-1}\beta\hat{D}^* + (I-\rho W^*)^{-1}\hat{\varepsilon}^* + (I-\rho W^*)^{-1}\hat{\mu}_O^*\right] \times \Delta^*\left[(I-\lambda W^*)^{-1}\hat{\eta}^* + (I-\lambda W^*)^{-1}\hat{\mu}_D^*\right] i^*}{i^T\left[(I-\rho W)^{-1}\hat{\varepsilon} + (I-\rho W)^{-1}\hat{\mu}_O\right]\Delta\left[(I-\lambda W)^{-1}\hat{\eta} + (I-\lambda W)^{-1}\hat{\mu}_D\right] i} \tag{5.33}$$

which is now a function of the aggregation level r, of the two variances of the error terms (σ_ε^2 and σ_η^2), of the two spatial correlation parameters and of the regression parameter β. In the present context we are interested, in particular, to studying how different levels of spatial dependence in the origin and destination variables may affect the mean flow when data are aggregated. However, the formal expression derived in Eq. (5.33) is highly nonlinear in the parameters' vector $\theta = (r,\sigma_\varepsilon^2,\sigma_\eta^2,\rho,\lambda,\beta)$ and, as such, the relationship between the spatial structure of O and D and the mean flow is not evident. To better visualize such a relationship in the next section we will consider the behavior of the RC function in some artificially generated data.

5.4 Analysis of Artificial Data

The aim of the present section is that of stressing the effects of spatial dependence on the MAUP emerging in nonlinear spatial interaction models. To achieve this aim we will consider artificially generated data laid on regular square lattice grids hierarchically arranged in squares of increasing dimensions. In the present context we will only consider the case of perfect aggregation, thus restricting only to the scale problem and neglecting, at least for the time being, the aggregation problem.

In our experiments, a regular square lattice grid 64-by-64 ($n = 4096$) is progressively aggregated by constituting groups of 4 neighbouring units into smaller lattices of increasing cell size r according to the following scheme: 32-by-32 ($m = 1024$, $r = 4$), 16-by-16 ($m = 256$, $r = 16$), 8-by-8 ($m = 64$, $r = 64$) and 4-by-4 ($m = 16$, $r = 1024$).

Our simulation exercise is deliberately kept at a very simple level to illustrate the essence of the problem. We consider the case of a regular square lattice and a constant criterion of aggregation of 4 adjacent cells at each step. Considering irregular lattices and different criteria of aggregation (like e.g. the NUTS 1,2 and 3 levels in the Eurostat classification of European regions, see EUROSTAT 2012) can lead to different conclusions, but should not dramatically modify the essence of them. With the aim of visualizing the effects of spatial dependence on aggregation, in our artificial data we considered the most general case where the origin and the destination variables are stochastic, spatially autocorrelated and mutually dependent according to the model formalization presented in Sect. 5.3.4. In particular we generated our observations for ε and, respectively, for η, drawn from two normal independent random variables and we introduced the results thus obtained into Eqs. (5.25)–(5.26). This procedure guarantees that the origin and destination variables are spatially correlated (with the desired level of intensity captured by the parameters λ and ρ) and mutually dependent (with a level of dependence controlled by the parameter β). Through the formal expressions derived in Sect. 5.3, we use such observations to model the variation of the observed mean flows when changing the level of scale. More specifically referring to the expression reported in Eq. (5.33), we considered the following parameters specification. First of all we considered a constant mean for the origin and destination, conventionally set to 1 ($\mu_O = \mu_D = 1$) and a constant value of the two dimensionality parameters k and h (also conventionally set to unity: $k = h = 1$). The hypothesis of an a priori constant mean may appear to be a limitation of our simulation exercise. However, the presence of a spatial structure in Eqs. (5.23)–(5.24) and of a linear dependence between the origin and the destination variables, has the effect of modelling more realistic scenarios. For instance if we refer to origin and destination variables proportional to the population size, we are able to reproduce a situation where highly densely populated areas are close in space thus producing ex post an uneven distribution which is closer to empirically observed phenomena. In addition, we considered the effects on scale of two levels of the variance of the random component ε in Eq. (5.23) (namely $\sigma_\varepsilon^2 = [4, 8]$), and a constant proportionality between the variances of the two random components expressed by $\sigma_\eta^2 = \sigma_\varepsilon^2/2$. As for the spatial dependence parameters we considered both the case of positive and negative values within the feasible range allowing $\rho, \lambda = [-0.24, -0.1, 0, 0.1, 0.24]$. Finally, in order to assess the effects on aggregation of the strength of the relationship between the origin and the destination variables, we considered two possible values of the regression coefficient corresponding to $\beta = [1, 3]$.

The choice of the simulation parameters μ_O and μ_D is purely conventional. The choice of the parameters σ_ε, σ_η and β is justified empirically: we have attempted several specifications and those reported here are enough to show the main effects. Finally the choice of the parameters λ and ρ are justified theoretically by the fact that in a regular square lattice grid with a weight matrix W row-standardized and defined according to the rooks case definition, they are restricted by the inequalities $|\lambda| < 0.25$ and $|\rho| < 0.25$ (see e.g. Cliff and Ord 1981).

Figures 5.1 and 5.2 plot the Relative Change of mean flow (RC) as a function of the level of spatial aggregation r observed at various levels of the spatial dependence parameters λ and ρ. The two Figures clearly show that the RC always increase monotonically with aggregation as it was expected. Since the flows are directly proportional to the size of the origin and the destination variables, higher levels of scale will produce an increase in the total flows between regions. The benchmarking values are represented by the solid line in Fig. 5.2, when both λ and

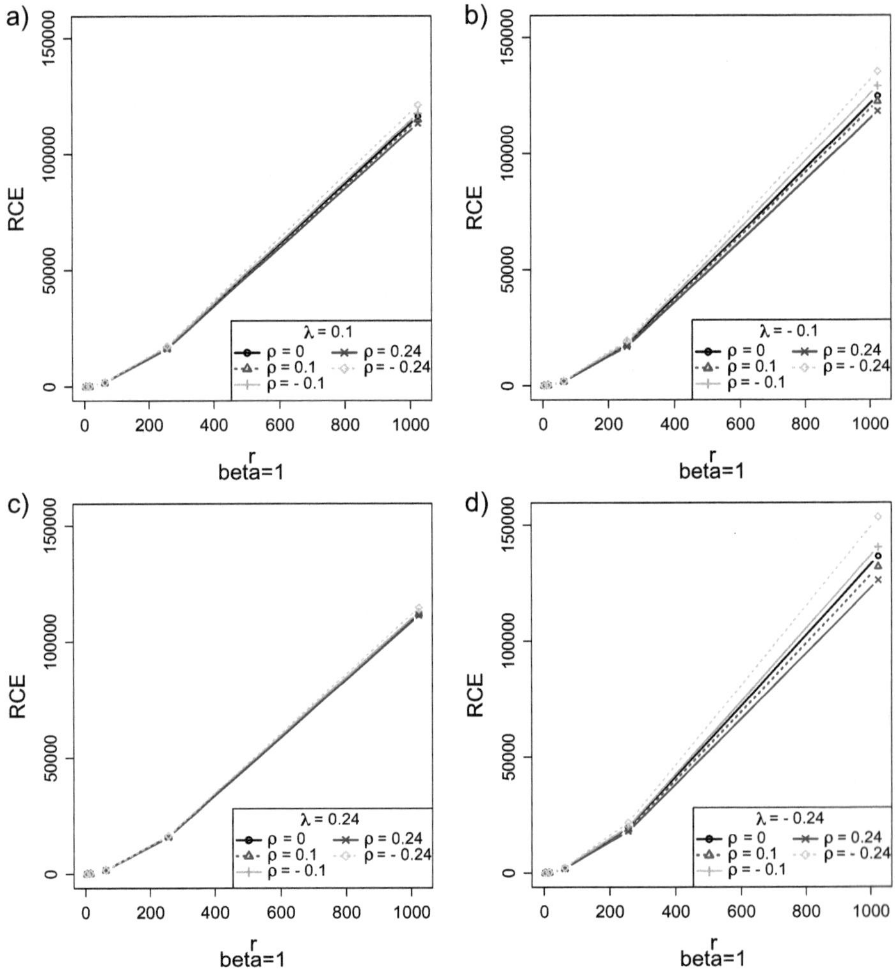

Fig. 5.1 Results of simulation of the model case d (Sect. 2.4) in the case of perfect aggregation. Behavior of the Relative Change in mean flow (RC) with respect to the aggregation level r at different values of the origin spatial dependence parameter *rho* (**a**) $\lambda = 0.1$; (**b**) $\lambda = -0.1$; (**c**) $\lambda = 0.24$; (**d**) $\lambda = -0.24$. Graph are based on 1000 simulations

ρ are equal to zero. At any given level of the parameter λ of spatial correlation in the destination variable, when the spatial correlation in the origin variable (the parameter ρ) is negative, we observe a more pronounced effect on the RC with a sharper increase when r increases, with respect to the case of no spatial correlation. On the contrary, the presence of positive values of the parameter ρ moderates the increase of RC observed with aggregation. These effects are more evident in the case of $\lambda = -0.24$ (see Fig. 5.1d) and are conversely negligible in the case of $\lambda = 0.24$ (see Fig. 5.1c). Figures 5.1 and 5.2 show how the RC generally increases

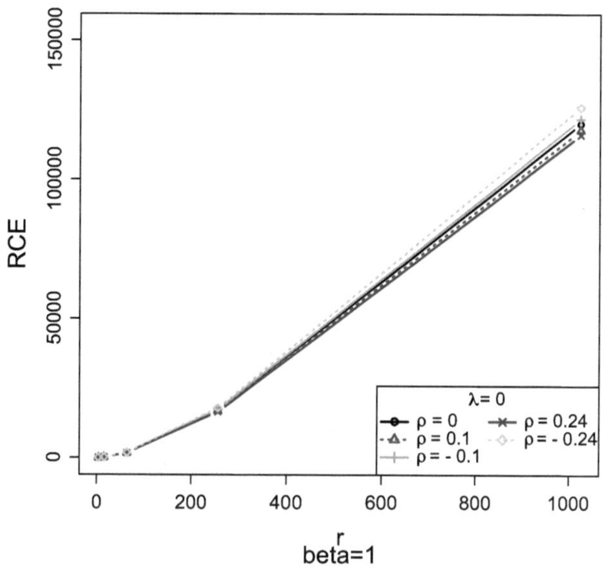

Fig. 5.2 Results of simulation of the model case d (Sect. 2.4) in the case of perfect aggregation. Behavior of the Relative Change in mean flow (RC) with respect to the aggregation level r at different values of the origin spatial dependence parameter ρ. Case of $\lambda = 0$. Graph are based on 1000 simulations

with the level of aggregation r, but it does not provide enough insights on how λ and ρ interact in determining it. For this reason we produced two more graphs reported in Figs. 5.3 and 5.4. In these figures we keep the level of scale fixed at $r = 256$ and we concentrate our attention on the joint effects of λ and ρ on RC in a three-dimensional graph. In the same graphs we also aim at assessing the effects of β and the influence of the variability of ε and η on the Relative Change of mean flow. Notice that Figs. 5.3 and 5.4 report only the mean of the RC with no reference to its simulation variability. These plots show that, when λ and ρ are both negative, we have a dramatic increase of the Relative Change of mean flow (higher values in the bottom left corner of Figs. 5.3 and 5.4 with respect to the case of spatial incorrelation $\lambda = \rho = 0$ (the central point of the figures). Conversely, when λ and ρ are both positive we observe a moderating effect on the level of RC (lower values in the upper right corner of Figs. 5.3 and 5.4).

These effects are consistent with the theoretical expectations. In fact, in the case of a negative spatial correlation observed in both the origin and the destination variables, the process of aggregation dramatically reduces the variability between the aggregated areas (Arbia 1989) thus increasing the overall mean flow and producing a higher level of flows between the areas. In contrast, when both λ and ρ are positive, the operation of aggregation involves the summation between values that are similar to one another so that the reduction of the variance is moderated and so it is the overall mean flow. This effect reduces the intensity of the inter-regional flows between the aggregated areas and therefore moderates the RC.

As an example, let us consider the case of interregional flows of traded goods modelled through Eq. (5.1) with the origin and the destination variables proportional to the size of the population in the various regions (e.g. the NUTS-3 European

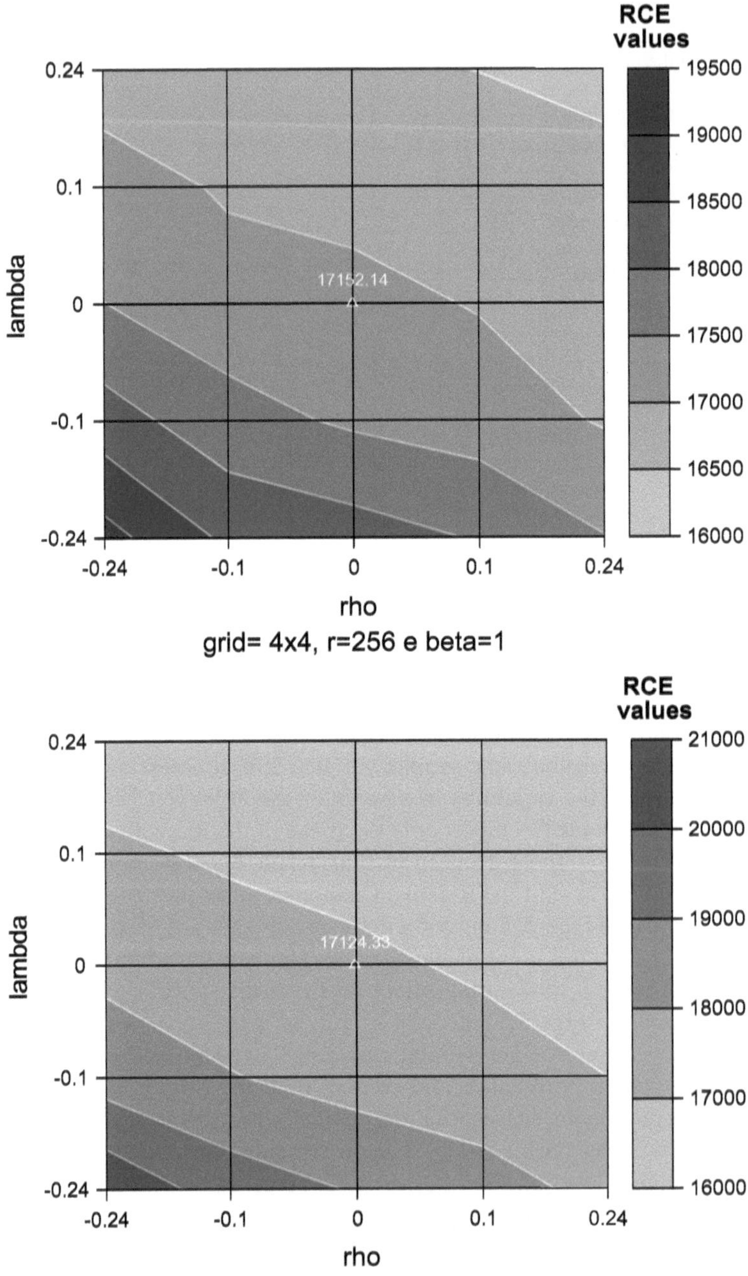

Fig. 5.3 Results of simulation of the model case d (Sect. 2.4) in the case of perfect aggregation for a fixed level of aggregation ($r = 256$) and $\sigma_\varepsilon^2 = 4$. Behavior of the Relative Change in mean flow (RC) with respect to different values of the origin and destination spatial dependence parameters ρ and λ. (**a**) $\beta = 1$; (**b**) $\beta = 3$. Graph are based on 1000 simulations

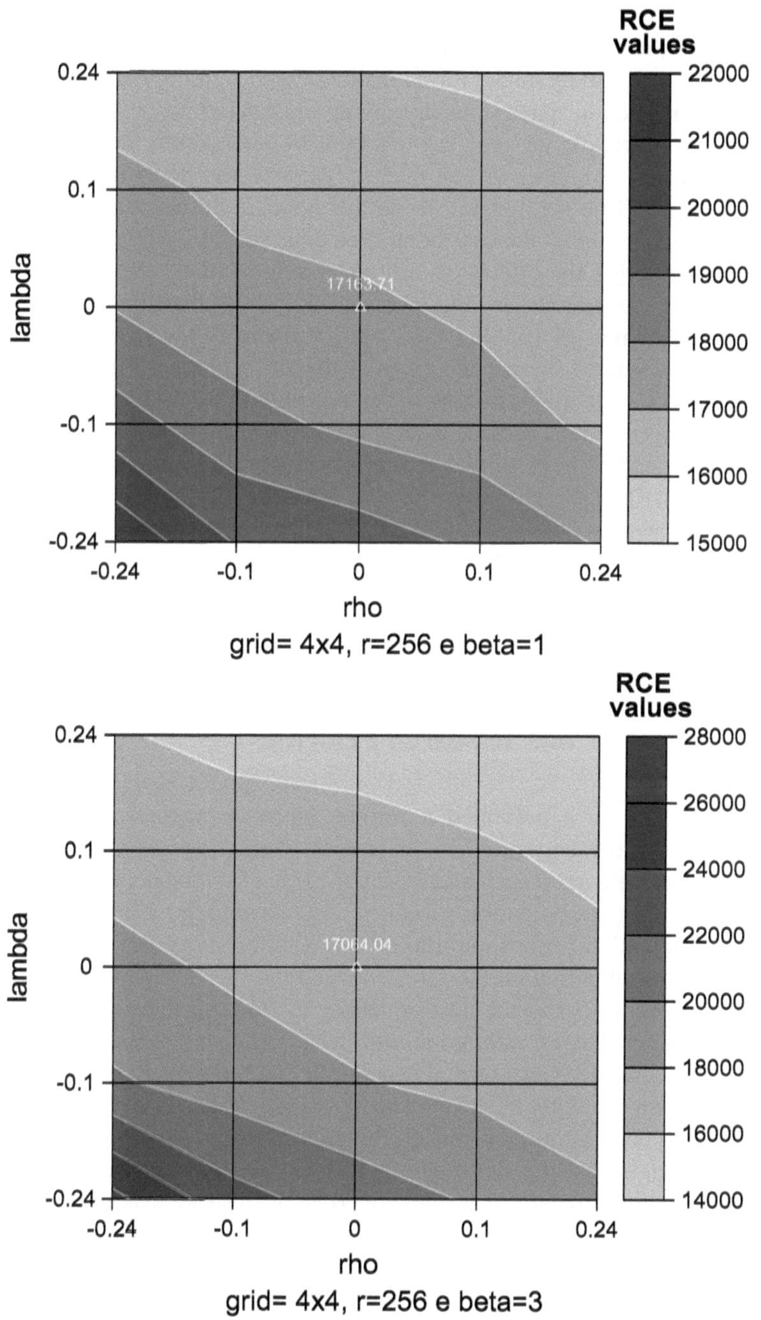

Fig. 5.4 Results of simulation of the model case d (Sect. 2.4) in the case of perfect aggregation for a fixed level of aggregation ($r = 256$) and $\sigma_\varepsilon^2 = 8$. Behavior of the Relative Change in mean flow (RC) with respect to different values of the origin and destination spatial dependence parameters ρ and λ. (**a**) $\beta = 1$; (**b**) $\beta = 3$. Graph are based on 1000 simulations

regions, see EUROSTAT 2012). An even distribution of the population in the space (corresponding to low variability) produces a high level of flows of goods among regions due to our gravity model formalization. On the contrary, if the population is unevenly distributed in space (thus displaying high variability connected to higher concentration of people in some regions than in others) only the flows of goods between overcrowded areas will be intense, whereas the flows involving (almost) empty regions will be negligible. So, on the average, the flows at the aggregated level will be lower than in the case of an even distribution.

When considering the effects of different levels of linear dependence between the origin and the destination, Figs. 5.3 and 5.4 show that higher values of the regression coefficient β, (linking the origin variable to the destination variable; see Eq. (5.25)), lead to sharper increases in the RC (compare Fig. 5.3a,b and also Fig. 5.4a,b. Notice the different grey scales levels in the right banners). This effect was also to be expected. In fact, when β is large, the origin and the destination variables will tend to have similar spatial structures thus emphasizing the effects previously described. Finally, Figs. 5.3 and 5.4 show that the Relative Change of mean flow is also emphasized by larger variances of ε and η due to the overall greater mean flow of the spatial system associated to larger variability (compare Figs. 5.3a with 5.4a and Figs. 5.3b and 5.4b by observing the different grey scales levels in the right banners).

5.5 Conclusions and Research Priorities

In this paper we have presented a formal approach to analyze the effects of the modifiable areal unit problem in spatial interaction gravity models. More specifically, we were interested in assessing the role of spatial dependence, observed in the origin and the destination variables, in determining the amount of the loss of information which is connatural to all aggregation processes. In particular, we concentrated our attention on the ratio between the mean quantity of flows at the more aggregated level and the mean quantity of flows at the more disaggregated level: a parameter that we referred to with term Relative Change of mean flow or RC. In Sect. 5.2 we derived a formal expression that links the RC to all the model's parameters when changing the level of spatial aggregation.

In synthesis our results show that, in the presence of positive spatial dependence in both the origin and the destination variables, the increase in the mean flow, (connatural with aggregation) is moderated. It is instead exacerbated when we observe a negative spatial correlation in both the origin and the destination variables.

The results obtained in this paper provide a useful tool to study the influence of spatial effects on aggregation in gravity models and they can contribute in various ways to substantial achievements in nonlinear spatial econometric studies.

A first important use of the formal expressions derived in the present context is in the identification of worst-case scenarios when data are aggregated and the amount of spatial dependence at the lower level of aggregation is unknown. This scenarios correspond to the cases where the spatial dependence parameters are negative.

A second use of the results derived in this paper is in suggesting statistical tools to infer the likely value of the mean flows at a finer level of aggregation when only data at a coarser level of aggregation are available. In this sense, one possible strategy consists in exploiting a Bayesian approach by using the formal expressions derived in this paper for the aggregated mean flows as the likelihood and imposing reasonable priors on the model parameters to derive the disaggregated mean flows.

In the present version we deliberately kept the presentation at the simplest possible level to make more clearly the point, but the results obtained here could be extended in the future to deal with more general cases like, e.g., the specification of models different from the simple gravity-like law, the case of more than one origin and destination variables and the case of non perfect aggregation thus considering also the aggregation problems occurring when different partitions at the same level scale are considered.

References

Arbia G (1989) Spatial data configuration in the statistical analysis of regional economics and related problems. Kluwer, Dordrecht

Arbia G, Petrarca F (2011) Effects of MAUP on spatial econometric models. Lett Spat Resour Sci 4(3):173–185

Cliff AD, Ord JK (1981) Spatial processes: models and applications. Pion, London

Cramer JS (1964) Efficient grouping, regression and correlation in Engel curve analysis. J Am Stat Assoc 59:233–50

EUROSTAT (2012) http://epp.eurostat.ec.europa.eu/portal/page/portal/nuts_nomenclature/introduction

Griffith DA (2009) Modeling spatial autocorrelation in spatial interaction data: empirical evidence from 2002 Germany journey-to-work flows. J Geogr Syst 11(2):117–140

Haitovsky J (1973) Regression estimation from grouped observations. Griffin's statistical courses and monographs, vol 33. Hafner Press, New York

LeSage J, Fisher M (2010) Spatial econometric methods for modeling origin-destination flows. In: Fischer MM, Getis A (eds) Handbook of applied spatial analysis. Springer, Dordrecht, pp 409–433

Openshaw S, Taylor PJ (1979) A million or so of correlated coefficients: three experiments on the modifiable areal unit problem. In: Wrigley N (ed) Statistical applications in the spatial sciences. Pion, London, pp 120–438

Orcutt G, Watts HW, Edwards JB (1968) Data aggregation and information loss. Am Econ Rev 58:773–87

Pesaran MH, Pierse RG, Kumar MS (1989) Econometric analysis of aggregation in the context of linear prediction models. Econometrica 57:861–888

Prais S, Aitchinson J (1954) The grouping of observations in regression analysis. Rev Int Stat Inst 22:1–22

Theil H (1954) Linear aggregation on economic relations. North-Holland Publishing, Amsterdam

Yule U, Kendall MS (1950) An introduction to the theory of statistics. Griffin, London

Zellner A (1962) An efficient method of estimating seemingly unrelated regression equations and tests for aggregation bias. J Am Stat Assoc 57:348–368

Part II
Specific Methodological Issues

Part II
Scientific Method Applied

Chapter 6
Dealing with Intraregional Flows in Spatial Econometric Gravity Models

Kazuki Tamesue and Morito Tsutsumi

Keywords Gravity • Intraregional flows • Spatial econometrics • Spatial interaction

JEL Classifications: C18, C40, C43, C51

6.1 Introduction

The gravity model, which employs the logic of the equation of gravity in physics, has been indispensable for the analysis of origin–destination flows, mostly owing to the simplicity of its mathematical form. Since the standard ordinary least squares (OLS) type gravity model assumes observed flows as independent and affected by spatial autocorrelation, LeSage and Pace (2008) proposed incorporating the spatial dependence of OD flows in the gravity model by using a spatial econometrics approach.

Recently, the number of applications for this spatial econometric gravity model has been increasing. LeSage and Polasek (2008) used the model in considering the highway network as a tool for spatial connectivity of commodity flows; Deng and Athanasopoulos (2011) extended the model to a dynamic panel model for investigating Australia's domestic and international demand for inbound tourism; de la Mata and Llano (2012, 2013) used the model to analyze the intra- and interregional trade flows in several sectors in Spain, analyzing spatial as well as social network dependence; Marrocu and Paci (2012) used it to analyze the demand and supply determinants of domestic tourism flows in Italian provinces; and Behrens et al. (2012) incorporated the techniques of spatial econometrics into the theory-based gravity model to take into account the interdependence between trade flows.

K. Tamesue (✉)
Graduate School of Systems and Information Engineering, University of Tsukuba, Tsukuba, Japan
e-mail: tamesue70@gmail.com

M. Tsutsumi
Faculty of Engineering, Information and Systems, University of Tsukuba, Tsukuba, Japan

R. Patuelli, G. Arbia (eds.), *Spatial Econometric Interaction Modelling*, Advances in Spatial Science, DOI 10.1007/978-3-319-30196-9_6

All these studies report that the empirical applications demonstrated the existence of spatial dependence in the OD flow data, and that the model is more effective than the classical OLS-type gravity model.

As in the case of other gravity models, there are some problems regarding the treatment of intraregional flows within the spatial econometric gravity model. Moreover, these problems are further complicated in this model as the model requires both interregional and intraregional flows, owing to the interdependent structure of the spatial weight matrices, as pointed out by Tsutsumi and Tamesue (2012) and Behrens et al. (2012). The objective of this paper is to discuss two main issues regarding intraregional flows within the spatial econometric gravity model: the definitions of intraregional distance and model estimation with unobserved intraregional flows. Some researchers may regard intraregional flows as nuisance information. However, in spatial econometrics context, where we consider spatial interdependence within observed phenomenon, information of intraregional flow is as important as interregional flows. Moreover, the realization of intraregional flows is similar to the modifiable areal unit problem, in that if OD regions are disaggregated to the lower level of spatial units, intraregional flows can be decomposed into the lower level of interregional flows and are no longer intraregional. Likewise, interregional flows can be treated as intraregional flows by considering larger contiguous areas.

In the next section, we briefly review the model specification of the spatial econometric gravity model and then introduce the estimation method employed in this study. In Sect. 6.3, we discuss the issues regarding intraregional flows in the model and introduce techniques or methodologies to deal with them. We apply these methods to Japanese migration data in Sect. 6.4 as an illustration. In Sect. 6.5, an experimental analysis about the difference between interregional and intraregional flows is carried out, and in Sect. 6.6, we conclude.

6.2 The Spatial Econometric Gravity Model

In this study, we consider LeSage and Pace's (2008) general unrestricted spatial lag model (SLM) for OD flows, which is expressed as follows:

$$\mathbf{y} = \rho_1 \mathbf{W}_1 \mathbf{y} + \rho_2 \mathbf{W}_2 \mathbf{y} + \rho_3 \mathbf{W}_3 \mathbf{y} + \mathbf{X}\boldsymbol{\beta} + \boldsymbol{\varepsilon}, \tag{6.1}$$

where $\mathbf{y}$ is the $n^2 \times 1$ vector of OD flows, and is sorted by an origin-centric ordering (LeSage and Pace 2008); $\mathbf{X}$ is the $n^2 \times (2 + p + q)$ matrix containing a constant term, p origin-specific variables, q destination-specific variables, and the $n^2 \times 1$ vector of distances; and $\boldsymbol{\varepsilon}$ is the $n^2 \times 1$ vector of disturbances with $\boldsymbol{\varepsilon} \sim N(0, \sigma^2 \mathbf{I}_N)$. The model differentiates the spatial contiguity between flows into three types by using a set of spatial weight matrices: origin-based ($\mathbf{W}_1 = \mathbf{W} \otimes \mathbf{I}_n$), destination-based ($\mathbf{W}_2 = \mathbf{I}_n \otimes \mathbf{W}$), and origin-to-destination based ($\mathbf{W}_3 = \mathbf{W} \otimes \mathbf{W}$), where $\mathbf{W}$ is the $n \times n$ spatial weight matrix of objective regions and $\mathbf{I}$ is the $n \times n$ identity matrix. Thereby, $\mathbf{W}_1\mathbf{y}$ expresses the weighted average of the flows from neighbors of an origin to a certain destination and $\mathbf{W}_2\mathbf{y}$ expresses the weighted average of the flows from a certain origin to neighbors of a destination. The last spatial lag $\mathbf{W}_3\mathbf{y}$ captures the spatial dependence of the flows from neighbors of an origin to neighbors of a destination. Setting several restrictions on the spatial lag coefficients (spatial parameters) would result in a family of nine models (LeSage and Pace 2008), which can consider different patterns of spatial dependencies.

To see how interregional and intraregional flows are treated in spatial weight matrices, let us consider a two-region case for simplicity. The spatial weight matrix of the target regions can be expressed as

$$\mathbf{W} = \begin{bmatrix} 0 & w_{12} \\ w_{21} & 0 \end{bmatrix}, \tag{6.2}$$

where we suppose that $w_{12} > 0$ and $w_{21} > 0$. For the basic binary contiguity definition, when each region is a neighbor of the other, w_{12} and w_{21} are equal to one. Using this $\mathbf{W}$ and two-dimensional identity matrix $\mathbf{I}$, three different spatial weight matrices can be constructed:

$$\mathbf{W}_o = \mathbf{W} \otimes \mathbf{I} = \begin{bmatrix} 0 & 0 & w_{12} & 0 \\ 0 & 0 & 0 & w_{12} \\ w_{21} & 0 & 0 & 0 \\ 0 & w_{21} & 0 & 0 \end{bmatrix}, \tag{6.3}$$

$$\mathbf{W}_d = \mathbf{I} \otimes \mathbf{W} = \begin{bmatrix} 0 & w_{12} & 0 & 0 \\ w_{21} & 0 & 0 & 0 \\ 0 & 0 & 0 & w_{12} \\ 0 & 0 & w_{21} & 0 \end{bmatrix}, \tag{6.4}$$

$$\mathbf{W}_w = \mathbf{W} \otimes \mathbf{W} = \begin{bmatrix} 0 & 0 & 0 & w_{12}w_{12} \\ 0 & 0 & w_{12}w_{21} & 0 \\ 0 & w_{12}w_{21} & 0 & 0 \\ w_{21}w_{21} & 0 & 0 & 0 \end{bmatrix}. \tag{6.5}$$

Consequently, an origin–destination flow matrix (logged) of these regions can be expressed as

$$\mathbf{Y} = \begin{bmatrix} y_{11} & y_{12} \\ y_{21} & y_{22} \end{bmatrix}, \tag{6.6}$$

and origin-centric vectorization would yield $\mathbf{y} = \begin{bmatrix} y_{11} & y_{12} & y_{21} & y_{22} \end{bmatrix}'$. Since y_{11} and y_{22} are intraregional flows, the first and the fourth rows and columns correspond to intraregional flows. As long as $w_{12} > 0$ and $w_{21} > 0$, intraregional flows have neighbor flows and interregional flows have intraregional flows as their neighbors, in the spatial weight matrices $\mathbf{W}_o$, $\mathbf{W}_d$, and $\mathbf{W}_w$.

The maximum likelihood estimation of higher order spatial econometric models would require solving the optimization problem involving the log-determinant ln $|\mathbf{I}_N - \rho_1\mathbf{W}_1 - \rho_2\mathbf{W}_2 - \rho_3\mathbf{W}_3|$. This is the most computationally demanding part of the estimation and would create computer memory problems as the number of origins and destinations rises (LeSage and Pace 2008). Thus, we employ an alternative estimation method, that is, spatial two-stage least squares (S2SLS) for parameter estimation. The S2SLS for higher-order spatial lag model, as in Eq. (6.1), is described in Badinger and Egger (2011), which is an extension of the S2SLS by Kelejian and Prucha (2010) into a higher-order model. In the first step, the predicted values of the spatial lags are estimated with an instrumental variable $\mathbf{H}$, where

$$\hat{\overline{\mathbf{Y}}} = \mathbf{H}\left(\mathbf{H}'\mathbf{H}\right)^{-1}\mathbf{H}'\overline{\mathbf{Y}} \tag{6.7}$$

and $\overline{\mathbf{Y}} = (\mathbf{W}_1\mathbf{y}, \mathbf{W}_2\mathbf{y}, \mathbf{W}_3\mathbf{y})$. The instrumental variable comprises explanatory variables $\mathbf{X}$ and a subset of linearly independent columns of terms of the sum $\sum_{m=1}^{M}\left(\sum_{r=1}^{3}\mathbf{W}_r\right)^m \mathbf{X}$ (Badinger and Egger 2011), because

$$E\left(\sum_{r=1}^{3}\mathbf{W}_r\mathbf{y}\right) = \sum_{r=1}^{3}\mathbf{W}_r\left[\mathbf{I} + \sum_{m=1}^{\infty}\left(\sum_{r'=1}^{3}\rho_{r'}\mathbf{W}_{r'}\right)^m\right]\mathbf{X}\boldsymbol{\beta}, \tag{6.8}$$

where $m = 2$ seems to be sufficient (Kelejian et al. 2004). Following Badinger and Egger (2011), we chose $\mathbf{H}$ to be,

$$\mathbf{H} = \left(\mathbf{X}, \mathbf{W}_1\mathbf{X}, \mathbf{W}_2\mathbf{X}, \mathbf{W}_3\mathbf{X}, \mathbf{W}_1^2\mathbf{X}, \mathbf{W}_2^2\mathbf{X}, \mathbf{W}_3^2\mathbf{X}, \mathbf{W}_1\mathbf{W}_3\mathbf{X}, \mathbf{W}_2\mathbf{W}_3\mathbf{X}\right). \tag{6.9}$$

In the second step, the predicted value $\hat{\overline{\mathbf{Y}}}$ is used in place of $\overline{\mathbf{Y}}$ in Eq. (6.1), and the ρ's and $\boldsymbol{\beta}$ are estimated via OLS since $\mathbf{H}$ and $\boldsymbol{\varepsilon}$ are uncorrelated.

6.3 Issues with Intraregional Flows

6.3.1 Intraregional Distance

One of the issues when dealing with intraregional flows is how to define the distances of intraregional flows, whereas defining the distances of interregional flows can be done without much difficulty. There are a number of studies approximating or determining the appropriate measure for internal distance, with Head and Mayer (2002) presenting a good review of these studies.

The first attempt to define internal distance was as the fraction of distance to the nearest neighboring regions (e.g., Wei 1996). However, this has been criticized because internal distance should depend only on the geography of a region and not of its neighbor (Nitsch 2000). An alternative and attractive approach is the area-based measure, in which each region is assumed to be a circular disk. This is a practical application of the analytical approach for approximating the average distances between and within zones (e.g., Vaughan 1984; Koshizuka and Kurita 1991), and the internal distance can be given as follows:

$$d_{ii} = c\sqrt{\frac{S_i}{\pi}}, \tag{6.10}$$

where S_i is an area of region i and c is the constant. $c = 1$ would be a good approximation of the average distance between two points in a population that is uniformly distributed across regions (e.g., Nitsch 2000), or $c = 2/3$ as in Head and Mayer (2000) and Redding and Venables (2004) for example. Behrens et al. (2012) and Tsutsumi and Tamesue (2012) use $c = 1/3$ and $c = 2/3$ to check the robustness of the estimation results.

6.3.2 *Unobserved Intraregional Flow Data*

6.3.2.1 The Heckit-Type Model

Another issue associated with intraregional flows is estimation of the model with data in which intraregional flows are unobserved. In many cases, intraregional flows tend to be missing values within the OD data. Some may think of simply setting zeros for these unknown flows. However, the inadequacy of this ad hoc method is clearly shown in the results of the empirical studies by LeSage and Fischer (2010), and Tsutsumi and Tamesue (2012), which imply that information about intraregional flows is as important as that of interregional flows. Another common approach, especially in migration flows, is to estimate intraregional flows as a difference between the total population of each region and net migration balance. Unfortunately, this will lead to overestimation of intraregional flows, because the flows obtained from this approach contain populations that did not move.

Another way would be to exclude the unobserved flows, a method known as listwise deletion. This method requires reconstructing the spatial weight matrices that are already constructed by the Kronecker products, and it may lead to bias estimates due to the arbitrary deletion of observed data. The latter is known among econometricians as the sample selection bias, and the Heckit model (Heckman 1979) is widely used to take the sample selection problem into account. The following equation (selection model) represents the selection mechanism:

$$\mathbf{z}^* = \mathbf{Q}\boldsymbol{\gamma} + \mathbf{u}, \tag{6.11}$$

where $\mathbf{z}^*$ are latent variables with $z_i = 1$, if flow i is observed, and $z_i = 0$, if flow i is unobserved. By assuming that $\boldsymbol{\varepsilon}$ in Eq. (6.1) and $\mathbf{u}$ in Eq. (6.11) have a bivariate normal distribution, with zero mean and correlation ψ, we can obtain the outcome model for our study:

$$E\left[y_i \middle| z_i = 1\right] = \left[\mathbf{I}_N - \sum_{r=1}^{3} \rho_r \mathbf{W}_r^*\right]_i^{-1} \left[\mathbf{X}_i\boldsymbol{\beta} + \psi\sigma_\varepsilon\lambda_i\left(\mathbf{Q}_i\boldsymbol{\gamma}\right)\right], \tag{6.12}$$

where $\lambda_i(\mathbf{Q}_i\boldsymbol{\gamma})$ is the inverse mills ratio (IMR) of observation i. $\mathbf{W}_r^*$ is the $n\ (n-1) \times n\ (n-1)$ spatial weight matrix, which excluded rows and columns corresponding to intraregional flows from $\mathbf{W}_r$. The parameters of the sample selection model can be estimated by maximum likelihood. However, Heckman (1979) provides a two-step estimation procedure as described below:

1. Estimate parameter $\boldsymbol{\gamma}$ of the probit model in Eq. (6.11). Then calculate λ_i for each observed flows.
2. Estimate parameters for ρ, $\boldsymbol{\beta}$ and $\beta_\lambda = \psi\sigma_\varepsilon$ in Eq. (6.12).

Therefore, Heckman's two-step estimation approach only requires adding the IMR (λ_i), which is derived from the first step, to the model and estimating parameters as though they were other explanatory variables. λ_i is also known as a bias correction term that addresses the selection bias caused by unobserved values, in this case intraregional flows. Thus, we can test the existence of the bias or effect of unobserved values by checking whether the estimate of β_λ is significant. If we cannot reject the hypothesis that $\beta_\lambda = 0$, we cannot reject the hypothesis that $\boldsymbol{\varepsilon}$ and $\mathbf{u}$ are uncorrelated.

6.3.2.2 EM Algorithm Model

While the Heckit-type model may correct the bias of unobservables, it requires reconstruction of the spatial weight matrices. Tsutsumi and Tamesue (2012) focused on the estimation problem of the spatial econometric gravity model with unobserved intraregional flow data. They proposed the use of the EM algorithm, which is a method for carrying out maximum likelihood estimation of incomplete data with iterative calculation, to help estimate parameters without modifying or reconstructing the model. The estimation procedure is as follows:

1. The initial values are set to unobserved intraregional flows.
2. Until convergence, the following steps are iterated:

   (a) parameter estimation with pseudo-complete data (M step)

(b) calculation of expectations of the intraregional flows with the estimated parameters (E step)

LeSage and Pace (2004) also discussed replacing missing spatial dependent data with the EM algorithm. However, the method used in Tsutsumi and Tamesue (2012) does not require model reconstruction, especially of the spatial weight matrix, and seems to be more practical when spatial weight matrices for OD flows are already constructed via the Kronecker products.

6.4 Empirical Application

6.4.1 Data

The OD flow data used in this study are the inter-prefectural migration flows (logged) in 2006, acquired from the basic resident register migration report of the Statistics Bureau of the Ministry of Internal Affairs and Communications in Japan. The number of prefectures in Japan is 47, which makes the number of observed flows to be $47^2 = 2209$. The 47×47 five-nearest neighbor spatial weight matrix $\mathbf{W}$ is used to construct the spatial weight matrices. To illustrate the size of the spatial units, a map of Japan is depicted in Fig. 6.1. Note that the study chose the data because it contains observed intraregional flows, so that we can compare and discuss the effectiveness of the methods. To show internal mobility of the migration, Fig. 6.1 also illustrates the proportion of internal migration flows against total in-migrations

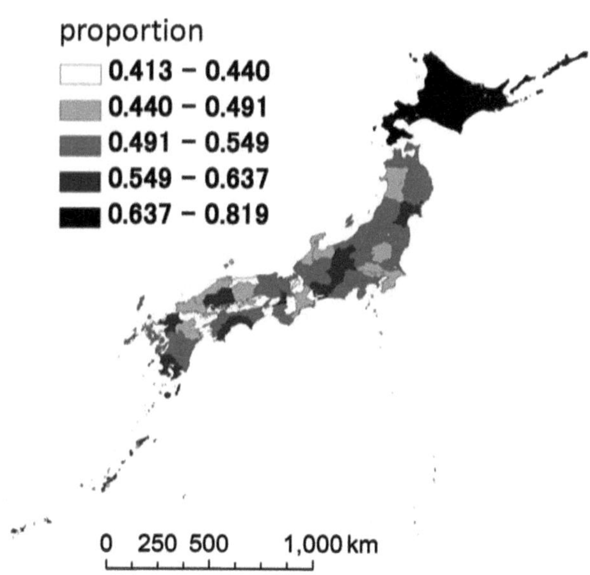

Fig. 6.1 Proportion of internal migration

Table 6.1 Descriptive statistics

Variable name	Description	Mean	Std. error	VIF
Dependent variable	Interprefectural migration flow (log)	5.792	1.760	
Pop	Population (log)	14.500	0.743	2.693
LivArea	Inhabitable land area (log)	12.229	0.581	2.083
U15Pop	Proportion of the population under age 14 years	0.134	0.010	1.264
UnempPop	Unemployment rate	0.030	0.006	1.825
TertiaryEmp	Proportion of tertiary industry employee	0.313	0.016	1.588
Income	Per capita income (log)	7.904	0.149	2.657
Distance	The great-circle distance between prefectures (log)	12.729	1.388	1.026

in each prefecture. The mean of the proportion is 0.52, which indicates that more than half of total migration flows consist of internal migrations.

For explanatory variables representing the characteristics of origin and destination regions, the following variables from 2005 are chosen, to replicate those used by LeSage and Pace (2008) and Tsutsumi and Tamesue (2012), starting with the log of population, the log of inhabitable land area (in square meters), the proportion of the population under 14 years, the proportion of the unemployed, the proportion of the tertiary industry employees, and finally, the log of per capita income (in thousands yen). We have decided to lag 1 year between the explained and explanatory variables to avoid endogeneity problem, if any. The study employs the great-circle distances (logged), between the centers of population for each prefecture as the distance variable, and the distances are calculated using ArcGIS software. All of the explanatory variables are from the Statistics Bureau of the Ministry of Internal Affairs and Communications, except the per capita income, which is from the Cabinet Office, Government of Japan. Descriptive statistics of each variable are shown in Table 6.1 along with the variance inflation factor (VIF) for indication of degrees of multicollinearity (e.g., O'Brien 2007). VIF of the jth variable can be calculated as $VIF_j = 1/\left(1 - R_j^2\right)$, where R_j^2 is the coefficient of determination of a regression of the jth explanatory variable on all other explanatory variables. 4 or 10 is commonly used as a rule of thumb for VIF, but the highest value of VIF in Table 6.1 is only 2.69 and does not exceed the rule of thumb. This implies that there is only a small possibility of collinearity among the explanatory variables.

6.4.2 Results

Tables 6.2, 6.3 and 6.4 illustrate the parameter estimates of three models: the standard SLM, Heckit-type model, and EM algorithm model. The standard SLM uses both intraregional and interregional observed flow data, and the remaining two models use only interregional flow data for estimation. Moreover, for simplicity, the

Table 6.2 Parameter estimates of standard SLM

	$c = 1/3$			$c = 2/3$		
Variables	Coefficient	t-Statistic	p-Value	Coefficient	t-Statistic	p-Value
Intercept	−5.903	−4.150	0.000	−5.702	−3.992	0.000
Origin Pop	0.473	12.906	0.000	0.501	13.591	0.000
Origin LivArea	−0.011	−0.239	0.811	−0.007	−0.169	0.866
Origin U15Pop	4.179	3.354	0.001	4.421	3.532	0.000
Origin UnempPop	11.068	4.233	0.000	11.815	4.497	0.000
Origin TertiaryEmp	6.118	6.740	0.000	6.460	7.082	0.000
Origin Income	−0.479	−3.674	0.000	−0.527	−4.023	0.000
Destination Pop	0.489	13.638	0.000	0.519	14.345	0.000
Destination LivArea	−0.007	−0.150	0.881	−0.003	−0.072	0.943
Destination U15Pop	6.593	5.255	0.000	6.994	5.547	0.000
Destination UnempPop	11.451	4.372	0.000	12.182	4.630	0.000
Destination TertiaryEmp	7.632	7.161	0.000	6.916	7.542	0.000
Destination Income	−0.140	−1.083	0.279	−0.168	−1.291	0.197
Distance	−0.504	−44.161	0.000	−0.552	−43.750	0.000
ρ_1	0.536	21.959	0.000	0.509	20.635	0.000
ρ_2	0.541	20.977	0.000	0.515	19.774	0.000
ρ_3	−0.565	−17.505	0.000	−0.543	−16.752	0.000
AIC	3532.848			3551.298		

study uses the explanatory variables of the probit model in the Heckit-type model to be the same as the outcome model ($\mathbf{Q} = \mathbf{X}$).

In each model, two internal distances obtained from Eq. (6.10) with $c = 1/3$ and 2/3 are used for estimation. The standard SLM in Table 6.2 indicates that $c = 1/3$ is preferable since it results in lower AIC than $c = 2/3$. Tables 6.3 and 6.4, however, show that the difference in AIC between the two distance measures are quite negligible in the Heckit-type and EM algorithm models. In the Heckit-type model, the internal distances only enter as an explanatory variable in the selection model to calculate the IMR. Thus, the parameter estimates are very much alike between the two, as shown in Table 6.3. All the same, parameter estimates are robust against the specification of internal distances in this study.

For all models, the signs of significant parameters show similar trends and are reflective of our intuition. The inhabitable land area of both origin and destination, and per capita income of destination are not significant for any model. Furthermore, the unemployment rate of origin and destination, population under 14 years of age at origin, and per capita income of origin prefectures are not significant at the 5 % level, when the EM algorithm model is used. Table 6.3 shows that estimates of the IMR coefficients are significant at the 5 % level, rejecting the hypothesis that there is no correlation between $\boldsymbol{\varepsilon}$ and $\mathbf{u}$. Thus, the result indicates that just deleting the unobserved intraregional flows and estimating the model would lead to biased results.

Table 6.3 Parameter estimates of Heckit-type model

	$c = 1/3$			$c = 2/3$		
Variables	Coefficient	t-Statistic	p-Value	Coefficient	t-Statistic	p-Value
Intercept	−0.229	−0.172	0.863	−0.235	−0.177	0.860
Origin Pop	0.161	4.109	0.000	0.161	4.118	0.000
Origin LivArea	0.008	0.192	0.847	0.008	0.193	0.847
Origin U15Pop	1.879	1.659	0.097	1.879	1.659	0.097
Origin UnempPop	4.366	1.806	0.071	4.378	1.811	0.070
Origin TertiaryEmp	2.732	3.194	0.001	2.738	3.201	0.001
Origin Income	−0.240	−1.989	0.047	−0.240	−1.990	0.047
Destination Pop	0.170	4.364	0.000	0.170	4.373	0.000
Destination LivArea	0.006	0.162	0.871	0.007	0.163	0.870
Destination U15Pop	2.535	2.178	0.030	2.537	2.179	0.029
Destination UnempPop	4.682	1.934	0.053	4.695	1.939	0.053
Destination TertiaryEmp	2.692	3.097	0.002	2.698	3.104	0.002
Destination Income	−0.116	−0.989	0.323	−0.116	−0.989	0.323
Distance	−0.254	−8.327	0.000	−0.254	−8.348	0.000
IMR	2.103×10^9	2.096	0.036	1.630×10^9	2.081	0.038
ρ_1	0.854	28.378	0.000	0.854	28.381	0.000
ρ_2	0.857	27.760	0.000	0.856	27.762	0.000
ρ_3	−0.890	−24.804	0.000	−0.890	−24.803	0.000
AIC	2944.532			2944.595		

In the standard SLM, absolute values of spatial parameters ρ_1, ρ_2, and ρ_3 are lower than those of the Heckit-type and EM algorithm models. This may be because the standard SLM includes intraregional flow data for estimation. Thereby, the spatial parameters of the standard SLM express the degree of spatial dependencies between all flows, whereas the spatial parameters of the other two models express the spatial dependencies between interregional flows. The fact that intraregional flows are much larger than interregional flows may have led to the underestimation of spatial dependencies among flows. We may also infer from the results that intraregional flows are different in nature compared to interregional flows. Therefore, some modeling strategies to explicitly differentiate between interregional and intraregional flows would be considered as desirable approaches (e.g. LeSage and Fischer 2010). In case of the EM algorithm model, however, specifying separate coefficients for inter and intraregional flows (missing data) will affect the convergence, such that it depends on initial values (Tsutsumi and Tamesue

Table 6.4 Parameter estimates of EM algorithm model

	$c = 1/3$			$c = 2/3$		
Variables	Coefficient	*t*-Statistic	*p*-Value	Coefficient	*t*-Statistic	*p*-Value
Intercept	−2.287	−1.653	0.098	−1.910	−1.379	0.168
Origin Pop	0.158	4.296	0.000	0.143	3.837	0.000
Origin LivArea	−0.010	−0.235	0.814	−0.010	−0.225	0.822
Origin U15Pop	2.002	1.699	0.090	1.897	1.609	0.108
Origin UnempPop	3.933	1.586	0.113	3.629	1.463	0.144
Origin TertiaryEmp	2.401	2.760	0.006	2.227	2.556	0.011
Origin Income	−0.162	−1.314	0.189	−0.155	−1.253	0.210
Destination Pop	0.170	4.730	0.000	0.154	4.246	0.000
Destination LivArea	−0.011	−0.259	0.796	−0.011	−0.255	0.799
Destination U15Pop	2.723	2.288	0.022	2.536	2.130	0.033
Destination UnempPop	4.379	1.762	0.078	4.075	1.639	0.101
Destination TertiaryEmp	2.396	2.737	0.006	2.202	2.508	0.012
Destination Income	−0.0376	−0.307	0.759	−0.040	−0.328	0.743
Distance	−0.179	−15.856	0.000	−0.170	−13.503	0.000
ρ_1	0.841	32.884	0.000	0.856	32.769	0.000
ρ_2	0.845	31.350	0.000	0.860	31.299	0.000
ρ_3	−0.861	−25.842	0.000	−0.876	−25.966	0.000
AIC	3283.361			3280.394		

2012). Thus, the model has to be specified to have same explanatory variables for inter and intraregional flows to enable the algorithm to converge appropriately.

6.5 Experimental Analysis of the Difference in Nature

Considering the difference in nature of interregional and intraregional flows, one way to model these is to add a dummy variable representing intraregional flows to capture fixed effect of intraregional flows. Other than this, LeSage and Pace (2008) and LeSage and Fischer (2010) suggest using separate explanatory variables for inter and intraregional flows, which they call as "adjusted model." The "adjusted model" can be expressed as

$$\mathbf{y} = \rho_1 \mathbf{W}_1 \mathbf{y} + \rho_2 \mathbf{W}_2 \mathbf{y} + \rho_3 \mathbf{W}_3 \mathbf{y} + \widetilde{\mathbf{X}} \boldsymbol{\beta} + \mathbf{X}^* \boldsymbol{\gamma} + \boldsymbol{\varepsilon}, \tag{6.13}$$

where $\mathbf{X}^*$ contains explanatory variables that correspond to intraregional flows and all other rows are set to zero. Similarly, $\widetilde{\mathbf{X}}$ contains only explanatory variables that correspond to interregional flows (see LeSage and Pace 2008 for more detail). This approach can be seen as a special case of the regime-switching model, in that Eq. (6.13) can be rewritten as

$$\begin{cases} \mathbf{y}_i = \rho_1 \mathbf{W}_{1i}\mathbf{y} + \rho_2 \mathbf{W}_{2i}\mathbf{y} + \rho_3 \mathbf{W}_{3i}\mathbf{y} + \widetilde{\mathbf{X}}_i \boldsymbol{\beta} + \boldsymbol{\varepsilon}_i & I_i(\bullet) = 1 \\ \mathbf{y}_i = \rho_1 \mathbf{W}_{1i}\mathbf{y} + \rho_2 \mathbf{W}_{2i}\mathbf{y} + \rho_3 \mathbf{W}_{3i}\mathbf{y} + \mathbf{X}_i^* \boldsymbol{\beta} + \boldsymbol{\varepsilon}_i & I_i(\bullet) = 0 \end{cases} \tag{6.14}$$

where $I_i(\bullet)$ is some indicator function. The adjusted model in Eq. (6.13) is to arbitrarily set the function $I_i(\bullet)$ as a dummy variable, indicating whether a flow is interregional or intraregional flow. This is equivalent to postulating the existence of non-linearity in the model between these two types of flows. Threshold regression proposed by Hansen (2000) remedies the above-mentioned arbitrary setting of the indicator function by introducing a threshold variable q_i into the indicator function. Threshold regression further provides us to estimate such a threshold that distinguishes between two regimes ($I_i\,(q_i > \alpha)$ and $I_i\,(q_i \leq \alpha)$) endogenously, using a simple estimation procedure. Estimation procedure of the threshold regression is as follows (e.g., Hansen 2000; Falvey et al. 2009)

1. Sort the dataset in ascending-order of the threshold variable (the distances of the flows)
2. Estimate parameters of model in Eq. (6.14) and calculate the sum of square errors (SSEs) for each q_i
3. Obtain the estimate of the threshold, $\hat{\alpha}$, that minimizes the SSE.

Going back to the introduction, where we have mentioned that intraregional flows can be seen as the aggregation of flows at a smaller spatial unit, we can assume that the non-linearity of the model may come from the difference between longer distance and shorter distance flows. To verify this hypothesis in our data, we employ the threshold regression with the distances of flows as the threshold variable, and estimate the threshold value that divides observed flows into two regimes. Since distances of intraregional flows are much lower than those of interregional flows, the threshold can be found at the maximum distance of intraregional flows, which would split the observations into interregional and intraregional clearly, if there exists the difference in nature of interregional and intraregional flows.

We used the same dataset as in Sect. 6.4 for simplicity. Figure 6.2 shows the transition of the SSE with the X-axis representing ascending-order of the threshold variable. Both $c = 1/3$ and $2/3$ are used for the internal distances, but the identical results are obtained. The minimum value of the SSE is obtained at 78th and 79th lowest distances. Since the maximum distance of intraregional flows is the 47th lowest distance, the result indicates that the estimated threshold of our data contains not only intraregional, but also some interregional flows that have shorter distances.

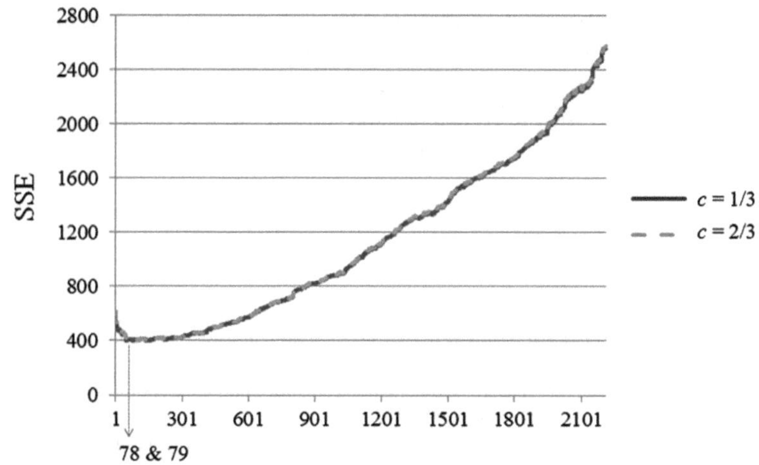

Fig. 6.2 Transition of SSE in ascending order of the distances

6.6 Conclusion

This study has considered and discussed the issues regarding intraregional flows with the spatial econometric gravity model. We mainly focused on two issues: the definition of intraregional distance and model estimation with unobserved intraregional flows. Heckman's two-step estimation approach and the EM algorithm approach were used to deal with unobserved intraregional flows. We demonstrated the above methodologies by using Japanese inter-prefectural migration data and examined the estimation results. The results of the Heckit-type model indicated that excluding intraregional flows would cause the sample selection bias. The Heckit-type and EM algorithm models gave similar results, and we concluded that both approaches are fairly valid. It is important to note that the Heckit-type model requires model specification of the outcome and the selection models (probit model). In this study, we used the same explanatory variables for the outcome and selection models. However, misspecification or alternative specification of the selection model may lead to different results. On the other hand, the EM algorithm model does not suffer from the aforementioned problem or require reconstruction of the model. This characteristic sounds attractive for a practical use, but to ensure the convergence of the algorithm, the model cannot consider heterogeneity between observed and unobserved samples.

Considering the different natures of interregional and intraregional flows is a stylized fact in much of the literature, but due to the limitation of the models, we have assumed homogeneity between these two flows in actual study. Although the result of the threshold regression in Sect. 6.5 suggests little evidence of any clear distinction between inter and intra, we think that ignoring the difference in nature may seriously affect the result, depending on a spatial scale of the data. For example, international flows rather than interregional flows in one country would likely suffer from heterogeneity due to the border effect and home bias caused by asymmetric information of foreign countries. The threshold regression can be used as a solution to test the existence of the difference in nature; however, it is limited to a case when both intraregional and interregional flows are observed.

References

Badinger H, Egger P (2011) Estimation of higher-order spatial autoregressive cross-section models with heteroscedastic disturbances. Pap Reg Sci 90:213–235

Behrens K, Ertur C, Koch W (2012) 'Dual' gravity: using spatial econometrics to control for multilateral resistance. J Appl Econ 27(5):773–794

De la Mata T, Llano C (2012) Spatial pattern and domestic tourism: an econometric analysis using inter-regional monetary flows by type of journey. Pap Reg Sci 91(2):437–470

De la Mata T, Llano C (2013) Social networks and trade of services: modeling interregional flows with spatial and network autocorrelation effects. J Geogr Syst. doi:10.1007/s10109-013-0183-6

Deng M, Athanasopoulos G (2011) Modelling Australian domestic and international inbound travel: a spatial–temporal approach. Tour Manag 32:1075–1084

Falvey R, Foster N, Greenaway D (2009) Trade, imitative ability and intellectual property rights. Rev World Econ 145:373–404

Hansen BE (2000) Sample splitting and threshold estimation. Econometrica 68:575–603

Head K, Mayer T (2000) Non-Europe: the magnitude and causes of market fragmentation in the EU. Weltwirtschaftliches Arch 136:284–314

Head K, Mayer T (2002) Illusory border effects: distance mismeasurement inflates estimates of home bias in trade. Working papers 2002-01, CEPII research center

Heckman JJ (1979) Sample selection bias as a specification error. Econometrica 47(1):153–161

Kelejian HH, Prucha IR (2010) Specification and estimation of spatial autoregressive models with autoregressive and heteroscedastic disturbances. J Econ 157(1):53–67

Kelejian HH, Prucha IR, Yuzefovich E (2004) Instrumental variable estimation of a spatial autoregressive model with autoregressive disturbances: large and small sample results. In: LeSage JP, Pace RK (eds) Advances in econometrics: spatial and spatiotemporal econometrics. Elsevier, New York

Koshizuka T, Kurita O (1991) Approximate formulas of average distances associated with regions and their applications to location problems. Math Program 52:99–123

LeSage JP, Fischer MM (2010) Spatial econometric methods for origin-destination flows. In: Fischer MM, Getis A (eds) Handbook of applied spatial analysis. Springer, Berlin

LeSage JP, Pace RK (2004) Models for spatially dependent missing data. J Real Estate Financ Econ 29:233–254

LeSage JP, Pace RK (2008) Spatial econometric modeling of origin-destination flows. J Reg Sci 48:941–967

LeSage JP, Polasek W (2008) Incorporating transportation network structure in spatial econometric models of commodity flows. Spat Econ Anal 3(2):225–245

Marrocu E, Paci R (2012) Different tourists to different destinations. Evidence from spatial interaction models. Tour Manag 39:71–83. doi:10.1016/j.tourman.2012.10.009

Nitsch V (2000) National borders and international trade: evidence from the European Union. Can J Econ 33:1091–1105

O'Brien RM (2007) A caution regarding rules of thumb for variance inflation factors. Qual Quant 41:673–690

Redding S, Venables AJ (2004) Economic geography and international inequality. J Int Econ 62:53–82

Tsutsumi M, Tamesue K (2012) Intraregional flow problem in spatial econometric model for origin-destination flows. Environ Plan B 39(6):1006–1015

Vaughan R (1984) Approximate formulas for average distances associated with zones. Transp Sci 18:231–244

Wei S (1996) Intra-national versus international trade: how stubborn are nations in global integration? Working paper 5531, National Bureau of Economic Research

Chapter 7
A Bayesian Spatial Interaction Model Variant of the Poisson Pseudo-Maximum Likelihood Estimator

James P. LeSage and Esra Satici

Keywords Bayesian • Gravity • Poisson pseudo-maximum likelihood • Spatial interaction

JEL: C11, C13, C18, R11

7.1 Advantages of PPML for Spatial Interaction Modeling

There are several econometric advantages to the Poisson pseudo-maximum likelihood (PPML) approach to estimating relationships involving flows (Santos Silva and Tenreyro 2010). One is that the coefficients on logged explanatory variables (X) in the (exponential) relationship involving non-logged flow magnitudes as the dependent variable (y) can be interpreted as the elasticity of the conditional expectation of y_i with respect to X_i. Since Jensen's inequality implies that $E(\ln y) \neq \ln E(y)$, heteroscedasticity in log-linear regression gravity models can lead to inconsistent elasticity estimates, which is not a problem with PPML estimates.[1] In addition to dealing with heteroscedasticity, PPML estimation procedures do not require taking logs of the flows, so avoid the problem of (logs) in the presence of zero flows. With regard to the zero problem, Santos Silva and Tenreyro (2010) also point out that zeros resulting from 'rounding down' small flows are likely to be associated with levels of the explanatory variables, which suggests an endogeneity issue.

[1]Santos Silva and Tenreyro (2010) note there is strong evidence that disturbances from log-linear gravity models are heteroscedastic.

J.P. LeSage (✉)
Department of Finance and Economics, McCoy College of Business Administration, Texas State University, San Marcos, TX 78666, USA
e-mail: james.lesage@txstate.edu

E. Satici
General Directorate of Turkish Highways, Ankara, Turkey

R. Patuelli, G. Arbia (eds.), *Spatial Econometric Interaction Modelling*, Advances in Spatial Science, DOI 10.1007/978-3-319-30196-9_7

The traditional gravity relationship takes the form in (7.1) for the case of n regions with an $n \times n$ matrix of flows. This can be written in the log-linear regression form shown in (7.2) (see LeSage and Pace 2009; Sen and Smith 1995).

$$\begin{aligned} Y_{ij} &= \beta_0 X_i^{\beta_i} X_j^{\beta_j} D_{ij}^{\gamma} \eta_{ij} && (7.1)\\ \ln(y) &= \ln(\beta_0)\iota_{n^2} + X_d\beta_d + X_o\beta_o + \ln(d)\gamma + \ln(\eta) && (7.2)\\ X_d &= \iota_n \otimes \ln(X), \quad X_o = \ln(X) \otimes \iota_n \\ \eta &\sim N(0, \sigma^2 I_{n^2}) \end{aligned}$$

In (7.2), y is an $n^2 \times 1$ vector representing columns of the $n \times n$ flow matrix (Y) stacked. Without loss of generality, the flows are organized so that element in the ith column represents flows from the ith (origin) region to all destination regions, with the i, ith diagonal element representing flows within the ith region. The $n \times 1$ vector ι_n contains all ones, $\otimes$ denotes the kronecker product, and X is an $n \times k$ matrix of explanatory variables describing characteristics of the n regions. The $n^2 \times 1$ vector d represents columns from the distance matrix (D) stacked. The disturbances in (7.1) are assumed to be such that $E(\eta_{ij}|X_i, X_j, D_{ij}) = 1$, and are statistically independent of the explanatory variables. Santos Silva and Tenreyro (2010) point out that if we assume η follows a log-normal, with $E(\eta_{ij}|X_i, X_j, D_{ij}) = 1$ and variance-covariance $\sigma_{ij}^2 = f(X_i, X_j, D_{ij})$, then the log-linearized version of these (normally distributed) version of these disturbances has $E(\ln(\eta_{ij})|X_i, X_j, D_{ij}) = -\frac{1}{2}\ln(1 + \sigma_{ij}^2)$, which exhibits dependence on the explanatory variables.

A theoretical motivation for the relationship $y_i = \exp(x_i\beta)$ is the constant elasticity relationship between y and x implied by the gravity relationship. This leads to a conditional expectation in (7.3), and the stochastic model relationship in (7.4) and (7.5), where we let $z_i = [\ln(1)\ \ln(X_i)\ \ln(X_j)\ \ln(D_{ij})]$ and $\delta = [\ln(\beta_0)\ \beta_i\ \beta_j\ \gamma]'$ (Smith 1975).

$$\begin{aligned} E(Y_{ij}|X_i, X_j, D_{ij}) &= \exp\{\ln(1) + \ln(X_i)\beta_i + \ln(X_j)\beta_j + \ln(D_{ij})\gamma\} && (7.3)\\ y_i &= z_i\delta + \varepsilon_i && (7.4)\\ y_i &= z_i\delta + \eta_i && (7.5)\\ \eta_i &= 1 + \varepsilon_i/\exp(z_i\delta) \\ E(\eta_i|z) &= 1 \end{aligned}$$

An important point is that consistent estimates based on the log-linear relationship require special conditions to produce a situation where $E(\ln(\eta_i)|z)$ is constant (homoscedasticity) (see Santos Silva and Tenreyro (2010) for details regarding these).

The non-linear pseudo-maximum likelihood estimator proposed by Gourieroux et al. (1984) is based on solving for $\hat{\delta}$ from the first-order conditions in (7.6), which only required that the conditional mean in (7.7) be specified correctly. In fact, Gourieroux et al. (1984) consider four different type of disturbance specifications and show that estimates based on this criterion have desirable properties.

$$\sum_{i=1}^{n} \left(y_i - \exp(z_i\hat{\delta})\right) z_i = 0 \tag{7.6}$$

$$E(y_i|z) = \exp(z_i\delta) \tag{7.7}$$

One of the four disturbance specifications considered in Gourieroux et al. (1984) produces the Poisson pseudo-maximum likelihood (PPML) estimator, hence the name given to this approach to estimation. For consistency, the data do not need to be Poisson distributed, nor do the values of y_i need to be integers. Both of these properties are attractive in the context of modeling flows, which may be non-integer as well as integer-valued (e.g., dollar values of flows versus counts of migrants).

Arvis and Shepherd (2013) have pointed out that the PPML model produces estimates such that the doubly constrained model of Wilson holds for the case of the log-linear model (that is, where the explanatory variables are log-transformed), *and* when fixed effects for origins and destinations are added to the model (as is conventional in the empirical trade literature). Fally (2012) argues that inclusion of importer and exporter fixed effects are consistent with general equilibrium conditions and the introduction of "multilateral resistance" indexes, along with other useful properties of fixed effects in the PPML model.

7.2 A Spatial Extension of the PPML Model

The regional science literature credits Alonso (1973, 1978) with development of a generalized gravity model (labeled Alonso's Theory of Movements or ATM) used in migration theory, whereas the international trade literature credits Anderson and van Wincoop (2003). A generalized version of the gravity model takes the form in (7.8), where the terms: $B_j^{-\alpha}$ and $A_i^{-\beta}$ were labeled "multilateral resistance" indexes by Anderson and van Wincoop (2003). (See de Vries et al. (2001) for an extensive review of the ATM).

$$Y_{ij} = A_i^{1-\alpha} X_i^{\beta_i} B_j^{1-\beta} X_j^{\beta_j} D_{ij}^{-\gamma} \tag{7.8}$$

$$A_i = \{\sum_j B_j^{1-\beta} X_j D_{ij}^{-\gamma}\}^{-1} \tag{7.9}$$

$$B_j = \{\sum_i A_i^{1-\alpha} X_i D_{ij}^{-\gamma}\}^{-1} \tag{7.10}$$

Alonso (1973, p. 11) described A^{-1} as 'opportunity', 'demand' or 'draw', noting that if many opportunities (for migrants) were available from one location (origin), the flow of out-migrants might be expected to increase overall, but the flow to any particular destination will decrease in response to the other attractive destinations. Similarly, B^{-1} was labeled ‘competition’, ‘congestion’, ‘potential pool of moves’, reflecting the fact that if a large number of migrants competed for opportunities at one location (destination), this should reduce the attractiveness and have a negative impact on flows.

In both the case of Alonso and Anderson and van Wincoop, the terms A_i, B_j reflect latent unobservable variables that require estimation. In the trade literature the “multilateral resistance” indexes have been proxied using origin- and destination-specific fixed effects (e.g., Feenstra 2004).

de Vries et al. (2001) point out that the ATM subsumes Wilson's (1967; 1970; 1974) family of spatial interaction models as special cases. For the case of $\alpha = 0, \beta = 0$, the doubly constrained model of Wilson arises. On the other hand, setting $\alpha = 1, \beta = 1$ produces the unconstrained gravity model, and $\alpha = 1, \beta = 0$ results in an ‘attraction-constrained’ model whereas $\alpha = 0, \beta = 1$ produces a ‘production-constrained’ model. Taking this view, the ATM model can be viewed as reflecting intermediate cases of the constrained models of Wilson, when we restrict α and β to lie between 0 and 1.

In the spirit of Alonso, we propose adding a linear combination of the ‘size’ variables from regions neighboring the origin as a proxy for ‘opportunity’ or ‘draw’ and a linear combination of the ‘size’ variables for regions neighboring the destination as a proxy for ‘competition’ or ‘congestion’. This can be accomplished by forming spatial lag variables that reflect neighbors to the origin and destination (Griffith and Jones 1980; Griffith 2007). LeSage and Pace (2008) point out that these take the form of: $W_o = (W \otimes I_n)$, $W_d = (I_n \otimes W)$, where W is an $n \times n$ spatial weight matrix for the n regions used to produce the $n \times n$ flow matrix. Returning to our vector notation we have:

$$y = \exp(\beta_0 \iota_{n^2} + X_d \beta_d + X_o \beta_o + \ln(d)\gamma + W_d X_d \theta_d + W_o X_o \theta_o) \qquad (7.11)$$

Consistent with Alonso's notion that changes in regions neighboring the origin and destination will impact flows, we have a local spatial spillover effect that arises in (7.11). Changes in (logged) characteristics of a single region i, $\ln(X_i)$ produce changes in this region viewed as both an origin and destination since: $X_o = (\ln(X) \otimes \iota_n), X_d = (\iota_n \otimes \ln(X))$, as well as regions neighboring the origin and destination region i whose characteristics have changed, since: $W_o X_o = W_o(\ln(X) \otimes \iota_n), W_d X_d = W_d(\iota_n \otimes \ln(X))$.

As noted in Sect. 7.1, an advantage of the PPML specification is that the coefficients (β_d, β_o on logged explanatory variables (X_d, X_o) in the (exponential) relationship involving non-logged flow magnitudes as the dependent variable (y) can be interpreted as the elasticity of the conditional expectation of y with respect to X_d, X_o. These reflect the usual interpretation where β_o^r measures the impact of changing the rth characteristic in the matrix X_o on outflows, and β_d^r measures the impact of changing the rth characteristic in the matrix X_d on inflows, (averaged across all observations as in a typical regression). The coefficients (θ_d, θ_o on logged explanatory variables $(W_d X_d, W_o X_o)$ reflect the ‘spillover’ impact of changing the rth characteristic in the matrices X_d, X_o flows involving neighboring regions. Specifically, θ_d^r measures the (elasticity) impact of changing the rth characteristic in X_d on flows *to* regions neighboring the (typical) destination, again averaged across all observations as in a typical regression. The coefficient θ_o^r measures the (elasticity) impact of changing the rth characteristic in X_o on flows *from* regions neighboring the (typical) origin (Thomas-Agnan and LeSage 2014).

As a concrete example, consider the case of commuting flows from places of residence to that of employment. We assume two explanatory variables in $X^{r=1}, X^{r=2}$, one measuring the population of residents in each region and another reflecting the number of jobs in each region. An increase in employment/jobs in the typical destination region $\Delta X_d^{r=2}$ should produce a direct (elasticity) impact ($\beta_d^{r=2}$) showing increased inflows to that region. As noted by Alonso, the competition or congestion impact (the spatial spillover impact in our model specification), should exert a negative impact on inflows to the typical neighboring destination as a result of the increase in employment. That is, we might expect $\theta_d^{r=2}$ to be negative. Similarly, an increase in residents living in a region should have a positive direct impact ($\beta_o^{r=1}$) on commuting outflows from the typical region, whereas the opportunity or draw impact on neighboring regions ($\theta_o^{r=1}$) would be negative. In our specification, the total impact is the sum of the direct plus indirect impacts. We would expect the congestion and opportunity impacts (θ_d, θ_o) to be 'second-order' impacts of lesser magnitude than the direct impacts, leaving us with a total impact consisting of the sum of the direct plus indirect impact that is still positive.

It would be possible to extend our specification to include second-order neighbors by adding $W_d^2 X_d$ and $W_o^2 X_o$ to the model (and associated coefficients). However, these variables are likely to be highly correlated with $W_d X_d$ and $W_o X_o$ as well as X_d, X_o. For this variant of the model, the spatial spillover (indirect) effects would be the sum of the coefficients on both set of variables $W_d X_d$, $W_d^2 X_d$ and $W_o X_o$, $W_o^2 X_o$. Since this is the case we have an analogy to vector autoregressive (VAR) models where Granger causality tests and impulse response functions depend on a sum of coefficients. This can lessen the impact of collinearity, since interest centers on a joint test of these coefficients in the case of Granger causality tests and impulse response functions. Another analogy to VAR models would be that a smoothness prior could be imposed to force the coefficients on successively higher powers of $W_d^k X_d$ to decay in magnitude. This topic is left as a subject for future research.

An important point is that PPML estimates are known to be robust with respect to omitted variables that *are not* correlated with the included variables X_d, X_o. However, variables such as $W_d X_d$, $W_o X_o$ are likely to be highly correlated with X_d, X_o for the case of regional data. For example, if X_d, X_o represent an economic measure of regional size related to income, then $W_d X_d$, $W_o X_o$ reflect linear combinations of income from regions that neighbor the destination and origin. Since regional income tends to exhibit clustering (e.g., spatial dependence) so that neighboring regions have similar levels of income, exclusion of these spatial lags when they are truly part of the data generating process should lead to bias in the PPML model. We explore this issue in the next section.

7.3 Estimating the PPML Model

Maximizing the objective function in (7.6) with respect the $\hat{\delta}$ is relatively straightforward and a numerical hessian calculation can be used to produce measures of dispersion. These can be used to create t-statistics.

An alternative approach is to use Markov Chain Monte Carlo (MCMC) estimation that relies on an independence random-walk proposal distribution for each coefficient in δ. Specifically, given the scalar coefficient at draw t, δ_i^t, we set the proposal value δ_i^{t+1} using: $\delta_i^{t+1} = \delta_i^t + c \cdot N(0, 1)$, where c is a tuning parameter and $N(0, 1)$ denotes the standard normal distribution. The tuning parameter is varied according to the acceptance rate such that $c' = c/1.1$ if the rate falls below 40 %, which should lead to an increase in the acceptance rate. If the acceptance rate rises above 60 %, we set $c' = (1.1)c$, which should lead to a decrease in the acceptance rate. The proposals were evaluated using the conditional distribution for each parameter, which takes the form: $p(\delta_i^{t+1}|\delta_{j\neq i}^t, y, z) = \sum_{k=1}^n \left(y_k - \exp(z_{k,i}\delta_i^{t+1} - \sum_{j\neq i}(z_{k,j}\delta_j^t)\right) z_{k,i}$, where the proposed parameter is accepted according to the Metropolis-Hastings algorithm.

A block-sampling MCMC approach was also explored, where pilot draws from the independence random-walk sampler described above were used to construct a variance-covariance matrix (Ω) for all parameters in δ. This matrix was used in conjunction with the random-walk scheme: $\delta^{t+1} = \delta^t + c \cdot N(\underline{0}, \Omega)$ to produce a proposal vector that was accepted or rejected as a block. This seems to make little difference in performance of the MCMC sampler.

Without prior distributions assigned to the coefficients, this approach to MCMC estimation should produce nearly identical estimates as maximization. One advantage of MCMC estimation is that the sequence of draws for the model parameters can be used to calculate measures of dispersion that can be used for inference. Difficulties that may arise using numerical hessian calculations to produce dispersion estimates should not arise for the case of MCMC estimates.

As with all non-linear optimization or MCMC estimation procedures, properly scaled data is important, so the X_d, X_o matrices and (logged) distance vector are standardized to reflect deviations from means divided by the standard deviation.

As a test of these estimation approaches as well as the spatial extension of the model specification we conducted a simulation experiment. This involved generating a vector of flows using the latitude-longitude coordinates of 60 regions in Toulouse, as well as the residential population and employment of each region as two explanatory variables, in addition to (logged) distance. The set of 3,600 (non-spatial) flow observations (y_{ns}) were producing using (7.12), where z_i, Z and δ are as defined in (7.3). The disturbance term η is a log-normal random deviate with mean 1 and non-constant variance σ_i^2. The $n \times n$ distance matrix D contains zeros on the main diagonal, so we add the identity matrix prior to taking logs, and the vec operator stacks columns of the distance matrix to form an $n^2 \times 1$ vector of (logged) distances that we denote d. Of course, $\beta_0 = \ln(\tilde{\beta}_0)$.

$$y_{ns} = \mu(Z\delta)\eta = (\tilde{\beta}_0[\iota_n \otimes \ln(X)]^{\beta_d}[\ln(X) \otimes \iota_n]^{\beta_o}[vec\ \ln(D + I_n)]^{\gamma})\eta \quad (7.12)$$

$$E(y|Z) = \exp(\beta_0 + X_d\beta_d + X_o\beta_o + d\gamma)$$

$$\text{Var}(\eta_i) = \sigma_i^2 = \mu(z_i\delta)^{-1}; \text{Var}(y_i|z_i) = \mu(z_i\delta)$$

$$E(y|Z) = \exp(\beta_0 + X_d\beta_d + W_dX_d\theta_d + X_o\beta_o + W_oX_o\theta_o + d\gamma) \quad (7.13)$$

The spatial variant of the model relied on expression (7.13) to produce a vector of flows that we label y_s. A reciprocal misspecification design was carried out using 100 trials. Four model were estimated using PPML estimates based on optimization, where a combination of the spatial and non-spatial dependent variables were used in conjunction with the spatial and non-spatial set of explanatory variables. That is, (y_s, Z_s), $(y_{ns}Z_{ns})$, (y_s, Z_ns), (y_{ns}, Z_s). We would expect correctly specified models based on (y_s, Z_s) and (y_{ns}, Z_{ns}) to perform best, but are interested in problems that arise in the face of the misspecified models: (y_s, Z_ns), (y_{ns}, Z_s). In addition to PPML estimates, ordinary regression estimates based on $\ln(y_s), \ln(y_{ns})$ were also part of the experiment. This was done to illustrate bias that arises from use of the log-transformation in conjunction with regression, a common practice.

Table 7.1 shows results for the four models estimated, with mean and median coefficient estimates calculated using the 100 trials as well as 0.05 and 0.95 intervals for the distribution of 100 outcomes. True values of the model coefficients used to generate the flow vectors y_s, y_{ns} are shown in the first column. As expected, results for the case of (y_{ns}, Z_{ns}) are excellent, with the mean and median for all coefficient estimates falling within the 0.05 and 0.95 intervals. This is consistent with other more extensive Monte Carlo evidence for the PPML model. We find similar results for our spatial extension of the model reported for the case of (y_s, Z_s) in Table 7.1.

The case of (y_s, Z_{ns}) should exhibit omitted variables bias, because the spatial lags of the explanatory variables used to generate y_s were excluded from the model. Although the PPML model is robust to omitted variables that are *uncorrelated* with included variables, this would not be the case for spatial lag variables such as W_dX_d, W_oX_o, since there are highly correlated with the included variables X_d, X_o.

On the other hand, it is well-known that including redundant variables does not lead to problems of bias. This appears for the case involving $(y_{ns}Z_s)$, where the estimates correctly indicate that none of the spatial lags of the explanatory variables are different from zero (based on the 0.05 and 0.95 intervals).

For the set of experiments reported in Table 7.1 there were no zero flow values generated. The PPML model specification can produce zero flow values by rounding flows down to the nearest integer. The notion here is that zero flows represent magnitudes that do not exceed a 'threshold' value. A second set of experiments was conducted where the flows were generated in the same way as before, but rounded down to the nearest integer. This produced 12.93 % zero flow values for the case of y_{ns} and 15.40 % zero values for y_s on average over the 100 trials. Estimation results are reported in Table 7.2 for this data generating process.

Table 7.1 PPML Monte Carlo results based on 100 trials

Coefficients	Lower 0.05	Mean	Median	Upper 0.95
	y_{ns}, Z_{ns}			
$\beta_0 = 2$	1.9877	1.9990	1.9997	2.0079
$\beta_{d1} = -0.8$	−0.8039	−0.8004	−0.8004	−0.7968
$\beta_{d2} = 1$	0.9940	0.9998	0.9996	1.0046
$\beta_{o1} = 1$	0.9902	0.9999	0.9998	1.0102
$\beta_{o2} = -0.5$	−0.5060	−0.4997	−0.4996	−0.4933
$\gamma = -0.5$	−0.5049	−0.5001	−0.5003	−0.4949
	y_s, Z_{ns}			
$\beta_0 = 2$	1.9939	2.0028	2.0029	2.0106
$\beta_{d1} = -0.8$	−1.1475	−1.1450	−1.1452	−1.1425
$\beta_{d2} = 1$	1.1915	1.1961	1.1962	1.1997
$\beta_{o1} = 1$	0.7679	0.7744	0.7742	0.7797
$\beta_{o2} = -0.5$	−0.5483	−0.5437	−0.5438	−0.5401
$\gamma = -0.5$	−0.6266	−0.6235	−0.6234	−0.6205
	y_{ns}, Z_s			
$\beta_0 = 2$	1.9887	1.9991	1.9999	2.0080
$\beta_{d1} = -0.8$	−0.8042	−0.8002	−0.8004	−0.7957
$\beta_{d2} = 1$	0.9943	0.9998	0.9997	1.0042
$\beta_{o1} = 1$	0.9884	0.9998	0.9994	1.0106
$\beta_{o2} = -0.5$	−0.5069	−0.4995	−0.4992	−0.4924
$\theta_{d1} = 0$	−0.0096	0.0003	0.0006	0.0083
$\theta_{d2} = 0$	−0.0075	−0.0005	−0.0001	0.0038
$\theta_{o1} = 0$	−0.0061	0.0005	0.0010	0.0057
$\theta_{o2} = 0$	−0.0074	−0.0006	−0.0002	0.0051
$\gamma = -0.5$	−0.5046	−0.5003	−0.5004	−0.4950
	y_s, Z_s			
$\beta_0 = 2$	1.9922	2.0001	2.0001	2.0066
$\beta_{d1} = -0.8$	−0.8042	−0.7999	−0.7998	−0.7960
$\beta_{d2} = 1$	0.9943	1.0001	1.0004	1.0043
$\beta_{o1} = 1$	0.9926	0.9999	0.9996	1.0069
$\beta_{o2} = -0.5$	−0.5056	−0.5000	−0.4998	−0.4951
$\theta_{d1} = -0.5$	−0.5085	−0.4999	−0.4998	−0.4936
$\theta_{d2} = -0.5$	−0.5053	−0.4999	−0.5001	−0.4934
$\theta_{o1} = -0.4$	−0.4040	−0.4004	−0.4002	−0.3968
$\theta_{o2} = -0.2$	−0.2042	−0.1996	−0.1997	−0.1959
$\gamma = -0.5$	−0.5033	−0.4999	−0.5000	−0.4961

These results are consistent with points made in the trade literature by Martinez-Zarzoso et al. (2007) and Martinez-Zarzoso (2013). The presence of zero values has an adverse impact on the PPML estimates, producing results that exhibit systematic bias. This is evident from the fact that the 0.05 and 0.95 intervals no longer

Table 7.2 PPML Monte Carlo results based on 100 trials, flows rounded down to nearest integer

Coefficients	Lower 0.05	Mean	Median	Upper 0.95
	y_{ns}, Z_{ns}			
$\beta_0 = 2$	1.9256	1.9350	1.9349	1.9449
$\beta_{d1} = -0.8$	−0.8110	−0.8077	−0.8076	−0.8046
$\beta_{d2} = 1$	1.0115	1.0173	1.0172	1.0229
$\beta_{o1} = 1$	1.0178	1.0265	1.0266	1.0373
$\beta_{o2} = -0.5$	−0.5192	−0.5127	−0.5133	−0.5051
$\gamma = -0.5$	−0.5152	−0.5099	−0.5099	−0.5044
	y_s, Z_{ns}			
$\beta_0 = 2$	1.9506	1.9587	1.9584	1.9686
$\beta_{d1} = -0.8$	−1.1542	−1.1518	−1.1519	−1.1491
$\beta_{d2} = 1$	1.2032	1.2071	1.2069	1.2119
$\beta_{o1} = 1$	0.7783	0.7833	0.7832	0.7879
$\beta_{o2} = -0.5$	−0.5517	−0.5481	−0.5480	−0.5444
$\gamma = -0.5$	−0.6309	−0.6275	−0.6275	−0.6239
	y_{ns}, Z_s			
$\beta_0 = 2$	1.9220	1.9317	1.9320	1.9421
$\beta_{d1} = -0.8$	−0.8163	−0.8114	−0.8114	−0.8065
$\beta_{d2} = 1$	1.0125	1.0182	1.0183	1.0242
$\beta_{o1} = 1$	1.0154	1.0251	1.0246	1.0344
$\beta_{o2} = -0.5$	−0.5197	−0.5118	−0.5121	−0.5036
$\theta_{d1} = 0$	−0.0113	0.0005	0.0009	0.0086
$\theta_{d2} = 0$	−0.0005	0.0061	0.0063	0.0122
$\theta_{o1} = 0$	−0.0037	0.0025	0.0027	0.0072
$\theta_{o2} = 0$	−0.0094	−0.0038	−0.0038	0.0018
$\gamma = -0.5$	−0.5149	−0.5094	−0.5094	−0.5037
	y_s, Z_s			
$\beta_0 = 2$	1.9434	1.9532	1.9534	1.9640
$\beta_{d1} = -0.8$	−0.8082	−0.8045	−0.8046	−0.8006
$\beta_{d2} = 1$	1.0034	1.0078	1.0076	1.0136
$\beta_{o1} = 1$	1.0057	1.0118	1.0119	1.0170
$\beta_{o2} = -0.5$	−0.5102	−0.5054	−0.5050	−0.5009
$\theta_{d1} = -0.5$	−0.5247	−0.5146	−0.5148	−0.5057
$\theta_{d2} = -0.5$	−0.5064	−0.5003	−0.5002	−0.4944
$\theta_{o1} = -0.4$	−0.4050	−0.4008	−0.4008	−0.3968
$\theta_{o2} = -0.2$	−0.2077	−0.2034	−0.2036	−0.1996
$\gamma = -0.5$	−0.5076	−0.5031	−0.5028	−0.4992

encompass the true parameter values used to generate the vectors y_{ns}, y_s. However, Santos Silva and Tenreyro (2011) point out that the PPML model works better than alternative approaches even in the face of a large proportion of zero flow values.

For the cases of no specification error (y_{ns}, Z_{ns}) and (y_s, Z_s), we see small biases in the estimation outcomes, with the largest bias occurring for the intercept coefficient which has no interpretative value. A much more important source of bias would be omission of spatial lags of the explanatory variables, as illustrated by the case of (y_s, Z_{ns}) in both Tables 7.1 and 7.2.

The bias arising from the presence of zero flows does not appear to inhibit the ability of the model estimates to detect the fact that coefficients on spatial lags of the explanatory variables are zero for the case of (y_{ns}, Z_s), which would be important in applied practice. All estimates for coefficients θ_d, θ_o on these spatially lags variables have 0.05 and 0.95 intervals that span zero, indicating they are not different from zero.

Table 7.3 presents results based on the common log-transformation of flows. We report results based on the best case scenario with no rounding of flows down to the nearest integer to produce zero flows. Here we see estimates across the board for all models (correctly and incorrectly specified) that exhibit bias. The 0.05 and 0.95 intervals do not encompass the true coefficient values used to generate the vectors of flows (y_{ns}, y_s) in any of the four sets of results. Further, three of the four coefficients θ_d, θ_o for the case of $(\ln y_s, Z_s)$ would lead to the incorrect conclusion regarding the significant of the spatial lag variables.

7.4 An Application to Commuting Flows

We illustrate estimation and interpretation of the model estimates using commuting-to-work flows for 60 regions (Quartiers) in Toulouse France, taken from the 1999 census from INSEE (The National Institute for Statistics and Economic Studies, France; LeSage and Thomas-Agnan 2015). Flows were constructed from the census home and work addresses provided by the actively employed population. These were aggregated from individual level information to the regional level. Workers in the defense sector and workers moving to variable sites or working at home were excluded from the individuals used in aggregating to the regional level. The distance matrix was formed using distance between centroids of the spatial units.

For the 60 region area studied, 52 % of workers in the region come from outside the region and 19 % of residents in the region work outside. These were excluded to form a system of flows between districts that includes only persons who both live and work in one of the 60 regions.

As explanatory variables we use the (logged) number of persons who work that reside in each district (*residents*), and the (logged) number of jobs located in each district (*employment*). These two vectors plus a constant and distance were used in the non-spatial model. The variables and distance were standardized, that is, put in deviation from means form and divided by the standard deviation. Use of the conventional log transformation of the two explanatory variables and distance allows us to interpret estimates as elasticities. We adopt an approach suggested by LeSage and Pace (2009, p. 223) that introduces a separate model for intraregional

Table 7.3 Regression Monte Carlo results based on 100 trials $\ln(y_{ns})$, $\ln(y_s)$

Coefficients	Lower 0.05	Mean	Median	Upper 0.95
	$\ln(y_{ns}), Z_{ns}$			
$\beta_0 = 2$	2.2236	2.2303	2.2302	2.2374
$\beta_{d1} = -0.8$	−0.7188	−0.7107	−0.7108	−0.7037
$\beta_{d2} = 1$	0.8532	0.8599	0.8598	0.8661
$\beta_{o1} = 1$	0.6810	0.6882	0.6881	0.6957
$\beta_{o2} = -0.5$	−0.3570	−0.3478	−0.3473	−0.3411
$\gamma = -0.5$	−0.4025	−0.3940	−0.3939	−0.3860
	$\ln(y_s), Z_{ns}$			
$\beta_0 = 2$	2.2613	2.2682	2.2683	2.2746
$\beta_{d1} = -0.8$	−0.7762	−0.7700	−0.7700	−0.7639
$\beta_{d2} = 1$	0.6925	0.7000	0.6996	0.7081
$\beta_{o1} = 1$	0.6298	0.6381	0.6376	0.6451
$\beta_{o2} = -0.5$	−0.4176	−0.4101	−0.4106	−0.4012
$\gamma = -0.5$	−0.2900	−0.2821	−0.2822	−0.2755
	$\ln(y_{ns}), Z_s$			
$\beta_0 = 2$	2.2236	2.2303	2.2302	2.2374
$\beta_{d1} = -0.8$	−0.7221	−0.7142	−0.7139	−0.7074
$\beta_{d2} = 1$	0.8531	0.8604	0.8605	0.8668
$\beta_{o1} = 1$	0.6785	0.6861	0.6861	0.6945
$\beta_{o2} = -0.5$	−0.3406	−0.3311	−0.3308	−0.3241
$\theta_{d1} = 0$	0.0190	0.0294	0.0300	0.0387
$\theta_{d2} = 0$	−0.0121	−0.0039	−0.0037	0.0034
$\theta_{o1} = 0$	0.0392	0.0479	0.0482	0.0557
$\theta_{o2} = 0$	−0.0725	−0.0633	−0.0628	−0.0562
$\gamma = -0.5$	−0.3982	−0.3906	−0.3903	−0.3827
	$\ln(y_s), Z_s$			
$\beta_0 = 2$	2.2613	2.2682	2.2683	2.2746
$\beta_{d1} = -0.8$	−0.7046	−0.6979	−0.6980	−0.6920
$\beta_{d2} = 1$	0.8239	0.8321	0.8318	0.8407
$\beta_{o1} = 1$	0.6782	0.6868	0.6866	0.6938
$\beta_{o2} = -0.5$	−0.3577	−0.3482	−0.3486	−0.3386
$\theta_{d1} = -0.5$	−0.3626	−0.3534	−0.3533	−0.3463
$\theta_{d2} = -0.5$	−0.4571	−0.4491	−0.4491	−0.4430
$\theta_{o1} = -0.4$	−0.3127	−0.3034	−0.3029	−0.2959
$\theta_{o2} = -0.2$	−0.2122	−0.2020	−0.2022	−0.1924
$\gamma = -0.5$	−0.3771	−0.3694	−0.3699	−0.3629

flows, which tend to have large values relative to interregional flows. This is done by creating an intercept for flows associated with the main diagonal of the flow matrix (intraregional flows), as well as a set of explanatory variables for these flows. The explanatory variables X_d, X_o are adjusted to have zero values for main diagonal elements of the flow matrix and a new variable which we label X_i is created that contains the *residents* and *employment* explanatory variables for each region to capture intraregional flow variation.

There were 15 % of the 3,600 flows with zero values. Interestingly, in the Monte Carlo experiments reported in the previous section, where the same explanatory variables and spatial weight matrix were used to generate a spatial y_s dependent variable that was rounded down to the nearest integer resulted in 15.40 % zero values. This suggests that rounding is a plausible explanation for the observed zero flows in this dataset.

The spatial model formed a spatial weight matrix W based on first-order contiguity of the 60 regions. Regions with borders that touched each region were equally weighted, and the matrix was row-standardized to have row-sums of unity.

Table 7.4 presents estimates for the non-spatial model. Ordinary regression results based on log-transformed flows (plus one to avoid taking logs of the zero values) are presented alongside PPML estimates based on optimization and the MCMC procedure. The MCMC procedure used a burn-in sample of 5,000 independence-based tuned random-walk univariate normal proposals to produce candidate values. The tuning adjusted the proposal distribution variance to achieve acceptance rates between 40 and 60 %. The set of 5,000 burn-in draws were used to calculate an empirical variance-covariance matrix that was used in conjunction with a multivariate normal proposal and block sampling of the parameters δ to produce another 5,000 draws. Posterior means and standard deviations were based on the last 5,000 draws. For comparability with the regression-based estimates and optimization-based PPML estimates, a pseudo t-statistic was calculated based on the posterior mean and standard deviation of the retained 5,000 draws.

From the table we see agreement between the optimization-based PPML estimates and MCMC-based PPML estimates to two decimal places. There is also a great deal of agreement regarding the dispersion of the estimates indicated by the similarity of the t-statistics based on the numerical hessian procedure for the optimization-based estimates versus the sequence of 5,000 retained draws from the MCMC procedure.

There is some disagreement between the regression estimates based on the log-transformation and both sets of PPML estimates, but nowhere near that seen in the Monte Carlo experiments from the previous section.

Turning attention to interpretation of the estimates, we would conclude that the positive and significant intercept for intraregional flows ($vec(I_n)$) points to higher flow levels within regions, and the positive and significant coefficients for intraregional residents and employment point to higher intraregional flows for regions where more residents and jobs are located. Specifically, a 10 % increase in residents in a region would lead to a 7.4 % increase in intraregional commuting flows, and a 10 % increase in employment is associated with a 4.8 % increase in commuting flows within the region (those that begin and end in the same region).

Increasing residents in a (work-place) destination reduces commuting inflows to those destination regions. A 10 % increase in residents would lead to a 1.29 % decrease of commuting inflows. Increasing employment/jobs in a (work-place) destination increases commuting inflows to those destination regions. A 10 % increase in jobs would lead to a 13.2 % increase of commuting inflows.

Table 7.4 Non-spatial estimates for Toulouse commuting flows

Variables	Coefficient	t-Statistic	t-Probability
	Regression using $ln(y+1)$		
Constant	2.3990	104.330	0.0000
$vec(I_n)$	8.0022	6.916	0.0000
Residents at destination	−0.1277	−5.962	0.0000
Employment at destination	1.3249	70.966	0.0000
Residents at origin	1.0508	49.053	0.0000
Employment at origin	−0.0325	−1.744	0.0811
Intraregional residents	0.7331	5.596	0.0000
Intraregional employment	0.4285	4.112	0.0000
ln(distance)	−0.3244	−21.104	0.0000
	PPML optimization		
Constant	2.4979	400.260	0.0000
$vec(I_n)$	7.8517	56.994	0.0000
Residents at destination	−0.1289	−26.049	0.0000
Employment at destination	1.3231	240.868	0.0000
Residents at origin	1.2104	150.458	0.0000
Employment at origin	−0.1266	−21.939	0.0000
Intraregional residents	0.7441	53.734	0.0000
Intraregional employment	0.4835	48.620	0.0000
ln(distance)	−0.3245	−87.558	0.0000
	PPML MCMC		
Constant	2.4980	384.315	0.0000
$vec(I_n)$	7.8701	52.969	0.0000
Residents at destination	−0.1293	−27.917	0.0000
Employment at destination	1.3225	229.913	0.0000
Residents at origin	1.2101	155.743	0.0000
Employment at origin	−0.1246	−22.994	0.0000
Intraregional residents	0.7416	52.057	0.0000
Intraregional employment	0.4841	49.680	0.0000
ln(distance)	−0.3247	−93.725	0.0000

Increasing residents in a (residential) origin produces a increase in commuting flows from those origin regions. A 10 % increase in residents would lead to an 12.1 % increase in commuting outflows from the origin.

Increasing employment/jobs in a (residential) origin produces a small decrease in commuting outflows from those origin regions. A 10 % increase in jobs located in an origin regions reduces outflows by 1.26 %.

Distance of course has a negative impact on commuting flows, such that a 10 % increase in distance would decrease commuting flows by 3.24 %.

Table 7.5 shows estimates from the spatial variant of the model. There are larger discrepancies between the regression-based estimates and the two sets of

Table 7.5 Spatial estimates for Toulouse commuting flows

Variables	Coefficient	t-Statistic	t-Probability
	Regression using $ln(y+1)$		
Constant	2.4021	105.788	0.0000
$vec(I_n)$	7.8144	6.839	0.0000
Residents at destination	−0.1112	−5.204	0.0000
Employment at destination	1.3210	68.748	0.0000
Residents at origin	1.0628	49.736	0.0000
Employment at origin	−0.0059	−0.307	0.7587
W_d (Residents at destination)	−0.0790	−4.218	0.0000
W_d (Employment at destination)	0.0144	0.800	0.4236
W_o (Residents at origin)	−0.0093	−0.499	0.6172
W_o (Employment at origin)	−0.0797	−4.421	0.0000
Intraregional residents	0.7480	5.782	0.0000
Intraregional employment	0.4448	4.317	0.0000
ln(distance)	−0.2600	−15.513	0.0000
	PPML optimization		
Constant	2.5036	401.562	0.0000
$vec(I_n)$	7.6710	55.690	0.0000
Residents at destination	−0.0969	−19.155	0.0000
Employment at destination	1.3300	240.957	0.0000
Residents at origin	1.2117	145.866	0.0000
Employment at origin	−0.0989	−16.075	0.0000
W_d (Residents at destination)	−0.1533	−11.922	0.0000
W_d (Employment at destination)	−0.0505	−5.526	0.0000
W_o (Residents at origin)	−0.0315	−2.643	0.0082
W_o (Employment at origin)	−0.1234	−11.264	0.0000
Intraregional residents	0.7562	54.729	0.0000
Intraregional employment	0.5045	50.659	0.0000
ln(distance)	−0.2431	−56.175	0.0000
	PPML MCMC		
Constant	2.5042	273.870	0.0000
$vec(I_n)$	7.6506	42.215	0.0000
Residents at destination	−0.0978	−19.370	0.0000
Employment at destination	1.3302	141.187	0.0000
Residents at origin	1.2089	84.908	0.0000
Employment at origin	−0.0979	−11.628	0.0000
W_d (Residents at destination)	−0.1534	−11.921	0.0000
W_d (Employment at destination)	−0.0502	−4.873	0.0000
W_o (Residents at origin)	−0.0312	−2.437	0.0116
W_o (Employment at origin)	−0.1236	−10.340	0.0000
Intraregional residents	0.7586	37.537	0.0000
Intraregional employment	0.5028	53.354	0.0000
ln(distance)	−0.2434	−54.300	0.0000

PPML estimates in this case. The PPML estimates indicate that spatial lags of the explanatory variables are significantly different from zero. Inclusion of these variables also impacts estimates for the other coefficients. For example, a 10 % increase in distance implies a 2.43 % reduction in commuting flows for the spatial model compared to the 3.24 % reduction noted above for the non-spatial model.

All of the estimates for the spatial lag variables are negative, consistent with Alonso's notion that regions neighboring origins represent opportunity or draw impact on regions neighboring the origin and a congestion or competition impact on regions neighboring the destination. As we would expect, the congestion and opportunity impacts are small, consistent with 'second-order' impacts of lesser magnitude than the direct impacts.

From the estimates, we would conclude that the positive and significant intercept for intraregional flows ($vec(I_n)$) points to higher flow levels within regions, and the positive and significant coefficients for intraregional residents and employment point to higher intraregional flows for regions where more residents and jobs are located. Specifically, a 10 % increase in residents in a region would lead to a 7.5 % increase in intraregional commuting flows, and a 10 % increase in employment is associated with a 5.0 % increase in commuting flows within the region (very similar to our inferences for the non-spatial model).

Increasing residents in a (work-place) destination reduces commuting inflows to those destination regions. A 10 % increase in residents would lead to a 0.96 % decrease of commuting inflows for the typical region. Regions neighboring the destination would also see a decrease in commuting inflows equal to 1.53 % in response to a 10 % increase in residents of the typical region. The non-spatial model assumes this magnitude equals zero. This would result in an underestimate of the *total* impact on commuting inflows arising from an increase in residents in the typical region by around one-half. The total impact is the sum of the direct plus indirect impact determined by the sum of the rth coefficients $\beta_d^r + \theta_d^r = 0.97 + 1.53 = 2.50$. If we compare this to the non-spatial model estimate of 1.29, the downward bias is evident.

Increasing employment/jobs in a (work-place) destination increases commuting inflows to those destination regions and reduces flow to regions neighboring those destinations. A 10 % increase in jobs would lead to a 13.3 % increase of commuting inflows for the typical region, while reducing inflows to neighboring regions by 0.5 % for a total impact of 12.8 %. This estimate would produce a nearly identical inference as the 13.2 estimate from the non-spatial model

Increasing residents in a (residential) origin produces a increase in commuting flows from those origin regions and reduces outflows from neighboring regions. A 10 % increase in residents would lead to an 12.1 % increase in commuting outflows from the origin, and a reduction in outflows from regions neighboring the typical origin by 0.31 %. As in the case of changes in jobs at the destination, inferences from the non-spatial and spatial models would not differ in a substantive way.

Increasing employment/jobs in a (residential) origin produces a small decrease in commuting outflows from those origin regions, while decreasing outflows from regions neighboring the typical origin. A 10 % increase in jobs located in a typical origin region reduces outflows by 0.98 %, and reduces outflows from neighboring regions by 1.23 %. The total impact estimate of −2.21 % suggests some downward bias in the non-spatial model estimate of −1.26 %. Again, this arises from omitting the spatial spillover impact.

Figure 7.1 shows the logged (non-zero) actual flows versus the logged predictions from the spatial PPML model for these non-zero flows. The log transformation was used to enhance scaling of the values in the figure.

For contrast, Fig. 7.2 shows the logged (non-zero) actual flows versus the predictions from the regression model based on *ln*(*flows* + 1) for contrast with the

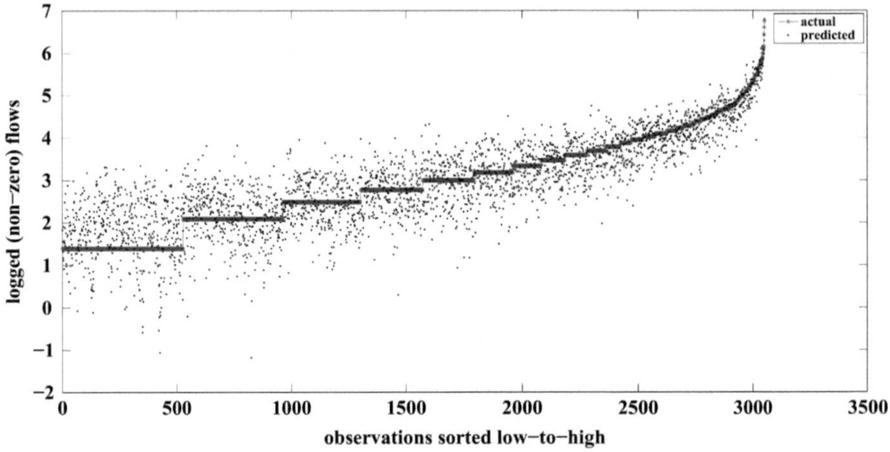

Fig. 7.1 Actual vs. predicted logged non-zero flows

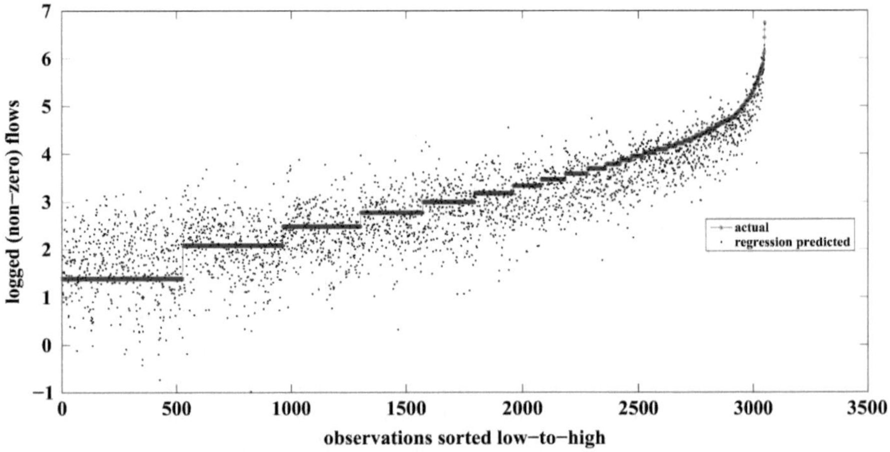

Fig. 7.2 Actual vs. regression predicted logged non-zero flows

PPML spatial model predictions. The log transformation was used for compatibility between the PPML and regression models.

As the figures suggest, the fit from both models is similar. The regression model mean squared error for the non-zero flows was 0.3282 and 0.3311 for the PPML model. The mean absolute error for the regression model was 0.4423 and 0.4386 for the PPML model.

7.4.1 *Higher-Order Neighbors*

The 60 regions used represent relatively small areas within Toulouse, so spatial spillover impact may extend beyond first-order (contiguous) neighboring regions.

Figure 7.3 shows a Moran scatterplot and Fig. 7.4 an associated map of jobs for the 60 regions in Toulouse. The scatterplot shows employment in deviation from means on the horizontal axis and average employment from neighboring regions on the vertical axis (also in deviation from means). Points associated with each region fall into four quadrants. Points in quadrant I indicate regions that have higher than average employment and whose neighboring regions also have higher than average employment. These points in the associated map show the location of these regions, which tend to be clustered in the center of Toulouse. The points in the third quadrant of the scatterplot show regions with lower than average employment whose neighboring regions also have lower than average levels

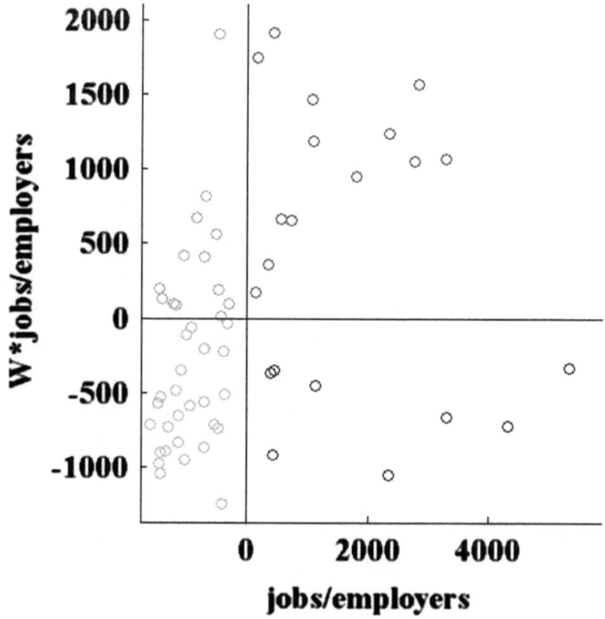

Fig. 7.3 Employment Moran scatterplot

Fig. 7.4 Employment Moran map

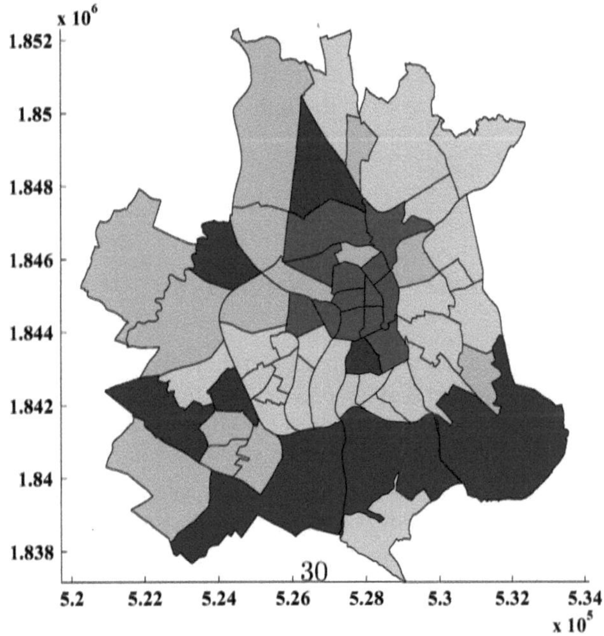

of employment. These regions are clustered on the map in locations surrounding the central Toulouse regions, where higher than average employment are located. Points in the fourth quadrant indicate regions with higher than average employment surrounded by regions with lower than average employment. These regions point to areas of outlying employment, interspersed with residential regions. A clear pattern of spatial clustering exists for the quadrant I, III and IV regions on the map, which contradicts the assumption made by the non-spatial interaction model that employment in one region is not systematically related to employment in nearby regions.

Figure 7.5 shows a Moran scatterplot and Fig. 7.6 an associated map of (working) residents for the 60 regions in Toulouse. Here we see quadrant I points indicating a cluster of regions to the east of the city center with higher than average residents whose neighboring regions also contain higher than average residents. The quadrant III points show regions with lower than average residents whose neighboring regions also contain lower than average residents, that tend to be clustered southwest of the city center. Quadrant IV and II points and associated regions on the map indicate areas where residences and employment are interspersed. This scatterplot and associated map also points to clusters of regions with high and low numbers of (working) residents which is inconsistent with the assumption of spatial independence of residents made by the non-spatial interaction model.

We test the spatial extent of spillovers by adding additional spatial lags of the explanatory variables to the model. Specifically, we test models that add second-

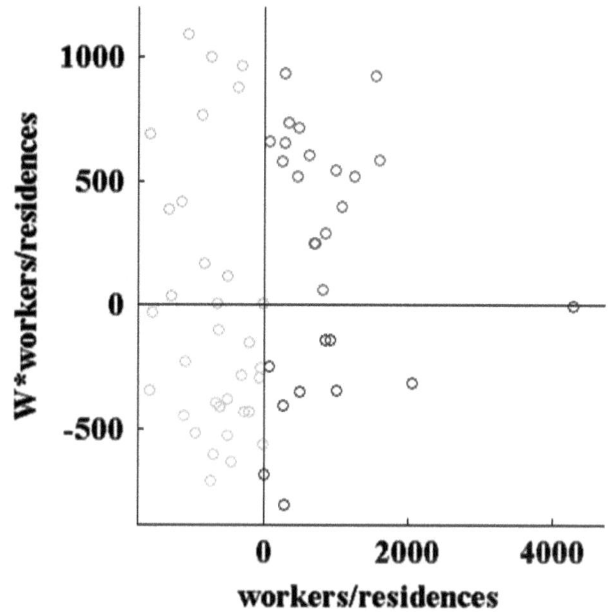

Fig. 7.5 Residents Moran scatterplot

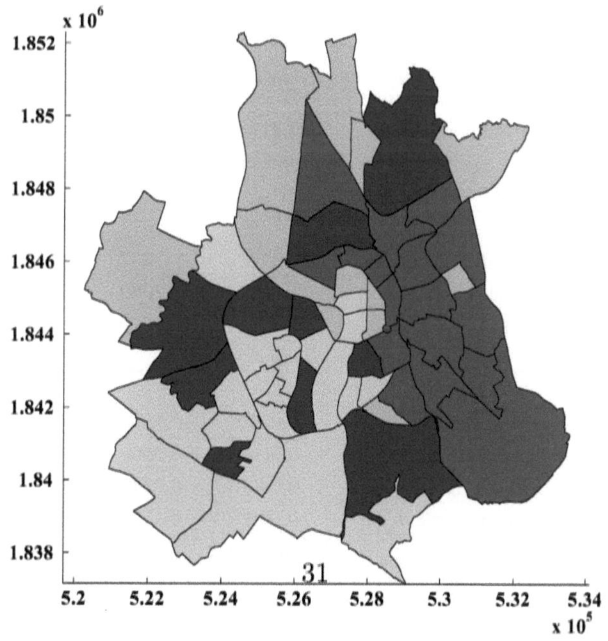

Fig. 7.6 Residents Moran map

through fourth order neighbors to the origin and destination regions. shown in (7.14).

$$E(y|Z) = \exp(\beta_0 + X_d\beta_d + X_o\beta_o + \sum_{j=1}^{4} W_d^j X_d \theta_{dj} + \sum_{j=1}^{4} W_o^j X_o \theta_{oj} + d\gamma) \tag{7.14}$$

Spillovers (or indirect effects) in these models are calculated using the sum of the coefficients: θ_{oj} and θ_{dj}. Table 7.6 reports two measures of model fit for the set of five different models that were estimated. The table indicates the five models using: $X, W^1X, \sum_{j=1}^{2} W^jX, \sum_{j=1}^{3} W^jX, \sum_{j=1}^{4} W^jX$ to denote the set of explanatory variables used. We note that some confusion has arisen in the literature due to Anselin and Smirnov (1996), who view *proper* higher order spatial lag operators *as if* they were time-series lag operators. They advocate an approach to calculating higher-order spatial lags that purges feedback loops, which are of course the hallmark of higher-order spatial lags that distinguishes them from time-series lag operators. The higher-order spatial lags in (7.14) contain the feedback loops implied

Table 7.6 Extended model estimates

	Measures of model fit				
Measure/model	X	W^1X	$\sum_{j=1}^{2} W^jX$	$\sum_{j=1}^{3} W^jX$	$\sum_{j=1}^{4} W^jX$
Root mean squared error	17.7268	16.1210	15.6687	15.3776	15.4545
Mean absolute error	9.8143	9.3447	9.2193	9.0947	9.1090
	Direct effects				
Variables/model	X	W^1X	$\sum_{j=1}^{2} W^jX$	$\sum_{j=1}^{3} W^jX$	$\sum_{j=1}^{4} W^jX$
Residents at destination	−0.1293	−0.0978	−0.0478	−0.0660	−0.0593
Employment at destination	1.3225	1.3302	1.3762	1.3673	1.3552
Residents at origin	1.2101	1.2089	1.2177	1.2477	1.2592
Employment at origin	−0.1246	−0.0979	−0.0615	−0.0988	−0.0953
	Indirect effects				
Variables/model	X	W^1X	$\sum_{j=1}^{2} W^jX$	$\sum_{j=1}^{3} W^jX$	$\sum_{j=1}^{4} W^jX$
Residents at destination	0.0000	−0.1534	−0.3807	−0.4745	−0.4826
Employment at destination	0.0000	−0.0502	−0.1349	−0.1740	−0.1302
Residents at origin	0.0000	−0.0312	−0.0620	−0.0360	0.0705
Employment at origin	0.0000	−0.1236	−0.2455	−0.3442	−0.4335
	Total effects				
Variables/model	X	W^1X	$\sum_{j=1}^{2} W^jX$	$\sum_{j=1}^{3} W^jX$	$\sum_{j=1}^{4} W^jX$
Residents at destination	−0.1293	−0.2512	−0.4284	−0.5405	−0.5419
Employment at destination	1.3225	1.2800	1.2414	1.1933	1.2250
Residents at origin	1.2101	1.1777	1.1557	1.2117	1.3297
Employment at origin	−0.1246	−0.2215	−0.3069	−0.4430	−0.5288

by spatial lags, and these matrix products must compete with lower-order spatial lags to improve the model fit.

An alternative approach would be to define $W = \sum_{i=1}^{m} \left(\phi^i N_i / \sum_{i=1}^{m} \phi^i\right)$, where N_i refers to a matrix containing non-zero elements for the ith nearest neighbor, and ϕ serves to weight the relative effect of the ith individual neighbor matrices, so that W depends on the parameter ϕ as well as m the number of neighbor matrices considered. To see the role played by the spatial decay parameter ϕ, note that $\phi = 0.87$ implies a decay profile where the sixth nearest neighbor receives less than one-half the weight of the nearest neighbor This approach would require estimation of the additional parameters m and ϕ. For an illustration of this see in another context, see LeSage and Pace (2009, Chapter 9).

Of course, the additional explanatory variables for modeling intraregional flows X_i and intercept term for these were also included in the model. The best fitting model included first, second, and third order neighboring regions. Both root mean squared error and mean absolute error were minimized for this model.

The direct effects reported in Table 7.6 represent coefficients on the set of explanatory variables associated with the matrix X, while the indirect effects estimates represent a sum of coefficients associated with the various orders of spatial lags used in the alternative models. For example, in the model containing only a single spatial lag (W^1X), the indirect effect estimates are the MCMC estimates reported in Table 7.5 for the variables: W_d (Residents at Destination), W_d (Employment at Destination), W_o (Residents at Origin), and W_o (Employment at Origin). For models containing higher-order neighbors, we sum over the coefficients for all orders. The total effects reported in the table are the sum of direct plus indirect effects.

From the table, we see that spatial spillovers may be larger than inferred from the simple model containing only contiguous neighbors. For the best-fitting model containing first through third order neighbors, the spillover magnitudes (for *Residents at Destination*, *Employment at Destination*, and *Employment at Origin* variables) are about three times that reported for the model containing only first-order neighbors. For the variable *Residents at Origin* the indirect effects/spillovers are the same for the first- and third-order models.

The conclusion drawn from this experiment with an extended version of the model is that inferences regarding spatial spillovers may be sensitive to the number of neighbors used, or more generally the spatial extent of the spillovers. Formal statistical methods for comparing models based on varying specifications with regard to neighboring regions included in the model seems an area for future research.

7.5 Conclusion

A problem that can invalidate use of maximum likelihood and Bayesian spatial autoregressive interaction models of the type described in LeSage and Pace (2008, 2009) is the presence of zero flow magnitudes. For datasets containing even a moderate number zero flows, this produces a situation where the assumption of normally distributed disturbances required for maximum likelihood estimation is not met.

Taking an approach used in modeling international trade flows based on an exponential specification in conjunction with pseudo Poisson maximum likelihood or Bayesian MCMC estimation appears to hold promise in these situations. A set of Monte Carlo experiments based on Toulouse commuting-to-work flows showed that the PPML model produce more accurate estimates that the conventional log-transformed regression model in the presence of zero flows.

A spatial extension of the model to include 'size' variables reflecting neighbors to origin and destination regressions was proposed. This type of extension appears consistent with Alonso's Theory of Movement, which generalizes the conventional regional gravity model.

An application to Toulouse commuting-to-work flows showed that ignoring spatial spillover impacts will lead to downward bias in estimates of the impacts associated with changes in characteristics of the regions.

Future work should explore issues pertaining to the spatial extent of spillovers. Extended specifications of the model can be used to introduce spillovers that extend beyond immediately neighboring regions. However, collinearity problems arise when introducing higher-order spatial lags in the model. Some type of Bayesian smoothness priors such as those proposed by Shiller (1973) might be applicable for the extended model.

Another area for future work would be consideration of Poisson modeling situations where spillovers are present in the conditional mean of y_i, which implies spatial clustering of high and low conditional variances. We note however that spatially lagged dependent variables considerably complicate interpretation of the model estimates in the case of a spatial Poisson regression (see LeSage and Thomas-Agnan 2015 on interpretation issues that arise for this type of model in a non-Poisson context).

There is also the potential for spatial dependence in the model disturbances, examined by Rathnun and Fei (2006) and Wakefield (2007), who consider Bayesian spatial Poisson regression models where spatial dependence is modeled in the residuals.

References

Alonso W (1973) National interregional demographic accounts: a prototype. Monograph 17, Institute of Urban and Regional Development, University of California, Berkeley

Alonso W (1978) A theory of movements. In: Hansen NM (ed) Human settlement systems: international perspectives on structure, change and public policy. Ballinger, Cambridge, MA, pp 197–211

Anderson JE, van Wincoop E (2003) Gravity with gravitas: a solution to the border puzzle. Am Econ Rev 93(1):170–192

Anselin L, Smirnov O (1996) Efficient algorithms for constructing proper higher order spatial lag operators. J Reg Sci 36(1):67–89
Arvis J-F, Shepherd B (2013) The Poisson quasi-maximum likelihood estimator: a solution to the 'adding up' problem in gravity models. Appl Econ Lett 20(6):515–519
de Vries JJ, Nijkamp P, Rietveld P (2001) Alonso's theory of movements: developments in spatial interaction modeling. J Geogr Syst 3:233–256
Fally T (2012) Structural gravity and fixed effects. Working paper available at: spot.colorado.edu/fally/Gravity_PPML.pdf
Feenstra R (2004) Advance international trade, Princeton University Press
Gourieroux C, Monfort A, Trognon A (1984) Pseudo maximum likelihood methods: applications to Poisson models. Econometrica 52:701–720
Griffith DA (2007). Spatial structure and spatial interaction: 25 years later. Rev Reg Stud 37(1):28–38
Griffith DA, Jones KG (1980) Explorations into the relationship between spatial structure and spatial interaction. Environ Plan A 12:187–201
LeSage JP, Pace RK (2008) Spatial econometric modeling of origin-destination flows. J Reg Sci 48(5):941–967
LeSage JP, Pace RK (2009) Introduction to spatial econometrics, CRC Press, Taylor & Francis Group, Boca Raton, FL
LeSage JP, Thomas-Agnan C (2015) Interpreting spatial econometric origin-destination flow models. J. Reg. Sci 55(2):188–208
Martinez-Zarzoso I (2013) The log of gravity revisited. Appl Econ 45:311–327
Martinez-Zarzoso I, Nowak-Lehmann D F, Vollmer S (2007) The log of gravity revisited, CeGE Discussion Papers 64, University of Goettingen. Available at http://papers.ssrn.com/sol3/papers.cfm?abstract_id=999908
Rathnun SL, Fei S (2006) A spatial zero-inflated Poisson regression model for oak regeneration. Environ Ecol Stat 13:409–426
Sen A, Smith TE (1995) Gravity models of spatial interaction behavior, Springer, Heidelberg
Smith TE (1975) A choice theory of spatial interaction. Reg Sci Urban Econ 5(2):137–176
Santos Silva JMC, Tenreyro S (2006) The log of gravity. Rev Econ Stat 88:641–658
Santos Silva JMC, Tenreyro S (2010) On the existence of the maximum likelihood estimates for Poisson regression. Econ Lett 107(2):310–312
Santos Silva JMC, Tenreyro S (2011) Further simulation evidence on the performance of the Poisson-PML estimator. Econ Lett 112(2):220–222
Shiller R (1973) A distributed lag estimator derived from smoothness priors. Econometrica 41(4):775–788
Thomas-Agnan C, LeSage JP (2014) Spatial econometric origin-destination flow models. In: Fischer MM, Peter Nijkamp (eds) Handbook of regional science. Springer, pp 1653–1673
Wakefield J (2007) Disease mapping and spatial regression with count data. Biostatistics 8(2):158–183
Wilson AG (1967) A statistical theory of spatial distribution models Transp Res 1:253–269
Wilson AG (1970) Entropy in urban and regional modelling. Pion, London
Wilson AG (1974) Urban and regional models in geography and planning. Wiley, Chichester

Chapter 8
The Space of Gravity: Spatially Filtered Estimation of a Gravity Model for Bilateral Trade

Roberto Patuelli, Gert-Jan M. Linders, Rodolfo Metulini, and Daniel A. Griffith

Keywords Bilateral trade • Spatial filtering • Unconstrained gravity model

JEL Codes: C14, C21, F10

8.1 Introduction

During the past two decades, scholars have shown renewed interest in the theoretical foundations and estimation of the gravity model for bilateral trade (e.g., Deardorff 1998; Anderson and van Wincoop 2003). The interest in modelling trade flows has increased with questions about the effectiveness of trade agreements (Baier and Bergstrand 2009) and the persistence of border and distance effects and largely unobserved trade costs (Anderson and van Wincoop 2004). The developments have re-affirmed the importance of accounting for relative trade costs in explaining patterns of trade. Yet, empirical application of the resulting gravity model framework that incorporates theoretically motivated multilateral resistance (MR) is not straightforward. The system of equations for MR involves non-linearities in the parameters and requires custom programming (Feenstra 2004).

R. Patuelli (✉)
Department of Economics, University of Bologna, Bologna, Italy

The Rimini Centre for Economic Analysis (RCEA), Rimini, Italy
e-mail: roberto.patuelli@unibo.it

G.-J.M. Linders
Ministry of Social Affairs and Employment, The Hague, The Netherlands

R. Metulini
Institute of Economics (LEM), Scuola Superiore Sant'Anna, Pisa, Italy

D.A. Griffith
School of Economic, Political & Policy Sciences, The University of Texas at Dallas, Richardson, TX, USA

R. Patuelli, G. Arbia (eds.), *Spatial Econometric Interaction Modelling*, Advances in Spatial Science, DOI 10.1007/978-3-319-30196-9_8

An alternative specification that circumvents the need to consider the full system of equations includes country-specific effects to control for omitted country-specific MR variables. However, both the system approach and the alternative using fixed effects impose restrictions on the empirical specification of the gravity model. They allow identification of the impact of bilateral trade barriers, but preclude (at least in a cross-section) the analysis of country-specific covariates that may affect patterns of trade.

This paper aims to contribute to the literature in providing an alternative solution to deal with omitted MR, which allows for parameter identification for country-specific covariates in a cross-section analysis of trade patterns. This solution hinges on the interpretation of spatial autocorrelation (SAC)[1] in trade flows as reflecting unobserved country-specific heterogeneity due to MR. Our approach is complementary to a related recent strand of literature that starts from the same interpretation in that we offer an alternative methodology to deal with SAC in trade flows, called spatial filtering (SF) estimation.

The literature review about trade costs by Anderson and van Wincoop (2004) suggests that the application of spatial econometric techniques in modelling origin-destination trade flows needs further exploration, to take into account the (auto)correlation in trade flows. Although the gravity model is essentially a model of spatial interaction, little attention has been paid to flows autocorrelation in the trade literature (Porojan 2001, is an exception). In part, this lack of attention was due to technical reasons. Spatial econometric modelling of origin-destination flows is complex and computationally taxing. Estimation of spatial lag and spatial error models in this context has long been impossible due to computing power limitations. Applications of spatial interaction modelling in regional science have recently made progress on this issue (see Fischer and Griffith 2008; LeSage and Pace 2008; Sellner et al. 2013). Applications in empirical trade and FDI modelling have followed shortly thereafter (see Baltagi et al. 2007; Behrens et al. 2012). These contributions show the relevance of autocorrelation in trade flows. However, spatial econometric origin-destination flow models remain complex and relatively taxing to apply empirically. In response to these concerns, several studies have applied an alternative spatial econometric technique, SF, which deals with autocorrelation in a different but equally effective way. The technique of SF has recently been applied to the origin-destination flow context in other fields, such as commuting and patent citations (Fischer and Griffith 2008; Griffith 2009). Instead of accounting for autocorrelation by spatial modelling, SF estimation deals with it by filtering the residuals. Because only an origin-specific and a destination-specific filter are needed in order to account for autocorrelation, the dimensionality of estimation is much less demanding than in the case of a spatial lag or spatial error origin-destination model.

---

[1]Spatial autocorrelation is the correlation that occurs among the values of a georeferenced variable, and that can be attributed to the proximity of the units. The concept of SAC can be related to the first law of geography, stating that 'everything is related to everything else, but near things are more related than distant things' (Tobler 1970, p. 236).

This paper follows up on this development by applying SF estimation to bilateral trade flows. We argue that the application of origin-specific and destination-specific filtering of residuals corresponds well to the theoretically expected importance of omitted origin-specific and destination-specific MR terms. Empirical results show that SF estimation can account well for autocorrelation in trade flows.

Moreover, SF estimation of an otherwise standard empirical gravity equation appears to go a long way in correcting for bias due to the origin- and destination-specific omitted variables predicted by the theoretical gravity model. The regression coefficients are close to the benchmark values in a specification using origin- and destination-specific indicator variables. This implies that SF estimation provides a relatively simple alternative to spatial econometric origin-destination flow models and custom-programmed non-linear estimation of the theoretical gravity model, which can be estimated using standard techniques such as ordinary least squares (OLS) or Poisson regression.[2]

Finally, the SF approach allows for a greater flexibility in the empirical specification of the gravity equation. Unlike the specification using indicator variables, we can include country-specific variables—so called push and pull factors—in the model. Moreover, a SF model is a significant improvement in terms of parsimony and efficiency compared to the indicator variables model. Compared to the theoretical gravity framework, we can relax the assumption that total trade depends exclusively and proportionately on the gross domestic product (GDP) of the trading countries. Other potential push and pull factors, such as landlockedness, land area, or per capita income can be included as well, and we do not have to assume a proportional relation between trade and GDP. Thus, SF estimation entails greater flexibility in specification choice compared to the stylized theoretical gravity model.

The paper proceeds as follows. In Sect. 8.2, we specify a theoretical gravity model following Anderson and van Wincoop (2003) and discuss some practical limitations of applying the theoretical framework. In Sect. 8.3, we illustrate the link between theoretical gravity and autocorrelation in trade flows. We present the approach of SF estimation to control for autocorrelation, and motivate that it allows controlling for unobserved MR. Section 8.4 outlines the empirical specifications and estimators that we compare, while Sect. 8.5 discusses the SAC tests that we use for post-estimation diagnostics. In Sect. 8.6, after an overview of data used, we turn to the estimation results and diagnostics. Section 8.7 concludes the paper.

8.2 The Gravity Model and Autocorrelation

We can divide the discourse over trade gravity modelling into two parts, regarding the theoretical and empirical approaches to the problem, respectively. The following sections attempt to provide such a discussion.

---

[2]The estimates presented in this paper have been carried out with the R statistical software (R Core Team 2015). The script necessary for running the SF estimations is available for download from the first author's personal homepage.

8.2.1 Theoretical Gravity

Gravity equations for analysing bilateral trade flows have been estimated since the 1960s (e.g., Tinbergen 1962; Pöyhönen 1963). The model describes the volume of bilateral trade as a function of push and pull factors, such as economic size of origins and destinations, and transactional distance between trade partners. It has been deployed for various purposes, such as analysing the determinants of trade patterns, testing trade theories, forecasting future flows or estimating missing data, and comparative static analysis of changes in trade costs. Recent applications increasingly emphasize the importance of estimating a gravity equation that is consistent with theoretical gravity (e.g., Anderson and van Wincoop 2003; Baier and Bergstrand 2009). The theoretical framework that is most influential has been developed by Anderson and van Wincoop (2003), in their paper on consistent estimation and assessment of the border effect in U.S.-Canadian regional trade flows.[3]

Anderson and van Wincoop derive a reduced-form gravity equation, assuming an N-country endowment economy, constant elasticity of substitution (CES) preferences, and symmetric bilateral trade costs. Their model explicitly takes into account the role played by country-specific price indices (MR terms). The gravity equation that results is specified as:

$$x_{ij} = \frac{y_i y_j}{y_w}\left(\frac{t_{ij}}{\Pi_i P_j}\right)^{1-\sigma}, \tag{8.1}$$

where x_{ij} is the value of the flow of goods from country i to country j, y is GDP (w stands for world) and t_{ij} is the bilateral trade cost factor. Finally, two variables enter that we discuss in greater detail later. Π_i measures outward MR of country i, and P_j measures inward MR of country j. The term σ is the elasticity of substitution ($\sigma > 1$).

Equation (8.1) shows that bilateral exports would be proportional to the size of the exporting market and the share of the import market in total demand, in the absence of bilateral trade costs (t_{ij}). Trade costs are of the iceberg type, and defined as a mark-up on the 'mill price' p_i ($t_{ij} \geq 1$). Hence, ($t_{ij} - 1$) is the ad-valorem tariff equivalent of bilateral trade costs. The bilateral delivered prices (p_{ij}) then equal:

$$p_{ij} = t_{ij} \cdot p_i. \tag{8.2}$$

A wide variety of covariates in the literature is used to represent bilateral trade costs. We include some of the most common bilateral explanatory variables. A multiplicative formulation of bilateral trade costs (see Deardorff 1998; Anderson

[3]Related theoretical derivations of a gravity equation for trade can be found in earlier literature as well, such as Bergstrand (1985) and Bröcker (1989).

and van Wincoop 2004) yields:

$$t_{ij} = D_{ij}^{\beta_1} \cdot e^{\beta_2 \cdot (1-CB_{ij})} \cdot e^{\beta_3 \cdot (1-CL_{ij})} \cdot e^{\beta_4 \cdot (1-CH_{ij})} \cdot e^{\beta_5 \cdot (1-FTA_{ij})} \cdot b_{ij}, \tag{8.3}$$

where D stands for geographical distance; CB stands for an indicator variable equal to 1 if two countries share a (land) border (and zero otherwise); CL, CH and FTA are a set of similar indicator variables indicating whether or not two countries share a common official language, common colonial history, and/or common free-trade agreement. The parameter b_{ij} reflects the impact of all remaining bilateral trade barriers on the bilateral trade cost factor, assumed independent from the included covariates. Based on economic intuition, we expect positive parameters for the covariates in the trade cost function.

Bilateral export does not depend on only bilateral trade cost and the (exogenously given) size of the trading economies. It also depends on the weighted average trade costs that an exporter and importer face in their export and import market, respectively. This is reflected by the MR terms entering the denominator of equation (8.1). Anderson and van Wincoop (2003) derive the set of equations for the MR terms Π_i and P_j,

$$\Pi_i^{1-\sigma} = \sum_{j=1}^{N} \left(\theta_j \left({}^{t_{ij}}\!/_{P_j} \right)^{1-\sigma} \right), \tag{8.4}$$

$$P_j^{1-\sigma} = \sum_{i=1}^{N} \left(\theta_i \left({}^{t_{ij}}\!/_{\Pi_i} \right)^{1-\sigma} \right), \tag{8.5}$$

where $\theta_i = y_i / y_w, \forall i$.

Note that the outward (inward) resistance term includes the GDP-share-weighted average of bilateral trade costs relative to the inward (outward) resistance terms across destinations (origins). Given bilateral trade costs t_{ij}, a high value for MR implies that other countries k are less attractive trading partners. Hence countries i and j will trade more with each other, as shown in Eq. (8.1).

8.2.2 *Practical Gravity*

The theoretical gravity model conveys an important message. Trade flows are not mutually independent. For a consistent econometric estimation of the parameters in the model, problems emerge if the regressor variables are correlated with the residuals. The theoretical model shows that this endogeneity bias is likely to emerge if we do not control for country-specific MR.

Despite the prominent position of this theoretical framework over the past years, many empirical studies continued to rely on a more pragmatic empirical gravity equation instead. Several plausible explanations for this come to mind. Estimating a theoretically consistent gravity equation involves dealing with Eqs. (8.4) and (8.5), which are nonlinear in their parameters. Developing the required estimation procedures involve some restrictive assumptions (see Baldwin and Taglioni 2006; Balistreri and Hillberry 2007), and work on deriving an analytical solution has only recently emerged (e.g., Straathof 2008).

Furthermore, the theoretical framework puts restrictions on the empirical specification that follows from the stylized model rather than from practical considerations. In fact, trade depends proportionately on the GDP of an origin and destination. Moreover, GDP variables are the only push and pull factors in the model to explain total external trade. While the theoretical model requires total exports to sum to an exporter's GDP, and total imports to sum to an importer's GDP, these constraints do not hold in practical applications.[4] First, trade and GDP are measured in different units. While trade is measured in gross output values, GDP is a measure of value added. Moreover, the model includes intranational trade while most practical applications only consider international trade flows in estimating the gravity equation, due to data limitations. This context implies that theoretically imposed constraints in the model are not generally valid in estimation. Second, the share of external trade in total expenditure and gross output may be different from the predictions in the theoretical model. The theoretical gravity model predicts that larger economies are less open to international trade and allocate a larger share of their expenditure on intranational trade, but the share of international trade on GDP is often constrained to a constant by imposing proportionality between the former and the latter.

Hence, practical considerations may provide a valid motivation to choose an unconstrained empirical gravity equation, which allows more flexibility in specification. An empirical gravity equation can include additional push and pull factors to capture variation in openness to international trade. For example, we may think of per capita income, landlockedness, and land area as factors determining a country's openness to international trade. Many of these variables have been used in empirical specifications of the gravity model for international trade (e.g., Frankel 1997; Raballand 2003; De Groot et al. 2004).

Taking theoretical and practical insight seriously, ideally we would need to combine the flexibility of the empirical gravity equation and the insights about omitted variable bias due to MR of the theoretical foundation of gravity. An often used practical solution to deal with country-specific omitted variable bias is to include country-specific indicator variables in the gravity equation (Bröcker and Rohweder 1990). As argued by Feenstra (2004), a model specification that includes origin- and destination-specific intercepts is consistent with theoretical concerns. Moreover, this solution has been widely applied in regional science to

[4]The MR terms obtained impose the constraints: $\sum_i x_{ij} = y_j$ and $\sum_j x_{ij} = y_i$. In similar applications of the model in regional science, this type of specification is known as a doubly-constrained gravity model (e.g., Wilson 1970; Fotheringham and O'Kelly 1989).

deal with the practical problems of estimating a gravity equation in which the total flows are not known (Sen and Smith 1995).[5] This solution is not completely satisfactory, though. It is rather drastic medicine to cure the patient. First, including origin- and destination-specific indicator variables reduces the statistical efficiency of econometric estimation. Second, it precludes the analysis of country-specific determinants of trade, which are interesting for empirical applications, and which explain cross-country variation in openness to international trade.

8.2.3 Consistent Estimation and Autocorrelation

The main insight from theoretically derived gravity is that regressor variables and residuals in the unconstrained gravity equation are likely to be correlated, because bilateral trade barriers also appear in the omitted MR terms. In empirical estimations, failure to control for MR might result in omitted variable bias in the parameter estimates of the bilateral regressors.

This paper proposes an alternative estimation approach that allows for the estimation of an unconstrained empirical specification of the gravity model, including push and pull factors, while offering a correction for origin- and destination-specific omitted variable bias. The approach starts from a specific interpretation of endogeneity bias as resulting from autocorrelation in trade flows. The argument for this interpretation has been made before in Behrens et al. (2012) and in Koch and LeSage (2009), and more generically relates to the recent revival in modelling SAC in bilateral flow data in the previously mentioned regional science literature. To the best of our knowledge, however, this paper is the first to link the theoretical MR effects to origin- and destination-specific filters, and to make use of SF techniques to accommodate autocorrelation in trade flows.

The argument starts by inspecting Eqs. (8.4) and (8.5). We propose that countries located in close spatial proximity tend to have similar MR. Similar geographical location implies similar geographical distance to trade partners across the world and a higher probability of shared neighbours. Likewise, shared languages tend to be more similar for countries closely located in space. Also, the logic of regional integration implies a higher likelihood of proximate countries being part of shared trade agreements with surrounding countries. This context implies that these spatial patterns in MR would induce autocorrelation in the residuals of the unconstrained gravity equation. As a result, the residuals and the bilateral trade cost variables are correlated, because similar reasoning to the preceding discussion suggests

[5] Although total international trade by country is generally known, or can be proxied by summing available bilateral flows, we do not have comparable direct observations for intranational trade. Hence, we would need to proxy for openness to trade of each country in estimating the gravity equation. This can be done either by including (additional) push and pull factors in the specification, or by using country-specific intercepts.

SAC would be in the regressor variables distance, contiguity, language and trade agreement. Omitted variable bias would result.

8.3 Recent Developments in Estimating the Theoretical Gravity Model of Trade

The theoretical gravity model shows that consistent estimation of the parameters requires us to take into account the price indices. As discussed in Feenstra (2004), the computational complexity of the non-linear estimation procedure has prevented its widespread use in the applied international trade literature. Still, Anderson and van Wincoop (2003) show that estimation of the more traditional empirical gravity equation (omitting the MR terms) yields inconsistent parameter estimates for the key regressor variables. A simple solution that results in consistent parameter estimates is to use a set of country-specific indicator variables for the exporting and importing countries (Bröcker and Rohweder 1990; Feenstra 2004). The indicator variables capture the country-specific MR terms, and control for omitted variable bias related to the country-specific intercepts. The main advantage of this formulation is that the resulting specification can be estimated by familiar methods such as OLS or Poisson regression.

However, the disadvantage of this solution is that the parameters of country-specific determinants of trade cannot be estimated. Variables such as GDP, per capita income, landlockedness, and land area are captured by the country-specific indicator variables. Still, empirical estimation of the effect of these variables may be relevant depending on the topic under investigation. Hence, a solution that would share the basic simplicity of estimation with the indicator variable specification, while allowing retention of the country-specific regressors, is needed.

Several recent developments in the trade gravity model literature focus on combining consistent estimation and flexibility in the specification of the gravity equation. Egger (2005) argues that a Hausman-Taylor approach, which allows for country-specific covariates, is consistent even if unobserved country-specific heterogeneity exists. This formulation provides an alternative to the indicator variables specification that controls for omitted variable bias due to omitted MR terms, and allows for the estimation of the parameters related to the country-specific variables. The method is based upon an approach similar to instrumental variables, which relies on instruments from inside the model.

In contrast, Baier and Bergstrand (2009) log-linearize the MR terms using a first-order Taylor series approximation. This yields *exogenous* bilateral multilateral-world-resistance (MWR) variables that proxy the endogenous country-specific MR variables in Anderson and van Wincoop (2003). The resulting reduced-form gravity equation can be estimated with OLS. This method is termed *bonus vetus* ('good-old') OLS (BV-OLS). The approach yields log-linear approximations of the MR terms, using Taylor series expansion around a centre of identical and symmetric trade costs, $t_{ij} = t$, but differing economic sizes ($\theta_i = y_i/y_w$).

Starting from a reformulated Eq. (8.1):

$$\ln x_{ij} = -\ln y_w + \ln y_i + \ln y_j - (\sigma - 1)\ln t_{ij} + (\sigma - 1)\ln P_i + (\sigma - 1)\ln P_j, \tag{8.6}$$

the equation that Baier and Bergstrand derive is:

$$\begin{aligned} \ln x_{ij} = & -\ln y_w + \ln y_i + \ln y_j - (\sigma - 1)\ln t_{ij} \\ & + (\sigma - 1)\left[\left(\sum_{j=1}^{N}\theta_j \ln t_{ij}\right) - \tfrac{1}{2}\left(\sum_{i=1}^{N}\sum_{j=1}^{N}\theta_i\theta_j \ln t_{ij}\right)\right] \\ & + (\sigma - 1)\left[\left(\sum_{i=1}^{N}\theta_i \ln t_{ji}\right) - \tfrac{1}{2}\left(\sum_{i=1}^{N}\sum_{j=1}^{N}\theta_i\theta_j \ln t_{ij}\right)\right]. \end{aligned} \tag{8.7}$$

The terms in square brackets are the MR terms. They contain a first component that captures multilateral trade frictions for each exporting or importing country, relative to a second part that reflects world trade costs.

A third approach to the consistent cross-sectional estimation of the gravity model is proposed in Behrens et al. (2012). Their approach is closely related to our approach. Starting from the Anderson and van Wincoop formulation of the theoretical gravity equation, they show that the MR terms can be shown to reflect a correlation structure between trade flows that can be modelled similarly to SAC. They suggest a spatial-autoregressive moving-average specification for the gravity model, which results in consistent estimates of the standard gravity equation parameters. At the same time, they argue that the baseline fixed-effects specification discussed previously does not fully succeed in capturing the MR dependencies in the error structure introduced by the general equilibrium nature of trade patterns modelling, and that its residuals still show a significant amount of autocorrelation (Behrens et al. 2012).

We now proceed to discuss the methodology followed in this paper. The alternative we propose, SF, combines two attractive features. First, it is fairly simple to apply, much like OLS with indicator variables; second, it takes into account the general equilibrium interdependence of trade flows that can be modelled as SAC, like spatial econometric origin-destination specifications.

8.4 Proposed Methodology: Spatial Filtering Estimation

The theoretical gravity model includes origin- and destination-specific MR variables that reflect the export and import accessibility of countries. Omitting these endogenous MR variables from the specification results in potential omitted variable bias, both for the trade cost variables and for the size variables in the gravity equation. Consistent estimation requires some way to capture the endogeneity between MR terms and standard regressors. We propose to make use of the fact that this dependency structure is likely to manifest as SAC in the residuals of the traditional specification of the gravity model. The reasoning is that many trade cost variables, such as geographical distance, adjacency, trade agreements, and common language, are spatially correlated: countries close in space are more likely to share the same (or similar) characteristics. This context likewise implies that both inward and outward accessibility are spatially correlated: close countries are likely to have more similar accessibility. We deal with SAC by using an origin- and a destination-specific spatial filter, which serve to capture the spatially autocorrelated parts of the residuals.

When including these spatial filters as additional origin- and destination-specific regressors (much like the origin and destination specific MR variables), the model can be estimated by standard regression techniques, such as OLS or Poisson regression, which are common in the literature about spatial interaction patterns. The parameters of the standard regressor variables are unrelated to the remaining residual term, and standard estimation yields consistent parameter estimates as a result. We refer to this estimation method as SF estimation of origin-destination models (see Griffith 2007; Fischer and Griffith 2008).

Basically, SF estimation of georeferenced data regressions (such as international trade) can reduce to defining a geographically varying mean and a variance on the basis of an exogenous spatial weights matrix. In other words, the spatially correlated residuals from an otherwise non-spatial regression model are partitioned into two synthetic variables: (1) a spatial filter which captures latent SAC; and, (2) a non-spatial variable (free of SAC), which will be the newly obtained residuals. The workhorse for this SF decomposition is a transformation procedure based upon eigenvector extraction from the matrix

$$\left(\mathbf{I}-\mathbf{1}\mathbf{1}^{\mathrm{T}}/n\right)\mathbf{W}\left(\mathbf{I}-\mathbf{1}\mathbf{1}^{\mathrm{T}}/n\right), \tag{8.8}$$

where $\mathbf{W}$ is a generic $n \times n$ spatial weights matrix; $\mathbf{I}$ is an $n \times n$ identity matrix; and, $\mathbf{1}$ is an $n \times 1$ vector containing 1s. The spatial weights matrix $\mathbf{W}$ defines the relationships of proximity between the n georeferenced units (e.g., points, regions, and countries). The transformed matrix appears in the numerator of Moran's coefficient (MC), which is a commonly used measure of SAC (see Sect. 8.5).

The eigenvectors of Eq. (8.8) represent distinct map pattern descriptions of SAC underlying georeferenced variables (Griffith 2003). Moreover, the first extracted eigenvector, say e_1, is the one showing the highest positive MC that can be achieved by any spatial recombination induced by $\mathbf{W}$. The subsequently extracted eigenvectors maximize MC while being orthogonal to and uncorrelated with the previously extracted eigenvectors. Finally, the last extracted eigenvector maximizes negative MC.

Having extracted the eigenvectors of Eq. (8.8), a spatial filter is constructed by judiciously selecting a subset of these n eigenvectors. In detail, for our empirical application, we select a first subset of eigenvectors (which we will call ‘candidate eigenvectors’) by means of the following threshold: $MC(e_i)/MC(e_1) > 0.25$. This threshold yields a spatial filter that approximately replicates the amount of variance explained by a spatial autoregressive model (SAR) (Griffith 2003).[6] Subsequently, a stepwise regression model may be employed to further reduce the first subset (whose eigenvectors have not yet been related to the data) to just the (smaller) subset of eigenvectors that are statistically significant as additional regressors in the model to be evaluated. The resulting group of eigenvectors is what we call our ‘spatial filter’. This estimation technique has been applied, both in autoregression and in traditional modelling terms, to various fields, including labour markets (Patuelli 2007), innovation (Grimpe and Patuelli 2011), economic growth (Crespo Cuaresma and Feldkircher 2013) and ecology (Monestiez et al. 2006).

The added challenge, with regard to the case at hand, is that trade data do not represent points in space, but flows between points. Therefore, the eigenvectors are linked to the flow data by means of Kronecker products: the product $\mathbf{E_K} \otimes \mathbf{1}$, where $\mathbf{E_K}$ is the $n \times k$ matrix of the candidate eigenvectors, may be linked to the origin-specific information (for example, GDP per exporting countries), while the product $\mathbf{1} \otimes \mathbf{E_K}$ may be linked to destination-specific information (again, for example, the GDP of importing countries) (Fischer and Griffith 2008). As a result, we have two sets of origin- and destination-specific variables, which aim to capture the SAC patterns commonly accounted for by the indicator variables of a doubly-constrained gravity model (Griffith 2009), therefore avoiding omitted variable bias.

The main advantages of the proposed estimation method are: (a) this approach can be applied to *any* type of regression, including simple OLS and generalized linear models (GLMs) such as Poisson or negative binomial regressions (although auto-Poisson and auto-negative binomial specifications cannot describe positive spatial dependence), for which usually dedicated spatial econometric applications do not exist; (b) by avoiding the use of indicator variables, we are able to save degrees of freedom, and, (c) the approach can be used to estimate regression parameters for origin- and destination-specific variables, such as GDP or trade agreement indicators.

For our case study, because of the nature of trade data, as suggested by Santos Silva and Tenreyro (2006), we estimate a count data model. While the natural choice would be Poisson regression, in order to take into account overdispersion in the data due to unobserved heterogeneity (which results in a sample variance which is much greater than the sample mean), we estimate a negative binomial model, which can explicitly account for such overdispersion by iteratively estimating the dispersion parameter. In subsequent comparisons regarding residual spatial autocorrelation, we consider, for the SF models, quasi-Poisson estimations as well.

---

[6]Recent research by Chun et al. (2016) proposes an estimation equation, based on residual SAC, to predict the ideal size of the candidate set.

8.5 Spatial Autocorrelation Diagnostics

When employing GLMs, traditional SAC indices may not be appropriate, as discussed below. In this section, we review the available alternatives.

In linear regression contexts, when analysing model residuals, an adapted Moran test (Cliff and Ord 1972, 1981) is commonly used, under a standard assumption of normality. A t test can be used to test the null hypothesis of spatial randomness of the residuals. The formula for the MC computed on the residuals is the following:

$$I = \frac{n\sum_{i,j} w_{ij}\varepsilon_i\varepsilon_j}{S_0\sum_i \varepsilon_i^2}, \tag{8.9}$$

where w_{ij} is the (i,j) element of a chosen spatial weight matrix $\mathbf{W}$, ε_i and ε_i are the related model residuals, and S_0 is the sum of all elements of $\mathbf{W}$. The expected value of this index is:

$$E(I) = \frac{n\,\mathrm{tr}\,(\mathbf{A})}{S_0\,(n-k)}, \tag{8.10}$$

where $\mathbf{A} = (\mathbf{X}^{\mathrm{T}}\mathbf{X})^{-1}\mathbf{X}^{\mathrm{T}}\mathbf{W}\mathbf{X}$ corresponds to the factor that accounts for the effect of the independent variables. $\mathbf{X}$ is the $n \times k$ matrix containing the values of the k independent variables included in the regression model.

A permutation-based Moran test has also been proposed (Cliff and Ord 1981) in order to improve the results of the approximate t test and to gain insights in its sampling distribution under spatial randomness.

Because the Moran test has been developed for linear models and normally distributed residuals, the use of MC calculated on the residuals of count data (Poisson, negative binomial) regression models is questionable (Schabenberger and Gotway 2005, p. 377), despite recent literature agreeing that it possesses good power against a wide array of autoregressive models and different distributions of the residuals (Anselin and Rey 1991).

Griffith (2010) studies the behaviour of the MC for non-normal random variables, and shows that, above moderate values of n (25–100), the MC is a suitable indicator in these cases as well. However, Griffith does not study the case of SAC diagnostics for regression residuals, in which we can consider the effect of the independent variables in the model.

Further, Moran's test may not be properly applied to the residuals of Poisson or negative binomial regression, whose distributional properties are not well known. In addition, because the test does not consider the heterogeneity of observations, its standard moments may not be appropriate under heteroscedasticity. For more details, one can refer to Oden (1995), who discusses this problem.

Lin and Zhang (2007) suggest that the MC can be used to test the residuals of a Poisson model by employing Pearson or deviance residuals under an asymptotic normality assumption. This approach is followed, among others, by Scherngell and

Lata (2013), who employ a panel SF modelling approach. However, this permutation test once again does not incorporate the effect of the independent variables of the model in constructing a reference distribution.

Fortunately, the standardized t statistic of Jacqmin-Gadda et al. (1997) can be applied in this context. This t statistic can be considered as an extension of standard SAC statistics into the domain of GLMs. It is derived in an analogous way to a score test based on generalized estimating equations (Prentice and Zhao 1991). As the condition of validity of the above test does not always hold, since the computation is intractable for large samples, a test based on the permutation distribution has been also proposed by the same authors.

Under the null hypothesis of no spatial autocorrelation, the t statistic is defined as:

$$t = \sum_{i=1}^{n} \sum_{j \neq i} w_{ij} \left(y_i - \hat{\mu}_i\right) \left(y_i - \hat{\mu}_j\right), \tag{8.11}$$

or, in matrix notation:

$$t = (\mathbf{Y} - \hat{\mu})^{\mathrm{T}} \mathbf{W} (\mathbf{Y} - \hat{\mu}), \tag{8.12}$$

where $\mathbf{Y}$ is the $n \times 1$ vector of the observations of the dependent variable, and $\hat{\mu}$ is the $n \times 1$ vector of the estimated means.

Using a first-order Taylor series expansion for the deviation of estimated means from the true means, Jacqmin-Gadda et al. (1997) show that the index's expectation and variance are as follows:

$$E(t) = \mathrm{tr}\,(\mathbf{RD})\,; \tag{8.13}$$

$$\mathrm{var}(t) = \sum_{i=1}^{n} R_{ii}^2 \left(\mu_{i(4)} - \mu_{i(2)}^2\right) + 2\mathrm{tr}\,(\mathbf{RDRD}), \tag{8.14}$$

where $\mathbf{R} = \mathbf{M}^{\mathrm{T}}\mathbf{W}\mathbf{M}$, $\mathbf{M} = \mathbf{I} - \mathbf{D}\mathbf{X}(\mathbf{X}^{\mathrm{T}}\mathbf{D}\mathbf{X})^{-1}\mathbf{X}^{\mathrm{T}}$, and $\mathbf{D}$ is the diagonal matrix whose elements are the variance of each observation. Consequently, R_{ii}^2 is the ith diagonal element of matrix $\mathbf{R}$, while $\mu_{i(2)}$ and $\mu_{i(4)}$ are the second and the fourth central moments of the ith observation, respectively. Jacqmin-Gadda et al. (1997) show that the standardized t statistic asymptotically follows the standard normal distribution.

The Jacqmin-Gadda (JG) test is a development of the statistic developed by le Cessie and van Houwelingen (1995), similarly derived as a score test in the spirit of Prentice and Zhao (1991), but not accounting for the effect of the independent variables. In fact, referring to Eq. (8.13), the component $\mathbf{R}$ in the le Cessie (LC) test is reduced to $\mathbf{R} = \mathbf{W}^{\mathrm{T}}\mathbf{W}$, while $\mathbf{D} = \mathrm{cov}(\mathbf{Y})$. In other words, the LC test does not incorporate the adjustment of estimating parameters, that is, the effect of independent variables is not considered in constructing a reference distribution. In summary, using the JG standardized t statistic, a test for spatial autocorrelation in the context of GLMs can be carried out.

8.6 Empirical Application

We apply the SF estimation to a cross-section of bilateral trade flows between 64 (major trading) countries for the year 2000 (a full list of countries is provided in the Appendix, Table 8.3). In this section, we discuss the empirical specification, data and the estimation results.

8.6.1 Data and Model Specification

For estimation, we follow a standard specification of the gravity equation of bilateral trade. Starting from the trade costs variables identified in Eq. (8.3), we further extend the specification with additional variables commonly mentioned in the literature (see, e.g., Frankel 1997; Raballand 2003). We use the following specification of the gravity equation:

$$\begin{aligned}\ln X_{ij} - \ln\left(GDP_i \cdot GDP_j\right) &= \alpha_0 + \alpha_1 \cdot \ln\left(GDPCAP_i \cdot GDPCAP_j\right) + \beta_1 \cdot \ln\left(D_{ij}\right) \\ &+ \beta_2 \cdot CB_{ij} + \beta_3 \cdot CL_{ij} + \beta_4 \cdot CH_{ij} + \beta_5 \cdot FTA_{ij} + \beta_6 \cdot ISL_i + \beta_7 \cdot ISL_j + \beta_8 \cdot \ln(Area)_i \\ &+ \beta_9 \cdot \ln(Area)_j + \beta_{10} \cdot LL_i + \beta_{11} \cdot LL_j + \delta_1 \cdot MWRD_{ij} + \delta_2 \cdot MWRCB_{ij} \\ &+ \delta_3 \cdot MWRCL_{ij} + \delta_4 \cdot MWRCH_{ij} + \delta_5 \cdot MWRFTA_{ij} + \varepsilon_{ij},\end{aligned} \tag{8.15}$$

where *GDPCAP* represents per capita GDP, *ISL* is an indicator variable that equals 1 if the country is an island, *Area* is the land area of a country, and *LL* equals 1 for landlocked countries, and in which:

$$MWRCB_{ij} = \left[\left(\sum_{j=1}^{N}\theta_j CB_{ij}\right) + \left(\sum_{i=1}^{N}\theta_i CB_{ij}\right) - \left(\sum_{i=1}^{N}\sum_{j=1}^{N}\theta_i\theta_j CB_{ij}\right)\right], \tag{8.16}$$

and likewise for the remaining *MWR* variables. The other variables are as defined earlier. The product of origin and destination GDPs is used as an offset variable.

The data for trade are from the World Trade Database compiled on the basis of COMTRADE data by Feenstra et al. (2005). GDP and per capita GDP data are from the World Bank's WDI database. Distance, language, colonial history, landlocked countries, and land area data are from the CEPII institute.[7] Whether pairs of countries take part in a common regional integration agreement (FTA) has been determined on the basis of OECD data about major regional integration agreements.[8] A dummy variable indicates whether a pair of countries has (membership

[7] See http://www.cepii.fr.

[8] See http://www.oecd.org/dataoecd/39/37/1923431.pdf.

in) at least one common FTA. Data on island status have been kindly provided by Hildegunn Kyvik-Nordas (from Jansen and Nordås 2004).

We first estimate Eq. (8.15) using negative binomial regression including country-specific indicator variables. GDP is used as an offset, which implies we move the log-sum of GDP to the left handside, assuming it has a proportional effect on trade with elasticity equal to 1 (Anderson and van Wincoop 2003). This is our first benchmark model, which, according to Feenstra (2004), yields consistent parameter estimates, but is criticized by Behrens et al. (2012). Secondly, we estimate Eq. (8.15), extending it with approximations of MR terms obtained using the Taylor series approximation proposed by Baier and Bergstrand (2009). This is our second benchmark model. These results, as well as the ones for the SF approach, are discussed in Sect. 8.6.2.

8.6.2 Estimation Results: Spatial Filtering and Benchmark Models

The first benchmark model includes origin- and destination-specific indicator variables. As shown in Anderson and van Wincoop (2003) and Feenstra (2004), this specification accounts for MR terms, and yields consistent parameter estimates. The disadvantage is that country-specific variables cannot be included, as their effect cannot be identified separately. This implies that explanatory variables that are potentially relevant for explaining variation in bilateral trade patterns, such as GDP per capita, land area and landlockedness, cannot be investigated empirically (if not ex post, by, e.g., regressing the indicator variable coefficients on them). A second disadvantage is the loss of degrees of freedom for estimation, because a substantial number of indicator variables ($2n-2$) is needed. Usually, however, the degrees of freedom remain large enough, since observations are bilateral (i.e., n^2-n).

The second benchmark model is the specification developed in Baier and Bergstrand (2009), which includes first-order Taylor series approximations of the MR terms. This specification follows from Eq. (8.6). Further manipulation [substituting Eq. (8.3) for bilateral trade costs] allows us to combine both terms between square brackets into a set of bilateral variables, one for each bilateral variable determining trade costs (such as geographical distance). The reduced-form double-log gravity equation is as follows:

$$\begin{aligned}\ln X_{ij} - \ln\left(GDP_i \cdot GDP_j\right) &= \alpha_0 + \alpha_1 \cdot \ln\left(GDPCAP_i \cdot GDPCAP_j\right) + \beta_1 \cdot \ln\left(D_{ij}\right)\\ &+ \beta_2 \cdot CB_{ij} + \beta_3 \cdot CL_{ij} + \beta_4 \cdot CH_{ij} + \beta_5 \cdot FTA_{ij} + \beta_6 \cdot ISL_i\\ &+ \beta_7 \cdot ISL_j + \beta_8 \cdot \ln(Area)_i + \beta_9 \cdot \ln(Area)_j + \beta_{10} \cdot LL_i + \beta_{11} \cdot LL_j\\ &+ \delta_1 \cdot MWRD_{ij} + \delta_2 \cdot MWRCB_{ij} + \delta_3 \cdot MWRCL_{ij} + \delta_4 \cdot MWRCH_{ij}\\ &+ \delta_5 \cdot MWRFTA_{ij} + \varepsilon_{ij},\end{aligned} \tag{8.17}$$

Baier and Bergstrand (2009) show that theory imposes the restrictions $\delta_k = -\beta_k$ for each k.

The equations specify the model in double-logarithmic transformation form. We estimated the benchmark models multiplicatively, using negative binomial regressions, aside from the BV model, which is estimated linearly. This method allows a direct treatment of the non-negative values of trade flows and of the zeros, and enables us to correct for overdispersion of trade flows (see Santos Silva and Tenreyro 2006).

The empirical estimation results are presented in Table 8.1. Model (1) presents the regression results for the first benchmark model, including country-specific indicator variables. Following Anderson and van Wincoop (2003), we estimate the model using GDP as an offset variable (i.e., restricting the coefficient of GDP variables to equal 1). The parameter estimates are in line with the findings elsewhere in the literature (see, e.g., Anderson and van Wincoop 2004; Disdier and Head 2008). Geographical distance has a negative effect on trade, with an estimated elasticity of -1.30. The effect of proximity on trade is reinforced by a positive and (marginally) significant effect of contiguity on trade. Proximity in terms of language and colonial links also positively affects bilateral trade, while preferential trade policy (i.e., enjoying common FTAs), appears to have a counterintuitive negative effect. These results—with the exception of the latter—confirm previous findings

Table 8.1 Estimation results

	(1) Fixed effects (GDP offset)	(2) Spatial filter	(3) BB-estimation (GDP offset)	(4) BB-estimation
Distance	–1.30***	–1.23***	–1.25***	–1.22***
Common border	0.24*	0.33**	0.23	0.25
Common language	0.36***	0.33***	0.32***	0.37***
Common history	0.86***	0.71***	0.79***	0.80***
Free trade	–0.14**	0.41	–0.27***	–0.22**
GDP exporter	–	0.75***	–	0.91***
GDP importer	–	0.92***	–	1.15***
GDP per cap. exporter	–	0.13***	–0.06**	0.02
GDP per cap. importer	–	0.12***	–0.04*	–0.16***
Island exporter	–	–0.41***	–0.29***	–0.28***
Island importer	–	–0.31***	0.08	0.20*
Area exporter	–	–0.00	–0.11***	–0.07***
Area importer	–	–0.17***	–0.22***	–0.28***
Landlocked exporter	–	0.23*	0.30**	0.26**
Landlocked importer	–	–0.58***	0.07	0.19*
Constant	–29.60***	–27.42***	–34.01***	–34.97***
AIC	101,713	47,805	102,485	102,436
Observations	4032	4032	4032	4032

Notes: BB stands for Baier-Bergstrand, and AIC for Akaike information criterion. ***, **, * denote parameter estimates statistically significant at 1 %, 5 % and 10 %, respectively

about the importance of these dimensions of transactional distance on trade (e.g., Obstfeld and Rogoff 2000; Loungani et al. 2002).

Model (3) compares these findings with the regression outcomes for the second benchmark model, the Baier-Bergstrand estimation. This method proxies for the endogenous and unobserved MR terms by including exogenous linear approximations based upon bilateral trade costs variables. Provided that the approximation is sufficiently adequate, this specification results in consistent estimates (Baier and Bergstrand 2009). Once again, GDP has been used as an offset variable, and the model is estimated by OLS. The obtained parameter estimates are comparable to the estimates for the first benchmark model [Model (1)], including the negative effect found for free-trade blocs. Additionally, on the one hand, the Baier-Bergstrand specification has an advantage, because it enables us to include country-specific regressors explicitly; on the other hand, the results do not always appear to be satisfactory.

Closer inspection of the Baier-Bergstrand estimation, dropping the offset assumption on the product of exporter and importer GDP in Model (4), yields qualitatively similar—and in some cases more plausible (e.g., for landlocked importers)—results, and a slightly better fit. For example, although a negative effect of GDP per capita variables on trade is not uncommon in some specifications (see, e.g., Anderson and Marcouiller 2002), the effect in Model (3) seems to be driven mainly by offsetting GDP, which imposes a GDP elasticity of trade of 1.

Summarizing, the two benchmark models yield somewhat different results. Although, as mentioned, some effects may be more plausible in the Baier-Bergstrand estimation results, the more traditional specification using country-specific indicator variables results in a slightly better model likelihood, as shown by the Akaike information criterion (AIC). The disadvantages of this model, though, are the loss of country-specific variables, and a diminished precision in the determination of the significance of variables, resulting from the loss of degrees of freedom in the model estimation.

Results emerging from the SF estimation of the gravity model, which combines the consistent estimation of the first benchmark model with the flexibility of specification of the second benchmark model, are shown for Model (2) in Table 8.1. The results presented here are obtained for a symmetrized k-nearest neighbours[9] spatial weights matrix $\mathbf{W}$, and for a negative binomial estimation, employed in order to cope with overdispersion in the trade flows. With regard to the coefficients of bilateral resistance variables, we note that with the exception of the one for FTA, they are highly significant, and their values are consistent with the ones found for Model (1). The FTA coefficient not being significantly negative anymore might be

[9]For the k-nearest neighbours definition of proximity, each country's neighbours are defined by selecting the k closest countries. Distance between the geographical centroids of the countries was used (Great Circle), setting $k = 3$ and forcing, for computational reasons, symmetry of the spatial weights matrix. As a result, the minimum number of neighbours per country is 3, while the maximum number is not constrained. Alternative definitions of proximity based upon, for example, simple rook contiguity or distance decay could be tested in order to assess the sensitivity of the model to the choice of spatial specification.

seen as a result that is more consistent with theoretical expectations. With regard to the importer- and exporter-specific variables, we are able to identify highly significant and positive coefficients for GDP, and GDP per capita is now significant and positive as well in both cases. This result is in contrast with the ones for the Baier-Bergstrand benchmarks [Models (3) and (4)], in which the same variable is either not significant or significantly negative. The SF estimation also allows us to estimate significant parameters for the variables identifying the geographical characteristics of importer and exporter countries. The signs obtained are mostly consistent with the ones found for the Baier-Bergstrand benchmarks. They show that larger and both landlocked and island countries tend to trade less. Noteworthy differences between the SF model and the benchmarks regard the negative and significant coefficients obtained for the importing patterns of island and landlocked economies (it was marginally positive or non-significant for the benchmarks). For islands, it may seem counterintuitive to find this result, although it should be considered that the sample of countries used excludes, because of non-reporting, most micro-island countries, while it includes all large island countries like the UK or Japan. In contrast, in the case of landlocked countries, a negative importing coefficient is more consistent with theoretical expectations.

Finally, the AIC of the SF model appears to vastly improve on the ones of the benchmark models, because of the high amount of variance explained by the origin- and destination-specific spatial filters, which are also highly significant from a statistical viewpoint (not shown in Table 8.1). In summary, the proposed SF approach to the estimation of a gravity model of trade allows identification of the regression parameters related to the bilateral variables, as well as those related to the origin- and destination-specific variables. Moreover, the model has a better likelihood (leading to improved AIC) than the competing models tested, and uses a limited number of degrees of freedom.

8.6.3 Testing for Spatial Autocorrelation

In Sect. 8.5, we discussed SAC statistics based on the score test [by le Cessie and van Houwelingen (1995) and Jacqmin-Gadda et al. (1997)], which are alternatives to the traditional MC in the case of GLMs, since the MC statistical distribution theory has been developed under linear regression assumptions.

Having an $n^2 \times n^2$ spatial weight matrix (obtained as $\mathbf{W} \otimes \mathbf{W}$) and the t statistic by Jacqmin-Gadda et al. (1997), residual SAC in Poisson and negative binomial regressions can be modelled by eigenvector SF within the same framework as standard spatial autocorrelation in regression residuals. The eigenvectors employed in Model (2) (see the preceding section) represent a certain level of SAC, given a spatial connectivity pattern, and by including them as proxy variables for such spatial autocorrelation, SAC that is not explained by independent variables is expected to be filtered out (at least partially) of the residuals, and transferred to the mean response.

Because eigenvectors are introduced as independent variables in a (forward or backward) stepwise manner, the adjustment of estimating parameters for independent variables developed in the Jacqmin-Gadda test seems to be desirable. Chun (2008) performs the test to evaluate SAC in a Poisson model in an analysis of migration flows. To the best of our knowledge, no one so far has used the test on a negative binomial model. We performed both the aforementioned score tests described in Sect. 8.5 to empirically detect the presence (or the absence) of SAC. We compare the tests on the model augmented with selected SF variables with the ones on the non-filtered model to verify if the introduction of the selected spatial filters lets the SAC be filtered out of the residuals. The tests are calculated on both quasi-Poisson[10] and negative binomial model residuals (estimating or offsetting GDP benchmark variables).

A further relevant question is whether adjusting the test for the presence of independent variables considerably changes SAC detection outcomes, or if this correction has just marginal effects. Table 8.2 presents the results for the different SAC tests. We start by reporting, in the first and second row of the table, the value of MC computed on the residuals as developed by Cliff and Ord for linear models. In the first row, we show the results of the basic, stand-alone, MC, while in the second row, the test accounts for the effect of independent variables. The presence of SAC is never rejected, even when we introduce the spatial filters in the model (despite the scores decreasing). Performing also the discussed MC permutation test, our findings do not change: the permutation score decreases after adding the spatial filters, but we never reject the SAC hypothesis.[11] In the third and the fourth rows of Table 8.2, the values for the LC and JG tests are reported. Using these tests, developed for GLMs, we can note how the SAC is effectively filtered out by the introduction of the selected spatial filters. The tests show significant SAC in the baseline model, which is filtered out by the spatial filter eigenvectors, especially when using negative binomial regression, for which the p-value stands to 0.239 (0.230 with offsets). Moreover, the results from LC and JG are quite similar, highlighting that the introduction of the correction for the independent variables in the JG test does not considerably change the test results. The general increase in t-scores obtained when the right-hand-side variables are taken into account may be explained by the fact that their inclusion pulls expected values slightly to the left (towards negative values).

These results seem to be comforting, and they lead to a positive confirmation of the initial theorized idea that we can account for spatial autocorrelation in the model by filtering out the residual spatial component by means of the selected

[10]Quasi-Poisson models are equivalent to standard Poisson models in terms of coefficient estimation, but because a dispersion parameter is estimated from the data, inference differs. For the purposes of eigenvector selection, AIC- or BIC-based selection is not possible (quasi-Poisson models have no likelihood), so it is manually performed by backward elimination (iteratively) of the eigenvector with the highest p-value.

[11]Results of the Moran permutation tests are available upon request.

Table 8.2 SAC with different statistics, for different models

		Quasi-Poisson		Negative binomial		Negative binomial (offset)	
		Non-spatial	Spatial filter	Non-spatial	Spatial filter	Non-spatial	Spatial filter
MC	Score	0.212	0.129	0.185	0.043	0.158	0.035
	t	39.99	24.61	34.93	8.08	30.06	6.74
	p-value	<2.2e–16	<2.2e–16	<2.2e–16	<2.2e–16	<2.2e–16	8.09e–12
MC (res.)	Score	0.168	0.119	0.429	0.277	0.375	0.283
	t	31.206	21.853	79.823	54.496	72.249	55.086
	p-value	<2.2e–16	<2.2e–16	<2.2e–16	<2.2e–16	<2.2e–16	<2.2e–16
LC	t	4.962	1.971	3.218	0.652	4.601	0.683
	p-value	3.49e–07	0.024	0.001	0.257	2.10e–06	0.247
JG	t	5.125	2.111	3.336	0.708	4.766	0.737
	p-value	1.49e–07	0.017	<0.001	0.239	9.41e–07	0.230

Notes: MC stands for the standalone Moran's I test, MC (res.) for the Moran's I test on regression residuals, LC for the le Cessie test, and JG for the Jacqmin-Gadda test

spatial filters, and that this is detectable only using a correct SAC test (specifically designed for GLMs).

8.7 Conclusions

Recent contributions to the modelling of bilateral trade have shown the importance of sound theoretical underpinnings for obtaining consistent parameter estimates for the determinants of trade in the gravity model of bilateral trade. This paper addresses the issue of how to achieve empirical consistency without the need to estimate a full general equilibrium system of equations, and without the loss of specification flexibility that results from the use of origin- and destination-specific indicator variables. We argue that endogeneity of regressors and residuals—due to omitted MR variables in the traditional gravity model—is likely to manifest in the form of autocorrelation in both regressors and residuals. By including an origin-specific and a destination-specific spatial filter as additional regressors, SF estimation of the gravity equation enables us to filter SAC out of the residuals, as demonstrated by the results obtained implementing appropriate SAC tests for nonlinear models. As a result, the residuals and the regressors are no longer correlated, and standard estimation methods can be applied to obtain consistent parameter estimates for the determinants of bilateral trade. We demonstrate the use of SF estimation in a negative binomial estimation of the gravity equation of bilateral trade. The comparison with two benchmark models, which are theoretically consistent in estimation, reveals that SF yields results that are highly comparable to the estimation using country-specific indicator variables. Moreover, SF estimation does not suffer from the drawbacks of using indicator variables. It allows explicit estimation of the effect of country-specific variables that are potentially important determinants of bilateral trade, such as GDP, per capita GDP and landlockedness.

Further analyses aimed at measuring the extent to which SAC is filtered out in SF estimation. We tested three different SAC tests, either from the linear modelling tradition (Moran's I tests) or specifically developed for GLMs (the le Cessie and Jacqmin-Gadda tests) on both quasi-Poisson and negative binomial model estimations. Our results confirm the 'filtering' effect of the spatial filters on the residuals. Such a finding is mostly evident with the GLM tests, which can be expected to be more suitable for analysing our models' residuals. On the other hand, the inclusion of right-hand-side variables in the computation of the SAC tests does not appear to considerably change our findings.

Future research should focus, on the methodological side, on expanding the analyses above to the SF network-autocorrelation approach first suggested by Chun (2008) and further employed in a panel framework (see, e.g., Scherngell and Lata 2013). Furthermore, quasi- or pseudo-Poisson estimation could be considered more extensively, by employing stepwise selection criteria which do not require likelihood-based indicators. In this regard, Krisztin and Fischer (2015) have very recently applied network-autocorrelation SF to a trade model, by including, among others, zero-inflated specifications. On the empirical side, it would be desirable to exploit the methodology proposed toward investigating specific research questions in the trade field, while a simulation study could help further extend the presented evidence on the adequacy of the SF approach for cross-sectional spatial interaction/gravity models.

Acknowledgements We thank Yongwan Chun for useful comments, as well as participants at the following conferences: Small Open Economies in a Globalized World II (Waterloo, ON); Summer Conference of the German Speaking Section of the European Regional Science Association (Kiel); 48th Conference of the European Regional Science Association (Liverpool); International Conference on Econometrics and the World Economy (Fukuoka); SSES Annual Meeting 2009 (Geneva).

Appendix

Table 8.3

Table 8.3 List of the countries used in the empirical application

Algeria	Angola	Argentina
Australia	Austria	Belgium
Brazil	Bulgaria	Canada
Chile	China	Colombia
Czech Republic	Denmark	Dominican Republic
Ecuador	Finland	France
Germany	Greece	Hungary
India	Indonesia	Iran
Ireland	Israel	Italy
Japan	Kazakhstan	Kuwait
Libya	Malaysia	Mexico
Morocco	Netherlands	New Zealand
Nigeria	Norway	Oman
Pakistan	Peru	Philippines
Poland	Portugal	Qatar
Romania	Russia	Saudi Arabia
Singapore	Slovakia	Slovenia
South Africa	South Korea	Spain
Sweden	Switzerland	Thailand
Tunisia	Turkey	United Arab Emirates
United Kingdom	United States	Venezuela
Vietnam		

References

Anderson JE, Marcouiller D (2002) Insecurity and the pattern of trade: an empirical investigation. Rev Econ Stat 84(2):342–352
Anderson JE, van Wincoop E (2003) Gravity with gravitas: a solution to the border puzzle. Am Econ Rev 93(1):170–192
Anderson JE, van Wincoop E (2004) Trade costs. J Econ Lit 42(3):691–751
Anselin L, Rey S (1991) Properties of tests for spatial dependence in linear regression models. Geogr Anal 23(2):112–131
Baier SL, Bergstrand JH (2009) Bonus vetus OLS: a simple method for approximating international trade-cost effects using the gravity equation. J Int Econ 77(1):77–85
Baldwin R, Taglioni D (2006) Gravity for dummies and dummies for gravity equations. NBER working paper series. National Bureau of Economic Research, Cambridge
Balistreri EJ, Hillberry RH (2007) Structural estimation and the border puzzle. J Int Econ 72(2):451–463
Baltagi BH, Egger P, Pfaffermayr M (2007) Estimating models of complex FDI: are there third-country effects? J Econ 140(1):260–281
Behrens K, Ertur C, Koch W (2012) 'Dual' gravity: using spatial econometrics to control for multilateral resistance. J Appl Econ 25(2):773–794
Bergstrand JH (1985) The gravity equation in international trade: some microeconomic foundations and empirical evidence. Rev Econ Stat 67(3):474–481
Bröcker J (1989) How to eliminate certain defects of the potential formula. Environ Plan A 21(6):817–830
Bröcker J, Rohweder HC (1990) Barriers to international trade. Ann Reg Sci 24(4):289–305
Chun Y (2008) Modeling network autocorrelation within migration flows by eigenvector spatial filtering. J Geogr Syst 10(4):317–344
Chun Y, Griffith DA, Lee M, Sinha P (2016) Eigenvector selection with stepwise regression techniques to construct eigenvector spatial filters. J Geogr Syst 18(1):67–85
Cliff A, Ord K (1972) Testing for spatial autocorrelation among regression residuals. Geogr Anal 4(3):267–284
Cliff AD, Ord JK (1981) Spatial processes: models & applications. Pion, London
Crespo Cuaresma J, Feldkircher M (2013) Spatial filtering, model uncertainty and the speed of income convergence in Europe. J Appl Econ 28(4):720–741
De Groot HLF, Linders G-J, Rietveld P, Subramanian U (2004) The institutional determinants of bilateral trade patterns. Kyklos 57(1):103–123
Deardorff AV (1998) Determinants of bilateral trade: does gravity work in a neoclassical world? In: Frankel JA (ed) The regionalization of the world economy. The University of Chicago Press, Chicago, pp 7–31
Disdier A-C, Head K (2008) The puzzling persistence of the distance effect on bilateral trade. Rev Econ Stat 90(1):37–48
Egger P (2005) Alternative techniques for estimation of cross-section gravity models. Rev Int Econ 13(5):881–891
Feenstra RC (2004) Advanced international trade: theory and evidence. Princeton University Press, Princeton
Feenstra RC, Lipsey RE, Deng H, Ma AC, Mo H (2005) World trade flows: 1962–2000. NBER working paper. National Bureau of Economic Research, Cambridge
Fischer MM, Griffith DA (2008) Modeling spatial autocorrelation in spatial interaction data: an application to patent citation data in the European Union. J Reg Sci 48(5):969–989
Fotheringham AS, O'Kelly ME (1989) Spatial interaction models: formulations and applications. Studies in operational regional science. Kluwer Academic, Dordrecht
Frankel JA (1997) Regional trading blocs in the World Economic System. Institute for International Economics, Washington

Griffith DA (2003) Spatial autocorrelation and spatial filtering: gaining understanding through theory and scientific visualization. Springer, Berlin
Griffith DA (2007) Spatial structure and spatial interaction: 25 years later. Rev Reg Stud 37(1):28–38
Griffith DA (2009) Spatial autocorrelation in spatial interaction: complexity-to-simplicity in journey-to-work flows. In: Reggiani A, Nijkamp P (eds) Complexity and spatial networks: in search of simplicity. Springer, Berlin, pp 221–237
Griffith DA (2010) The Moran coefficient for non-normal data. J Stat Plan Inference 140(11):2980–2990
Grimpe C, Patuelli R (2011) Regional knowledge production in nanomaterials: a spatial filtering approach. Ann Reg Sci 46(3):419–451
Jacqmin-Gadda H, Commenges D, Nejjari C, Dartigues J-F (1997) Tests of geographical correlation with adjustment for explanatory variables: an application to Dyspnoea in the elderly. Stat Med 16(11):1283–1297
Jansen M, Nordås HK (2004) Institutions, trade policy and trade flows. CEPR discussion paper 4416. Centre for Economic Policy Research (CEPR), London
Koch W, LeSage JP (2015) Latent multilateral trade resistance indices: theory and evidence. Scot J Polit Econ 62(3):264–290
Krisztin T, Fischer MM (2015) The gravity model for international trade: specification and 758 estimation issues. Spat Econ Anal 10(4):451–470
le Cessie S, van Houwelingen HC (1995) Testing the fit of a regression model via score tests in random effects models. Biometrics 51(2):600–614
LeSage JP, Pace RK (2008) Spatial econometric modeling of origin-destination flows. J Reg Sci 48(5):941–967
Lin G, Zhang T (2007) Loglinear residual tests of Moran's I autocorrelation and their applications to Kentucky Breast Cancer Data. Geogr Anal 39(3):293–310
Loungani P, Mody A, Razin A (2002) The global disconnect: the role of transactional distance and scale economies in gravity equations. Scott J Polit Econ 49(5):526–543
Monestiez P, Dubroca L, Bonnin E, Durbec JP, Guinet C (2006) Geostatistical modelling of spatial distribution of Balaenoptera physalus in the Northwestern Mediterranean Sea from sparse count data and heterogeneous observation efforts. Ecol Model 193(3-4):615–628
Obstfeld M, Rogoff K (2000) The six major puzzles in international macroeconomics: is there a common cause? NBER Macroecon Annu 15:339–390
Oden N (1995) Adjusting Moran's I for population density. Stat Med 14(1):17–26
Patuelli R (2007) Regional labour markets in Germany: statistical analysis of spatio-temporal disparities and network structures. Ph.D. thesis, Department of Spatial Economics, VU University Amsterdam, Amsterdam
Porojan A (2001) Trade flows and spatial effects: the gravity model revisited. Open Econ Rev 12(3):265–280
Pöyhönen P (1963) A tentative model for the volume of trade between countries. Weltwirtschaftliches Arch 90(1):93–99
Prentice RL, Zhao LP (1991) Estimating equations for parameters in means and covariances of multivariate discrete and continuous responses. Biometrics 47(3):825–839
R Core Team (2015) R: A language and environment for statistical computing. R Foundation for Statistical Computing, Vienna
Raballand G (2003) Determinants of the negative impact of being landlocked on trade: an empirical investigation through the central Asian case. Comp Econ Stud 45(4):520–536
Santos Silva JMC, Tenreyro S (2006) The log of gravity. Rev Econ Stat 88(4):641–658
Schabenberger O, Gotway CA (2005) Statistical methods for spatial data analysis. Chapman & Hall/CRC, Boca Raton
Scherngell T, Lata R (2013) Towards an integrated european research area? findings from eigenvector spatially filtered spatial interaction models using european framework programme data. Pap Reg Sci 92(3):555–577

Sellner R, Fischer MM, Koch M (2013) A spatial autoregressive Poisson gravity model. Geogr Anal 45(2):180–201

Sen A, Smith TE (1995) Gravity models of spatial interaction behavior. Advances in spatial and network economics series. Springer, Heidelberg

Straathof SM (2008) Gravity with gravitas: comment. CPB discussion paper 111. Netherlands Bureau for Economic Policy Analysis, The Hague

Tinbergen J (1962) Shaping the World Economy: suggestions for an International Economic Policy. Twentieth Century Fund, New York

Tobler W (1970) A computer movie simulating Urban growth in the Detroit region. Econ Geography 46(supplement):234–240

Wilson AG (1970) Entropy in Urban and regional modelling. Pion, London

Chapter 9
A Spatial Interaction Model with Spatially Structured Origin and Destination Effects

James P. LeSage and Carlos Llano

Keywords Bayesian hierarchical models • Commodity flows • Spatial autoregressive random effects • Spatial connectivity of origin-destination flows

JEL: C21, R11, R32

9.1 Introduction

We introduce a Bayesian hierarchical regression model that includes latent spatial effects structured to follow a spatial autoregressive process to investigate commodity flows between origin and destination regions. The sample data involves $n = 18$ Spanish regions where the commodity flows have been organized as an n by n "origin-destination (OD) flow matrix" that we label Y. Without loss of generality, the row elements of the matrix $Y_{ij}, i = 1, \ldots, n$ reflect the dollar value (in millions of Euros) of commodity flows originating in region j that were shipped to destination regions $i = 1, \ldots, n$. We therefore treat the columns as "origins" of the commodity flows and the rows are "destinations" of the flows.

*This paper has been previously published in the Journal of Geographical Systems. Special Issue on "Advances in the Statistical Modelling of Spatial Interaction Data", Vol. 15, Number 3/July 2013, ©Springer-Verlag Berlin Heidelberg, pp. 265–289.

J.P. LeSage (✉)
Fields Endowed Chair of Urban and Regional Economics, McCoy College of Business Administration, Department of Finance and Economics, Texas State University, San Marcos, TX 78666, USA
e-mail: james.lesage@txstate.edu

C. Llano
Departamento de Análisis Económico, and CEPREDE, Universidad Autónoma de Madrid, 28049 Madrid, Spain
e-mail: carlos.llano@uam.es

R. Patuelli, G. Arbia (eds.), *Spatial Econometric Interaction Modelling*, Advances in Spatial Science, DOI 10.1007/978-3-319-30196-9_9

The term 'spatial interaction models' has been used by Sen and Smith (1995) and others to label models that focus on flows between origins and destinations. These models seeks to explain variation in the level of flows across the sample of $N = n^2$ OD pairs by relying on a function of distance between the origin and destination regions as well as explanatory variables consisting of origin and destination characteristics of the regions. Conventional spatial interaction models assume that using distance as an explanatory variable will eradicate the spatial dependence among the sample OD pairs allowing use of least-squares estimation methods. We note that use of least-squares also requires a normal distribution for the dependent variable magnitudes contained in the vectorized flow matrix $y = vec(Y)$ for valid inference using traditional regression t-tests and measures of statistical significance. However, unbiased estimates for the slope parameters can still be obtained for non-normal disturbances and associated distribution for the y variable. We assume a normal distribution for the disturbances to be the case in developing our model which rules out use of our methodology in cases where the flow matrix is sparse containing a large number of zero entries reflecting a lack of interaction between regions. Sparse flow matrices typically arise when regions are defined using a fine spatial scale or a short time period over which observed flow information is collected.

A spatial autoregressive structure is used to structure two latent regional effects vectors, one for regions reflecting origins of the commodity flows and a second for the destination regions. The spatial autoregressive prior structure reflects a prior belief that the latent origin effects levels should be similar to those from regions that neighbor the region where commodity flows originate. A second regional effects vector imposes the same prior belief regarding the effects levels of destination regions and their neighbors. Intuitively, the missing covariates for the origin region that contribute to model heterogeneity may have a spatial character, so that the same missing covariates would influence nearby regions. The same intuition applies to the destination regions, missing covariates are likely to exert similar heterogeneity as those from neighboring destinations.

We use posterior estimates of the origin and destination latent effects to identify regions that exhibit positive and negative effects magnitudes. Since the effects parameters have a prior mean of zero, positive and negative posterior effects estimates can be interpreted as measuring the magnitude and influence of missing covariates or latent unobservable factors on the commodity flow process.

The hierarchical regression model utilizes recent work by Smith and LeSage (2004) that introduced Bayesian Markov Chain Monte Carlo (MCMC) estimation methods for these models where the regional effects parameters are modelled using data augmentation. There is a large literature on Bayesian hierarchical spatial models (see Besag et al. 1991; Besag and Kooperberg 1995; Cressie 1995; Banerjee et al. 2004), that relies on the conditional autoregressive (CAR) spatial prior to structure the regional effects parameters. In contrast, our approach utilizes the spatial autoregressive process (SAR) from Smith and LeSage (2004) as a prior structure on the regional effects parameters.

Individual effects estimates are notoriously difficult to estimate with precision in conventional hierarchical linear models (Gelfand et al. 1995). Our approach to structuring two sets of regional/spatial effects parameters overcomes these problems in two ways.

First, the spatial autoregressive structure placed on the latent effects parameters for the origin depend on one hyperparameter measuring the strength of spatial dependence and another representing a scalar variance parameter. These two parameters are introduced in the context of a sample of $n^2 = N$ observations, where $n = 18$ regions and $N = 324$ represents the sample of origin-destination pairs that arise from vectorizing the origin-destination flow matrix. As noted above, the $N = n^2$ sample size arises from vectorizing an n by n origin-destination flow matrix Y, where the rows of the matrix Y reflect commodity flow destinations and the columns reflect regions where the commodity flows originate. We estimate only n latent regional "origin" effects parameters, one for each region treated as an origin, allowing us to rely on n sample data observations *for each* of the $i = 1, \ldots, n$ origin effect parameter estimates. In fact, since the n origin effects parameters are derived from the two hyperparameters that completely determine the spatial autoregressive process assigned to govern these effects, we could view this as relying on a sample of N observations to estimate two parameters. A similar situation holds for the case of the n "destination" effects estimates for the destination regions. Again, we rely on the larger sample of N observations to produce estimates of the two parameters specifying the spatial autoregression assigned to these n effects parameters.

Second, the spatial autoregressive (SAR) structure assumed to govern the origin and destination effects introduces additional sample data information in the form of an n by n spatial contiguity matrix that describes the spatial connectivity structure of the sample regions. This additional spatial structure in conjunction with the spatial autoregressive process assumption provides a parsimonious parameterization of the regional effects parameters. This is in contrast to the typical assumption of a normal distribution with zero mean and constant scalar variance assigned as a prior for non-spatial latent effects parameters. Our approach of estimating two sets of n latent effects based on a sample of size $N = n^2$ also differs from the conventional approaches that estimate a latent effect parameter for all sample observations, which would be N in our case.

As noted above, use of a spatial autoregressive process as a prior for the latent effects parameters also differs from most hierarchical spatial linear models that rely on a conditional autoregressive (CAR) process prior, or an intrinsic conditional autoregressive (ICAR) process. In this regard, we follow Smith and LeSage (2004) who introduced spatially structured SAR priors for latent effects in the context of a probit model. There are numerous advantages to the SAR prior over the CAR. We will have more to say about this in Sect. 9.2 where details regarding the model specification are provided.

Section 9.2 of the paper describes the conventional spatial interaction model along with our extension of this model to include the latent origin and destination regional effects parameters. Section 9.3 applies the method to a data generated example where the true parameters are known in order to illustrate and assess the proposed methodology, and Sect. 9.4 applies the method to a sample of commodity flows during the year 2002 between 18 Spanish regions.

9.2 Empirical Modeling of Commodity Flows

In Sect. 9.2.1 we review the traditional gravity or spatial interaction model that assumes the OD flows contained in the dependent variable vector $y = vec(Y)$ are independent, consistent with the Gauss-Markov assumptions for least-squares. Section 9.2.2 describes our extension to this model that introduces spatially structured regional effects parameters.

9.2.1 Conventional Gravity Models

A conventional gravity or spatial interaction model would rely on an n by k matrix of explanatory variables that we label X, containing k characteristics for each of the n regions and the flow matrix Y vectorized, so that each column of the matrix Y is stacked. Given the origin-destination format of the vector y, where observations 1 to n reflect flows from origin 1 to all n destinations, the matrix X would be repeated n times to produce an N by k matrix representing destination characteristics that we label X_d (see LeSage and Pace 2008). We note that X_d equals $\iota_n \otimes X$, where ι_n is an n by 1 vector of ones. A second matrix can be formed to represent origin characteristics that we label X_o. This would repeat the characteristics of the first region n times to form the first n rows of X_o, the characteristics of the second region n times for the next n rows of X_o and so on, resulting in an N by k matrix that we label $X_o = X \otimes \iota_n$. The distance from each origin to destination is also included as an explanatory variable vector in the gravity model. We let G represent the n by n matrix of distances between origins and destinations, and thus $g = vec(G)$ is an N by 1 vector of these distances from each origin to each destination formed by stacking the columns of the origin-destination distance matrix into a variable vector.

This results in a regression model of the type shown in (9.1).[1]

$$y = \alpha\iota_N + X_d\beta_d + X_o\beta_o + \gamma g + \varepsilon \tag{9.1}$$

In (9.1), the explanatory variable matrices X_d, X_o represent N by k matrices containing destination and origin characteristics respectively and the associated k by 1 parameter vectors are β_d and β_o. The scalar parameter γ reflects the effect of distance g, and α denotes the the constant term parameter. The N by 1 vector ε

[1]If one starts with the standard gravity model and applies a log-transformation, the resulting structural model takes the form of (9.1) (c.f., Eq. (6.4) in Sen and Smith (1995)).

represent disturbances and we assume $\varepsilon \sim N[0, \sigma^2 I_N]$, where we use $N_k[\mu, \Sigma]$ to represent a k-variate normal distribution with mean μ and variance-covariance Σ.

One problem encountered in modeling the n by n matrix of flows, which we designate using Y is that main diagonal elements reflect intraregional flows and are typically large relative to the off-diagonal elements that represent interregional flows. LeSage and Pace (2008) suggest creating a separate model for intraregional flows from the main diagonal of the flow matrix. They do this by setting all elements of the covariate matrices X_d, X_o corresponding to the main diagonal of the flow matrix to zero, and moving these elements to a new N by k matrix which we label X_i. The matrix X_i has zeros except for those elements associated with the main diagonal of the flow matrix. This which prevents the variables in X_d, X_o from entering the interregional flow model, creating a separate set of explanatory variables to explain this variation in the matrix X_i. In our applied illustration we use a vector for the matrix X_i containing the main diagonal flow elements from a previous time period. In many circumstances previous period flows may not be available, necessitating the approach of LeSage and Pace (2008). We note that one need not employ all variables in the matrix X, since a subset of these might work well to explain intraregional flows. For example, the area of a region, the income level and population might work well to explain the magnitude of flows within the region. It is typically the case that intraregional flows are considered a nuisance in these models, since the focus is on explaining variation in interregional flows. Introduction of the separate models for inter- and intraregional flows allows the parameter estimates for β_d, β_o to better reflect the impact of origin and destination characteristics on the interregional flow levels. The conventional gravity model approach allows the large main diagonal flow elements to influence these parameter estimates. A frequent practice in applied modeling is to set the diagonal elements of the flow matrix to zero (see Tiefelsdorf 2003 and Fischer et al. 2006). In a spatial context where neighboring regions are not independent, setting these elements to zero will exert an impact on the pattern of spatial dependence.

A second problem that arises is the need to store sample data information in the N by k matrices, X_d, X_o, X_i, which can consume a large amount of computer memory when n is large. For example, a model involving 3,000 US county-level flows would require three 9 million by k matrices. We extend the moment matrix approach of LeSage and Pace (2008) to our model. They point out that rather than work with matrices $X_d = \iota_n \otimes X, X_o = X \otimes \iota_n$, it is possible to work with smaller k by k matrices $X'X$.

This can be accomplished for the least-squares model by letting:

$$y = Z\delta + \varepsilon \tag{9.2}$$

where: $Z = \begin{bmatrix} \iota_N & \tilde{X}_d & \tilde{X}_o & X_i & g \end{bmatrix}$, and $\delta = \begin{bmatrix} \alpha & \beta_d & \beta_o & \beta_i & \gamma \end{bmatrix}'$.

We assume the matrix X is in deviation from means form, and define the n by n matrix G to contain the interregional distances (in deviation from means form). Based on the introduction of the matrix X_i described above, the matrices: $\tilde{X}_d = X_d - X_i$, $\tilde{X}_o = X_o - X_i$, where $X_d = I_n \otimes X, X_o = X \otimes I_n$. The resulting moment matrices take the form:

$$Z'Z = \begin{bmatrix} N & 0 & 0 & 0 & 0 \\ 0 & (n-1)X'X & -X'X & 0 & X'\mathrm{d}(G) - X'G\iota_n \\ 0 & -X'X & (n-1)X'X & 0 & X'\mathrm{d}(G) - X'G\iota_n \\ 0 & 0 & 0 & X'X & X'\mathrm{d}(G) \\ 0 & \iota_n' G'X - \mathrm{d}(G')X & \iota_n' G'X - \mathrm{d}(G')X & \mathrm{d}(G')X & tr\left(G^2\right) \end{bmatrix}$$

Where $\mathrm{d}(G)$ is an n by 1 vector containing the diagonal elements of the matrix G. For the case of the $Z'y$ we have that: $(X_d - X_i)'y = (I_n \otimes X)'y - X_i'y = X'Y\iota_n - X'\mathrm{d}(Y)$ and $(X_o - X_i)'y = X_o'y - X_i'y = X'Y'\iota_n - X'\mathrm{d}(Y)$, yielding:

$$\begin{aligned} Z'y &= \left[\iota_n' Y \iota_n \; (X_d - X_i)'y \; (X_o - X_i)'y \; X_i'y \; tr(GY)\right]' \\ &= \left[\iota_n' Y \iota_n \; X'Y\iota_n - X'\mathrm{d}(Y) \; X'Y'\iota_n - X'\mathrm{d}(Y) \; X'\mathrm{d}(Y) \; tr(GY)\right] \end{aligned}$$

Least-squares estimates for the model can now be produced using: $(Z'Z)^{-1}Z'y$, which involves inversion of the $3k + 2$ by $3k + 2$ matrix $Z'Z$.

9.2.2 A Bayesian Hierarchical Gravity Model

LeSage and Pace (2008) point to the implausible nature of the assumption that OD flows contained in the dependent variable vector y exhibit no spatial dependence. They note that the gravity model makes an attempt at modeling spatial dependence between observations using distance, but if each region exerts an influence on its neighbors this might be inadequate. For example, neighboring origins and destinations may exhibit estimation errors of similar magnitude if underlying latent or unobserved forces are at work or missing covariates exert a similar impact on neighboring observations. They point out that agents located at origins nearby in space may experience similar transport costs and profit opportunities when evaluating alternative destinations.

We extend the model from (9.1) by introducing two n by 1 vectors of regional effects parameters, one for each region treated as an origin θ and another for destination regions ϕ. This model can be expressed as:

$$y_j = z_j\delta + v_j\theta + w_j\phi + \varepsilon_j \quad \varepsilon \sim N_N[0, \sigma_\varepsilon^2 I_N] \tag{9.3}$$

$$y = Z\delta + V\theta + W\phi + \varepsilon$$

$$\theta = \rho_o D\theta + u_o, \quad u_o \sim N_n[0, \sigma_o^2 I_n] \tag{9.4}$$

$$\phi = \rho_d D\phi + u_d \quad u_d \sim N_n[0, \sigma_d^2 I_n] \tag{9.5}$$

Where $z_j = \left[1 \; \tilde{x}_{j,d} \; \tilde{x}_{j,o} \; x_{j,i} \; g_j \right]$, with $\tilde{x}_{j,d}, \tilde{x}_{j,o}, x_{j,i}$ representing row elements from the corresponding matrices: $\tilde{X}_d, \tilde{X}_o, X_i$. The vector, $v_j = (v_{j1}, \ldots, v_{jn})$ identifies region j as an origin region and $w_j = (w_{j1}, \ldots, w_{jn})$ identifies destination regions. Given our configuration for the commodity flow matrix with columns as origins and rows as destinations, the matrices $W = I_n \otimes \iota_n$ and $V = \iota_n \otimes I_n$ such that v_j and w_j represent the jth row of these mutually exclusive N by n matrices.

For the spatial effects parameters we rely on the spatial autoregressive priors shown in (9.4) and (9.5), where D is an n by n row-normalized first-order spatial contiguity matrix. This matrix reflects the spatial configuration of the regions in terms of common borders, with row-sums of unity by virtue of the row-normalization.

We provide an economic motivation for inclusion of the spatial effects vectors θ and ϕ in the model in the sequel. Bonacich (1987) introduced a centrality measure in the context of social networking that has come to be known as the Bonacich centrality index. In our context, we can view the spatial weight matrix D as an n by n adjacency matrix related to the spatial configuration or network of our observations/regions. The Bonacich index for region i counts the total number of paths in the network defined by our spatial contiguity weight matrix D that start at region i. These consist of the sum of all loops from region i to itself, and the sum of all outer paths from region i to every other region $j \neq i$. Specifically, Bonacich defines a vector: $(I_n - \rho_d D)^{-1}\iota_n = (\sum_{k=0}^{\infty} \rho_d^k D^k)\iota_n$, that sums up the elements of $(I_n - \rho_o D)^{-1}$. The i,jth element represents a count of the number of paths in our regional configuration that start at region i and end at j, with paths of length k weighted by the parameter ρ^k.[2] We note that the SAR structure placed on the origin (destination) effects parameters reflect a weighted variant of the Bonacich network centrality measure: $\theta = (I_n - \rho_o D)^{-1} u_o$, where the heterogenous vector u_o replaces the homogenous ι_n vector.[3] The centrality measure indicates regions with more/less contiguous neighbors, and therefore posits large/smaller effects estimates for regions in accordance with this. For example, regions on the edge of Spain as well as (physically) large regions would have less contiguous neighbors, and we would expect to see smaller (in absolute value terms) effects estimates. This is in fact consistent with our empirical findings, an issue taken up when presenting a map of the effects estimates.

Abstracting from any economic motivation, when $\rho_o > 0$,the SAR prior structure leads to larger origin and destination effects parameters θ associated with regions that exhibit greater "network centrality", when regions are viewed as origins or destinations of commodity flows.

An economic motivation for the vectors θ, ϕ on which we place the SAR prior structure is provided by a result from Ballester et al. (2006). They show that in a noncooperative network game with linear quadratic payoffs as a return to effort,

---

[2]For our conventional spatial contiguity matrix D which has zeros on the diagonal and row-sums of unity, the inverse is well defined for $\rho < 1$.

[3]Of course for the destination effects parameters we have: $\phi = (I_n - \rho_d D)^{-1} u_d$.

the Nash equilibrium effort exerted by each player is proportional to the Bonacich centrality of the player's situation in the network. The game involves efforts that exhibit local complementarity with efforts of other players.

Drawing on their result, we can posit the existence of unobservable inputs, that play the role of effort exerted in Ballester et al. (2006). These inputs can be related to intra- and interregional commodity flows using a strictly concave bilinear payoff function. The unobservable inputs are not reflected in the regional characteristics measured by X_d, X_o, X_i or the distances g, on which the model is already conditioned. Ballester et al. (2006) show that for the case of a simultaneous move n player game there is a unique (interior) Nash equilibrium (see Theorem 1, Remark 1, Ballester et al. 2006) for effort exerted. The equilibrium (effort, or in our case unobservable input usage) is proportional to our weighted variant of the Bonacich network centrality measure. They establish that this result applies to both symmetric and asymmetric structures of complementarity across the regions represented by the n by n matrix D, and the matrix D is required to obey the usual spatial autoregressive process restrictions.[4]

This result motivates that when we model a cross-section of observed commodity flows at a particular point in time, after conditioning on observable regional factors in the explanatory variable matrices X_d, X_o, X_i and g, unobservable factors are likely to exhibit the SAR structure we use as a prior for the vectors θ and ϕ

Turning to specification of the remaining priors for parameters in our model, we assign an uninformative inverse-gamma (IG) prior for the parameters σ_o^2, σ_d^2 and σ_ε^2, taking the form:

$$\pi(\sigma_o^2), \pi(\sigma_d^2), \pi(\sigma_\varepsilon^2) \sim IG(\nu_1, \nu_2) \tag{9.6}$$

Where in the absence of prior information, it seems reasonable to rely on the same prior for σ_o^2, σ_d^2 and σ_ε^2. It also seems reasonable to assign values $\nu_1 = 2, \nu_2 = 1$ which reflects an uninformative prior with mean = 1, mode = 0.33, and infinite variance.

The spatial dependence parameters are known to lie in the stationary interval: $[\kappa_{\max}^{-1}, \kappa_{\min}^{-1}]$ where $\kappa_{\min} < 0, \kappa_{\max} > 0$ denote the minimum and maximum eigenvalues of the matrix D, (see for example, Lemma 2 in Sun et al. 1999). We rely on a uniform distribution over this interval as our prior for ρ_o, ρ_d, that is:

$$\pi(\rho_o), \pi(\rho_d) \sim U[\kappa_{\max}^{-1}, \kappa_{\min}^{-1}] \propto 1 \tag{9.7}$$

Solving for θ and ϕ in terms of u_o and u_d suggests a normal prior for the origin and destination spatial effects vectors taking the form:

$$\theta | \rho_o, \sigma_o^2 \sim N_n[0, \sigma_o^2 (B_o' B_o)^{-1}]$$

[4]Row-sums of unity and zeros on the main diagonal.

$$\phi|\rho_d, \sigma_d^2 \sim N_n[0, \sigma_d^2(B_d'B_d)^{-1}]$$
$$B_o = (I_n - \rho_o D)$$
$$B_d = (I_n - \rho_d D)$$

We note that B_o, B_d are non-singular for conventional row-normalized first-order spatial contiguity matrices D and the spatial dependence parameters ρ_o, ρ_d in the interval: $[\kappa_{\max}^{-1}, \kappa_{\min}^{-1}]$. This leads to a proper prior distribution in contrast to the well-known intrinsic CAR prior introduced by Besag and Kooperberg (1995).

We also point out that when the parameters $\rho_o = \rho_d = 0$, our model collapses to the special case of a normal prior for the random effects vectors with means of zero for both effects and constant scalar variances σ_o^2 and σ_d^2, so our SAR prior specification subsumes this as a special case. It should be noted that estimates for these two sets of random effects parameters are identified, since a set of n mutually exclusive sample data observations are aggregated through the vectors v_i and w_i to produce each estimate θ_i, ϕ_i in the vector of parameters θ and ϕ.

Finally, we use a normal prior distribution for the parameters $\delta = \left[\alpha\ \beta_o\ \beta_d\ \beta_i\ \gamma\right]'$ associated with the covariates in the explanatory variables matrix $X = \left[\iota\ X_d\ X_o\ X_i\ g\right]$ centered on zero with a large standard deviation:

$$\pi(\delta|\psi) \sim N_{3k+2}[0, T] \tag{9.8}$$

Where $3k + 2$ denotes the number of explanatory variables in the matrix Z, $T = \omega^2 I_{3k+2}$, with $\omega^2 = 1{,}000$.

9.2.3 *Related Spatial Effects Models*

In place of the SAR prior, we could rely on variants of the CAR prior that result in proper priors, Sun et al. (2000) among others. Other examples of the SAR prior in the context of random spatial effects are Smith and LeSage (2004), and LeSage et al. (2007).

Banerjee et al. (2000) model the timeliness of postal service flows using a binary response indicator for on-time or delayed mail as the dependent variable in place or our flows. Their model replaces the origin and destination effects terms: $v_j\theta$ and $w_j\phi$ with dummy variables (fixed effects) and associated parameter estimates. They then proceed to model the disturbances ε_j using a spatial process model. This type of approach focuses on disturbance heterogeneity and covariance which can be modeled in an effort to improve the precision of the estimates.

We note the contrast with our model where introduction of the spatially structured effects parameters will have a direct impact on the resulting estimates $\beta_d, \beta_o, \beta_i$ and γ. To see this consider the conditional distribution of δ:

$$\begin{aligned}\delta|\theta, \phi, \rho_d, \rho_o, \sigma_u\sigma_o, \sigma_\varepsilon &= (Z'Z)^{-1}Z'(y - V\theta - W\phi) \\ &= (Z'Z)^{-1}Z'[y - V(I_n - \rho_d D)^{-1}u_d - W(I_n - \rho_o D)^{-1}u_o]\end{aligned} \quad (9.9)$$

in contrast to that from a model where V and W represent fixed effects, and θ, ϕ the associated parameters, with the disturbances modeled by a spatial process whose variance-covariance structure we represent by Ω:

$$\tilde{\delta}|\theta, \phi, \rho_d, \rho_o, \sigma_u\sigma_o, \sigma_\varepsilon = (Z'\Omega Z)^{-1}Z'\Omega(y - V\theta - W\phi) \quad (9.10)$$

In the fixed effects model (9.10), $E(\tilde{\delta}) = (Z'Z)^{-1}Z'(y - V\theta - W\phi)$, so the spatial process model for the disturbances has no impact on the parameter estimates $\tilde{\delta}$. If we eliminated the spatial autoregressive priors in (9.12) and (9.13) and estimated coefficient vectors θ, ϕ for the model: $y = Z\delta + V\theta + W\phi + \varepsilon$, we would have a fixed effects model.[5]

In contrast, the model containing SAR structured effects results in destination or origin specific shocks, (u_d, u_o), exerting an influence on the parameter estimates. The amount of influence is described by the weighted Bonacich centrality measures: $(I_n - \rho_d D)^{-1}u_d$ and $(I_n - \rho_o D)^{-1}u_o$.

Intuitively, the existence of spatially clustered unobserved latent influences should lead to an adjustment in the response of commodity flows (y) to destination and origin region characteristics (X_d, X_o) as well as distance (g) and the intraregional model variables (X_i), captured in the parameters δ associated with each of these explanatory variables. Further, the magnitude of adjustment will depend on the weighted Bonacich centrality of the region where unobserved latent influences are operating.

9.2.4 MCMC Estimation of the Model

For notational convenience in the following discussion we restate the observation-level expression (9.3) of our model in matrix form:

$$\begin{aligned}y &= Z\delta + V\theta + W\phi + \varepsilon \\ \theta &= \rho_o D\theta + u_o \\ \phi &= \rho_d D\phi + u_d\end{aligned} \quad (9.11)$$

[5] Of course, one of the regions would need be eliminated from each of the matrices V, W to avoid have a perfect linear combination of dummy variables.

$$\pi(\theta|\rho_o, \sigma_o^2) \sim (\sigma_o^2)^{n/2}|B_o|\exp\left(-\frac{1}{2\sigma_o^2}\theta' B_o' B_o \theta\right) \quad (9.12)$$

$$\pi(\phi|\rho_d, \sigma_d^2) \sim (\sigma_d^2)^{n/2}|B_d|\exp\left(-\frac{1}{2\sigma_d^2}\phi' B_d' B_d \phi\right) \quad (9.13)$$

Where the expressions (9.12) and (9.13) reflect the implied prior for the spatial effects vector θ conditional on ρ_o, σ_o^2 and that for ϕ conditional on ρ_d, σ_d^2.

We use the normal linear model from (9.11) as the starting point to introduce the conditional posterior distributions that form the basis of an MCMC estimation scheme for our model. The basic scheme involves the following steps.

1. sample the regression parameters δ given $\theta, \phi, \rho_o, \rho_d, \sigma_o^2, \sigma_d^2, \sigma_\varepsilon^2$.
2. sample the noise variance σ_ε^2 given $\delta, \theta, \phi, \rho_o, \rho_d, \sigma_o^2, \sigma_d^2$.
3. sample the regional effects parameters θ, ϕ given $\rho_o, \rho_d, \sigma_o^2, \sigma_d^2, \delta, \sigma_\varepsilon^2$.
4. sample the spatial dependence parameters ρ_o, ρ_d given σ_o^2, σ_d^2.
5. sample the spatial effects variances σ_o^2, σ_d^2 given ρ_o, ρ_d.

Given the assumed prior independence of $\delta, \rho_o, \rho_d, \sigma_o^2, \sigma_d^2, \sigma_\varepsilon^2$, we have a joint posterior density for δ shown in (9.14).

$$\begin{aligned} p(\delta|\theta, \phi, \rho_o, \rho_d, \sigma_\varepsilon^2) &\propto \pi(\delta) \\ &\cdot \exp\{-\frac{1}{2\sigma_\varepsilon^2}(y - Z\delta - V\theta - W\phi)'(y - Z\delta - V\theta - W\phi)\} \\ &\propto \exp\{-\frac{1}{2\sigma_\varepsilon^2}(y - Z\delta - V\theta - W\phi)'(y - Z\delta - V\theta - W\phi)\} \\ &\cdot \exp\{-\frac{1}{2}\delta' T^{-1}\delta\} \end{aligned} \quad (9.14)$$

In appendix, we show that this results in a multivariate normal conditional posterior distribution for δ taking the form shown in (9.15).

$$\begin{aligned} \delta|\theta, \phi, \rho_o, \rho_d, \sigma_o^2, \sigma_d^2, \sigma_\varepsilon^2, y, Z &\sim N_k[\Sigma_\delta^{-1}\mu_\delta, \Sigma_\delta^{-1}] \\ \mu_\delta &= \sigma_\varepsilon^{-2} Z'(y - V\theta - W\phi) \\ \Sigma_\delta &= (\sigma_\varepsilon^{-2} Z'Z + T^{-1}) \end{aligned} \quad (9.15)$$

As already noted when discussing the least-squares variant of the model, it is not computationally efficient to work with the n^2 by $3k + 2$ matrix Z which involves repeating the smaller n by k sample data information matrix X through the use of kronecker product. We can rely on a similar moment matrix approach as set forth for the case of least-squares.[6]

Taking a similar approach to that for δ, we have a joint posterior density for θ of the form:

$$\begin{aligned} p(\theta|\delta,\phi,\rho_o,\rho_d,\sigma_\varepsilon^2) &\propto \pi(\theta|\rho_o,\sigma_o^2) \\ &\cdot \exp\{-\frac{1}{2\sigma_\varepsilon^2}[V\theta-(y-Z\delta-W\phi)]'[V\theta-(y-Z\delta-W\phi)]\} \\ &\propto \exp\{-\frac{1}{2\sigma_\varepsilon^2}[V\theta-(y-X\delta-W\phi)]'[V\theta-(y-Z\delta-W\phi)]'\} \\ &\cdot \exp\{-\frac{1}{2\sigma_o^2}\theta' B_o' B_o \theta\} \end{aligned}$$

Which we show in appendix leads to a multivariate normal as the conditional posterior distribution for θ:

$$\begin{aligned} \theta|\delta,\phi,\rho_o,\rho_d,\sigma_o^2,\sigma_d^2,\sigma_\varepsilon^2,y,Z &\sim N_n[\Sigma_\theta^{-1}\mu_\theta,\Sigma_\theta^{-1}] \\ \mu_\theta &= \sigma_\varepsilon^{-2}V'(y-Z\delta-W\phi) \\ \Sigma_\theta &= (\frac{1}{\sigma_o^2}B_o'B_o+\frac{1}{\sigma_\varepsilon^2}V'V) \end{aligned} \tag{9.16}$$

Similarly for the spatial effects vector ϕ we have:

$$\begin{aligned} \phi|\delta,\theta,\rho_o,\rho_d,\sigma_o^2,\sigma_d^2,\sigma_\varepsilon^2,y,Z &\sim N_n[\Sigma_\phi^{-1}\mu_\phi,\Sigma_\phi^{-1}] \\ \mu_\phi &= \sigma_\varepsilon^{-2}W'(y-Z\delta-V\theta) \\ \Sigma_\phi &= (\frac{1}{\sigma_d^2}B_d'B_d+\frac{1}{\sigma_\varepsilon^2}W'W) \end{aligned} \tag{9.17}$$

The joint posterior distributions for ρ_o,ρ_d take the forms:

$$\begin{aligned} p(\rho_o|\delta,\theta,\phi,\sigma_o^2,\sigma_d^2,\rho_d,\sigma_\varepsilon^2,y) &\propto \pi(\theta|\rho_o,\sigma_o^2)\pi(\rho_o) \\ &\propto |B_o|\exp\left(-\frac{1}{2\sigma_o^2}\theta' B_o' B_o\theta\right) \\ p(\rho_d|\delta,\theta,\phi,\sigma_o^2,\sigma_d^2,\rho_o,\sigma_\varepsilon^2,y) &\propto \pi(\phi|\rho_d,\sigma_d^2)\pi(\rho_d) \\ &\propto |B_d|\exp\left(-\frac{1}{2\sigma_d^2}\phi' B_d' B_d\phi\right) \end{aligned} \tag{9.18}$$

[6]For clarity of presentation, we set forth conditional distributions involved in our sampling scheme in vector-matrix notation rather than the moment matrix form.

Which as noted in Smith and LeSage (2004) are not reducible to a standard distribution. We rely on a Metropolis-Hastings sampler for these parameters with a tuned normal random-walk distribution as the proposal density. We note that the determinant term $|B_o| = |I_n - \rho_o D|$, is calculated using the sparse matrix methods of Barrya and Paceb (1997) to compute and store tabled values for this determinant over a grid of q values for ρ_o in the interval $[\kappa_{\min}^{-1}, \kappa_{\max}^{-1}]$. This is done prior to beginning the MCMC sampling loop with table look-up used during sampling, allowing rapid evaluation of candidate values during sampling.

The joint posterior densities for σ_o^2, σ_d^2 take the form:

$$p(\sigma_o^2|\delta,\theta,\phi,\rho_o,\rho_d,\sigma_\varepsilon^2,y,Z) \propto \pi(\theta|\rho_o,\sigma_o^2)\pi(\sigma_o^2)$$
$$\propto (\sigma_o^2)^{-n/2}\exp\left(-\frac{1}{2\sigma_o^2}\theta' B_o' B_o \theta\right)(\sigma_o^2)^{-\frac{q}{2}+\nu_1+1}$$

Which results in an inverse gamma distribution for the conditional posterior. A similar result applies to σ_d^2, with details provided in appendix.

$$\begin{aligned}
\sigma_o^2|\delta,\theta,\phi,\rho_o,\rho_d,\sigma_d^2,\sigma_\varepsilon^2 &\sim IG(a,b)\\
a &= (n/2)+\nu_1\\
b &= \theta' B_o' B_o \theta + 2\nu_2 \qquad (9.19)\\
\sigma_d^2|\delta,\theta,\phi,\rho_o,\rho_d,\sigma_o^2,\sigma_\varepsilon^2 &\sim IG(c,d)\\
c &= (n/2)+\nu_1\\
d &= \phi' B_d' B_d \phi + 2\nu_2 \qquad (9.20)
\end{aligned}$$

Finally, the conditional posterior distribution for the noise variance parameter σ_ε^2 takes the form of an inverse gamma distribution:

$$\begin{aligned}
\sigma_\varepsilon^2|\delta,\theta,\phi,\rho_o,\rho_d,\sigma_d^2,\sigma_o^2,y,Z &\sim IG(e,f)\\
e &= (n/2)+\nu_1\\
f &= \nu'\nu + 2\nu_2 \qquad (9.21)\\
\nu &= y - Z\delta - V\theta - W\phi
\end{aligned}$$

9.3 A Data Generated Example

To illustrate our method, a sample of flows were generated using the model from (9.11) with the latitude-longitude coordinates from our sample of 18 Spanish regions used to produce a spatial weight matrix based on 5 nearest neighbors. The parameters of the model were set to: $\sigma_\varepsilon^2 = 1.5, \sigma_o^2 = 0.75, \sigma_d^2 = 0.5, \rho_o = 0.6, \rho_d = 0.7$.

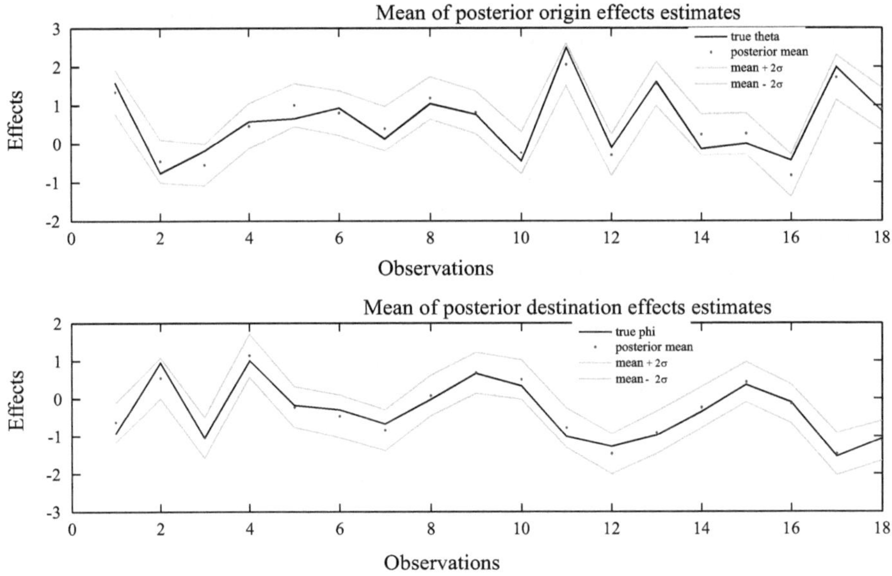

Fig. 9.1 Posterior estimates for origin/destination regional effects parameters

Table 9.1 Posterior estimates for δ

Parameter	Posterior mean	Posterior median	Posterior standard deviation
δ_{o1}, truth $= 1$	0.9907	0.9912	0.0610
δ_{o2}, truth $= -1$	-1.0073	-1.0095	0.0745
δ_{d1}, truth $= -1$	-1.0760	-1.0752	0.0598
δ_{d2}, truth $= 1$	0.9167	0.9179	0.0740

The parameters δ were associated with matrices X_o, X_d which reflected a random normal n by 2 matrix X repeated to form: $X_d = \iota_n \otimes X$ and $X_o = X \otimes \iota_n$. The parameters $\delta = (\delta_o, \delta_d)$ were set to: $\begin{pmatrix} 1 & -1 & -1 & 1 \end{pmatrix}$.[7]

The MCMC sampler was run to produce 5,500 draws with the first 2,500 discarded for burn-in of the sampler. Figure 9.1 shows the posterior means for the spatially structured regional origin and destination effects parameters along with a two standard deviation upper and lower limit. True effects parameters are also shown in the figure, where we see that the posterior means are within the two standard deviation limits.

The posterior means and medians for the parameters δ along with their standard deviations and the true values are presented in Table 9.1. All of the estimates are within two standard deviations of the true values used to generate the data. The medians are near the means, indicating a symmetric posterior distribution.

[7]We exclude the intraregional model from the data generating process as well as estimation procedure.

Table 9.2 Least-squares estimates for δ

Parameter	OLS $\hat{\delta}$	Standard deviation
δ_{o1}, truth = 1	1.0076	0.0861
δ_{o2}, truth = −1	−0.6739	0.1034
δ_{d1}, truth = −1	−1.1367	0.0861
δ_{d2}, truth = 1	0.7416	0.1034

Table 9.3 Posterior estimates for the spatial dependence parameters

Parameter	Posterior mean	Posterior median	Posterior standard deviation
ρ_d, truth = 0.6	0.5701	0.5834	0.2002
ρ_o, truth = 0.7	0.6290	0.6572	0.1986

Table 9.4 Posterior estimates for the variance parameters

Parameter	Posterior mean	Posterior standard deviation
σ_d^2, truth = 0.5	0.5273	0.2041
σ_o^2, truth = 0.75	0.7546	0.2793
σ_ε^2, truth = 1.5	1.4107	0.1122

An interesting contrast to the accurate estimates from the Bayesian hierarchical spatial model are those from ordinary least-squares, shown in Table 9.2. Here, we see two of the four parameter estimates more than two standard deviations away from the true values used to generate the sample data. We note that the spatially structured regional effects vectors θ and ϕ were generated to have a mean of zero, so we would not expect bias in the least-squares estimates. Nevertheless, this appears to be the case here. The least-squares noise estimate for σ_ε^2 was 2.76, with the true value used to generate the data equal to 1.5.

Table 9.3 shows estimates for the parameters ρ_o, ρ_d, and Table 9.4 presents results for the variance parameters $\sigma_o^2, \sigma_d^2, \sigma_\varepsilon^2$. All of these posterior mean estimates are reasonably close to the true values used to generate the sample data.

9.4 An Application to Commodity Flows Between Spanish Regions

Here we present results from applying our methodology to the logged year 2002 commodity flows measured in Euros between 18 Spanish NUTS 2 regions.

9.4.1 The Data

In Spain, like in many other countries, there are no official data on the interregional trade flows. However, there are different estimates produced with alternative methodologies (Oliver et al. 2003; Ghemawat et al. 2010). The data used in this article corresponds to recent estimates produced in the C-intereg project (www.c-intereg.es), by combining the most accurate data on Spanish transport flows of goods by transport modes (road, rail, ship and plane) with additional information regarding export price vectors, one per each region of origin, transport mode and type of product. The methodology also includes a process for debugging the original transport flows database, which allows the identification and reallocation of multi-modal transport flows and international transit flows hidden in the interregional flows. This procedure results in initial estimates of interregional trade flows in tons and euros. Finally, a process of harmonization is applied to produce final figures in tons and euros coherent with figures of total output from the Spanish Industrial Survey and the National Accounts. At each stage the methodology relies on the lowest level of disaggregation available.

The dependent variable was (logged) year 2002 flows within and between the 18 Spanish regions. Explanatory variables used in the model were characteristics of the origin and destination regions: the log of 1995 GDP, the log of year 1995 population density, the log of year 2002 kilometers of motorways in the region standardized by area of the region, foreign exports and imports measured in millions of Euros. In addition, the log of distance between regions constructed as a vectorized version of the OD distance matrix was added.

The population density and 1995 GDP were included to capture size, urban agglomeration and income effects. Foreign export and import trade variables were included as a proxy for openness to trade by the regions. We would expect that more foreign exports at the origin would lead to more interregional flows since this suggests firms have in place administrative structures to facilitate export trade. More foreign imports at the destination might also be positively related to interregional flows because this should correlate with intermediate-final requirements, as well as firms administrative structures to facilitate foreign imports. Since around 90 % of Spanish interregional trade is moved by road, a motorways variable was included to capture regional infrastructure effects of these on commodity flows.

Least-squares estimates are presented in Table 9.5. Posterior estimates from the Bayesian hierarchical model in Table 9.6 are presented using t-statistics and associated probabilities constructed using the posterior means and standard deviations of the MCMC draws for ease of comparison with the least-squares estimates. The r-squared for least-squares was 0.8, suggesting a good fit to the data. All but three of the explanatory variables were significant at the 95 % level or above. Origin and destination GDP in 1995 were both positive and near unity which indicates that interregional trade flows are roughly proportional to this measure of economic size of the regions, consistent with the underlying premise of the gravity model relationship. More foreign exports at the origin exert a positive

Table 9.5 Least-squares gravity model estimates

Variable	Coefficient	*t*-Statistic	*t*-Probability
Constant	−16.1051	−9.505	0.0000
D_GDP95	1.5018	17.262	0.0000
D_PopDensity	−0.1653	−2.238	0.0259
D_Motorways	0.2675	3.308	0.0010
D_Imports	0.3985	2.425	0.0158
D_Exports	−0.0392	−0.271	0.7864
O_GDP95	1.0589	12.172	0.0000
O_PopDensity	0.0237	0.321	0.7482
O_Motorways	0.0603	0.745	0.4564
O_Imports	−0.5913	−3.598	0.0003
O_Exports	0.6057	4.182	0.0000
log(Distance)	−1.2206	−14.995	0.0000

Table 9.6 Bayesian model posterior estimates

Variable	Mean	*t*-Statistic	*t*-Probability
D_GDP95	1.3287	14.3966	0.0000
D_PopDensity	−0.5699	−7.0965	0.0000
D_Motorways	−0.1280	−1.3884	0.1660
D_Imports	0.2137	1.2046	0.2293
D_Exports	−0.0927	−0.5707	0.5686
O_GDP95	0.7356	8.0480	0.0000
O_PopDensity	−0.2437	−2.9809	0.0031
O_Motorways	−0.0399	−0.4220	0.6733
O_Imports	−0.8621	−4.7029	0.0000
O_Exports	0.6992	4.1297	0.0000
log(Distance)	−1.5071	−17.5146	0.0000

impact on interregional exports as expected, whereas more foreign imports at the origins have a negative impact on the interregional deliveries. By contrast, more foreign imports at the destination implies more interregional imports, while foreign exports at the destinations have not significant effects on interregional imports. These results are coherent with previous findings (Llano et al. 2010) that suggest that regions with higher levels of foreign imports (exports) are associated with higher interregional imports (exports). Furthermore, as it was suggested in such previous analysis, the non-significant results for 'D_Exports' and the negative and significant for 'O_imports' are coherent with the inverse signs of the interregional and international trade balance obtained for some regions such as Castilla y León, Castilla-La Mancha, Comunidad-Valenciana, Cataluña or Madrid.

Motorways at the destination have a positive and significant impact on trade flows, while motorways at the origin are not significant. Finally, population density at the destination has a negative impact on interregional trade flows while that for origins is not significant. This suggest less interregional trade flows going to more densely populated regions where we would expect more intraregional flows to take place. Note that small (in surface) but dense populated and single-provincial regions such as Ceuta y Melilla, Madrid, Asturias or the Islands (Canarias and Baleares) are in this group. The insignificant coefficient for origin region population density is probably explained by the fact that some of the largest exporting regions to the rest of Spain are also big regions in terms of surface (Cataluña, País Vasco, Comunidad Valenciana, Castilla y León or Andalucía), whose population density are not among the largest in the country. Logged distance between regions has the expected negative impact on interregional trade flows.

Bayesian estimates are reasonably similar to those from least-squares, with a few exceptions that may be important. Origin and destination 1995 GDP was positive and significant with coefficients near one, but smaller in magnitude than the least-squares estimates. These estimates suggest that destination GDP is nearly twice as important in explaining interregional flows than origin GDP. Motorways are not significant at either the origin or destination, in contrast to least-squares where this coefficient was positive and significant for the destination. Population density at both the origin and destination were negative and significant, perhaps suggesting more intraregional flows for high population density regions and less interregional flows. Like in least-squares, origin region foreign imports exert a negative and significant impact on interregional flows. Origin region foreign exports are positive and significant, suggesting that openness to foreign trade is positively associated with more interregional exports to the rest of the country. Destination region foreign imports and exports are not significant in terms of their influence on interregional trade flows.

A question of interest is whether the origin and destination individual effects exhibit spatial dependence. Table 9.7 shows the posterior estimates for the spatial dependence parameters. Posterior means, medians and standard deviations are presented along with t-statistics constructed using the standard deviations.

From the table we see that destination effects exhibit positive and significant spatial dependence, while origin effects exhibit positive but weak and possibly not significant dependence. These positive dependence estimates indicate that latent or unobserved variables are at work at destinations to create effects estimates that are similar to those from regions neighboring the destinations. In our view, this result is in line with the geographical structure of the Spanish interregional flows, where: (1) some regions, such as Cataluña, Madrid, Comunidad Valenciana or País Vasco, accumulate a large share of the outflows and are not surrounded by other regions

Table 9.7 Bayesian model posterior estimates

Parameter	Mean	Median	Standard deviation	t-Statistic
ρ_d	0.4883	0.5080	0.2208	2.2115
ρ_o	0.3386	0.3035	0.2239	1.5123
σ_d^2	0.3743		0.1841	2.0331
σ_o^2	0.8551		0.3681	2.3230
σ_ε^2	1.9850		0.1602	12.3908

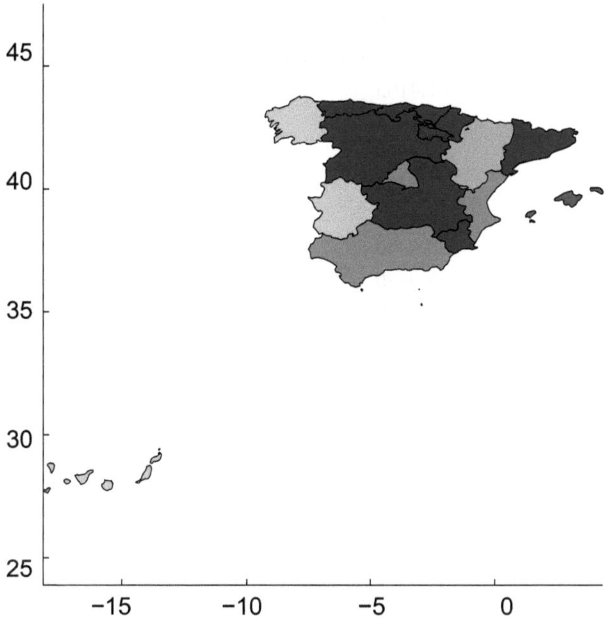

Fig. 9.2 Map of posterior estimates for origin effects parameters

with strong interregional exports; (2) while the main importing regions are clustered together in the western and southern part of the country. This spatial pattern will be clear in Figs. 9.2 and 9.4.

The posterior mean origin and destination effects estimates by regions are presented in Tables 9.8 and 9.9 along with 0.05 and 0.95 credible intervals for these parameters constructed using the sample of draws. A positive effects parameter for the origin (destination) suggests that unobserved forces would lead to higher commodity flow levels at origin (destination) than predicted by the explanatory variables reflecting regional characteristics. Regions that have positive origin and destination effects parameters are those that exhibit higher levels of commodity flows not explained by their characteristics alone. These regions could have some natural advantage or benefit from spatial spillovers. In contrast, regions with negative effects parameters experience levels of commodity flows lower than would be expected given their regional characteristics. These regions could be experiencing a natural disadvantage or suffer from adverse spatial spillovers.

In terms of the origin effects parameters shown in Table 9.8, (also mapped in Fig. 9.2 with accompanying legend in Fig. 9.3) we see six negative and significant regional effects (Aragón, Balears, Castilla Y León, Castilla-La Mancha, Extremadura and Ceuta y Melilla) and no positive and significant effects. The map makes it clear that the negative and significant effects estimates are pointing to two island regions (Balears, Canarias) and two other peripheral regions located on the eastern border of Spain (Extremadura and Galicia). This is consistent with the

Table 9.8 Bayesian model posterior origin effects estimates

Region	0.05 HPDI interval	Mean	0.95 HPDI interval
Andalucia	−1.4105	−0.7045	0.0015
Aragon	−1.9017	−1.2078	−0.5140
Asturias (Principado de)	−0.8699	−0.1944	0.4811
Balears (Illes)	−3.0338	−2.3332	−1.6327
Canarias	−0.7961	−0.0276	0.7408
Cantabria	−0.8440	−0.1659	0.5122
Castilla y leon	−2.0980	−1.3756	−0.6532
Castilla-La Mancha	−2.0612	−1.3581	−0.6550
Cataluña	−0.8102	−0.0977	0.6148
Comunidad Valenciana	−1.0164	−0.3483	0.3199
Extremadura	−2.3244	−1.5877	−0.8511
Galicia	−0.5959	0.0695	0.7348
Madrid (Comunidad de)	−0.8803	−0.1110	0.6583
Murcia (Region de)	−0.9732	−0.2563	0.4605
Navarra (C. Foral de)	−1.0243	−0.3735	0.2774
Pais Vasco	−0.4113	0.2529	0.9172
Rioja (LA)	−1.3142	−0.5724	0.1694
Ceuta y Melilla	−2.3218	−1.4922	−0.6625

Table 9.9 Bayesian model posterior destination effects estimates

Region	0.05 HPDI interval	Mean	0.95 HPDI interval
Andalucia	0.0766	0.7187	1.3608
Aragon	−0.5562	0.0653	0.6868
Asturias (Principado de)	−0.3995	0.2126	0.8247
Balears (Illes)	−1.2403	−0.6190	0.0024
Canarias	0.0614	0.7607	1.4600
Cantabria	−0.1628	0.4704	1.1037
Castilla y Leon	−1.0215	−0.3497	0.3221
Castilla-La Mancha	−0.6487	−0.0163	0.6161
Cataluña	0.1153	0.7621	1.4088
Comunidad Valenciana	0.1845	0.8258	1.4672
Extremadura	−0.9758	−0.2921	0.3915
Galicia	0.0091	0.6146	1.2201
Madrid (Comunidad de)	−0.2086	0.4573	1.1232
Murcia (Region de)	−0.5898	0.0513	0.6923
Navarra (C. Foral de)	−0.6849	−0.0870	0.5110
Pais Vasco	0.0345	0.6742	1.3138
Rioja (La)	−0.5113	0.1601	0.8316
Ceuta y Melilla	−0.7844	−0.0317	0.7211

Fig. 9.3 Histogram legend for origin effects parameters

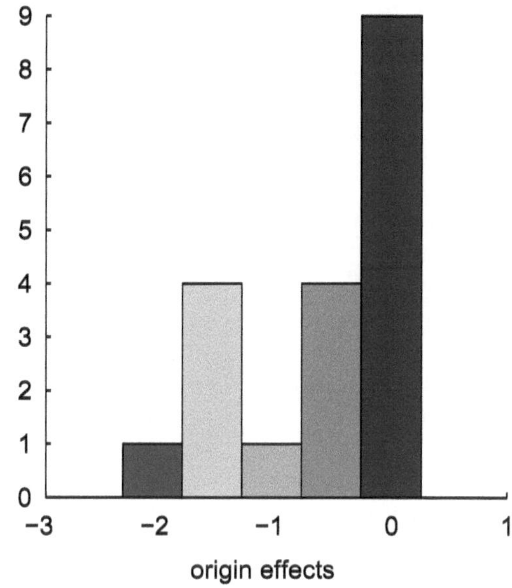

notion that the regional effects estimates point to regions with physical/geographical disadvantages regarding origins of interregional trade flows. The negative and significant effects suggests that interregional flows originating from these regions are smaller than one would expect given regional characteristics and distance alone. Of course, our model does not include an explanatory variable indicating the friction that arises for the two island locations. Consistent with earlier comments regarding the relationship of our spatial autoregressive prior and Bonacich centrality, the map shows effects magnitudes that are near zero (not significantly different from zero) for regions located more centrally in Spain, and the negative effects for eastern border regions is also consistent with a lack of centrality (Table 9.10).

The destination effects in Table 9.9 (also mapped in Fig. 9.4 with accompanying legend in Fig. 9.5) show only positive and significant regional effects for six regions (Andalucía, Canarias, Cataluña, Comunidad Valenciana, Galicia and País Vasco). However, the map shows that negative but not significant effects are indicated for the island region of Balears and the eastern border region Castilla Y León.

The positive effects observed in País Vasco, Cataluña and Comunidad Valenciana may be explained by the importance of their ports. Moreover, both País Vasco and Cataluña play a role as importing hubs from international markets, being surrounded by other important importing regions such as Cantabria, Navarra, Castilla y León or la Rioja (for the País Vasco), or Aragón and Comunidad Valenciana (for Cataluña). The sectoral and geographical specificities of these regions may explain the higher interregional imports of their neighbors, resulting in flows that would be higher than predicted by the destination characteristics included in the X_d matrix of explanatory variables. Of course, Cataluña is the home of Barcelona, and the main entree-door to the rest of Europe by road.

Table 9.10 Bayesian model posterior origin + destination effects estimates

Region	0.05 HPDI interval	Mean	0.95 HPDI interval
Andalucia	−0.9518	0.0142	0.9802
Aragon	−2.1025	−1.1425	−0.1826
Asturias (Principado de)	−0.8983	0.0182	0.9347
Balears (Illes)	−3.9166	−2.9522	−1.9879
Canarias	−0.3131	0.7331	1.7792
Cantabria	−0.6434	0.3045	1.2525
Castilla y Leon	−2.7152	−1.7254	−0.7355
Castilla-La Mancha	−2.3331	−1.3743	−0.4156
Cataluña	−0.2762	0.6644	1.6051
Comunidad Valenciana	−0.4600	0.4776	1.4152
Extremadura	−2.8785	−1.8799	−0.8813
Galicia	−0.2394	0.6841	1.6075
Madrid (Comunidad de)	−0.6813	0.3463	1.3740
Murcia (Region de)	−1.1733	−0.2050	0.7632
Navarra (C. Foral de)	−1.3549	−0.4604	0.4341
Pais Vasco	−0.0037	0.9271	1.8579
Rioja (La)	−1.4412	−0.4122	0.6167
Ceuta y Melilla	−2.6561	−1.5238	−0.3916

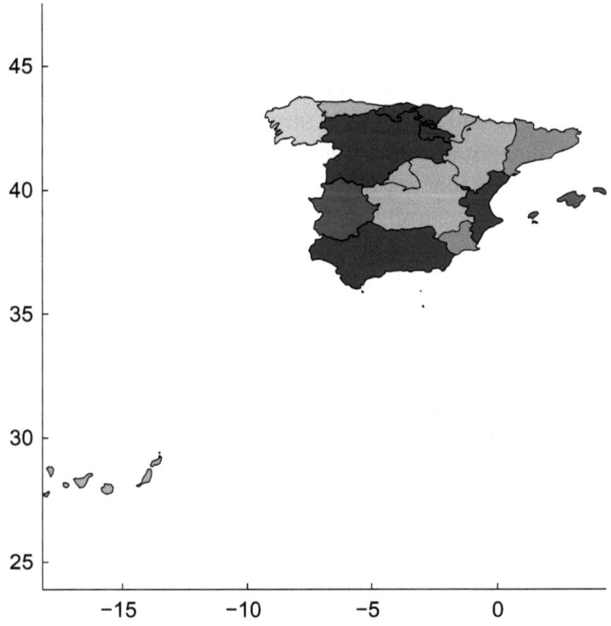

Fig. 9.4 Map of posterior estimates for destination effects parameters

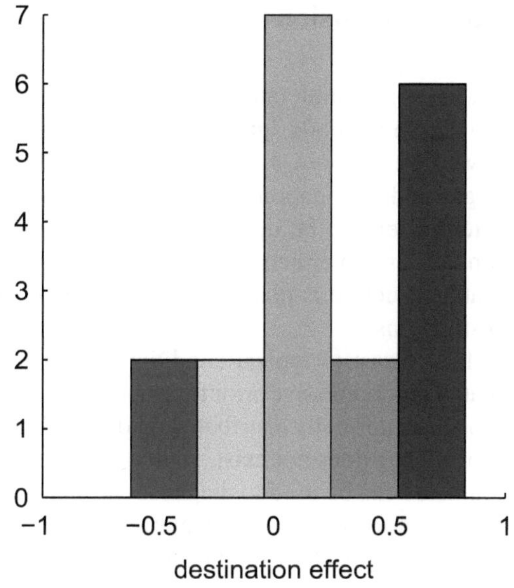

Fig. 9.5 Histogram legend for destination effects parameters

In addition to the two tables presenting origin and destination effects estimates a third table shows the posterior mean for the sum of both origin and destination effects along with 0.05 and 0.95 credible intervals. This was constructed using the sum of the draws for both origin and destination effects. Positive values for these combined parameter estimates provide us with an indication of which regions benefit from unobserved positive forces at work that lead to high levels of interregional commodity flows that originate and terminate in the region. Similarly, negative combined values for these parameters point to regions that suffer disadvantages leading to lower interregional commodity flow levels.

The combined effects in Table 9.10 shows six negative and no positive and significant effects parameters. Consistent with the discussion above, this final picture may capture the presence of possible disadvantages in those regions characterized by a relative backwardness in terms of income and accessibility that are located relatively far from the main axis of development (Mediterranean Arc; Ebro-Valley) and the most powerful regions in terms of production and trade (Madrid, Cataluña, Andalucía, Comunidad Valenciana).

In conclusion, the spatial effects estimates based on our model of commodity flows aggregated across all commodity types seem plausible in that they were able to capture the most salient feature of Spanish interregional trade. This is seen in the concentration of flows within the eastern part of the country. In addition, the model demonstrated the significance of distance and the origin-destination characteristics of regions in explaining variation in the flows. (Nearly 80 % of the variation in flows was explained by the model.)

Future work based on specific types of commodities as well as classification of goods into final or intermediate products may be important.

9.5 Conclusions

Gravity or spatial interaction models have traditionally relied on least-squares estimation methods, ignoring the issue of spatial dependence between interregional flows. We propose a modeling methodology that introduces spatially structured origin and destination region effects parameters. These parameters allow spatial heterogeneity to be modeled in such a way that regions treated as origins exhibit similar random effects levels to those of regions that neighbor the origins. A similar spatial structure is placed on random effects parameters for the regions viewed as destinations.

In contrast to typical conditional autoregressive spatial structure we rely on a spatial autoregressive prior to structure the random effects parameters. Our approach subsumes normally distributed random effects models as a special case when spatial dependence does not exist, so that $\rho_o = \rho_d = 0$. In addition, the effects parameter estimates can be used to diagnose the presence of positive or negative unobservable latent factors that influence interregional commodity flows.

In an application of the method to commodity flows among a sample of 18 Spanish regions, we found that least-squares estimates of the role played by regional characteristics differ greatly from those found by our Bayesian hierarchical spatial effects model. Introduction of the spatially structured random effects that account for heterogeneity across the regions appear to produce more efficient parameter estimates for the characteristics parameters.

Appendix: Details Regarding the MCMC Sampler

First, we show that the conditional posterior for δ takes the multivariate form presented in the text.

$$
\begin{aligned}
p(\delta|\theta, \phi, \rho_o, \rho_d, \sigma_o^2, \sigma_d^2, \sigma_\varepsilon^2) &\propto \pi(\delta) \\
&\cdot \exp\{-\frac{1}{2\sigma^2\varepsilon}(y - Z\delta - V\theta - W\phi)'(y - Z\delta - V\theta - W\phi)\} \\
&\propto \exp\{-\frac{1}{2\sigma^2\varepsilon}(y - Z\delta - V\theta - W\phi)'(y - Z\delta - V\theta - W\phi)\} \\
&\cdot \exp\{-\frac{1}{2\sigma^2\varepsilon}\delta' T^{-1}\delta\} \\
&\propto \exp\left(-\frac{1}{2\sigma^2\varepsilon}[\delta'(Z'Z + T^{-1})\delta - 2Z'(y - V\theta - W\phi)'\delta]\right) \\
&\propto \exp\left(-\frac{1}{2\sigma^2\varepsilon}[\delta - \Sigma_\delta^{-1}\mu_\delta]'\Sigma_\delta[\delta - \Sigma_\delta^{-1}\mu_\delta]\right)
\end{aligned}
$$

Where as reported in the text:

$$\mu_\delta = \frac{1}{\sigma^2 \varepsilon} Z'(y - V\theta - W\phi)$$
$$\Sigma_\delta = \frac{1}{\sigma^2 \varepsilon}(Z'Z + T^{-1})$$

In this appendix we follow Smith and LeSage (2004) in deriving the conditional posterior for the spatial autoregressive effects parameters θ. They note that:

$$\begin{aligned} p(\theta|\ldots) &\propto \exp\left(-\frac{1}{2\sigma_\varepsilon^2}[V\theta - (y - Z\delta - W\phi)]'[V\theta - (y - Z\delta - W\phi)]\right) \\ &\cdot \exp\left(-\frac{1}{2\sigma_o^2}\theta' B_o' B_o \theta\right) \\ &\propto \exp\left(-\frac{1}{2\sigma_\varepsilon^2}[\theta' V' V\theta - 2(y - Z\delta - W\phi)' V\theta + \theta'(\sigma_o^{-2} B_o' B_o)\theta]\right) \\ &= \exp\left(-\frac{1}{2\sigma_\varepsilon^2}[\theta'(\sigma_o^{-2} B_o' B_o + V'V)\theta - 2(y - Z\delta - W\phi)' V\theta]\right) \end{aligned}$$

from which it follows that:

$$\begin{aligned} \theta|\delta, \phi, \rho_o, \rho_d, \sigma_o^2, \sigma_d^2, \sigma_\varepsilon^2, y, Z &\sim N_n[\Sigma_\theta^{-1}\mu_\theta, \Sigma_\theta^{-1}] \\ \mu_\theta &= \sigma_\varepsilon^{-2} V'(y - Z\delta - W\phi) \\ \Sigma_\theta &= (\frac{1}{\sigma_o^2} B_o' B_o + \frac{1}{\sigma_\varepsilon^2} V'V) \end{aligned} \tag{9.22}$$

The conditional posteriors for σ_o^2, σ_d^2:

$$\begin{aligned} p(\sigma_o^2|\ldots) &\propto \pi(\theta|\rho_o, \sigma_o^2)\pi(\sigma_o^2) \\ &\propto (\sigma_o^2)^{-n/2} \exp\left(-\frac{1}{2\sigma_o^2}\theta' B_o' B_o \theta\right)(\sigma_o^2)^{\nu_1+1} \exp\left(-\frac{\nu_2}{\sigma_o^2}\right) \\ &\propto (\sigma_o^2)^{-(\frac{n}{2}+\nu_1+1)} \exp[-\theta' B_o' B_o \theta + \frac{2\nu_2}{2\sigma_o^2}] \end{aligned}$$

Which is proportional to the inverse gamma distribution reported in the text. A similar approach leads to $p(\sigma_d^2|\ldots)$, and the conditional posterior for σ_ε^2:

$$p(\sigma_\varepsilon^2|\ldots) \propto (\sigma_\varepsilon^2)^{-n/2}\exp\left(-\frac{1}{2\sigma_\varepsilon^2}e'e\right)(\sigma_\varepsilon^2)^{\nu_1+1}\exp\left(-\frac{\nu_2}{\sigma_\varepsilon^2}\right)$$

$$\propto (\sigma_\varepsilon^2)^{-(\frac{n}{2}+\nu_1+1)}\exp[-e'e+\frac{2\nu_2}{2\sigma_\varepsilon^2}]$$

$$e = y - Z\delta - V\theta - W\phi$$

References

Ballester C, Calvó-Armengol A, Zenou Y (2006) Who's who in networks. Wanted: the key player. Econometrica 74:1403–1417

Banerjee S, Gelfand AE, Polasek W (2000) Geostatistical modelling for spatial interaction data with application to postal service performance. J Stat Plan Infer 90:87–105

Banerjee S, Carlin BP, Gelfand AE (2004) Hierarchical modeling and analysis for spatial data. Chapman & Hall/CRC, Boca Raton

Barrya RP, Paceb RK (1997) Kriging with large data sets using sparse matrix techniques. Commun Stat Simulat 26:619–629

Besag JE, Kooperberg CL (1995) On conditional and intrinsic autoregressions. Biometrika 82:733–746

Besag JE, York JC, Mollie A (1991) Bayesian image restoration, with two applications in spatial statistics (with discussion). Ann Inst Stat Math 43:1–59

Bonacich PB (1987) Power and centrality: a family of measures. Am J Sociol 92:1170–1182

Cressie N (1995) Bayesian smoothing of rates in small geographic areas. J Reg Sci 35:659–673

Fischer MM, Scherngell T, Jansenberger E (2006) The geography of knowledge spillovers between high-technology firms in Europe: evidence from a spatial interaction modeling perspective. Geogr Anal 38(3):288–309

Gelfand AE, Sahu S, Carlin BP (1995) Efficient parameterizations for normal linear mixed models. Biometrika 82(3):479–488

Ghemawat P, Llano-Verduras C, Requena-Silventre F (2010) Competitiveness and interregional as well as and international trade: the case of Catalonia. Int J Ind Organ 28:415–422

LeSage JP, Pace RK (2008) Spatial econometric modeling of origin-destination flows. J Reg Sci 48(5):941–967

LeSage JP, Fischer MM, Scherngell T (2007) Knowledge Spillovers across Europe, evidence from a poisson spatial interaction model with spatial effects. Pap Reg Sci 86(3):393–421

Llano C, Esteban A, Pulido A, Pérez J (2010) Opening the interregional trade black box: the c-intereg database for the spanish economy (1995–2005). Int Reg Sci Rev 33:302–337

Oliver J, Luria J, Roca A, Pérez J (2003) In: lo Blanch T (ed) en La apertura exterior de las regiones en España: evolución del comercio interregional e internacional de las Comunidades Autónomas, 1995–1998. Institut dÉstudis Autonòmics, Generalitat de Catalunya, Valencia

Sen A, Smith TE (1995) Gravity models of spatial interaction behavior. Springer, Heidelberg

Smith TE, LeSage JP (2004) A Bayesian probit model with spatial dependencies. In: LeSage JP, Pace RK (eds) Advances in econometrics: spatial and spatiotemporal econometrics, vol 18. Elsevier, Oxford, pp 127–160

Sun D, Tsutakawa RK, Speckman PL (1999) Posterior distribution of hierarchical models using car(1) distributions. Biometrika 86:341–350

Sun D, Tsutakawa RK, Kim H, He Z (2000) Bayesian analysis of mortality rates with disease maps. Stat Med 19:2015–2035

Tiefelsdorf M (2003) Misspecifications in interaction model distance decay relations: a spatial structure effect. J Geogr Syst 5:25–50

Chapter 10
Bayesian Variable Selection in a Large Vector Autoregression for Origin-Destination Traffic Flow Modelling

Minfeng Deng

Keywords Bayesian • Variable selection • Vector autoregressive model • Traffic

JEL Classifications: C11, C21, R41

10.1 Introduction

Modelling and forecasting of traffic conditions are very important for everyday life in metropolitan areas, particularly for large cities. For commuters, obtaining reliable real time traffic information and accurate short term traffic forecasts allow for a smoother ride on the road. In fact, when a person checks Google Maps for real time traffic conditions, she is implicitly making her own traffic forecasts using current traffic conditions as predictors. The directed nature of traffic flow also implies that certain upstream or downstream traffics are more important as predictors than others, and it would be beneficial for a commuter to know which ones they are. For urban planners, it is important to know where and why congestions occur regularly in certain parts of the traffic network, so that road network infrastructure improvements can be made. For the police, it might be of great interest to simulate scenarios in which a part of the traffic network is blocked off due to road accidents or signal faults. Traffic network sensitivity analysis of this kind can be performed if a complete stochastic model for the traffic network is available.

It is noted that traffic flow modelling faces a number of non-trivial methodological challenges. Firstly, both temporal and spatial dependence are important. It is possible that a street that was congested 10 min ago could still be congested. It is also possible that when all the streets within a 1 km radius are congested your current street could be congested too. The need to jointly account for temporal and spatial

M. Deng (✉)
Department of Statistics, Data Science & Epidemiology, Faculty of Health, Arts & Design, Swinburne University of Technology, Melbourne, VIC, Australia
e-mail: gary.dengmf@gmail.com

R. Patuelli, G. Arbia (eds.), *Spatial Econometric Interaction Modelling*, Advances in Spatial Science, DOI 10.1007/978-3-319-30196-9_10

dependence has lead to the application of the so-called space-time autoregressive integrated moving average (STARIMA) methodology in traffic flow forecasting, for instance see Kamarianakis and Prastacos (2005), Kamarianakis et al. (2005), and Ding et al. (2011). The STARIMA methodology was originally due to Pfeifer and Deutsch (1980a, b, 1981a, b) and is a multivariate extension of the univariate ARIMA (autoregressive integrated moving average) methodology. To illustrate, assume that there are N traffic flows under consideration, and for simplicity assume that they are all stationary, mean-deviated, absent of seasonality, and containing only first order lagged dynamics, a STARIMA(1_1,0,1_1) model for traffic flow forecasting can be written as:

$$y_t = \phi_{10} y_{t-1} + \phi_{11} W_1 y_{t-1} + \varepsilon_t - \theta_{10}\varepsilon_{t-1} - \theta_{11} W_1 \varepsilon_{t-1}, \quad t = 1, \ldots, T \qquad (10.1)$$

where y_t is an $(N \times 1)$ vector of observed traffic flows at time t. W_1 is known as the spatial weights matrix and is of dimension $(N \times N)$. W_1 identifies the first order spatial relationships between the N traffic series, and $W_{1,ij}$ takes on a nonzero value when traffic series i and j are spatially contiguous in some sense. Typically, the closer i and j are, the larger $W_{1,ij}$ is. Thus, the inclusion of y_{t-1} and ε_{t-1} accounts for own lagged dynamics, and the inclusion of $W_1 y_{t-1}$ and $W_1 \varepsilon_{t-1}$ accounts for lagged dynamics of spatial neighbours. $\{\phi_{10}, \phi_{11}, \theta_{10}, \theta_{11}\}$ are all scalar coefficients. The above STARIMA model provides a parsimonious model that captures both temporal and spatial dynamics, and it has been shown to produce more accurate traffic flow forecasts when compared with univariate alternatives.

Another important feature of a traffic network is its origin-destination (OD) flow structure. Every traffic flow has an origin and a destination, and for any two connected traffic flows, one flow's destination is another flow's origin. The connected nature of a traffic network is important, as it provides useful information on the direction in which high level of correlation is expected to exist. While the STARIMA model accounts for both temporal and spatial dynamics, it uses averages of spatial neighbourhood values as predictors and therefore it does not explicitly recognize the connected origin-destination flow nature of the data. It is noted that OD flow regression modelling has a long history and has its origin in spatial interaction models. For instance, Bolduc et al. (1989) and Bolduc et al. (1992) provide excellent examples of OD travel flow modelling, and Griffith (2007) provides an extensive review of the literature. Following the notation of Bolduc et al. (1992), an OD travel flow model can be written as follows:

$$y_{ij} = \beta_0 + N_{ij}\beta_1 + S_i\beta_2 + S_j\beta_3 + \varepsilon_{ij} \qquad (10.2)$$

where y_{ij} is the observed flow from origin i to destination j. N_{ij} contains network-specific explanatory factors, S_i contains origin-specific factors, and S_j contains destination-specific factors. Porojan (2001), LeSage and Pace (2008), LeSage and Polasek (2008), and LeSage and Fischer (2010) provide detailed discussions on the econometric framework. The OD model of Eq. (10.2) has the advantage of explicitly accounting for the directed nature of flow data. However, empirically

OD flow modelling has been applied primarily in a cross-sectional setting. Deng and Athanasopoulos (2010) is one of the few exceptions, where origin-destination international inbound tourism flows are modelled using a dynamic spatial panel.

10.1.1 A VAR Model for Traffic Flows

Given the importance of both temporal dependence and origin-destination connectivity of a traffic network, one might consider specifying traffic flow as a function of temporally lagged values of all other traffic flows in the system. In doing so, one would have arrived at a vector autoregression (VAR) model. Specifically,

$$y_t = \mathrm{M} + \Phi_1 y_{t-1} + \Phi_2 y_{t-2} + \cdots + \Phi_p y_{t-p} + \varepsilon_t, \quad t = 1, \ldots, T \tag{10.3}$$

where y_t contains N observed traffic flows at time t and is explained by up to p temporally lagged values of y_t. ε_t is an $(N \times 1)$ vector of independently, identically and normally distributed errors with variance-covariance matrix Σ, i.e., $\varepsilon_t \sim iidN(0, \Sigma)$. $\Phi_l\ (l = 1, \ldots, p)$ are $(N \times N)$ matrices of unknown coefficients and M is an $(N \times 1)$ vector of intercepts. Pfeifer and Bodily (1990) and Giacomini and Granger (2004) show that the STARIMA model is a restricted case of vector autoregressive integrated moving average (VARIMA) models, which includes the VAR model of Eq. (10.3).

The literature on VAR, originally due to Sims (1972, 1980), is extensive and will not be reviewed in great detail in this paper. VAR models offer a flexible and easy to use alternative to multivariate time series modelling, but the problem of 'overfitting' of VAR has often limited its empirical application to a small number of equations. It is clear that the number of unknowns in Eq. (10.3) grows geometrically with N and proportionally with lag length p, and a serious consequence of 'overfitting' is imprecise estimation of Φ_l, which could lead to wildly inaccurate forecasts. This is bad news for traffic flow modelling and forecasting, since in any realistic empirical application the number of flows in a traffic system would be sizable.

10.1.2 Bayesian VARs

Litterman (1980, 1986) advocates a Bayesian approach to VAR estimation as a solution to 'overfitting' of VAR in the context of macroeconomic forecasting. In particular, the so-called Minnesota prior (Doan et al. 1984; Litterman 1986) relies on well-known statistical properties of macroeconomic time series and imposes stylized priors on elements of Φ_l. Specifically, prior means are set to unity for own lags while zero for other lags, reflecting the belief that many macroeconomic series follow a random walk and that own lags are more important as predictors than other lags. Furthermore, a small number of hyper parameters are used to control the tightness of the priors around their means. As a result, generally speaking more recent lags are given more weight than distant lags, and own lags are given more weight than lags of other variables. Assuming that this prior information is neither too vague nor too informative, it will only be overwhelmed by 'signal' instead of 'noise' in the data. Empirically, it has been shown that Bayesian VAR with Minnesota prior often performs well in forecasting, for instance see Alvarez and Ballabriga (1994). Amongst others, Kadiyala and Karlsson (1997) provide important extensions to the Bayesian VAR literature, where numerical estimation methods are derived for different forms of priors.

Specifications of the Minnesota prior, while suitable for macroeconomic data, may have little relevance or are ill-suited in another context. It is interesting to note that, for regional studies a spatial prior for Bayesian VARs has been developed in Pan and LeSage (1995), LeSage and Pan (1995), and LeSage and Krivelyova (1999). Specifically, prior means on the Φ matrix are derived directly from the spatial contiguity structure and are equal to the spatial average of neighbouring region coefficients, while prior variances are controlled by a small number of hyper parameters to reflect the decreasing importance of higher lags in both spatial and temporal dimensions. Their formulation offers an attractive alternative to VAR estimation when spatial contiguity is inherent in the data. They show that empirically VARs with spatial priors produce more accurate forecast than traditional Minnesota priors.

Essentially, VARs are heavily parameterized models, and Bayesian estimators with varying forms of priors are shrinkage methods that reduce the risks associated with 'overfitting' by shrinking unlikely predictors towards zero. However, there might be cases where more precise identification of the model space is needed. For instance, it might be of great interest to urban planners to know exactly the directions in which congestion builds up in a traffic network so that they could implement infrastructural changes. Moreover, the directed nature of a traffic network means that even amongst neighbouring flows of the same order of contiguity there could be drastically different degrees of importance. For instance, it is often the case that in any traffic network there are a number of predominant traffic flow directions, and the identification of these directions (in the sense of identifying specific upstream and downstream neighbours) becomes important. Bayesian priors that apply equal shrinkage to lags of the same spatial and temporal order may fail to identify those directions precisely, as they only capture an average spatial effect.

10.1.3 Bayesian Variable Selection

Therefore, there appears to be a need for variable selection in VAR modelling, in the sense that one would want to completely zero out a large number of elements in Φ_l in Eq. (10.3). An extensive literature exists on variable selection in Bayesian statistics, a complete survey of which is beyond the scope of this paper. In a univariate setting, George and McCulloch (1993), Smith and Kohn (1996), Geweke (1996), and Cui and George (2008) provide detailed discussions on sampling procedures for Bayesian variable selection. Liang et al. (2008) provide a comprehensive summary of state of the art Bayesian methods involving mixtures of Zellner's g prior (1986) for Bayesian variable selection. In a multivariate setting, Brown and Vannucci (1998) illustrate the application of multivariate Bayesian variable selection in compositional analysis of three sugars with 160 infra-red absorbances as regressors. Korobilis (2013) is perhaps the only example in which Bayesian variable selection is used explicitly in VAR forecasting.

In this paper, a complete Bayesian variable selection methodology for VAR will be developed, with specific application in, though in theory not limited to, traffic flow modelling. Markov Chain Monte Carlo sampling procedure will be discussed at length. A simulation study demonstrates that the estimated posterior distribution over the model space corresponds closely to the true connectivity of the underlying traffic network, and the posterior distribution of the coefficient vector largely avoids the issues associated with 'overfitting'.

10.2 Bayesian Variable Selection in VAR

10.2.1 The Model

To illustrate the proposed method for Bayesian variable selection in VAR, consider the closed traffic network in Fig. 10.1.

There are six intersections and $N = 14$ traffic flows in total (not allowing for U-turns). For the sake of simplicity and without loss of generality, let temporal lag effect be limited to order 1, we have a VAR(1) model:

$$y_t = \mathrm{M} + \Phi_1 y_{t-1} + \varepsilon_t, \quad t = 1, \ldots, T \tag{10.4}$$

where y_t is (14×1). ε_t is iid normal with a (14×14) variance-covariance matrix Σ. In particular, Σ needs not be diagonal, and its nonzero off-diagonal elements capture important contemporaneous correlations between traffic flows. M is a (14×1) vector of intercepts. Φ_1 is a (14×14) coefficient matrix. Even in this simple example, the total number of unknowns (excluding the nuisance parameters in Σ) is $(14^2 + 14)$ and is sizable, making precise estimation difficult.

The first step is to utilize the connectivity of the traffic network to zero out some of the elements in Φ_1. Define $y_{ij,t}$ as the traffic flow from intersection i to intersection j at time t, and suppose that we can reasonably assume that only: (1) own lagged traffic flow, i.e., $y_{ij,t-1}$; (2) lagged traffic flows of immediate upstream neighbours, i.e., $y_{li,t-1}, l \neq i$; (3) lagged traffic flows of immediate downstream neighbours, i.e., $y_{jl,t-1}, l \neq j$; are considered potential predictors, we arrive at a full set of potential predictors as listed in the third column in Table 10.1.

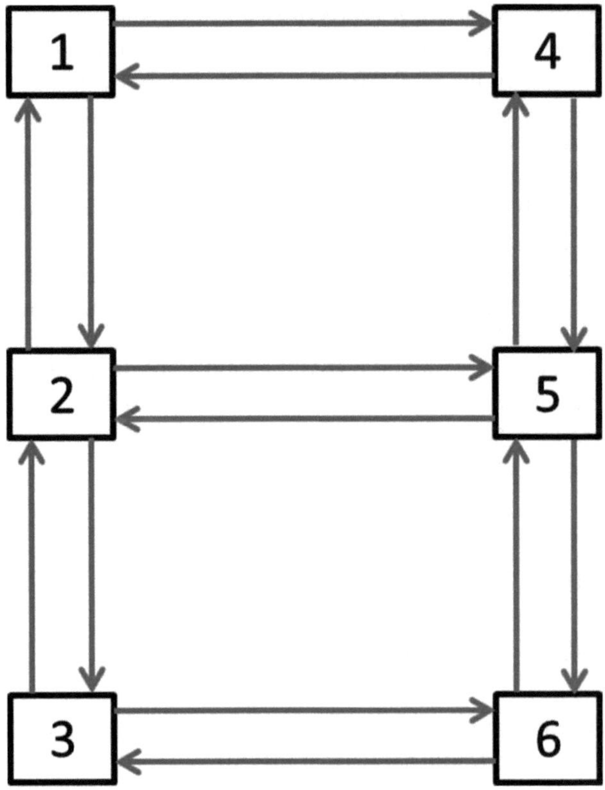

Fig. 10.1 A hypothetical traffic network, with 6 intersections and 14 traffic flows in total

For example, for traffic flow $y_{25,t}$, its potential predictors are: (1) own lag $\{y_{25,t-1}\}$; (2) lagged upstream neighbours $\{y_{12,t-1}; y_{32,t-1}\}$; (3) lagged downstream neighbours $\{y_{54,t-1}; y_{56,t-1}\}$. By utilizing the known structure of the traffic network, the total number of predictors in the VAR model (equivalently the number of unknowns in Φ_1), has been reduced from 14^2 to 54 (the total number of predictors listed in the third column in Table 10.1), which is still a sizable number.

Now suppose that the 'true' traffic conditions are as shown in Fig. 10.2, in which the dashed arrows represent dominant traffic flow in one direction, and the solid arrows represent a second dominant traffic flow in another direction.

While the example is meant to be a stylized representation of a traffic network, one could imagine a scenario where: (1) office buildings are positioned near both intersection 1 and 3 while residential units near intersection 6, thus creating traffic leaving work for home along the dashed arrows; (2) a football stadium is positioned near intersection 1, thus creating traffic going from the residential units towards the stadium along the solid arrows. If we further assume that traffics on any street are allowed to clear within discrete time period t and that the own lagged values are not important, the set of 'true' predictors for this traffic network can be found in

Table 10.1 The second column contains all 14 traffic flows in the system as specified in Fig. 10.1

Flow ID	$y_{ij,t}$	$X_{ij,t}$: full set of potential predictors	$X_{ij,t}$: upstream	$X_{ij,t}$: downstream
1	$y_{12,t}$	$y_{12,t-1}, y_{41,t-1}, y_{23,t-1}, y_{25,t-1}$		$y_{25,t-1}$
2	$y_{23,t}$	$y_{23,t-1}, y_{12,t-1}, y_{32,t-1}, y_{36,t-1}$		
3	$y_{36,t}$	$y_{36,t-1}, y_{23,t-1}, y_{65,t-1}$		
4	$y_{65,t}$	$y_{65,t-1}, y_{36,t-1}, y_{52,t-1}, y_{54,t-1}$		$y_{54,t-1}$
5	$y_{54,t}$	$y_{54,t-1}, y_{65,t-1}, y_{25,t-1}, y_{41,t-1}$	$y_{65,t-1}$	$y_{41,t-1}$
6	$y_{41,t}$	$y_{41,t-1}, y_{54,t-1}, y_{12,t-1}$	$y_{54,t-1}$	
7	$y_{14,t}$	$y_{14,t-1}, y_{21,t-1}, y_{45,t-1}$		
8	$y_{45,t}$	$y_{45,t-1}, y_{14,t-1}, y_{52,t-1}, y_{56,t-1}$		
9	$y_{56,t}$	$y_{56,t-1}, y_{45,t-1}, y_{25,t-1}, y_{63,t-1}$	$y_{25,t-1}$	
10	$y_{63,t}$	$y_{63,t-1}, y_{56,t-1}, y_{32,t-1}$		
11	$y_{32,t}$	$y_{32,t-1}, y_{63,t-1}, y_{21,t-1}, y_{25,t-1}$		$y_{25,t-1}$
12	$y_{21,t}$	$y_{21,t-1}, y_{32,t-1}, y_{52,t-1}, y_{14,t-1}$		
13	$y_{25,t}$	$y_{25,t-1}, y_{12,t-1}, y_{32,t-1}, y_{54,t-1}, y_{56,t-1}$	$y_{12,t-1}, y_{32,t-1}$	$y_{56,t-1}$
14	$y_{52,t}$	$y_{52,t-1}, y_{45,t-1}, y_{65,t-1}, y_{21,t-1}, y_{23,t-1}$		

The third column contains a full list of potential predictors in the VAR. The fourth and fifth columns contain 'true' upstream and downstream predictors respectively

the fourth and fifth column in Table 10.1 for upstream and downstream neighbours respectively. Thus, the 'true' set of predictors only contains 10 variables, and the main methodological issue is to judiciously and consistently select 'true' predictors from the full set of potential predictors, in this case identifying these 10 variables from 54 potential variables.

One could think of many other ways to specify traffic conditions. Moreover, one could easily relax the assumption of a closed system and allow for traffic to merge in and out of the network through tertiary roads. This would not increase the level of modelling difficulty, as auxiliary traffic flows can be treated as additional exogenous predictors on the right-hand side and become part of the model selection process.

One could rewrite the system of equations, in the order the 14 traffic flows are listed in the second column in Table 10.1, as:

$$\begin{bmatrix} y_{12} \\ y_{23} \\ \vdots \\ y_{52} \end{bmatrix} = \begin{bmatrix} 1 & 0 & \cdots & 0 \\ 0 & 1 & \cdots & 0 \\ \vdots & \vdots & \ddots & \vdots \\ 0 & 0 & \cdots & 1 \end{bmatrix} \begin{bmatrix} M_{12} \\ M_{23} \\ \vdots \\ M_{52} \end{bmatrix} + \begin{bmatrix} X_{12} & 0 & \cdots & 0 \\ 0 & X_{23} & \cdots & 0 \\ \vdots & \vdots & \ddots & \vdots \\ 0 & 0 & \cdots & X_{52} \end{bmatrix} \begin{bmatrix} \beta_{12} \\ \beta_{23} \\ \vdots \\ \beta_{52} \end{bmatrix} + \begin{bmatrix} \varepsilon_{12} \\ \varepsilon_{23} \\ \vdots \\ \varepsilon_{52} \end{bmatrix} \tag{10.5}$$

where $y_{ij} = \left[y_{ij,1}, y_{ij,2}, \ldots, y_{ij,T}\right]'$ is a $(T \times 1)$ vector of the observed traffic flow from intersection i to intersection j. 1 is a $(T \times 1)$ vector of 1's. M_{ij} is a scalar constant for the intercept in the equation for y_{ij}. X_{ij} is a $\left(T \times K_{ij}\right)$ matrix of potential predictors, in which the included elements vary and K_{ij} is not constant across equations. For example, for traffic flow y_{25}, $X_{25} = \{y_{25}(-1), y_{12}(-1); y_{32}(-1), y_{54}(-1); y_{56}(-1)\}$ and $K_{25} = 5$. β_{ij} is a $\left(K_{ij} \times 1\right)$

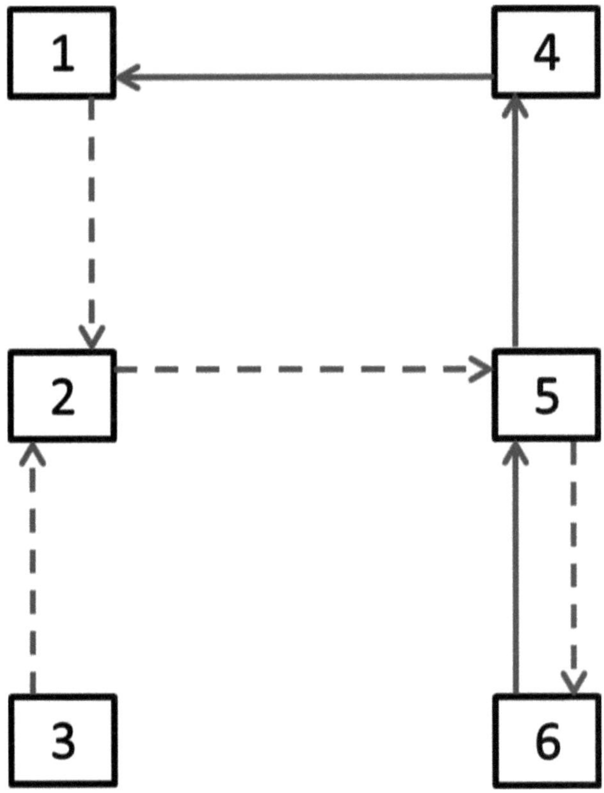

Fig. 10.2 The *dashed arrows* and the *solid arrows* point towards two different dominant traffic flow directions in this hypothesized traffic system

vector of unknown parameters. $\varepsilon_{ij} = \left[\varepsilon_{ij,1}, \varepsilon_{ij,2}, \ldots, \varepsilon_{ij,T}\right]'$ is a $(T \times 1)$ vector of errors terms, which are serially uncorrelated but cross-sectionally correlated, and $\varepsilon_t = [\varepsilon_{12,t}, \varepsilon_{23,t}, \ldots, \varepsilon_{52,t}]' \sim iidN\,(0, \Sigma)$.

Equation (10.5) can be written more succinctly as:

$$Y = \mathbf{1}\mathrm{M} + \mathrm{XB} + E \tag{10.6}$$

where Y is $(NT \times 1)$, $\mathbf{1}$ is $(NT \times N)$, M is $(N \times 1)$, X is $\left(NT \times \sum_{ij} K_{ij}\right)$, B is $\left(\sum_{ij} K_{ij} \times 1\right)$, and E is $(NT \times 1)$. In this example, $\sum_{ij} K_{ij} = 54$. $\varepsilon_t \sim iidN\,(0, \Sigma)$ implies that $E \sim N\,(0, \Sigma \otimes I_T)$.

10.2.2 The Latent Binary Selection Vector

Finally, variable selection will be introduced in the sense of George and McCulloch (1993). Define a latent binary vector γ of dimension $\left(\sum_{ij} K_{ij} \times 1\right)$, where $\gamma_j = 1$ if the jth predictor in **X** is included and $\gamma_j = 0$ otherwise. This γ vector is of great importance, as it allows us to perform selection and make probabilistic statements about the model space of Eq. (10.6). The number of 1's in γ translates directly to the complexity of the selected model. At one extreme, the most complex model contains all potential predictors, in which case $\sum_j \gamma_j = \sum_{ij} K_{ij}$ and the degrees of freedom is the lowest. At another extreme, the most simple model contains zero predictors, in which case $\sum_j \gamma_j = 0$, leaving Eq. (10.6) with just the intercept **1M** and the noise term E. As the number of nonzero elements in γ increases, the fit of the model increases through increased number of predictors, but the trade-off is such that imprecision of coefficient estimates also increases.

10.2.3 The Priors

Bayesian estimation of Eq. (10.6) requires suitably specified prior distributions of the unknown parameters $(\mathrm{M}, \mathrm{B}, \Sigma, \gamma)$. Assuming prior independence between M and B, and between Σ and γ, the joint prior can be broadly decomposed into:

$$p\left(\mathrm{M}, \mathrm{B}, \Sigma, \gamma\right) = p\left(\mathrm{M}\middle|\Sigma\right) \cdot p\left(\mathrm{B}\middle|\Sigma, \gamma\right) \cdot p\left(\Sigma\right) \cdot p\left(\gamma\right) \tag{10.7}$$

The prior for the intercepts vector M is relatively straightforward. Let

$$p\left(M - \overline{M}\middle|\Sigma\right) = N\left(h, \Sigma\right) \tag{10.8}$$

where $\overline{M}$ is an arbitrarily chosen prior mean of M. Brown and Vannucci (1998) show that in the case of a weak prior, h can be set to be large and the intercepts vector can be ignored in the variable selection process. This will be the approach taken in this study, and for notational simplicity for the remainder of this paper the intercept vector will be omitted.

For B and Σ, a vast literature has been devoted to the identification of their suitable priors for Bayesian VAR, a complete survey of which is beyond the scope of this paper. The Minnesota prior (Doan et al. 1984; Litterman 1986) is rooted in macroeconomic theory and seems ill-suited in the current context. The diffuse prior of Kadiyala and Karlsson (1997)

$$p\left(\mathrm{B}, \Sigma\right) \propto \mid \Sigma\mid^{-\frac{N+1}{2}} \tag{10.9}$$

is shown to be computationally straightforward and imposes no restrictions on the structure of the variance-covariance matrix Σ. However, it does not allow for incorporation of our prior belief that a large number of elements in B should be shrunk towards zero. Moreover, as highlighted in Berger and Pericchi (2001) and Liang et al. (2008), improper priors for B are usually not permitted in the context of model selection, as they lead to indeterminate model probabilities and Bayes factors. Another popular choice is the mathematically convenient conjugate Normal-Wishart prior of Kadiyala and Karlsson (1997)

$$p\left(\mathrm{B}\middle|\Sigma\right) = N\left(\overline{\mathrm{B}}, \Sigma \otimes \overline{\Omega}\right), p\left(\Sigma\right) = iW\left(\overline{\Sigma}, \alpha\right) \tag{10.10}$$

where the prior of B is normal with unconditional mean $\overline{\mathrm{B}}$ and variance $(\alpha - N - 1)^{-1}\overline{\Sigma} \otimes \overline{\Omega}$, and the prior of Σ is inverse-Wishart with mean $(\alpha - N - 1)^{-1}\overline{\Sigma}$ and $\alpha > N + 1$ degrees of freedom. In a conventional VAR setting, the Normal-Wishart prior allows for a convenient analytical solution for the marginal posterior of B being a multivariate t-distribution. Unfortunately, as pointed out in Kadiyala and Karlsson (1997), it is also restrictive in a sense that the prior variance-covariance matrix of B requires symmetrical treatments of all equations in the VAR. More specifically, it eliminates the possibility of having different zero restrictions in different equations, which is precisely what we need in the case of traffic flow modelling, as significant upstream/downstream neighbours are most likely different for different parts of the traffic network.

Yet another potential candidate is the Normal-Diffuse prior of Zellner (1971) and Kadiyala and Karlsson (1997)

$$p\left(\mathrm{B}\right) = N\left(\overline{\mathrm{B}}, \overline{\Omega}\right),\ p\left(\Sigma\right) \propto \left|\Sigma\right|^{-(N+1)/2} \tag{10.11}$$

which assumes prior independence between B and Σ and thus avoids restrictions on the variance-covariance matrix of B. This is also the approach taken in Korobilis (2013).

It should be noted that, in model selection in a univariate framework, Zellner's g prior (1986):

$$p\left(\beta\middle|\sigma^2\right) = N\left(0, g\sigma^2(X'X)^{-1}\right) \tag{10.12}$$

has been widely used due to its computational efficiency and conceptual interpretability. In particular, the prior variance-covariance matrix of β corresponds to a scalar multiple of the Fisher information matrix. g is typically set to be equal to sample size N, and it can be shown that $g/(1+g)$ can be interpreted as the shrinkage factor applied to β. The relationship between g and shrinkage is intuitive. The smaller the sample size the smaller g is, which means $g/(1+g)$ becomes smaller and a larger amount of shrinkage will be applied to β. In other words, when sample information is insufficient, we place less "trust" on the coefficient estimates and shrink them more towards 0. On the other hand, when sample size is large, $g/(1+g) \approx 1$ and close to no shrinkage will be applied.

Finally, in terms of the prior for the model space, as defined by the latent binary vector γ, a popular option, for example in Korobilis (2013), is:

$$p\left(\gamma_j = 1\right) = 0.5, \ \forall j \tag{10.13}$$

which is seemingly innocuous and uninformative. However, it should be noted that a probabilistic statement for individual γ_j does not translate to the same probabilistic statement for the complexity of the model space of γ. If one defines model complexity in terms of the size of γ, denoted as q_γ, then Eq. (10.13) implies a substantially high probability weight on mid-size q_γ, for the simple reason that there are a lot more combinations of $\gamma_j^{'}s$ that could give the same mid-size q_γ than there are for small-size and/or large-size q_γ. As an example, for a model involving 500 potential predictors, Eq. (10.13) gives a prior probability in excess of 99.9 % for all the models where $q_\gamma \in [200, 300]$, which is highly informative and practically eliminates any small-size models.

One viable alternative, originally proposed in George and McCulloch (1993), is to assume a flat prior on model complexity q_γ. Specifically,

$$p\left(q_\gamma\right) = uniform\,(0, q) \tag{10.14}$$

where q is the maximum size of γ, which is equal to $\sum_{ij} K_{ij}$. When $q_\gamma = 0$, it gives the null model that includes only an intercept term. When $q_\gamma = q$, it gives a full model. A flat prior on q_γ implies that models of any size have the same prior probability of being chosen.

In this paper, given the focus on variable selection, a modified version of Zellner's g prior will be proposed for B:

$$p\left(\mathrm{B}_\gamma \middle| \Sigma, \gamma\right) = N\left(0, g\left[\mathrm{X}_\gamma'(\Sigma \otimes I_T)^{-1}\mathrm{X}_\gamma\right]^{-1}\right) \tag{10.15}$$

where the subscript γ indicates that only elements in B and columns in X corresponding to $\gamma_j = 1$ are included, thus X_γ is $\left(NT \times q_\gamma\right)$. The Fisher information matrix is adjusted to account for cross-equation correlation via $(\Sigma \otimes I_T)^{-1}$. g is set to be sample size NT, as there are T observations on N traffic flows.

And an inverse-Wishart prior will be proposed for Σ:

$$p(\Sigma) = iW\left(\overline{\Sigma},\ \alpha\right) \tag{10.16}$$

where $\overline{\Sigma}$ is set to be equal to the variance-covariance matrix of the residuals from equation-by-equation OLS. Following Kadiyala and Karlsson (1997), degrees of freedom is set to be $\alpha = N + 2$.

Finally, for γ, the first option is to impose a flat prior on model complexity in the form of Eq. (10.14). Interestingly, an additional possibility arises for VAR models, where model complexity can be specified for each equation of the VAR individually. In this case, one could write:

$$p\left(q_{\gamma,n}\right) = uniform\left(0, q_n\right), \quad \forall\, n = 1, \ldots, N \tag{10.17}$$

where $q_{\gamma,n}$ is the size of γ for the nth equation and q_n is the maximum size of γ for the nth equation. Both priors will be tested in the simulation study.

10.2.4 The Posterior

The joint posterior distribution of the parameters conditional on the data is obtained via Bayes rule as:

$$\begin{aligned} p\left(\mathrm{B}, \Sigma, \gamma \middle| Y\right) &= \frac{p\left(\mathrm{Y} \middle| \mathrm{B}, \Sigma, \gamma\right) p(\mathrm{B}, \Sigma, \gamma)}{p(Y)} \\ &\propto p\left(\mathrm{Y} \middle| \mathrm{B}, \Sigma, \gamma\right) \cdot p\left(\mathrm{B}_\gamma \middle| \Sigma, \gamma\right) \cdot p(\Sigma) \cdot p(\gamma) \end{aligned} \tag{10.18}$$

where $p\left(\mathrm{Y} \middle| \mathrm{B}, \Sigma, \gamma\right)$ is the likelihood function. Substituting the proposed priors into the above, and integrating out B_γ, one can obtain an analytical expression for the joint posterior $p\left(\Sigma, \gamma \middle| Y\right)$ (see Appendix 1):

$$\begin{aligned} p\left(\Sigma, \gamma \middle| Y\right) &\propto (1+g)^{-\frac{q_\gamma}{2}} \cdot |\Sigma|^{-\frac{T+\alpha+N+1}{2}} \cdot exp\left\{-\tfrac{1}{2} tr\left(\overline{\Sigma}\Sigma^{-1}\right)\right\} \cdot \\ exp&\left\{-\tfrac{1}{2} Y' \left\{(\Sigma \otimes I_T)^{-1} - (\Sigma \otimes I_T)^{-1} \mathrm{X}_\gamma \left[\left(\tfrac{1+g}{g}\right) \mathrm{X}_\gamma' (\Sigma \otimes I_T)^{-1} \mathrm{X}_\gamma\right]^{-1} \right.\right. \\ &\left.\left. \mathrm{X}_\gamma' (\Sigma \otimes I_T)^{-1} \right\} Y \right\} \cdot p(\gamma) \end{aligned} \tag{10.19}$$

which can be simplified no further.

10.2.5 The Sampling Procedure

Even in this simple example, there are $2^{54} \approx 1.8e+16$ different combinations of the latent binary vector γ, or equivalently 2^{54} potential models to choose from. The cardinality of the model space grows exponentially with $q\left(=\sum_{ij} K_{ij}\right)$, which makes it impossible to enumerate all possible configurations of γ. However, Markov Chain Monte Carlo (MCMC) methods can be used for posterior inference. A Gibbs sampler similar to that of Smith and Kohn (1996) will be used to sequentially generate iterates from conditional posterior $p\left(\gamma_i \middle| Y, \Sigma, \gamma_{j\neq i}\right)$ for $i = 1, \ldots, q$.

Specifically, define $\gamma_i^0 = (\gamma_1, \ldots, \gamma_{i-1}, \gamma_i = 0, \gamma_{i+1}, \ldots, \gamma_q)'$ and $\gamma_i^1 = (\gamma_1, \ldots, \gamma_{i-1}, \gamma_i = 1, \gamma_{i+1}, \ldots, \gamma_q)'$. And let the value of Σ at the current kth step in the MCMC sampler be Σ_k, which is assumed to be positive-definite. In the first part of the sampler, the conditional posterior $p\left(\gamma_i \middle| Y, \Sigma_k, \gamma_{j\neq i}\right)$ can be expressed as:

$$p\left(\gamma_i \middle| Y, \Sigma_k, \gamma_{j\neq i}\right) = \left(1 + BF_{\gamma_i^0:\gamma_i^1}\middle|\Sigma_k\right)^{-1} \frac{p\left(\gamma_i = 1 \middle| \gamma_{j\neq i}\right)}{p\left(\gamma_i = 0 \middle| \gamma_{j\neq i}\right)} \tag{10.20}$$

where $BF_{\gamma_i^0:\gamma_i^1}\big|\Sigma_k$ is the Bayes factor of the model given by γ_i^0 relative to the model given by γ_i^1, conditional on Σ being a known quantity at the kth step as Σ_k. Following a similar approach to Liang et al. (2008), after some algebra one obtains

$$\begin{aligned}
&BF_{\gamma_i^0:\gamma_i^1}\Big|\Sigma_k \\
&= (1+g)^{\frac{1}{2}} \cdot exp\left\{-\tfrac{1}{2}\left\{Y'(\Sigma_k \otimes I_T)^{-1}\left\{\left(\tfrac{g}{1+g}\right)\mathrm{X}_{\gamma_i^1}\left[\mathrm{X}'_{\gamma_i^1}(\Sigma_k \otimes I_T)^{-1}\mathrm{X}_{\gamma_i^1}\right]^{-1}\mathrm{X}'_{\gamma_i^1}\right\}\right.\right. \\
&(\Sigma_k \otimes I_T)^{-1}Y - Y'(\Sigma_k \otimes I_T)^{-1}\left\{\left(\tfrac{g}{1+g}\right)\mathrm{X}_{\gamma_i^0}\left[\mathrm{X}'_{\gamma_i^0}(\Sigma_k \otimes I_T)^{-1}\mathrm{X}_{\gamma_i^0}\right]^{-1}\mathrm{X}'_{\gamma_i^0}\right\} \\
&\left.\left.(\Sigma_k \otimes I_T)^{-1}Y\right\}\right\} = (1+g)^{\frac{1}{2}} \cdot exp\left\{-\tfrac{1}{2}\left(ESS_{\gamma_i^1}\middle|\Sigma_k - ESS_{\gamma_i^0}\middle|\Sigma_k\right)\right\}
\end{aligned} \tag{10.21}$$

where $ESS_{\gamma_i^1}\big|\Sigma_k$ and $ESS_{\gamma_i^0}\big|\Sigma_k$ can be interpreted as the explained sum of squares adjusted for shrinkage (due to the presence of shrinkage factor $\left(\frac{g}{1+g}\right)$ in the projection matrix), conditional on Σ_k, and for model γ_i^0 and γ_i^0 respectively. Thus the inclusion probability of the ith predictor is meaningfully related to the extra amount of fit the additional ith predictor adds to the model.

On the other hand, under the flat prior on model complexity and using combinatorics, $\frac{p\left(\gamma_i=1\middle|\gamma_{j\neq i}\right)}{p\left(\gamma_i=0\middle|\gamma_{j\neq i}\right)}$ in Eq. (10.19) can be shown to be (see Appendix 2)

$$\frac{p\left(\gamma_i = 1\middle|\gamma_{j\neq i}\right)}{p\left(\gamma_i = 0\middle|\gamma_{j\neq i}\right)} = \frac{q_{\gamma_i^0} + 1}{q - q_{\gamma_i^0}} \tag{10.22}$$

where $q_{\gamma_i^0}$ is the size of γ_i^0. The Gibbs sampler will sample through γ_i conditional on Σ_k and $\gamma_{j\neq i}$ for $i = 1, \ldots, q$ and preferably in a random order.

In the second part of the sampler, the so-called Metropolisized hit-and-run sampler, originally due to Schmeiser and Chen (1991) and Chen and Schmeiser (1993), and extended for the reference prior in Yang and Berger (1994), will be used to generate Σ from the conditional posterior $p\left(\Sigma\middle|Y, \gamma\right)$. Firstly, define $\Sigma^* = log\left(\Sigma\right)$, or equivalently $\Sigma = \exp\left(\Sigma^*\right)$, in the sense of Leonard and Hsu (1992), that

$$\Sigma = \sum_{i=0}^{\infty} \frac{\left(\Sigma^*\right)^i}{i!} \tag{10.23}$$

The Metropolisized hit-and-run sampler proceeds as follows:

1. For the current value of the variance-covariance matrix Σ_k, compute $\Sigma_k^* = log\left(\Sigma_k\right)$.
2. Generate a random direction symmetric matrix $\Psi\left(N \times N\right)$, where $\psi_{ij} = z_{ij}/\sqrt{\sum_{l<m} z_{lm}^2}$, and $z_{ij} \sim N\left(0, 1\right)\ \forall\ i < j$. The rest of the elements in Ψ are defined by symmetry, i.e., $\psi_{ji} = \psi_{ij}$.
3. Generate $\lambda \sim N\left(0, 1\right)$.
4. Generate a proposal $\Sigma_k^{*\dagger} = \Sigma_k^* + \lambda\Psi$.
5. Set

$$\Sigma_{k+1} = \begin{cases} \Sigma_k^{\dagger}, \text{ with probability } min\left(1, \frac{p\left(\Sigma_k^{\dagger}\middle|Y,\gamma\right)}{p\left(\Sigma_k\middle|Y,\gamma\right)}\right) \\ \Sigma_k, \text{ otherwise} \end{cases}$$

where $\Sigma_k^{\dagger} = exp\left(\Sigma_k^{*\dagger}\right)$. Note that as the proposal is generated in terms of Σ^* but the conditional posterior is evaluated in terms of Σ, the Jacobian term $|\Sigma|$ needs to be included in the computation of the conditional posterior.

The procedure alternates and samples recursively between two conditional posteriors, $p\left(\gamma \middle| Y, \Sigma\right)$ and $p\left(\Sigma \middle| Y, \gamma\right)$, and forms a Markov Chain, which for a sufficiently large number of iterations can be regarded as draws of (Σ, γ) from the true joint posterior distribution from $p\left(\Sigma, \gamma \middle| Y\right)$ as defined in Eq. (10.19). Marginal densities of interest can be obtained easily with corresponding MCMC sample averages.

10.3 A Simulation Study

The traffic network in Fig. 10.1 and dominant traffic flow directions in Fig. 10.2 will be used in this simulation study. There are 14 traffic flows in total and 54 potential predictors to choose from in the entire system. Let there be $T = 30$ observations in the time dimension. Let the intercept be five for all traffic flows, and the nonzero elements of β_{ij} in Eq. (10.5) correspond to values in Table 10.2, where the coefficients are given in the brackets. Finally, let $E\left(\varepsilon_{n,t}^2\right) = 1\ \forall\ n = 1, \ldots, N,\ t = 1, \ldots, T$ and $E\left(\varepsilon_{l,t}\varepsilon_{m,t}\right) = 0.5\ \forall\ l \neq m,\ t = 1, \ldots, T$.

Figure 10.3 illustrates a typical simulation run of the traffic flows in this system. Traffic volumes along the dominant flow directions are much higher, and both contemporaneous and lagged correlations are significantly present.

To see the danger of 'overfitting' in a large system of equations, suppose Eq. (10.6) was estimated with generalized least squares (GLS), the estimation results can be found in Table 10.3 for a typical simulation run. Twice as many predictors are found to be statistically significant. A large number of the coefficient estimates report a counter-intuitive negative sign, and for some of the 'insignificant' predictors, for example $x_{54,t}$, the coefficient estimate is still sizable (0.259). Imprecise coefficient estimates that are sensitive to noise and inability to distinguish between genuine and false predictors are symptomatic of model overfitting.

Turning to the Bayesian VAR method proposed in this paper, the sampler was run for 5000 iterations, and the simulation exercise was repeated 100 times and averaged results are reported. Starting values for γ were randomly selected with 10 % inclusion probability. Starting value for Σ was chosen to be the variance-covariance matrix of the residuals from equation-by-equation OLS. Moreover, two

Table 10.2 Coefficient values used in the simulation study

Flow ID	$y_{ij,t}$	$X_{ij,t}$: upstream	$X_{ij,t}$: downstream
1	$y_{12,t}$		$y_{25,t-1}(0.6)$
4	$y_{65,t}$		$y_{54,t-1}(0.6)$
5	$y_{54,t}$	$y_{65,t-1}(0.4)$	$y_{41,t-1}(0.4)$
6	$y_{41,t}$	$y_{54,t-1}(0.6)$	
9	$y_{56,t}$	$y_{25,t-1}(0.6)$	
11	$y_{32,t}$		$y_{25,t-1}(0.6)$
13	$y_{25,t}$	$y_{12,t-1}(0.3), y_{32,t-1}(0.3)$	$y_{56,t-1}(0.3)$

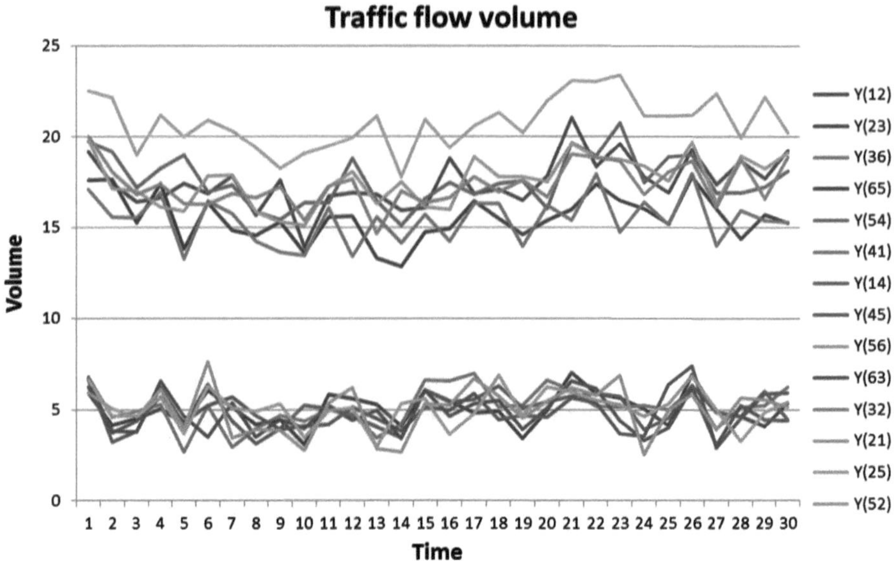

Fig. 10.3 A typical simulation run of the traffic flows in the system. It can be seen that traffic volumes are much higher along the dominant directions, and both contemporaneous and lagged correlations are significantly present

types of priors on model complexity: (a) flat prior on overall model complexity; (b) flat prior on model complexity for each equation in the VAR, are investigated.

Firstly, the marginal posterior probabilities for components in γ, i.e., $p\left(\gamma_i = 1 \middle| Y\right)$, $i = 1, \ldots, 54$, under both priors, are plotted in Fig. 10.4. The green columns represent the known 'true' predictors, and it can be seen that the spikes of the marginals, which represent high inclusion probabilities in the MCMC sample, correspond very closely to the green columns. The marginals under both types of priors on model complexity yield very similar results, with the second type giving slightly higher inclusion probabilities overall. The average inclusion probabilities of 'true' predictors and 'false' predictors under both types of priors can be found in Table 10.4. The average inclusion probabilities for the 'true' predictors are very high and at 0.782 and 0.828 respectively, and the average inclusion probabilities for the 'false' predictors are very low and at 0.153 and 0.202 respectively.

For decision makers, it is often more important to be able to select the best model than to know on average which models could be better. For instance, urban planners may want to know exactly which roads need to be widened to relieve traffic congestion. To this end, it is informative to look at the posterior mode of γ, which corresponds to the model picked most often by the sampler. The average inclusion probabilities of the posterior mode are plotted in Fig. 10.5. A very similar picture emerges, in which the modal model's inclusion probabilities correspond very closely to the true model. The modal model's average inclusion probabilities of 'true' predictors and 'false' predictors under both types of priors can be found in

Table 10.3 GLS estimates are listed

True predictor	Predictor	Estimate	Std Error	t-value	P-value	
No	X1	0.025	0.100	0.254	0.799	
No	X2	−0.090	0.117	−0.767	0.443	
No	X3	0.218	0.168	1.293	0.196	
Yes	X4	0.660	0.090	7.357	0.000	***
No	X5	0.017	0.185	0.094	0.925	
No	X6	−0.004	0.035	−0.128	0.899	
No	X7	−0.310	0.192	−1.614	0.107	
No	X8	0.139	0.122	1.144	0.252	
No	X9	−0.100	0.140	−0.713	0.476	
No	X10	−0.050	0.152	−0.329	0.742	
No	X11	0.032	0.047	0.672	0.502	
No	X12	−0.159	0.058	−2.714	0.007	***
No	X13	0.623	0.122	5.119	0.000	***
No	X14	−0.492	0.149	−3.298	0.001	***
Yes	X15	0.675	0.049	13.831	0.000	***
No	X16	−0.042	0.091	−0.456	0.648	
Yes	X17	0.280	0.121	2.313	0.021	**
No	X18	−0.002	0.087	−0.023	0.982	
Yes	X19	0.604	0.132	4.567	0.000	***
No	X20	−0.012	0.098	−0.118	0.906	
Yes	X21	0.494	0.085	5.821	0.000	***
No	X22	0.021	0.089	0.238	0.812	
No	X23	0.153	0.118	1.302	0.193	
No	X24	−0.298	0.095	−3.150	0.002	***
No	X25	−0.206	0.103	−1.990	0.047	**
No	X26	−0.365	0.164	−2.223	0.026	**
No	X27	0.412	0.194	2.119	0.034	**
No	X28	−0.483	0.213	−2.274	0.023	**
No	X29	−0.052	0.049	−1.063	0.288	
No	X30	0.106	0.069	1.546	0.122	
No	X31	0.083	0.106	0.781	0.435	
Yes	X32	0.508	0.055	9.299	0.000	***
No	X33	−0.040	0.106	−0.380	0.704	
No	X34	−0.073	0.121	−0.601	0.548	
No	X35	0.073	0.134	0.547	0.584	
No	X36	−0.086	0.139	−0.616	0.538	
No	X37	−0.055	0.078	−0.713	0.476	
No	X38	0.023	0.107	0.215	0.830	
No	X39	−0.002	0.094	−0.021	0.983	
Yes	X40	0.620	0.060	10.274	0.000	***
No	X41	−0.111	0.163	−0.686	0.493	

Table 10.3 (Continued)

True predictor	Predictor	Estimate	Std Error	t-value	P-value	
No	X42	−0.035	0.051	−0.690	0.490	
No	X43	−0.635	0.216	−2.939	0.003	***
No	X44	0.316	0.182	1.736	0.083	*
No	X45	−0.087	0.081	−1.079	0.281	
Yes	X46	0.552	0.151	3.669	0.000	***
Yes	X47	−0.132	0.159	−0.834	0.404	
No	X48	0.079	0.091	0.868	0.385	
Yes	X49	0.527	0.167	3.157	0.002	***
No	X50	−0.520	0.195	−2.666	0.008	***
No	X51	−0.001	0.092	−0.008	0.993	
No	X52	−0.042	0.045	−0.936	0.349	
No	X53	0.118	0.094	1.251	0.211	
No	X54	0.259	0.192	1.351	0.177	

Twice as many predictors were identified as statistically significant. And the coefficients are imprecisely estimated, fluctuating between large positive and large negative values
Significance levels are at 10 %, 5 %, and 1 % for *, **, and *** respectively

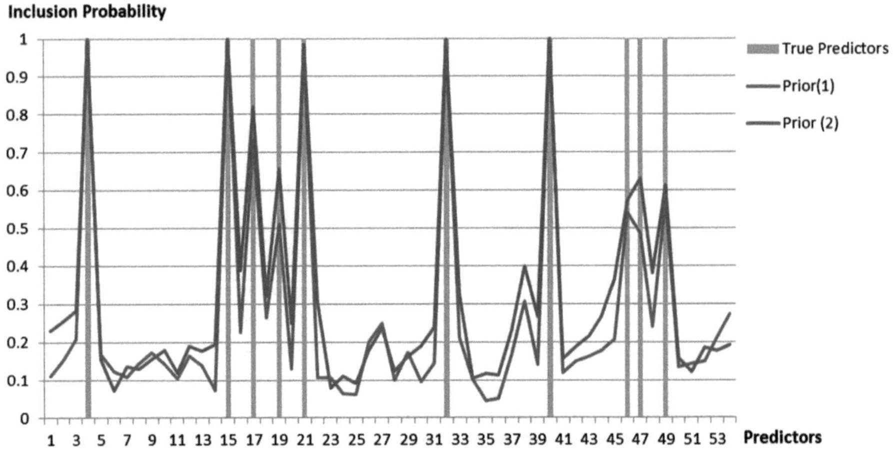

Fig. 10.4 Average marginal posterior probabilities of components in γ. Under both priors, the inclusion probabilities correspond very closely to the 'true' model

Table 10.4 Average inclusion probabilities of 'true' predictors and 'false' predictors based on the marginals for both types of priors

Marginal	Prior (1)	Prior (2)
P(True)	0.782	0.828
P(False)	0.153	0.202

Table 10.5. While the true inclusion probabilities remain similar for both types of priors, the false inclusion probabilities are even lower.

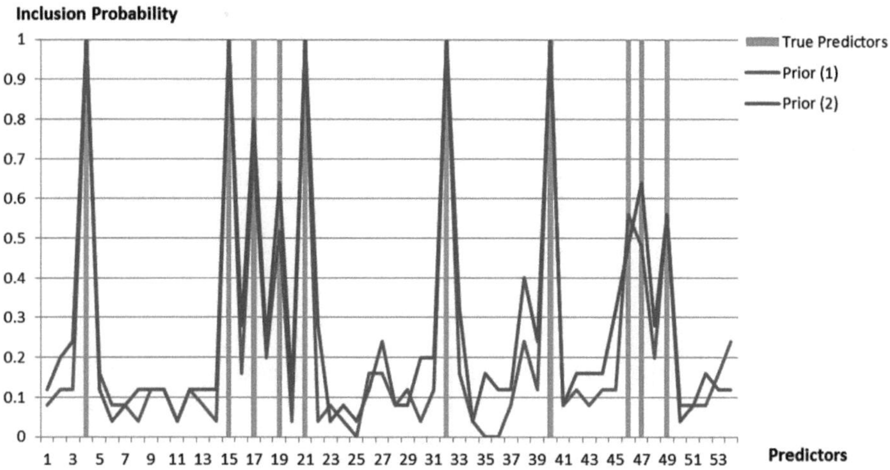

Fig. 10.5 Average inclusion probabilities of posterior modes of γ. Under both priors, the inclusion probabilities correspond very closely to the 'true' model

Table 10.5 Average inclusion probabilities of 'true' predictors and 'false' predictors based on the posterior modes for both types of priors

Modal	Prior (1)	Prior (2)
P(True)	0.784	0.812
P(False)	0.100	0.151

It is also informative to look at the marginal posterior distribution for B, i.e., $p\left(\mathrm{B}\middle|Y\right)$. While B was integrated out in Eq. (10.19), given the MCMC sample of (Σ, γ) the conditional posterior of $p\left(\mathrm{B}\middle|Y, \Sigma, \gamma\right)$ can be viewed as a valid approximation to the true $p\left(\mathrm{B}\middle|Y\right)$. Figure 10.6 compares the GLS estimates with the sample mean of estimates of B from both types of priors for a typical simulation run. It is interesting to see that, large negative GLS estimates have largely disappeared under the Bayesian model. As the modified g prior shrinks coefficient estimates towards 0, when genuine signal is not present for a potential predictor its effect size is by designed forced towards zero. This provides further support to the claim of this paper that Bayesian variable selection provides a superior option to making statistical inferences over a large model space.

Overall, it appears that the choice between the two priors on model complexity makes only a small difference to the estimation outcome in this simulation study, with the second prior giving slightly larger models on average. However, it would be interesting to examine what happens when the number of potential predictors differs substantially for different equations. For instance, the hubs of a traffic network might have a lot more potential predictors than the far ends of the network. In that case,

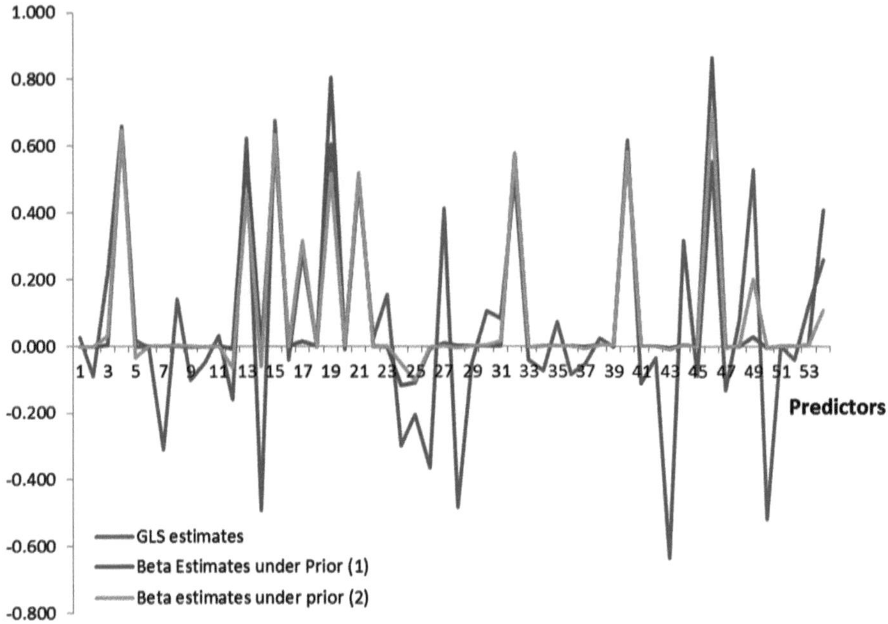

Fig. 10.6 Comparison of GLS estimates and Bayesian VAR estimates of B. Large fluctuations that are symptomatic of 'overfitting' have mostly disappeared for Bayesian VAR estimates

model complexity might be dominated by potential connections to the hubs and equation-specific model complexity assumptions may add more value.

10.4 Concluding Remarks

VAR models have been used extensively in macroeconomic modelling and forecasting. A growing literature also exists for Bayesian variable selection in VAR. In this paper, the methodology has been adapted to the specific context of traffic flow modelling. In particular, shrinkage prior in the form of Zellner's g prior (1986) has been modified for VAR modelling, the flat prior on model complexity in the form of George and McCulloch (1993) has been modified to account for equation-specific model complexity assumptions, and an MCMC sampling procedure is developed at length. A small scale simulation study shows that the marginal posterior distribution of the inclusion indicator vector γ corresponds very closely to the 'true' underlying model space, and the marginal posterior distribution of the effects vector B centres around the 'true' values of B, and in comparison to conventional GLS estimates it largely avoids the problems of 'overfitting'.

It should be noted that the topic of impulse response analysis has not been covered in this paper. As noted in Koop and Korobilis (2009), in the absence of natural conjugate priors and analytical solutions, which is the case for the model presented in this paper, posterior distributions of impulse response functions have to be obtained through Monte Carlo integration and is not trivial. The presence of the latent selection vector γ further complicates matters. As the main goal of this paper is to propose a Bayesian variable selection method for VAR model identification and estimation in the context of traffic flow modelling, the topic of impulse response analysis will be left for future research.

Finally, contemporary spatial dependence in the form of spatially weighted contemporary values of y_t (i.e., ρWy_t) is also not being considered in this manuscript. In the literature of Bayesian shrinkage and variable selection, all predictors are assumed to be either predetermined or exogenous thus far. Introduction of endogenous predictors to the right-hand side introduces significant challenges to the modelling framework and will be left for future research.

Appendix 1

Recall that the joint posterior is

$$p\left(\mathrm{B}, \Sigma, \gamma \middle| Y\right) \propto p\left(\mathrm{Y} \middle| \mathrm{B}, \Sigma, \gamma\right) \cdot p\left(\mathrm{B}_\gamma \middle| \Sigma, \gamma\right) \cdot p\left(\Sigma\right) \cdot p\left(\gamma\right)$$

To integrate out B

$$\begin{aligned}
p\left(\Sigma, \gamma \middle| Y\right) &= \int_{\mathrm{B}} p\left(\mathrm{B}, \Sigma, \gamma \middle| Y\right) d\mathrm{B} \\
&\propto \int_{\mathrm{B}} p\left(\mathrm{Y} \middle| \mathrm{B}, \Sigma, \gamma\right) \cdot p\left(\mathrm{B}_\gamma \middle| \Sigma, \gamma\right) \cdot \left[p\left(\Sigma\right) \cdot p\left(\gamma\right)\right] d\mathrm{B} \\
&\propto \int_{\mathrm{B}} p\left(\mathrm{Y} \middle| \mathrm{B}, \Sigma, \gamma\right) \cdot p\left(\mathrm{B}_\gamma \middle| \Sigma, \gamma\right) d\mathrm{B} \cdot p\left(\Sigma\right) \cdot p\left(\gamma\right) \\
&\propto \int_{\mathrm{B}} (2\pi)^{-\frac{NT}{2}} \cdot |\Sigma|^{-\frac{T}{2}} \cdot exp\left\{-\tfrac{1}{2}\left(Y - \mathrm{X}_\gamma \mathrm{B}_\gamma\right)' \left(\Sigma \otimes I_T\right)^{-1} \left(Y - \mathrm{X}_\gamma \mathrm{B}_\gamma\right)\right\} \\
&\quad \cdot (2\pi)^{-\frac{q_\gamma}{2}} \cdot g^{-\frac{q_\gamma}{2}} \cdot \left|\mathrm{X}_\gamma' \left(\Sigma \otimes I_T\right)^{-1} \mathrm{X}_\gamma\right|^{\frac{1}{2}} \\
&\quad \cdot exp\left\{-\tfrac{1}{2}\mathrm{B}_\gamma' \left[\left(\tfrac{1}{g}\right) \mathrm{X}_\gamma' \left(\Sigma \otimes I_T\right)^{-1} \mathrm{X}_\gamma\right] \mathrm{B}_\gamma\right\} d\mathrm{B} \cdot \left[p\left(\Sigma\right) \cdot p\left(\gamma\right)\right]
\end{aligned}$$

Complete the squares and divide and multiply

$$\begin{aligned}
&\int_{B} p\left(\mathrm{B}, \Sigma, \gamma \middle| Y\right) d\mathrm{B} \\
&\propto |\Sigma|^{-\frac{T}{2}} \cdot exp\left\{-\tfrac{1}{2} Y'(\Sigma \otimes I_T)^{-1} Y\right\} \cdot \int_{B} (2\pi)^{-\frac{q_\gamma}{2}} \cdot \left|\mathrm{X}_\gamma'(\Sigma \otimes I_T)^{-1}\mathrm{X}_\gamma\right|^{\frac{1}{2}} \cdot \left(\tfrac{g}{1+g}\right)^{-\frac{q_\gamma}{2}} \\
&\cdot exp\left\{-\tfrac{1}{2}\left[\left(\tfrac{1+g}{g}\right)\mathrm{B}_\gamma'\mathrm{X}_\gamma'(\Sigma \otimes I_T)^{-1}\mathrm{X}_\gamma \mathrm{B}_\gamma - 2\mathrm{B}_\gamma'\mathrm{X}_\gamma'(\Sigma \otimes I_T)^{-1} Y \right.\right. \\
&\qquad \left.\left. + Y'(\Sigma \otimes I_T)^{-1}\mathrm{X}_\gamma\left[\left(\tfrac{1+g}{g}\right)\mathrm{X}_\gamma'(\Sigma \otimes I_T)^{-1}\mathrm{X}_\gamma\right]^{-1}\mathrm{X}_\gamma'(\Sigma \otimes I_T)^{-1} Y\right]\right\} d\mathrm{B} \\
&\cdot exp\left\{\tfrac{1}{2} Y'(\Sigma \otimes I_T)^{-1}\mathrm{X}_\gamma\left[\left(\tfrac{1+g}{g}\right)\mathrm{X}_\gamma'(\Sigma \otimes I_T)^{-1}\mathrm{X}_\gamma\right]^{-1}\mathrm{X}_\gamma'(\Sigma \otimes I_T)^{-1} Y\right\} \\
&\cdot (1+g)^{-\frac{q_\gamma}{2}} \cdot [p(\Sigma) \cdot p(\gamma)]
\end{aligned}$$

Let

$$\widetilde{\mathrm{B}}_\gamma = \left(\frac{g}{1+g}\right)\left[\mathrm{X}_\gamma'(\Sigma \otimes I_T)^{-1}\mathrm{X}_\gamma\right]^{-1}\mathrm{X}_\gamma'(\Sigma \otimes I_T)^{-1} Y$$

and let

$$(\mathrm{B}_\gamma - \widetilde{\mathrm{B}}_\gamma) \sim N\left(0, \left(\frac{g}{1+g}\right)\left[\mathrm{X}_\gamma'(\Sigma \otimes I_T)^{-1}\mathrm{X}_\gamma\right]^{-1}\right)$$

then

$$\begin{aligned}
&(\mathrm{B}_\gamma - \widetilde{\mathrm{B}}_\gamma)'\left[\left(\tfrac{1+g}{g}\right)\mathrm{X}_\gamma'(\Sigma \otimes I_T)^{-1}\mathrm{X}_\gamma\right](\mathrm{B}_\gamma - \widetilde{\mathrm{B}}_\gamma) \\
&= \left[\left(\tfrac{1+g}{g}\right)\mathrm{B}_\gamma'\mathrm{X}_\gamma'(\Sigma \otimes I_T)^{-1}\mathrm{X}_\gamma \mathrm{B}_\gamma - 2\mathrm{B}_\gamma'\mathrm{X}_\gamma'(\Sigma \otimes I_T)^{-1} Y\right. \\
&\qquad \left. + Y'(\Sigma \otimes I_T)^{-1}\mathrm{X}_\gamma\left[\left(\tfrac{1+g}{g}\right)\mathrm{X}_\gamma'(\Sigma \otimes I_T)^{-1}\mathrm{X}_\gamma\right]^{-1}\mathrm{X}_\gamma'(\Sigma \otimes I_T)^{-1} Y\right]
\end{aligned}$$

is easily recognized as the kernel of the integral over B. Thus

$$\begin{aligned}
&p\left(\Sigma, \gamma \middle| Y\right) \\
&\propto |\Sigma|^{-\frac{T}{2}} \cdot (1+g)^{-\frac{q_\gamma}{2}} \cdot exp\left\{-\tfrac{1}{2} Y'(\Sigma \otimes I_T)^{-1} Y\right\} \\
&\quad \cdot exp\left\{\tfrac{1}{2} Y'(\Sigma \otimes I_T)^{-1}\mathrm{X}_\gamma\left[\left(\tfrac{1+g}{g}\right)\mathrm{X}_\gamma'(\Sigma \otimes I_T)^{-1}\mathrm{X}_\gamma\right]^{-1}\mathrm{X}_\gamma'(\Sigma \otimes I_T)^{-1} Y\right\} \\
&\qquad \cdot [p(\Sigma) \cdot p(\gamma)]
\end{aligned}$$

Finally, substitute the prior density of

$$p(\Sigma) = iW\left(\overline{\Sigma},\, \alpha\right) = \frac{\left|\overline{\Sigma}\right|^{\frac{\alpha}{2}}}{|\Sigma|^{\frac{\alpha+N+1}{2}} \cdot 2^{\frac{\alpha N}{2}} \cdot \Gamma_N\left(\frac{\alpha}{2}\right)} \cdot exp\left\{-\frac{1}{2}tr\left(\overline{\Sigma}\Sigma^{-1}\right)\right\}$$

Into the above, Eq. (10.19)

$$\begin{aligned} p\left(\Sigma, \gamma \middle| Y\right) &\propto (1+g)^{-\frac{q_\gamma}{2}} \cdot |\Sigma|^{-\frac{T+\alpha+N+1}{2}} \cdot exp\left\{-\tfrac{1}{2}tr\left(\overline{\Sigma}\Sigma^{-1}\right)\right\} \cdot \\ & exp\left\{-\tfrac{1}{2}Y'\left\{(\Sigma\otimes I_T)^{-1} - (\Sigma\otimes I_T)^{-1}\mathrm{X}_\gamma\left[\left(\tfrac{1+g}{g}\right)\mathrm{X}'_\gamma(\Sigma\otimes I_T)^{-1}\mathrm{X}_\gamma\right]^{-1}\right.\right. \\ & \left.\left.\mathrm{X}'_\gamma(\Sigma\otimes I_T)^{-1}\right\} Y\right\} \cdot p(\gamma) \end{aligned}$$

is obtained.

Appendix 2

Define $q_{\gamma_i^0}$ as the size of γ excluding element i, one can write

$$p\left(\gamma_i = 1 \middle| \gamma_{j\neq i}\right) = \frac{p\left(q_{\gamma_i^0}+1\right)}{p\left(q_{\gamma_i^0}\right) + p\left(q_{\gamma_i^0}+1\right)}$$

Using combinatorics, as defined for the same prior in Cui and George (2008), one could write

$$\begin{aligned} p\left(\gamma_i = 1 \middle| \gamma_{j\neq i}\right) &= \frac{p\left(q_{\gamma_i^0}+1\right)}{p\left(q_{\gamma_i^0}\right)+p\left(q_{\gamma_i^0}+1\right)} \\ &= \frac{\left(\frac{1}{q+1}\right)\binom{q}{q_{\gamma_i^0}}^{-1}}{\left(\frac{1}{q+1}\right)\binom{q}{q_{\gamma_i^0}}^{-1} + \left(\frac{1}{q+1}\right)\binom{q}{q_{\gamma_i^0}+1}^{-1}} \end{aligned}$$

which, after some algebra, yields

$$p\left(\gamma_i = 1 \middle| \gamma_{j\neq i}\right) = \frac{q_{\gamma_i^0}+1}{q+1}$$

which implies

$$p\left(\gamma_i = 0 \middle| \gamma_{j \neq i}\right) = \frac{q - q_{\gamma_i^0}}{q + 1}$$

It is straightforward to show that Eq. (10.19)

$$\frac{p\left(\gamma_i = 1 \middle| \gamma_{j \neq i}\right)}{p\left(\gamma_i = 0 \middle| \gamma_{j \neq i}\right)} = \frac{q_{\gamma_i^0} + 1}{q - q_{\gamma_i^0}}$$

holds.

References

Alvarez JL, Ballabriga FC (1994) BVAR models in the context of cointegration: A Monte Carlo experiment. Bank of Spain Working Paper No. 9405 (Madrid)

Berger JO, Pericchi L (2001) Objective Bayesian methods for model selection: introduction and comparison. In: Lahiri P (ed) Model selection. Institute of Mathematical Statistics, Hayward, pp 135–193

Bolduc D, Dagenais MG, Gaudry MJ (1989) Spatially autocorrelated errors in origin-destination models: A new specification applied to urban travel demand in Winnipeg. Transp Res B 23(5):361–372

Bolduc D, Laferriere R, Santarossa G (1992) Spatial autoregressive error components in travel flow models. Reg Sci Urban Econ 22:371–385

Brown PJ, Vannucci M (1998) Multivariate Bayesian variable selection and prediction. J R Stat Soc Ser B 60(3):627–641

Chen H, Schmeiser B (1993) Monte Carlo estimation for guaranteed-coverage nonnormal tolerance intervals. Proceedings of the winter simulation conference, 509–515

Cui W, George EI (2008) Empirical Bayes vs fully Bayes variable. J Stat Plan Inference 138:888–900

Deng M, Athanasopoulos G (2010) Modelling Australian Domestic and International Inbound Travel: a spatial-temporal approach. In: Tourism management, vol 32(5). Pergamon, Oxford, pp 1075–1084

Ding Q, Wang X, Zhang X, Sun Z (2011) Forecasting traffic volume with space-time ARIMA model. Adv Mater Res 156–157:979–983

Doan T, Litterman R, Sims C (1984) Forecasting and conditional projections using realist prior distributions. Econ Rev 3(1):1–100

George EI, McCulloch RE (1993) Variable selection via Gibbs sampling. J Am Stat Assoc 88:881–889

Giacomini R, Granger, Clive WJ (2004) Aggregation of space-time processes. J Econ 118(1/2):7–26

Griffith DA (2007) Spatial structure and spatial interaction: 25 years later. Rev Reg Stud 37(1):28–38

Geweke J (1996) Variable selection and model comparison in regression. In: Bernardo JM, Berger JO, Dawid AP, Smith AFM (eds) Bayesian statistics 5: proceedings of the fifth Valencia international meeting. Oxford University Press, Oxford, pp 609–620

Kadiyala KR, Karlsson S (1997) Numerical methods for estimation and inference in Bayesian VAR models. J Appl Econ 12:99–132
Kamarianakis Y, Kanas A, Prastacos P (2005) Modelling traffic volatility dynamics in an urban network. Transportation Research Record: Journal of the Transportation Research Board No. 1923. Transportation Research Board of the National Academies, Washington, pp 18–27
Kamarianakis Y, Prastacos P (2005) Space-time modelling of traffic flow. Comput Geosci 31:119–133
Koop G, Korobilis D (2009) Bayesian multivariate time series methods for empirical macroeconomics. Found TrendsR Econ 3(4):267–358
Korobilis D (2013) VAR forecasting using Bayesian variable selection. J Appl Econ 28:204–230
Leonard T, Hsu J (1992) Bayesian inference for a covariance matrix. Ann Stat 20(4):1669–1696
LeSage JP, Fischer MM (2010) Spatial econometric methods for modelling origin–destination flows. In: Fischer MM, Getis A (eds) Handbook of applied spatial analysis: software tools, methods and applications. Springer, Berlin, pp 413–437
LeSage JP, Krivelyova A (1999) A spatial prior for Bayesian vector autoregressive models. J Reg Sci 39(2):297–317
LeSage JP, Pan Z (1995) Using spatial contiguity as Bayesian prior information in regional forecasting models. Int Reg Sci Rev 18:33–53
LeSage JP, Pace RK (2008) Spatial econometric modelling of origin-destination flows. J Reg Sci 48(5):941–967
LeSage JP, Polasek W (2008) Incorporating transportation network structure in spatial econometric models of commodity flows. Spat Econ Anal 3(2):225–245
Liang F, Paulo R, Monila G, Clyde MA, Berger JO (2008) Mixture of g priors for Bayesian variable selection. J Am Stat Assoc 103(148):410–425
Litterman R (1980) Techniques for forecasting with vector autoregressions. PhD Dissertation, University of Minnesota, Minneapolis
Litterman R (1986) Forecasting with Bayesian vector autoregressions: five years of experience. J Bus Econ Stat 4:25–38
Pan Z, LeSage JP (1995) Using spatial contiguity as prior information in vector autoregressive models. Econ Lett 47:137–142
Pfeifer PE, Deutsch SJ (1980a) A three-stage iterative procedure for space–time modelling. Technometrics 22(1):35–47
Pfeifer PE, Deutsch SJ (1980b) Identification and interpretation of first-order space–time ARMA models. Technometrics 22(3):397–403
Pfeifer PE, Deutsch SJ (1981a) Variance of the sample-time autocorrelation function of contemporaneously correlated variables. SIAM J Appl Math Ser A 40(1):133–136
Pfeifer PE, Deutsch SJ (1981b) Seasonal space–time ARIMA modelling. Geogr Anal 13(2):117–133
Pfeifer PE, Bodily SE (1990) A test of space-time ARMA modelling and forecasting of hotel data. J Forecast 9(3):255–272
Porojan A (2001) Trade flows and spatial effects: the gravity model revisited. Open Econ Rev 12:265–280
Schmeiser BW, Chen MH (1991) On Hit-and-Run Monte Carlo sampling for evaluating multidimensional integrals. Technical Report, 91-39, Dept. Statistics, Purdue University
Sims C (1972) Money, income and causality. Am Econ Rev 62(1):540–553
Sims C (1980) Macroeconomics and reality. Econometrica 48:1–48
Smith M, Kohn R (1996) Nonparametric regression using Bayesian variable selection. J Econ 75:317–343
Yang R, Berger JO (1994) Estimation of a covariance matrix using the reference prior. Ann Stat 22(3):1195–1211
Zellner A (1971) An introduction to Bayesian inference in econometrics. Wiley, New York
Zellner A (1986) On assessing prior distributions and Bayesian regression analysis with g-Prior distributions. In: Goel PK, Zellner A (eds) Bayesian inference and decision techniques: essays in Honor of Bruno de Finetti, North-Holland/Elsevier, Amsterdam, pp 233–243

Chapter 11
Double Spatial Dependence in Gravity Models: Migration from the European Neighborhood to the European Union

Michael Beenstock and Daniel Felsenstein

Keywords European Union • Gravity • Migration • Spatial dependence • Spatial interaction

JEL Classifications: C33, F22, O15

11.1 Introduction: 150 Years of Gravity

Gravity modeling emerged over a century ago as an attempt to harness Newtonian physics in the explanation of socio-economic processes. Ravenstein's Law of Migration (1885) and Reilly's Law of Retail Gravitation (1929) are but two examples of the mechanistic straightjacket of early social physics. With the expansion of applications to spatial consumer choice, commuting patterns and housing choice, a more behavioral gravity model emerged. This embraced the principles of minimum effort (Zipf 1949) intervening opportunities (Stouffer 1960) and demographic potential (Stewart 1948). Over time, the use of gravity models in spatial analysis veered away from social physics and contemporary spatial gravity modeling is now part of a toolkit of spatial interaction techniques that run from entropy maximization (Wilson 1971) through to neural network modeling (Fischer et al. 2003).

A major juncture in the development of gravity modeling developed 50 years ago in the field of bilateral trade flows with the pioneering work of Tinbergen (1962) and Pöyhönen (1963). In its basic form, the gravity model hypothesizes that bilateral transactions between origins and destinations vary inversely with the distance between them, as well as with pull factors in destinations and push factors in origins. Although gravity modeling was initially applied to international trade, it was subsequently extended to the study of international capital flows and

---

M. Beenstock (✉) • D. Felsenstein
Hebrew University of Jerusalem, Jerusalem, Israel
e-mail: michael.beenstock@mail.huji.ac.il

R. Patuelli, G. Arbia (eds.), *Spatial Econometric Interaction Modelling*, Advances in Spatial Science, DOI 10.1007/978-3-319-30196-9_11

international migration. Gravity modeling has also been applied intranationally, e.g. in the study of internal migration. Indeed, the gravity model has served as a methodological work-horse in numerous empirical studies involving origins and destinations. Most probably the number of published papers using gravity modeling runs into the thousands.

Although the basic gravity assumption, the strength of attraction between origins and destinations varies inversely with distance between them, makes intuitive sense, it was not until the late 1970s that the theoretical underpinnings of gravity in international trade were formulated (Anderson 1979). Subsequently trade theorists have disputed whether gravity is consistent with the old theory of international trade based on Heckscher–Ohlin or the new theory of international trade based on imperfect competition (Bergstrand 1985, 1989; Deardorff 1998; Evenett and Keller 2002).

It took another 20 years for the theoretical underpinnings of gravity in international trade and migration to be formulated in terms of Multilateral Resistance (Anderson and van Wincoop 2003, 2004; Feenstra 2004), according to which traders or migrants face a discrete choice problem in choosing to trade with or emigrate to alternative destinations. The common denominator to these theories is that goods in the case of trade, and domiciles in the case of migration are imperfect substitutes and that trade and migration involve frictions. In this chapter, however, our concern does not lie with gravity theory but with its econometric aspects. Surprisingly, the latter have attracted little attention, except until recently.

In gravity models the dependent variable is bilateral from an origin to a destination. If there are N locations or nodes there must be N(N-1) bilateral observations. The standard econometric assumption made in innumerable studies has been that these bilateral observations are independent, which enables the use of ordinary least squares (OLS) to estimate the parameters of the gravity model. Denoting the residuals from the gravity model by u_{od} (where o labels origins and d labels destinations), OLS assumes that u_{od} is independent of u_{do}. For example, Italian exports to Israel are independent of Italian imports from Israel. This assumption may be contravened for a variety of reasons.[1] OLS also assumes the u_{od} is independent of $u_{od'}$ where d′ is another destination. If, for example d′ refers to Greece and the economies of Israel and Greece are related directly through international trade or indirectly through third countries, Italian exports to Israel may not be independent of Italian exports to Greece. OLS further assumes that u_{od} is independent of $u_{o'd}$ where o′ is another origin. If, for example, o′ refers to France and the economies of France and Israel are related, Israel's exports to Italy may not be independent of Israel's exports to third countries such as France. In short, the assumption that the residuals are independent may be incorrect.

If the gravity residuals are dependent, OLS estimates of the gravity model parameters are inefficient but consistent and unbiased, because according to the classical OLS assumptions dependence between residuals induces inefficiency

[1] For example, Israel swimsuit exports use fabrics made in Italy.

but does not constitute a threat to consistency and unbiasedness.[2] Since OLS is inefficient there may be many results that are incorrectly reported as being statistically significant. In principle robust standard errors may be calculated which take account of the dependence between the gravity residuals. Driscoll and Kraay (1998) have suggested such a procedure for spatially correlated residuals in panel data. More generally, the solution to this problem would be seemingly-unrelated regression (SUR) in which the estimated standard errors are calculated under the assumption that the gravity residuals are dependent. However, SUR is only feasible in the case of panel data.

The issue of dependence runs deeper than this; it does not merely concern the gravity residuals, but the specification of the gravity model itself. Since trade, capital flows and immigration are essentially multilateral, a bilateral specification is miss-specified. The trade flows between Italy and Israel do not only depend on push and pull factors in these countries, but also on these factors in third countries. For example, an increase in GDP in France might affect bilateral trade between Italy and Israel. In principle, the gravity model should specify all $N - 2$ push-pull factors. Since in practice gravity models do not specify third country effects, numerous studies may have omitted variables that are empirically relevant. If these omitted variables are correlated with the variables in the gravity model, the parameter estimates of the gravity model will be biased and inconsistent. This criticism applies to hundreds of studies that have been published during the last 50 years.

Econometric theory for gravity modeling only began to receive attention in the last few years. LeSage and Pace (2008) were the first to draw attention to the problem. Although the problem is essentially multilateral, LeSage and Pace assume that the data are spatially dependent. This simplification enables them to draw upon spatial econometric theory by specifying spatially lagged dependent variables in the gravity model, and by allowing the gravity residuals to be spatially autocorrelated. They specify separate spatial connectivity matrices for origins and destinations. If multilateralism happens to be spatial this solution is fine. However, it might not be. In the case of trade, for example, Israel's high-tech exports to Italy may be multilaterally related to Israel's competitors in the US and Finland, which are remote, rather than to Israel's immediate neighbors in the Middle East. Behrens et al. (2012) have adapted LeSage and Pace (2008) to multilateral resistance theory by giving spatial connectivity matrices a multilateral rather than a spatial interpretation.[3] Recently this attention to spatial dependence has been extended to the case where 'latent' spatial effects are estimated for both the origin and destination (LeSage and Llano 2013). This involves the estimation of a Bayesian

[2]This is the spatial counterpart to the time series result that auto-correlated residuals induce inefficiency but do not threaten consistency, unless the model includes lagged dependent variables.

[3]Behrens et al. assume that because income and the number of product varieties vary directly with scale, larger economies are more likely to trade with each other than smaller ones. According, spatial weights are defined in terms of the relative size of regions as reflected in population shares. Their identification strategy assumes that internal migration is independent of trade.

hierarchical model that uses the SAR structure as a spatial prior to structure the regional effects parameters.

It should be clear by now that econometric theory for gravity has lagged substantially behind the economic theory of gravity. Indeed, the econometric theory for gravity is in its infancy. Economists have been preoccupied instead with other econometric problems that arise in gravity models, and especially how to deal with the fact that many bilateral flows are zero, and their implications for testing hypotheses about extensive and intensive margins. Helpman et al. (2008) specify a probit selection model for zero trade flows, and Burger et al. (2009) apply a zero-inflation methodology. In our opinion this a second order problem; the main methodological problem stems from the fact that gravity is essentially multilateral rather than bilateral.

We have noted that dependence between gravity residuals affects the efficiency but not consistency of OLS estimates of gravity parameters. Matters are different regarding the nonlinear maximum likelihood estimators used to handle zero bilateral flows. Dependence between residuals in probit and zero-inflating estimators induces inconsistency. Having solved one problem, Helpman et al. and others might have created another. It is difficult to know whether OLS that ignores zero bilateral flows is inferior to ML which does not ignore zeros, but which ignores dependence between gravity residuals.

Griffith and Fischer (2013) suggest treating spatial dependence by using spatial filtering. This involves screening the origin–destination data for spatial association by transferring SAC effects from residuals to the mean or intercept. This creates dependence-free data suitable for Poisson estimation. The Poisson regression interprets the flows as dependent on the origin and destination specific effects. Spatial filtering treats spatiality as a nuisance parameter that may be "concentrated out" of the data to estimate the parameters of interest. We have remarked elsewhere (Beenstock and Felsenstein 2007) that spatial filtering is only legitimate if the parameters of interest are independent of the spatial nuisance parameters. If they are not, spatial filtering may induce pre-test bias, and in the limit the effect of a parameter of interest may be completely filtered away.[4] Indeed, since trade and migration are inherently multilateral, spatial filtering inappropriately treats parameters of interest as nuisances.

In this chapter we make the following methodological contributions to the econometrics of gravity modeling. First, we consider the case in which origins and destinations are not mutual, i.e. countries or spatial units are either origins or destinations, but not both, so bilateral relations are one-way. Second, we propose a lagrange multiplier test for spatial autocorrelation among origins and among destinations, which may be used to check whether OLS gravity residuals are spatially independent. Third, we also propose a test for spatial autoregressive conditional heteroscedasticity (SpARCH) between origins and destinations. SpARCH

[4]Temporal filtering (seasonal adjustment) of time series data is usually avoided because seasonality cannot be assumed to be independent of the parameters of interest.

exists when error variances are spatially autocorrelated; it is the spatial counterpart to ARCH in time series, and it is the counterpart to spatial autocorrelation for variances.[5] More generally, whereas spatial econometric analysis has been almost exclusively concerned with spatial dependence between means, as e.g. in the spatial lag model, we draw attention to potential spatial dependence between second moments as well as between first moments. We illustrate these concepts empirically with an application to migration from European Neighborhood Countries (EN) to members of the European Union (EU). Since migration from EN to EU is one-way, EN countries serve as origins and EU countries serve as destinations.

A limitation is that multilateralism is assumed here to be spatial. This means, for example, that when Egyptians emigrate to France their decision is not independent of local alternative destinations to France, such as Germany. However, it is independent of distant alternatives, such as the United States. It also means that when Libyans emigrate to France their decision is not independent of their Egyptian neighbors' decisions to emigrate to France. However, their decisions are independent of emigration decisions in origins remote from Libya, such as Ukraine. The implicit assumption in spatial multilateralism is that, everything else given, destinations are closer substitutes the nearer they are, and that shocks are likely to be more correlated among origins the closer they are.

This implicit assumption is no doubt too restrictive because multilateralism is not merely spatial. Quebec may be a closer substitute to France for francophone Algerians than Germany regardless of distance. Also, the emigration decisions of Israelis and Egyptians are unlikely to be correlated just because they happen to be in the Middle East. If decision making in migration and trade is hierarchal or nested, then spatial effects are likely to be important. However, if it is direct and unmediated, we can assume that relations are multilateral.

11.2 Theory

11.2.1 Origins and Destinations

Let y_{od} denote the bilateral flow between origin o and destination d. There are N_o origins, N_d destinations and $N = N_d N_o$ one-way bilateral flows. Let y_o denote an N_d-length vector of bilateral flows from origin o to all destinations. These vectors

[5]SpARCH is not to be confused with the spatial GARCH model in Willcocks (2010) in which the variance in location i at time t depends on the variance of location j at time t-1. Nor should it be confused with the SEARCH model of Caporin and Paruolo (2005) in which the residuals are spatially autocorrelated in a regular ARCH model, i.e. $u_{it} = Wu_{it} + e_{it}$ where e is an ARCH process.

are stacked, as in panel data, to form an N-length vector of bilateral flows y:

$$y' = (y'_1\ y'_{2.} \ldots . y'_{N_o})$$

The first N_d elements of y refer to flows from origin 1 to all destinations, the second N_d elements refer to flows from origin 2 to all destinations, and so on until the last N_d elements refer to flows from origin N_o to all destinations. W_o is a square N_o-matrix of spatial weights in the origins with zeros along the leading diagonal, and row-summed to one:

$$W_o = \begin{bmatrix} 0 & w_{12} & .. & w_{1N_0} \\ w_{21} & 0 & .. & w_{2N_0} \\ .. & .. & .. & .. \\ w_{N_o1} & w_{N_o2} & .. & 0 \end{bmatrix}$$

W_d is a square N_d-matrix of spatial weights in the destinations with zeros along the leading diagonal, and row-summed to one:

$$W_d = \begin{bmatrix} 0 & w_{12} & .. & w_{1N_d} \\ w_{21} & 0 & .. & w_{2N_d} \\ .. & .. & .. & .. \\ w_{N_d1} & w_{N_d2} & .. & 0 \end{bmatrix}$$

The elements w_{ij} are zero if i and j are spatially unconnected.[6] Define $D = I_{N_o} \otimes W_d$ and $\Omega = W_o \otimes I_{N_d}$, which are N × N matrices. D is block diagonal with W_d along the leading diagonal and zeros elsewhere. Ω has zeros along the leading diagonal and $w_{od}I_{Nd}$ elsewhere. The vector of spatial lags in origins and destinations may be defined as:

$$\tilde{y}_o = \Omega y \tag{11.1a}$$

$$\tilde{y}_d = Dy \tag{11.1b}$$

For example, y_{od} is the flow from origin o to destination d. Let o be Egypt and d be France. Flows from Egypt to France might be related to flows from Libya (Egypt's neighbor among origins) to France. This spatial lag component is included in $\tilde{y}_o$ because Libya and Egypt are origins with common destinations. Flows from Egypt to France might be related to flows from Egypt to Germany. This spatial lag

[6]Subscripts i and j refer to origins in W_o and destinations in W_d.

component is included in $\tilde{y}_d$ because France and Germany are destinations with common origins.

11.2.2 Spatial Gravity

The generalized spatial lag model with origins and destinations (GSOD) is:

$$\begin{aligned}
y &= \alpha i_N + X_o^*\beta_o + X_d^*\beta_d + \delta C + \tilde{X}_o^*\gamma_o + \tilde{X}_d^*\gamma_d + \rho_o\tilde{y}_o + \rho_d\tilde{y}_d + u \\
X_o^* &= X_o \otimes i_{N_d} \\
X_d^* &= i_{N_o} \otimes X_d \\
\tilde{X}_o^* &= W_oX_o \otimes i_{N_d} \\
\tilde{X}_d^* &= i_{N_o} \otimes W_dX_d
\end{aligned} \tag{11.2}$$

where C is an N-vector of distances between origins and destinations with elements c_{od}, X_o is an $N_o \times K_o$ matrix of push factors in the origins, X_d is an $N_d \times K_d$ matrix of pull factors in the destinations, and $\tilde{X}_o = W_oX_o$ and $\tilde{X}_d = W_dX_d$ are their spatial "Durbin" lag counterparts. Greek symbols are parameters to be estimated where α and δ are scalars, β_o and γ_o are K_o-vectors of push parameters, β_d and γ_d are K_d-vectors of pull parameters, and ρ_o and ρ_d are spatial lag coefficients in origins and destinations. Finally, u is an N-vector of residuals. Equation (11.2) states that flows, e.g. from Egypt to France depend on push factors in Egypt through α, push factors in Libya through δ, pull factors in France through β, and pull factors in Germany through π. They also depend on flows from Libya to France via ρ_o, and from France to Germany via ρ_d.

There are several economic justifications for specifying spatial dynamics in Eq. (11.2). First, there may be mutual causal effects between neighboring origins and destinations. For example, the decision by Libyans to emigrate to France might induce Egyptians to emigrate to France because neighbors influence one another. Second, if the specification of the pull (X_d) and push (X_o) factors is incomplete spatial lagged dependent variables might capture omitted variables. For example, if Libya and Egypt share common omitted variables they will be picked up by ρ_o. Third, Libyans and Egyptians might be complements or substitutes in common labor markets such as France. In the former case Libyans and Egyptians crowd-in one another in France; in the latter case they crowd-out one another. In the case of illegal immigration there is likely to be crowding-out unless Libyans and Egyptians share common social networks and logistics.

Similar economic justifications for ρ_d apply in the destinations. There might be a causal effect of Egyptian immigration to Belgium on Egyptian immigration to France through demonstration effects; Egyptian immigration to Belgium induces Egyptians to consider emigration to France. Omitted variables might be picked-up by Egyptian immigration to Belgium. Finally, if Belgium accepts more Egyptians this might deflect Egyptian emigration to France.

11.2.3 Spatial Multilateralism

The general solution for y is obtained by substituting Eq. (11.2) into Eq. (11.3) to obtain:

$$\begin{aligned} y &= \Theta\left[\alpha i_N + X_o^* \beta_o + X_d^* \beta_d + \delta C + \tilde{X}_o^* \gamma_o + \tilde{X}_d^* \gamma_d + u\right] \\ \Theta &= \left(I_N - \rho_o \Omega - \rho_d D\right)^{-1} \end{aligned} \tag{11.3}$$

We assume that ρ_o and ρ_d are less than one in absolute value otherwise y would be spatially nonstationary (Beenstock et al. 2012). This ensures that Θ is invertible. The N^2 elements of Θ, denoted by $\theta_{od.o'd'}$, describe the partial derivative of y_{od} with respect to immigration shocks from origin o′ to destination d′. These shocks propagate spatially so that to a greater or lesser degree all bilateral flows are related. This means for example that immigration from Morocco to Spain depends on shocks to immigration from Ukraine to Finland. Similarly, shocks to push factors in Morocco and pull factors in Spain affect immigration from Ukraine to Finland. It also means that $\theta_{od.od}$ does not necessarily equal unity as it would in a standard gravity model. Indeed, if the spatial dynamics are positive $\theta_{od.od} > 1$ because shocks propagate spatially back onto their origins. For example, an immigration shock from Morocco to Spain reverberates back onto Morocco via its effect on immigration from other origins to other destinations.

The spatial specification of the gravity model "multilateralizes" it from being purely bilateral. In short, GSOD specifies a rich range of spatial dynamics of the autoregressive and moving average varieties through ρ_o and ρ_d, and γ_o and γ_d respectively.

11.3 The Econometrics of Spatial Gravity Modeling

11.3.1 Double Spatial Lagged Dependent Variables

Since GSOD involves a double spatial lag, estimation is not straightforward because the likelihood function involves the determinant $|I_N - \rho_o \Omega - \rho_d D|$. If $\rho_o = \rho_d$ matters are simplified and the determinant reverts to its standard form involving a single spatial lag, in which case standard estimators available in Matlab etc. may be used. The likelihood has to be maximized with respect to ρ_o and ρ_d as well as other GSOD parameters. We use the double spatial lag estimator developed by Elhorst et al. (2012) to estimate the parameters of GSOD.

11.3.2 Spatial Autocorrelation

The GSOD residuals (u) are assumed to be iid random variables that are asymptotically normal. Spatial autocorrelation in GSOD residuals may arise either because the residuals are spatially correlated among origins, or because they are spatially correlated among destinations. For example, spatial autocorrelation among origins arises when the residuals for Egyptian flows to France and other destinations are correlated with Libya's residuals with respect to France as well as other destinations. Spatial autocorrelation among destinations arises when the residuals for Egyptian flows to France are correlated with Egypt's residuals with respect to Germany and other destinations.

We suggest the following auxiliary regression to test for both types of spatial autocorrelation:

$$\begin{aligned}\hat{u} &= X_o \otimes i_{N_d}\psi_o + i_{N_o} \otimes X_d\psi_d + \lambda_o\tilde{u}_o + \lambda_d\tilde{u}_d + \varepsilon \\ \tilde{u}_o &= \Omega\hat{u} \\ \tilde{u}_d &= D\hat{u}\end{aligned} \tag{11.4}$$

where $\hat{u}$ are the GSOD residuals estimated by ML, and ε is iid. The absence of spatial autocorrelation means that λ_o and λ_d are zero, in which case ψ_o and ψ_d must be zero. The lagrange multiplier statistic is $LM = NR^2$ where R^2 is for Eq. (11.4). It has a chi-square distribution with 2 degrees of freedom for the two independent restrictions regarding λ_o and λ_d.

If the GSOD residuals happen to be spatially autocorrelated, this may indicate that the GSOD model is spatially misspecified, or it may suggest that it is correctly specified but the residuals just happen to be spatially autocorrelated. A straightforward common factor test (Anselin 1988) may be used to distinguish between these alternatives. If there is a spatial common factor the model would be spatially misspecified. If in the former event, λ_o only is statistically significant the spatial misspecification arises among the origins, and if λ_d only is statistically significant the spatial misspecification arises among the destinations.

11.3.3 Spatially Robust Standard Errors for Gravity Models

Spatial autocorrelation may be inherent or it might be induced by the misspecification of Eq. (11.2). In the latter case the remedy involves specifying the model correctly. In the former case the parameter estimates are unbiased but inefficient in linear models, but are inconsistent in nonlinear models such as ML estimates of spatial lag models. In this section we assume that the true model is not spatial so that $\rho_o = \rho_d = \gamma_o = \gamma_d = 0$, but the gravity residuals are spatially autocorrelated.

Equation (11.2) is rewritten compactly as Eq. (11.5a):

$$y = Q\omega + u \tag{11.5a}$$

$$u = (\lambda_o\Omega + \lambda_d D)\, u + \varepsilon \tag{11.5b}$$

where $Q = (X_o{}^*\ X_d{}^*\ C)$ refers to the $K_o + K_d + 1$ regressors in Eq. (11.2) and $\omega = (\beta_o\ \beta_d\ \delta)$ their coefficients. Equation (11.5b) is the SAC model for the gravity residuals. The solution for u is:

$$\begin{aligned} u &= A\varepsilon \\ A &= (I_N - \lambda_o\Omega - \lambda_d D)^{-1} \end{aligned} \tag{11.6}$$

The spatially robust covariance matrix of the OLS estimate of ω is:

$$\begin{aligned} \Sigma_\omega &= (Q'Q)^{-1}\left(Q'\hat{\Theta}Q\right)(Q'Q)^{-1} \\ \hat{\Theta} &= \hat{A}\hat{\Sigma}_\varepsilon\hat{A}' \end{aligned} \tag{11.7}$$

If ε is homoscedastic $\Theta = \sigma_\varepsilon{}^2 AA'$. To implement Eq. (11.7) consistent estimates of A and Σ_ε based on estimates of λ_o, λ_d and ε obtained from Eq. (11.4) are substituted into Eq. (11.7). If ε is heteroskedastic $\Theta = A\ \Xi\ A'$ where Ξ is a diagonal matrix with diagonal elements $\hat{u}^2_{od}$.

General least squares (GLS) jointly estimates the parameters of the error model and the structural parameters consistently and efficiently. By contrast, the estimate of Σ_ω in Eq. (11.7) is consistent but not efficient because it is derived from OLS parameter estimates which are less informative than their GLS counterparts. Therefore a superior alternative to the use of spatially robust standard errors is to estimate Eq. (11.2) by GLS, which involves the joint estimation of the parameters in Eq. (11.2) together with λ_o and λ_d. This argument applies generally and is not specific to spatial models.[7] Indeed, the preference for robust standard errors is typically motivated by convenience.

11.3.4 Spatial Autoregressive Conditional Heteroskedasticity (SpARCH)

Another type of potential dependence concerns variances. We suggest that the spatial counterpart to the ARCH (autoregressive conditional heteroskedasticity) that

[7] See e.g. Greene (2012), pp. 325 and 960.

arises in time series may be specified as:

$$\hat{u}^2 = \phi + \phi_o \tilde{u}_o^2 + \phi_d \tilde{u}_d^2 \tag{11.8}$$

The spatial ARCH (SpARCH) parameters are ϕ_o and ϕ_d, which might differ between origins and destinations. Equation (11.8) assumes that volatility may be transmitted spatially, and that the conditional variance of u_{od} depends on volatility in the vicinity of *o* among origins, and in the vicinity of *d* among destinations. These variances are therefore conditionally heteroskedastic. By contrast, the unconditional variance is:

$$\sigma_e^2 = \phi[I_N - \phi_o \Omega - \phi_d D]^{-1}$$

Since this does not depend on o or d the unconditional variance is the same for all gravity residuals (u_{od}). The LM test for SpARCH involves using the estimated GSOD residuals to estimate Eq. (11.8). The test statistic is NR^2 and has a chi-squared distribution with 2 degrees of freedom.

Whereas unconditional homoskedasticity is one of the classical assumptions required for OLS, conditional heteroskedasticity does not violate these assumptions.[8] Therefore, evidence of SpARCH does not matter for efficiency in OLS contexts because the residuals remain unconditionally homoskedastic. With nonlinear estimators matters are different because it is well known that ARCH interferes with consistency. Since the spatial lag parameters in GSOD obtained by ML are nonlinear, SpARCH induces inconsistency in the estimates of the GSOD parameters.

11.4 The European Neighborhood

The European Neighborhood (EN) is a geopolitical concept (see map) as defined by EU foreign policy in general and the European Neighborhood Policy (ENP) in particular.[9] It includes countries that are not candidates for EU membership, hence Turkey is not included in the EN. EN includes all countries in North Africa with coasts on the Mediterranean. It includes countries in the Middle East (Israel, Jordan, Lebanon and Syria), countries in South Caucasia (Georgia, Armenia, Azerbaijan), and countries in the former USSR (Ukraine, Belorussia and Moldova), making 16 countries in all. The EU regards EN countries as their political and economic hinterland. These EN countries serve as origins in the present study.

[8] See e.g. Greene (2012), p. 972.

[9] ENP involves concessions to EN countries regarding trade, investment and migration. It also obliges neighboring countries to adapt local legislation to EU norms thereby extending integration without formal enlargement (Harpaz, 2014).

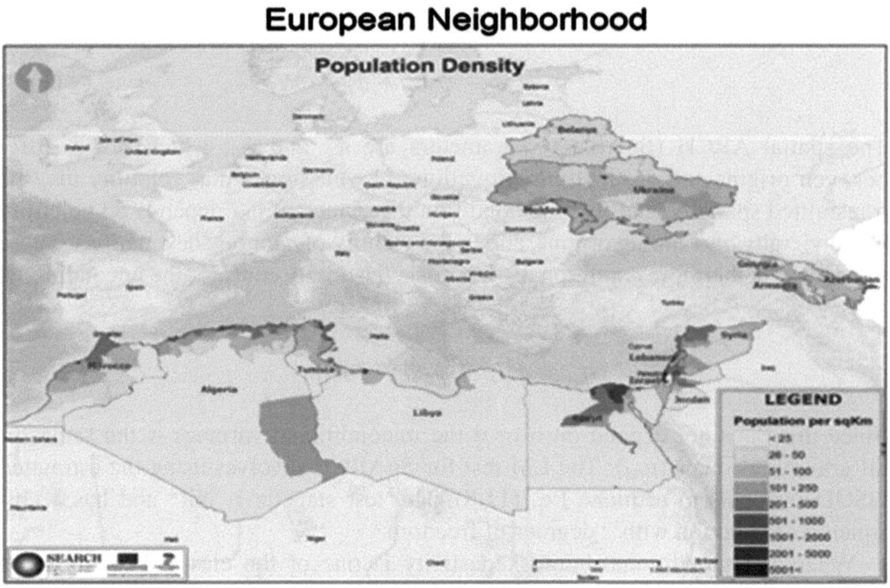

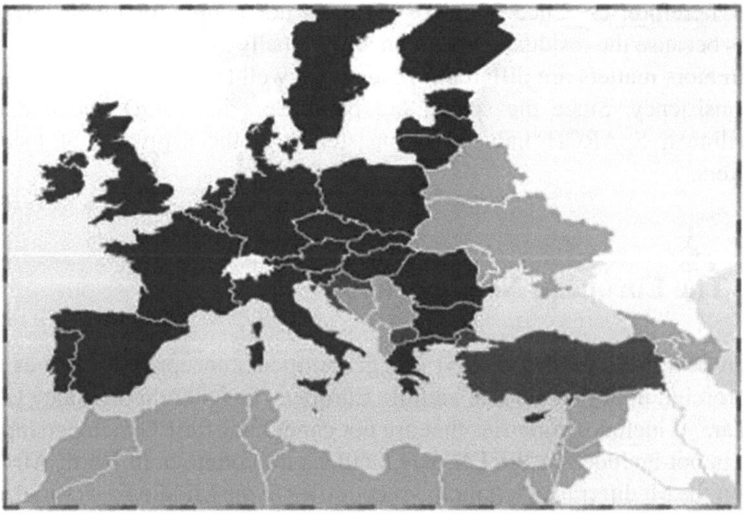

Dealing with migration flows from the ENP countries is high on the EU policy agenda. While this chapter deals with immigration over the period 2000–2010, i.e. prior to the current immigration crisis in the EU, the issues of cross-border controls with the EN countries remain a pervasive issue. The EU shares a 5000 + km border with the EN countries to the east and a similar length (albeit maritime) border with the EN countries to the south. EU policy relating to migration from the EN countries has been articulated in various agreements such as the Amsterdam Treaty and the Tampere, Hague and Stockholm Programs. Migration policy with respect to EN countries is part of an EU attempt to regulate border security in three areas: illegal (or irregular) migration, combating trafficking and smuggling of human beings and cross-border management practice.

The EU currently has 28 members, including countries such as Latvia, Romania and Croatia that have joined recently. In principle these countries serve as the destinations. However, we restrict the EU destinations to the 15 members prior to the recent enlargement for two reasons. First, the study period refers to immigration during the first decade of the twenty-first century. Since countries such as Romania and Bulgaria were not members in 2000 they are omitted from the study. Secondly, it turns out that there were no immigrants from EN in the 10 omitted EU members. Dropping these countries conveniently means that we may ignore the problem of treating zero bilateral flows. Therefore, N_o is 16 and N_d is 15.

We use the Global Bilateral Migration Database (GBMD, World Bank) which provides estimates of the number of foreign-born by all origins of the world in all destinations.[10] Table 11.1 presents these data in 2000 for our 16 origins in the 15 destinations. Notice that with the exception of Portugal these population stocks are non-zero. GBMD is decennial starting from 1960. Since GBMD refers to population stocks, we define immigration flows from origins to destinations by the stock in 2010 minus the stock in 2000. GBMD in principle covers people who returned to their country of origin by 2010 or migrated to third countries. However, foreign-born who died between 2000 and 2010 would be registered as a decrease in the number of foreign-born. Therefore, our definition of immigration flows is an underestimate because GBMD does not identify the deceased. This partly explains why the estimated flows of immigrants (Table 11.2) are occasionally negative. Table 11.2 expresses changes in foreign-born during 2000–2010 as a percentage of the stock in 2000. Some of these estimated rates are very large especially in destinations where foreign-born in 2000 was small (e.g. Portugal)

11.5 Immigration Theory

This paper tests the welfare-motivation pull factor hypothesis of migration. The basic idea that immigration is driven by income differentials between origins and destinations is usually attributed to Hicks (1932) and Sjaastad (1962). However, Adam Smith argued that migration is driven by wage differentials, and regarded policies to limit internal migration in England as unjust and economically harmful.[11] The development of the welfare state during the twentieth century created a new motivation for immigration. Immigrants are attracted to destinations where welfare

[10]See Özden et al. (2011) for methodological details how GBMD was constructed.

[11]Smith (1776) argued that the Law of Settlements, enacted to prevent inter-parish welfare-chasing, restricted internal migration and was responsible for spatial wage inequality. "The very unequal price of labour which we frequently find in England in places at no great distance from one another, is probably owing to the obstruction which the law of settlements gives to a poor man who would carry his industry from one parish to another without a certificate" (p. 142). Smith called for the repeal of the Law of Settlements and the promotion of internal migration.

Table 11.1 Foreign-born in 2000

Origin	Destination														
	Austria	Belgium	Denmark	Finland	France	Germany	Greece	Ireland	Italy	Luxembourg	Netherlands	Portugal	Spain	Sweden	UK
Algeria	546	8004	932	456	1,057,135	20,295	267	861	15,861	347	3873	0	23,269	1664	40,555
Armenia	654	195	569	89	2961	21,695	7438	52	280	6	252	19	2502	448	15
Azerbaijan	140	13	125	41	382	2055	102	43	99	4	423	2	144	249	2
Belarus	373	45	239	154	791	3813	336	610	1680	42	71	5	667	590	46
Egypt	6661	724	1247	388	5060	14,208	7156	620	43,477	107	9381	0	1631	2062	26,975
Georgia	332	254	110	47	15,420	75,104	21,977	150	318	12	113	105	1341	174	82
Israel	1696	1679	1423	442	4919	9351	335	285	2561	74	4314	0	912	1500	7729
Jordan	412	289	961	133	635	11,007	646	137	2983	6	827	0	1202	1056	636
Lebanon	544	1016	11,982	283	11,033	51,611	1228	151	4163	92	3060	0	1657	19,817	11,219
Libya	357	61	167	68	413	831	188	737	3382	15	466	0	438	370	136
Morocco	827	110,962	4776	998	262,462	84,619	521	302	286,498	557	151,254	1094	253,173	4443	20,878
Moldova	308	135	109	65	2608	13,736	5492	958	6680	15	22	2947	1833	97	180
Russia	4895	1129	2669	10,527	217,690	978,793	16,847	2695	14,864	461	23,439	1462	11,316	8579	15,053
Syria	825	690	1328	183	5550	26,114	5334	153	3411	33	5662	0	2720	14,005	5646
Tunisia	1710	3762	728	292	310,949	25,260	225	125	75,808	237	3800	0	1005	2698	9948
Ukraine	2534	540	1056	878	11,687	58,163	13,082	1566	13,755	204	225	9843	18,491	1919	783

Table 11.2 Foreign-born growth rates (%) 2000-2010

Origin	Destination														
	Austria	Belgium	Denmark	Finland	France	Germany	Greece	Ireland	Italy	Luxembourg	Netherlands	Portugal	Spain	Sweden	UK
Algeria	34.4	169.2	27.4	68.6	−13.6	3.9	41.6	125.9	85.9	16.7	−1.0		172.2%	33.6	−61.5
Armenia	−9.9	491.3	30.8	66.3	389.1	−28.5	17.9	159.6	97.9	16.7	658.7	310.5	395.1%	98.2	5160.0%
Azerbaijan	40.0	753.8	50.4	68.3	−8.4	1032.1	52.9	160.5	156.6	25.0	566.9	700.0	295.1%	117.3	37450.0
Belarus	48.5	1102.2	134.3	66.2	36.3	664.1	61.0	88.2	230.1	21.4	625.4	3620.0	474.1%	120.8	3260.9
Egypt	79.9	258.6	37.3	80.2	453.8	47.0	28.9	134.8	108.1	20.6	20.5		156.6%	36.9	4.2
Georgia	98.5	63.8	43.6	57.4	−92.5	−75.8	90.3	144.0	313.8	16.7	732.7	89.5	698.1%	121.3	800.0
Israel	27.8	126.6	40.8	80.5	77.3	50.6	124.2	128.4	18.4	21.6	20.7		225.9%	45.7	75.1
Jordan	32.0	115.6	38.8	80.5	51.0	42.4	49.7	144.5	24.7	16.7	5.4		96.9%	50.6	548.7
Lebanon	175.6	332.2	28.3	79.5	312.0	19.3	206.1	148.3	143.7	20.7	9.6		110.9%	23.3	39.2
Libya	17.9	549.2	38.9	82.4	268.3	437.8	55.9	138.7	−41.7	20.0	26.8		293.8%	49.5	8802.9
Morocco	41.5	55.6	34.4	59.5	220.4	28.2	36.1	95.0	66.1	19.7	10.6	74.5	207.5%	40.5	−40.2
Moldova	45.5	167.4	74.3	66.2	−72.1	26.9	34.4	248.1	1235.1	20.0	590.9	45.5	857.5%	173.2	238.3
Russia	77.4	2794.5	91.8	66.6	−80.2	−69.4	125.4	150.0	88.3	18.9	−74.9	124.8	442.2%	58.1	121.3
Syria	162.8	323.9	71.0	80.3	192.3	54.5	99.1	105.9	34.9	18.2	18.4		100.5%	38.5	−2.2
Tunisia	60.7	195.8	34.2	76.4	−2.8	46.7	58.2	99.2	60.5	19.4	11.4		170.7%	33.8	−59.1
Ukraine	68.7	265.4	486.4	66.6	29.6	248.2	89.8	221.1	1154.6	20.6	610.2%	56.8	377.4%	76.8	3090.2

benefits in cash and in kind are more generous.[12] Empirical evidence in favor of this hypothesis has been found for the EU (Péridy 2006; De Giorgi and Pellizzari 2006; Docquier and Marfouk 2006; Razin et al. 2011) and for internal migration in the US (Borjas 1999; McKinnish 2007). In recent work we found that while immigration does not depend on the level of welfare generosity, it varies directly with changes in generosity (Beenstock et al. 2015). More benevolent countries do not necessarily attract more immigration but if a country become more welfare-generous that will have a positive effect on migration. Razin et al. argue that welfare generosity disproportionately attracts unskilled immigrants because skilled immigrants are deterred by the higher taxation required to finance this generosity. In all of these studies it is assumed that bilateral migration flows are independent.

11.5.1 Stocks and Flows

Immigration flows during time t to t + 1 are hypothesized to be determined according to Sjaastad's stock adjustment model in which the levels of push and pull factors at time t and their changes during times t to t + 1 are hypothesized to determine immigration. For example, if GDP per head is a pull factor, immigration varies directly with the level of GDP per head at time t and the change in GDP per head between times t and t + 1. If the immigrant stock was at its equilibrium level in time t, the stock-adjustment model predicts that immigration during times t and t + 1 should only depend on changes in the push and pull factors. The stock adjustment model predicts that immigration during t and t + 1 should vary inversely with the stock of immigrants at time t. If, however, incumbent immigrants provide new immigrants with social network amenities, the stock of immigrants at time t might also increase immigration.

Let Y_{odt} denote the stock of immigrants, or foreign-born, from origin o in destination d in time t, and Y^*_{odt} denote its equilibrium counterpart. The stock adjustment model predicts that the flow of immigrants between times t and t + 1 is:

$$y_{odt} = \eta\left(Y^*_{odt} - Y_{odt}\right) + \varphi\Delta Y^*_{odt+1} \tag{11.9}$$

where η and φ are stock adjustment coefficients with values between zero and one, and Y* depends on the levels of push and pull factors:

$$Y^*_t = X^*_d\zeta + X^*_o\xi \tag{11.10}$$

[12]Adam Smith would have been familiar with this theory since the Law of Settlements prevented individuals from migrating to parishes where the poor laws were administered more generously.

Substituting Eq. (11.10) into Eq. (11.9) and dropping subscript t gives:

$$y = \eta \left(X_d^* \zeta + X_o^* \xi \right) + \varphi \left(\Delta X_d^* \zeta + \Delta X_o^* \xi \right) - \eta Y_{od} \tag{11.11}$$

Therefore in Eq. (11.2) immigration depends on the levels and the changes in push and pull factors.

11.5.2 Push and Pull Factors

In gravity models immigration is assumed to depend on GDP per head in origins and destinations, as well as measures of cultural and ethnic difference. For example, if o and d share a common language immigration from o to d is likely to be greater. Also, immigration is hypothesized to vary inversely with the geographical distance between o and d. If immigrants are positively selected (Borjas 1987) they are attracted by income inequality since they expect to earn more where there is more wage dispersion. If so, immigration should vary directly with the gini coefficient in d.

We also investigate whether immigration is motivated by welfare. Legal immigrants benefit from social security and other benefits received by natives. Apart from pecuniary benefits, such as unemployment benefit and income support, we attach importance to benefits in kind including health, education and housing. Given everything else, we expect that d will be a more attractive destination to immigrants the more generous are its benefits.

The case of illegal or irregular immigrants is more complicated. Procedures for dealing with political refugees vary by country; they may be more or less lenient. If country d is more lenient it is likely to attract more immigrants. Illegal immigrants either did not apply for refugee status, or if they did and were refused, they go underground. Countries also vary by their alacrity in expelling illegal immigrants. Finally, countries vary by the legal rights of illegal immigrants and their children in terms of their access to health services and schooling. Countries that are more lenient and generous in their treatment of illegal immigrants are expected to be more attractive as destinations. We are unaware of empirical studies of the effects of immigration policy on illegal immigration. Indeed, Yoshida and Woodland (2005) signally do not cite such studies.[13]

We have collected data on the rights of legal and irregular immigrants, as well as on the way countries treat irregular immigrants. We use data on expulsions and apprehensions to calculate expulsion and apprehension rates (in terms of the population at risk) in EU destinations. These rates are of the order of one percent except in Greece where they approach 30 % (see data Appendix). We also report

[13]Their concern is with the effects of illegal immigration on natives and policies designed to achieve the socially optimum amount of illegal immigration.

in the data appendix an index (MIPEX) of the treatment of legal immigrants in EU destinations in terms of the assistance they get to integrate economically, socially and politically.

11.6 Results

The dependent variable in Eq. (11.2) is defined as the rate of immigration that took place between 2000 and 2010, i.e. it is the data in Table 11.2. The push factors in origins (X_o) include GDP per head in 2000 and its rate of growth during 2000–2010. The push factors in destination (X_d) include GDP per head in 2000 and its rate of growth during 2000–2010, the gini coefficient for household income, social spending per head in 2000 and its rate of growth during 2000–2010, spending per head on primary education, expulsion and apprehension rates, and the treatment index of immigrants. We also control for distances between origins and destinations, common official languages, and immigrant stocks in 2000.

Most of these variables did not turn out to be statistically significant. Model 1 in Table 11.3 retains the variables which survived a specification search process in which insignificant variables were successively omitted. Since Model 1 is estimated by OLS it is assumed that the observations are spatially independent. The signs of the parameters in Model 1 are "correct" but they are not statistically significant at conventional levels. Since the LM test statistic for heteroskedasticity is highly significant, we also use robust standard errors.

Variables that do not feature in Model 1 include GDP per head and its growth in the EU destinations as well as the treatment index of immigrants. Immigration flows vary inversely with apprehension rates, and GDP per head and its growth in the EN origins, and they vary directly with social spending per head, spending on education and income inequality. When model 1 is estimated using data for 1990–2000 its explanatory power is even smaller than it is for 2000–2010, none of the estimated parameters is statistically significant, and many parameters change their signs. In short, model 1 is not robust and depends on the observation period.

The LM statistics reported in Table 11.4 indicate that the residuals of model 1 are not spatially autocorrelated, and the SpARCH coefficients are not significantly different from zero. When spatially lagged dependent variables are specified in models 2 and 3, the spatial lag coefficients are statistically significant. In model 2 the spatial lag coefficients are restricted to be identical in origins and destinations. Although in model 3 these coefficients are unrestricted, their estimates turn out to be similar, but different to their counterpart in model 2. Table 11.4 shows that when spatially lagged dependent variables are specified, the SAC and SpARCH coefficients are statistically significant between 2000 and 2010 as represented by the data in Table 11.2.

Table 11.3 Estimates of the migration model: 2000–2010

	Model 1: OLS		Model 2: ML		Model 3: ML	
	Coefficient	t statistic	Coefficient	t statistic	Coefficient	t statistic
Intercept	−0.66	−0.58	−0.558	−0.56	−0.54	−0.53
Immigrant stock 2000*	0.013	1.53	0.0091	1.39	−0.000387	−0.06
GDP per head in origin 2000*	−0.0314	−1.31	−0.00174	0.08	−0.00373	−0.18
Growth of GDP per head in origin	−0.0137	−0.99	−0.00735	−0.61	−0.00292	−0.24
Gini	1.709	1.95	1.115	1.54	0.7435	0.99
Social spending per head*	0.3283	0.31	0.0243	0.25	0.00384	0.40
Spending per pupil in primary education	0.0111	1.65	0.00477	0.94	0.00422	0.83
Apprehension rate	−3.02	−1.22	0.1129	0.25	0.3263	0.71
Common language	0.141	1.76	0.0968	1.41	0.0393	0.57
Distance	−0.000035	−1.50	−0.0000376	−1.86	−0.0000179	−0.90
Spatial lag: origin					0.500119	13.85
Spatial lag: destination			0.09897	2.4675	0.569238	16.65
R^2 adj	0.0632		0.0592		0.0677	

Dependent variable is the rate (percent) of migration from ENC to EU during 2000–2010. Asterisked variables are in logarithms

Table 11.4 SAC and SpARCH coefficients

Model	1	2	3
SAC			
Origin	0.0504 (0.23)	−0.4768 (−2.06)	−0.9941 (−9.16)
Destination	−0.0511 (−0.63)	−0.0840 (−0.37)	−0.9725 (−8.90)
LM	2.6015	24.209	81.399
SpARCH			
Origin	0.6596 (0.59)	0.9152 (4.18)	0.5922 (4.33)
Destination	0.0167 (0.25)	0.2350 (2.44)	0.5961 (6.91)
LM	0.408	25.536	61.968

Notes: LM refers to lagrange multiplier statistics for SAC and SpARCH. Their critical values ($p = 0.05$) are χ^2 ($df = 2$) = 5.991. t-statistics for SAC and SpARCH coefficients reported in parentheses

11.7 Conclusions

We have tried to make two contributions, methodological and substantive. Standard econometric analysis of gravity models has typically assumed that the observations are independent. This assumption is surprising because it implies that transactions from a given origin to alternative destinations are independent. It also assumes that transactions from different origins to the same destination are independent. We suggest a lagrange multiplier statistic to test origin–destination independence. We also model origin–destination dependence using recently developed double spatial lag estimators.

Our substantive contribution uses data on migration flows from European Neighborhood countries to EU destinations during the first decade of the twentieth century to test key hypotheses concerning the determinants of international migration. These include the hypotheses that migration is driven by income differentials, income inequality, welfare generosity in the destination countries, and policies to deter irregular immigration.

During the first decade of the twentieth century there is little if any evidence that migration from European Neighborhood Countries to the European Union depended on determinants that have been high-lighted in the theoretical literature. Neither the level of GDP per head in EU countries nor its rate of growth, explain migration from EN to EU. Therefore, the recent economic recession in EU is unlikely to deter migration from EN. There is some weak evidence that GDP per head and its growth in the EN countries deter migration. There is also some evidence that migrants prefer to migrate to EU countries where there is greater economic inequality. If immigrants are positively selected they stand to gain more in countries where incomes are more unequal.

There is no evidence that immigrants engage in welfare-chasing. This is true when welfare generosity is measured by social spending per head in the EU countries, when it is measured by per capita spending on primary schooling, or when expert indices are used. Nor does physical distance or common languages, which are standard variables in gravity models, significantly explain immigration from EN to EU. Indeed, immigration does not seem to be explained by any of the standard hypotheses regarding international migration. However, there is weak evidence that immigration policy, as measured by apprehension rates among irregular immigrants, deters immigration.

These results may be disappointing as far as policy recommendations are concerned. Social welfare policy and policy towards illegal migrants in EU destinations do not seem to impact the flow of migrants from the ENP countries. The paper also addresses the extent to which destination choices within the EU are complements and substitutes. This has policy ramifications with respect to the spillover of migration pressure points within the EU. A parochial policy which, for example, restricts migration in one country might deflect immigration to its neighbors. Also a policy which encourages immigration in one country might induce immigration to its neighbors. Thus immigration policy would need to be designed globally rather than parochially.

On the other hand, the methodological results are more salient. They show that results obtained using conventional econometric methods which assume gravity flows are independent are over-turned when these flows are specified to be dependent. Specifically, gravity models in which spatial lags are specified produce different results to standard gravity models. Moreover, separate spatial lags are specified among destination countries in the EU and origin countries in the EN. The coefficients on these spatial lags are about 0.5–0.6, implying that there are strong spillover effects in migration between neighboring origins as well as destinations. Indeed, these effects cancel out almost all the substantive effects to which reference has already been made.

Appendix: Data Sources

Variable	Unit	Definition	Source	Link
Immigration stock	Persons	Stock of persons born in country A living in country B at time t	World Bank—Global Bilateral Migration Database	http://data.worldbank.org/data-catalog/global-bilateral-migration-database
Immigration flow	Persons	Stock of persons born in country A living in country B at time t minus stock of persons born in country A living in country B at time t-1	World Bank—Global Bilateral Migration Database	http://data.worldbank.org/data-catalog/global-bilateral-migration-database
GDP	U.S. dollars, current prices	Gross domestic product per capita	IMF—World Economic Outlook Databases	http://www.imf.org/external/pubs/ft/weo/2012/02/weodata/download.aspx
Education expenditure	%	Public expenditure per pupil as a % of GDP per capita	UNESCO	http://stats.uis.unesco.org/unesco/TableViewer/document.aspx?ReportId=143&IF_Language=eng
Inequality	Gini coefficient		OECD	http://stats.oecd.org/
Social expenditure	U.S. dollars, constant PPPs (2000)	Expenditure per head	OECD	http://stats.oecd.org/
Common language	–	Common official language	CEPII Geodist dyadic dataset	http://www.cepii.fr/anglaisgraph/bdd/distances.htm
Distance	Km	Simple distance between most populated cities	CEPII Geodist dyadic dataset	http://www.cepii.fr/anglaisgraph/bdd/distances.htm

(continued)

Variable	Unit	Definition	Source	Link
Labour market mobility	Index	Experts index on the labour market mobility of immigrants	MIPEX—Migrant Integration Policy Index	http://www.mipex.eu/sites/default/files/downloads/mipexrawdata_final_13_02_2012.xlsx
Family reunion	Index	Experts index on the possibility of family reunion of immigrants	MIPEX—Migrant Integration Policy Index	http://www.mipex.eu/sites/default/files/downloads/mipexrawdata_final_13_02_2012.xlsx
Education	Index	Experts index on the special attention given to immigrant s needs in the education system	MIPEX—Migrant Integration Policy Index	http://www.mipex.eu/sites/default/files/downloads/mipexrawdata_final_13_02_2012.xlsx
Political participation	Index	Experts index on the level of political participation of immigrants	MIPEX—Migrant Integration Policy Index	http://www.mipex.eu/sites/default/files/downloads/mipexrawdata_final_13_02_2012.xlsx
Long term residence	Index	Experts index on the long term residency possibilities for immigrants	MIPEX—Migrant Integration Policy Index	http://www.mipex.eu/sites/default/files/downloads/mipexrawdata_final_13_02_2012.xlsx
Access to nationality	Index	Experts index on access to nationality possibilities for immigrants	MIPEX—Migrant Integration Policy Index	http://www.mipex.eu/sites/default/files/downloads/mipexrawdata_final_13_02_2012.xlsx
Anti-discrimination	Index	Experts index on anti-discrimination regulations to protect immigrants	MIPEX—Migrant Integration Policy Index	http://www.mipex.eu/sites/default/files/downloads/mipexrawdata_final_13_02_2012.xlsx

Toleration of residence	Index	Index based on policy options for persons not removed due to practical or technical obstacles	FRA (European Union Agency for Fundamental Rights)—Fundamental rights of migrants in an irregular situation in the European Union	http://research.icmpd.org/fileadmin/Research-Website/FRA/FRA_irregular_migration/Final_Reports-FRA_published_2011/FRA_2011_Migrants_in_an_irregular_situation_EN.pdf
Crime	Index	Index based on whether irregular entry/stay considered a crime?	FRA (European Union Agency for Fundamental Rights)—Fundamental rights of migrants in an irregular situation in the European Union	http://research.icmpd.org/fileadmin/Research-Website/FRA/FRA_irregular_migration/Final_Reports-FRA_published_2011/FRA_2011_Migrants_in_an_irregular_situation_EN.pdf
Housing	Index	Index based on the level of punishment for renting shelter to migrants in an irregular situation	FRA (European Union Agency for Fundamental Rights)—Fundamental rights of migrants in an irregular situation in the European Union	http://research.icmpd.org/fileadmin/Research-Website/FRA/FRA_irregular_migration/Final_Reports-FRA_published_2011/FRA_2011_Migrants_in_an_irregular_situation_EN.pdf
Healthcare	Index	Index based on the general healthcare entitlements for migrants in an irregular situation	FRA (European Union Agency for Fundamental Rights)—Fundamental rights of migrants in an irregular situation in the European Union	http://research.icmpd.org/fileadmin/Research-Website/FRA/FRA_irregular_migration/Final_Reports-FRA_published_2011/FRA_2011_Migrants_in_an_irregular_situation_EN.pdf

(continued)

Variable	Unit	Definition	Source	Link
Education	Index	Index based on the right to education for undocumented children	FRA (European Union Agency for Fundamental Rights)—Fundamental rights of migrants in an irregular situation in the European Union	http://research.icmpd.org/fileadmin/Research-Website/FRA/FRA_irregular_migration/Final_Reports-FRA_published_2011/FRA_2011_Migrants_in_an_irregular_situation_EN.pdf
Apprehensions	%	% of the number of foreign nationals apprehended/found to be illegally staying vs. the migrant stock in the destination country	EMN (European Migration Network)—Annual Report on Migration and International Protection Statistics 2003–2009	http://ec.europa.eu/dgs/home-affairs/what-we-do/networks/european_migration_network/reports/migrationstatistics/index_en.htm
Refusals	%	% of the number of foreign nationals refused entry vs. the migrant stock in the destination country	EMN (European Migration Network)—Annual Report on Migration and International Protection Statistics 2003–2009	http://ec.europa.eu/dgs/home-affairs/what-we-do/networks/european_migration_network/reports/migrationstatistics/index_en.htm
Removed	%	% of the number of foreign nationals removed vs. the migrant stock in the destination country	EMN (European Migration Network)—Annual Report on Migration and International Protection Statistics 2003–2009	http://ec.europa.eu/dgs/home-affairs/what-we-do/networks/european_migration_network/reports/migrationstatistics/index_en.htm

References

Anderson JE (1979) A theoretical foundation for the gravity equation. Am Econ Rev 69:105–116
Anderson J, van Wincoop E (2003) Gravity with gravitas: a solution to the border puzzle. Am Econ Rev 93:170–192
Anderson J, van Wincoop E (2004) Trade costs. J Econ Lit 42:691–751
Anselin J-L (1988) Spatial econometrics: methods and models. Kluwer, Dordrecht
Beenstock M, Felsenstein D (2007) Spatial vector autoregressions. Spat Econ Anal 2(2):167–196
Beenstock M, Feldman D, Felsenstein D (2012) Testing for unit roots and cointegration in spatial cross-section data. Spat Econ Anal 7:203–222
Beenstock M, Felsenstein D, Rubin Z (2015) Immigration to the European Union from its neighborhoods. Int J Manpow 36(4):491–517
Behrens K, Ertur C, Koch W (2012) "Dual gravity": using spatial econometrics to control for multilateral resistance. J Appl Econ 27:773–794
Bergstrand JH (1985) The gravity equation in international trade: some microfoundations and empirical evidence. Rev Econ Stat 67:474–481
Bergstrand JH (1989) The generalized gravity equation, monopolistic competition, and the factor proportions theory of international trade. Rev Econ Stat 71:143–153
Borjas GS (1987) Self selection and the earnings of immigrants. Am Econ Rev 77:531–533
Borjas GS (1999) Heaven's door: immigration policy and the American economy. Princeton University Press, Princeton
Burger M, van Oort F, Linders G-J (2009) On the specification of the gravity model of trade: zeros, excess zeros and zero-inflated estimation. Spat Econ Anal 4(2):167–190
Caporin M, Paruolo P (2005) Spatial effects in multivariate ARCH, discussion paper. Universita dell' Insurbia, Varese
De Giorgi G, Pellizzari M (2006) Welfare migration in Europe and the cost of harmonized social assistance. IZA discussion paper 2094
Deardorff AV (1998) Determinants of bilateral trade: does gravity work in a neoclassical world? In: Frankel JA (ed) Regionalization of the world economy. University of Chicago Press, Chicago, pp 7–32
Docquier F, Marfouk A (2006) International migration by education attainment, 1990–2000. In: Ozden C, Schiff M (eds) International migration, remittances, and the brain drain. Palgrave Macmillan, New York
Driscoll JC, Kraay AC (1998) Consistent covariance matrix estimation with spatially dependent panel data. Rev Econ Stat 80:549–560
Elhorst JP, Lacombe DJ, Piras G (2012) On model specifications and parameter space definitions in higher order spatial econometric models. Reg Sci Urban Econ 42:211–220
Evenett S, Keller W (2002) On theories explaining the gravity equation. J Polit Econ 110:281–316
Feenstra RC (2004) Advanced international trade: theory and evidence. Princeton University Press, Princeton
Fischer MM, Reismann M, Hlavackova-Schindler K (2003) Neural network modelling of constrained spatial interaction flows: design, estimation and performance issues. J Reg Sci 43(1):35–61
Greene WA (2012) Econometric analysis, 7th edn. Pearson, Boston
Griffith DA, Fischer MM (2013) Constrained variants of the gravity model and spatial dependence: model specification and estimation issues. J Geogr Syst 15:291–317
Harpaz G (2014) Approximation of laws under the European Neighbourhood Policy: the challenges that lie ahead. Eur Foreign Aff Rev 19(3):429–452
Helpman E, Melitz M, Rubinstein Y (2008) Estimating trade flows: trading partners and trading values. Q J Econ 132:441–487
Hicks JR (1932) The theory of wages. Macmillan, London
LeSage JP, Llano C (2013) A spatial interaction model with spatially structured origin and destination effects. J Geogr Syst 15:265–289

LeSage J, Pace RK (2008) Spatial econometric modeling of origin–destination flows. J Reg Sci 48:941–967
McKinnish T (2007) Welfare-induced migration at state borders: new evidence. J Public Econ 91:437–450
Özden C, Parsons CR, Schiff M, Walmsley T (2011) Where on earth is everybody? The evolution of global bilateral migration 1960–2000. World Bank Econ Rev 25:12–56
Péridy N (2006) The European Union and its new neighbors: an estimation of migration potentials. Econ Bull 6:1–11
Pöyhönen P (1963) A tentative model for the volume of trade between countries. Wetwirtschaftliches Archiv (Rev World Econ) 90:92–100
Ravenstein EG (1885) The laws of migration. J R Stat Soc 48:163–235
Razin A, Sadka E, Suwankiri B (2011) Migration and the welfare state. MIT Press, Cambridge
Reilly WJ (1929) Methods for the study of retail relationships, University of Texas Bulletin, 2944. University of Texas, Austin
Sjaastad LA (1962) The costs and returns of human migration. J Polit Econ 70:80–93
Smith A (1776) In: Sutherland K (ed) An inquiry into the nature and causes of the wealth of nations. Oxford University Press, Oxford
Stewart JQ (1948) Demographic gravitation: evidence and application. Sociometry 11:31–58
Stouffer A (1960) Intervening opportunities and competing migrants. J Reg Sci 1:1–20
Tinbergen J (1962) An analysis of world trade flows. In: Tinbergen J (ed) Shaping the world economy. Twentieth Century Fund, New York
Willcocks G (2010) Conditional variances in UK regional house prices. Spat Econ Anal 5(3): 339–354
Wilson AG (1971) A family of spatial interaction models and associated developments. Environ Plan A 3:1–32
Yoshida C, Woodland AD (2005) The economics of illegal immigration. Palgrave Macmillan, New York
Zipf GK (1949) Human behavior and the principle of least effort. Addison-Wesley, Reading

Chapter 12
Multilateral Resistance and the Euro Effects on Trade Flows

Camilla Mastromarco, Laura Serlenga, and Yongcheol Shin

Keywords Multilateral resistance • The factor-based and the spatial-based panel gravity models • Cross-section dependence • The Euro effects on trade and integration

JEL: C33, F14

12.1 Introduction

With the formation of the Euro in 1999, the literature on the common currency effects on trade has been rapidly growing. By eliminating exchange rate volatility and reducing the costs of trade, a currency union is expected to boost trade among member countries. An important policy issue is identifying the right magnitude and the nature of the Euro's trade impact, which is not only important for member countries but also for EU members that have not joined yet. Baldwin (2006) provides an extensive survey, establishing that the infamous Rose effect is severely (upward) biased. As an earlier evaluation of the Euro effect, Micco et al. (2003) find that the common currency increases trade among Euro zone members by 4 % in the short-run and 16 % in the long-run. See also de Nardis and Vicarelli (2003), Flam and Nordström (2006), and Berger and Nitsch (2008), from which we find that the estimated Euro effects are very wide from 2 % to over 70 %.

C. Mastromarco
Dipartimento di Scienze dell'Economia, University of Salento, CESIfo and RCEA., 73100 Lecce, Italy
e-mail: camilla.mastromarco@unisalento.it

L. Serlenga
Department of Economics, University of Bari, IZA, 70124 Bari, Italy
e-mail: laura.serlenga@uniba.it

Y. Shin (✉)
Department of Economics and Related Studies, University of York, Heslington, York YO10 5DD, UK
e-mail: yongcheol.shin@york.ac.uk

R. Patuelli, G. Arbia (eds.), *Spatial Econometric Interaction Modelling*, Advances in Spatial Science, DOI 10.1007/978-3-319-30196-9_12

However, most of existing studies make an implicit assumption, which does not hold in practice, that bilateral trade flows are independent of the rest of the trading world. Anderson and van Wincoop (2003) highlight an importance of controlling for the regional interaction structure in estimating gravity equation systems. They propose including multilateral resistance terms that capture the fact that bilateral trade flows depend on bilateral barriers as well as trade barriers across all trading partners. Acknowledging such an important issue, an investigation of unobserved multilateral resistance terms together with omitted trade determinants has assumed a prominent role in measuring the Euro's trade effects (Baldwin 2006; Baldwin and Taglioni 2006).

To address this important issue of how best to model (unobserved and time-varying) multilateral resistance and bilateral heterogeneity, simultaneously, in this paper, we implement two recently proposed methodologies: the factor-based approach proposed by Serlenga and Shin (2013, hereafter SS) and the spatial-based techniques developed by Behrens et al. (2012, hereafter BEK). The first approach extends the cross-sectionally dependent panel gravity models advanced by Serlenga and Shin (2007) and Baltagi (2010), which can control for time-varying multilateral resistance and trade costs through using both observed and unobserved factors with heterogenous loadings. The spatial model by BEK is derived from a structural gravity equation, and it allows both trade flows and error terms to be cross-sectionally correlated with the spatial weight matrix derived directly from economic theory. Chudik et al. (2011) show that the factor-based models account for strong cross section dependence while the spatial-based model addresses weak dependence. Following SS, we combine these estimators with the instrument variables estimators advanced by Hausman and Taylor (1981), Amemiya and McCurdy (1986), and Breusch et al. (1989), and develop a methodology which allows us to consistently estimate the impacts of (potentially endogenous) bilateral resistance barriers such as border and language effects.

We apply these methodologies to the dataset over 1960–2008 for 190 country-pairs. This is an extended dataset analysed by SS by enlarging the control group. Though the Euro-area economies have become more integrated with a trade boost within the region, this positive currency-union effect can be greatly mitigated by multilateral trade costs associated with the larger control group of non-Euro countries. This may help us to better disentangle the effect of the Euro on trade within and outside currency union by introducing a substitutability between intra-EU and extra-EU trade flows (Anderson and van Wincoop 2003, 2004).

Our main empirical findings are summarized as follows: First, when we control for time-varying multilateral resistance and trade costs through cross-sectionally correlated unobserved factors, we find that the Euro impact on trade amounts to 4–5 %. This magnitude is generally consistent with comprehensive evidence compiled by Baldwin (2006). We also find that the custom union effect is substantially reduced to 11 %. Next, we find that the impacts of the Euro and the custom union on trades are estimated at about 20 % and 30 %, respectively, under the spatial-based SARAR models. These magnitudes are substantially larger than those obtained under the factor-based models, but rather close to the values estimated under the basic model without controlling for cross-section dependence. Furthermore, when applying the cross-section dependency (CD) test advanced by Pesaran (2004), we find that the null of no cross-sectional dependence is strongly rejected for all of the spatial-based gravity models. Therefore, we may conclude that trade flows are likely to be better modelled by allowing for a strong form of cross section dependence rather than weak dependence.

Finally, we investigate another important issue of the Euro effect on trade integration by estimating time-varying coefficients of bilateral resistance terms, and find that border and language effects declined more sharply after the introduction of the Euro in 1999. The implication of these findings is that the Euro helps to reduce trade effects of bilateral resistance and to promote the EU integration. On the other hand, distance impacts have been rather stable, showing no pattern of downward trending. This generally supports broad empirical evidence that the notion of the death of distance is difficult to identify in current trade data (Disdier and Head 2008; Jacks 2009).

The paper is organised as follows: Sect. 12.2 provides a brief literature review on the Euro's Trade Effects. Section 12.3 describes two alternative cross-sectionally dependent panel gravity models. Section 12.4 presents main empirical findings. Section 12.5 concludes.

12.2 Literature Review

Recently, there has been an intense policy debate on the effects of the Euro on trade flows. Rose (2000) was the first to introduce common currency variables in the gravity model, and documented evidence that countries in a currency union trade three times as much, using the data for 186 countries over the period, 1970–1990. It is widely acknowledged that Rose's huge estimate of the currency union effect on trade is severely (upward) biased. In particular, his estimates are heavily inflated by the presence of very small countries (Frankel 2008). Thus, whether one can uncover similar findings for the European monetary union with the substantially large economies, is an important policy issue.

The main critiques against Rose's (2000) original gravity approach are classified as follows: inverse causality or endogeneity, missing or omitted variables, and incorrect model specification (nonlinearity or threshold effects). Once these methodological issues have been appropriately addressed, the currency union effects appear to be far less than those estimated earlier by Rose and others. Baldwin (2006) presents an extensive survey, highlighting that recent studies report relatively smaller trade effects of the Euro. See also Micco et al. (2003), de Nardis and Vicarelli (2003), Flam and Nordström (2006) and Berger and Nitsch (2008).

Another important issue is the omitted variables bias. Omitted pro-bilateral trade variables are likely to be correlated with the currency union dummy, as the formation of currency unions is driven by factors which are omitted from the gravity specification. If so, the Euro effect may capture general economic integration among the member states, not merely the currency impact. Anderson and van Wincoop (2003) develop the micro foundation of the gravity equation by introducing the multilateral resistance terms, which are bilateral trade barriers relative to average trade barriers that both countries face with all of their trading partners. In this regard, the gravity model produces seriously misleading results, if multilateral resistance terms and trade costs are neglected. Baldwin (2006) also stresses an importance of taking into account time-varying multilateral resistance terms such as trade costs (Anderson and van Wincoop 2004), and criticises against the use of the fixed effect estimation as it may still leave a times-series trace in the residuals, which is likely to be correlated with the currency union dummy.[1]

In retrospect, a large number of existing studies have already highlighted an importance of taking into account unobserved and time-varying multilateral resistance and bilateral heterogeneity, simultaneously. This raises an immediate important issue of controlling for cross section dependence or correlation among trade flows in a coherent manner. Only recently, a small number of studies have begun to explicitly address this issue, e.g., Serlenga and Shin (2007, 2013), Herwartz and Weber (2010), Behrens et al. (2012), and Camaero et al. (2012).

SS follow recent developments in panel data studies (Pesaran 2006; Bai 2009), and extend the cross-sectionally dependent panel gravity models advanced by Serlenga and Shin (2007). The desirable feature of this approach is to control for time-varying multilateral resistance, trade costs and globalisation trends explicitly through the use of both observed and unobserved factors, which are modelled as (strong) cross-sectionally correlated. Applying the proposed model to the dataset over the period 1960–2008 for 91 country-pairs amongst 14 EU member countries, SS find that the Euro's trade effect amounts to 3–4 %, even after controlling for trade diversion effects, and conclude that these small effects of currency union provide a support for the hypothesis that the trade increase within the Euro area may reflect a continuation of a long-run historical trend of economic integrations in the EU (e.g. Berger and Nitsch 2008).

Alternatively, BEK propose the modified spatial techniques by adopting a broader definition of the spatial weight matrix, which can be derived directly from the theoretical structural gravity model. By capturing (cross-sectionally correlated) multilateral resistance through the spatial effects, they find that the measured Canada-US border effects are significantly lower than paradoxically large estimates reported by McCallum (1995). Thus, in an analysis of the trade-creation effects of a single currency, it is important to specify an estimation procedure that account for distribution of data in space. The spatial dependence may arise due to the so-called third country (neighbour) effects, which is increasingly playing a central role

[1]In particular, Bun and Klaassen (2007), and Berger and Nitsch (2008) simply introduce time trends with heterogeneous coefficients, and find that the Euro effect on trade falls dramatically. However, Baldwin et al. argue that including time trends in an ad hoc manner is not the satisfactory empirical approach. SS also show that simply introducing heterogeneous time trends is not yet sufficiently effective in capturing any upward trends in omitted trade determinants, which suggests that such diverse measures might be better described by stochastic trending factors (e.g. Herwartz and Weber 2010).

in examining the spatial dependence structure in the closely linked literature on foreign direct investment and multinational enterprises, e.g., Baltagi et al. (2007, 2008), Blonigen et al. (2007), and Hall and Petroulas (2008), and Camaero et al. (2012).

12.3 Cross Sectionally Dependent Panel Gravity Models

All of the discussions in Sect. 12.2 suggest that a Euro effect on trade flows be carefully examined under the appropriate econometric framework that is expected to deal with time-varying and cross-sectionally correlated multilateral resistance terms in a robust manner.[2] In what follows, we will describe two alternative approaches to the panel gravity model of the trade flows: the spatial-based techniques developed by BEK and the factor-based approach proposed by SS.

We first consider a factor-based panel data model as follows:

$$y_{it} = \boldsymbol{\beta}'\mathbf{x}_{it} + \boldsymbol{\gamma}'\mathbf{z}_i + \boldsymbol{\pi}_i'\mathbf{s}_t + \varepsilon_{it},\ i = 1,\ldots,N,\ t = 1,\ldots,T, \tag{12.1}$$

$$\varepsilon_{it} = \alpha_i + \boldsymbol{\varphi}_i'\boldsymbol{\theta}_t + u_{it}, \tag{12.2}$$

where $\mathbf{x}_{it} = (x_{1,it},\ldots,x_{k,it})'$ is a $k \times 1$ vector of variables that vary across individuals and over time periods, $\mathbf{s}_t = (s_{1,t},\ldots,s_{s,t})'$ is an $s \times 1$ vector of observed factors, $\mathbf{z}_i = (z_{1,i},\ldots,z_{g,i})'$ is a $g \times 1$ vector of individual-specific variables, $\boldsymbol{\beta} = (\beta_1,\ldots,\beta_k)'$, $\boldsymbol{\gamma} = (\gamma_1,\ldots,\gamma_g)'$ and $\boldsymbol{\pi}_i = (\pi_{1,i},\ldots,\pi_{s,i})'$ are the associated column vectors of parameters, α_i is an individual effect that might be correlated with regressors, $\mathbf{x}_{it}$ and $\mathbf{z}_i$, $\boldsymbol{\theta}_t$ is the $c \times 1$ vector of unobserved common factors with the loading vector, $\boldsymbol{\varphi}_i = (\varphi_{1,i},\ldots,\varphi_{c,i})'$, and u_{it} is a zero mean idiosyncratic disturbance with constant variance. Notice that the cross-section dependence in (12.1) is explicitly allowed through heterogeneous loadings, $\boldsymbol{\varphi}_i$. Chudik et al. (2011) show that these factor models exhibit the strong form of cross section dependence (hereafter, CSD) since the maximum eigenvalue of the covariance matrix for ε_{it} tends to infinity at rate N.[3] We thus expect that this factor-based panel gravity model will capture the time-varying pattern of unobserved multilateral resistance effects in a robust manner.

To avoid the potential biases associated with the cross-sectionally dependent factor structure, (12.2), SS propose using two leading approaches developed by

[2]The multilateral resistance function and trade costs, both of which affect bilateral trade flows, are not only difficult to measure, but also are likely to vary over time. A number of ad hoc approaches have been proposed in the literature. Simply, fixed time dummies or time trends are added as a proxy for time-varying effects in the gravity equation, e.g. Baldwin and Taglioni (2006), Bun and Klaassen (2007) and Berger and Nitsch (2008). Alternatively, some studies include regional remoteness indices (e.g. Melitz and Ghironi 2007).

[3]Bailey et al. (2012) also discuss that the extent of cross-sectional dependence crucially depends on the nature of factor loadings. The degree of cross-sectional dependence will be strong if φ_i is bounded away from 0 and the average value of φ is different from zero.

Pesaran (2006) and Bai (2009). Hence, we consider the following cross-sectionally augmented regression of (12.1):

$$y_{it} = \boldsymbol{\beta}'\mathbf{x}_{it} + \boldsymbol{\gamma}'\mathbf{z}_i + \boldsymbol{\lambda}_i'\mathbf{f}_t + \tilde{\alpha}_i + \tilde{u}_{it}, \ i = 1, \ldots, N, \ t = 1, \ldots, T, \tag{12.3}$$

where $\mathbf{f}_t = \left(\mathbf{s}_t', \bar{y}_t, \bar{\mathbf{x}}_t'\right)' \left\{= (f_{1,t}, \ldots, f_{\ell,t})'\right\}$ is the $\ell \times 1$ vector of augmented factors with $\ell = s + 1 + k$ and $\boldsymbol{\lambda}_i = (\lambda_{1,i}, \ldots, \lambda_{\ell,i})'$, $\bar{y}_t = N^{-1}\sum_{i=1}^{N} y_{it}$, $\bar{\mathbf{x}}_t = N^{-1}\sum_{i=1}^{N} \mathbf{x}_{it}$, $\boldsymbol{\lambda}_i' = \left(\boldsymbol{\pi}_i' - (\varphi_i/\bar{\varphi})\,\bar{\boldsymbol{\pi}}', (\varphi_i/\bar{\varphi}), -(\varphi_i/\bar{\varphi})\,\boldsymbol{\beta}'\right)'$ with $\bar{\varphi} = N^{-1}\sum_{i=1}^{N}\varphi_i$ and $\bar{\boldsymbol{\pi}} = N^{-1}\sum_{i=1}^{N}\boldsymbol{\pi}_i$, $\tilde{\alpha}_i = \alpha_i - (\varphi_i/\bar{\varphi})\,\bar{\alpha} - (\varphi_i/\bar{\varphi})\,\boldsymbol{\gamma}'\bar{\mathbf{z}}$ with $\bar{\alpha} = N^{-1}\sum_{i=1}^{N}\alpha_i$ and $\bar{\mathbf{z}} = N^{-1}\sum_{i=1}^{N}\mathbf{z}_i$, and $\tilde{u}_{it} = u_{it} - (\varphi_i/\bar{\varphi})\,\bar{u}_t$ with $\bar{u}_t = N^{-1}\sum_{i=1}^{N} u_{it}$. Using (12.3), we can derive Pesaran's Pooled Common Correlated Effects (PCCE) estimator of $\boldsymbol{\beta}$ by (12.4) below. Alternatively, we can estimate $\boldsymbol{\beta}$ consistently by Bai's (2009) principal component (PC) estimator in which case the cross section averages are replaced by the estimated factors $\left(\hat{\boldsymbol{\theta}}_t\right)$ such that $\mathbf{f}_t = \left(\mathbf{s}_t', \hat{\boldsymbol{\theta}}_t'\right)'$.[4] Thus, we obtain the CSD-consistent estimator of $\boldsymbol{\beta}$ by

$$\hat{\boldsymbol{\beta}}_{CSD} = \left(\sum_{i=1}^{N}\mathbf{x}_i'\mathbf{M}_T\mathbf{x}_i\right)^{-1}\left(\sum_{i=1}^{N}\mathbf{x}_i'\mathbf{M}_T\mathbf{y}_i\right), \ \hat{\boldsymbol{\beta}}_{CSD} = \hat{\boldsymbol{\beta}}_{PCCE} \ or \ \hat{\boldsymbol{\beta}}_{PC} \tag{12.4}$$

where $\mathbf{y}_i = (y_{i1}, \ldots, y_{iT})'$, $\mathbf{x}_i = (\mathbf{x}_{i1}, \ldots, \mathbf{x}_{iT})'$, $\mathbf{M}_T = \mathbf{I}_T - \mathbf{H}_T\left(\mathbf{H}_T'\mathbf{H}_T\right)^{-1}\mathbf{H}_T'$, $\mathbf{H}_T = (\mathbf{1}_T, \mathbf{f})$, $\mathbf{1}_T = (1, \ldots, 1)'$ and $\mathbf{f} = \left(\mathbf{f}_1', \ldots, \mathbf{f}_T'\right)'$.

Alternatively, we will investigate the issue of CSD among trade flows by employing spatial techniques. This approach assumes that the structure of cross section correlation is related to the location and the distance among units on the basis of a pre-specified weight matrix.[5] Hence, cross section correlation is represented mainly by means of a spatial process, which explicitly relates each unit to its neighbours. A number of approaches for modeling spatial dependence have been suggested in the spatial literature. The most popular ones are the Spatial Autoregressive (SAR), the Spatial Moving Average (SMA), and the Spatial Error Component (SEC) specifications. The spatial panel data model is estimated using the maximum likelihood (ML) or the generalized method of moments (GMM) techniques (e.g., Elhorst 2011). We follow BEK and consider a spatial panel data gravity (SARAR) model, which combines a spatial lagged variable and a spatial autoregressive error term:

$$y_{it} = \rho y_{it}^{*} + \boldsymbol{\beta}'\mathbf{x}_{it} + \boldsymbol{\gamma}'\mathbf{z}_i + \tilde{\alpha}_i + v_{it}, \ i = 1, \ldots, N, \ t = 1, \ldots, T, \tag{12.5}$$

$$v_{it} = \lambda v_{it}^{*} + u_{it} \tag{12.6}$$

[4] We estimate $\boldsymbol{\theta}_t$ consistently using the Bai and Ng (2002) procedure.

[5] Pesaran and Tosetti (2011) argue that proximity does not have to be measured in terms of physical space. Rather, it can be defined in terms of other types of metric such as economic, policy or social cost and distance (e.g., Conley and Topa 2002).

where $y_{it}^{*} = \sum_{j\neq i}^{N} w_{ij}y_{jt}$ is the spatial lagged variable, and $v_{it}^{*} = \sum_{j\neq i}^{N} w_{ij}v_{jt}$ is the spatial autoregressive error term, w_{ij}'s are the spatial weight with the row-sum normalisation, $\sum_i w_{ij} = 1$, and u_{it} is a zero mean idiosyncratic disturbance with constant variance. This approach is especially designed to deal with CSD across both variables and error terms in which ρ is the spatial lag coefficient and λ refers to the spatial error component coefficient. These coefficients capture the spatial spillover effects and measure the influence of the weighted average of neighboring observations on cross section units. Chudik et al. (2011) show that a particular form of a weak cross dependent process arises when pairwise correlations take non-zero values only across finite units that do not spread widely as the sample size rises. A similar case occurs in the spatial processes, where the local dependency exists only among adjacent observations. In particular, Pesaran and Tosetti (2011) show that spatial processes commonly used, such as the SAR or the SMA process, can be represented by a process with an infinite number of weak factors and no idiosyncratic error terms.

Both the factor- and the spatial-based models cannot estimate the coefficients, $\boldsymbol{\gamma}$ on time-invariant variables in the presence of fixed effects. In this regard, we follow SS and combine these estimators with the instrumental variables estimation proposed by Hausman and Taylor (1981, HT), Amemiya and McCurdy (1986, AM), and Breusch et al. (1989, BMS). We denote such estimators by the PCCE-HT, PCCE-AM, PCCE-BMS, PC-HT, PC-AM, PC-BMS, SARAR-HT, SARAR-AM, and SARAR-BMS estimators, respectively.

We now decompose $\mathbf{x}_{it} = \left(\mathbf{x}_{1it}', \mathbf{x}_{2it}'\right)'$ and $\mathbf{z}_i = \left(\mathbf{z}_{1i}', \mathbf{z}_{2i}'\right)'$, where $\mathbf{x}_{1it}$, $\mathbf{x}_{2it}$ are $k_1 \times 1$ and $k_2 \times 1$ vectors, and $\mathbf{z}_{1i}$, $\mathbf{z}_{2i}$ are $g_1 \times 1$ and $g_2 \times 1$ vectors. Then, we estimate $\boldsymbol{\gamma}$ consistently using instrumental variables in the following regression:

$$d_{it} = \boldsymbol{\gamma}_1'\mathbf{z}_{1i} + \boldsymbol{\gamma}_2'\mathbf{z}_{2i} + \tilde{\alpha}_i + \tilde{u}_{it} = \mu + \boldsymbol{\gamma}'\mathbf{z}_i + e_{it},\ i = 1, \ldots, N,\ t = 1, \ldots, T. \tag{12.7}$$

We construct d_{it} as follows, for the factor models, we obtain

$$d_{it} = y_{it} - \boldsymbol{\beta}'\mathbf{x}_{it} - \boldsymbol{\lambda}_i'\mathbf{f}_t,$$

where $\mu = E(\tilde{\alpha}_i)$, and $e_{it} = (\tilde{\alpha}_i - \mu) + \tilde{u}_{it}$ is a zero mean process. Next, for the spatial-based model, we have

$$d_{it} = y_{it} - \rho y_{it}^{*} - \boldsymbol{\beta}'\mathbf{x}_{it},$$

where $\mu = E(\tilde{\alpha}_i)$, and $e_{it} = (\tilde{\alpha}_i - \mu) + v_{it}$ is a zero mean process. In matrix notation, we have:

$$\mathbf{d} = \mu\mathbf{1}_{NT} + \mathbf{Z}_1\boldsymbol{\gamma}_1 + \mathbf{Z}_2\boldsymbol{\gamma}_2 + \mathbf{e}, \tag{12.8}$$

where $\mathbf{d} = \left(\mathbf{d}_1', \ldots, \mathbf{d}_N'\right)'$, $\mathbf{d}_i = \left(d_{i1}, \ldots, d_{iT}\right)'$, $\mathbf{Z}_j = \left((\mathbf{z}_{j1}' \otimes \mathbf{1}_T)', \ldots, (\mathbf{z}_{jN}' \otimes \mathbf{1}_T)'\right)'$, $j = 1, 2$, $\mathbf{1}_{NT} = \left(\mathbf{1}_T', \ldots, \mathbf{1}_T'\right)'$, $\mathbf{1}_T = \left(1, \ldots, 1\right)'$, and $\mathbf{e} = \left(\mathbf{e}_1', \ldots, \mathbf{e}_N'\right)'$ with $\mathbf{e}_i =$

$\left(e_{i1},\ldots,e_{iT}\right)'$. Replacing $\mathbf{d}$ by its consistent estimate, $\hat{\mathbf{d}} = \left\{\hat{d}_{it}, i = 1,\ldots,N, t = 1,\ldots,T\right\}$:[6]

$$\hat{\mathbf{d}} = \mu\mathbf{1}_{NT} + \mathbf{Z}_1\boldsymbol{\gamma}_1 + \mathbf{Z}_2\boldsymbol{\gamma}_2 + \mathbf{e}^{\dagger} = \mathbf{C}\boldsymbol{\delta} + \mathbf{e}^{\dagger}, \tag{12.9}$$

where $\mathbf{e}^{\dagger} = \mathbf{e} + \left(\hat{\mathbf{d}} - \mathbf{d}\right)$, $\mathbf{C} = (\mathbf{1}_{NT}, \mathbf{Z}_1, \mathbf{Z}_2)$ and $\boldsymbol{\delta} = \left(\mu, \boldsymbol{\gamma}_1', \boldsymbol{\gamma}_2'\right)'$.

To deal with nonzero correlation between $\mathbf{Z}_2$ and $\boldsymbol{\alpha}$, we should find the $NT \times (1 + g_1 + h)$ matrix of instrument variables:

$$\mathbf{W} = \left[\mathbf{1}_{NT}, \mathbf{Z}_1, \mathbf{W}_2\right],$$

where $\mathbf{W}_2$ is an $NT \times h$ matrix of instrument variables for $\mathbf{Z}_2$ with $h \geq g_2$ for identification. To this end, we follow SS and obtain the $NT \times (k_1 + \ell)$ HT, the $NT \times (k_1 + \ell + Tk_1 + T\ell)$ AM and the $NT \times (k_1 + \ell + Tk_1 + T\ell + Tk_2)$ BMS instrument matrices as: $\mathbf{W}_2^{HT} = \left[\mathbf{PX}_1, \mathbf{P}\hat{\boldsymbol{\xi}}_1, \ldots, \mathbf{P}\hat{\boldsymbol{\xi}}_\ell\right]$, $\mathbf{W}_2^{AM} = \left[\mathbf{W}_2^{HT}, (\mathbf{QX}_1)^{\dagger}, \left(\mathbf{Q}\hat{\boldsymbol{\xi}}_1\right)^{\dagger}, \ldots, \left(\mathbf{Q}\hat{\boldsymbol{\xi}}_\ell\right)^{\dagger}\right]$, and $\mathbf{W}_2^{BMS} = \left[\mathbf{W}_2^{AM}, (\mathbf{QX}_2)^{\dagger}\right]$, where $\mathbf{P} = \mathbf{D}(\mathbf{D}'\mathbf{D})^{-1}\mathbf{D}'$ is the $NT \times NT$ idempotent matrix, $\mathbf{D} = \mathbf{I}_N \otimes \mathbf{1}_T$, $\mathbf{I}_N$ is an $N \times N$ identity matrix, $\hat{\boldsymbol{\xi}}_j = \left(\hat{\lambda}_{j,1}\mathbf{f}_j', \ldots, \hat{\lambda}_{j,N}\mathbf{f}_j'\right)'$, $j = 1,\ldots,\ell$, where $\mathbf{f}_j = \left(f_{j,1}, \ldots, f_{j,T}\right)'$ with $\hat{\lambda}_{j,i}$ being consistent estimate of heterogenous factor loading, $\lambda_{j,i}$, $\mathbf{Q} = \mathbf{I}_{NT} - \mathbf{P}$, $(\mathbf{QX}_1)^{\dagger} = (\mathbf{QX}_{11}, \mathbf{QX}_{12}, \ldots, \mathbf{QX}_{1T})$ is the $NT \times k_1 T$ matrix with $\mathbf{QX}_{1t} = (\mathbf{QX}_{11t}, \ldots, \mathbf{QX}_{1kt})'$, and $(\mathbf{QX}_2) = (\mathbf{QX}_{21}, \ldots, \mathbf{QX}_{2T})$.

To derive the consistent estimator of $\boldsymbol{\delta}$, we premultiply $\mathbf{W}'$ by (12.9)

$$\mathbf{W}'\hat{\mathbf{d}} = \mathbf{W}'\mathbf{C}\boldsymbol{\delta} + \mathbf{W}'\boldsymbol{\varepsilon}^{+}. \tag{12.10}$$

Therefore, the GLS estimator of $\boldsymbol{\delta}$ is obtained by

$$\hat{\boldsymbol{\delta}}_{GLS} = \left[\mathbf{C}'\mathbf{W}\mathbf{V}^{-1}\mathbf{W}'\mathbf{C}\right]^{-1}\mathbf{C}'\mathbf{W}\mathbf{V}^{-1}\mathbf{W}'\hat{\mathbf{d}}, \tag{12.11}$$

where $\mathbf{V} = Var\left(\mathbf{W}'\mathbf{e}^{\dagger}\right)$. We obtain the feasible GLS estimator by replacing $\mathbf{V}$ by its consistent estimator. In practice, estimates of $\boldsymbol{\delta}$ and $\mathbf{V}$ can be obtained iteratively until convergence. The HT-IV estimator employs only the mean of $\mathbf{X}_1$ to be uncorrelated with the effects whereas the AM-IV estimator exploits such moment conditions to be held at every time period. Hence, the AM instruments requires

[6] For the factor-based models, d_{it} is consistently estimated by $\hat{d}_{it} = y_{it} - \hat{\boldsymbol{\beta}}_{CSD}'\mathbf{x}_{it} - \hat{\boldsymbol{\lambda}}_i'\mathbf{f}_t$, where $\hat{\boldsymbol{\lambda}}_i$ are the OLS estimators of $\boldsymbol{\lambda}_i$ consistently estimated from the regression of $\left(y_{it} - \hat{\boldsymbol{\beta}}_{CSD}'\mathbf{x}_{it}\right)$ on $\left(1, \mathbf{f}_t\right)$ for $i = 1,\ldots,N$. Next, for the spatial-based models, d_{it} is consistently estimated by $\hat{d}_{it} = y_{it} - \hat{\rho}_{SARAR}y_{it}^{*} - \hat{\boldsymbol{\beta}}_{SARAR}'\mathbf{x}_{it}$, where $\hat{\rho}_{SARAR}$ and $\hat{\boldsymbol{\beta}}_{SARAR}$ are the ML estimators of ρ and β in (12.5) and (12.6).

the stronger exogeneity assumption for $\mathbf{X}_1$, under which the AM-IV estimator is more efficient. Furthermore, the BMS instruments require uncorrelatedness of $\mathbf{X}_2$ with fixed effects separately at every point in time. The validity of AM and BMS instruments can be easily tested using the Hausman statistics testing for the difference between HT-IV and AM-IV and between AM-IV and BMS-IV, both of which follow the asymptotic χ^2_g null-distribution with the degree of freedom g, being the number of coefficients tested, see SS for details.

12.4 Empirical Results

We extend the dataset analysed by Serlenga and Shin (2007, 2013) to cover the longer period 1960–2008 (49 years) for 190 country-pairs amongst 14 EU member countries (Austria, Belgium-Luxemburg, Denmark, Finland, France, Germany, Greece, Ireland, Italy, Netherlands, Portugal, Spain, Sweden, the United Kingdom) plus six OECD member countries (Australia, Canada, Japan, Norway, Switzerland and the US). By considering the larger control group of countries that do not belong to the currency union, we can check for the robustness of the previous empirical results reported in SS. These additional countries constitute the meaningful control group such that we can better identify the trade effect of currency union within and outside the Euro area by introducing substitutability between them (Anderson and van Wincoop 2003, 2004). The US is still the leading trade partner of the EU, though its role has recently been challenged by China and Russia. Norway and Switzerland constitute a coherent control group since these non-member countries share with similar historical ties to the Euro-area countries and experience similar legislation and regulation. Australia, Japan and Canada also belong to the large global traders.

Our sample period consists of many important economic integrations such as the Custom Union in 1958, the European Monetary System in 1979 and the Single Market in 1993.[7] Given that the Euro effect should be analysed as an ongoing process (Berger and Nitsch 2008), we will examine the Euro's trading effect more carefully by applying the two alternative cross-sectionally correlated panel data gravity models described in Sect. 12.3.

We first estimate the panel data model of gravity, (12.1) and (12.2). First, we consider the basic model without unobserved time-varying factors in order to facilitate the comparison with most of existing studies. Secondly, we consider the factor-based model with both unobserved time-varying factors, $\varphi_i\theta_t$, and linear time trends, $s_t = \{t\}$, as a single observed factor. Following Serlenga and Shin (2007), we focus on the augmented gravity model specification in which trade flows depend on (1) gravity determinants (countries' economic mass and geographical distance); (2) time-varying covariates such as bilateral real exchange rates, free trade agreements and common currency union; and (3) time-invariant dummies that proxy common language and common border. Finally, in line with the New Trade Theory

[7] See Table 12.1 in SS for the key summary figures of EU trade shares and growths.

Table 12.1 Estimation results for the panel gravity model without cross-section dependence

	OLS	FE	RE	HT	AM
gdp	1.6861**	1.9207**	1.9049**	1.9208**	1.9150**
	[0.008]	[0.010]	[0.010]	[0.010]	[0.010]
sim	1.0006**	0.8803**	0.9833**	0.8807**	0.9301**
	[0.011]	[0.037]	[0.031]	[0.037]	[0.034]
rfl	−0.0030	0.0156**	0.0207**	0.0157**	0.0175**
	[0.005]	[0.006]	[0.006]	[0.006]	[0.006]
rer	−0.0079*	0.0211**	0.0177**	0.0191**	0.0192**
	[0.003]	[0.007]	[0.006]	[0.006]	[0.006]
emu	0.2659**	0.2109**	0.2060**	0.2105**	0.2079**
	[0.032]	[0.018]	[0.018]	[0.018]	[0.018]
cee	0.3811**	0.3860**	0.3867**	0.3851**	0.3860**
	[0.019]	[0.014]	[0.014]	[0.014]	[0.014]
dis	−0.7026**		−0.7864**	−0.7587**	−0.8090**
	[0.008]		[0.040]	[0.090]	[0.056]
bor	0.2711**		0.1220	0.8341	−0.0298
	[0.028]		[0.164]	[1.038]	[0.251]
lan	0.5171**		0.4849**	−0.8909	0.7316**
	[0.023]		[0.133]	[1.880]	[0.277]
CD		126.13			
p-value		0.00			

Notes: Using the annual data over 1960–2008 for 190 country-pairs, we estimate the model (12.1) and (12.2) without including time specific factors, where the dependent variable is the logarithm of real total trade flows and the regressors are $\mathbf{x}'_{it} = \{RER, TGDP, RLF, SIM, CEE, EMU\}_{it}$ and $\mathbf{z}_i = \{DIS, BOR, LAN\}_i$. POLS stands for the pooled OLS estimator, FE for fixed effects estimator and RE for random effects estimator, respectively. For the HT and the AM estimates we consider the following set of instruments: IV $= \{RER_{it}, RLF_{it}\}$. Figures in $[\cdot]$ indicate the standard error. **, * and + denote 1, 5, and 10 % level of significance, respectively. *CD* denotes the diagnostic test statistic for the null of no cross-section dependency advanced by Pesaran (2004)

(e.g., Krugman, 1979; Helpman, 1987), we add two more variables: relative factor endowment and similarity in size. See the Data Appendix for more details with a priori expectations about the signs of their impacts on trade flows

Table 12.1 presents the estimation results for the basic model with individual effects only, using the alternative estimation methodologies. The random effects model (REM) assumption that there is no correlation between regressors and individual effects is convincingly rejected in all cases considered. Therefore, we focus on the fixed effects model (FEM) results. The FEM estimation results are all statistically significant and consistent with our a priori expectations. The impact of *GDP* (the sum of home and foreign country GDPs) on trade is positive. The impact of relative difference in factor endowments between trading partners (*RLF*) is significant and positive whilst similarity in size (*SIM*) boosts trade flows significantly. A depreciation of the home currency (increase in *RER*) increases trade flows as the export component of the total trade is larger than the import.

Importantly, we find that trade and currency union memberships (*CEE* and *EMU*) significantly boost trade flows, but their magnitudes appear to be substantial at 0.39 and 0.21. This finding confirms our main concern that upward trends in omitted trade determinants may cause them to be upward-biased.[8] We now turn to the estimated impacts of individual-specific bilateral trade barriers. Under the maintained assumption that *LAN* is the only variable correlated with individual effects (as a proxy for cultural and historical proximity), we select the final set of instruments containing *RER* and *RLF*, after conducting a sequence of the Sargan tests for the validity of over-identifying restrictions. As the Hausman test does not reject the legitimacy of the AM-IV estimates, we focus on more efficient AM results, and find that impacts of *DIS* and *LAN* are significant (−0.81 and 0.73) while the border impact is insignificant and negligible.

Given that (unobserved) multilateral resistance terms and trade costs are likely to exhibit history and time dependence in a complex manner (e.g. Herwartz and Weber 2010), we turn to the factor-based panel gravity models proposed by SS. In Table 12.2, we report two consistent estimators, the PCCE and PC.[9] The stylised findings are summarised as follows: First, the impact of *RLF* becomes significant and negative,[10] confirming our expectations that its impact on total trade flows (the sum of inter- and intra-industry trades) may not necessarily be unambiguous (e.g. Helpman and Krugman 1985). Secondly, similarity turns out to have a larger effect. Combined together, the intra-industry trade appears to have been the main part of the total EU trade.[11] More importantly, the impacts of *CEE* and *EMU* are substantially smaller albeit still significant. The *CEE* impact falls to 0.114 and 0.117 for PCCE and PC estimators while the Euro impact drops sharply to 0.039 and 0.048 for PCCE and PC. Turing to HT-IV and AM-IV estimates of the impacts of time-invariant regressors,[12] we find that the impacts of distance dummy and language dummy

---

[8]When comparing with the estimation results reported in SS for the smaller dataset with 91 country-pairs among 14 EU countries, we find the following notable difference that the impacts of EMU and CEE increase from 0.21 and 0.14 to 0.39 and 0.31, respectively.

[9]For the PCCE estimation we consider $\mathbf{f}_t = \{\overline{TRADE}_t, \overline{TGDP}_t, \overline{SIM}_t, \overline{RLF}_t, \overline{CEE}_t\}'$ and $\mathbf{s}_t = \{t\}$ in (12.3), where the bar over variables indicates their cross-sectional average. For the PC estimation, we first extract six common PC factors using the Bai and Ng (2002) procedure, and use them as $\mathbf{f}_t$ in (12.3) together with $\mathbf{s}_t = \{t\}$. See SS for more details about a selection of the final specification on the basis of statistical significance and empirical coherence.

[10]This result is crucially different from those reported in SS. This may be due to the fact that we now employ a larger number of country-pairs. In particular, the OECD dataset includes large countries such as the US, Japan and Canada, that have recently experienced a steady growth in the intra-industry trade. The presence of those countries might help to better identify the effect of relative factor endowments by fostering intra-industry trade, see OECD (2010).

[11]We observe form Table 12.1 in SS that the share of the intra-trade increase from 37.2 % in 1960 to around 60 % from 1990 onwards.

[12]Assuming that *LAN* is the only time invariant variable correlated with individual effects, we use the same instrument variables, $IV = \{RER_{it}, RLF_{it}\}$. We also consider an additional instrument set, denoted $IV1 = \left\{IV, \hat{\xi}_{it}\right\}$, where $\hat{\xi}_{it} = \hat{\lambda}_i f_t$, and $\hat{\lambda}_i$ are estimated loadings. See SS for more details about a selection of the final set of HT and AM instrument variables.

Table 12.2 Estimation results for the panel gravity model with cross section dependence and heterogeneous trends

	PCCE					PC				
gdp	2.192 **					2.042 **				
	[0.022]					[0.065]				
sim	1.374 **					1.298 **				
	[0.024]					[0.078]				
rlf	−0.012**					−0.015**				
	[0.006]					[0.004]				
rer	0.017 **					0.034 *				
	[0.003]					[0.018]				
emu	0.039 **					0.048 *				
	[0.004]					[0.018]				
cee	0.114 **					0.117 **				
	[0.003]					[0.013]				
	OLS	HT	HT1	AM	AM1	OLS	HT	HT1	AM	AM1
con	0.702 **	0.88 **	0.918 **	0.835 **	0.883 **	6.434 **	6.667 **	6.796 **	6.55 **	6.602 **
	[0.459]	[0.58]	[0.52]	[0.488]	[0.493]	[0.423]	[0.582]	[0.524]	[0.438]	[0.448]
dis	−0.881**	−0.91**	−0.917**	−0.902**	−0.91**	−0.835**	−0.874**	−0.895**	−0.853**	−0.862**
	[0.057]	[0.09]	[0.067]	[0.062]	[0.063]	[0.053]	[0.086]	[0.067]	[0.056]	[0.057]
bor	−0.034	−0.46	−0.552	−0.274	−0.399	0.069	−0.491	−0.803	−0.171	−0.298
	[0.235]	[1.04]	[0.373]	[0.297]	[0.297]	[0.216]	[1.015]	[0.089]	[0.262]	[0.277]

lan	0.441 *	1.23	1.397 *	0.849 *	1.084 **	0.456 *	1.49	2.067**	0.881 **	1.118 **
	[0.191]	[1.96]	[0.574]	[0.361]	[0.366]	[0.176]	[1.908]	[0.547]	[0.312]	[0.332]
Sargan		$\chi_1^2 = 0.92$	$\chi_7^2 = 7.12$	$\chi_{53}^2 = 66.31$	$\chi_{58}^2 = 67.79$		$\chi_1^2 = 2.552$	$\chi_7^2 = 6.10$	$\chi_{48}^2 = 57.40$	$\chi_{56}^2 = 61.8$
p value		0.338	0.416	0.104	0.178		0.11	0.528	0.166	0.276
Hausman				H1:$\chi_3^2 = 0.09$	H1:$\chi_3^2 = 0.71$				H1:$\chi_3^2 = 0.13$	H1:$\chi_3^2 = 5.682$
p value				0.999	0.951				0.999	0.224
CD	2.75					1.257				
p value	0.006					0.271				

Notes: We estimate the model (12.1)–(12.2) with cross section dependence, CCEP denotes the Pesaran (2006) PCCE estimation whereas PC denotes the PC estimator proposed by Bai (2009). In the CCEP $\mathbf{f}_t = \{\overline{TRADE}_t, \overline{TGDP}_t, \overline{SIM}_t, \overline{RLF}_t, \overline{CEE}_t\}$ plus linear trend whereas in PC $\mathbf{f}_t$ are six factors extracted using Bai and Ng (2002) procedure plus linear trend. For the HT and the AM estimates we consider the following sets of instruments: IV $= \{RER_{it}, RLF_{it}\}$ and IV1 $= \left\{IV, \widehat{\boldsymbol{\lambda}}_i \mathbf{f}_t\right\}$. H denotes the Hausman statistic under the null of no correlation between explanatory variables and individual effect. H1 denotes the Hausman statistic testing for the legitimacy of the AM estimates above the corresponding *p*-values. Sargan denotes the statistic testing for the validity of over-identifying restrictions above the corresponding *p*-values. *CD* denotes the diagnostic test statistic for the null of no cross-section dependency advanced by Pesaran (2004)
**, * and + denote 1, 5 and 10 % level of significance

are significantly negative and positive whilst the border impact is still insignificant, a finding consistent with SS. Furthermore, the Hausman test does not reject the hypothesis that the AM-IV estimates are more efficient.

Similar to the results reported in SS for a smaller EU dataset, we also confirm that both the PCCE and the PC estimation results are remarkably similar. First, the coefficient of *TGDP* converges at around 2.[13] Secondly, both the Euro and the CEE impacts are significant but considerably smaller (around 0.04 and 0.11) than those reported in Table 12.2 without considering time-varying unobserved factors. This is generally consistent with the predictions of most recent studies and survey evidence (Baldwin 2006) as reviewed in Sect. 2. Finally, focussing on efficient AM-IV estimates, we find that distance and common language dummies exert significantly negative and positive impacts on trade. But, the border impact appears to be insignificant.

Tables 12.3 and 12.4 display the estimation results for SARAR models with endogenous interaction effects among the dependent variables (spatial lag effects) and the interaction effects among the disturbance terms (spatial error component effects). To examine the robustness of the estimation results, we consider four different spatial weight matrices so as to capture potentially complex spatial interactions: namely, the population-, the trade-, the border- and the distance-based ones. Following BEK, we first construct the population-based weight matrix, which is designed to capture the concept of multilateral resistance with respect to country-pair trade flows; namely, the weight for the pair of countries i and j is given by $\frac{L_k}{L}$ where L_k is the third country population/trade for $k \neq i$ and $k \neq j$, and $L = \sum_k L_k$ is the total population. To examine the robustness of the estimation results, we consider the trade-based weight matrix, following the global macroeconometric modelling (e.g. Greenwood-Nimmo et al. 2013). Further, as commonly used in the spatial econometric literature, we also consider the distance-based weight matrix by employing the inverse squared distance using the geographical coordinates of countries pair capitals, and the border-based one on the basis of contiguity. Hence, for the pair of countries i and j, the distance and the border matrices capture the geographical proximity between countries j and k. In all four weight matrices, our prior is a negative spatial autoregressive coefficient, ρ.[14] We find that the impacts of *GDP*, *SIM* and *RLF* are significantly positive. A depreciation of the home currency (increase in *RER*) leads to an increase in trade flows for the case of $W = border$ and

[13]Serlenga (2005) estimates coefficients on GDP_h and GDP_f, using the triple index model, where h and f indicate home and foreign countries, and finds that the sum of their coefficients are close to the coefficient on $TGDP_{hf}$ obtained from the double index model.

[14]We expect ρ to be negative because it measures the multilateral trade resistance. For example, if the trade barriers between country k and country j ($k \neq i$ and $k \neq j$) are reduced, then the trade flow between country j and country k increases while the trade flow between the country i and j decreases. Indeed we find that the autocorrelation coefficient between y and Wy is -0.014 for $W = trade$, -0.019 for $W = population$, -0.218 for $W = distance$, and -0.165 for $W = border$.

Table 12.3 Estimation results for the panel gravity SARAR model with W = Pop and W = Trade

	W=Pop			W=Trade		
gdp	2.3967**			2.1667**		
	[0.059]			[0.060]		
sim	0.9871**			1.231**		
	[0.054]			[0.042]		
rfl	0.0239**			0.0026		
	[0.0051]			[0.0051]		
rer	−0.0173**			−0.0235**		
	[0.0057]			[0.0059]		
emu	0.1879**			0.1907**		
	[0.0216]			[0.022]		
cee	0.3955**			0.3856**		
	[0.0149]			[0.015]		
Spatial	−0.1692**			−0.0806**		
rho	[0.0256]			[0.0265]		
lambda	0.7531**			0.7503**		
	[0.0137]			[0.0156]		
	OLS	HT	AM	OLS	HT	AM
con	5.062 **	4.359 **	5.118 **	2.852 **	3.743 **	5.118 **
	[0.601]	[1.176]	[0.667]	[0.450]	[0.554]	[0.667]
dis	−1.067**	−0.949**	−1.076**	−0.874**	−0.856**	−1.076**
	[0.075]	[0.176]	[0.087]	[0.056]	[0.082]	[0.087]
bor	−0.296	1.395	−0.451	0.057	0.319	−0.451
	[0.308]	[2.080]	[0.332]	[0.231]	[1.024]	[0.332]
lan	0.481 *	−2.643	0.776 *	0.519 **	0.035	0.776 *
	[0.251]	[3.686]	[0.361]	[0.188]	[1.868]	[0.361]
Sargan		$\chi_1^2 = 0.005$	$\chi_{50}^2 = 58.31$		$\chi_1^2 = 0.095$	$\chi_{50}^2 = 59.75$
p value		0.941	0.196		0.761	0.162
Hausman			H1:$\chi_3^2 = 0.092$			H1:$\chi_3^2 = 0.084$
p value			0.901			0.999
CD	9.961			7.089		
p value	0.000			0.000		

Notes: Using the annual data over 1960–2008 for 190 country-pairs, we estimate the SARAR model (12.11) and (12.12). Figures in [.] indicate the standard error. **, * and + denote 1, 5, and 10 % level of significance, respectively. The weight matrices used in the estimations are: Population and Trade. See also note to Table 12.1

Table 12.4 Estimation results for the panel gravity SARAR model with W = Border and W = Distance

	W=Border			W=Distance		
gdp	2.0393**			2.3647**		
	[0.0132]			[0.0390]		
sim	0.7594**			0.8778**		
	[0.0351]			[0.0417]		
rfl	0.0059			0.0120**		
	[0.0052]			[0.0049]		
rer	0.0321**			0.0960**		
	[0.0072]			[0.0081]		
emu	0.2267**			0.2201**		
	[0.0207]			[0.0198]		
cee	0.3261**			0.3683**		
	[0.0143]			[0.0148]		
Spatial	−0.0786**			−0.2100**		
rho	[0.0092]			[0.0198]		
lambda	0.3842**			0.6184**		
	[0.0125]			[0.0121]		
	OLS	HT	AM	OLS	HT	AM
con	5.262 **	4.937 **	5.353 **	5.172 **	5.198 **	5.449 **
	[0.480]	[0.732]	[0.496]	[0.622]	[0.751]	[0.675]
dis	−0.910**	−0.855**	−0.923**	−0.971**	−0.975**	−1.011**
	[0.060]	[0.109]	[0.064]	[0.078]	[0.110]	[0.087]
bor	0.091	0.874	−0.043	−0.212	−0.274	−0.610
	[0.246]	[1.266]	[0.259]	[0.318]	[1.324]	[0.468]
lan	0.510*	−0.937	0.721*	0.440*	0.555	1.057*
	[0.200]	[2.268]	[0.309]	[0.259]	[2.465]	[0.399]
Sargan		$\chi_1^2 = 1.816$	$\chi_{50}^2 = 59.51$		$\chi_1^2 = 9.303$	$\chi_{50}^2 = 56.81$
p value		0.177	0.167		0.002	0.236
Hausman			H1:$\chi_3^2 = 0.866$			H1:$\chi_3^2 = 0.671$
p value			0.923			0.954
CD	7.497			3.571		
p value	0.000			0.000		

Notes: Using the annual data over 1960–2008 for 190 country-pairs, we estimate the SARAR model (12.11) and (12.12). Figures in [.] indicate the standard error. **, * and + denote 1, 5, and 10 % level of significance, respectively. The weight matrices used in the estimations are: Border and Distance. See also note to Table 12.1

$W = distance$, but a decrease in trade for $W = trade$ and $W = pop$.[15] We also find that trade and currency union memberships (*CEE* and *EMU*) boost real trade flows significantly.

We now follow LeSage and Fisher (2010), and discuss the estimation results for the spatial gravity model in terms of direct and indirect effects. To this end we rewrite (12.5) as follows:

$$\mathbf{y}_t = \rho \mathbf{W}\mathbf{y}_t + \mathbf{X}_t\boldsymbol{\beta} + \mathbf{Z}\boldsymbol{\gamma} + \boldsymbol{\varepsilon}_t,\ t = 1, \ldots, T \tag{12.12}$$

where $\mathbf{y}_t = (y_{1t}, \ldots, y_{Nt})'$, $\mathbf{W} = \{w_{ij}\}_{i,j=1}^{N}$ is the $N \times N$ spatial weight matrix, $\mathbf{X}_t = (\mathbf{x}'_{1t}, \ldots, \mathbf{x}'_{Nt})$ is the $N \times k$ matrix of time-varying regressors, $\mathbf{Z} = (\mathbf{z}'_1, \ldots, \mathbf{z}'_N)$ is the $N \times g$ matrix of time-invariant regressors,and $\boldsymbol{\varepsilon}_t = (\varepsilon_{1t}, \ldots, \varepsilon_{Nt})'$ with $\varepsilon_{it} = \tilde{\alpha}_i + v_{it}$. We then rewrite (12.12) as

$$\mathbf{y}_t = (\mathbf{I}_N - \rho \mathbf{W})^{-1} (\mathbf{X}_t\boldsymbol{\beta} + \mathbf{Z}\boldsymbol{\gamma} + \boldsymbol{\varepsilon}_t). \tag{12.13}$$

Then, the impacts of a change in the rth time-varying regressor corresponds to the following $N \times N$ matrix of partial derivatives:

$$\frac{\partial \mathbf{y}_t}{\partial X_{rt}} = (\mathbf{I}_N - \rho \mathbf{W})^{-1} \beta_r,\ r = 1, \ldots, k \tag{12.14}$$

Notice that diagonal elements of (12.14) (direct impacts), are different across cross-section units; off-diagonal terms (indirect impacts) differ from zero, and the matrix is not symmetric. We now have N direct effects and $N(N-1)$ indirect effects. To avoid such an interactive heterogeneity issue, LeSage and Pace (2009) suggest to employ only three scalar measures to summarise information contained in the matrix (12.14): the average of the N diagonal elements as a measure of direct effects, the average of the $N(N-1)$ off-diagonal elements as the average of the cumulative indirect effects and the average total effect as the mean of total effects.

From Table 12.5 we find that the direct effects are always positive while the indirect effects are mostly negative and significant.[16] Thus, the estimated total effects are smaller than the main estimates reported in Tables 12.3 and 12.4. As discussed in footnote 16, we also notice that the signs of impacts of real exchange rates on trades are different across different spatial weights. Furthermore, we find

[15]These contradictory findings can be explained as follows: When we use $W = border$ and *distance*, the spatial matrices capture the effect of proximity and distance on trade flow, and therefore, a depreciation of the home currency leads to an increase in trade flow, especially as the distance rises. On the other hand, when we employ $W = trade$ and *pop*, the spatial matrices control for multilateral resistance in which case it would prevent the trade flow (exports) to increase as *RER* rises.

[16]For example, the indirect spillover effects of *GDP*, *SIM*, *EMU* and *CEE* are all negative and significant. Where indirect effects are positive, they are insignificant or negligible.

Table 12.5 Direct and indirect effects for the panel gravity SARAR model

	W=Trade direct	W=Pop direct	W=border direct	W=distance direct	W=Trade indirect	W=Pop indirect	W=border indirect	W=distance indirect
gdp	2.1667**	2.3967**	2.0393**	2.3647**	−0.162**	−0.349**	−0.103**	−0.423**
	[0.060]	[0.059]	[0.0132]	[0.0390]	[0.049]	[0.049]	[0.013]	[0.037]
sim	1.231**	0.9871**	0.7594**	0.8778**	−0.092**	−0.144**	−0.039**	−0.158**
	[0.042]	[0.054]	[0.0351]	[0.0417]	[0.027]	[0.022]	[0.005]	[0.016]
rfl	0.0026	0.0239**	0.0059	0.0120**	0.000	−0.004**	0.000	−0.002 *
	[0.0051]	[0.0051]	[0.0052]	[0.0049]	[0.000]	[0.001]	[0.000]	[0.001]
rer	−0.0235**	−0.0173**	0.0321**	0.0960**	0.002 *	0.003 **	−0.002**	−0.017**
	[0.0059]	[0.0057]	[0.0072]	[0.0081]	[0.001]	[0.001]	[0.000]	[0.002]
emu	0.1907**	0.1879**	0.2267**	0.2201**	−0.015**	−0.028**	−0.012**	−0.040**
	[0.022]	[0.0216]	[0.0207]	[0.0198]	[0.004]	[0.004]	[0.002]	[0.004]
cee	0.3856**	0.3955**	0.3261**	0.3683**	−0.029**	−0.058**	−0.017**	−0.066**
	[0.015]	[0.0149]	[0.0143]	[0.0148]	[0.008]	[0.008]	[0.002]	[0.006]
Spatial	−0.0806**	−0.1692**	−0.0786**	−0.2100**				
rho	[0.0265]	[0.0256]	[0.0092]	[0.0198]				
lambda	0.7503**	0.7531**	0.3842**	0.6184**				
	[0.0156]	[0.0137]	[0.0125]	[0.0121]				

Notes: Following LeSage and Pace (2009), we compute the average of the N diagonal elements of the matrix in (12.14) as the direct effects, and the average of the $N(N-1)$ off-diagonal elements as the average of the (cumulative) indirect effects indirect effects. The average total effect is then the sum of average direct and average indirect effects. Figures in [.] indicate the standard error. **, * and + denote 1, 5, and 10 % level of significance, respectively. Standard errors in parenthesis. The weight matrix used in the estimations are: Trade, Population, border and distance

that indirect spillover effects of *RFL* are significantly negative only for $W = Pop$ and *Distance*.

Comparing the estimation results for the spatial-based panel gravity models in Tables 12.3 and 12.4 with those for the factor-based models in Table 12.2, we notice the following important differences: The impact of *RLF* is rather positive and significant for $W = pop$ and $W = distance$. Secondly, as explained above, the effect of depreciation of home currency depends on the way we model spatial spillover effects. Thirdly, the impacts of *EMU* and *CEE* are around 0.2 and 0.3 and substantially higher than those obtained by the factor-based models. These values are rather close to the estimates obtained under the basic model specification without controlling for cross-section dependence. To investigate this issue further, we apply the cross-section dependency (CD) test advanced by Pesaran (2004) to the residuals obtained from the spatial-based gravity models, we find that the null of no cross-sectional dependence is strongly rejected for all of the models as reported in Tables 12.3 and 12.4. On the other hand, we find from Table 12.2 that the null hypothesis is only marginally rejected for the factor-based models. Overall evidence may suggest that the spatial model does not fully accommodate the potential correlation between regressors and unobserved individual and time effects.

Given that most of existing studies neglect an important issue of evaluating the currency union effects on trade through bilateral resistance channels, SS propose an alternative way to testing the Euro effect on trade integration by testing the validity of the hypothesis that the Euro might have caused a fall in trade impacts of bilateral trade barriers, if it had a positive effect on internal European trade (by reducing overall trade costs). In particular, we will examine whether the coefficients on bilateral resistance proxies (γ) tend to be more downward-sloping after the introduction of the Euro in 1999 than before. If so, this implies a (indirect) positive effect of the Euro on the European Integration. To this end, we re-estimate the model, (12.9), by the cross-section regressions for each time period. After consistently estimating $\hat{d}_{it}$ in (12.9) by the factor-based PCEE and PC estimators or the spatial-based SARAR estimators, we apply the more efficient AM-IV estimation and perform the following cross section regression for each t:

$$d_{it} = a_i + \boldsymbol{\gamma}_t' \mathbf{z}_i + e_{it},\ i = 1, \ldots, N,$$

where $\mathbf{z}_i$ includes Dis_i, Bor_i and Lan_i.

Figures 12.1 and 12.2 display the estimation results for the time-varying coefficients of $\hat{\boldsymbol{\gamma}}$. Overall, we find that the downward slopes of coefficients are steeper for both border and language effects after 1999 than before 1999.[17] Also, their decreases

[17]Close inspection of Figs. 12.1 and 12.2 reveals that here are the following (minor) differences among six different estimation results: The decrease in border and language effects is slightly more pronounced for the PCCE estimator than the PC estimator. Turning to the spatial models, we find that the time-varying patterns for $W = Population$ and $W = Distance$ are similar whereas the spatial

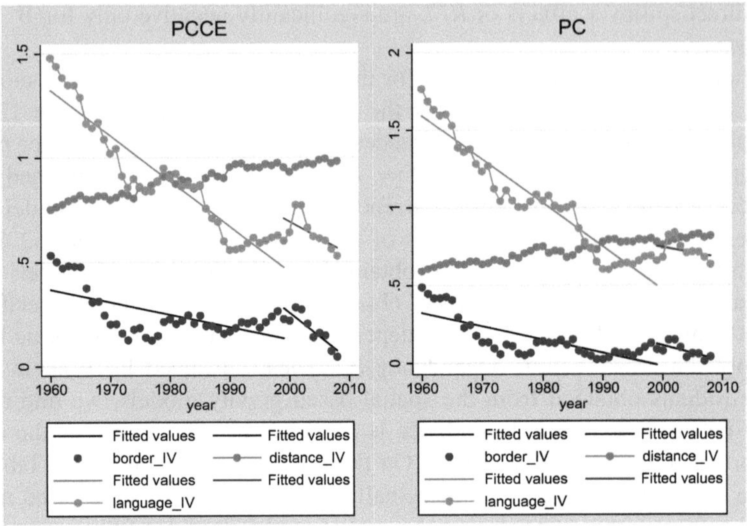

Fig. 12.1 Time-varying trade impacts of bilateral trade barriers for the factor-based gravity models. Notes: We estimate the time-varying impacts of bilateral trade barriers (distance, border and language) on trade flows by applying the two-step AM-IV estimators as follows: In the first-step, we estimate the factor-based gravity model, (12.1)–(12.2), by PCCE or PC estimators as in Table 12.2. Then, in the second-step, we estimate (12.9) by the cross-section regression at each time period. See SS for details. To enhance visibility, we super-impose the fitted relative slopes

turn out to be sharp and monotonic. The declining language impacts may reflect the progressive lessening of restrictions on labor mobility within EU (e.g. Rauch and Trindade 2002). Importantly, the monotonically declining border impacts especially after 2000 suggest that the Euro help to reduce border-linked trade costs. Finally, we find that the distance effects on trade have been more or less stable or slightly increasing over the full sample period. This evidence provides support for the studies by Disdier and Head (2008) and Jacks (2009), who document that the notion of the death of distance has been difficult to identify in the present-day trade data.[18] Overall, these findings suggest that the introduction of the Euro helps to reduce trade effects of bilateral trade barriers and promote more integration among the EU countries.

models with $W = \mathit{Trade}$ and $W = \mathit{Border}$ produce similar results. Further, the fall in language effect is sharper for $W = \mathit{Distance}$.

[18]On the basis of our most preferred specification with unobserved factors (strong CSD) and endogeneity (AM-IV estimates), we are able to document a negative albeit the lower impact of distance on trade.

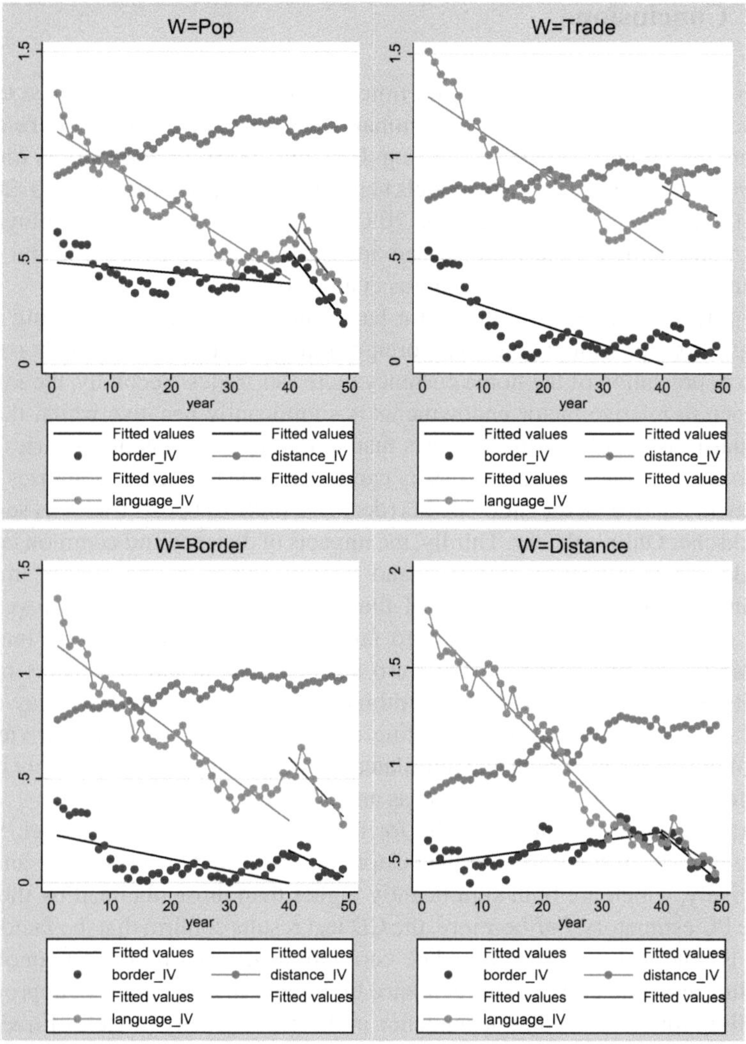

Fig. 12.2 Time-varying trade impacts of bilateral trade barriers for the spatial-based gravity models. Notes: We estimate the time-varying impacts of bilateral trade barriers (distance, border and language) on trade flows by applying the two-step AM-IV estimators as follows: In the first-step, we estimate the spatial-based gravity model, (12.11)–(12.12), by SARAR estimators with W = Pop, Trade, Border and Distance as in Tables 12.3 and 12.4. Then, in the second-step, we estimate (12.9) by the cross-section regression at each time period. See SS for details. To enhance visibility, we super-impose the fitted relative slopes

12.5 Conclusion

The investigation of unobserved and time-varying multilateral resistance terms in conjunction with omitted trade determinants has assumed a prominent role in the literature on the Euro's trade effects (e.g. Baldwin 2006). To address this important issue we apply the panel gravity models to the dataset over the period 1960–2008 (49 years) for 190 country-pairs amongst 20 OECD member countries, employing two recent methodologies: the factor-based approach proposed by SS and the spatial-based techniques developed by Behrens et al. (2012).

The estimation results for the factor-based model provide the following stylised findings: First, the sum of home and foreign country GDPs significantly boosts trade while a depreciation of the home currency increases trades. Secondly, the impact of difference in relative factor endowments is significantly negative whilst the effect of similarity is positive. This suggests that similarity (in terms of countries' *GDP*) helps to ease the integration process by capturing trade ties across countries and the diversity in relative factor endowments (decrease in *RFL*) boosts trades as suggested by Heckscher Ohlin's theory. Thirdly, the impacts of distance and common language on trade are significantly negative and positive whereas the border impact is insignificant. Further investigation of their time-varying coefficients reveals that border and language effects started to fall more sharply after 1999. Finally and importantly, we find that both the Euro and the custom union impacts on trade amounts only to 4–5 % and 11 %. Combined together, these findings may support the idea that the potential trade-creating effects of the Euro should be viewed in terms of the proper historical and multilateral perspective rather than simply in terms of the formation of a monetary union as an isolated event.

Next, from the estimation results for the spatial-based gravity model, we find that the impacts of the Euro and the custom union on trade rises to 20 % and 30 %, respectively, which are both significantly higher than those obtained by the PCCE and the PC estimators. Furthermore, the CD test results confirm that the factor-based model is able to better accommodate correlation between regressors, unobserved individual and time effects. This evidence highlights an importance of appropriately controlling for cross-section dependence in the panel gravity models of trade flows through the use of both observed and unobserved factors in order to account for time-varying multilateral resistance, trade costs and globalisation trends.

12.6 The Data Appendix

Here we revise and update the data appendix of Serlenga and Shin (2007) for the sake of completeness.

All variables are converted into constant dollar prices with 2005 as the base year. The dependent variable is the logarithm of real total trade given by $Trade_{it} = \ln\left(X_{hft}^R + M_{hft}^R\right)$, where X_{hft}^R is the bilateral real export from country h to country

f, and M^R_{hft} are bilateral real imports from country h to country f, at time t with i denoting the country-pair.

Regressors can be divided into two categories: time-varying and time-invariant variables. First, the time-varying regressors are:

TGDP is the (log of) total GDP defined as $TGDP_{it} = \ln\left(GDP^R_{ht} + GDP^R_{ft}\right)$, where GDP^Rs are defined as gross domestic products at constant (2005) dollar prices for home and foreign countries, respectively. *TGDP* proxies overall economic mass of the trading pair countries, and it is expected to exert a positive effect on bilateral trade.

SIM is the measure of countries' similarity in size constructed as

$$SIM_{it} = \ln\left[1 - \left(\frac{GDP^R_{ht}}{GDP^R_{ht} + GDP^R_{ft}}\right)^2 - \left(\frac{GDP^R_{ft}}{GDP^R_{ft} + GDP^R_{ht}}\right)^2\right];$$

This index is bounded between zero (absolute divergence) and 0.5 (equal size). The SIM effect on trade is expected to be positive.

RLF is a measure of countries' difference in relative factor endowments, constructed as

$$RLF_{it} = \ln\left|PGDP^R_{ft} - PGDP^R_{ht}\right|,$$

where $PGDP^R$ is per capita GDP. The higher is *RLF*, the larger is difference between their factor endowments, resulting in the higher volume of inter-industry trade and the lower share of intra-industry trade. Therefore, the total impact of *RLF* on trade flows (sum of inter- and intra-industry trades) might not be unambiguous.

RER is the real exchange rate in constant (2005) dollars, defined as $RER_{it} = NER_{it} \times XPI_{US}$, where NER_{it} is nominal exchange rate between currencies h and f in terms of the U.S. dollars, XPI_{US} is the exports price index. *RER* is the price of the foreign currency per the home currency unit and is meant to capture the relative price effects. A depreciation of the home currency relative to the foreign currency (an increase in *RER*) should lead to more export and less import for home country. The effect of real exchange rates on trade flows will be positive if the export is significantly larger than the import, and vice versa, e.g., Egger and Pfaffermayr (2003).

CEE is the European Community dummy, which is equal to one when both countries belong to the European Community, and it is expected to exert a positive impact. See also De Sousa and Desdier (2005) and Cheng and Wall (2005) for an analysis of the effects of regional trading blocks.

EMU is the European Monetary Union dummy which is equal to one when both trading partners adopt the Euro. Given that an official motivation behind the EMU is that the single currency will reduce the transaction costs of trade, the impact of *EMU* on trade flows is expected to be positive.

Next, we consider the following time-invariant variables:

LAN is the dummy for common language, which is equal to one when both countries speak the same official language. As *LAN* is supposed to capture similarity in cultural and historical backgrounds of trading countries, it is expected to display a positive effect.

BOR is a dummy for common border which is equal to one when the trading partners share a border. Its effect on bilateral trade flows is expected to be positive.

DIS is the (log of) distance between countries, where the distance is measured as the (log) of great circle distance between national capitals in kilometers. The effect of geographical distance on trade flows is expected to be negative.

Acknowledgements We are grateful to the coeditor, Roberto Patuelli, an anonymous referee, Badi Baltagi, Peter Burridge, Matthew Greenwood-Nimmo, George Kapetanios, Minjoo Kim, Hashem Pesaran, Ron Smith, Takashi Yamagata, the seminar participants at Universities of Bari and York, and the conference delegates at the Fifth Italian Congress of Econometrics and Empirical Economics, 2013 and Cross-sectional Dependence in Panel Data Models, May 2013 at Cambridge for their helpful comments. The usual disclaimer applies.

References

Amemiya T, McCurdy T (1986) Instrumental variables estimation of an error components model. Econometrica 54:869–880

Anderson J, van Wincoop E (2003) Gravity with gravitas: a solution to the border puzzle. Am Econ Rev 93:170–192

Anderson J, van Wincoop E (2004) Trade costs. J Econ Lit 42:691–751

Bai J (2009) Panel data models with interactive fixed effects. Econometrica 77:1229–1279

Bai J, Ng S (2002) Determining the number of factors in approximate factor models. Econometrica 70:191–221

Bailey N, Kapetanios G, Pesaran MH (2012) Exponent of cross-sectional dependence: estimation and inference. IZA Discussion Paper No. 6318

Baldwin RE (2006) In or out: Does it matter? An evidence-based analysis of the Euro's trade effects. CEPR, London

Baldwin RE, Taglioni D (2006) Gravity for dummies and dummies for gravity equations. NBER Working Paper 12516

Baltagi BH (2010) Narrow replication of Serlenga and Shin (2007) gravity models of intra-EU trade: application of the PCCE-HT estimation in heterogeneous panels with unobserved common time-specific factors. J Appl Econ 25:505–506

Baltagi BH, Egger P, Pfaffermayr M (2007) Estimating models of complex FDI: Are there third-country effects? J Econ 140:260–281

Baltagi BH, Egger P, Pfaffermayr M (2008) Estimating regional trade agreement effects on FDI in an interdependent world. J Econ 145:194–208

Behrens K, Ertur C, Kock W (2012) Dual gravity: using spatial econometrics to control for multilateral resistance. J Appl Econ 27:773–794

Berger H, Nitsch V (2008) Zooming out: the trade effect of the euro in historical perspective. J Int Money Financ 27:1244–1260

Blonigen BA, Davies RB, Waddell GR, Naughton HT (2007) FDI in space. Eur Econ Rev 51:1303–1325

Breusch T, Mizon G, Schmidt P (1989) Efficient estimation using panel data. Econometrica 57:695–700

Bun M, Klaassen F (2007) The Euro effect on trade is not as large as commonly thought. Oxf Bull Econ Stat 69:473–496

Camaero M, Gómez-Herrera E, Tamarit C (2012) The Euro impact on trade. long run evidence with structural breaks. Working Papers in Applied Economics, University of Valencia, WPAE-2012-09

Cheng I, Wall HJ (2005) Controlling heterogeneity in gravity models of trade and integration. Federal Reserve Bank St Louis Rev 87:49–63

Chudik A, Pesaran MH, Tosetti E (2011) Weak and strong cross-section dependence and estimation of large panels. Econ J 14:45–90

Conley TG, Topa G (2002) Socio-economic distance and spatial patterns in unemployment. J Appl Econ 17:303–327

de Nardis S, Vicarelli C (2003) Currency unions and trade: the special case of EMU. World Rev Econ 139:625–649

De Sousa J, Desdier A (2005) Trade, border effects and individual characteristics: a proper specification. In: Mayer T, Muchielli JL (eds) Multinational firms' location and new economic geography. Edward Elgar, Cheltenham, pp 59–75

Disdier A, Head K (2008) The puzzling persistence of the distance effect on bilateral trade. Rev Econ Stat 90:37–48

Egger P, Pfaffermayr M (2003) The proper panel econometric specification of the gravity equation: a three-way model with bilateral interaction effects. Empir Econ 28:571–580

Elhorst JP (2011) Spatial panel models. University of Groningen, Mimeo, Department of Economics, Econometrics and Finance

Flam H, Nordström H (2006) Trade volume effects of the Euro: aggregate and sector estimates. Seminar Papers 746, Stockholm University, Institute for International Economic Studies

Frankel JA (2008) The estimated effects of the euro on trade: Why are they below historical effects of monetary unions among smaller countries? NBER Working Paper 14542

Greenwood-Nimmo MJ, Nguyen VH, Shin Y (2013) Measuring the Connectedness of the Global Economy, Mimeo University of Melbourne, Department of Economics

Hall SG, Petroulas P (2008) Spatial interdependencies of FDI locations: a lessening of the Tyranny of distance? Bank of Greece Working Paper No.67

Hausman JA, Taylor WE (1981) Panel data and unobservable individual effect. Econometrica 49:1377–1398

Helpman E, Krugman P (1985) Market structure and international trade. MIT Press, Cambridge

Helpman E (1987) Imperfect competition and international trade: evidence from fourteen industrialized countries. J Jpn Int Econ 1:62–81

Herwartz H, Weber H (2010) The Euro's trade effect under cross-sectional heterogeneity and stochastic resistance. Kiel Working Paper No. 1631, Kiel Institute for the World Economy, Germany

Jacks DS (2009) On the death of distance and borders: evidence from the nineteenth century. NBER Working Paper 15250

Krugman PR (1979) Increasing returns, monopolistic competition and international trade. J Int Econ 9:469–479

LeSage JP, Pace RK (2009) Introduction to spatial econometrics. CRC Press, Boca Raton

McCallum J (1995) National borders matter: Canada-U.S. regional trade patterns. Am Econ Rev 85:615–623

Melitz M, Ghironi F (2007) Trade flow dynamics with heterogeneous firms. Am Econ Rev 97:356–361

Micco A, Stein E, Ordoñez G (2003) The currency union effect on trade: early evidences from EMU. Econ Policy 37:317–356

OECD (2010) Measuring globalisation: OECD economic globalisation indicators. OECD, Paris

Pesaran MH (2004) General diagnostic tests for cross section dependence in panels. IZA Discussion Paper No. 1240

Pesaran MH (2006) Estimation and inference in large heterogeneous panels with a multifactor error structure. Econometrica 74:967–1012

Pesaran MH, Tosetti E (2011) Large panels with common factors and spatial correlation. J Econ 161:182–202

Rauch J, Trindade V (2002) Ethnic Chinese networks in international trade. Rev Econ Stat 84:116–130

Rose A (2000) Currency unions and trade: the effect is large. Econ Policy 33:449–461

Serlenga L (2005) Three essays on the panel data approach to an analysis of economics and financial data. Unpublished Ph.D. dissertation, University of Edinburgh

Serlenga L, Shin Y (2007) Gravity models of intra-EU trade: application of the PCCE-HT estimation in heterogeneous panels with unobserved common time-specific factors. J Appl Econ 22:361–381

Serlenga L, Shin Y (2013) The Euro effect on intra-EU trade: evidence from the cross sectionally dependent panel gravity models, Mimeo, University of York

Part III
Applications

Chapter 13
The Effects of World Heritage Sites on Domestic Tourism: A Spatial Interaction Model for Italy

Roberto Patuelli, Maurizio Mussoni, and Guido Candela

Keywords Cultural tourism • Domestic tourism • Italy • Spatial competition • Spatial interaction model • World Heritage Sites

JEL Classifications: C23, L83, R12, Z10

13.1 Introduction

Culture is gaining increasing importance in the modern tourism industry, and represents a significant force of attraction for tourists (both domestic and international). Cultural tourism allows destinations and regions to: (1) expand their customer base; (2) diversify their offer; (3) extend the stay of the tourists (overnight stays) and reduce seasonality. For these reasons, national governments and regions make great efforts to obtain official designation for their historical and cultural attractions, for example through the United Nations Educational, Scientific and Cultural Organization (UNESCO) World Heritage Sites (WHS) label.

Such aspect seems particularly relevant for a country like Italy, which is internationally renowned for its abundance of historical and cultural resources, as shown by its high number of entries in the WHS list, and where regions take an active role in promoting tourism. As of 2011, the UNESCO WHS list included 936

This paper has been previously published in the *Journal of Geographical Systems*. Special Issue on "Advances in the Statistical Modelling of Spatial Interaction Data", Vol. 15, Number 3/July 2013, ©Springer-Verlag Berlin Heidelberg, pp. 369–402.

R. Patuelli (✉) • M. Mussoni
Department of Economics, University of Bologna, Bologna, Italy

The Rimini Centre for Economic Analysis (RCEA), Rimini, Italy
e-mail: roberto.patuelli@unibo.it

G. Candela
Department of Economics, University of Bologna, Bologna, Italy

R. Patuelli, G. Arbia (eds.), *Spatial Econometric Interaction Modelling*, Advances in Spatial Science, DOI 10.1007/978-3-319-30196-9_13

sites: 725 were cultural, 183 natural, and 28 mixed, in 153 countries (UNESCO 2011). Italy hosted the greatest number of WHS to date, with 47 sites, corresponding to 5.02 % of the total.

Tourism is one of the fastest growing and most profitable sectors of the Italian economy: in 2010, with 43.6 million international tourist arrivals, and international tourism receipts estimated at US$ 38.8 billion, Italy was the fifth highest tourism earner and the fifth most visited country in the world (UNWTO 2011), behind France, Spain, United States, and China.

In this paper, we analyse Italian 'domestic tourism', which, according to the United Nations, is defined as tourism involving residents of a given country travelling only within the country itself (UNWTO 1994).[1] Recently, the tourism industry has shifted from the promotion of inbound tourism to the promotion of domestic tourism, because many countries are experiencing increasing competition on the inbound tourism market. Some national policymakers have shifted their priority to the promotion of domestic tourism to contribute to the local economy. Domestic tourism, historically speaking, is in fact the first form of tourism, and today continues to account by far for most of this activity: it is estimated that worldwide, out of the 4.8 billion tourist arrivals per year (2008 figures), 4 billion (83 %) correspond to domestic tourism (Pierret 2011). Likewise, UNWTO scholars estimate that, globally, domestic tourism represents:

- 73 % of total overnight stays;
- 74 % of arrivals and 69 % of overnight stays at hotels;
- 89 % of arrivals and 75 % of overnight stays in other (non-hotel) accommodations.

In Italy, it represents the greatest share of the entire tourism sector, and produces a remarkable macroeconomic impact in terms of value added and labour force. In 2007, domestic tourism provided, on a regional scale, up to 88 and 90 % of arrivals and overnight stays, respectively (Massidda and Etzo 2011).

Several studies have investigated whether or not WHS endowment, or more generally cultural offer, increases tourism demand. However, the empirical evidence on this issue is mixed. A number of studies claim that the cultural heritage and attractions of a country are important determinants of tourism demand (see, e.g., Carr 1994; Alzua et al. 1998; Vietze 2008), while others conclude that it is not possible to find a clear positive relationship between cultural endowment and tourism flows (see, e.g., Cuccia and Cellini 2007; Cellini and Cuccia 2013). Regarding specifically WHS endowment, UNESCO declares that obtaining a WHS designation provides significant economic benefits to the host countries (UNESCO 2012). Nevertheless, there is no agreement on this finding in the scientific literature,

[1]The UNWTO also derived different categories of tourism by combining the three basic forms of tourism: 'internal tourism', which comprises domestic tourism and inbound tourism; 'national tourism', which comprises domestic tourism and outbound tourism; and 'international tourism', which consists of inbound tourism and outbound tourism.

and the debate, focusing on international tourism, is still open (see, e.g., Arezki et al. 2009; Yang et al. 2010; Cellini 2011; Yang and Lin 2011).

On the basis of the above discussion, the aim of this paper is to investigate the determinants of Italian domestic tourism flows, with particular reference to the specific contribution of the endowment in WHS. The main concern of this paper is to investigate the importance of the regional endowment in WHS for domestic tourism. We analyse how and to what extent WHS designation affects the flows of tourists between each pair of Italian regions (i.e., between any origin and destination region). The domestic tourism setting, using regional data, provides a more fitting framework for analysing spatial interaction and spatial competition phenomena. We do not analyse international tourism flows (to and from Italy), because of lack of data (for consistency with the modelling framework employed, data on international flows to and from each Italian region would be necessary).

To the best of our knowledge, two specific research questions remain unanswered in the literature on the relationship between WHS endowment and tourism: (1) How differently does the WHS endowment of the origin and destination regions influence tourism flows (i.e., in a push/pull perspective)? (2) Does WHS endowment generate spatial substitution or complementarity between regions?

Accordingly, the objectives of this paper are: (1) to separate the effects on tourism flows of WHS located in the residence region of the tourist (the origin region) and in the destination region; and (2) to take into account potential spatial substitution or spatial complementarity between regions due to their WHS endowment.

Specifically, our first research question, regarding the origin- and destination-level effects of WHS endowment, can be further stated as follows:

- Does the origin region's WHS endowment push the inhabitants to travel more (or less), influencing tourism outflows (the 'push effect')?
- Does the destination region's WHS endowment attract greater tourism inflows (the 'pull effect')?

In addition to the effect of WHS endowment on inflows and outflows, we are interested in evaluating how the tourists' choices are influenced by the spatial distribution of the WHS. In particular, our second research question can be declined as follows:

- Does the WHS endowment of the regions surrounding the tourist's origin region create a substitution between 'recordable' tourism (arrivals, which involve overnight stays) and daily trips of excursionists (e.g., within the origin region)?
- Does the WHS endowment of the regions surrounding each possible destination region cause spatial competition for tourism demand or spatial complementarity (mutual beneficial effects deriving by trip-chaining) between regions? This question may be particularly relevant from a policy perspective, since regions could use WHS designation for competition or towards joint benefits.

With regard to our second research question, we provide an interpretative framework for the potentially varying effects of WHS endowment of 'neighbouring' destination regions on tourism flows, which is followed by a spatial sensitivity analysis.

To answer the above questions, we set up a spatial interaction model for tourism flows recorded between the 20 Italian regions over the years 1998–2009 (i.e., a 12-year panel). We divide the possible determinants of domestic tourism flows into 'push variables', 'pull variables', and 'deterrence (bilateral) variables', and carry out two Poisson-based (negative binomial) estimations: a two-way fixed effects (FE) model and a spatial filtering-augmented model (including origin and destination FE and a network autocorrelation spatial filter).

The paper is organized as follows. Section 13.2 briefly reviews the literature on the application of the spatial interaction model in tourism studies. Section 13.3 briefly presents the literature on the relationship between cultural heritage and tourism, and more specifically between WHS endowment and tourism. Section 13.4 describes the model and the variables used, the estimation strategy and an interpretative model for the spatial sensitivity analysis offered. Section 13.5 describes the data set used in this study, and presents our empirical findings and their interpretation. Section 13.6 provides concluding remarks and future research directions.

13.2 Modelling Tourism Flows: Spatial Interaction Models

The spatial interaction model (or gravity model; for an overview, see Haynes and Fotheringham 1984; Sen and Smith 1995), is a modelling framework commonly used in many fields, like commuting, migration, trade, leisure activities, and also tourism. In the case of the latter, it is often used for studying tourism flows between regions or countries (e.g., Uysal and Crompton 1985; Witt and Witt 1995; Khadaroo and Seetanah 2008).

Gravity equations have been estimated since the 1960s for analysing bilateral trade flows (e.g., Tinbergen 1962; Pöyhönen 1963; Anderson 1979; Colwell 1982), and recent applications increasingly emphasize the importance of estimating a theoretically consistent model (e.g., Anderson and van Wincoop 2003; Baier and Bergstrand 2009). The spatial interaction model describes the interaction flow (T_{ij}) between the origin region i and the destination region j as a function of repulsive forces/push factors at i (R_i) and attractive forces/pull factors at j (A_j), such as the economic size of the origins and destinations, and separation variables referring to the (i, j) pair, such as an inverse function of the friction/distance between the regions i and j (D_{ij}). A generic formulation of the spatial interaction model can be as follows:

$$T_{ij} = \frac{f\left(R_i, A_j\right)}{f\left(D_{ij}\right)}. \tag{13.1}$$

Formally, a spatial interaction model is specified as:

$$T_{ij} = G\frac{R_i^{\alpha} A_j^{\beta}}{D_{ij}^{\theta}}, \tag{13.2}$$

where G is a proportionality constant, and α, β and θ are the specific weights of R_i, A_j and D_{ij} respectively. This multiplicative model is typically estimated after rendering it linear in parameters through log-linearization, or through nonlinear optimization techniques, when constraints are applied in order to respect marginal totals (Wilson 1967, 1970).

Likewise, applications of the spatial interaction model to tourism (see, e.g., Armstrong 1972; Crampon and Tan 1973; Malamud 1973; McAllister and Klett 1976; Swart et al. 1978; Saunders et al. 1981) express bilateral tourism flows (T_{ij}) as a function of the characteristics of the regions of origin i and destination j (X_i and X_j)—factors that augment or distort tourism flows—and of distance, which acts as a proxy for transportation costs. More specifically, in the tourism context, repulsive forces/push factors are associated with leaving i for tourism reasons (tourism outflows), while attractive forces/pull factors are related to going to j for tourism reasons (tourism inflows).

Within this framework, tourism flows (in particular arrivals) can be seen in a similar fashion to migration or commuting flows (e.g., Lowry 1966). Accordingly, tourism flows could be related, for example, to the number of WHS available in the destination, and to other control variables evaluated at the same location, like crime indices and other cultural proxies. On the other hand, flows could also be dependent on the number of WHS available in the origin, as well as on the population basin or per capita income, and finally on the distance between the origin and the destination. An alternative interpretation of the spatial interaction model for tourism consists of applying a 'commodity version' of the model, according to which tourism is essentially seen as a form of trade, and tourism flows are treated as traded services (Leamer and Levinsohn 1995; Eilat and Einav 2004; Yang et al. 2010).

In the empirical literature on international and domestic tourism (e.g., Sheldon and Var 1985; Calantone et al. 1987; Kim and Fesenmaier 1990; Gardini 1998; Zhang and Jensen 2007; Nicolau 2008; Keum 2010; de la Mata and Llano-Verduras 2011), the most frequently used dependent variables have been tourist arrivals or overnight stays, as well as tourist expenditures or receipts. Regarding the explanatory variables, there is undoubtedly a wide range of possible determinants of tourism demand, the most prominent being income (GDP at the macro level), relative tourism prices, transportation costs, exchange rates, and qualitative factors in destination regions.

In particular, the level of income of the potential tourist affects his/her capability to pay for travel (Sheldon and Var 1985), while GDP (observed both at the origin and at the destination) is used as a proxy for market size, and represents push and pull factors, which influence the value of tourism flows.[2] Other important determinants of tourism demand are: the relative prices of goods and services purchased by tourists in the destination, compared with the origin and the competing destinations (see, e.g., Gerakis 1965; Edwards 1976; Bond et al. 1977); transportation costs (usually proxied for by distance), which refer to the cost of round-trip travel between

[2]Further specifications in the literature have used population (Linnemann 1966) in order to capture size effects.

the origin and destination regions; the exchange rates between the currencies of origin and destination (mostly relevant in the case of international tourism). Demand for travel to a particular destination is expected to be positively related to both income in the origin and exchange rates, and negatively related to both transportation costs and relative tourism prices.

Further explanatory variables included in tourism demand models (for an overview, see Sheldon and Var 1985; Lim 1997) are: trip motive or frequency; destination attractiveness and endowment (climate and temperature, natural environment, pollution and environmental quality, culture and history, cultural heritage, WHS); political, social, cultural and sporting events in the destination; destination marketing or promotional expenditures (information, tourist services, public expenditure for culture activities and events, etc.); supply/capacity constraints of tourist accommodations (carrying capacity); supply-side variables, like tourism and transport infrastructure of the destination; social variables capturing the role of public safety, such as the diffusion of small and/or violent crime (Eilat and Einav 2004; Massidda and Etzo 2011); a time trend variable capturing long-run change in tourist tastes (Barry and O'Hagan 1972) or the steady change in the tourist mix (Fujii et al. 1985, 1987); lagged variables accounting for dynamics, such as the previous values of income, relative prices, exchange rates, and foreign investment; proxies for business travels, such as trade, foreign direct investment, or capital outflows. Finally, a large number of qualitative factors (typically accommodated by means of dummy variables) may influence the decision to demand tourism, including the tourists' attributes (gender, age, education level, and employment/profession), which may affect leisure time availability or similar constraints.

In this paper, we choose as a dependent variable the bilateral tourism flows (in terms of arrivals) between each pair of Italian regions, while, in terms of explanatory variables we consider the main determinants outlined above. Our variable of interest is the number of WHS existing in each Italian region. Finally, on the basis of the preceding discussion, we argue that the spatial interaction model is a suitable tool for investigating the research questions proposed in this paper. We build our model starting from a standard spatial interaction model for tourism, and we subsequently augment it by including key variables related to WHS.

To further investigate our research questions, the next section briefly presents the literature and the ongoing debate on the relationship between cultural heritage and tourism, and more specifically between WHS endowment and tourism.

13.3 Cultural Heritage, WHS Endowment and Tourism: The Evidence

13.3.1 Cultural Heritage and Tourism

Many studies aim to investigate whether the cultural endowment and heritage of a country can be considered as an important determinant of tourism demand, for either domestic or international tourism. Several studies claim that cultural heritage and attractions, in many developed countries, are becoming a major driving force for further growth of the tourism market, and that the abundance and diversity of cultural resources are essential assets for a country to develop its tourism industry (see, e.g., Carr 1994; Markwell et al. 1997; Alzua et al. 1998; McIntosh and Prentice 1999; Herbert 2001; Vietze 2008). According to these studies, all combinations of natural, cultural, and manmade elements are closely related to the demand for tourism, since they are unique to the single tourism destinations and cannot be transferred or reproduced in other locations (Dritsakis 2004). Consequently, a location endowed with natural landscapes, historical sites, cultural traditions, and heritage could have a competitive advantage when it comes to attracting tourists. Moreover, from the viewpoint of domestic tourism, heritage tourism is recognized as an effective way of achieving the educational function of tourism (Light 2000; Dean et al. 2002).

However, other studies stress that cultural sites and attractions are not effective in attracting tourism flows (see, e.g., Cuccia and Cellini 2007). Cellini and Cuccia (2013) find evidence that tourism flows Granger-cause cultural sites attendance, while the reverse does not hold, that is, a unidirectional long-run causal link emerges, but running from tourism flows to cultural sites attendance. Consequently, it would not be possible to sustain the hypothesis that cultural attractions can promote tourism in the long run, at least at the aggregate level, and, at most, the role of cultural sites would be limited to being a marginal product within a destination's tourism basket or a possible solution towards decreasing seasonality. Moreover, contrasting evidence on the relationship between attendance of cultural attractions and tourism flows was found for other 'cultural goods' as well, such as temporary arts exhibitions (Di Lascio et al. 2011) or museums and monuments (Cellini and Cuccia 2013).

13.3.2 WHS Endowment and Tourism

We focus on the effects of UNESCO's WHS designations on Italian domestic tourism flows, rather than on the overall effects of 'cultural heritage',[3] or of generic cultural sites and attractions. According to UNESCO, there are significant economic benefits to obtaining a WHS designation. This is due to an 'increase in public awareness of the site and of its outstanding values', which would in turn spark an increase in tourist activities and visitation to the area, with related economic benefits

[3] 'Cultural heritage' is defined in Article 1 of the *Convention concerning the Protection of the World Cultural and Natural Heritage* (adopted by UNESCO in 1972) as monuments, groups of buildings and sites that are of 'outstanding universal value from the point of view of history, art or science' and form the 'aesthetic, ethnological or anthropological point of view'.

not only for the destinations hosting the cultural and natural sites, but also for the local economy (UNESCO 2012).

There is a large body of literature that investigates the impact of WHS endowment on tourism, although no final evidence appears to have been reached. The literature on this topic can be divided into four main streams, depending on the conclusions on the impact of WHS endowment on tourism: (1) the literature which generally suggests a positive effect; (2) the empirical studies that claim that WHS designation has a positive but relatively small effect; (3) the recent studies which find an insignificant effect for tourism but an important effect in terms of protection of heritage; and (4) the literature on the overall negative aspects of WHS designation.

The early literature focuses mainly on the benefits of WHS designation. Its primary motivation was the protection and preservation of outstanding natural and cultural sites, but since the mid 1990s the literature began to analyse also its potential socio-economic benefits, mostly in terms of possible increases of tourism flows and revenues (Ashworth and Tunbridge 1990; Drost 1996; Pocock 1997; Shackley 1998; Thorsell and Sigaty 2001). The main conclusions were generally that WHS designation increases the popularity of a location, acts as a 'magnet for visitors', and is 'virtually a guarantee that visitor numbers will increase' (Shackley 1998, Preface). Therefore, according to this strain of the literature, WHS designation helps building a 'destination image'. Moreover, according to more recent studies (Arezki et al. 2009; Yang et al. 2010; Yang and Lin 2011), WHS are increasingly becoming one of the main touristic resources in many countries. The UNESCO WHS label would provide a surplus value to the sites, with respect to the generic cultural, historical and natural sites of a country, as it is expected to have a (strong) impact on tourism demand, and therefore on tourist arrivals, revenues and jobs creation, all important aspects for regional development. For example, WHS labels are nowadays widely used in marketing campaigns to promote tourism, and to increase the visibility of destinations.

A second stream of (empirical) literature focuses on the quantification of the impact of WHS designation on tourism flows and revenues. These studies provide mixed results, and generally suggest that WHS designation has a positive but relatively small impact on tourism flows (see, e.g., Buckley 2004; van der Aa 2005; Blacik 2007; Soares et al. 2007; Bové Sans and Laguado Ramírez 2011; VanBlarcom and Kayahan 2011). These studies find a positive association between WHS designation and tourism flows, but in some cases the evidence presented is not conclusive. Di Giovine (2009) argues that WHS designations are not 'impotent political performances that lead to the commercialization of local monuments', but instead are the building blocks of a new social and economic system. Other studies analyse the relationship between WHS endowment and tourism for specific countries; for example, Buckley (2004) for Australia, Blacik (2007) for Africa, Soares et al. (2007) for Portugal, VanBlarcom and Kayahan (2011) for Canada, and Bové Sans and Laguado Ramírez (2011) for Spain. Most of the sites reported an average increase of 1–5 % per year in tourists since the designation. However, the causal link between WHS designation and increased tourism flows above existing tourism trends is found to be relatively weak, particularly for sites that were already major attractions prior to their designation. In fact, according to VanBlarcom and Kayahan (2011), sites that are globally well known appear to benefit less from WHS designation relative to sites with a lower global profile. Furthermore, Bové Sans and Laguado Ramírez (2011) claim that, in order to exploit a WHS for tourism, it is necessary to enforce policies of external promotion and communication, in order to clearly position the destination within the tourism market as a 'cultural heritage destination'. Finally, according to van der Aa (2005), WHS status leads in particular to an increase in the number of international tourists, who tend to stay longer and spend more than domestic tourists.

A third and more recent stream of literature finds an insignificant impact of WHS designation in terms of tourism flows, but an important effect in terms of heritage protection (see, e.g., Hall and Piggin 2001; Hall 2006; Cellini 2011). Cellini claims that the effects of the WHS designation on tourism demand are far from clear-cut and robust. As a consequence, the main motivation for WHS recognition would only be a better protection of heritage, through the availability of additional funds. Hall (2006) states that the common perception is that WHS designation leads to increased commitment and tourism flows, and to increased public support for site maintenance and preservation. However, he notes that there are many other implications of a WHS designation, including 'potential changed access and use of the site and related environmental issues, new regulatory structures and altered economic flows'. The author concludes that much attention has been given to WHS designation, rather than to how effectively the designation has been implemented.

Finally, a fourth stream of literature suggests an overall negative impact of WHS designation (see, e.g., Mossetto 1994; Gamboni 2001; Meskell 2002; Frey and Steiner 2011). In particular, according to some studies (Li et al. 2008; Yang et al. 2010), WHS designation might have a negative impact on heritage conservation, since the sites could attract an excessive number of visitors, carrying the danger of seriously compromising the environmental and cultural integrity of the sites.

An alternative stream of literature focuses on the costs of WHS designation, in comparison with the related benefits, and conducts cost-benefit analyses (CBA). PriceWaterhouseCoopers LLP (2007) carries out a CBA of WHS designation in the UK, and finds an increase in tourism flows by 0–3 %, compared to an increase in costs around £500 K, including bidding costs, cost of the management plan and management costs of the WHS. Research Consulting Ltd and Trends Business Research Ltd (2009) report that approximately 70–80 % of WHS sites appear to be doing little or nothing to exploit the WHS designation towards significant socio-economic impacts. The authors conclude that management organization, marketing promotion and stakeholders' perception of WHS status matter. They argue that the small-to-null economic impacts of WHS designation found in the early literature are not surprising, since most of the sites analysed lack the motivation to promote their WHS designation in order to generate economic gains. VanBlarcom and Kayahan (2011) find evidence consistent with the conclusions of Research Consulting Ltd and Trends Business Research Ltd (2009): the economic impact of WHS labels is site-specific, and is subject to overall tourism trends affecting the level of tourism flows. In other words, WHS designation alone is not sufficient to stimulate transformational change, so the local policymakers must enforce policies aimed at capitalizing upon it, and invest in the other links within the tourism chain to gain benefits through a 'ripple' effect.

On the basis of the above discussion, we believe that it is highly relevant to further investigate and assess the extent to which WHS endowment attracts tourists, in order to gather information that can be critical towards implementing effective tourism policies, in terms of both promoting cultural tourism and managing potential damages caused by the overloading of tourists. In particular, we aim to shed light on the role of WHS endowment in trip generation and assignment, that is, on its influence over the outflows and inflows of tourists. The studies reviewed above investigate the impact of WHS endowment on tourism by applying a variety of econometric models. However, none of them faces the problem from a spatial interaction perspective. In addition, the current applied literature does not provide empirical evidence on how the spatial distribution of amenities (in our case, WHS) affects tourists' trips, in a competing destinations (Fotheringham 1983) or trip-chaining perspective. Following these reflections, the subsequent section outlines the empirical model used in this paper, and further specifies our research questions and their operationalization.

13.4 Model and Estimation Strategy

13.4.1 Model

Most applications of the spatial interaction model in the tourism domain regard international tourism. Nevertheless, models for international or domestic tourism do not differ in their fundamentals, but with respect to the set of explanatory variables considered. In the international domain, exchange rates, institutional factors, trade intensity, and common characteristics of countries (such as language) are important drivers of tourism flows. For domestic tourism, such variables are generally not relevant (institutions and language tend to be invariant within a country, and interregional trade is seldom measured) or indirectly related (e.g., the substitution effects generated by exchange rate variations may alter the distribution of domestic tourism). On the other hand, variables relating to demand (e.g., GDP or per capita GDP) or supply (e.g., kms of coastline, investment in recreational activities, cultural offer) can easily be interpreted in a domestic setting as well.

We start from a standard spatial interaction model, by considering two types of variables: origin-related and destination-related. In addition, bilateral variables are frequently given in the context of international tourism, while geographical distance remains a variable of interest in the domestic context as well. In particular, although most origin or destination variables can be reformulated (and reinterpreted) in a bilateral fashion (i.e., in terms of differentials), in our modelling framework we prefer to maintain the bidimensionality of our information, so to differentiate the effect of the characteristics of the origins on outgoing flows, and of destination characteristics on incoming flows.

Our model can be written as follows:

$$T_{ij} = f\left(X_i, WHS_i, L.WHS_i, X_j, WHS_j, L.WHS_j, D_{ij}\right), \quad (13.3)$$

where T_{ij} is the flow of tourists from region i to region j, X_i and X_j are the vectors of values for the origin (push) and destination (pull) variables given above, respectively, and D_{ij} is the geographical distance between the two regions.[4] We exploit the full origin-destination (OD) matrix, therefore including all cases of $i = j$ (i.e., intra-regional flows). Because of data availability, most variables are lagged, in the empirical specification, by 1 or 2 years. By means of Eq. (13.3), we can separate the main effect (direct effect) of WHS endowment of the origin and destination on tourism flows (WHS_i and WHS_j) from the indirect effect of WHS endowment of their surrounding regions ($L.WHS_i$ and $L.WHS_j$; see below for discussion).

We model interregional tourism flows, measured as arrivals in hotels and other accommodation structures, as a function of a number of control variables incorporating push and pull factors, including regional population and GDP, evaluated at both the origin and destination regions, in order to capture information on market size and income (i.e., GDP conditional to market size), respectively. For the origin region, these variables are commonly expected to be associated with a positive effect on tourism flows. For the destination region, GDP can still be interpreted in a market size fashion, to account for the share of business trips over total flows, and both GDP and population may have an influence on the choice of destination both as a positive effect, proxying for the level of economic development, and as a negative effect, since tourists could prefer visiting less-industrialized (or less dense) and more relaxing areas (see, e.g., the 'snob effect', in Candela and Figini 2012). Because income tends to influence consumption choices with a delay, we use lagged GDP.

Furthermore, we control for the price dynamics in the origin and destination regions, to cope with variations in the costs of living. More precisely, we use a price index computed regionally and specifically for the hotels and restoration sector.[5] Destination prices are commonly used in the tourism modelling literature and are expected to negatively affect inflows, while origin prices may be expected to have the opposite effect, pushing tourists out in search of price-effectiveness. In

[4] A further (binary) variable, simply indicating a relationship of spatial contiguity (shared border) between the origin and destination regions could be employed, if it is of interest to parcel this component out from the average effect of distance. We choose not to follow this approach, so to maintain the most general estimate for distance deterrence.

[5] One would prefer to use regional power-purchasing-parity (PPP) price indices to account for relative consumption prices. However, such indices are not available from the Italian National Statistical Agency and have been computed only in one study (ISTAT, Unioncamere and Istituto Tagliacarne 2010). Additionally, the FE estimators used in this paper would render the long-run levels of relative price irrelevant (they are absorbed into the FE), so that only short-run inflation trends would be identified (as for the variable used here).

other applications, the ratio between destination and origin prices is used to permit substitution between the choice of a destination and the local tourism/stay-home hypothesis (or, in the international tourism framework, between foreign destinations and domestic tourism; Witt and Witt 1995).

We include in the model further regional characteristics, aiming to account for the diffusion of crime, public spending in recreational activities, regional reliance on the tourism industry and seasonal concentration of tourism, public transport efficiency, cultural demand, and environmental quality. In detail, with regard to crime diffusion, we employ two indices, which denote small crime and violent crime, respectively. With regard to the destination, regions with high crime rates may be expected to show a diminished interest from tourists, all being equal, because of safety concerns. On the other hand, a region with renowned tourism sites may actually attract further criminals seeking potential victims (Eilat and Einav 2004; Dhariwal 2005), therefore incorporating the medium-long run level of local tourism demand. As far as the origins are concerned, we may expect residents of high-crime regions to be more likely to travel, in order to alleviate, at least temporarily, their risky condition. However, this effect may indeed be difficult to catch, even conditionally to per capita income, if the income distribution is strongly unequal (that is, a vast share of the population would not be able to afford travelling). Finally, to control for possible endogeneity of the tourism-crime relationship, we enter the small crime and violent crime variables in the model in lagged form.

In order to account for the different tourism 'vocation' of regions, and their reliance on this sector, we include a variable reporting the share of regional value added of the macro-sector including commerce, hotels and restaurants, transports and communications over total value added. Similarly, we account for the share of regional public spending invested in recreational, cultural and religious activities. A third variable accounts for the regions' reliance on off-season tourism.

We may expect the tourism specialization variable to account, for destination regions, for most of past unobservable factors that make a region a staple in (domestic) tourism, and therefore to be positively correlated with flows. With regard to origin regions, sign expectation is ambiguous. On the one hand, residents of tourism-relying regions might tend to have repulsion for traditional (hotel) tourism. On the other hand, a phenomenon of tourism 'addiction' *à la* Becker (1996) might be observed, for which the residents of such regions would appear to travel more, on average. Public spending in recreational/cultural activities represents, in our model, the investment of local administrations towards attracting tourists. As such, we should expect a positive effect on flows with regard to destination regions. However, this spending can also be seen as the administrations' attempt to face a medium-term scarcity in tourism demand, eventually showing a possible negative correlation with tourism flows. A similar reasoning goes for the origin region, where the residents may be more likely to stay or to undertake shorter (1-day) trips, if local recreational and cultural activities generate a significant interest, while if spending efforts are made in order to catch up with more successful regions, we might observe greater tourism outflows. Finally, the variable for the number of off-season tourists (per inhabitant) accounts for the regions' success in extending their period of touristic consumption, for example by diversifying their touristic offer. Regions with higher off-season tourism are expected to experience greater inflows, while a sign expectation at the origin level can hardly be formulated. For both tourism specialization and recreational spending, we include the variables in lagged form, to allow for habit formation and the fact that, for example, longer periods of time are needed for public events to develop a 'reputation'.

On the supply side, more variables are included, namely the share of satisfied customers of the regional railway service, and the percentage of coastline unsuitable for bathing. The former accounts for the provision and quality of transport infrastructure, which can be expected to influence flows both at the origin and at the destination. The latter is an indicator of the quality of waters for coastal regions (in Italy, 15 of 20 regions have access to the sea), and therefore should be expected to negatively influence flows to the destination region, and positively influence outflows from the origin region.[6]

On the demand side, we account for the quality of the cultural offer by including the average number of visitors per state museums, and the number of tickets sold per inhabitant for theatrical and musical events. Both variables can be expected to have a positive effect on inflows of tourists, while the expected sign at the origin is unclear: on the one hand, higher quality attractions in the region of residence may diminish outflows; on the other hand, we might again observe a phenomenon of 'addiction', for which the residents of a cultural endowed region might travel more to experience further cultural goods.

The first research question we aim to answer is whether the regional endowment in WHS has a measurable effect on domestic tourism flows, and how this (potential) effect can be decomposed in an origin-level effect and a destination-level effect. More precisely, we aim to evaluate whether WHS-endowed regions (1) generate more or less recordable outflows, and (2) attract greater inflows.

With respect to the first case, both a positive and a negative effect may be expected. On the one hand, we might expect regions which are endowed in WHS to experience lesser tourist outflows, if the residents' opportunity cost linked to travelling is evaluated on the basis of the lower opportunity cost of visiting local valuable cultural sites. As a result, if potential tourists prefer to travel locally, in particular by daily excursions, recorded flows—which are collected at hotels and other accommodations—would be diminished, leading to a negative push effect. On the other hand, a positive push effect might be found if the region's residents tend to be more curious, and therefore to generally travel more, when they are locally surrounded by cultural sites (because of love for variety). The second case is more straightforward, that is, WHS endowment allowing regions to attract a greater number of tourists. We expect a positive sign for this effect, since a negative

[6]The variable for the share of coast unsuitable for bathing should ideally be complemented by a variable for the length of the coast, in order to account for landlocked regions. As for other time-invariant variables (e.g., indicator variables for regions bordering with other countries), it is not possible to include them in our models (unless interacted with time-varying variables), as their effect is accounted for by the FE.

one could only be justified by a crowding out effect of international tourists (not considered here) on domestic tourists.

The paper's second research question deals with the tourists' behaviour with respect to the spatial distribution of the WHS endowment of the regions. As above, we can subdivide it in two subquestions: (1) Does the WHS endowment of the regions surrounding the origin influence tourists outflows? (2) Does the WHS endowment of the regions surrounding a destination influence its inflows?

The first subquestion can be reconducted to the justification of the similar question we introduced above with respect to the WHS endowment of the origin region. We hypothesize that, the higher a WHS endowment is available in nearby regions, the more potential tourists could be induced to substitute 'traditional' tourism (i.e., hotel arrivals, involving overnight stays, and therefore recordable) with 'daily excursions', inducing a negative effect on recorded outflows. The second subquestion has both an empirical interest and a policy one. Fotheringham (1983) has shown, in his work on competing destinations theory, that the spatial interaction model is better specified when the clustering of possible destinations is explicitly taken into account within the theoretical model leading to a multinomial logit (at the individual level). In other words, he showed that the individual does not have perfect information on the characteristics of all destinations, and that he/she will consider, for each possible destination, alternatives clustered in its proximity. Eventually, this boils down to incorporating in the spatial interaction model an additional variable describing the alternative destinations, usually in terms of accessibility. In tourism modelling, an attempt to include such aspects in an empirical model is made by Khadaroo and Seetanah (2008), who, in a study on international tourism, include a binary variable for the presence of nearby alternative destinations.

With regard to our case study, we model accessibility to alternative destinations by considering the WHS endowment of the regions surrounding each destination (i.e., we use a rook contiguity definition of proximity[7]). We hypothesize that the tourist's set of information—for the purposes of evaluating a destination's attractiveness—is limited to just the set of all neighbouring alternative destinations. We may frame this approach within the more general framework of the prominence models described in Sen and Smith (1995), which includes, among others, Fotheringham's model of competing destinations (Fotheringham 1983). An estimated positive effect for the endowment of neighbouring destinations would therefore imply that a phenomenon of trip-chaining exists (spatial complementarity), in which the tourists consider potential visits to WHS outside of the destination region (but relatively close). On the other hand, a negative sign would instead imply that the 'competition' of alternative WHS decreases a region's inflows (spatial competition). This aspect assumes great relevance from a policy perspective, in a framework like

[7]When a contiguity rule is applied to define proximity, two regions are defined as neighbours if they share a border. In rook contiguity, the common border has to have length greater than zero, while in queen contiguity common borders of length zero are allowed as well.

the one of Italy, where regional agencies are in charge of promoting tourism, and where lobbying activities for the designation of additional WHS is strong.

The two research questions outlined above are operationalized in a spatial interaction model by including, for the first research question, two variables, WHS_i and WHS_j, accounting for the WHS endowment of each origin and destination region, respectively. With regard to the second question, we include the average WHS endowment of regions contiguous to each origin and destination. The new variables, $L.WHS_i$ and $L.WHS_j$, are computed as $\mathbf{W} * WHS_i$ and $\mathbf{W} * WHS_j$, respectively, where $\mathbf{W}$ is a 20×20 row-standardized spatial weights matrix defining contiguity relations of proximity between all regions.

The inclusion of spatial lags of other independent variables is equally interesting and useful from an econometric viewpoint, as it helps accounting for omitted spatial dependence. In a linear estimation framework, this has been shown to result in spatially correlated model residuals and model parameter estimates which are inefficient and potentially biased (LeSage and Pace 2009). Theoretically, spatial lags could be computed for all explanatory variables in the model, therefore covering as much omitted information as possible. At the same time, accessibility to all other destination characteristics, as modelled for WHS, can be of interest to the analyst, in particular when considering the possibility that tourists simultaneously consider various characteristics of neighbouring destinations in forming their ideal trip (e.g., combining a seaside vacation with some cultural activities in a nearby region). We spare this additional analysis for model parsimony and to focus on our interest variable.

The following sections describe the empirical estimation method and provide an interpretative framework for the varying direct and indirect effects of WHS endowment on tourism flows, according to a spatial sensitivity analysis.

13.4.2 Estimation

We estimate our model for a panel of all 20 Italian regions, and 12 years (1998–2009). Considering the time dimension, we can again generically write Eq. (13.3) for estimation purposes, as follows:

$$T_{ijt} = f\left(\alpha_{ij}, year_t, X_{it}, WHS_{it}, L.WHS_{it}, X_{jt}, WHS_{jt}, L.WHS_{jt}\right), \qquad (13.4)$$

where α_{ij} is a vector of individual FE coefficients (or random effects if, e.g., suggested by a Hausmann test), and $year_t$ is the vector of time FE, included to account for the business cycle. The model constant is excluded if all time effects are estimated. In an estimation framework including individual FE, time-invariant variables (like distance) cannot be identified, and are dropped.

Since the spatial interaction model is multiplicative (see Sect. 13.2), a typical choice—as for any other multiplicative model, like production functions—is to render it linear in parameters through log-linearization (see, e.g., Lim 1997). In panel applications, the individual FE act as surrogates for the omitted explanatory variables, similarly to the case of international trade models (in which price indices are unobserved; see Anderson and van Wincoop 2003). In this paper, we estimate the spatial interaction model in its multiplicative form, by means of count data regression techniques, in order to account for Jensen's inequality and potential overdispersion. Santos Silva and Tenreyro (2006) have shown, in a widely popular article, that many problems are associated with the log-linearization of multiplicative models in the presence of heteroskedasticity (e.g., because of the zero trade problem in international trade, or because of the typical presence of a small number of flows much greater than the average), and suggested the use of count data regression models. Following Santos Silva and Tenreyro's contribution, Burger et al. (2009) have expanded this discussion by considering a wider family of Poisson-type models. In this regard, the negative binomial model is suggested as a solution to the problem of overdispersion in the data due to unobserved heterogeneity, which hinders the hypothesis at the basis of the Poisson regression model of equal sample mean and variance. Overdispersion phenomena are typical of dyadic data (e.g., in trade, commuting, migration), whose statistical distribution shows a multitude of small flows and a small number of much greater flows. On the basis of the above considerations, we carry out negative binomial two-way FE estimations. Formally, the estimated model can now be written as follows:

$$T_{ijt} = \exp\left(\alpha_{ij} + year_t + X_{it} + WHS_{it} + L.WHS_{it} + X_{jt} + WHS_{jt} + L.WHS_{jt}\right) + \varepsilon_{ijt}, \tag{13.5}$$

where ε_{ijt} is the regression residual for the generic flow from region i to region j at time t. A dispersion parameter φ is iteratively estimated. It should be noted that, because of the inclusion of the FE, the effect of any WHS that obtained its designation *before* our observation period is null, so that the WHS variables employed here produce exactly the same results as alternative WHS variables where previously designated WHS are omitted. A similar reasoning can be applied to the control variables.

Finally, with the purpose of empirically evaluating the effect of distance, we set up a further model by means of an alternative estimation approach, that is, a panel spatial filtering-based negative binomial model. In this model specification, the individual (pair-level) FE are substituted by two sets of origin and destination dummy variables and a network autocorrelation filter. The former components include, in a common FE manner, all time-invariant information specific to the origin and destination regions (for example, the average level of GDP). The latter component incorporates spatial and network dependence due to omitted variables. Because the FE are moved from the pair-level to the origin- and destination-level, time-invariant bilateral variables can be identified, allowing the estimation of a regression coefficient for the distance variable.[8] The spatial filter is included in the

[8]Internal distances are computed as $\sqrt{area/\pi}$ (see, e.g., Leamer 1997; Nitsch 2000).

regression model as a set of eigenvectors related to the chosen spatial weights matrix (see Sect. 13.4.1).[9]

The model with distance and spatial filter is the following one:

$$T_{ijt} = \exp\Big(\alpha_i + \alpha_j + year_t + X_{it} + WHS_{it} + L.WHS_{it} + X_{jt} + WHS_{jt} + L.WHS_{jt} + D_{ij} + \sum\nolimits_k e_{k,ij}\Big) + \varepsilon_{ijt}, \tag{13.6}$$

where α_i and α_j are the origin and destination FE, and e_k is value for the (i, j) pair of the kth network autocorrelation eigenvector selected (and composing the spatial filter).

13.4.3 Spatial Sensitivity Analysis: An Interpretative Framework

We now expand on our second research question, by providing an interpretative framework aimed at understanding how and to what extent the effects of the neighbouring (competing) destinations' WHS endowment on tourism flows (the indirect effect discussed above) may vary depending on the assumptions we make on the tourist's capacity to compare alternative destinations in his/her choice set. In this regard, a spatial sensitivity analysis according to the average number of neighbours k is offered in the paper.

In the case of no neighbours ($k = 0$), all regions are isolated destinations ('islands' in a relational sense). In this case, all additional flows T due to an interest in visiting the new WHS reach the corresponding region independently of the WHS endowment of other regions. In the case of one neighbour ($k = 1$), the regions are not isolated anymore, but have a possible spatial competitor (each), with which they compete on the basis of their WHS endowment. Given that the competitor is perceived by the tourists as 'close', it may now represent a valid alternative, all else being equal. Following the same line of reasoning, in the case of two neighbours ($k = 2$), we hypothesize that the tourists evaluate each destination against its two possible spatial competitors based on WHS, and so on for higher numbers of neighbours.

To build a general model, we make three assumptions. First, in order to test the corresponding effect, *ceteris paribus*, on tourism flows, we assume that a new WHS is designated in a region (i.e., a change in the region's WHS endowment).

The second assumption is that the designation of a WHS can cause two main opposite direct effects on tourism flows: (1) a negative crowding-out effect ($E \geq 0$, in

[9] Because the implementation of a panel spatial filtering model is not the main focus of this paper, we refer to Chun and Griffith (2011) and Lionetti and Patuelli (2009) for methodological and implementation details.

absolute value), as a result of which some tourists may dismiss the destination since the new WHS may entail some constraints, costs and limitations in site accessibility, such as restrictions on visiting flows, management costs yielding a price increase, or tourism pressure. In fact, these reasons could persuade some tourists (with different motivations or different capability to spend) to leave the destination; (2) a positive attractiveness effect ($T_1 > 0$), which on average dominates the negative crowding-out effect ($T_1 > E \geq 0$), so that the overall direct effect of WHS designation on tourism flows is positive. As a matter of fact, were the direct effect of WHS designation negative ($E > T_1 > 0$), applying for it would not be desirable for a rationale destination within an objective function aiming to maximize tourism flows.

The third assumption concerns the possible spatial interaction effect on tourism flows (indirect effect) between neighbouring regions due to their WHS endowment, $T_2(k)$, which can be of (1) spatial competition or (2) spatial complementarity. There is spatial competition when a region's tourism inflows are diminished by the WHS endowment of regions which are perceived as substitute destinations ($T_2(k)$ is negative and may be expected to increase with the number of neighbours k), while there is spatial complementarity when a region receives a benefit, in terms of inflows, from the WHS endowment of 'close' regions (e.g., mutual beneficial effects may derive by trip chaining, so that $T_2(k)$ is positive and expected to increase with the number of neighbours k). In other words, according to this third assumption, WHS-induced flows are conditional on the number of destinations perceived as substitutes or complements by the tourist. Such competition (complementarity) effect may be expected to vary monotonically with the number of neighbours considered, until a threshold is reached after which regions further away are not perceived anymore as substitutes (complements) by tourists.

We can now outline a simple model for the relationship between WHS-induced tourism inflows and the number k of alternative destinations considered by the tourist. We can describe the tourism flows T towards a single destination as depending on other destination characteristics (T_0, given by the generic X in the model) and on WHS endowment, which generates a positive direct effect on inflows T_1. In addition to T_1, a second indirect effect $T_2(k)$ may be included, for the overall interplay of spatial complementarity and competition effects, which depends on the number of neighbours k. By assumption, $T_2(0) = 0$, while for $k > 0$, $T_2(k) > 0$ denotes a dominance of spatial complementarity, while $T_2(k) < 0$ denotes a dominance of spatial competition. Exploiting the Poisson-type estimation framework of the paper, and omitting origin-level variables for notation simplicity, the total tourism inflows of a region j from a region i can be written as:

$$T_{ij} = \exp\left(T_{0,ij}\right) \exp\left[(T_1 - E)\, WHS_j + T_2(k) L.WHS_j\right], \qquad (13.7)$$

with $T_1 > E \geq 0$, and where T_0 are inflows due to the control variables, on the scale of the linear predictor. In regression terms, $\beta_1 = T_1 - E$ is the regression coefficient estimated for the *WHS* variable, while $\beta_2 = T_2(k)$ is the coefficient of the spatial lag of *WHS* (i.e., $\mathbf{W} * WHS = L.WHS_j$). We can now analyse how tourism inflows change conditional to the number of neighbours k. Since by assumption $dT_1/dk = 0$

and $T_2(0) = 0$, then the sign of the overall effect of WHS on domestic tourism depends only on the assumptions made on the behaviour of $T_2(k)$.

To further investigate the indirect effect, we can specify $T_2(k)$ as the difference between two separate effects:

$$T_2(k) = T_{2.1}(k) - T_{2.2}(k), \tag{13.8}$$

where $T_{2.1}(k) \geq 0$ is the spatial complementarity effect, and $T_{2.2}(k) \geq 0$ is the spatial competition effect. By construction, $T_{2.1}(0) = T_{2.2}(0) = 0$, and we may hypothesize that both effects increase with k ($T_{2.1}'(k) > 0$ and $T_{2.2}'(k) > 0$), with $T_{2.1}''(k) < 0$ and $T_{2.2}''(k) > 0$, resulting in two functions crossing each other at the value k^* that implies an overall null indirect effect [$T_{2.1}(k^*) = T_{2.2}(k^*)$], as suggested in Fig. 13.1.[10] Here, we hypothesize that competition effects eventually dominate complementarity effects for greater values of k.

The above model can explain the mixed empirical evidence in the current literature on the effects of WHS endowment on tourism flows (see Sect. 13.3). In fact, even though a region's WHS endowment can potentially attract additional tourists (direct effect T_1; not shown in Fig. 13.1), the indirect effect on tourism flows $T_2(k)$ can be both positive, if it is dominated by spatial complementarity, and negative in the case of a prevailing competitive relationship (spatial competition). Nevertheless, even in the latter case, the overall effect, given T_1, can be positive, negative or null, depending on the number of spatial competitors (neighbours). Since T_2 depends on k, $dT_2/dk < 0$ (for k large enough) implies tendencies towards spatial competition as the number of neighbours considered increases, while tendencies towards spatial complementarity are found in the opposite case. Discussing the most problematic case, that is, the competitive relationship, we note that in general a number of neighbouring destinations k always exists which compensates the direct tourism flows growth induced by WHS increase. Furthermore, if spatial competition is very strong, there will be no advantage whatsoever for destinations deriving from WHS designation, but only potential losses in terms of tourism flows.

The present interpretative framework is particularly fitting for Italian domestic tourism, because of the many WHS, which are well distributed over the different regions (only 2 small regions out of 20 do not have any). Without a precise motivational analysis of the tourists, E, T_1, $T_{2.1}$ and $T_{2.2}$ are not directly observable. However, the observed regional tourism flows allow us to test a crucial assumption of the model, that is, whether $T_2(k)$ is increasing in k, which implies tendencies towards a dominance of spatial complementarity, or decreasing in k, implying tendencies towards spatial competition.

Furthermore, in the case of spatial competition, we can test: (1) for $k = 0$, if the direct effect of a new WHS designation is positive ($T_1 > E$) or null ($T_1 = E$); and (2) for $k > 0$, if it is possible to identify the number of competitors cancelling out the

[10] Alternatively, we could hypothesize $T_{2.2}''(k) < 0$. We consider the case of the intersecting functions more interesting and we limit ourselves to discussing the latter.

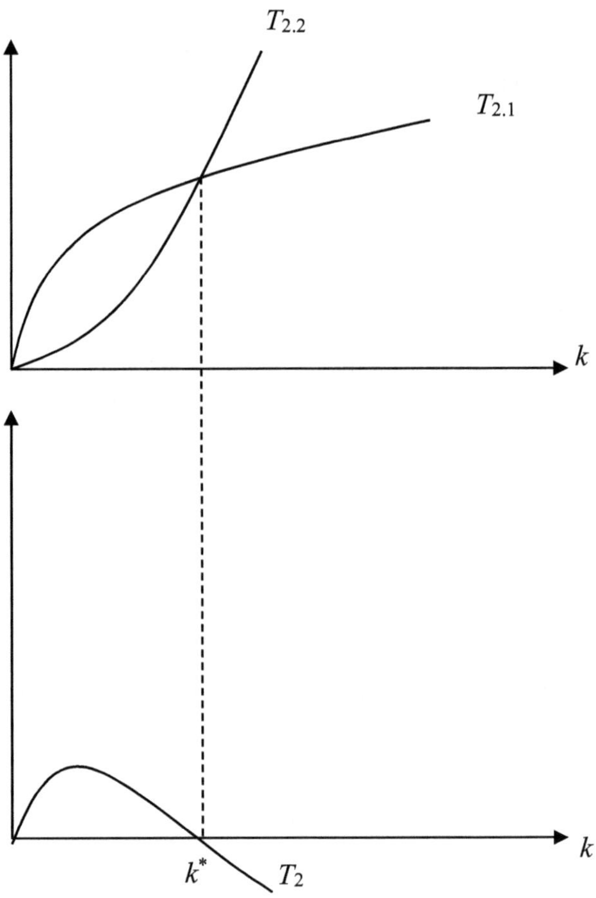

Fig. 13.1 Spatial complementarity and spatial competition effects within $T_2(k)$

positive direct effect of WHS endowment, and to justify why with a higher number of competitors the destination can eventually lose tourists. The following section reports our findings.

13.5 Empirical Application

13.5.1 Data

Our empirical application to tourism flows between the 20 Italian regions employs data from the Italian Statistical Agency (ISTAT). The dependent variable, that is, regional arrivals from and to all Italian regions for the period 1998–2009, is provided within the publication '*Statistiche del Turismo*', and collected through the accommodation structures survey. Traditional hotel accommodations, as well

Table 13.1 Explanatory variables

Variable	Description	Source
WHS	Number of WHS	UNESCO
GDP	Regional GDP (1-year lag, in logs)	ISTAT
SpecTour	Specialization in tourism (= share of value added generated from accommodation and restaurants, commerce, transport, etc.) (2-year lag, in logs)	ISTAT
ExpRecr	Share of public spending in recreational, cultural and religious activities (2-year lag, in logs)	ISTAT
PricesH&R	Price index for hotels and restaurants (in logs)	ISTAT
Pop	Regional population (in logs)	ISTAT
CrimDiff	Small crime index (= thefts and robberies × 1000 inhabitants) (1-year lag, in logs)	ISTAT
CrimVio	Violent crime index (= violent crimes × 10,000 inhabitants) (2-year lag, in logs)	ISTAT
SatisTrain	Train service satisfaction index (= share of customers who declare to be satisfied with train service) (in logs)	ISTAT
CultDem	Cultural demand index (= visitors to state antiquities and arts museums x institute) (1-year lag, in logs)	ISTAT
DiffShows	Diffusion of theatrical and musical shows (= theatrical and musical shows tickets sold × 100 inhabitants) (1-year lag, in logs)	ISTAT
NonBath	Coast unsuitable for bathing (= share of coast kms which are unsuitable for bathing due to pollution) (1-year lag)	ISTAT
OffSeas	Deseasoning index (= overnight stays in off-season months × inhabitant) (1-year lag, in logs)	ISTAT
Distance	Distance between regional centroids (in km, in logs)	Own calculation

as complementary accommodations and privately rented houses, are included in the survey.

Our key variable, the number of regional WHS, is obtained directly from UNESCO's World Heritage Convention website (http://whc.unesco.org/), which provides a list of all WHS by country, year of inclusion and nature of the site. All further variables used in this paper are obtained by ISTAT, and are published on: '*Conti Economici Regionali*', '*Prezzi al Consumo*', and '*Banca Dati Territoriale per le Politiche di Sviluppo*'. Table 13.1 provides a concise description of the variables used in our empirical application, while Table 13.6 in the Appendix provides the related correlation matrix. All variables are expressed in logs, aside from 'WHS' and "NonBath', which include a share of zeros.

Our interest variable, the number of sites inscribed in UNESCO's WHS list, is clearly not uniformly distributed across regions, as some have acquired over time a relatively large number of WHS, while others still have zero or very few (see Table 13.2). When looking at the WHS acquired during our observation period (1998–2009), some regions increased their (relative) quota of WHS considerably. The geographical allocation of WHS and of newly acquired WHS is provided in

Table 13.2 Italian WHS in 1998 and 2009

Region	1998	2009	Diff. (1998–2009)
Abruzzo	0	0	0
Basilicata	1	1	0
Calabria	0	0	0
Campania	5	5	0
Emilia-Romagna	3	3	0
Friuli-Venezia Giulia	1	2	1
Lazio	1	4	3
Liguria	1	2	1
Lombardia	3	6	3
Marche	1	1	0
Molise	0	0	0
Piemonte	1	2	1
Puglia	2	2	0
Sardegna	1	1	0
Sicilia	2	5	3
Toscana	5	6	1
Trentino-Alto Adige	0	1	1
Umbria	0	1	1
Valle d'Aosta	0	0	0
Veneto	3	5	2

Fig. 13.2. In addition to WHS, we also provide, in Fig. 13.3, maps for regional population and GDP, which are expected to act as the main control variables for size effects in the spatial interaction model. From the maps, it can be observed that, while the most populated regions are distributed in different parts of the country, a larger part of the overall GDP is produced in the northern part of the country, supporting the hypothesis that both variables could be employed together in our modelling exercise, in order to identify, in addition to population, the effect of per capita GDP.

13.5.2 Model Results

We start by estimating a benchmark model, that is, a standard tourism spatial interaction model, including only the control variables described in Sects. 13.4.1 and 13.5.1. Empirical estimates, according to Eq. (13.5), are provided in Table 13.3.

Model (1) in Table 13.3 confirms most of our basic assumptions. Regional inflows are positively influenced by supply factors, like the quality of the museum offer (CultDem) and the diffusion of cultural events (DiffShows), and negatively influenced by the level of prices of the restoration/accommodation sector (PricesH&R). Furthermore, regions which deseasonalize (OffSeas) enjoy greater

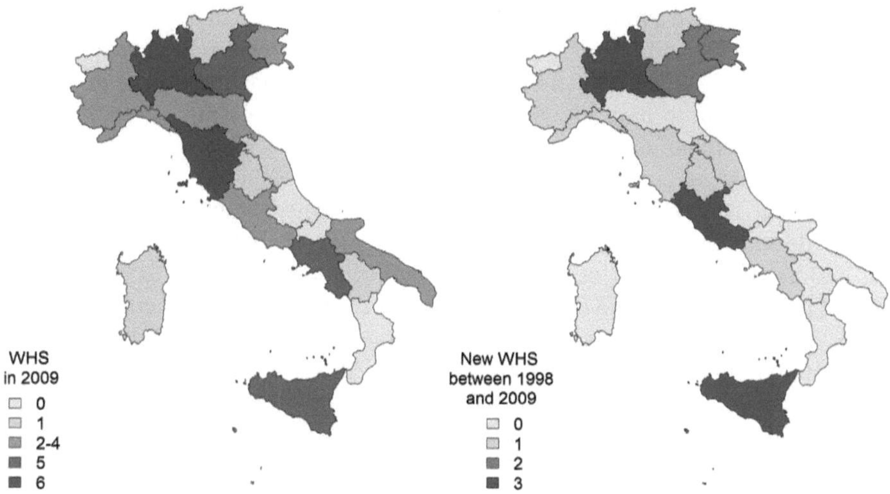

Fig. 13.2 Geographical distribution of WHS in 2009 and WHS acquired between 1998 and 2009

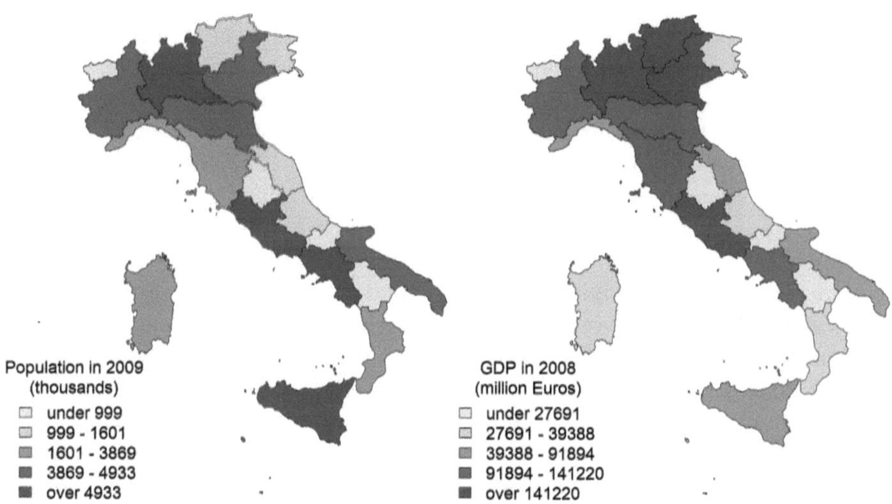

Fig. 13.3 Geographical distribution of population and regional GDP in 2009

inflows. Public spending in recreational activities (ExpRecr), instead, does not appear to have a significant impact. Finally, greater inflows are associated with lower GDP, suggesting that tourists look for less developed, more relaxing destinations. With regard to the regional outflows, GDP, which conditional to population identifies per capita income, is surprisingly not significant as a push effect.[11] Crime

[11]The results concerning GDP and population are stable independently of the number of contextual variables added to the basic framework of the spatial interaction model (supply and demand size

levels appear to have a role also in pushing tourists (out), since they positively affect outflows (CrimVio and CrimDiff), implying that residents of at-risk areas tend to get away in search of safer destinations. The residents of regions specialized in tourism (SpecTour) appear to have a higher propensity to travel, possibly according to an 'addiction to tourism' effect or as a refuge from the summer crowding.

We can now augment the benchmark model by including our variables of interest, that is, 'WHS' and 'L.WHS', again evaluated both at the origins and at the destinations. Model (2) in Table 13.3 provides empirical estimates for Eq. (13.5). The inclusion of the WHS variables allows to retain the findings of Model (1), while providing evidence for an effect of WHS endowment on tourism flows. We find that, with regard to the destinations, WHS are positively associated with inflows (this being the direct effect of WHS on tourism, and including, if existent, crowding-out effects). An increase of one WHS, for a generic destination, would imply, with a 95 % confidence interval, an inflows increase between 2.9 and 4.3 % [exp(0.0355) = 1.0361]. The effects of the WHS endowment of neighbouring destinations (the indirect effects of complementarity and competition) are also found to be significant, but negative, suggesting the existence of spatial competition between contiguous regions induced by WHS endowment. Clearly, a complementarity effect could exist as well, but appears to be dominated by the competition effect. Our finding implies that an increase of one WHS, on average, in the surrounding regions of a generic destination (an acceptable assumption in the long run) would lead to a decrease of arrivals, for the above destination, of about 10 % [exp(−0.1035) = −0.9017]. As the marginal effects of 'WHS dest' and 'L.WHS dest' cannot be considered separately, we conclude that, for an increase of one WHS in every region, the overall effect on tourism flows would be negative (around 6 %) when competing destinations are defined by shared borders.

With regard to the origin regions, we find a negative and significant sign (suggesting that outflows would decrease with the increase in WHS endowment) for both the direct and the indirect effects, reinforcing the hypothesis that the availability of WHS near the tourist's residence may lead to substitution between hotel arrivals (traditional tourism) and daily excursions, both within the residence region and to nearby (alternative) destinations. The decrease of outflows is numerically consistent with the decrease of inflows discussed above. From a statistical perspective, Model (2) improves significantly on the reliability of the benchmark model [Model (1)], as suggested by the improvements in terms of AIC, BIC and pseudo-R^2, as well as by a χ^2-based likelihood ratio (LR) test between the two models, which is highly significant.

Finally, Model (3) presents the results from an eigenvector spatial filtering model specification [Eq. (13.6)], carried out in order to evaluate the tourists' demand elasticity with respect to distance. With regard to the control variables, only selected

---

variables and distance as a deterrence variable). Only if the individual FE are excluded from the model GDP and population appear with the usual (expected) coefficient values between 0 and 1, which leads us to assume that in our panel specifications the 'size' effects are picked up by the FE.

Table 13.3 Empirical estimates

	Estimate (Std error)	p-value	Estimate (Std error)	p-value	Estimate (Std error)	p-value
	(1)		(2)		(3)	
GDP orig	0.2101 (0.3498)	0.5481	0.1834 (0.3481)	0.5983	0.3470 (0.6337)	0.5840
GDP dest	−2.2471 (0.3636)	<0.0001	−2.4442 (0.3670)	<0.0001	−2.2774 (0.6524)	0.0005
SpecTour orig	0.2823 (0.1098)	0.0101	0.2973 (0.3670)	0.0070	0.3177 (0.2408)	0.1870
SpecTour dest	0.3686 (0.1373)	0.0072	0.1753 (0.1407)	0.2128	0.1701 (0.2692)	0.5275
ExpRecr orig	0.0846 (0.0670)	0.2068	0.0422 (0.0667)	0.5272	0.0469 (0.1254)	0.7085
ExpRecr dest	−0.0681 (0.0552)	0.2174	−0.0832 (0.0595)	0.1617	−0.0632 (0.1246)	0.6118
PricesH&R orig	0.2101 (0.2610)	0.4207	0.2307 (0.2646)	0.3832	0.3454 (0.4700)	0.4624
PricesH&R dest	−0.8296 (0.2405)	0.0006	−1.1275 (0.2453)	<0.0001	−1.3658 (0.4594)	0.0030
Pop orig	−0.4803 (0.4571)	0.2933	−0.1232 (0.4522)	0.7853	−0.7002 (0.7332)	0.3396
Pop dest	0.3004 (0.2860)	0.2936	0.6503 (0.2590)	0.0120	0.3365 (0.5801)	0.5619
CrimDiff orig	0.1159 (0.0533)	0.0298	0.1153 (0.0533)	0.0304	0.1139 (0.0992)	0.2508
CrimDiff dest	−0.0237 (0.0279)	0.3966	−0.0044 (0.0280)	0.8755	0.0117 (0.0733)	0.8731
CrimVio orig	0.0522 (0.0264)	0.0480	0.0563 (0.0270)	0.0373	0.0577 (0.0492)	0.2412
CrimVio dest	−0.0214 (0.0251)	0.3951	0.0099 (0.0255)	0.6987	−0.0010 (0.0500)	0.9837
SatisTrain orig	0.0696 (0.0450)	0.1226	0.0292 (0.0460)	0.5251	0.0677 (0.1073)	0.5282
SatisTrain dest	0.0551 (0.0514)	0.2837	0.0627 (0.0499)	0.2088	0.1059 (0.1059)	0.3176
CultDem orig	−0.0356 (0.0222)	0.1089	−0.0305 (0.0223)	0.1722	−0.0234 (0.0456)	0.6080
CultDem dest	0.1879 (0.0223)	<0.0001	0.2073 (0.0233)	<0.0001	0.1971 (0.0452)	<0.0001
DiffShows orig	0.0574 (0.0390)	0.1409	0.0656 (0.0391)	0.0929	0.0818 (0.0689)	0.2350
DiffShows dest	0.0967 (0.0309)	0.0017	0.0868 (0.0317)	0.0062	0.0818 (0.0624)	0.1902
NonBath orig	0.0007 (0.0027)	0.7851	0.0011 (0.0027)	0.6691	0.0003 (0.0048)	0.9547
NonBath dest	0.0006 (0.0027)	0.8140	0.0016 (0.0028)	0.5562	0.0016 (0.0060)	0.7864
OffSeas orig	−0.0033 (0.0393)	0.9335	0.0020 (0.0389)	0.9599	0.0230 (0.0778)	0.7677
OffSeas dest	0.4093 (0.0521)	<0.0001	0.3915 (0.0514)	<0.0001	0.3541 (0.0927)	0.0001
WHS orig	–	–	−0.0164 (0.0079)	0.0387	−0.0203 (0.0159)	0.2009
L.WHS orig	–	–	−0.0451 (0.0198)	0.0227	−0.0516 (0.0364)	0.1567
WHS dest	–	–	0.0355 (0.0067)	<0.0001	0.0420 (0.0147)	0.0044
L.WHS dest	–	–	−0.1035 (0.0204)	<0.0001	−0.0983 (0.0365)	0.0071
Distance	–	–	–	–	−1.0165 (0.0362)	<0.0001
AIC	71,705	–	71,660	–	75,689	–
BIC	74,136	–	74,116	–	76,369	–
Res. dof	2977	–	2973	–	3263	–
McFadden's pseudo-R^2	0.4068	–	0.4073		0.1199	–
ANOVA (χ^2 LR test)	–	–	52.9132	<0.0001	–	–

destination-level variables are found to be significant (GDP, PricesH&R, CultDem, and OffSeas). The 'WHS' and 'L.WHS' variables, again for destination regions only, are significant and similar in estimated effect size to Model (2). The regression coefficient for the effect of distance is close to 1 (a unitary elasticity), suggesting, for example, that all else being equal, a destination region being 20 % farther away than another from a specified origin region will receive 20 % less tourists.[12]

13.5.3 Spatial Sensitivity Analysis

The analyses presented in the preceding section are based on a generic assumption of spatial competition/complementarity happening along regional borders. In particular, it is assumed that in evaluating the attractiveness of each region the tourist considers all other regions with which the destination shares a border (rook contiguity definition of proximity). This assumption is a common practice in the spatial econometric literature, but can be explicitly tested against alternative specifications of the spatial weights matrix.

We carry out a spatial sensitivity analysis to test the robustness of our findings to different hypotheses on the nature and geographical extent of spatial interaction, according to the interpretative framework described in Sect. 13.4.3. In particular, we aim to test to what extent the overall effect of WHS endowment on tourism flows may vary, in particular with regard to the (indirect) effect of WHS endowment in neighbouring regions and the average number of possible spatial competitors.

From a methodological viewpoint, the effect size and statistical significance of the indirect effect of WHS endowment may be sensitive to the definition of 'neighbours' used, that is, to the choice of the spatial weights matrix **W**. In Models (2) and (3) of Table 13.3, we define **W** by rook contiguity. According to this criterion, the average number of neighbours per region is 3.1, ranging from 0 to 6.

To carry out a spatial sensitivity analysis, we test different specifications of **W** for an increasing number of assigned neighbours, according to two additional definitions of proximity:

- k-nearest neighbours, based on Great Circle distance, for $k = 0, 1, \ldots, 4$;
- distance thresholds, based on distance bands computed as $h * \min(dist)$, with $h = 0, 2, \ldots, 4$.

[12]A sensitivity analysis testing polynomial specifications for the distance term shows that a cubic specification provides slight fitting advantages (for example, in terms of BIC). The negative-positive-negative signs for the three terms of the polynomial suggest that a destination's distance from the tourist's residence region becomes a positive tourism reinforcing factor only after a certain threshold (after which the destination appears to be 'exotic'), and up to a second threshold level, after which the distance deterrence effect again becomes dominant.

Table 13.4 *k*-nearest neighbours results for WHS dest and L.WHS dest

k-Nearest neighbours	0	1	2	3	4
WHS dest	0.0395***	0.0394***	0.0390***	0.0372***	0.0357***
L.WHS dest	–	−0.0153	−0.0210	−0.0320	−0.0731***
AIC	71,762	71,758	71,757	71,755	71,736
LR (χ^2) test – H_0: $k=0$	–	8.04**	9.14**	10.62***	30.41***
LR (χ^2) test – H_0: $\beta_{\text{WHS dest}} + \beta_{\text{L.WHS dest}} = 0$	–	–	–	–	1.48

*** and ** denote 1 and 5 percent significance levels, respectively

Table 13.5 Distance-threshold results for WHS dest and L.WHS dest

Distance threshold	0	2 * min(dist) (1.3 neigh.)	3 * min(dist) (3.3 neigh.)	4 * min(dist) (5.1 neigh.)
WHS dest	0.0395***	0.0366***	0.0371***	0.0398***
L.WHS dest	–	–0.0317**	–0.0484**	–0.1386***
AIC	71,762	71,757	71,749	71,714
LR (χ^2) test – H_0: $k=0$	–	8.83**	16.80***	52.51***
LR (χ^2) test – H_0: $\beta_{\text{WHS dest}} + \beta_{\text{L.WHS dest}} = 0$	–	0.07	0.20	13.99***

*** and ** denote 1 and 5 percent significance levels, respectively

Table 13.4 provides the empirical estimates for the effect of the destinations' WHS endowment on tourist inflows according to the *k*-nearest neighbours criterion, and presents the direct and indirect effect estimates (for variables 'WHS dest' and 'L.WHS dest'). In addition to effect size estimates, Table 13.4 provides AIC values and two χ^2-based likelihood ratio (LR) tests against (1) the hypothesis of equivalence between the $k>0$ models and the $k=0$ model (i.e., with no 'L.WHS' variables), and (2) the hypothesis that the overall effect of WHS endowment is null.

Table 13.4 shows that, when applying a *k*-nearest neighbours definition of proximity, the direct effect of WHS endowment is positive and numerically stable over estimations (around 4 %), confirming the results of Sect. 13.5.2. The WHS indirect effect is negative and increases in size with the number of neighbours, although it becomes significant only with $k \geq 4$. The LR χ^2 tests against the $k=0$ model always reject the hypothesis of equivalence, suggesting that the characteristics of competing destinations should indeed be considered in our modelling framework. Moreover, the LR test against the hypothesis that the overall effect of WHS endowment is null, which is not computed when a direct effect only is found, is not significant for $k=4$, that is, when 4 neighbours per region are considered, the direct effect of WHS endowment is cancelled by the (negative) effect of WHS-based competition.

Finally, Table 13.5 provides the estimated effect sizes of WHS endowment according to distance-threshold models, with $\min(dist) = 67$ km. Several distance bands (for $h = 0$, 2, 3, 4) are tested, corresponding each to a different neighbours list.

The distance-threshold models show again a positive and stable direct effect of WHS endowment (and always close to 4 %), while the indirect effect is significant and negative starting from the first bandwidth, and increasing with distance, like in the k-nearest neighbours case. The LR tests against the neighbourless model always reject the hypothesis of equivalence, as before, while the LR test against the hypothesis of null overall effect of WHS endowment is not significant for the first two bandwidths tested, while it becomes significant for $h \geq 4$, for an overall negative effect over greater distances.

Finally, with regard to the interpretative model provided in Sect. 13.4.3, we can note that the hypothesis of a tendency towards the dominance of spatial competition over spatial complementarity is confirmed. However, our results, showing first a non-significant indirect effect and then a negative one, do not allow us to shed light on the possibility, suggested in Fig. 13.1, of a sign inversion of the indirect effect over increasing values of k, and therefore on the sign of $T_{2.2}''(k)$.

In summary, our sensitivity analysis shows that the assumption made over the geographical extent at which regions may compete for tourists in terms of their WHS endowment matters. Among all the models tested above, the model with the best fit (in terms of AIC) is the one with the largest distance bandwidth, although Model (2) from Table 13.3, based on rook contiguity, has the best overall fit. Our findings suggest that, when comparing destinations on the basis of their WHS endowment, the tourist uses a potentially large number of alternative destinations.

13.6 Conclusions

In this paper, we analysed the relationship between domestic tourism and cultural endowment measured in terms of the number of sites enlisted in UNESCO's World Heritage List (WHS). We carried out an empirical application for 20 Italian regions for the years 1998–2009, employing data on the interregional tourism flows recorded as arrivals in hotels and other types of accommodation structures.

Our objectives can be framed within the ongoing debate on the relevance of cultural—and more specifically WHS—endowment for tourism. Our contribution appears to support the view that such a relationship exists, and that its numerical extent is non-negligible.

The first research question we aimed to answer was whether the regional WHS endowment affects tourism flows. On the one hand, we find that regions which are endowed in WHS are able to attract a greater number of tourists, all else being equal. More in detail, an increase of one WHS in a region's endowment implies a 4 % increase in tourist inflows. On the other hand, we found a negative effect of WHS endowment on regional outflows, that is, on the emissiveness of the tourists' residence regions. The estimated effect, around $-1.6\,\%$ is most likely due to substitution between arrivals (traditional—and recordable—tourism) and daily excursions.

Our second research question regarded the spatial behaviour of tourists, and the potential substitution or complementarity between tourism destinations. We found that the WHS endowment of the regions surrounding a hypothetical destination (i.e., sharing a border with it) has a negative effect on its inflows of tourists. We estimated this effect at about 10 % for an average increase of one WHS in a destination's neighbours. We may then speculate that, consistently with a competing destinations framework (Fotheringham 1983), tourists appear to consider, in forming their travelling choices, the WHS endowment of alternative destinations, generating a phenomenon of spatial substitution. The overall effect of a generalized increase of one unit in the WHS endowment of the regions would then lead—on average—to a negative balance (−6 %) in inflows. Consistently with the above results, we find that tourism outflows appear to be constrained also by the endowment of the origin region's neighbours.

Finally, in order to investigate the robustness of our findings to different hypotheses on the nature and geographical extent of spatial interaction, we carried out a spatial sensitivity analysis. In particular, we applied two further definitions of proximity, according to the *k*-nearest neighbours method and to distance thresholds.

With regard to the effect of WHS endowment on inflows (i.e., towards the destination regions), the result of a positive direct effect was confirmed in all cases. The negative indirect effect of the WHS endowment of neighbouring destinations (up to −13 %) was confirmed as well, showing in particular that the spatial competition effect becomes significant when a greater geographical extent is considered. The overall effect is therefore: first (1) positive and equal to about 4 % (when only 1 or 2 neighbouring regions are considered), then (2) non-significantly different from zero (when the number of spatial competitors is 3), and finally (3) negative (−9 % for the greatest distance bandwidth considered). This result may help explaining the mixed empirical evidence found in the literature, and suggests that spatial competition appears to dominate spatial complementarity (i.e., a cultural district effect is not observable, at least at the regional spatial scale).

Altogether, we can conclude that the spatial sensitivity analysis confirmed the robustness of our results. Furthermore, for all the definitions of proximity tested, the models including indirect effects outperformed in terms of AIC the model with only direct effects, confirming the empirical relevance of our second research question.

From a policy viewpoint, our findings have two main implications: (1) WHS endowment does appear to influence arrivals to tourism destinations for Italian domestic tourism,[13] providing a justification for local policymakers' lobbying towards the national government for obtaining WHS designations; (2) however, spatial competition may reduce the positive direct effect down to an overall negative effect, suggesting that the desirability of WHS designation depends on the expected spatial extent of competition. This last result strengthens the importance of WHS endowment, since it implies that competition among regions on the basis of WHS can be justified. In fact, given that the positive effects of trip-chaining are

[13]Our results might not carry over to international tourism.

outweighed by spatial competition, regions could indeed use WHS designations to gain competitive advantages over other regions, which also outlines the critical role of regional tourism promotion agencies in effectively managing the designated sites to cater to the cultural tourism demand.

Further improvements, from a methodological viewpoint, could involve the estimation of our model in a dynamic panel framework, to account for inertia mechanisms, as well as in its doubly-constrained form, so as to provide a view on the spatial substitution/complementarity effects under the hypothesis of constant overall tourism flows. From an empirical viewpoint, it would be desirable to augment the model specification by introducing physical variables (e.g., length of coastline, overall area, mean elevation) and further proxies of cultural offer, in order to further improve the identification of the WHS endowment's contribution to tourism. Moreover, our sensitivity analysis findings regarding the use of different distance bandwidths call for further testing by means of more realistic distance/opportunity cost metrics, such as the actual driving distance or travelling time between the regional centroids. Finally, including international tourist flows to and from each Italian region, and extending the analyses to additional regions outside of Italy, to account for the effects of WHS on international tourism, is also desirable in the future.

Acknowledgments The authors wish to thank Roberto Cellini (University of Catania) and two anonymous referees for useful comments, as well as session participants and seminar attendees at: the 2011 NECTAR Conference (Antwerp), the 51st European Congress of the Regional Science Association International (Barcelona), the Fifth European Workshop on Applied Cultural Economics (Dublin), the SNSF International Exploratory Workshop on 'Advances in the Statistical Modelling of Spatial Interaction Data' (Lugano), the 2nd International Conference on the Measurement and Economic Analysis of Regional Tourism (Bilbao), the Toulouse School of Economics of the Université Toulouse 1 Capitole (Toulouse), the Workshop on 'The Economics and Management of Leisure, Travel and Tourism' (Rimini), and the Workshop on 'UNESCO World Heritage: Economic and Policy Issues' (Turin).

Appendix

Table 13.6.

Table 13.6 Correlation matrix

WHS	1.00												
GDP	0.40	1.00											
Spectour	0.09	0.33	1.00										
ExpRecr	0.06	0.14	0.28	1.00									
PriceH&R	0.32	0.26	−0.06	−0.11	1.00								
Pop	0.77	0.63	0.03	0.01	0.23	1.00							
CrimDiff	0.49	0.43	0.47	0.28	0.22	0.58	1.00						
CrimVio	0.50	0.20	0.03	−0.03	0.57	0.48	0.32	1.00					
SatisTrain	0.03	0.30	0.49	0.26	−0.29	0.02	0.21	−0.21	1.00				
CultDem	0.33	0.09	0.07	0.40	0.20	0.22	0.19	0.21	0.18	1.00			
DiffShows	0.27	0.47	0.50	0.44	0.19	0.22	0.67	0.00	0.47	0.40	1.00		
NonBath	0.31	−0.08	0.04	−0.39	0.16	0.28	0.07	0.45	0.01	0.06	−0.16	1.00	
OffSeas	−0.25	0.39	0.49	0.48	−0.01	−0.30	−0.02	−0.16	0.40	−0.10	0.32	−0.31	1.00

References

Alzua A, O'Leary JT, Morrison A (1998) Cultural and heritage tourism: identifying niches for international travellers. J Tourism Studies 9(2):2–13

Anderson JE (1979) A theoretical foundation for the gravity equation. Am Econ Rev 69(1):106–116

Anderson JE, van Wincoop E (2003) Gravity with gravitas: a solution to the border puzzle. Am Econ Rev 93(1):170–192

Arezki R, Cherif R, Piotrowski J (2009) Tourism specialization and economic development: evidence from the UNESCO World Heritage List. IMF, Washington

Armstrong GWG (1972) International tourism: coming or going: the methodological problems of forecasting. Futures 4(2):115–125

Ashworth GJ, Tunbridge JE (1990) The tourist-historic city. Belhaven Press, London

Baier SL, Bergstrand JH (2009) Bonus Vetus OLS: a simple method for approximating international trade-cost effects using the gravity equation. J Int Econ 77(1):77–85

Barry K, O'Hagan J (1972) An econometric study of British tourist expenditure in Ireland. Econ Soc Rev 5:143–161

Becker GS (1996) Accounting for tastes. Harvard University Press, Cambridge

Blacik L (2007) A critical assessment of the impact of World Heritage Site designation in Sub-Saharan Africa. ISP Collection Paper 150

Bond D, Cohen B, Schachter G (1977) The spatial distribution of tourism demand and exchange rate variation: OECD European countries. Tour Rev 32(1):13–17

Bové Sans M, Laguado Ramírez R (2011) Image destination analysis for Tarragona's cultural heritage. Paper presented at the Economics and Management of Leisure, Travel and Tourism, Rimini

Buckley R (2004) The effects of World Heritage listing on tourism to Australian National Parks. J Sustain Tour 12(1):70–84

Burger M, van Oort F, Linders G-J (2009) On the specification of the gravity model of trade: zeros, excess zeros and zero-inflated estimation. Spat Econ Anal 4(2):167–190

Calantone RJ, Di Benedetto CA, Bojanic D (1987) A comprehensive review of the tourism forecasting literature. J Travel Res 26(2):28–39

Candela G, Figini P (2012) The economics of tourism destinations. Springer, Berlin

Carr EAJ (1994) Tourism and heritage: the pressures and challenges of the 1990s. In: Ashworth GJ, Larkham PJ (eds) Building a new heritage: tourism, culture, and identity in the New Europe. Routledge, London, pp 69–89

Cellini R (2011) Is UNESCO recognition effective in fostering tourism? A comment on Yang, Lin and Han. Tour Manage 32(2):452–454

Cellini R, Cuccia T (2013) Museum and monument attendance and tourism flow: a time series analysis approach. Appl Econ 45(24):3473–3482

Chun Y, Griffith DA (2011) Modeling network autocorrelation in space–time migration flow data: an eigenvector spatial filtering approach. Ann Assoc Am Geogr 101(3):523–536

Colwell PF (1982) Central place theory and the simple economic foundations of the gravity model. J Regional Sci 22(4):541–546

Crampon LJ, Tan KT (1973) A model of tourism flow into the pacific. Tour Rev 28(3):98–104

Cuccia T, Cellini R (2007) Is cultural heritage really important for tourists? A contingent rating study. Appl Econ 39(2):261–271

de la Mata T, Llano-Verduras C (2012) Spatial pattern and domestic tourism: an econometric analysis using inter-regional monetary flows by type of journey. Regional Sci 99(2):437–470

Dean A, Morgan D, Tan TE (2002) Service quality and customers' willingness to pay more for travel services. J Travel Tour Marketing 12(2-3):95–110

Dhariwal R (2005) Tourist arrivals in India: how important are domestic disorders? Tour Econ 11(2):185–205

Di Giovine MA (2009) The heritage-scape: UNESCO, World Heritage, and Tourism. Lexington Books, Lanham

Di Lascio FML, Giannerini S, Scorcu AE, Candela G (2011) Cultural tourism and temporary art exhibitions in Italy: a panel data analysis. Published in 2011 in: Stat Method Appl 20(4):519–542

Dritsakis N (2004) Cointegration analysis of German and British tourism demand for Greece. Tour Manage 25(1):111–119

Drost A (1996) Developing sustainable tourism for World Heritage Sites. Ann Tour Res 23(2):479–484

Edwards AD (1976) International tourism development: forecasts to 1985. Economist Intelligence Unit, London

Eilat Y, Einav L (2004) Determinants of international tourism: a three-dimensional panel data analysis. Appl Econ 36(12):1315–1327

Fotheringham AS (1983) A new set of spatial-interaction models: the theory of competing destinations. Environ Plann A 15:15–36

Frey BS, Steiner L (2011) World Heritage List: does it make sense? Int J Cul Policy 17(5):555–573

Fujii ET, Khaled M, Mak J (1985) An almost ideal demand system for visitor expenditures. J Transp Econ Policy 19(2):161–171

Fujii ET, Khaled M, Mak J (1987) An empirical comparison of systems of demand equations for tourist expenditures in resort destinations. Philipp Rev Econ 24(1-2):79–102

Gamboni D (2001) World Heritage: shield or target? Conservation 16(2):5–11

Gardini A (1998) L'Analisi della Domanda e della Produzione di Servizi Turistici. CLUEB, Bologna

Gerakis AS (1965) Effects of exchange-rate devaluations and revaluations on receipts from tourism. Staff Pap Int Monetary Fund 12(3):365–384

Hall CM (2006) Implementing the World Heritage convention: what happens after listing? In: Leask A, Fyall A (eds) Managing World Heritage Sites. Butterworth-Heinemann, Oxford, pp 20–34

Hall CM, Piggin R (2001) Tourism and World Heritage in OECD countries. Tour Recreat Res 26(1):103–105

Haynes KE, Fotheringham AS (1984) Gravity and spatial interaction models. Sage Publications, Beverly Hills

Herbert D (2001) Literary places, tourism and the heritage experience. Ann Tour Res 28(2):312–333

ISTAT, Unioncamere, Istituto Tagliacarne (2010) Le Differenze nel Livello dei Prezzi al Consumo tra i Capoluoghi delle Regioni Italiane. ISTAT Unioncamere Istituto Tagliacarne, Rome

Keum K (2010) Tourism flows and trade theory: a panel data analysis with the gravity model. Ann Regional Sci 44(3):541–557

Khadaroo J, Seetanah B (2008) The role of transport infrastructure in international tourism development: a gravity model approach. Tour Manage 29(5):831–840

Kim S-I, Fesenmaier DR (1990) Evaluating spatial structure effects in recreation travel. Leisure Sci 12(4):367–381

Leamer EE (1997) Access to Western Markets and Eastern Effort. In: Zecchini S (ed) Lessons from the economic transition: central and Eastern Europe in the 1990s. Kluwer Academic Publishers, Norwell Dordrecht, pp 503–526

Leamer EE, Levinsohn J (1995) International trade theory: the evidence. In: Grossman GM, Rogoff K (eds) Handbook of international economics, vol III. North Holland, Amsterdam, pp 1339–1394

LeSage JP, Pace RK (2009) Introduction to spatial econometrics. CRC Press, Boca Raton

Li M, Wu B, Cai L (2008) Tourism development of World Heritage Sites in China: a geographic perspective. Tour Manage 29(2):308–319

Light D (2000) Gazing on communism: heritage tourism and post-communist identities in Germany, Hungary and Romania. Tour Geogr 2(2):157–176

Lim C (1997) Review of international tourism demand models. Ann Tour Res 24(4):835–849

Linnemann H (1966) An econometric study of international trade flows. North-Holland, Amsterdam
Lionetti S, Patuelli R (2009) Trading cultural goods in the era of digital piracy. Quaderno della Facoltà di Scienze Economiche 09/07. University of Lugano, Lugano
Lowry IS (1966) Migration and metropolitan growth: two analytical models. Chandler, San Francisco
Malamud B (1973) Gravity model calibration of tourist travel to Las Vegas. J Leisure Res 5(1):13–33
Markwell S, Bennett M, Ravenscroft N (1997) The changing market for heritage tourism: a case study of visits to historic houses in England. Int J Herit Stud 3(2):95–108
Massidda C, Etzo I (2012) The determinants of Italian domestic tourism: a panel data analysis. Tour Manage 33(3):603–610
McAllister DM, Klett FR (1976) A modified gravity model of regional recreation activity with an application to Ski Trips. J Leis Res 8(1):21–34
McIntosh AJ, Prentice RC (1999) Affirming authenticity: consuming cultural heritage. Ann Tour Res 26(3):589–612
Meskell L (2002) Negative heritage and past mastering in archaeology. Anthropol Quart 75(3):557–574
Mossetto G (1994) The economic dilemma of heritage preservation. In: Peacock A, Rizzo I (eds) Cultural economics and cultural policies. Kluwer Academic Publishers, Dordrecht, pp 81–96
Nicolau JL (2008) Characterizing tourist sensitivity to distance. J Travel Res 47(1):43–52
Nitsch V (2000) National borders and international trade: evidence from the European Union. Can J Economics/Revue canadienne d'économique 33(4):1091–1105
Pierret F (2011) Some points on domestic tourism. http://unwto.org/en/opinion/some-points-domestic-tourism
Pocock D (1997) Some reflections on World Heritage. Area 29(3):260–268
Pöyhönen P (1963) A tentative model for the volume of trade between countries. Weltwirtsch Arch 90:93–100
PriceWaterhouseCoopers LLP (2007) The costs and benefits of World Heritage Site status in the UK: case studies. Department for Culture, Media and Sport, London
Research Consulting Ltd, Trends Business Research Ltd (2009) World Heritage Status: is there opportunity for economic gain? Lake District World Heritage Project, Kendal
Santos Silva JMC, Tenreyro S (2006) The log of gravity. Rev Econ Stat 88(4):641–658
Saunders PR, Senter HF, Jarvis JP (1981) Forecasting recreation demand in the Upper Savannah River Basin. Ann Tour Res 8(2):236–256
Sen A, Smith TE (1995) Gravity models of spatial interaction behavior. Springer, Heidelberg
Shackley ML (1998) Visitor management: case studies from World Heritage Sites. Butterworth Heinemann, Oxford
Sheldon PJ, Var T (1985) Tourism forecasting: a review of empirical research. J Forecasting 4(2):183–195
Soares JO, Neves J, Fernandes F (2007) The impact of World Heritage classification on the development of tourist destinations: the Sintra case study. Paper presented at the Advances in Tourism Economics, Vila Nova de Sto André
Swart WW, Var T, Gearing CE (1978) Operations research applications to tourism. Ann Tour Res 5(4):414–428
Thorsell J, Sigaty T (2001) Visitor human use in World Heritage natural sites: a global inventory. Tour Recreat Res 26(1):85–101
Tinbergen J (1962) Shaping the world economy: suggestions for an international economic policy. Twentieth Century Fund, New York
UNESCO (2011) World Heritage List. http://whc.unesco.org/en/list
UNESCO (2012) The World Heritage Convention. http://whc.unesco.org/en/convention#Benefits-of-Ratification. Accessed 19 April 2012
UNWTO (1994) Recommendations on tourism statistics. Statistical Papers. UNWTO, New York

UNWTO (2011) Facts and figures: information, analysis and know-how. http://www.unwto.org/facts/menu.html

Uysal M, Crompton JL (1985) An overview of approaches used to forecast tourism demand. J Travel Res 23(4):7–15

van der Aa BJM (2005) Preserving the heritage of humanity? Obtaining World Heritage Status and the impacts of listing. Ph.D. thesis, University of Groningen, Groningen

VanBlarcom BL, Kayahan C (2011) Assessing the economic impact of a UNESCO World Heritage Designation. J Herit Tour 6(2):143–164

Vietze C (2008) Cultural effects on inbound tourism into the USA: a gravity approach. Jena Economic Research Papers 2008-037. Friedrich Schiller University and Max Planck Institute of Economics, Jena

Wilson AG (1967) A statistical theory of spatial distribution models. Transport Res 1:253–269

Wilson AG (1970) Entropy in urban and regional modelling. Pion, London

Witt SF, Witt CA (1995) Forecasting tourism demand: a review of empirical research. Int J Forecast 11(3):447–475

Yang C-H, Lin H-L (2011) Is UNESCO recognition effective in fostering tourism? A comment on Yang, Lin and Han: Reply. Tour Manage 32(2):455–456

Yang C-H, Lin H-L, Han C-C (2010) Analysis of international tourist arrivals in China: the role of World Heritage Sites. Tour Manage 31(6):827–837

Zhang J, Jensen C (2007) Comparative advantage: explaining tourism flows. Ann Tour Res 34(1):223–243

Chapter 14
Testing Transport Mode Cooperation and Competition Within a Country: A Spatial Econometrics Approach

Jorge Díaz-Lanchas, Nuria Gallego, Carlos Llano, and Tamara de la Mata

Keywords Border effect • Distance • Inter-provincial trade • Logistics • Multi-modal transport flows

JEL Classifications: F14, R40, C21

14.1 Introduction

In most countries, information concerning interregional commodity flows is scarce and incomplete (Jackson et al. 2006). One of the most common ways to obtain it is to look at transport flows within the country. Many of these analyses are found in the literature on border effects, where the trade intensity within one country (or region) is measured against with the trade flows develop with other countries (or regions of the same country). Directly connected to our paper, some authors have focused on the national level and computed a country's home bias, defined as how much some regions (provinces) trade with itself than with any other region (province) of the same country. Wolf (1997, 2000) and Yilmazkuday (2012) did it for the United States; Helliwell (1996, 1997, 1998) for Canada; Helble (2007) and Nitsch (2002) for Germany; Combes et al. (2005) for France; and Garmendia et al. (2012) for

J. Díaz-Lanchas • N. Gallego • C. Llano (✉)
Departamento de Análisis Económico: Teoría Económica e Historia Económica, Facultad de Ciencias Económicas y Empresariales, Universidad Autónoma de Madrid, Campus Cantoblanco, 28049 Madrid, Spain
e-mail: jorge.diaz@uam.es; nuria.gallego@uam.es; carlos.llano@uam.es

T. de la Mata
Departamento de Análisis Económico: Teoría e Historia Económic, Universidad Autónoma de Madrid, 28049 Madrid, Spain

CEPREDE, Madrid, Spain
e-mail: tamara.delamata@uam.es

R. Patuelli, G. Arbia (eds.), *Spatial Econometric Interaction Modelling*, Advances in Spatial Science, DOI 10.1007/978-3-319-30196-9_14

Spain. In most of these studies, interregional transport flows or deliveries as reported by the exporting firm (Hillberry and Hummels 2008) are used as the best proxy for internal bilateral trade (as in fact it is).

In principle, a commercial transaction implies the shipment of a good, but shipment can mean single-mode or multimodal transport. It might be simple door-to-door delivery, or it might encompass a range of intermediation activities, such as multimodal nodes, logistics platforms, warehouses and wholesale operations. The same single trade transaction could be registered in any number of ways by different trade and transport surveys; there could thus be coherence or divergence between the surveyed records of the various intervening agents (exporter, importer, transporter, customs, etc.). Assuming a good match between transport and trade information, it is standard to identify the origin of a transport flow with the point of production and the destination with the point of consumption.

In this regard, recent literature on transport economics, geography, global management and logistics points to a rise in economic and logistical complexity (Van Klink and van den Berg 1998; Woudsma 1999; Rodrigue 2003; Hesse and Rodrigue 2004; Rodrigue et al. 2009; Rodrigue and Notteboom 2010), which may introduce a number of misrepresentations in the observation of specific dyadic records, for both international and intra-national transport flows. Thus behind any given interprovincial flows across one single country, a number of factors could contravene the previous hypothesis. Indeed, it is a commonplace to call into question anyone's work in this literature for the bias induced by bilateral transport flows within a country (or between countries) precisely because of this logistical complexity (see McCallum 1995; Henderson and Millimet 2008, and Combes et al 2005, for specific comments on the limitations of their datasets in relation to this point, both when using datasets for Canada and the U.S., and France).

The aim of this paper is to analyze the complexity of modal cooperation and competition behind *apparently standard* deliveries within a country. We will evaluate some of the aforementioned biases attributable to logistics infrastructures, warehouses and wholesale activities as well as to *hub-spoke structures* and international transit flows. We will use a novel dataset that contains 16 sector-specific flows, by four modes of transport (truck, train, ship, and aircraft), between 50 provinces. Our dataset—which includes 160,000 origin–destination deliveries (50*50*4*16) for the single year of 2007, along with a comprehensive set of regressors and rich distance measures based on Spain's actual transportation network—is notable both for its size and for its quality. We then introduce a novel index to address the presence of hub-spoke structures within a country. We analyze this index with GIS techniques using the actual transport network for each mode. Finally, we feed our data into various specifications of the gravity model that incorporate spatial autocorrelation elements when modeling flows for each transport mode and its competition effects with regards to the other modes. We also use a gravity equation with a spatial autocorrelation term (SAR) for tackling network dependence attributable to hub-spoke structures. Our hypothesis is that "*re-exportation schemes*" constitute an additional source of cross-sectional correlation between dyadic commodity flows to the sources already described in the literature (LeSage and Pace 2008, 2009; Fischer and Griffith 2008). To the best of our knowledge, no one has analyzed this type of relationship in the same detail.

The rest of the paper is structured as follows: Sect. 14.2 describes some important links between trade, transportation and logistics and briefly reviews the state of the art in the analysis of these complexities in Spain and elsewhere. Section 14.3 describes a conceptual framework that will be the base for our empirical strategy—revised in Sect. 14.4—for modeling flows within a country in presence of this logistic complexity. Section 14.5 describes the dataset. Section 14.6 comprises our descriptive and Section 14.7 the results for the econometric analysis. A final section concludes.

14.2 Trade, Transport Flows and Logistics

As certain authors (Rodrigue 2003; Hesse and Rodrigue 2004; Rodrigue and Notteboom 2010) have posited, freight flows at the local level result from global and regional economic processes. Internationally, with the division of the production chain and the development of door-to-door distribution schemes, distribution networks have expanded. The development of hub structures, gateways and corridors is also connected as global supply chains have sprouted up, firms have sought out optimal locations in more stable and free-entry situations for foreign investment and multi-location firms have surged. These developments have modified freight-distribution systems and spurred a proliferation of new transport terminals and distribution centers in new locations.

The same author (Rodrigue 2003) defines an "*articulation point*" as "a location that promotes the continuity of circulation in a transportation system servicing a supply chain. Such concept expands the traditional "*hub*" concept as it includes the consideration of terminal facilities, distribution centers, warehouses and finance". He also suggests that an articulation point's relevance depends on the volume and nature of the traffic it handles, which in turn suggest that the characterization of such points depends on the type of flow (international versus intra-national) as well as on the transport modes used. In line with such concepts, Hesse and Rodrigue (2004) provide an insightful description of the evolution of logistics as it pertains to the core dimensions of transport geography (flows, nodes/locations and networks).

In a related paper, Rodrigue and Notteboom (2010) compared the North American and European freight transport systems, showing that the two regions were following alternative patterns of transport and logistics networks. To explain this polarity, the authors cited three main factors: globalization, economic integration and intermodal transport. Intermodalism results from high integration between transport modes and tends to produce complex transport networks.

So much for international freight flows within large regional areas (Europe vs. North America). What about equivalent systems within single countries? These, it turns out, are similarly complex, although, because of a lack of statistical sources, perhaps more opaque. Our paper focuses on this more opaque part of the problem.

Another interesting result in the literature on logistics and transport geography is the idea of transport-mode competition and cooperation. Some stimulating papers have analyzed these relationships within Spain with micro-founded general equilibrium and model-choice approaches, both for freight and person movements (Monzón and Rodríguez-Dapena 2006; Cantos-Sánchez et al. 2009; Álvarez-SanJaime et al. 2013a, b). Similarly, Feo-Valero et al. (2011) focuses on the empirical evidence regarding modal-choice determinants for the inland leg of maritime shipments. The paper analyzes modal choice between road and rail transport on the inland leg of Spanish maritime freight shipments through an error components mixed logit discrete choice model, with the aim of evaluating the potential of rail transport to connect ports with their respective hinterlands. In most European countries, rail freight departing from or bound for ports accounts for the bulk of the rail-freight market. But its share is much smaller in Spain. The authors' main contribution is to have produced an empirical study of door-to-port/port-to-door freight traffic. Their results confirm the role that frequency plays in the relative competitiveness of rail transport.

Taking a more empirical approach, a certain number of papers have combined gravity equations and spatial econometric techniques in order to deal with some of the issues mentioned above. We will discuss two examples here. First, LeSage and Polasek (2008) modeled commodity flows with an extended gravity model that incorporates information on the highway network into the spatial connectivity structure of the spatial autoregressive econometric model. Their results pointed to better model fits and higher likelihood-function values. They also found different types of origin and destination connectivity between regions when considering the links between trading regions and their neighbors, as defined by the actual highway network.

Second, and more recently, Alamá-Sabater et al. (2013a) analyzed whether transport connectivity affects trade flows. Using first-order contiguity and incorporating logistics-network-structure dependence in a spatial autoregressive model, they considered flows between 15 landlocked regions (Nuts 2) of Spain and sector-specific flows by road. Their results provided evidence for the role of logistics-platform location in satisfying existing demand for transport structures in Spain. Their approach relied mainly on the definition of two different connectivity concepts. First, they considered a purely geographical effect, using contiguous regions as an ad-hoc structure for spatial autocorrelation effects. Then, they built an index that captured the relative presence of logistics platforms in each region. By considering the endowment of such platforms in regions adjacent to trading partners, they expected to capture part of the previously defined logistical complexity. In line with previous papers (Lesage and Llano 2013) confirms the presence of spatial-dependence effects for the Spanish case. In addition, the weighted matrix defined by the index of logistics platforms generated poor results for aggregate flows but interesting insights for certain industry-specific deliveries. The authors have also developed a working paper that uses similar techniques, as well as transport flows by road, to analyze the same effects at NUTS-3 level in Spain. Our paper explores a wider set of flows (50 NUTS-3 provinces and four transport modes instead of one) and considers alternative effects (hub-spoke structures, international transit flows and wholesale activity).

14.3 A Conceptual Framework for Competition and Cooperation Between Transport Modes

Let us start by considering a country with I provinces ($I = 50$ for Spain). Without loss of generality, all types of bilateral trade flows from province i to province j could be defined as Y_{ji}. If $i = j$ we have intra-provincial trade flows, while if $i \neq j$ we have inter-provincial, intra-national trade flows. International exports and imports from each province can be denoted Y_{RoWi} and Y_{jRoW} respectively. Note that such flows can correspond to products delivered to the point of final or intermediate demand.

Let us now consider that each bilateral aggregated flow can be decomposed into a set of sector-specific flows for every set of tradable goods k,[1] which can be delivered by four alternative transport modes (m): road (R), train (T), ship (S) and aircraft (A). Therefore, for the most general case of aggregate trade flow, Y_{ji} can be decomposed as:

$$Y_{ji}^{k} = Y_{ji}^{kR} + Y_{ji}^{kT} + Y_{ji}^{kS} + Y_{ji}^{kA} \tag{14.1}$$

where Y_{ji}^{kR} is the bilateral trade flow in current € of commodity k delivered from province i to province j within Spain. The capital letters R, T, S, A denote the transport mode used for the delivery.

In principle, an inter-provincial trade flow by road of product k from province i to province j (that is, Y_{ji}^{kR}) corresponds to a transport movement with similar characteristics, which could itself be denoted F_{ji}^{kR} (F for freight). Under normal circumstances it is standard to assume that $Y_{ji}^{k} = F_{ji}^{k}$. However, as described in the previous section, economic complexity and modern logistics can introduce certain alterations into this match between trade flows (usually non-observable within a country) and transport flows for each mode (sometimes observable within a country). In some cases $Y_{ji}^{k} \neq F_{ji}^{k}$, because behind two or more "*apparent*" transport flows ($F_{ni}^{k}, F_{mn}^{k'}, \ldots F_{jc}^{k''}$) there is just one trade flow Y_{ji}^{k}.

[1]Although in some parts of this paper the terms *goods*, *products* and *sectors* are used interchangeably, we prefer the term *sector-specific flows*. This reason is the limited number of products (15) available in our dataset. For the sake of rigor, we have discarded alternative expressions such as: *industry-specific flows* (because of the inclusion of agricultural products) and *commodity flows* (because *commodity* can be identified with raw materials and non-transformed products, which are not included here).

14.3.1 Transport Mode Competition

Before we analyze the main reasons why $Y_{ji}^{k} \neq F_{ji}^{k}$, it is convenient to briefly discuss the concept of "transport competition".

Firms located in province i have access to a range of transport-mode mixes with which to deliver a given product k to some other province j, both within the country or abroad. All these transport modes differ in price, security and speed. Since each product type has its own nature and characteristics (volume, value, perishability, demand, etc.), there is a preferred transport mix by sector and province. Given the geographical location of firms, final markets and actual transportation networks, similar products can be shipped in parallel by alternative transport modes. The likelihood of competition will differ by product k and dyad i-j. When it comes to island provinces, for example, ships and aircraft may compete for certain products but not for others. For a given pair of landlocked provinces i-j, competition between road and train will depend on the actual transport network and the nature of the products. Moreover, the transport network will be endogenous to preexisting demand for a certain transport mode between the countries of a dyad (Fig. 14.1).

14.3.2 Transport-Mode Cooperation

In this section we focus on transport mode cooperation. With this aim, we start considering the general case where a trade flow (transaction) is linked to more than one concatenated transport flow (physical movement of a good), and therefore where $Y_{ji}^{k} \neq F_{ji}^{k}$. This re-exporting scheme generates what can be described as *transit flows* between the initial delivery from i and the final destination j. In this paper, a *transit*

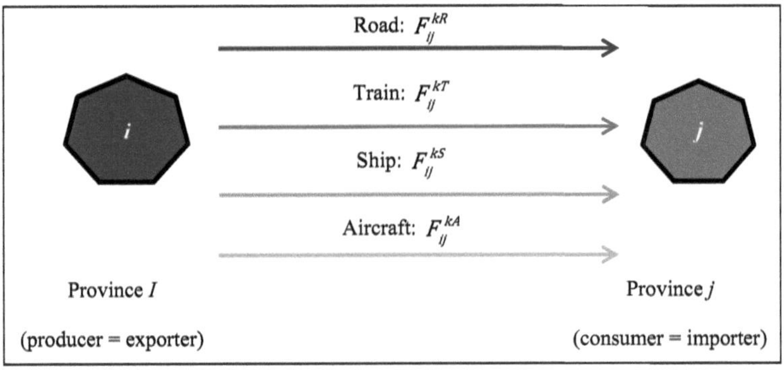

Fig. 14.1 Domestic transport-mode competition scheme

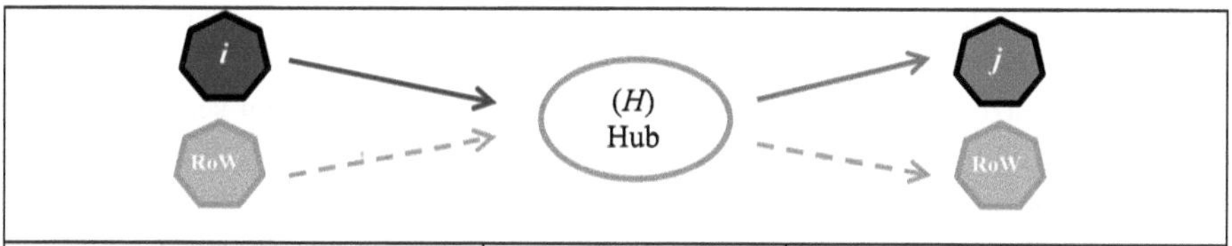

▪ F^{km}_{Hi} **Intra-national transit flows:** A Spanish province *H* receives product *k* from another Spanish province *i*, which is the true producer (i.e., exporter). The load is then re-exported from *H* to *j* within the country. For generality, we use superscript m to denote any transport mode (or the aggregate) ▪ $F^{km}_{H,RoW}$ **International transit flow:** a Spanish province *H* receives *k* products from abroad, which are then re-exported to another province *j* within the country.	▪ Province *H* is the Hub, where the logistics, warehouse, wholesale facilities are. ▪ A Hub province could also be one with a port, airport or large train station.	▪ F^{km}_{jH} **Intra-national transit flows:** a Spanish province *H* delivers product *k* to final destination *j*, which is the true consumer (i.e., importer). The load has been produced not in *H* but in *i*. ▪ $F^{km}_{RoW,H}$ **International transit flow:** a Spanish province *H* delivers product *k* to final destination *j*. This load has been produced not in *H* but abroad.

Fig. 14.2 Transport mode cooperation: "hub-spoke" structure with national and international "transit flows"

flow can imply multimodality or not. Generally, then, *transit flow* refers to flows that satisfy either of the following two conditions:

- The transport flow's point of departure ($F^k{}_{jH}$) is not the point of production but the *Hub* (*H*). In this case, logistics platforms, warehouses and wholesale activities located in the province of delivery accumulate certain amounts of a product *k*, which has been produced elsewhere within the country (intra-national transit flow) or abroad (inter-national transit flow).
- The transport flow's point of destination ($F^k{}_{Hi}$) is not the point of consumption but the *Hub* (*H*). That is, shipments arrive at a province where a logistics platform, warehouse or wholesale activity is located.

We can thus depict a *transit flow* with the following scheme (Fig. 14.2):

In summary, in this paper the term *transit flow* implies that two or more concatenated flows correspond to the same commodity ($k_1 = k_2$). In principle, any province can serve as a *Hub*, for both intra-national and inter-national flows. In this general definition of the *hub-spoke* relationship, no additional conditions are set regarding the transport mode used for the initial *inflow* to the *Hub* and the subsequent *outflow* from the *Hub*. Multiple combinations are possible, each explicable in terms of location (*i*, *H*, *j*) and the specific product in question (*k*). For example, we can account for (transit) flows entering or leaving a province (*H*) in at least one of two ways: by the presence of logistics platforms, warehouses and wholesales infrastructures[2] or by the presence of "*multimodal*

[2]Moreover, inflows to and outflows from the warehouse could be different in nature: (a) the warehouse could be owned by a logistics company offering services to the producer or to retailers.

platforms". The latter case is not expressly considered in this paper due to lack of space.

We emphasize that, in principle, any province of a country can serve as a *Hub*. In fact, any i and any j in a given system of bilateral flows can play that role. For simplicity, we will assume that there is no interconnection between *transit flows*—in other words, that a flow i_1-H-j_1 is not connected to another flow i_2-H-j_2 such that $j_1 = i_2$ becomes a new Hub (H), and so on.

As we will see in the next sections, spatial econometrics techniques allow us to identify and control for potential connections between flows departing from or arriving at any i and j from any other location in the system. To this end, our empirical approach assumes a typical situation: the statistical system of a developed country, where trade and transport bilateral flows are reported separately, with little connection between them. Moreover, transport bilateral flows within the country are stated on an isolated basis by transport mode, with no information about their relationship with the actual point of production/consumption or about any previous or subsequent delivery using the same or an alternative mode (Boonstra 2011). Perfect identification of such links between *concatenated flows* would, of course, require a very detailed dataset on the products and specific locations of each flow. Since such data is, to the best of our knowledge, unavailable anywhere, we have developed our empirical strategy in such a way as to describe an average EU country while taking full advantage of a very rich dataset for Spain. This is the next best thing, and far better than nothing at all.

14.4 The Empirical Strategy

In this section we define the empirical models we will use to embody the main concepts described before regarding competition and cooperation between the transport flows within a country.

The simplest gravity equation for modelling commodity flows between a set of n provinces within a country is described in Eq. (14.2):

$$\ln F_{ji}^{km} = \alpha i_N + X_i\beta_1 + X_j\beta_2 + \ln d_{ji}\beta_3 + Intra\beta_4 + Adj\beta_5 + \ln\left(gdp_i{}^{*}gdp_j\right)\beta_6 + \varepsilon_{ji} \qquad (14.2)$$

Where F_{ji}^{km} is the bilateral flow of product k (or the aggregate) in current euros with origin in province i and destination in province j, which has been delivered

Therefore, although there is no transformation of product k when it is delivered to the warehouse, the outflows and inflows truly correspond to "trade flows"; (b) however, if the warehouse is owned by the producer or the retailer, product k's entry into or departure from that infrastructure does not necessarily imply a trade flow between i and j but, perhaps, an "intra-firm" displacement of products with the aim of getting said products closer to the final market. An additional problem is that the products could be produced abroad and only moved within the country.

using transport mode m (or the aggregate). Flows F_{ji}^{km} have been organized into an $n \times n$ ($N = 50 \times 50 = 2500$, in our case) destination–origin (*j-i*) flow matrix, which contains intra-regional flows in the on-diagonal elements, and inter-provincial in the off-diagonal ones. By vectorizing the matrix, we obtain a column vector *F* with dimensions $n^2 \times 1$. Thus, using the terminology of LeSage and Pace (2009), this column vector is *destination-based*. Thus, the first *n* (50) observations correspond to interprovincial flows exported by province $i = 1$, the next *n* (50) to exports departing from $i = 2$, and so on. The term i_N is an $n^2 \times 1$ vector of ones. A dummy variable, *Intra*, is included to control for the potentially different nature of flows occurring within a province and between provinces. This dummy variable takes the value of one if the flow's origin and destination are the same province and zero otherwise. The anti-log of the coefficient linked with this dummy variable can be interpreted as the *provincial home bias* discussed in the introduction. We add a dyadic dummy, *Adj*, to control for trading-partner adjacency. X_i and X_j contain different characteristics of province *i* and *j*, as the production capacity of province *i* or the absorption capacity in province *j*. More specifically the main variables considered in these two matrices are described below. Moreover, in order to disentangle the effect of the previous monadic variables and the economic size of the exporting and importing province, we have opted for introducing the gross domestic product of the trading provinces as a dyadic variable, by computing the log of their product ($gdp_i * gdp_j$). By doing this, we avoid that the monadic variables will compete with the gdp's. All specifications also add two dummy variables $Island_i$ and $Island_j$ to control for the specific characteristics of being an Island province, both as an exporter or as an importer. Thus, for example, $Island_i$ is a dummy variable identifying the three island provinces of Spain (Islas Baleares, Las Palmas and Santa Cruz de Tenerife) as exporting provinces. To conclude, all models add the bilateral distance (d_{ji}) between the exporting and importing province (the best available proxy for transport cost by transport mode and commodity type). All the variables considered—except the dummies—are expressed in logarithms. ε. is an $n^2 \times 1$ vector of normally distributed constant variance disturbances. For the sake of generality, although due to a lack of space some of our specifications are just tested for aggregate flows at the sectoral and transport mode level, the equations are defined using superscripts *k* and *m*.

It is common to depart from this basic equation and introduce variables that help to account for other factors affecting the direction and intensity of flows. Inadequate specification of the forces driving flow intensity can induce problems of cross-sectional autocorrelation, rendering the estimation method unsuitable. In line with the general goal of this paper, after testing a basic specification of the simplest gravity equation, we add the following variables with the aim of capturing the logistical capacity of trading partners (logistics platforms, warehouses, wholesale activities) and potential controls for international transit flows[3]:

[3]For simplicity, we now define these variables only for exporting province i (there is an equivalent set of variables for importing province *j*).

- *Ln(wholesales* pc_i*)*: the ratio between the number of wholesale activities in province *i* (La Caixa 2013) relative to the population of *i*. It is expressed as a log and used as an alternative to the "platform infrastructure" in Alamá-Sabater et al. (2013a, b).
- *Border int. core* EU_i: a dummy variable identifying Spanish provinces that share an international border with France and Andorra in the north. This variable—taking the value one for border provinces and zero otherwise—is meant to control for expected higher flows departing from/arriving at these provinces as *gateways* for trade with the EU core. A positive and significant coefficient for the variable should be interpreted as a *symptom* that these border provinces are behaving as *Hubs* for international flows; in other words, their exports exceed expected inter-provincial flows (relative to their size, remoteness, etc.) because they are receiving from the EU core international imports of product *k*, which will be subsequently re-exported domestically (generating an *apparent inter-provincial flow*). Note that by including an equivalent dummy for importing provinces *j*, we also control for the potential of border provinces to behave as *Hubs* and receive domestic imports for subsequent re-exportation to the EU core.
- *Border int.* $other_i$: a dummy variable meant to control for the same effect as the previous variable but for Spanish provinces that share an international border with countries to the southeast: that is, Portugal and countries in Africa. Although the aim is equivalent, the importance of the EU core and these other markets, along with the size of Spain's border provinces, make it worthwhile to consider the effects separately.
- *Ln(imp. int. all/*gdp_i*)*: a further variable added to take into account the bias introduced by ambushed international flows within domestic flows. In addition to controlling for Spanish provinces bordering on foreign markets, this variable is the logarithm of the total products, measured in euros, imported by *i* (origin province of the domestic flow) regardless of transport mode. The variable is introduced in relative terms to i's GDP, so we can measure relative openness to foreign markets, at the same time that we avoid multicollinearity problems with the other variables that are associated with the size of the province. The idea is to acknowledge that even a non-border province can behave as a *Hub* (in this case, not as a *gateway*, since it is not a border-province), thanks to, say, a large maritime port (e.g., Barcelona, Bilbao, Valencia). Thus a positive and significant coefficient for this variable indicates that interprovincial product exports from *i* are positively associated with the province's absorption capacity for *international imports*. Note that by including an equivalent variable, *Ln(exp. int. all/*gdp_j*)*, for importing provinces *j*, we also control for the contrary case, where the large capacity for importing interprovincial Spanish flows of a province *j* is associated with its high intensity of international exports regardless of transport mode.

Moreover, for those of our specifications that use sector-specific flows as endogenous variables, the previous variables *Ln(imp. int. all/*gdp_i*)* and *Ln(exp. int. all/*gdp_j*)* are redefined much more precisely as *Ln(imp. int.*all^k*/*gdp_i*)* and *Ln(exp. int.* all^k*/*gdp_j*)*. In these cases, although all transport modes are considered together, international exports and imports are *k-specific*. We thus expect to disentangle the very cases of *hub-spoke* structures (which implies international re-exportation of exactly the same product k that was previously unloaded in the exporting province and produced elsewhere in the country), and an alternative situation where a province is an important international exporter (of all products) and a great importer of a specific product k produced in another province within the country.

Taking a cue from the literature, our empirical strategy is based on several alternative gravity-equation specifications some of which embed spatial econometric terms. For the sake of clarity, each specification is defined along with each of the previously described possible relationships between competing or cooperative transport modes.

14.4.1 Transport Mode Competition

14.4.1.1 A Basic Gravity Equation for Testing Transport Mode Competition

To consider the presence of transport-mode competition within the country, we first estimate a non-spatial model, as in Eq. (14.3):

$$\begin{aligned}\ln F_{ji}^{kR} &= \alpha i_N + X_i\beta_1 + X_j\beta_2 + \ln d_{ji}\beta_3 + Intra\beta_4 + Adj\beta_5 \\ &+ \ln F_{ji}^{kT}\beta_6 + \ln F_{ji}^{kS}\beta_7 + \ln F_{ji}^{kA}\beta_8 + \ln\left(gdp_i{}^{*}gdp_j\right)\beta_9 + \varepsilon_{ji}\end{aligned} \tag{14.3}$$

Where F_{ji}^{kR} is the bilateral flow of product k (or the aggregate) by road with origin i and destination j. Elements αi_N, X_i, X_j, d_{ji}, *Intra* and *Adj* are the same as in Eq. (14.2). In addition, Eq. (14.3) includes three new elements, $F_{ji}^{kT}; F_{ji}^{kS}; F_{ji}^{kA}$, each of them corresponding to equivalent (same k) flows between i and j by alternative transport modes ($T = train$, $S = ship$, $A = aircraft$).[4] By means of these new elements we expect to measure whether the trade flows of one mode are, on

[4]Similarly, we estimate alternative combinations such as:

$$\begin{aligned}\ln F_{ji}^{kT} &= \alpha i_N + X_i\beta_1 + X_j\beta_2 + \ln d_{ji}\beta_3 + Intra\beta_4 + Adj\beta_5 + \ln F_{ji}^{kR}\beta_6 + \ln F_{ji}^{kS}\beta_7 + \ln F_{ji}^{kA}\beta_8 \\ &+ \ln\left(gdp_i{}^{*}gdp_j\right)\beta_9 + \varepsilon_{ji}\end{aligned}$$

$$\begin{aligned}\ln F_{ji}^{kS} &= \alpha i_N + X_i\beta_1 + X_j\beta_2 + \ln d_{ji}\beta_3 + Intra\beta_4 + Adj\beta_5 + \ln F_{ji}^{kR}\beta_6 + \ln F_{ji}^{kT}\beta_7 + \ln F_{ji}^{kA}\beta_8 \\ &+ \ln\left(gdp_i{}^{*}gdp_j\right)\beta_9 + \varepsilon_{ji}\end{aligned}$$

$$\begin{aligned}\ln F_{ji}^{kA} &= \alpha i_N + X_i\beta_1 + X_j\beta_2 + \ln d_{ji}\beta_3 + Intra\beta_4 + Adj\beta_5 + \ln F_{ji}^{kR}\beta_6 + \ln F_{ji}^{kS}\beta_7 + \ln F_{ji}^{kT}\beta_8 \\ &+ \ln\left(gdp_i{}^{*}gdp_j\right)\beta_9 + \varepsilon_{ji}\end{aligned}$$

average, compatible with those of the others for the full range of products (aggregate flow) and for each separately (k-specific).

14.4.1.2 An Extended Gravity Equation with Cross-Sectional Dependence

The use of least-squares would imply to assume that the bilateral flows are considered to be independent. The validity of this assumption has long been questioned by various authors (Griffith and Jones 1980; Black 1992; Bolduc et al. 1992; LeSage and Pace 2008), who have shown how potential spatial and network dependence can affect different types of bilateral flows. LeSage and Pace (2008) suggested, among other potential causes, the variable-omission problem. According to Black (1992), network and spatial autocorrelation could bias the classical estimation procedures for spatial interaction models. He suggested that "autocorrelation may [. . .] exist among random variables associated with the links of a network". Bolduc et al. (1992) suggested that classical gravity models did not consider the socioeconomic and network variables adjacent to the bilateral origin–destination regions i and j, arguing that these too should be incorporated into the relationship that attempts to explain flows (F_{ji}) between these provinces. They emphasized that the omission of neighboring variable values would give rise to spatial autocorrelation in regression errors. Sources of spatial autocorrelation among errors included model misspecification and omitted explanatory variables to capture effects related to the physical and economic characteristics (distances between zones, zone sizes, lengths of frontiers between adjacent zones, etc.) of a region. More recently, LeSage and Pace (2008) challenged the assumption that the classical gravity model's origin and destination (OD) flows contained in the dependent variable vector F_{ji} exhibited no spatial dependence.

For most socioeconomic spatial interactions (migration, trade, commuting, etc.), there are several explanations for these effects. For example, neighboring origins (exporting provinces) and destinations (importing provinces) could exhibit estimation errors of similar magnitude if underlying latent or unobserved forces were at work, so that missing covariates exerted a similar impact on neighboring observations. Agents located at contiguous provinces could experience similar transport costs and profit opportunities when evaluating alternative nearby destinations. This similar positive/negative influence among neighbors could also be explained in terms of common factor endowments, complementary/competitive sectoral structures, etc.

As explained in the previous section, in many cases two or more bilateral transport flows might be anything but independent, being the end of the one the beginning of the next. Transport infrastructures (the network itself, but also ports, airports and logistics facilities) are usually not included as explanatory variables in trade-flow models. Moreover, the actual transport mode used for delivery and transport-mode competition/cooperation schemes is often overlooked in models of aggregate flows and sector-specific deliveries. All these omitted variables can easily become additional sources of spatial and network autocorrelation effects affecting spatial interaction models. In the next section, we formally test an extended gravity-model specification that accounts for such cross-sectional autocorrelation effects in models of inter-provincial flows with Spain. The extended model subsumes models that exclude such dependence as special cases of the more elaborate model.

Departing from these previous comments, we now extend the model described by Eq. (14.3) for testing the presence of transport mode competition by adding a spatial lag component in the spirit of LeSage and Pace (2008). The aim of this spatial model is to determine whether competing structures exist in neighboring provinces (neighbors to the origins and destinations of the observed transport flows). The economic rationale behind this extension could be, for example, that if a province i delivers products to a province j by a specific transport mode (e.g., *train*), it would raise the price of that mode for this specific trip (dyad i-j). Thus neighboring provinces of i (n_i) [or of j (n_j)] could gain by using an alternative transport mode (e.g., road) for their deliveries to j (or from i).[5] We therefore test the data for such effects with a spatial autocorrelation model (SAR), described in Eq. (14.4):

$$\begin{aligned}\ln F_{ji}^{kR} &= \alpha i_N + X_i\beta_1 + X_j\beta_2 + \ln d_{ji}\beta_3 + Intra\beta_4 + Adj\beta_5 \\ &+ \ln F_{ji}^{kT}\beta_6 + \ln F_{ji}^{kS}\beta_7 + \ln F_{ji}^{kA}\beta_8 + \ln\left(gdp_i{}^{*}gdp_j\right)\beta_9 + \rho_1 W \ln F_{ji}^{kR} + \varepsilon_{ji}\end{aligned} \tag{14.4}$$

This model includes all the explanatory variables from the previous models, allowing them to subsume non-spatial regression models as special cases. The main novelty lies in the spatial lag term $\rho_1 WF_{ji}^{kR}$, where W represents a spatial weight matrix of the form suggested by LeSage and Pace (2008).

In a typical cross-sectional model with n provinces, where each pair of provinces represents an observation, spatial regression models rely on an $n \times n$ non-negative weight matrix that describes the connectivity structure between the n provinces. For example, $W_{ji} > 0$ if province i is contiguous to province j. By convention, $W_{ii} = 0$ to prevent an observation's being defined as a neighbor to itself, and the matrix W is typically row-standardized. In the case of bilateral flows, where we are working with $\mathrm{N} = \mathrm{n}^2$ observations ($50 \times 50 = 2500$ in our case), LeSage and Pace (2008), Chun (2008), Chun and Griffith (2011) and Fischer and Griffith (2008) suggest using $W = W_j + W_i$, where $W_j = I_n \otimes W_s$ represents an $\mathrm{N} \times \mathrm{N}$ spatial weight matrix (2500*2500 in our case) that captures connectivity between the importing province and its neighbor, and $W_i = W_s \otimes I_n$ is another $\mathrm{N} \times \mathrm{N}$ spatial weight matrix that captures connectivity between the exporting province and its neighbor.[6] W_s

[5]Or, on the other hand, it could be that, thanks to economics of scale in freight (by train in this example), the very fact that a province i delivers product k to j by train could increase the probability that i or j will become a "Hub", since neighboring regions to i or j might prefer to ship their products to i in order to enjoy less expensive deliveries by train to j, than to ship them directly by an alternative mode (say, road). If this were the case, the preceding model would fail (non-significant results would be expected), and we would have a Hub-spoke structure (see the next family of models described in this paper).

[6]We use the symbol ⊗ to denote a Kronecker product.

describes spatial connectivity between n provinces. This W_s matrix is symmetric, so it has a real eigenvalue and n orthogonal eigenvectors. We row-standardize the matrix W to form a spatial lag of the $N \times 1$ dependent variable.

LeSage and Pace (2008) note that the spatial lag variable captures both 'destination'- and 'origin'-based spatial dependence using an average of flows from neighbors to each origin (exporting) and destination (importing) province. Specifically, this means that flows from any origin to a particular destination may exhibit dependence on flows from the origin's neighbors to the same destination. LeSage and Pace (2008) call this origin-based dependence. The spatial lag matrix, W, also captures destination-based dependence, the term used in LeSage and Pace (2008) to reflect dependence between flows from a particular origin province to neighbors of the destination province.

As suggested above, origin- and/or destination-based dependence could be present for purely spatial reasons (long-lat. coordinates, temperature, factor endowments, etc.), or because of unobserved factors that are also conditioned by space. Moreover, as some papers (de la Mata and Llano 2013) have described, other non-pure spatial correlations could also appear. In the next sections we address certain such correlations connected with the idea of *hub-spoke* relations and multimodal links between subsequent trips.

To help elucidate the next sections, we remind the reader that, as in LeSage and Pace (2009), the spatial model in Eq. (14.4) can be described as filtering for spatial dependence related to the destination- and origin-based effect, as described in Eq. (14.5):

$$\left(I_N - \rho_j W_j\right)\left(I_N - \rho_i W_i\right) \ln F_{ji}^{kR} = \alpha i_N + X_i\beta_1 + X_j\beta_2 + \ln d_{ji}\beta_3 + Intra\beta_4 + Adj\beta_5 \\ + \ln F_{ji}^{kT}\beta_6 + \ln F_{ji}^{kS}\beta_7 + \ln F_{ji}^{kA}\beta_8 + \ln\left(gdp_i{}^{*}gdp_j\right)\beta_9 + \varepsilon_{ji} \qquad (14.5)$$

Again, the $N \times N$ weight matrix W is obtained by adding the destination- and origin-based matrices ($W = W_j + W_i$). The matrix W_j can be expressed as a Kronecker product, as in Eq. (14.6):

$$W_j = I_n \otimes W_s = \begin{pmatrix} W_s & 0_n & \cdots & 0_n \\ 0_n & W_s & & \vdots \\ \vdots & & \ddots & \\ 0_n & & & W_s \end{pmatrix} \qquad (14.6)$$

Similarly, origin-based connectivity can be defined as $W_i = W_s \otimes I_n$. An important characteristic of these expressions is that, for example, in a system of five provinces, where province 2 is contiguous to province 1, W_s is structured as follows[7]:

$$W_s = \begin{pmatrix} 0\,1\,0\,0\,0 \\ 1\,0\,0\,0\,0 \\ 0\,0\,0\,0\,0 \\ 0\,0\,0\,0\,0 \\ 0\,0\,0\,0\,0 \end{pmatrix} \tag{14.7}$$

14.4.2 Hub-Spoke Structures and Transit Flows

As previously described, a *hub-spoke* structure exists where an apparent transport flow *i-j* is connected with a preceding flow (with i serving as a Hub: $i = H$) or a subsequent one (with j serving as a Hub: $j = H$). For simplicity, we focus on the latter case, and we assume that there is no concatenation of two *transit flows*. We also assume that *transit flows* can be associated with any combination of transport modes (R, T, S, A).

With this approach, any i or j in a system of N (n × n) bilateral flows *i-j* can behave as a *Hub*. With this idea in mind, we formulate an approach linked to the gravity equation and the spatial autocorrelation effects described before. This strategy for modeling transit flows in *hub-spoke* structures assumes that every province j is a potential *Hub* (H). Thus, much as in the previous case, if we wish to explain a flow by road from i (Barcelona) to j (Zaragoza), we should consider the possibility that j (Zaragoza) will become H—that is, that it will re-export the same load, or some part of it, to a third province d (Madrid). Thus, j's absorption capacity (i.e., Zaragoza's GDP) should be reinforced with variables explaining the possibility of j's being H (Zaragoza). This possibility is based on, among other factors, the number of potential re-exporting flows of the same product k that is delivered from j to other destinations in the country (in this case, Madrid as a final destination). As we will see in Eq. (14.8), we can easily put this intuition to use in the standard structure of an SAR model, but using a special version of the weight matrix, labeled W_H (H for *Hub*):

$$\begin{aligned} \ln F_{ji}^{km} = {} & \alpha i_N + X_i\beta_1 + X_j\beta_2 + \ln d_{ji}\beta_3 + Intra\beta_4 + Adj\beta_5 + \ln\left(gdp_i{}^{*}gdp_j\right)\beta_6 \\ & + \rho_2 W_H \ln F_{ji}^{km} + \varepsilon_{ji} \end{aligned} \tag{14.8}$$

where $\rho_2 W_H \ln F_{ji}^{km}$ is a spatial lag term similar to the one in Eq. (14.4). The main difference lies in weight matrix W_H, which, unlike $W = W_i + W_j$ (defined on a purely spatial basis), is defined on the basis of actual trade flows for a given sector

[7]Remember that the OD matrix used for the endogenous variable is expressed with "destinations" in rows and "origins" in columns.

k and a given transport mode m (the aggregate in our empirical application). The goal of W_H is to capture all flows departing from a given destination j to any other province d in the system. To be more restrictive, we consider all potential (final) destinations d with the exception of i. Thus, we exclude the possibility that an initial flow of product k from region i to region j will be re-exported afterwards (with no further transformation) from j to i. The procedure to obtain this W_H matrix is as follows:

First, it is convenient to remember that the structure of all of our observations is *destination-based*, using the terminology of LeSage and Pace (2009). Thus, we produce W_H as a matrix with n block matrices each one of it referring to each exporting province i. This W_H matrix is defined in such a way as to capture every (subsequent) flow *departing* from the destination province j of a given dyad $i \to j$. Three alternative criteria are used to fill in this matrix W_H:

Option A: As described in Eq. (14.9), the first version of these matrices is W_{Ha}, which contains a set of n rectangular matrices A_n where all potential flows departing from H to any third destination j (except i) have a one, or otherwise a zero. The matrix thus links every flow $i \to H$ with every flow $H \to j$ (j being any province in the system except i).

$$W_{Ha} = \begin{pmatrix} A_1 \\ A_2 \\ \vdots \\ A_n \end{pmatrix} \tag{14.9}$$

To better illustrate our approach, the structure of three matrices ($A_1, A_2, \ldots A_5$) corresponding to a system of n = 5 provinces is described below.

$$A_1 = \begin{pmatrix} 0\,1\,1\,1\,1\,0\,0\,0\,0\,0\,0\,0\,0\,0\,0\,0\,0\,0\,0\,0\,0\,0\,0\,0\,0 \\ 0\,0\,0\,0\,0\,0\,1\,1\,1\,1\,0\,0\,0\,0\,0\,0\,0\,0\,0\,0\,0\,0\,0\,0\,0 \\ 0\,0\,0\,0\,0\,0\,0\,0\,0\,0\,0\,1\,1\,1\,1\,0\,0\,0\,0\,0\,0\,0\,0\,0\,0 \\ 0\,0\,0\,0\,0\,0\,0\,0\,0\,0\,0\,0\,0\,0\,0\,0\,1\,1\,1\,1\,0\,0\,0\,0\,0 \\ 0\,0\,0\,0\,0\,0\,0\,0\,0\,0\,0\,0\,0\,0\,0\,0\,0\,0\,0\,0\,0\,1\,1\,1\,1 \end{pmatrix}$$

$$A_2 = \begin{pmatrix} 1\,0\,1\,1\,1\,0\,0\,0\,0\,0\,0\,0\,0\,0\,0\,0\,0\,0\,0\,0\,0\,0\,0\,0\,0 \\ 0\,0\,0\,0\,0\,1\,0\,1\,1\,1\,0\,0\,0\,0\,0\,0\,0\,0\,0\,0\,0\,0\,0\,0\,0 \\ 0\,0\,0\,0\,0\,0\,0\,0\,0\,0\,1\,0\,1\,1\,1\,0\,0\,0\,0\,0\,0\,0\,0\,0\,0 \\ 0\,0\,0\,0\,0\,0\,0\,0\,0\,0\,0\,0\,0\,0\,0\,1\,0\,1\,1\,1\,0\,0\,0\,0\,0 \\ 0\,0\,0\,0\,0\,0\,0\,0\,0\,0\,0\,0\,0\,0\,0\,0\,0\,0\,0\,0\,1\,0\,1\,1\,1 \end{pmatrix} \ldots$$

$$A_5 = \begin{pmatrix} 1\,1\,1\,1\,0\,0\,0\,0\,0\,0\,0\,0\,0\,0\,0\,0\,0\,0\,0\,0\,0\,0\,0\,0\,0 \\ 0\,0\,0\,0\,0\,1\,1\,1\,1\,0\,0\,0\,0\,0\,0\,0\,0\,0\,0\,0\,0\,0\,0\,0\,0 \\ 0\,0\,0\,0\,0\,0\,0\,0\,0\,0\,1\,1\,1\,1\,0\,0\,0\,0\,0\,0\,0\,0\,0\,0\,0 \\ 0\,0\,0\,0\,0\,0\,0\,0\,0\,0\,0\,0\,0\,0\,0\,1\,1\,1\,1\,0\,0\,0\,0\,0\,0 \\ 0\,0\,0\,0\,0\,0\,0\,0\,0\,0\,0\,0\,0\,0\,0\,0\,0\,0\,0\,0\,1\,1\,1\,1\,0 \end{pmatrix}$$

Note that with this procedure, and for every j-i flow in the system, we consider j as a potential *Hub* (so we denote them with an H, while j is used just to denote the final destination of the subsequent re-exportation flows). Therefore W_{Ha} can be described as a variation on a pure *destination-based dependence* like W_j in LeSage and Pace (2008, 2009). It is also important to note that the previous matrix, W_{Ha}, gives the same weight to all potential re-exported flows from H (the potential *Hub*) to any subsequent final destination j (except i). Such an approach could be considered naive, since the farther H is with regards to the final destination j the lower the likelihood that such flow is a re-exportation of a previous one. This is the reason why two alternative definitions of hub-spoke schemes are defined below.

Option B: A more restrictive way to define this hub-spoke structure is described by W_{Hb} in Eq. (14.10). Now, the matrix W_{Hb} contains n rectangular matrices of type B_n, which contain ones for the flows from H to its contiguous regions n_H, and zeros otherwise. We thus link every flow $i \rightarrow H$ with every flow $H \rightarrow n_H$. Following with the previous example of a system with five provinces, a flow from $1 \rightarrow 2$ is connected only to the flow from 2 (the potential *Hub*) to its contiguous province {1; 4}, setting to zero the other three elements. This situation is captured by a matrix W_{Hb}, which has a similar structure than W_{Ha}, but has just ones when the destination province of the first flow is re-exporting to its contiguous provinces.[8] Note also that the perfect-loop elements have also a zero.

$$W_{Hb} = \begin{pmatrix} B_1 \\ B_2 \\ \vdots \\ B_n \end{pmatrix} \tag{14.10}$$

Option C: Our final version of weight matrix is based on Eq. (14.11), where W_{Hc} contains a set of n rectangular matrix C_n. Here as in W_{Ha}, we link every flow $i \rightarrow H$

[8]Note that, by means of W_{Hb}, flow $i \rightarrow j$ is associated with (subsequent) flow $j \rightarrow n_j$. This "network autocorrelation scheme", which is explained by "re-exporting" activity within a "hub-spoke" structure, is different from the typical "destination-base" spatial autocorrelation scheme (LeSage and Pace 2008, 2009), where, by means of matrix W_j, flow $i \rightarrow j$ is associated with the flow from the same origin i to the neighbor of destination j (here labeled n_j).

with every flow $H \rightarrow j$ (except i) but assigning a different weight to each potential re-exportation flow. The weight structure is based on the inverse of the distance from the *Hub* (H) to the final destination (j). Thus the closer is H to j, the larger the weight for the potential re-exporting flow $H \rightarrow j$.

$$W_{Hc} = \begin{pmatrix} C_1 \\ C_2 \\ \vdots \\ C_n \end{pmatrix} \tag{14.11}$$

Following with our previous example's flow F_{21} in a system of five provinces, the first block rectangular matrix C_1 will be as the one below, where the flow F_{21} is associated with all the flows delivered from the potential Hub ($H = 2$) to the remaining destinations $\{F_{22}, F_{32}, F_{42}, F_{52}\}$, again with the exclusion of the perfect loop (F_{12}). Now, however, the weight of each of these *potential re-exporting flows* depends on the inverse of the distance to the potential Hub (d_{22}; d_{32}; d_{42}; d_{52}).

$$C_1 = \begin{pmatrix} 0 & 1/d_{12} & 1/d_{13} & 1/d_{14} & 1/d_{15} & 0 & 0 & 0 & 0 & 0 & \cdots 0 & 0 & 0 & 0 & 0 \\ 0 & 0 & 0 & 0 & 0 & 0 & 1/d_{22} & 1/d_{23} & 1/d_{24} & 1/d_{25} & \cdots 0 & 0 & 0 & 0 & 0 \\ 0 & 0 & 0 & 0 & 0 & 0 & 0 & 0 & 0 & 0 & \cdots 0 & 0 & 0 & 0 & 0 \\ 0 & 0 & 0 & 0 & 0 & 0 & 0 & 0 & 0 & 0 & \cdots 0 & 0 & 0 & 0 & 0 \\ 0 & 0 & 0 & 0 & 0 & 0 & 0 & 0 & 0 & 0 & \cdots 0 & 1/d_{52} & 1/d_{53} & 1/d_{54} & 1/d_{55} \end{pmatrix}$$

Finally, it is worth mentioning that in none of the previous specifications, which are based in the SAR model, we are able to deal with *inter-modal* hub-spoke structures (multimodality: combination of different transport modes between two concatenated flows). Such option, is beyond the scope of this paper, and will be made in future research. However, since some of our specifications use aggregate flows (all transport modes analyzed together), it can be argued that multimodal transport relations are somehow present in these examples.

For the sake of clarity, Fig. 14.3 summarizes the different models and weight matrices considered in this paper.

14.5 Data

The dataset used in this paper to feed in the endogenous variable (flows) is based on the most accurate data on Spanish transport flows of goods by transport mode (road, train, ship, aircraft), in addition to 50 specific export price vectors, one for each province of origin, transport mode and product type. This rich dataset was collected and filtered in accord with the methodology described in Llano et al. (2010) and

Model	Endogenous variable	Exogenous variables (just the variables for the exporting province are reported)	Weight matrix
Baseline Models			
M1	All modes (aggreg.)	**Monadic:** *Island_i*; **Dyadic:** $Ln\ (d_{ij})$; *Intra*; *Adj*; $Ln\ (gdp_i{*}gdp_j)$	None
M2	Road	As in M1	None
M3	Train	As in M1	None
M4	Ship	As in M1	None
M5	Aircraft	As in M1	None
M6	All modes (aggreg.)	**Monadic:** *Ln (wholesales_pc_i)*; *Island_i*; *Border_int_coreEU_i*; *Border_int_other_i*; *Ln (imp_int_all_gdp_i)* ***Dyadic:*** $Ln\ (d_{ij})$; *Intra*; *Adj*; $Ln\ (gdp_i{*}gdp_j)$	None
M7	Road	**Monadic:** As in M6 **Dyadic:** Idem than in M6 + $Ln(FT_{ij})$; $Ln(FS_{ij})$; $Ln(FA_{ij})$;	None
Transport Mode Competition			
M8	Road	**Monadic:** As in M6 **Dyadic:** Idem than in M6 + $Ln(F^T{}_{ij})$; $Ln(F^S{}_{ij})$; $Ln(F^A{}_{ij})$;	Spatial *W*
M9	Train	**Monadic:** As in M6 **Dyadic:** Idem than in M6 + $Ln(F^R{}_{ij})$; $Ln(F^S{}_{ij})$; $Ln(F^A{}_{ij})$;	Spatial *W*
M10	Ship	**Monadic:** As in M6 **Dyadic:** Idem than in M6 + $Ln(F^R{}_{ij})$; $Ln(F^T{}_{ij})$; $Ln(F^A{}_{ij})$;	Spatial *W*
M11	Aircraft	**Monadic:** As in M6 **Dyadic:** Idem than in M6 + $Ln(F^R{}_{ij})$; $Ln(F^T{}_{ij})$; $Ln(F^S{}_{ij})$;	Spatial *W*
Transport Mode Cooperation: hub-spoke structures			
M12	All modes (aggreg.)	As in M6	W_{Ha}
M13	All modes (aggreg.)	As in M6	W_{Hb}
M14	All modes (aggreg.)	As in M6	W_{Hc}
Transport Mode Cooperation: hub-spoke structures with sector specific flows			
M14	All modes (by sector)	As in M6. Note that some variables are *k* specific	W_{Hc}

W for controlling for origin + destination base spatial autocorrelation: $W = W_i + W_j$

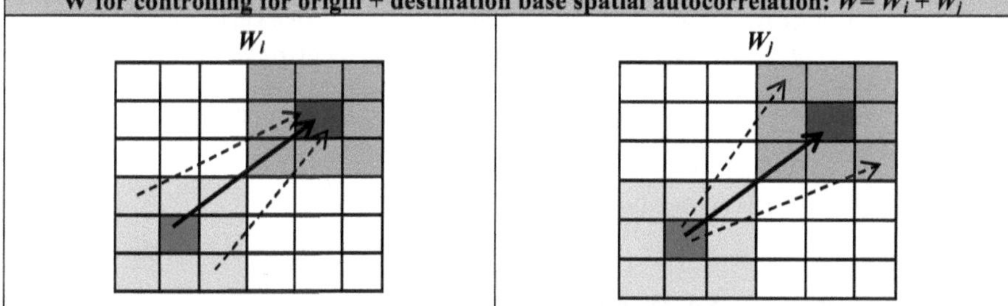

W_H matrices to control for *hub-spoke structures*

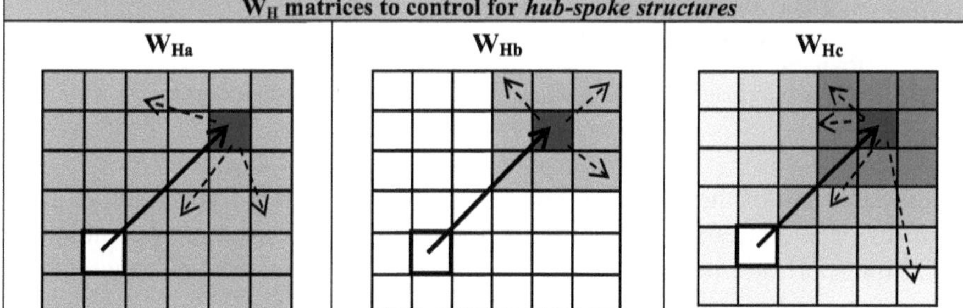

Fig. 14.3 Scheme describing the empirical strategy

Table 14.1 Transport statistics used to estimate Spanish interregional trade

Mode	Description and main features
Road	***Permanent Survey on Goods Transport by Road*** **(*Encuesta Permanente de Mercancías por Carretera*)** • **Source**: Ministerio de Fomento (Spanish Ministry of Public Works) • **Product Disaggregation**: 160 products (class. NSTR-3 digits) • **Availability**: 1995–present **Remarks**: • Permanent survey on the activity of a large sample of trucks in Spain: each trip includes origin–destination, product type, volume, distance (km), etc. • Survey may also include international transit flows from ports/airports to final destinations • It should be noted that figures obtained from truck surveys can be inconsistent with figures on production/purchases from firms/household surveys
Train	***RENFE Statistics on Complete Wagon and Container Flows*** • **Source**: *Statistics Department of RENFE* • **Product Disaggregation**: approx. 40 categories (RENFE classification) **Remarks**: • Every domestic flow recorded: high quality, low product detail • No information on products transported by container (30 % of rail flows)
Ship	***Statistics from Spanish Ports*** **(*Puertos del Estado*)** *Indirect estimation of interregional flow matrices using optimization procedure based on*: (a) *Tons loaded/unloaded per Spanish port, flow type, product type* • **Source**: **Statistical Yearbook. Puertos del Estado** • **Data**: Annual. 27 Spanish ports • **Product Disaggregation**: 40 products (Puertos del Estado classification) (b) *Set of Spanish domestic flow matrices with Ports of Origin and Destination.1989* • **Source**: Domestic maritime flows by Origin and Destination. 1989. Puertos del Estado • **Data**: Annual. 38 largest Spanish ports (at the time) • **Product Disaggregation**: 52 products (CSTE)
Aircraft	*O/D matrices of domestic flows of goods by airport of origin and destination 1995. AENA* • **Source**: AENA & Ministerio de Fomento • **Data**: Annual. Main Spanish Airports • **Product Disaggregation**: None **Remarks**: • No information on sectoral disaggregation of domestic flows by air

published as part of the C-intereg project (www.c-intereg.es).[9] The result is initial estimates of interprovincial trade flows in current euros, based on a combination of the transport and price databases. At each stage up to the final aggregation,

[9]The data used in this paper is not exactly the same than the official figures generated by C-intereg project. The reason is that in this paper, we want to be as close as possible to the original statistical source, rather than to use the C-intereg ones, which has been object of several final adjustments with regards to the Spanish national accounts and industrial business surveys.

Table 14.2 Variables

Name (variables for importing regions are reported in parentheses)	Description	Source
$F_{ji}^{kR}; F_{ji}^{kT}; F_{ji}^{kS}; F_{ji}^{kA}$	Inter-provincial flows in Spain by transport mode (R, T, S and A) and sector (k = all sectors, or product specific flows for 15 sectors)	Several sources reported in Table 14.1. Prepared for the C-intereg project
Pop_i (Pop_j)	Population of province *i* (Population of province *j*)	INE. Regional accounts
GDP_i (GDP_j)	Gross Domestic Product of province *i* (Gross Domestic Product of province *j*)	INE. Regional accounts
d_{ij}	• For distance within the Iberian Peninsula: actual distance traveled by trucks on their deliveries (EPTMC) • For distance between provinces within the Iberian Peninsula and islands: actual distance to main ports + actual distance from ports to islands by ship	• EPTMC. Ministerio de Fomento • Puertos del Estado
Intra	Dummy variable that takes value 1 if $i = j$ and 0 otherwise	Authors
Adj	Dummy variable that takes value 1 if *i* and *j* share a common border within Spain and 0 otherwise	Authors
Wholesales pc_i (*Wholesales* pc_j)	Ratio between number of wholesale activities in province *i* (*j*) and population of same province	La Caixa et al. 2013
$Island_i$ ($Island_j$)	Dummy variable that takes value 1 if exporting region *i* (importing province *j*) is an island province: Islas Baleares; Las Palmas and Santa Cruz de Tenerife	Authors
Imp. int. all/gdp_i (*Exp. int. all*/gdp_i)	International imports of all products in province *i* regardless of transport mode (Idem for exports in province *j*)	Official international trade data. AEAT
Imp. int.all^k/gdp_i (*Exp. int. all*^{k}/gdp_j).	International imports of product *k* in province *i* regardless of transport mode (Idem for exports in province *j*)	Official international trade data. AEAT
Border int. core EU_i (*Border int. core* EU_j)	Dummy variable that takes value 1 for Spanish provinces bordering on France or Andorra and 0 otherwise. (Idem for province *j*)	Authors
Border int. $other_i$ (*Border int.* $other_j$)	Dummy variable that takes value 1 for Spanish provinces bordering on Portugal or Africa and 0 otherwise. (Idem for province *j*)	Authors

the methodology relies on the lowest level of disaggregation available. Table 14.1 provides a summary of the original information used for each transport mode, while Table 14.2 describes the variables used as regressors.

14.6 Descriptive Analysis

The aim of this section is to describe the dataset. Our initial exploration aims to describe as thoroughly as possible the logistical complexity previously introduced. We will define a general index and explain our use, through GIS software, of some very rich information about the actual transportation network. The starting point of this analysis is found in Fig. 14.4, which depicts total inter-provincial flows for each province in 2007.

As shown, the main inter-provincial flows stem from Spain's richest provinces: Madrid, Barcelona, Valencia, Sevilla and Zaragoza. The northeast shows high trade volume; the west and south, low. As we will see later, this localization of trade flows is driven by network infrastructure (road, port and rail networks), which determine the transport mode used in each province.

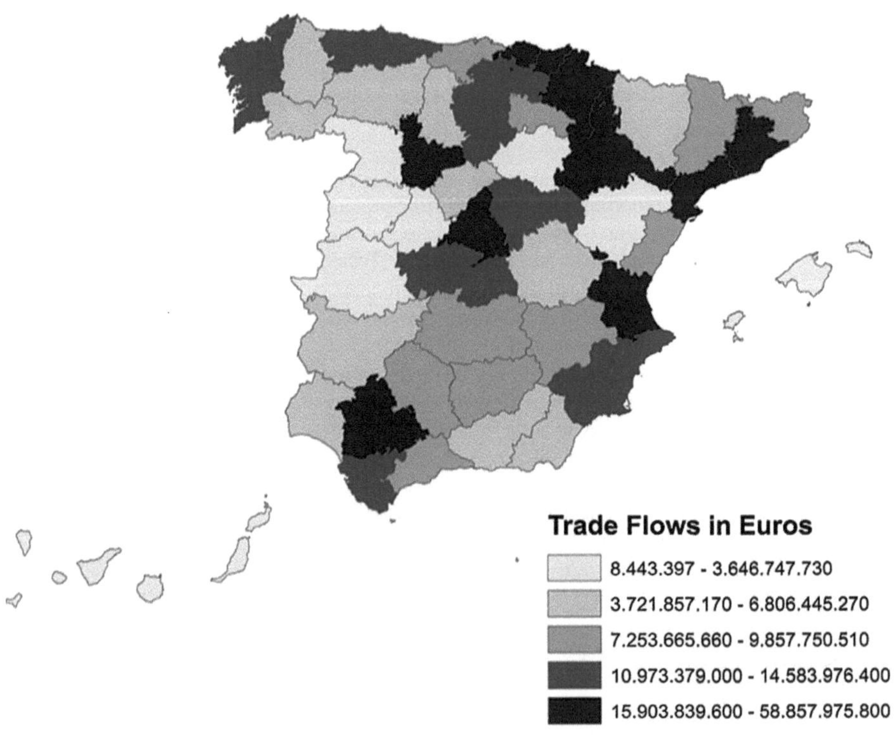

Fig. 14.4 Total trade flows (exports) by provinces (2007). Euros

This previous map breaks down trade flows by transport mode composition in order to bring out the transport specialization of each province. Our exploratory analysis aims to determine which provinces maintain high-level exporting and importing flows for each transport mode. A high intensity of inflows and outflows for a specific sector could be due to intra-industry trade, where interchanges between the production and consumption of goods occur within the same place and sector, or to product re-exporting flows, where third regions act as intermediate trade points between the actual origin and destination provinces (i.e., regions which receive and dispatch the same sector's inflows and outflows through the same transport mode).

To this end, we propose the "*Intra-Mode Re-exporting Index* (*IMRI*)" described in Eq. (14.12). It identifies provinces that can be considered as re-exporting points (hub-regions). The *IMRI* represents provinces that maintain a significant level of intra-mode trade flows: i.e., that move significant exports and imports by the same transport mode (m).

$$IMRI_i^m = \frac{1}{K}\sum_{k=1}^{K}\left(\frac{F_{.i}^{km} + F_{.i}^{km}}{\max\left(F_{j.}^{km} + F_{.j}^{km}\right)}\left(1 - \frac{\left|F_{i.}^{km} - F_{.i}^{km}\right|}{F_{i.}^{km} + F_{.i}^{km}}\right)\right) \tag{14.12}$$

This index is a version of the well-known Grubel and Lloyd (1975) index, which is the standard tool for measuring intra-industry trade between countries. Here, instead of international trade flows (regardless of transport mode), we use inter-provincial freight flows split by transport mode, where the variable $F_{.i}$ represents total freight flows with an origin in province i and a destination elsewhere in the country, freight flows within i itself is excluded. Conversely, the variable $F_{i.}$ represents the total inter-provincial freight flows that arriving at that province from elsewhere in the country. As a first step, the index focuses strictly on each transport mode m in sector k. The authors proposed their index to evaluate the extent to which intra-industry trade was more important than inter-industry trade between countries. As our definition of the index shows, the Grubel-Lloyd index is implemented on the last term on the right-hand side of the equation. We have included a term to weight the importance of exports and imports, in freight flows, of region i in sector k by transport mode m, relative to the maximum level of exports plus imports observed in the data for sector k and transport mode m.

If total importing freight flows for province i in sector k ($F_{i.}^{km}$) are equal to province i's total exporting freight flows ($F_{.i}^{km}$), the ratio of the second term of the *IMRI* index is zero, and the whole term equals one. On the other side, if a province receives or sends freight flows only within the same sector and transport mode—i.e., buys or sells goods only from sector k—the second term of the *IMRI* index equals zero. Finally, to summarize the information, we take the average mean for the 15 sectors to obtain one unique index by transport mode for each province. If the index for a specific province and transport mode approaches the value one, the province is, in relation to the rest of Spain, a re-exporting province (potential "Hub") with a high intensity of trade flows by that transport mode. By contrast, if the index is

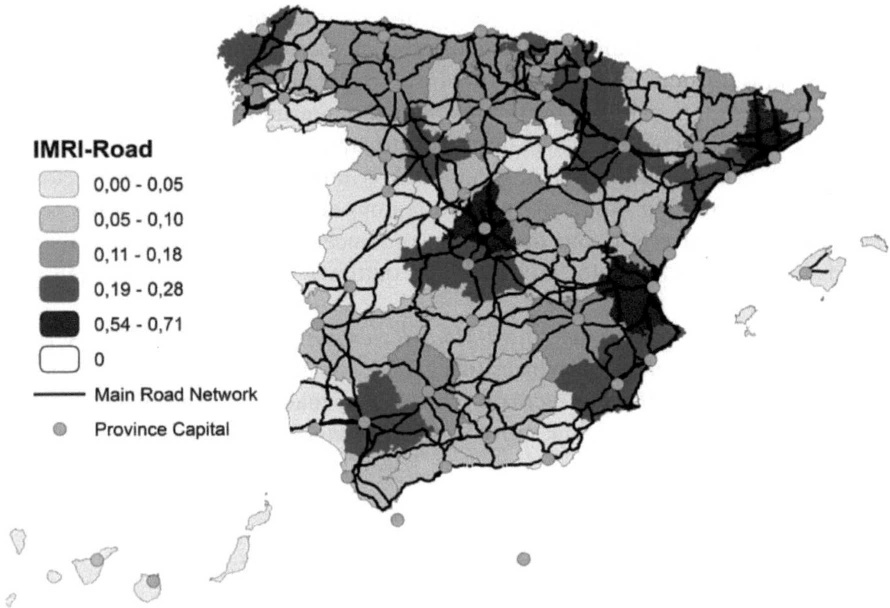

Fig. 14.5 IMRI for road freight flows (2007)

closer to zero, the province could be a site of consumption or of production without re-exporting flows.

The following maps show this index, highlighting each transport mode. Figure 14.5, showing the main road network in Spain (highways and national routes), reflects the *IMRI* for road by province. At a glance, the index identifies three main "*Hubs*" (Madrid, Barcelona and Valencia) when the "*road*" transport mode is considered alone. These regions present the widest road-crossing intensity, with a positive correlation between re-exporting flows by road and the *actual road network*, especially for regions crossed by main highways. Other provinces (Zaragoza, Sevilla, Valladolid and the three provinces of the País Vasco), which show a high volume of trade flows in Fig. 14.4, are not as important in terms of re-exporting intensity. As we will see later, this could be because other transport modes account for their trade-flow intensity.

Figure 14.6 reflects the *IMRI* for rail and the main Spanish rail network. Again, there exists a high correlation between the rail network and re-exporting trade flows by train. Here the potential "*Hubs*" are Madrid, Barcelona, Valencia and Vizcaya in the north of Spain, with important provinces to the northeast and the south. Indeed, there exists a positive correlation between provinces that re-export by rail and provinces that re-export by road.

As for trade flows by ship (Fig. 14.7), as expected, only provinces with ports (the islands, Cádiz in the south and, at lower intensity, Valencia and Barcelona on the Mediterranean coast) appear to be potential "*Hubs*", since they receive high-

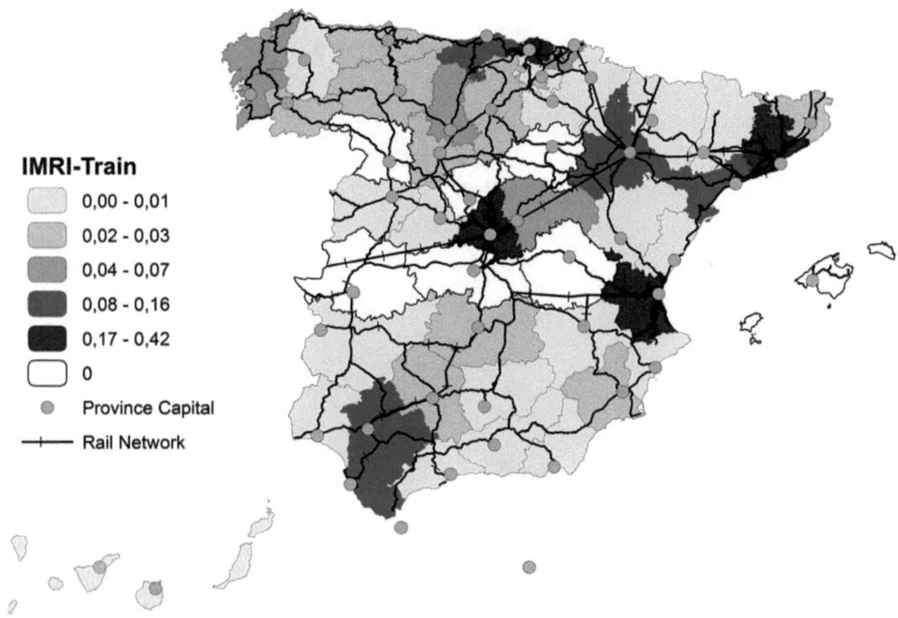

Fig. 14.6 IMRI for train freight flows (2007)

intensity inflows from the rest of Spain for export outflows to the islands (Islas Baleares and Islas Canarias) or to other provinces with ports. Anecdotally, it is interesting to highlight that some landlocked provinces show slight (but not null) intensity of inflows/outflows by ship. This is because trade-flow statistics with the Islas Canarias are, as explained in the Annex, official statistics from the AEAT, which collects the data that establishes the main transport mode used in the freight flow. That is, a freight flow originating in a landlocked province and proceeding by road to a port before taking a ship is nevertheless recorded as a delivery by ship from the landlocked province.

Finally, Fig. 14.8 presents the *IMRI* for aircraft flows, along with the location of the main Spanish commercial airports. Again, Madrid, Valencia and Barcelona appear to be the potential "Hubs", with Madrid's Barajas airport, one of the largest in Europe, playing a particularly important role and maintaining high-frequency freight flows with the Islas Canarias (Las Palmas and Santa Cruz de Tenerife). Here the Islas Baleares and the Islas Canarias are also important hub-provinces for airplanes, because most of their re-exporting flows occur between the small islands forming each province (e.g., the single province of the Islas Baleares, which includes such islands as Mallorca, Menorca, Ibiza and Cabrera) and use planes as the most efficient transport mode. For inland provinces with airplane freight flows but no airport, we advance the same explanation as in the case of ship flows, although freight-flow volumes tend to be insignificant in these provinces.

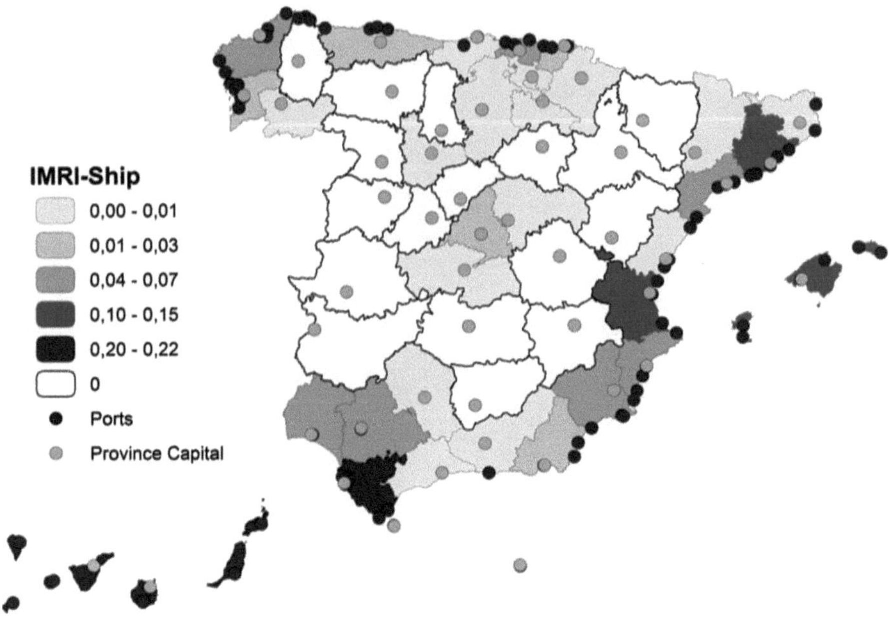

Fig. 14.7 IMRI for ship freight flows (2007)

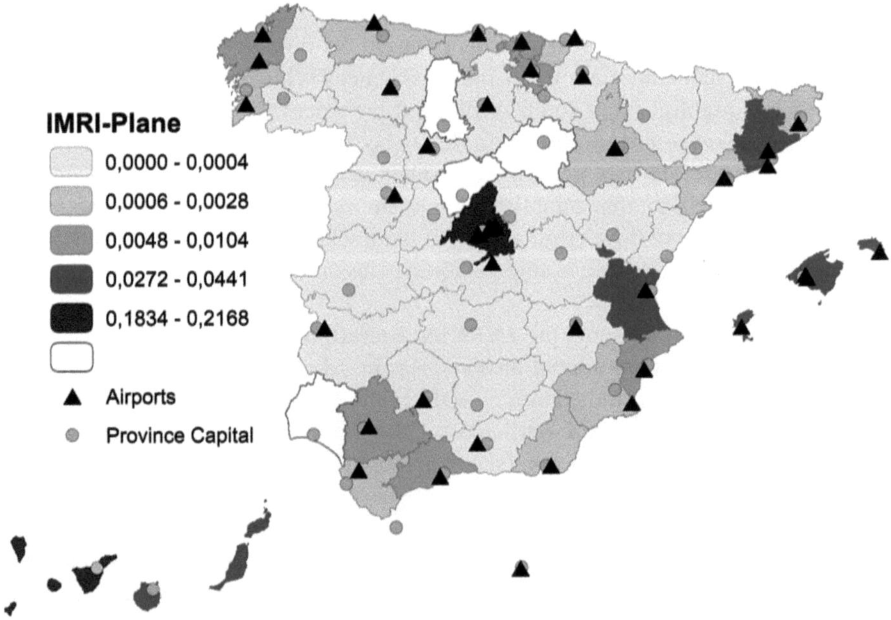

Fig. 14.8 IMRI for aircraft freight flows (2007)

14.7 Econometric Analysis

In this section we present estimates for the expressions in Sect. 14.4. The analysis is divided into two parts. First, we present a set of models to consider flows that are aggregated from the sectoral perspective but (sometimes) disaggregated from the transport-mode perspective. Then, focusing on the *hub-spoke* structures, we complement this analysis with an additional section where sector specific flows are analyzed in light of our main models. For each model it is important to consider the entry of endogenous variables, as well as aggregate or sector-specific factors considered regressors. We want to remark at this point that the number of alternative—an interesting—specifications is very large. Due to the nature of this contribution, we explore the main ones, leaving others for further developments.

14.7.1 Aggregate Flows by Modes

Our analysis begins with basic specifications of the gravity equation, with aggregate flows and OLS estimation procedure. The results are reported in Table 14.3 correspond to the results obtained using Eqs. (14.2) and (14.3). The first five columns (M1–M5) present the results for aggregate trade flows. In the case of M1 all transport modes are analyzed together, while the other four columns contain the results for each mode-specific delivery. In all cases, the most basic gravity model is taken into account. Models M6 and M7 reflect estimations for an augmented gravity model, including, among other variables, the per-capita wholesale variable for the origin and the destination. M6 uses aggregate flows by all modes while M7 focuses on flows by road, and tests cross-relationships between this mode and the other three.

The results for aggregate flows are in line with the standard results of the gravity-model literature for interregional trade flows; we find significant and negative coefficients for distance and positive and significant coefficients for the product of the GDP of the trading provinces. The positive and significant result for the *Intra* dummy also confirms that intra-provincial flows are much higher than inter-provincial flows; this result is consistent with the *border-effect* and *regional home bias* literature for almost all countries and circumstances. The coefficient observed for the *Adj* (contiguity) variable is also positive and significant in all models, indicating that adjacent provinces tend to trade above average. For transport-mode-specific (but still sectorally aggregated) flows, and for flows by road (the most relevant) and train, we find consistent results with M1, although for road flows (M2) island geography and distance have a much higher negative impact on trade. It is also remarkable that the positive coefficient obtained for some modes is slightly similar to the one for *Intra* (road and train), but considerable smaller for the other two (ship and aircraft).

Table 14.3 Ordinary least squares

	M1	M2	M3	M4	M5	M6	M7
Dependent variable	All (aggreg.) $Ln(F_{ji})$	Road $Ln(F^{R}{}_{ji})$	Train $Ln(F^{T}{}_{ji})$	Ship $Ln(F^{S}{}_{ji})$	Aircraft $Ln(F^{A}{}_{ji})$	All (aggreg.) $Ln(F_{ji})$	Road $Ln(F^{R}{}_{ji})$
Rbar-squared	0.2659	0.3327	0.2473	0.4261	0.5687	0.2935	0.3678
sigma^2	28.2454	31.5186	31.3485	22.8288	7.0719	27.1812	29.8597
Const	−10.327***	−4.859**	−36.268***	−39.314***	−22.989***	−21.988***	−9.518**
	(−5.047)	(−2.248)	(−16.824)	(−21.371)	(−22.453)	(−6.387)	(−2.431)
Ln (wholesales_pc_i)						0.496	0.891*
						(1.053)	(1.789)
Island_i	−3.065***	−7.002***	−4.09***	6.323***	5.719***	−2.49***	−7.691***
	(−6.224)	(−13.462)	(−7.884)	(14.283)	(23.21)	(−4.97)	(−12.822)
Border_int_coreEU_i						0.12	0.233
						(0.327)	(0.606)
Border_int_other_i						−0.547*	−0.582*
						(−1.835)	(−1.856)
Ln (imp_int_all_gdp_i)						0.994***	0.712***
						(7.784)	(5.211)
Ln (wholesales_pc_j)						2.139***	2.836***
						(4.688)	(5.882)
Island_j	0.498	−3.615***	−3.188***	9.032***	7.808***	−0.907	−7.017***
	(1.012)	(−6.949)	(−6.146)	(20.402)	(31.69)	(−1.548)	(−9.962)
Border_int_coreEU_j						−0.86**	−0.569
						(−2.377)	(−1.493)
Border_int_other_j						−0.338	−0.617**
						(−1.133)	(−1.97)
Ln (exp_int_all_gdp_j)						−0.453***	−0.559***
						(−3.62)	(−4.176)

Ln (d_{ji})	−2.02***	−2.722***	−0.611**	1.819***	0.93***	−1.977***	−2.887***
	(−8.748)	(−11.16)	(−2.511)	(8.764)	(8.052)	(−8.537)	(−11.587)
Intra	3.176***	2.701***	2.996***	6.871***	1.212***	3.258***	2.269**
	(3.575)	(2.878)	(3.201)	(8.603)	(2.728)	(3.717)	(2.427)
Adj	2.71***	2.347***	2.521***	2.587***	0.788***	2.718***	2.007***
	(5.92)	(4.854)	(5.227)	(6.286)	(3.441)	(6.024)	(4.184)
Ln($F^T{}_{ji}$)							0.049**
							(2.424)
Ln($F^S{}_{ji}$)							0.01
							(0.436)
Ln($F^A{}_{ji}$)							0.218***
							(5.056)
Ln (*gdpi***gdpj*)	2.04***	1.963***	2.33***	1.57***	0.943***	1.591***	1.137***
	(23.884)	(21.762)	(25.889)	(20.447)	(22.061)	(15.139)	(9.121)

***$p < 0.01$, **$p < 0.05$, *$p < 0.1$, all variables except the dummies in log form

For ship (M4) and aircraft (M5) flows, we obtain new and promising results. In these regressions, the *distance* and *island* variables present signs opposite to those obtained previously in the literature. We find a positive effect for both variables, thereby confirming the heterogeneity of trade, distance, transport costs and transport-mode competition. This result, in our view, confirms that the use of these two modes increases with the distance between origin and destination, something that usually occurs for an island. Concretely, for some locations (islands) aircraft and ships are the only transport modes available for trade. Consequently, the *distance* and *island* dummy variables have a positive sign. The intra-region dummy variable also presents a positive sign, because ships and aircraft are the main transport modes used to supply other locations (smalls islands) within the same province.

The M6 and M7 regressions present the augmented gravity model specifically including international trade flows (exports and imports) and dummy variables that indicate a border with a European core-country (basically France) or with other countries to the south, such as Portugal and Morocco. Both columns show consistent results, where the product of GDPs, distance and islands have the expected impact on trade. More interestingly, international imports seem to be positively correlated with the capacity of exporting within the country, which can be interpreted as a large content of international imports on inter-provincial exports, or as a sign of a pure international *hub-spoke* structure. However, international exports intensity has a negative and significant coefficient, indicating that the larger the foreign exports of a region relative to its gdp, the lower their inter-provincial imports. Another interesting point of reference is the result for the dummy variable controlling for *border provinces*, which have no significant impact on trade except if the origin trade-flow province shares a border with a country other than a European core country (in which case the effect is in fact negative). This result is crucial for anyone using our dataset, or the official freight flows considered in this paper, since it indicates that the risk incurred when including international transit flows in the inter-provincial flows is non-significant for the border provinces, and just can be possible in the interprovincial exports of non-border provinces. Moreover, the negative sign found in many cases (significant only for *Border int. other*$_i$) also suggests a certain degree of international isolation in the Spanish border provinces, which indeed show a negative correlation between their international importing/exporting capacity and their inter-provincial exporting/importing deliveries. This result makes sense in light of the political tensions some of these border provinces have suffered with their international neighbors in the past and their tendency to be overshadowed by other, larger nearby Spanish provinces (e.g., Girona vs. Barcelona, Guipuzcoa vs. Vizcaya, Cáceres vs. Sevilla).

We move now to the other variables of interest in these models: namely, those that capture the role of logistics, warehouses and wholesale activity in each trading province. In M6 (aggregate flows by sectors and modes), just *Ln*(*wholesales_pc_j*) has a positive and significant coefficient. Conversely, in M7, where just flows by road are modeled, the two variables capturing the number of *wholesale per capita* for the exporting and importing provinces show a positive and significant impact on trade. Finally, it is interesting to remember that M7 accounts for the interrelation between three transport modes in the flows by road (endogenous variable). Remarkably, train and aircraft flows show a positive and significant effect on road flows, while ship flows present no significant impact. Such results suggest that pairs of provinces with intense flows by road can also have intense bilateral flows by train and aircraft and could be a sign of competition between transport modes, at least when all products are analyzed together.

All these regressions lead us to perform a set of tests to determine the existence of spatial autocorrelation in our model. Table 14.4 reflects various spatial tests, such as Moran's I, the LM error test, the LM lag test, the robust version of these tests and a combination of them. We have performed them for Eq. (14.4) the M6–M7 regressions, using the three pure spatial weight matrices separately (W_i, W_j, $W_i + W_j$). As we can observe, all tests reject the null hypotheses for the non-existence of spatial autocorrelation effects based on the origin, the destination and both. We have tested alternative spatial models on the basis of these results and found the spatial lag model to be the most suitable.

Table 14.5 reports the results for modeling aggregate flows from a sectoral perspective with spatial autoregressive effects considered. The first four models (M8–M11) use pure spatial dependence structures, defined by $W = W_i + W_j$ matrices. In all these models, then, we are testing for the presence of origin- and

Table 14.4 Spatial autocorrelation tests. Model 6–7

	M6			M7		
	W_i	W_j	$W = W_i + W_j$	W_i	W_j	$W = W_i + W_j$
Moran's I—test for spatial autocorrelation in the residuals						
Moran's I	0.132	0.1769	0.171	0.108	0.155	0.137
Moran's I-statistic	10.031	13.324	17.574	8.318	11.735	14.248
Marginal probability	0.000	0.000	0.000	0.000	0.000	0.000
LM error test for spatial autocorrelation in the residuals						
LM value	94.9614	169.780	290.659	64.155	130.352	187.921
Marginal probability	0.000	0.000	0.000	0.000	0.000	0.000
LM error test for spatial autocorrelation in the dependent variable						
LM value	15.410	62.529	215.827	12.626	78.528	142.281
Marginal probability	0.000	0.000	0.000	0.000	0.000	0.000
Robust LM error test						
LM value	129.540	143.787	77.667	88.230	56.664	48.780
Marginal probability	0.000	0.000	0.000	0.000	0.000	0.000
Robust LM lag test						
LM value	49.989	36.536	2.835	36.701	4.840	3.140
Marginal probability	0.000	0.000	0.092	0.000	0.027	0.07638727
Combined LM lag and LM error test						
LM value	144.951	206.317	293.494	100.856	135.192	191.061
Marginal probability	0.000	0.000	0.000	0.000	0.000	0.000

Table 14.5 Spatial autoregressive models

	M8	M9	M10	M11	M12	M13	M14
Mode flow type	Road $Ln(F^R{}_{ji})$	Train $Ln(F^T{}_{ji})$	Ship $Ln(F^S{}_{ji})$	Aircraft $Ln(F^A{}_{ji})$	All $Ln(F_{ji})$	All $Ln(F_{ji})$	All $Ln(F_{ji})$
W type	$W = W_i + W_j$	$W = W_i + W_j$	$W = W_i + W_j$	$W = W_i + W_j$	W_{Ha}	W_{Hb}	W_{Hc}
Rbar-squared	0.3565	0.2655	0.4527	0.6034	0.3036	0.2956	0.3097
sigma^2	27.636	26.7907	10.3381	5.0591	26.1254	26.9732	26.0934
log-likelihood	−6853.5281	−6824.9845	−5771.4396	−4766.837	−6764.5553	−6799.6221	−6768.5024
const	−14.757***	−30.879***	−11.401***	−11.987***	−18.386***	−22.414***	−20.586***
	(−3.885)	(−8.068)	(−4.966)	(−7.397)	(−5.367)	(−6.459)	(−6.036)
log(wholesales_pc_i)	0.702	−0.152	−1.143***	0.704***	0.99**	0.462	0.977**
	(1.461)	(−0.315)	(−3.905)	(3.431)	(2.113)	(0.973)	(2.083)
Island_i	−5.646***	−4.407***	0.824**	2.739***	−2.352***	−2.46***	−2.251***
	(−9.439)	(−7.589)	(2.254)	(11.661)	(−4.786)	(−4.928)	(−4.577)
Border_int_coreEU_i	−0.055	−0.503	−0.472**	−0.616***	0.046	0.154	0.06
	(−0.147)	(−1.371)	(−2.085)	(−3.897)	(0.128)	(0.421)	(0.167)
Border_int_other_i	−0.308	−0.547*	0.474**	0.022	−0.584**	−0.562*	−0.565*
	(−1.019)	(−1.836)	(2.569)	(0.167)	(−1.996)	(−1.892)	(−1.932)
Ln (imp_int_all_gdp_i)	0.591***	0.729***	0.389***	−0.127**	1.06***	0.99***	1.055***
	(4.485)	(5.617)	(4.835)	(−2.242)	(8.45)	(7.784)	(8.414)
Ln (wholesales_pc_j)	2.37***	0.031	−0.91***	0.646***	0.699	2.225***	1.054**
	(5.093)	(0.066)	(−3.176)	(3.225)	(1.46)	(4.869)	(2.257)
Island_j	−5.657***	−4.657***	2.102***	2.743***	1.094*	−0.92	−0.376
	(−8.248)	(−6.905)	(4.998)	(9.893)	(1.769)	(−1.576)	(−0.651)
Border_int_coreEU_j	−0.625*	−0.992***	−0.38*	−0.465***	−0.443	−0.88**	−0.544
	(−1.705)	(−2.747)	(−1.694)	(−2.968)	(−1.237)	(−2.44)	(−1.526)

Border_int_other_j	−0.376	0.344	0.565***	−0.011	0.105	−0.356	−0.034
	(−1.246)	(1.159)	(3.067)	(−0.086)	(0.354)	(−1.199)	(−0.116)
Ln(exp_int_all_gdp_j)	−0.477***	0.141	0.501***	−0.281***	−0.552***	−0.444***	−0.525***
	(−3.695)	(1.101)	(6.372)	(−5.159)	(−4.48)	(−3.558)	(−4.275)
Ln (d_{ji})	−1.976***	−0.44*	−0.267*	0.103	−1.995***	−1.998***	−2.076***
	(−7.903)	(−1.793)	(−1.753)	(0.985)	(−8.785)	(−8.65)	(−9.132)
Intra	2.37***	1.63*	2.568***	−0.348	3.284***	3.216***	3.374***
	(2.634)	(1.834)	(4.69)	(−0.9)	(3.82)	(3.681)	(3.927)
Adj	1.438***	1.438***	−0.15	−0.149	2.717***	6.906***	2.692***
	(3.103)	(3.142)	(−0.527)	(−0.751)	(6.142)	(19.108)	(6.089)
$Ln(F^{R}_{ji})$		0.042**	−0.008	0.024***			
		(2.231)	(−0.704)	(2.943)			
$Ln(F^{T}_{ji})$	0.043**		0.037***	0.044***			
	(2.228)		(3.1)	(5.379)			
$Ln(F^{S}_{ji})$	−0.004	0.044*		0.039***			
	(−0.17)	(1.939)		(4.034)			
$Ln(F^{A}_{ji})$	0.204***	0.261***	0.125***				
	(4.903)	(6.38)	(4.922)				
*log(gdpi*gdpj)*	1.016***	1.348***	0.704***	0.472***	1.305***	1.603***	1.316***
	(8.428)	(11.277)	(9.585)	(9.135)	(11.981)	(15.168)	(12.062)
ρ_1 (for M8-M11)	0.373***	0.443***	0.887***	0.572***	0.442***	−0.265***	0.433***
ρ_2 (for M12-M14)	(12.911)	(14.436)	(56.734)	(221.826)	(8.759)	(−15.66)	(8.37)

$^{***}p<0.01$, $^{**}p<0.05$, $^{*}p<0.1$; all variables except dummies in log form

destination-based spatial autocorrelation effects affecting flows by road (M8), train (M9), ship (M10) and aircraft (M11). In all cases, ρ_1 is positive and significant, indicating that the exporting and importing province's neighbors exert, on average, an enhancing effect on the trading dyads' bilateral flows. This result is consistent with previous papers and similar datasets in Spain (LeSage and Llano 2013; de la Mata and Llano 2013; Alamá-Sabater et al. 2013a, b). Results for the standard variables also meet expectations based on previous specifications. Among the exceptions is the variable *Border int. core EU* for the exporting and importing province, which, being negative and significant in more cases than previously, reinforces our previous conclusions. The special results for ships and aircraft also find confirmation. More interestingly, the four models include the flows of the other three. For road (M8) we find enhancing effects, as before, with trains and aircraft. For trains (M9), we find a positive correlation with road, ships and aircraft. As expected, for ships (M10) we find positive coefficients with trains and aircraft but not with road. Finally, for aircraft (M11) we obtain positive results with all other modes.

The last three columns of Table 14.5 reports the results when the flows for all transport modes are modeled with Eq. (14.8), designed specifically to deal with *hub-spoke* structure using a SAR-like structure. The only difference between the three models is the weight matrix used for capturing the re-exporting scheme of importing province *j* when it can be assumed to be serving as a *Hub* within the country. M12 uses W_{Ha}, M13 uses W_{Hb}, and M14 uses W_{Hc}. In M12 and M14, a positive and significant ρ_2 is obtained. Inversely, in M13, which uses the narrowest definition of re-exporting scheme, a negative and significant ρ is obtained. Focusing on the first two, in all humility and prudence, one cannot affirm when using aggregate flows that this result unequivocally proves the presence of a "hub-spoke" structure in the country. What it indicates is that, on average, with these two alternative measures for the re-exportation scheme, there is a positive and significant relation between inflows received by road at province *H* and exports dispatched by road from *H* to other provinces *j*. Again, with aggregate flows, this could be a sign of a hub-spoke structure, but it could also be an effect of intra-industry trade or an indication of strong urban provinces with intense inflows and outflows. Clearly, a more detailed analysis using sector specific flows is needed.

14.7.2 Product-Specific Flows

In Table 14.6 we report the results of using Eq. (14.8) and W_{Hc} to model sector-specific flows by the aggregate for all transport modes. This approach reduces the number of zeroes for each sector specific flow, a factor that could harm our strategy using a Maximum Likelihood estimator for our SAR specifications. As a robustness check, we have produced a number of alternative estimates, which are not reported for brevity. Such analyses are expected to be published in forthcoming articles extending this approach.

Table 14.6 Sector-specific analysis

	S1	S2	S3	S4	S5	S6	S7	S8	S9	S10	S11	S12	S13	S14
Rbar-squared	0.3299	0.3737	0.3518	0.2285	0.3225	0.3237	0.3852	0.3388	0.3032	0.3588	0.3909	0.3687	0.4431	0.2901
sigma^2	43.5777	36.8471	43.8939	15.0027	13.0625	33.1249	32.0619	39.9239	37.0921	34.7756	43.2212	20.884	31.9405	42.7168
log-likelihood	−7401.407	−7193.0653	−7415.9189	−6066.6078	−5898.014	−7059.5079	−7018.2147	−7291.8754	−7197.7467	−7121.6174	−7390.9612	−6482.6645	−7013.9386	−7380.3831
constant	−9.837**	−10.047*	−38.583***	−21.555***	−22.196***	−40.211***	−49.772***	−28.331***	−34.737***	−19.393***	−60.96***	−29.547***	−42.882***	−43.338***
	(−2.329)	(−1.658)	(−8.273)	(−7.965)	(−7.809)	(−8.082)	(−10.658)	(−5.757)	(−7.781)	(−4.232)	(−10.16)	(−8.731)	(−10.432)	(−7.569)
Ln(wholesale_pc_i)	−1.708***	−0.026	−0.102	0.835**	1.216***	2.507***	2.192***	0.917	2.035***	2.728***	4.16***	2.3***	1.431***	3.219***
	(−2.998)	(−0.047)	(−0.159)	(2.241)	(3.812)	(4.967)	(4.303)	(1.642)	(3.816)	(5.258)	(7.131)	(5.816)	(2.653)	(5.397)
Island_i	−0.11	1.233**	0.066	1.264***	4.017***	0.852	0.295	−0.936	−1.474**	−0.513	1.914***	4.58***	2.188***	3.619***
	(−0.177)	(2.125)	(0.101)	(3.436)	(11.542)	(1.526)	(0.524)	(−1.424)	(−2.547)	(−0.881)	(2.996)	(10.274)	(4.07)	(5.803)
Border_int_coreEU_i	−0.093	−2.172***	−0.906**	−0.698**	−1.216***	−1.658***	−0.325	−1.637***	−0.184	−1.18***	−0.261	−0.707**	−1.006**	−0.573
	(−0.202)	(−5.124)	(−1.961)	(−2.554)	(−4.83)	(−4.131)	(−0.823)	(−3.716)	(−0.432)	(−2.873)	(−0.57)	(−2.213)	(−2.541)	(−1.255)
Border_int_other_i	0.427	−0.111	0.27	−0.309	−0.295	0.134	−1.184***	−1.222***	−2.014***	−1.749***	0.017	0.141	−0.406	−0.233
	(1.121)	(−0.315)	(0.702)	(−1.392)	(−1.416)	(0.396)	(−3.639)	(−3.258)	(−5.768)	(−5.165)	(0.044)	(0.515)	(−1.249)	(−0.622)
Ln(imp_int_gdp-p_i)	−0.543	0.643	4.311***	0.103	0.651	7.586***	1.611*	−2.399*	1.497	−1.618	6.087***	1.851***	2.279***	5.305***
	(−0.883)	(0.484)	(3.283)	(0.109)	(0.875)	(6.654)	(1.698)	(−1.894)	(1.396)	(−1.529)	(4.46)	(2.601)	(3.626)	(3.367)
Ln (wholesale_pc_j)	−0.478	−1.25**	−0.476	0.489	0.628*	0.198	0.06	−0.991*	0.67	−0.179	−0.977	0.28	−0.606	−0.925
	(−0.842)	(−2.358)	(−0.797)	(1.377)	(1.921)	(0.368)	(0.115)	(−1.76)	(1.194)	(−0.334)	(−1.638)	(0.689)	(−1.157)	(−1.547)
Island_j	4.869***	4.552***	4.344***	2.992***	2.631***	2.231***	4.29***	4.26***	0.738	4.387***	3.206***	3.954***	5.196***	4.135***
	(7.772)	(5.496)	(6.125)	(7.49)	(5.365)	(3.514)	(6.905)	(6.663)	(1.118)	(6.231)	(4.759)	(8.719)	(9.304)	(5.553)
Border_int_coreEU_j	−1.274***	0.265	−1.421***	−0.355	−0.449*	−0.853**	−0.724*	−0.498	−0.508	−1.615***	−0.177	−0.372	−1.731***	−0.805*
	(−2.783)	(0.6)	(−2.958)	(−1.322)	(−1.758)	(−2.026)	(−1.84)	(−1.128)	(−1.201)	(−3.876)	(−0.381)	(−1.166)	(−4.361)	(−1.754)

(continued)

Table 14.6 (continued)

	S1	S2	S3	S4	S5	S6	S7	S8	S9	S10	S11	S12	S13	S14
Border_int_other_j	−0.133	0.612*	−0.03	0	−0.181	−1.036***	−0.252	−0.439	−0.395	0.133	−0.222	−0.172	−0.196	0.37
	(−0.347)	(1.729)	(−0.079)	(0.002)	(−0.864)	(−3.123)	(−0.774)	(−1.21)	(−1.132)	(0.38)	(−0.588)	(−0.653)	(−0.594)	(0.98)
Ln (exp_int_gdp-p_j)	−0.567	−1.837	1.745**	−1.271***	−1.018**	−0.978	−0.448	−0.259	−1.722***	−1.207*	−1.486*	−0.928**	−0.362	−1.364
	(−0.986)	(−1.411)	(2.207)	(−2.855)	(−2.509)	(−1.518)	(−0.738)	(−0.447)	(−2.732)	(−1.678)	(−1.738)	(−2.109)	(−0.81)	(−1.389)
Ln (d_{ji})	−2.908***	−2.281***	−2.375***	−0.586***	0.159	−1.604***	−1.532***	−1.371***	−2.191***	−2.473***	−2.297***	−0.164	−1.084***	−1.931***
	(−9.975)	(−8.494)	(−8.071)	(−3.407)	(0.988)	(−6.255)	(−6.036)	(−4.86)	(−8.133)	(−9.48)	(−7.56)	(−0.805)	(−4.213)	(−6.569)
Intra	7.206***	11.918***	6.6***	3.895***	5.685***	12.169***	5.8***	9.769***	7.744***	8.513***	8.466***	16.527***	14.468***	6.183***
	(6.503)	(11.702)	(5.93)	(5.982)	(9.358)	(12.566)	(6.075)	(9.182)	(7.57)	(8.592)	(7.573)	(21.493)	(15.12)	(5.609)
Adjac	7.195***	8.774***	6.37***	1.327***	1.862***	7.344***	2.388***	5.854***	3.752***	6.327***	6.34***	4.37***	8.267***	3.147***
	(12.633)	(16.753)	(11.125)	(3.959)	(5.952)	(14.733)	(4.863)	(10.694)	(7.127)	(12.418)	(11.046)	(11.047)	(16.806)	(5.548)
*Ln (gdpi*gdpj)*	2.449***	1.887***	2.682***	1.13***	0.669***	1.372***	2.574***	2.475***	2.06***	1.651***	2.881***	0.835***	2.325***	2.009***
	(17.84)	(12.409)	(17.506)	(14.104)	(8.031)	(10.24)	(21.957)	(17.243)	(15.746)	(12.354)	(20.161)	(8.585)	(17.921)	(13.26)
ρ_2	0.204***	0.257***	0.373***	0.086***	0.297***	0.241***	0.221***	0.201***	0.039***	0.286***	0.196***	0.233***	0.239***	0.334***
	(70.104)	(6.384)	(7.616)	(45.412)	(9.358)	(6.612)	(72.895)	(69.527)	(30.489)	(7.027)	(68.658)	(74.924)	(7.008)	(9.321)

Endogenous variable: all transport modes $Ln(F_{ji})$. Spatial autoregressive model using: W_{Hc}

***$p<0.01$, **$p<0.05$, *$p<0.1$; all variables except dummies in log form

We now focus on Table 14.6. Remember that W_{Hc} is probably the finest definition of a "hub-spoke" structure considered here, since by means of this weight matrix, for every given $i \rightarrow j$ dyad, re-exporting flows of product k from j to any other provinces is considered, but weighting each by the distance between the potential hub H and the final destination j (See Tables 14.7 and 14.8 in the Appendix of this chapter to find out the results when is used WHa and WHb "hub-spoke" structure, respectively). The results show certain heterogeneity, which is a sign of the richness and complexity of the phenomenon being modeled at the sectoral level. To facilitate this analysis we schematically focus on the main variables:

- As in the case of aggregate flows (M14, Table 14.5), ρ_2 is significant and positive for every sector. This indicates that, on average, provinces that are strong importers of product k from other provinces in the country are strong exporters of the same product k to other provinces, and with a higher intensity to its closest provinces.
- Size of trading regions: for all sectors, also de product of the GDPs of the trading partners has a positive and significant effect on the intensity of inter-provincial flows.
- Variables capturing the relevance of trading provinces in terms of logistics, warehouses and wholesale facilities—*Ln*(*wholesale* pc_i) and *Ln*(*wholesale* pc_j)—generate interesting results. In the case of the exporting province (*Ln*(*wholesale* pc_i)), with all other variables controlled for, ten sectors show significant and positive coefficients, indicating that provinces with large ratios of such facilities per capita are positively associated with a larger capacity for export to other provinces than one might expect given their gross output in this sector. The exceptions are: S1, which shows a negative and significant coefficient; S2 and S3, also attaining negative (but non-significant) coefficients; and S8, with positive but non-significant coefficient. By contrast, the equivalent variable for the importing province (*Ln*(*wholesale* pc_i)) generates completely different results. None of the inter-provincial sector-specific flows are enhanced by a high/low per-capita ratio of wholesale facilities in the importing province. More surprisingly, the coefficient for S2 is negative and significant.
- Results obtained with variables controlling for international trade flows entering or living the country are also worth mentioning:
  - Results obtained with the four border-province variables (*Border int. core* EU_i, *Border int. core* EU_j, *Border int. other*$_j$, *Border int. other*$_i$) confirm that border provinces are not operating as *gateways* to foreign markets—or, better yet, their inflows and outflows are not inflated by their border geography, because of *international transit flows* of the same product k. Furthermore, in several cases a negative and significant coefficient is found, which indicates that bordering province are exporting (or importing) less than the provincial average, ceteris paribus. This can be, in part, caused by a certain level of substitution of national for international destinations by some of the merchandise produced in these border regions.
  - The results of contrasting inter-provincial flows with international flows for the same k are not so clear. For example, with *Ln*(*imp int.all*^{k}/*gdp*$_i$) some

sectors (S3; S6; S7; S11; S12; S13; S14) show positive and significant associations between their international inflows of product *k* by all transport modes and, at the same time, their strong interprovincial exports within Spain. This could be a sign that international transit flows can be induced by strong demand for intermediate products imported from abroad (usually included under the same rubric at this rough, fifteen-sector disaggregation). In other cases, such as S8 (Chemicals), both effects can be dismissed, since the coefficient obtained is negative and significant. Further research is needed on this point.

- By contrast, the results obtained for $Ln(exp.int.all^k/gdp_j)$ are more surprising. In any case, positive and significant coefficient between the international outflows and the internal inflows of *k* in a given province is just found for sector S3 (Food and Beverages). In fact, in most cases the coefficients are negative, and just in five cases both significant and negative. This result also points to a low risk of having international transit flows (exports) hidden in our interprovincial flows.
- Finally, it is interesting to comment briefly the heterogeneous results obtained for the *Distance*, *Intra* and *Adjacency* variables. *Distance* has a negative and significant effect in all cases. However, the elasticity shows a clear heterogeneity, even when we consider only one transport mode and a medium-size country like Spain. Further research will analyze the variability of mixing the four available transport modes and the nature of each product-specific flow (value/weight; transportability, etc.). The coefficient estimates for *Intra*, the variable related with the *home bias*, is also positive and significant in all cases, with large values for some sectors, as in previous papers using similar datasets (Garmendia et al. 2012). *Adjacency* remains an enhancing force for inter-provincial flows in all sectors.

14.8 Conclusions

Local freight flows result from global and regional economic processes. Internationally, distribution networks have expanded, in line with the division of the production chain and the development of door-to-door distribution schemes. The proliferation of hub structures, gateways and corridors is growing in most parts of the world. Such developments are behind the rise of efficiency in logistics. However, their complexity is compounding the already difficult task of producing accurate trade analyses within and between countries.

Many papers comparing international and interregional flows use transport flows as the best proxy for internal bilateral trade, assuming no transit flows or re-exportation activities. However, very few have seriously addressed the difficulties that the growing complexity of logistics poses for the identification of production and consumption sites with the points of origin and destination of flows.

The aim of this paper is to analyze the complexity of modal cooperation and competition, modeling interprovincial flows within a country and in the presence of logistics infrastructures, warehouses and wholesale activities, as well as hub-spoke structures and multimodal internal and international transit flows. It develops various gravity models incorporating spatial and network autocorrelation effects, and conducts tests upon a rich dataset with aggregate and sector-specific flows between 50 provinces by four alternative transport modes (road, trains, ships, and aircraft) in Spain.

The results are rich and promising, but not conclusive. The bottom line is that our paper suggests a new strategy to deal with the growing complexity in logistics, and finds significant results regarding the presence of transport mode cooperation and competition within Spain using a rich dataset. In addition, the paper has reached at least four important conclusions: (1) certain transport modes compete with other modes within the country (road, trains and aircraft); (2) the effect of distance on trade becomes positive and significant when the focus is ships and aircraft (i.e., the preferred modes for long distances and access to islands); (3) as our results suggest, our dataset is free (to a large extent) of international transit flows, for we find no "inflation" of inter-provincial flows at border provinces attributable to their status as *gateways* or *corridors* to important foreign markets; (4) on average, with aggregate and sector-specific flows, provinces receiving strong inter-provincial imports in Spain are also strong exporters to other provinces in the country. This important result is robust with (almost all) the definitions used here for capturing "*hub-spoke*" structures and the use of aggregated and disaggregated data. However, rather than clearly confirm the presence of "*hub-spoke*" *structures*, it could also be symptomatic of other, equally plausible phenomena, such as intra-industry trade or intermediate-final linkages formed by the presence of a multiple-stage production process within the country. Further research is needed to refine the modeling strategy, as well as the empirical assessment for Spain and other countries. In the meantime, our results can be considered a first attempt to tackle this complex topic.

Appendix

Tables 14.7, 14.8 and 14.9

Table 14.7 Sector-specific analysis

	S1	S2	S3	S4	S5	S6	S7	S8	S9	S10	S11	S12	S13	S14
Rbar-squared	0.3257	0.3691	0.3467	0.2259	0.3137	0.3203	0.3807	0.3356	0.3028	0.3532	0.3872	0.3639	0.438	0.2814
sigma^2	43.7048	37.0774	44.0033	14.9937	12.8042	33.1574	31.9273	40.0628	37.0949	34.9254	43.2757	20.7903	31.9325	42.6123
log-likelihood	−7403.6012	−7198.4217	−7415.2219	−6066.0046	−5876.3605	−7059.6314	−7012.8656	−7294.9755	−7197.8082	−7124.0063	−7391.4333	−6477.4844	−7012.6435	−7375.4849
constant	−9.581**	−8.185	−37.814***	−21.16***	−20.737***	−40.238***	−48.76***	−29.365***	−34.959***	−19.367***	−60.049***	−28.223***	−41.822***	−43.818***
	(−2.266)	(−1.356)	(−8.051)	(−7.831)	(−7.655)	(−7.992)	(−10.099)	(−5.945)	(−7.827)	(−4.195)	(−10.061)	(−7.898)	(−10.054)	(−7.675)
Ln(wholesale_pc_i)	−1.751***	−0.066	−0.095	0.878**	1.286***	2.459***	2.345***	0.875	2.025***	2.652***	4.163***	2.359***	1.529***	3.087***
	(−3.07)	(−0.121)	(−0.148)	(2.359)	(4.133)	(4.868)	(4.525)	(1.563)	(3.797)	(5.101)	(7.141)	(5.915)	(2.814)	(5.208)
Island_i	−0.19	1.133*	−0.05	1.25***	4.044***	0.775	0.219	−0.972	−1.495***	−0.584	1.873***	4.554***	2.137***	3.518***
	(−0.304)	(1.948)	(−0.076)	(3.399)	(11.75)	(1.388)	(0.389)	(−1.476)	(−2.582)	(−1.001)	(2.93)	(10.235)	(3.979)	(5.648)
Border_int_coreEU_i	−0.101	−2.182***	−0.93**	−0.71***	−1.231***	−1.669***	−0.367	−1.644***	−0.184	−1.18***	−0.268	−0.73**	−1.039***	−0.588
	(−0.218)	(−5.13)	(−2.01)	(−2.599)	(−4.942)	(−4.154)	(−0.929)	(−3.725)	(−0.434)	(−2.867)	(−0.585)	(−2.29)	(−2.625)	(−1.289)
Border_int_other_i	0.418	−0.13	0.247	−0.315	−0.298	0.127	−1.215***	−1.223***	−2.017***	−1.76***	0.006	0.118	−0.432	−0.25
	(1.094)	(−0.368)	(0.64)	(−1.421)	(−1.444)	(0.377)	(−3.742)	(−3.256)	(−5.776)	(−5.186)	(0.015)	(0.432)	(−1.33)	(−0.668)
Ln(imp_int_gdp-p_i)	−0.569	0.699	4.33***	0.051	0.535	7.719***	1.52	−2.283*	1.504	−1.489	6.115***	1.784**	2.234***	5.613***
	(−0.923)	(0.525)	(3.294)	(0.054)	(0.734)	(6.771)	(1.6)	(−1.799)	(1.403)	(−1.405)	(4.485)	(2.494)	(3.544)	(3.577)
Ln (wholesale_pc_j)	−0.482	−1.25**	−0.683	0.43	0.244	0.133	−0.13	−0.862	0.701	−0.11	−1.081*	−0.002	−0.701	−1.297**
	(−0.848)	(−2.355)	(−1.132)	(1.213)	(0.762)	(0.243)	(−0.237)	(−1.525)	(1.249)	(−0.203)	(−1.815)	(−0.004)	(−1.321)	(−2.132)
Island_j	5.565***	5.055***	5.696***	3.275***	2.942***	3.107***	5.442***	4.825***	0.893	5.026***	3.641***	4.14***	5.945***	4.934***
	(8.871)	(6.166)	(8.014)	(8.201)	(6.998)	(4.988)	(8.671)	(7.534)	(1.353)	(6.961)	(5.402)	(8.349)	(10.922)	(6.757)
Border_int_coreEU_j	−1.355***	0.14	−1.434***	−0.267	−0.194	−0.751*	−0.586	−0.321	−0.494	−1.686***	−0.209	−0.231	−1.59***	−0.638
	(−2.954)	(0.325)	(−2.978)	(−0.994)	(−0.782)	(−1.743)	(−1.485)	(−0.726)	(−1.168)	(−4.038)	(−0.449)	(−0.715)	(−3.959)	(−1.386)
Border_int_other_j	−0.078	0.58	0.049	0.034	−0.164	−1.063***	−0.066	−0.389	−0.376	0.126	−0.142	0.066	−0.008	0.355
	(−0.203)	(1.636)	(0.129)	(0.152)	(−0.793)	(−3.201)	(−0.198)	(−1.071)	(−1.078)	(0.357)	(−0.377)	(0.25)	(−0.025)	(0.942)

Ln (exp_int_gdp-p_j)	−0.588	−2.623**	1.893**	−1.293***	−0.632	−1.122*	−0.418	−0.26	−1.736***	−1.387*	−1.62*	−0.743*	−0.469	−0.957
	(−1.022)	(−2.13)	(2.4)	(−2.905)	(−1.575)	(−1.709)	(−0.688)	(−0.449)	(−2.755)	(−1.929)	(−1.896)	(−1.692)	(−1.052)	(−0.978)
Ln (d_{ji})	−2.836***	−2.183***	−2.26***	−0.563***	0.172	−1.525***	−1.433***	−1.307***	−2.172***	−2.392***	−2.251***	−0.116	−1.01***	−1.799***
	(−9.713)	(−8.137)	(−7.694)	(−3.279)	(1.085)	(−5.951)	(−5.664)	(−4.624)	(−8.063)	(−9.154)	(−7.411)	(−0.569)	(−3.935)	(−6.131)
Intra	7.143***	11.786***	6.517***	3.892***	5.562***	12.052***	5.83***	9.699***	7.739***	8.371***	8.372***	16.332***	14.324***	6.151***
	(6.437)	(11.537)	(5.849)	(5.979)	(9.251)	(12.441)	(6.122)	(9.099)	(7.565)	(8.434)	(7.486)	(21.291)	(14.978)	(5.586)
Adjac	7.203***	8.799***	6.385***	1.337***	1.862***	7.37***	2.461***	5.879***	3.761***	6.346***	6.35***	4.382***	8.275***	3.213***
	(12.629)	(16.75)	(11.137)	(3.99)	(6.018)	(14.777)	(5.023)	(10.718)	(7.144)	(12.427)	(11.06)	(11.1)	(16.828)	(5.671)
*Ln (gdpi*gdpj)*	2.466***	1.898***	2.675***	1.11***	0.636***	1.4***	2.49***	2.495***	2.063***	1.684***	2.878***	0.802***	2.274***	2.065***
	(17.94)	(12.525)	(17.394)	(13.871)	(8.136)	(10.458)	(18.969)	(17.356)	(15.774)	(12.568)	(20.138)	(7.839)	(16.921)	(13.875)
ρ_2	0.185***	0.222***	0.395***	0.148***	0.565***	0.29***	0.321***	0.199***	0.043***	0.249***	0.202***	0.368***	0.294***	0.414***
	(45.023)	(49.349)	(7.384)	(40.254)	(79.108)	(5.654)	(7.15)	(46.67)	(21.608)	(6.053)	(46.941)	(6.342)	(6.36)	(9.359)

Endogenous variable: all transport modes $Ln(F_{ji})$. Spatial autoregressive model using: W_{Ha}
$^{***}p<0.01$; $^{**}p<0.05$; $^{*}p<0.1$; all variables except dummies in log form

Table 14.8 Sector-specific analysis

	S1	S2	S3	S4	S5	S6	S7	S8	S9	S10	S11	S12	S13	S14
Rbar-squared	0.3279	0.3736	0.3495	0.229	0.3218	0.3194	0.3841	0.3423	0.303	0.3574	0.3909	0.3662	0.4418	0.2883
sigma^2	43.961	37.2944	44.9268	15.0344	13.2871	33.5334	32.5659	40.3083	37.0947	35.3442	43.6609	21.1274	32.4008	44.0981
log-likelihood	−7410.0924	−7204.4729	−7437.4607	−6068.8735	−5916.447	−7071.6625	−7035.0059	−7301.7332	−7197.7832	−7137.4103	−7401.4805	−6494.2769	−7028.6975	−7414.1605
constant	−9.481**	−5.262	−47.126***	−23.205***	−27.633***	−46.91***	−58.007***	−37.215***	−36.27***	−25.229***	−70.53***	−35.764***	−48.99***	−58.944***
	(−2.236)	(−0.866)	(−10.025)	(−8.518)	(−9.727)	(−9.423)	(−11.763)	(−7.348)	(−8.068)	(−5.471)	(−10.96)	(−10.278)	(−11.749)	(−10.012)
Ln(wholesale_pc_i)	−2.217***	−0.294	−1.175*	0.653*	0.874***	2.224***	1.527***	0.054	1.931***	2.146***	3.514***	1.915***	0.76	2.027***
	(−3.853)	(−0.533)	(−1.848)	(1.746)	(2.723)	(4.351)	(2.881)	(0.094)	(3.611)	(4.123)	(5.839)	(4.773)	(1.397)	(3.349)
Island_i	−0.203	1.064*	−0.039	1.207***	3.777***	0.752	0.172	−0.717	−1.47**	−0.505	1.919***	4.535***	1.964***	3.36***
	(−0.324)	(1.823)	(−0.059)	(3.276)	(10.769)	(1.34)	(0.303)	(−1.085)	(−2.536)	(−0.86)	(2.983)	(10.11)	(3.627)	(5.291)
Border_int_coreEU_i	−0.012	−2.141***	−0.765	−0.672**	−1.206***	−1.628***	−0.247	−1.54***	−0.141	−1.059**	−0.148	−0.619*	−0.916**	−0.534
	(−0.025)	(−5.017)	(−1.636)	(−2.456)	(−4.75)	(−4.027)	(−0.618)	(−3.474)	(−0.331)	(−2.557)	(−0.321)	(−1.928)	(−2.298)	(−1.147)
Border_int_other_i	0.448	−0.143	0.335	−0.298	−0.277	0.177	−1.139***	−1.076***	−2.023***	−1.732***	0.08	0.193	−0.358	−0.144
	(1.17)	(−0.405)	(0.862)	(−1.341)	(−1.318)	(0.523)	(−3.47)	(−2.854)	(−5.786)	(−5.071)	(0.21)	(0.701)	(−1.094)	(−0.379)
Ln(imp_int_gdp-p_i)	−0.688	1.087	5.502***	0.345	1.258*	8.152***	2.102**	−0.602	1.641	−0.707	7.272***	2.39***	2.761***	7.511***
	(−1.113)	(0.814)	(4.167)	(0.364)	(1.683)	(7.09)	(2.171)	(−0.472)	(1.527)	(−0.665)	(5.245)	(3.326)	(4.39)	(4.718)
Ln (wholesale_pc_j)	−0.369	−1.114**	0.413	0.65*	0.982***	0.925*	1.2**	−0.482	0.925	0.866*	0.133	1.04**	0.273	0.354
	(−0.646)	(−2.092)	(0.683)	(1.826)	(2.998)	(1.754)	(2.27)	(−0.838)	(1.639)	(1.649)	(0.212)	(2.531)	(0.522)	(0.583)
Island_j	5.008***	3.664***	5.031***	3.366***	4.919***	3.042***	4.759***	4.334***	0.675	4.007***	3.451***	5.429***	6.086***	5.589***
	(7.956)	(4.431)	(7.065)	(8.415)	(11.467)	(4.856)	(7.601)	(6.745)	(1.022)	(5.653)	(5.098)	(11.886)	(11.098)	(7.562)
Border_int_coreEU_j	−1.559***	−0.364	−2.334***	−0.396	−0.794***	−1.47***	−0.873**	−0.8*	−0.547	−2.142***	−0.461	−0.596*	−2.076***	−1.021**
	(−3.388)	(−0.839)	(−4.927)	(−1.472)	(−3.135)	(−3.571)	(−2.2)	(−1.802)	(−1.292)	(−5.173)	(−0.984)	(−1.859)	(−5.23)	(−2.186)
Border_int_other_j	−0.127	0.513	−0.193	−0.035	−0.313	−1.267***	−0.612*	−0.713*	−0.502	−0.507	−0.304	−0.034	−0.313	0.052
	(−0.33)	(1.444)	(−0.503)	(−0.159)	(−1.484)	(−3.82)	(−1.867)	(−1.955)	(−1.436)	(−1.48)	(−0.803)	(−0.127)	(−0.941)	(0.135)

Ln (exp_int_gdp-p_j)	−0.822	−4.682***	3.399***	−1.325***	−0.911**	−0.116	−0.856	−0.245	−1.837***	−1.769**	−1.358	−0.871**	−0.55	−0.628
	(−1.423)	(−3.756)	(4.379)	(−2.972)	(−2.225)	(−0.183)	(−1.395)	(−0.421)	(−2.914)	(−2.453)	(−1.565)	(−1.966)	(−1.223)	(−0.625)
Ln (d_{ji})	−2.87***	−2.134***	−2.188***	−0.554***	0.332**	−1.5***	−1.429***	−1.255***	−2.194***	−2.401***	−2.243***	−0.074	−0.96***	−1.723***
	(−9.802)	(−7.92)	(−7.348)	(−3.213)	(2.049)	(−5.799)	(−5.535)	(−4.41)	(−8.13)	(−9.129)	(−7.223)	(−0.357)	(−3.689)	(−5.695)
Intra	7.03***	11.809***	6.581***	3.897***	5.822***	12.016***	5.783***	9.752***	7.686***	8.287***	8.335***	16.294***	14.328***	6.225***
	(6.317)	(11.523)	(5.839)	(5.977)	(9.494)	(12.321)	(5.994)	(9.111)	(7.511)	(8.299)	(7.38)	(21.036)	(14.846)	(5.534)
Adjac	8.437***	9.094***	9.963***	1.154***	0.654**	6.584***	2.117***	7.444***	4.255***	7.728***	6.494***	5.048***	7.475***	1.677**
	(6.102)	(8.266)	(18.245)	(3.442)	(2.092)	(13.205)	(4.279)	(13.753)	(5.371)	(7.257)	(6.379)	(12.728)	(15.191)	(2.042)
*Ln (gdpi*gdpj)*	2.685***	2.006***	3.12***	1.204***	0.862***	1.527***	2.914***	2.92***	2.113***	1.933***	3.214***	1.023***	2.621***	2.572***
	(19.287)	(13.077)	(21.509)	(14.984)	(10.819)	(11.52)	(24.426)	(20.056)	(16.089)	(14.891)	(22.126)	(10.458)	(21.167)	(18.189)
ρ_2	−0.154	−0.056	−0.341***	0.133***	0.969***	0.185***	0.067***	−0.238***	−0.111	−0.191	−0.023	−0.263***	0.163***	0.323***
	(−1.007)	(−0.319)	(−17.752)	(11.136)	(29.629)	(13.133)	(7.889)	(−14.826)	(−0.852)	(−1.52)	(−0.205)	(−15.656)	(12.303)	(2.701)

Endogenous variable: all transport modes $Ln(F_{ji})$. Spatial autoregressive model using: W_{Hb}
***$p<0.01$; **$p<0.05$; *$p<0.1$; all variables except dummies in log form

Table 14.9 Sectoral classification

Sector	CNAE-93	Description
1	AA,BB	Agriculture, fishing
2	CA,CB	Mining industry
3	DA	Food and beverages
4	DB	Textile
5	DC	Shoes
6	DD	Wood
7	DE	Paper, edition
8	DG	Chemical industry
9	DH	Plastic
10	DI	Non-metallic minerals
11	DJ	Metallurgy and metallic products
12	DK	Machinery and mechanical equipment
13	DL	Electronic and electrical material
14	DM	Transport material
15	DN	Other industries

Comments on the Data

a) *Transport flows by road* (Q_{ji}^{kR})
The Permanent Survey on Commodity Transport by Road (PSCTR), published by the Spanish Ministry of Public Works (*Ministerio de Fomento*), is one of the key sources for our original database on transport flows in tons (more than 80 % of commodity flows in Spain take place by road). From this key survey, we obtain a large set of OD matrices of flows in tons, one per product type ($i = 160$). In order to get as close as possible to the concept of trade flow, we have removed intra-municipal flows from the road-transport database.[10] In addition, we have depurated the original flows recorded by the PSCTR to prevent the inclusion of international transit flows hidden within interregional deliveries.

b) *Transport flows by train* (Q_{ji}^{kT})
Information on commodity flows by train is provided by Spain's national rail network RENFE, the main operator and a former national monopoly. The statistics include commodities transported in 'complete wagon' or in 'containers' (30 % of total tonnage transported by ***CNT***). The latter are more clearly subject to ambushing multimodal transport strategies.

c) *Transport flows by ship* (Q_{ji}^{kS})
Owing to the absence of an up-to-date set of OD matrices by ship with the required sectoral breakdown, we have estimated these by a method commonly

[10]In some cases, intra-municipal flows do not correspond to economic transactions but to the capillary distribution of commodities stocked and distributed within each municipality for final consumption. The elimination of such flows will prevent the double counting of intra-regional flows.

used in the literature to update old inter-sectoral structures with new data for margin totals. The method, based on previous works, uses Long-Scale Optimization to update the most recent OD matrices available with new data on the volume of commodities loaded/unloaded at each port (Statistical Yearbook. Puertos del Estado[11]). Details in Llano et al. (2010).

d) *Transport flows by aircraft* (Q_{ji}^{kA})
On the basis of an aggregated OD matrix of total domestic flows by aircraft in tons in Spain, we have obtained a full set of OD matrices for domestic flows by product using the expected structure of flows by product observed on international flights for each airport of origin (r) and year (t). In this estimation we assume that if a specific region has interregional exports of goods shipped by aircraft, then the sectoral structure of its domestic outflows to any of its destinations will be the same as those observed in international exports from the same airport. To increase the plausibility of this assumption, we have considered only the international trade of Spanish regions with the nearest countries (France, Portugal, Germany, Italy and Morocco), where the same competition structures in terms of transport modes operate. The flows are divided into the 160 categories considered in the NSTR-3 digits used for road flows.

First Debugging Procedure for Transport Flows in Tons

a) *Debugging interregional flows from international transit flows (ITF)*
Although all the information described so far refers to interregional flows in tons taking place within the country, the transported products may have an international origin/destination. As a result, international trade may be double-counted and the interregional trade of some specific regions may be overvalued. In the case of Spain, the highest risk for that is associated with maritime-road and maritime-railway intermodal connections.[12] The identification and elimination of ITF have focused solely on transport flows by road (which account for more than 90 % of flows in Spain) and are detailed in Llano et al. (2010).

b) *Allocation of multi-modal flows*
Another key difficulty in the estimation of interregional trade with transport flows is that of identifying intermodal flows that correspond to the same transaction. The risk of intermodal connections is mainly associated with interregional trade between the mainland, the islands (Islas Baleares, Islas Canarias) and Ceuta and Melilla (in Africa). Owing to the existence of special fiscal regimes in some of these territories (Islas Canarias, Ceuta and Melilla), we have been able to access detailed fiscal information on the mainland's interregional trade with

[11]Puertos del Estado: http://www.puertos.es/es/estadisticas/index.html.

[12]In Spain, most international trade with non-European countries uses shipping as the transport mode. Trade by road tends to use international freight services, which are not included in our database.

the Islas Canarias as well as with Ceuta and Melilla (Spanish Tax Authority, www.aeat.es). Consequently, for these two cases, the quality of interregional flows within Spain is similar to that of international trade flows. One of the similarities stems from the procedure for reporting the main transport mode used for deliveries. For these extra-peninsular regions, our dataset includes flows by road between inner Spanish regions and overseas provinces. These flows imply a combination of road and ship modes, and can therefore be considered typical multimodal examples.

Estimating Interregional Trade Prices

Trade prices are estimated on the basis of *value/volume* relations deduced from detailed statistics in the Spanish Branch Surveys, Agricultural Price Survey and International Trade databases. For each year, transport mode and product type, the objective is to estimate 52 export price vectors (one per Spanish province, NUTS-3), at the lowest level of disaggregation, to capture price/quality differences between regions for the same product. For the sake of simplicity, we use a superscript m to denote the four transport modes considered (R, T, S, A).[13] Regional (NUTS-2) and national prices have been used in the absence of provincial data. Our estimation method is explained in detail in Llano et al. (2010).

References

Alamá-Sabater L, Márquez-Ramos L, Suárez-Burguet C (2013a) Trade and transport connectivity: a spatial approach. Appl Econ 45:2563–2566

Alamá-Sabater L, Márquez-Ramos L, Suárez-Burguet C, Navarro-Azorín JM (2013b) Interregional trade and transport connectivity: an analysis of spatial and networks dependence by using a spatial econometric flow model at NUTS3 level. Working paper

Álvarez-SanJaime O, Cantos-Sánchez P, Moner-Colonques R, Sempere-Monerris JJ (2013a) Vertical integration and exclusivities in maritime freight transport. Transp Res E 51:50–61

Álvarez-SanJaime O, Cantos-Sánchez P, Moner-Colonques R, Sempere-Monerris JJ (2013b) Competition and horizontal integration in maritime freight transport. Transp Res E 51:67–81

Black WR (1992) Network autocorrelation in transport network and flow systems. Geogr Anal 24(3):207–222

Bolduc D, Laferriere R, Santarossa G (1992) Spatial autoregressive error-components in travel flow models. Reg Sci Urban Econ 22(3):371–385

Boonstra HJH (2011) Macro-integration with inequality constraints: an application to the integration of transport and trade statistics. Statistica Neerlandica 65(4):407–431

Cantos-Sánchez P, Moner-Colonques R, Sempere-Monerris JJ, Álvarez-SanJaime O (2009) Alternative pricing regimes in interurban passenger transport with externalities and modal competition. Reg Sci Urban Econ 39:128–137

[13]Note that the pipe (P) was used only to reallocate apparent exports by road and truck.

Chun Y (2008) Modeling network autocorrelation within migration flows by eigenvector spatial filtering. J Geogr Syst 10(4):317–344

Chun Y, Griffith DA (2011) Modeling network autocorrelation in space–time migration flow data: an eigenvector spatial filtering approach. Ann Assoc Am Geogr 101(3):523–536

Combes PP, Lafourcade M, Mayer T (2005) The trade-creating effects of business and social networks: evidence from France. J Int Econ 66(1):1–29

De la Mata T, Llano C (2013) Social networks and trade of services: modelling interregional flows with spatial and network autocorrelation effects. J Geogr Syst 15(3):319–367

Feo-Valero M, García-Menéndez L, Sáez-Carramolino L, Furió-Pruñonosa S (2011) The importance of the inland leg of containerised maritime shipments: an analysis of modal choice determinants in Spain. Transp Res E 47:446–460

Fischer MM, Griffith DA (2008) Modeling spatial autocorrelation in spatial interaction data: an application to patent citation data in the European Union. J Reg Sci 48(5):969–989

Garmendia A, Llano-Verduras C, Requena-Silventre F (2012) Networks and the disappearance of the intranational home bias. Econ Lett 116:178–182

Grubel HG, Lloyd PJ (1975) Intra-industry trade: the theory and measurement of intra-industry trade in differentiated products. Macmillan, London

Griffith DA, Jones KG (1980) Explorations into the relationship between spatial structure and spatial interaction. Environ Plan A 12(2):187–201

Helble M (2007) Border effect estimates for France and Germany. Rev World Econ 143(3):433–463

Helliwell JF (1998) How much do national borders matter? Brookings Institution Press, Washington

Helliwell JF (1997) National borders, trade and migration. Pac Econ Rev 2(3):165–185

Helliwell JF (1996) Do national borders matter for Quebec's trade? Can J Econ 29(3):507–522

Henderson DJ, Millimet DL (2008) Is gravity linear? J Appl Econ 23:137–172

Hesse M, Rodrigue J-P (2004) The transport geography of logistics and freight distribution. J Transp Geogr 12(3):171–184

Hillberry R, Hummels D (2008) Trade responses to geographic frictions: a decomposition using micro-data. Eur Econ Rev 52(3):527–550

Jackson R, Schwarm WR, Okuyama Y, Islam S (2006) A method for constructing commodity by industry flow matrices. Ann Reg Sci 40:909–920

La Caixa (2013) Anuario Económico de España. Estudios y Análisis Económico. Caixa Bank Research

LeSage JP, Llano C (2013) A spatial interaction model with spatially structured origin and destination effects. J Geogr Syst 15(3):265–289

LeSage JP, Polasek W (2008) Incorporating transportation network structure in spatial econometric models of commodity flows. Spat Econ Anal 3:225–245

LeSage JP, Pace RK (2008) Spatial econometric modeling of origin–destination flows. J Reg Sci 48(5):941–967

LeSage JP, Pace RK (2009) Introduction to spatial econometrics. Chapman & Hall/CRC Press, Boca Raton

Llano C, Esteban A, Pulido A, Pérez J (2010) Opening the interregional trade black box: the C-intereg database for the Spanish economy (1995–2005). Int Reg Sci Rev 33:302–337

McCallum J (1995) National borders matter: Canada-U.S. regional trade patterns. Am Econ Rev 85:615–623

Monzón A, Rodríguez-Dapena A (2006) Choice of mode of transport for long-distance trips: solving the problem of sparse data. Transp Res A 40:587–601

Nitsch V (2002) Border effects and border regions: lessons from the German unification. Banakgesellschaft, Berlin

Rodrigue JP (2003) Freight, gateways and mega-urban regions: the logistical integration of the Bostwash corridor. Tijdschrift voor Economische en Sociale Geografie 95(2):147–161

Rodrigue J-P, Notteboom T (2010) Comparative North American and European gateway logistics: the regionalism of freight distribution. J Transp Geogr 18:497–507

Rodrigue J-P, Comtois C, Slack B (2009) The geography of transport systems. Routledge, New York

Van Klink H, van den Berg G (1998) Gateways and intermodalism. J Transp Geogr 6:11–19

Wolf HC (2000) Intranational home bias in trade. Rev Econ Stat 82(4):555–563

Wolf HC (1997) Patterns of intra- and inter-state trade. NBER Working Paper 5939. National Bureau of Economic Research, Cambridge

Woudsma C (1999) NAFTA and Canada-US crossborder freight transportation. J Transp Geogr 7:105–119

Yilmazkuday H (2012) Understanding interstate trade patterns. J Int Econ 86:158–166

Chapter 15
Modeling the Effect of Social-Network on Interregional Trade of Services: How Sensitive Are the Results to Alternative Measures of Social Linkages

Carlos Llano and Tamara de la Mata

Keywords Bayesian spatial autoregressive regression model • Border effect • Gravity models • Internal tourism • Social networks • Spatial connectivity of origin-destination flows • Trade in services • Trade of services

JEL Classifications: C21, F12, F14, L83, R23

15.1 Introduction

The recent literature on border effects shows that, despite decreases in transport costs, countries still engage in more internal trade than external trade (McCallum 1995; Helliwell 1996; Wolf 2000; Chen 2004; Okubo 2004; Evans 2006; Ghemawat et al. 2010). To explain this, research has increasingly focused on informal barriers to trade. One such barrier is the lack of information about international trade and investment opportunities (Rauch and Casella 2003). Social and business networks

---

This article is an updated and extended version of the paper "Social Network and Trade of Services: Modelling Interregional Flows with Spatial and Network Autocorrelation Effects" by the same authors previously published in the *Journal of Geographical Systems*, Special Issue on "Advances in the Statistical Modelling of Spatial Interaction Data", Volume 15, Number 3/July 2013, pp. 319–367.

C. Llano (✉)
Departamento de Análisis Económico, Teoría Económica e Historia Económica and Instituto L.R. Klein, Universidad Autónoma de Madrid, 28049 Madrid, Spain

T. de la Mata
Departamento de Análisis Económico: Teoría e Historia Económic, Universidad Autónoma de Madrid, 28049 Madrid, Spain

CEPREDE, Madrid, Spain
e-mail: tamara.delamata@uam.es; TDelamata@iese.edu

R. Patuelli, G. Arbia (eds.), *Spatial Econometric Interaction Modelling*, Advances in Spatial Science, DOI 10.1007/978-3-319-30196-9_15

are seen as possible ways to overcome such barriers and increase the volume of international trade (Portes and Rey 2005). Evidence supporting such channels has been found for business groups operating across national borders (Belderbos and Sleuwaegen 1998), immigrants (Gould 1994) and long-settled ethnic minorities that maintain co-ethnic business societies.

This literature distinguishes two main mechanisms through which bilateral trade could be promoted by immigration. The first relates to the 'idiosyncratic' preferences of immigrants, or 'taste effect', where the positive impact of immigrants on trade intensity reflects their taste for goods from their countries of origin. The second relates to the reduction of transaction costs, or 'information effects', due to migration; migrant familiarity with the preferences, social institutions, language and legal institutions of both countries reduces communication costs and cultural barriers. Communication between migrants and those living in their country of origin is facilitated by social and business networks, which in turn account for higher bilateral trade flows.

Some authors have tried to quantify the relevance of social and business networks on trade in goods between countries.[1] However, few papers have examined the role of migration in determining patterns of trade flows within a single country (i.e. Helliwell 1997; Combes et al. 2005; Millimet and Osang 2007; Garmendia et al. 2012). Helliwell (1997) has argued that, because institutions, flavors, culture, etc. might differ more in from country to country than between the regions of a single country, the trade-creation effect of migrants should be more intense on international than on interregional trade. Despite these results, there remain several reasons to expect larger effects on trade in services. First, domestic trade in services far outstrips domestic trade in goods in all OCDE countries[2]; second, immigration flows can be more intense, and at times more persistent, within countries than between countries; third, because services require face-to-face contact for the interchange to take place (also called 'proximity burden'), information is more important for trade in services than for trade in goods, so we can expect social-network–driven reductions in transaction costs to be larger; finally, in focusing on interregional tourism-related trade flows in services, we must consider (apart from information and taste effects operating in goods) the potential reduction of lodging costs for tourists who take advantage of second homes and accommodations owned by relatives and friends, a reduction most likely to occur within single countries, as tourists travel back to the regions of their birth. Note that at least in some Mediterranean countries, like Spain, Italy and France, this phenomenon is far from sporadic, and may be occurring almost every weekend. However, most of the studies focus on trade in goods, without considering interregional trade in services or the role of interregional migration flows.

[1]Among others: Gould (1994), Head and Ries (1998), Dunlevy and Hutchinson (1999, 2001), Wagner et al. (2002), Rauch and Trindade (2002), Girma and Yu (2002) and White and Tadesse (2008).

[2]For example, according to the Spanish National Accounts, more than 60 % of Spain's GDP is produced by services, and more than 70 % of Spain's total output is consumed within the country.

Then, we consider that an analysis of these effects on services and at the regional level is in order, and for several reasons. First, it is well known that services account for the largest share of total economic activity in all developed countries. Second, the lack of information on bilateral trade in services has stymied empirical work that quantifies border effects on services. Third, as mentioned, given the characteristics of services, we can reasonably expect information and tastes to have a greater effect on trade in services than on trade in goods. And, finally, because of data restrictions, most studies have focused on the link between international migration and international trade, ignoring the fact that most flows in both people and trade take place between the regions of single countries. There are, then, intuitively obvious reasons to analyze the relationships between trade flows in services sectors and immigrant stocks at the interregional level, but a lack of information has limited such analysis. To help fill this gap, we have already investigated—in de la Mata and Llano (2013)—whether similar results exist for regional trade in services linked with tourism[3]: Accommodations, Restaurants and Travel Agencies.

An additional novelty in de la Mata and Llano (2013) that is also explored in the present work is the use of spatial-econometrics techniques, which have elsewhere been used to analyze various topics in international economics, such as the determinants of foreign direct investment (Ledyaeva 2009) and the effects of bilateral agreements (Porojan 2001; Egger and Larch 2008). It is important to include the geographical perspective in such analyses in order to control for the spatial dependence caused by spatial aggregation, spatial externalities, spillover effects and spatial heterogeneity (Anselin 1988). Finally, Behrens et al. (2012) derived a structural gravity-equation system in which both trade flows and error terms were cross-sectionally correlated and estimable by means of techniques from the spatial-econometrics literature. According to their findings, directly controlling for cross-sectional interdependence reduces border-effect measurements by capturing 'multilateral resistance', which origin- and destination-specific fixed effects do not totally control for. As for social networks, we find—in addition to the trade-creation effects that the literature traditionally ascribes to emigrants and immigrants—potential sources of cross-section autocorrelation in the regional concentration of interregional emigration and immigration stocks. These sources, which we have labeled 'network autocorrelation' or 'demography-based autocorrelation', could also affect bilateral flows between two regions, as explained in Sect. 15.2.

In de la Mata and Llano (2013) we explored various models that allowed us to incorporate both spatial and demographic cross-sectional dependence. We estimated three versions of the Spatial Durbin Model (SDM), four versions of the General Spatial Model (SAC) and a Spatial Autoregressive Model that simultaneously incorporated two spatial lags (SAR): based on contiguity and based on regional demographic structure. All these models were estimated for different specifications

[3]There exist a few studies that analyze internal tourism flows, but they use input–output models (Eriksen and Ahmt 1999) or time-series approaches (Athanasopoulus and Hyndman 2008). None use a gravity model with cross-sectional data or pay attention to network effects.

and given robustness checks with a past-migration-flows variable, given by (a) a matrix of migration stocks in 1981 and (b) a second version of the same 1981 matrix that restricted the concept of 'neighbor' to the most intense demographic links. Our main conclusions can be summarized as follows: the distance coefficient turned out to have a negative sign, and therefore a negative effect, but the effect was mitigated when we controlled for intraregional flows and migration stocks, because the coefficient, while retaining the negative sign, became numerically smaller; the trade creation effect of social networks was confirmed, although the directionality of this effect (whether it was significant for emigrants, immigrants or both) depended on the spatial model used; the best performing model was the SAC model, which used a restricted version of the matrix (defining demographic neighbors by 1981 migrant stocks, so as to account for the spatial autocorrelation of the dependent variable) and a contiguity matrix (to control for the spatial autocorrelation in residuals). This confirmed a certain level of complementarity between the two types of autocorrelation, although the demography-based "network" autoregressive term was non-significant.

On the basis of these recent approaches and the results of our analysis in de la Mata and Llano (2013), in this paper we study the relationship between interregional trade flows in Accommodations and Restaurants as generated by travel. We use a gravity model that relies on conventional distance measures that are thought to inhibit flows and alternative social network-measures. For estimation purposes, we relied on spatial-econometric methods, incorporating cross sectional dependence based on contiguity and social-network dependence. The last one being measured by a spatial weight structure that links regions based on the stock of interregional immigrants living in each region. This type of interregional dependence is contrasted with more conventional weight structures based on the geographical proximity of regions. As in de la Mata and Llano (2013), we exploit recent estimates of intra- and interregional trade flows in tourism-related service sectors between Spanish regions (de la Mata and Llano 2012b). We have used Maximum Likelihood (ML) estimation to test four alternative spatial-model specifications: namely, a spatial lag model (SAR), a spatial error model (SEM), a spatial Durbin model (SDM) and a spatial general model (SAC).[4] Some of these specifications have been defined in such a way as to embed two different weight matrices, which attempt to capture (separately or simultaneously) the two previously described autocorrelation effects: spatial and demographic. We also report additional robustness analyses, using alternative measures that are thought to capture the pro-trade effect of variables representing different types of social networks, as described in Sect. 15.4.

One of the novelties of this paper is that we include only domestic flows linked with trips. This allows us to measure home-bias—defined as how many more times a region trades within itself than with any other region, once other factors are controlled for—in the domestic trips of Spanish residents at the regional level,

[4]These models have been estimated using the spatial econometrics toolbox provided by James P. LeSage (www.spatial-econometrics.com).

as well as the extent to which strong social networks over short distances can explain the observed internal border effect. Interestingly, once social networks are controlled for, the home-bias of domestic trips tends to decrease or, in some cases, even disappear. With this analysis we confirm that social networks do, by various measurements, exert a trade-creation effect and that in most cases, once social networks are controlled for, the negative effect of distance vanishes. We also confirm the spatial autocorrelation of flows and test it with two complementary matrices: contiguity and main relative social networks.

In Sect. 15.2 we discuss trade in services and network influences on its flows. Section 15.3 presents an empirical gravity model, detailing a series of increasingly complex specifications that control for spatial/geographical as well as network dependencies. In Sect. 15.4 we present and discuss our empirical results by applying the model to intra-and interregional trade flows associated with tourism in Spain. Section 15.4 includes an additional analysis with the model preferred, but instead of social-network variables we use different variables that try to capture other ways that social networks can be created.

15.2 Trade and Social Networks: Background and Definitions

An economic network has been defined as a group of agents that pursue repeated, enduring exchange relations with one another (Podolny and Page 1998). Using this definition, several authors have analyzed the impact on bilateral trade between origin and destination regions of the stock of immigrants in or emigrants from the importing and exporting region. Rauch (2001) pointed out in his review that any positive impact of immigration on trade may simply reflect immigrant preferences for goods from their countries of origin or a correlation of immigration with the trade-promoting characteristics of the country of origin or destination (e.g., geographic proximity). As other authors have shown, however, apart from these 'taste effects', there also exists a 'network effect' induced by social links that immigrants maintain with their countries of origin. Such links may lead to important reductions in transaction cost, which may in turn boost bilateral trade flows.

For our purposes, an immigrant is an individual born in a region ('homeland') different from his current region of residence ('host region'). Note also that, when considering interregional monetary flows in tourism-related sectors, we define the 'exporting region' as the one producing the service: in this case, the region receiving the tourists. Within these sectors are several channels that may lead to a positive relationship between the intensity of trade and the presence of social networks. We classify these channels into two groups, differentiating between relations that affect the trading regions ('emigrant and immigrant effects', as they have been traditionally labeled in the literature) and relations that affect the neighbors of trading regions (cross-section autocorrelation).

The empirical literature on the trade-creation effect of social networks identifies two main channels between our tourism-linked trade flows and interregional migration stocks:

1. Immigrants select their destination for internal (domestic) touristic trips in accord with family ties in their homeland (home region). Since tourists take advantage of vacations to visit their homeland, they may own homes or have access to property there. Thus the larger the stock of emigrants in a region, the greater the flow of exports from the emigrants' birth regions to their host regions. We call this the '*emigrant effect*'.
2. Conversely, non-migrant relatives and friends may tend to visit immigrants in their host regions, since these visits are made easier by access to information and to less-expensive accommodations than in other tourist destinations. Thus the larger the stock of immigrants in a region, the greater the flow of exports from the host region to the migrant homeland. We call this the '*immigrant effect*'.

Apart from these two effects, which appear to enhance bilateral flows and have traditionally been analyzed in the literature on trade, there are additional channels of influence that could affect bilateral trade flows in tourism-related sectors. These additional channels arise from what we might consider cross-sectional autocorrelation due to 'spatial' or 'demographic' neighboring, and they tend to connect each bilateral trade flow of services with outflows from or inflows to the neighboring exporting or importing regions under consideration.

For origin and destination flows, Lesage and Pace (2008) described an 'origin-based dependence' and a 'destination-based dependence'. The former associates flows from i to j with flows from i's neighbors to j, whereas the latter associates flows from i to j with flows from i to j's neighbors.[5]

Moreover, we could define a 'neighboring region' in terms of geographic proximity/spatial contiguity, as in Lesage and Pace (2008), or, more generally, in terms of proximity as measured by population and demography.

There could be **cross-sectional dependence** between a given flow and a flow from the exporting region's spatial neighbor (**contiguous region**) to the importing region (exporting-based dependence) and another flow from the exporting region itself to a neighbor of the importing region (importing-based dependence):

1. Export flows from a region i to a region j can be correlated with exports from i's neighbors to j. This spatial dependence could be caused by:
   (a) The 'taste effect', in which exports of tourism-related services from one region and its contiguous neighbors to some other region are related because people living in the importing region may select any or all of the exporting

[5]LeSage and Pace (2008) described a third 'origin–destination–based dependence', which related flows between the neighbours of i and the neighbours of j. This paper, like Fischer and Griffith (2008), does not consider this relationship.

regions as their destination for their similar characteristics (weather, culture, etc.).
   (b) People are more likely to have information about the tourism options of regions contiguous to the destination region and shared infrastructure often reinforces this channel.

2. Conversely, from the perspective of the importing region, there could also be some correlation between exports from a given region i to j and between the exports of the same region i and the neighbors of j. The mechanisms behind this spatial autocorrelation are equivalent to those described for the regions where flows originate (tourist destinations) but with the forces acting in the opposite direction.

For **cross-section autocorrelation** based on regional **demographic structure** (network dependence), we can also delineate two such mechanisms (on the basis of emigration from and immigration to each region):

1. The first relates a region's historical patterns of emigration with current tourist decisions through 'importing-based dependence'. If a given region's emigrants have concentrated in a group of host regions, then a social network between home and host regions is likely to appear. People in this social network (e.g., members of one family living in different regions) may decide to travel periodically as tourists to the same region. Thus the imports of one region are not independent of the imports of its demographic neighbor. This cross-relation between a region's demographic neighbors may introduce effects that enhance or compete with the positive relation of migrants and trade in our three services sectors. As noted earlier, immigration is influenced by gravity, so 'demographic neighbors' could coincide with 'spatial neighbors'. However, alternative situations might also arise.
2. A second situation could give rise to 'exporting-based dependence'. If one region's emigrants are highly concentrated in another region, exports from the homeland to any other region j will be correlated with exports from the host region to region j. The mechanisms that explain this dependence on flows are similar to those explained before but act in a different direction, toward the trip destination (the exporting region).

Finally, it is important to highlight that immigrants could also affect the 'tourism decisions' of non-immigrants living in the same region. Since a large number of immigrants start families with their host region's natives, it is easy to imagine an influence arising from tastes and family ties that acts not only on immigrant tourism decisions but on non-immigrant tourism decisions as well. Moreover, an immigrant's relatives and friends still living in the homeland (but remaining in regular contact) could also spread their travel experiences and tastes to fellow inhabitants of the homeland. Although information and preferences would spread mainly within each of the two regions (homeland and host region), it could also gradually spread to neighboring regions. In Combes et al. (2005), this effect is described as the main force driving the relation between the 'information effect'

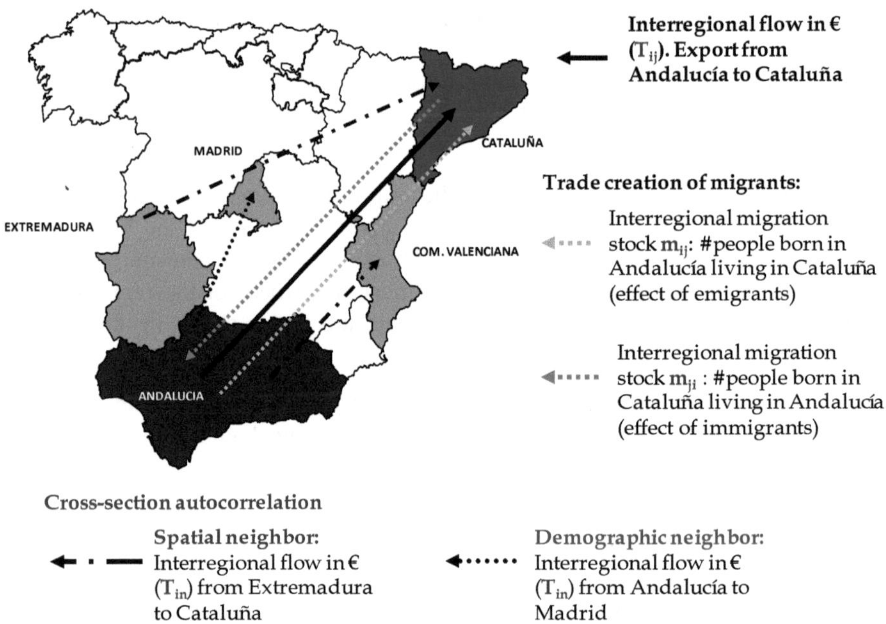

Fig. 15.1 Intuitive scheme showing the relation between trade flows in services and migration stocks

and the ‘border effect’ for interregional trade in goods. In this paper, the effect is mixed with and strengthened by the effects described above.

In conclusion, we have described how the stock of immigrants and emigrants can influence bilateral flows between two regions through different channels, but also how a given region’s trade flow can be related to the flows to and from contiguous regions and demographic neighbors (where a relatively large concentration of emigrants from one region lives in the other, or where a large share of a region’s immigrants have been born in the other). We have described, furthermore, how all these influences could affect both immigrant and non-immigrant tourism decisions. These effects are summarized in Figs. 15.1 and 15.2.

15.3 The Empirical Model

In this section, we first discuss the cross-section dependence of flows based on spatial and demographic neighboring and how they relate to our spatial econometric model. We set forth a series of alternative, increasingly complex specifications and compare them.

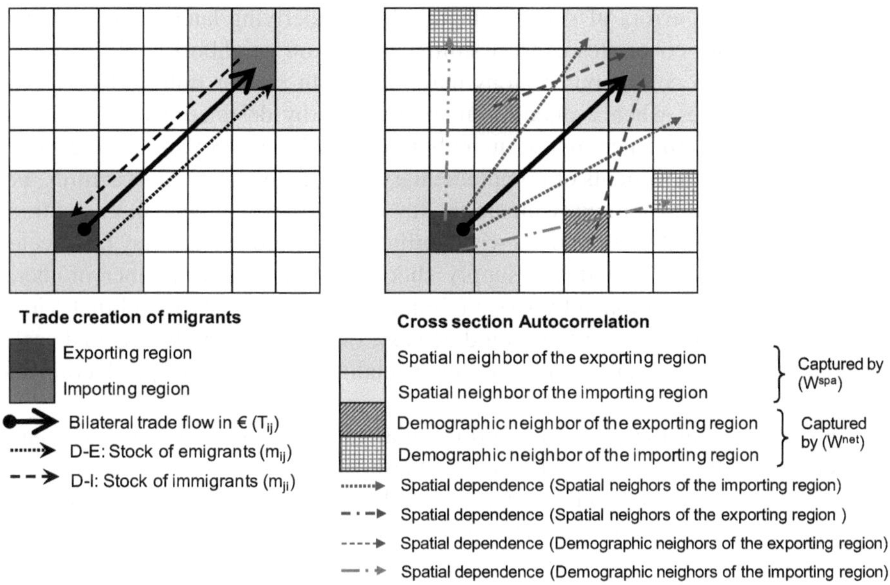

Fig. 15.2 Scheme summarizing spatial and network effects on bilateral flows

15.3.1 Spatial and Demographic Dependence Affecting Gravity-Model Estimates

Black (1992) suggested that network and spatial autocorrelation may bias the classical estimation procedures for spatial interaction models. He suggested that "autocorrelation may [. . .] exist among random variables associated with the links of a network". Bolduc et al. (1992) suggested that classical gravity models do not consider the socioeconomic and network variables adjacent to bilateral origin–destination regions *i* and *j*, arguing that these should also be incorporated into the equation that attempts to explain flows (T_{ij}) between these regions. He emphasized that omission of neighboring variable values gives rise to spatial autocorrelation in the regression errors. The sources of spatial autocorrelation errors include model misspecification and omitted explanatory variables to capture effects related to a region's physical and economic characteristics (distances between zones, size of zones, length of frontiers between adjacent zones, etc.).

More recently, LeSage and Pace (2008) challenged the assumption that the origin and destination (OD) flows in the classical gravity model contained in the dependent variable vector T_{ij} exhibit no spatial dependence. They note that the use of distance alone in a gravity model may be inadequate for the modeling of spatial dependence between observations. Most socioeconomic spatial interactions (migration, trade, commuting, etc.) have several explanations. For example, neighboring origins (exporting regions) and destinations (importing regions) may exhibit estimation errors of similar magnitude if underlying latent or unobserved forces or missing covariates exert a similar impact on neighboring observations. Agents located in contiguous regions may meet with similar transport costs and profit opportunities when evaluating alternative nearby destinations. This similar positive/negative influence among neighbors could also be explained in terms of common factor endowments or complementary/competitive sectoral structures. For example, if natural factor endowments are key variables explaining patterns of trade specialization, neighboring regions with similar factor endowments may be affected in similar ways by demand and supply shocks. Since a large number of factor endowments are conditioned by space (similar natural resources and climate, joint transport infrastructures, etc.), it would be easy, on a sufficiently fine spatial scale, to find spatial autocorrelation in the sector specialization of regional production and trade.

As explained in the previous section, bilateral trade flows of tourism-related services could themselves be affected by these sources of spatial dependence. In the next section, we formally test an extended gravity-model specification that accounts for spatial and network (in our case, demographic) autocorrelation effects in interregional trade flows. The extended model subsumes models that exclude spatial and network dependence as special cases of the most elaborate model, and provides a simple empirical test for the presence of significant spatial and network dependence.

Our empirical model will be based on several alternative specifications that allow us to consider the interdependence of flows between two regions and of flows to and from their neighbors. In this respect, we have defined two different types of neighbors: one based on geography and regional borders (the contiguity matrix) and a second based on the relative importance of certain past migration flows, which allow us to take into account the interdependence of flows caused by the existence of social networks.

15.3.2 Introducing Spatial and Network Effects in the Gravity Model

A conventional least-squares gravity-model specification is shown in Eq. (15.1), where bilateral flows (T_{ij}) between exporting region i and importing j are modeled as a function of a set of explanatory variables reflecting the economic size of the two regions and the distance (d_{ij}) between them. T_{ij} denotes the $n \times n$ matrix of exports in monetary units (current euros) of the services produced by Restaurants + Accommodations between each region i and imported by each region j. The size of the origin of the flow (exporting region) is proxied by the hospitality-industry gross value added in region i (gva_i), while the size of importing region j is modeled as depending on population (pop_j) and income (inc_j). A dummy variable $ownreg_{ij}$, taking the value one when trade is intraregional and zero otherwise, has been included to control for the different nature of intraregional trade flows (flows generated by trips within the region of residence), T_{ii}. Past studies (McCallum 1995; Helliwell 1997; Wolf 2000; Chen 2004; Okubo 2004; Combes et al. 2005; Requena and Llano 2010) have interpreted the coefficient associated with this dummy variable as an 'internal border effect' or 'home bias'. Once we have controlled for other factors (size, bilateral distance, presence of a social network), we interpret the coefficient linked with this dummy variable, γ, as the number of times one region tends to trade more within itself than with any other region in the country. We measure the trade creation effect of social networks by introducing the variables m_{ij} and m_{ij}. The former captures the effect of emigrants on trade exports from region i to j; similarly, the latter captures the variation in flows due to the stock of immigrants hailing from region j but living in region i. In a first specification we imposed the value of zero on both coefficients, while in a second we obtained both effects simultaneously. For simplicity we are not using alternative specifications with just one of the coefficients set to zero and thus estimating the 'emigrant' and 'immigrant' effect separately. We have already carried out this analysis, although with slightly different data, in de la Mata and Llano (2013).

$$T_{ij} = \alpha i_N + gva_i\beta_1 + pop_j\beta_2 + inc_j\beta_3 + d_{ij}\beta_4 + ownreg_{ij}\gamma + m_{ij}\beta_5 + m_{ji}\beta_6 + \varepsilon_{ij} \tag{15.1}$$

One may wish to consider the presence of potential multicolinearity problems caused by a high correlation between emigrant and immigrant bilateral flows. To cope with this limitation, Eq. (15.2) uses a single vector for bilateral "net migration" $m\_net_{ij} = \left(m_{ji} + m_{ij}\right)$ with which to capture the aggregate effect of immigrants + emigrants on trade. This third specification will be considered also for the forthcoming augmented models, which will include spatial and network effects.

$$T_{ij} = \alpha i_N + gva_i\beta_1 + pop_j\beta_2 + inc_j\beta_3 + d_{ij}\beta_4 + ownreg_{ij}\gamma + m\_net_{ij}\beta_7 + \varepsilon_{ij} \tag{15.2}$$

15.3.3 Alternative Spatial Models for Origin and Destination Flows

To determine whether spatial dependence on the bilateral flows discussed in previous sections is consistent with the data, we follow the approach set forth in LeSage and Pace (2008) and make our next spatial regression models rely on the spatial lags of the dependent variable. These models also include all the explanatory variables from the previous models, allowing them to subsume the non-spatial regression models as special cases. We include a spatial lag of the dependent variable (WT_{ij}), the independent variables (WX_{ij}), the error term (Wu_{ij}), or some combination thereof, where W represents a spatial weight matrix of the form suggested by LeSage and Pace (2008).

In a typical cross-sectional model with n regions, where each pair of regions represents an observation, spatial regression models rely on an $n \times n$ non-negative weight matrix that describes the connectivity structure between the n regions. For example, $W_{ij} > 0$ if region i is contiguous with region j. By convention, $W_{ii} = 0$ to prevent an observation from being defined as a neighbor to itself, and the matrix W is typically row-standardized. In the case of bilateral flows, where we work with $N = n^2$ observations, LeSage and Pace (2008), Chun (2008), Chun and Griffith (2011) and Fischer and Griffith (2008) suggest using $W^{spa} = W_j^{spa} + W_i^{spa}$, where $W_j^{spa} = I_n \otimes W_s$ represents an $N \times N$ spatial weight matrix that captures connectivity between the importing region and its neighbor, and $W_i^{spa} = W_s \otimes I_n$ is another $N \times N$ spatial weight matrix that captures connectivity between the exporting region and its neighbor.[6] We row-standardize the matrix W^{spa} to form a spatial lag of the dependent variable.

LeSage and Pace (2008) note that the spatial lag variable captures both 'destination-' and 'origin-based' spatial-dependence relations using an average of flows from neighbors to each origin (exporting) and destination (importing) region. Specifically, this means that flows from any origin to a particular destination region may exhibit dependence on flows from the origin's neighbors to the same destination—a situation that LeSage and Pace (2008) call origin-based dependence. The spatial lag matrix, W^{spa}, also captures destination-based dependence, which is a term used by LeSage and Pace (2008) to reflect dependence between flows from a particular origin region to neighboring regions of the destination region.

We take a similar approach to produce a network-dependence weight matrix, W^{net}, which captures network autocorrelation effects. As in the case of W^{spa}, the W^{net} matrix is formed as a sum of two matrices that specify 'demographic neighbors' to the origin and destination regions, specifically $W^{net} = W_i^{net} + W_j^{net}$. The matrix $W_j^{net} = I_n \otimes W_{81-sym}^{net}$, where W_{81-sym}^{net} is constructed on the basis of regions with the strongest demographic links as shown by past migration-stock patterns, is an $N \times N$ weight matrix that captures connectivity between the importing region and its demographic neighbors. Details on the procedure used to build this matrix are provided in the next section. Similarly, $W_i^{net} = W_{81-sym}^{net} \otimes I_n$, and the matrix W^{net} is row-standardized. This allows us to include in this model a network lag of the dependent variable shown in Eqs. (15.1) and (15.2).

We will now present our econometric models, which allow us to account for the different structures of the flows' spatial dependence.

15.3.3.1 A Spatial Lag Model

Equation (15.3) is a spatial lag model, including: (1) a spatial lag of the dependent variable (WT_{ij}), in which T_{ij} is the $N \times 1$ vector representing the $n \times n$ flows matrix

[6]We use the symbol $\otimes$ to denote a Kronecker product.

transformed into a vector, W is one of the previously described matrices used to capture spatial autocorrelation based on contiguity or demographic structures; i_N is an $N \times 1$ vector of ones; *gva*, *pop* and *inc* are $N \times 1$ vectors containing the explanatory variables; d is the $n \times n$ matrix of interregional distances transformed to an $N \times 1$ vector appropriate for each bilateral flow; $ownreg_{ij}$ is an identity matrix of order n controlling for intraregional flows that has been transformed into an $N \times 1$ vector; m_{ij} and m_{ji} are two $n \times n$ matrices of interregional migration stocks transformed into a pair of $N \times 1$ vectors and ε is an $N \times 1$ vector of normally distributed constant variance disturbances.

The scalar parameter ρ denotes the strength of spatial dependence in flows. When it takes the value of zero the model in Eq. (15.3) becomes the independent regression model. This allows us to carry out a simple empirical test for the statistical significance of spatial dependence in the flows.

$$\begin{aligned} T_{ij} = {} & \alpha i_N + \rho W T_{ij} + gva_i \beta_1 + pop_j \beta_2 + inc_j \beta_3 + d_{ij} \beta_4 + ownreg_{ij} \gamma \\ & + m_{ij} \beta_5 + m_{ji} \beta_6 + \varepsilon_{ij} \end{aligned} \tag{15.3}$$

Then, as in Eq. (15.3), a new Eq. (15.4) can be defined, where immigrant and emigrant effects are added in a single net migration vector.

$$\begin{aligned} T_{ij} = {} & \alpha i_N + \rho W T_{ij} + gva_i \beta_1 + pop_j \beta_2 + inc_j \beta_3 + d_{ij} \beta_4 + ownreg_{ij} \gamma \\ & + m\_net_{ij} \beta_7 + \varepsilon_{ij} \end{aligned} \tag{15.4}$$

15.3.3.2 A Spatial Error Model

The spatial error model is appropriate when the error terms of particular regions are can be expected to be linked. The parameter λ captures the presence of spatial dependence in the residuals of the bilateral flows.

$$\begin{aligned} lT_{ij} &= \alpha i_N + gva_i \beta_1 + pop_j \beta_2 + inc_j \beta_3 + d_{ij} \beta_4 + ownreg_{ij} \gamma + m_{ij} \beta_5 + m_{ji} \beta_6 + u_{ij} \\ u_{ij} &= \lambda W u_{ij} + \varepsilon_{ij} \\ \varepsilon_{ij} &\sim \left(0, \sigma^2 I_N\right) \end{aligned} \tag{15.5}$$

For the sake of simplicity, in this and the following models we do not include a new equation to describe the corresponding models in which the "net migration" vector would be used instead of their emigrant and immigrant counterparts. However, we analyze the corresponding results in the next section.

Now we briefly describe two of the models that allow us to test for more elaborate structures of dependence in the flows: the spatial Durbin model and the spatial general model.

15.3.3.3 A Spatial Durbin Model

This model, described in LeSage and Fischer (2008) and elsewhere, has been applied in the context of gravity equations by Angulo et al. (2011). In contrast to the previous models, it assumes spatial dependence in the dependent and independent variables, as described in Eq. (15.6):

$$T_{ij} = \alpha i_N + \rho_1 W T_{ij} + X\beta + WX\gamma + \varepsilon_{ij} \tag{15.6}$$

Where *WX* is the spatial lag of all the independent variables included in *X*. Note that, in contrast to previous specifications included in this paper, only one weight matrix is used at a time, but it generates two sources of spatial dependence. An SDM gravity model with two alternative W matrices has not been reported in the literature. Here, however, we depart from this common specification and estimate three alternative models using the following weight matrices, as in de la Mata and Llano (2013): (1) $W_1 = W^{spat}$, (2) $W_2 = W^{net}$, (3) $W_3 = W^{spa} + W^{net}$.

15.3.3.4 A Spatial General Model

The last model, based on the spatial general model (SAC) described in LeSage and Pace (2009, p. 32), considers spatial dependence in both the dependent variable and the disturbance term, as described in Eq. (15.7):

$$\begin{aligned} T_{ij} &= \alpha i_N + \rho W_1 T_{ij} + gva_i\beta_1 + pop_j\beta_2 + inc_j\beta_3 + d_{ij}\beta_4 + ownreg_{ij}\gamma \\ &\quad + m_{ij}\beta_5 + m_{ji}\beta_6 + u_{ij} \\ u_{ij} &= \lambda W_2 u_{ij} + \varepsilon_{ij} \\ \varepsilon_{ij} &\sim \left(0, \sigma^2 I_N\right) \end{aligned} \tag{15.7}$$

Note that the model described in Eq. (15.7) considers two different weight matrices, W_1 and W_2, each capturing the effects on the dependent variable and the disturbance term. Following the recommendations of LeSage and Pace (2009, p. 32), we will consider four alternative cases, without imposing a preferred structure to the data in advance: (1) $W_1 = W^{spa}$, $W_2 = W^{net}$; (2) $W_1 = W^{net}$, $W_2 = W^{spa}$; (3) $W_1 = W_2 = W^{spa}$; (4) $W_1 = W_2 = W^{net}$.

15.4 An Application to Spanish Domestic Trade in Certain Service Sectors

15.4.1 The Data

Like most countries, Spain has no official data on monetary interregional trade flows associated with the two tourism-related sectors we are considering here: Restaurants and Accommodations. To group these sectors between the Spanish regions, our application takes advantage of recent estimates of intra- and interregional trade flows. To generate our dataset for 2000–2009 (de la Mata and Llano 2012b)—a dataset constructed as part of a larger research project (www.c-intereg.es)—we improved on the methodology presented for 2001 in Llano and de la Mata (2009) and analyzed in De la Mata and Llano (2012a). Schematically, the methodology comprises two steps:

1. Estimation of the portion of each region's output that is consumed by Spanish citizens (i.e., that is not exported internationally);
2. Determination of the bilateral distribution of each region's non-internationally-exported output. This second step uses existing information on the daily expenses of domestic travelers in the destination region and origin and destination matrices (Familitur surveys and Occupancy Surveys) that capture the overnight stays and displacements of Spanish residents, depending on the accommodation types available in destination regions. The estimation uses different daily expenses in 'Accommodations' and 'Restaurants and the Like' for hotels, apartments, campsites, rural tourism, the homes of friends and relatives, second residences and excursions, covering all possible trip motives (leisure, work, education, etc.). We have performed separate estimations for Accommodations and Restaurants. By not including expenses for transport, shopping or any other goods or services in our data, we avoid endogeneity problems between interregional trade flows of tourist services and transport costs related to bilateral distance.
3. Proportional adjustment of bilateral flows for Accommodations to total output, and adjustment of the sum of interregional exports for '*Restaurants and the Like*' to output, under the assumption that the difference is the daily consumption in this sector.[7]

In summary, the estimates for the interregional monetary flows of the two service sectors analysed (Accommodations and Restaurants) use the most accurate statistical sources available in Spain, obtaining figures that are constrained by the regional and national output of the sector (Instituto Nacional de Estadística, INE), the Balance of Payment (Bank of Spain) and the widest available sample of

[7] In de la Mata and Llano (2013) we included the consumption for restaurants not linked to trips and travel agencies. These two types of consumption only increase intraregional flows, but since they have a different nature, we have in this case preferred to keep them out of the analysis. Note that we have nevertheless retained intraregional flows generated by trips within the region of residence.

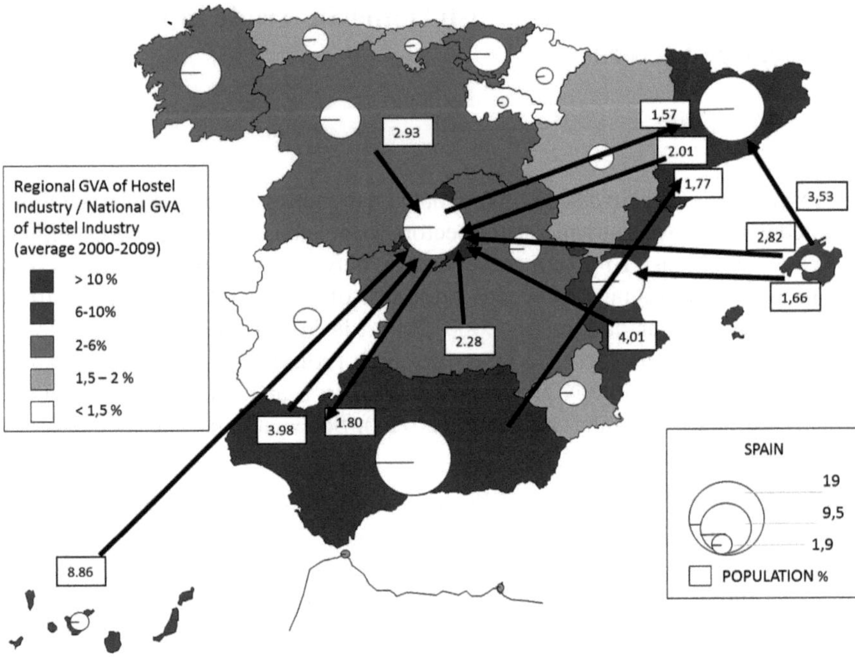

Fig. 15.3 Main interregional flows (€) for accommodations and restaurants % of total interregional flows (average for 2000–2009)

surveys on people movements within the country (Familitur, Instituto de Estudios Turísticos).

To provide an overview of internal flows for the Spanish sectors considered in this work, Fig. 15.3 shows the largest average interregional monetary flows in Accommodations and Restaurants, as well as the distribution of the population and the location coefficient for the 'Hotels and Restaurants' sector (LCRegion = Regional Hospitality Industry GVA/National Hospitality Industry GVA). Arrows from eastern coastal regions (Andalucía, C. Valenciana and Cataluña) to the landlocked region of Madrid show that a large share of interregional exports (in current euros) in Accommodation and Restaurants flow from these regions to Madrid. This is a consequence of the large number of travelers from Madrid to Andalucía. It is easy to see from the figure that the major exporting regions are located along the coast, with the largest importers located in the most populous high-income regions. There are also large exports from the islands to populous regions (Canarias to Madrid and Baleares to Madrid and Cataluña). In addition, there are many flows between the largest regions, such as exports from Cataluña to Madrid and Madrid to Cataluña or Andalucía. Note also that some of the largest interregional flows occur between distant regions. Finally, there are strong flows from the landlocked larger regions to contiguous, richer regions (Castilla y León and Castilla–La Mancha to Madrid). These results can be explained first by the size of the regions (in terms of population and income or gross domestic product) and second by important social networks that have arisen as a result of historical bilateral migration flows.

For the remaining variables, we use the hospitality—industry gross value added (*gva*), regional income (*inc*) from the Spanish Regional Accounts (INE) and population (*pop*) from the Spanish Register (INE). The interregional migration matrices are also obtained from the Spanish Register (INE), which offers information on the stock of region inhabitants born in other regions. The direct effects captured by the m_{ij} and the m_{ji} terms enter as two independent column vectors.

Distances are obtained from the 2001 Movilia survey (Ministerio de Fomento); these are the actual distances travelled by Spanish residents in their displacements, both within and between regions. The inclusion of both inter- and intraregional distance is one of the most interesting features of this measure. In line with Head and Mayer (2010), then, we are able to escape from the a priori quantification of intraregional distances assumed in other papers. Moreover, the distance used is an average of the actual distance travelled in each of the more than 500 million displacements estimated by the 2001 Movilia survey. These displacements cover all motives, so that reported distance is not constrained to the distance between capitals, which, while perhaps predominant for business trips, does not reflect the distances between peripherally located tourist spots (beaches, skiing resorts, the countryside, etc.).

The spatial weight matrices have been built to take into account first-order contiguity relations based on shared borders, with islands treated as having no adjacent regions. The demographic network weight matrix W_{81}^{net} is built to depart from an OD matrix of the stock of immigrants born in one region and living in another, with diagonal elements set to zero. We obtain this weight matrix through the following steps: (1) We create a matrix containing the stock of interregional migrants in 1981 as reported in the Spanish census. (2) For $W_{81\_born}^{net}$ we use every home region's share of interregional immigrants with respect to every host region's total (forming the rows), while for $W_{81\_residence}^{net}$ we use the every host region's share of interregional emigrants with respect to each home region's total (forming the columns). (3) Next, we compute the 90th percentile in the distribution of the shares of interregional migration for each *home* and *host region*. We then consider two regions to be neighbors when the threshold defined by the 90th percentile is lower than the corresponding share. In this case, the corresponding W matrix will either contain this share or have a value of zero. Note that by obtaining our two matrices, $W_{81\_residence}^{net}$ and $W_{81\_born}^{net}$, in this way, we ensure that every region has a positive number of neighbors and that the neighbor relation depends not on the size of both regions but on the relative weight that each region represents in the overall demographic structure of all the regions.[8] (4) Adding these two matrices,

[8]For example, emigrants from the Islas Canarias, with their small population, do not represent more than 2 % of interregional immigrants living in any other region. The largest shares are found in Andalucía, Baleares and Murcia. In these regions, immigrants from the Islas Canarias represent a 1.4, 1.2 and 1.3 % of total interregional immigrants. Their relative weight is higher in those regions than in Madrid (although in absolute terms are higher in Madrid), where they represent just the 0.2 % of total interregional immigrants. According to our definition, then, Canarias is a

Region (NUTS 2)	1	2	3	4	5	6	7	8	9	10	11	12	13	14	15	16	17
1				X	X			O	X		⊗			O			
2							O	O	⊗	O					⊗		O
3						⊗	⊗					⊗					
4	X				X				X	X				X			
5	X			X								X	X				
6			⊗				⊗									⊗	
7		O	⊗			⊗		O			O	⊗	⊗			⊗	O
8	O	O					O			⊗	⊗		⊗	O			
9	X	⊗		X						O							
10		O		X				⊗	O					⊗			
11	⊗						O	⊗					X			X	
12			⊗		X		⊗										
13					X		⊗	⊗			X						
14	O			X				O		⊗							
15		⊗														⊗	⊗
16						⊗	⊗				X				⊗		⊗
17							O								⊗	⊗	

Region (NUTS 2)	Code	Region (NUTS 2)	Code	Region (NUTS 2)	Code
Andalucía	1	Castilla y León	7	Madrid (Comunidad de)	13
Aragón	2	Castilla-La Mancha	8	Murcia (Región de)	14
Asturias (Principado de)	3	Cataluña	9	Navarra (Comunidad Foral de)	15
Baleares (Islas)	4	Comunidad Valenciana	10	País Vasco	16
Canarias	5	Extremadura	11	Rioja (La)	17
Cantabria	6	Galicia	12		

Fig. 15.4 Comparison of the neighboring pattern with the contiguity matrix and the demography-link matrix

we obtain a general matrix $W_{81}^{net} = W_{81_{born}}^{net} + W_{81_{residence}}^{net}$. (5) Then we add the W_{81}^{net} matrix to its transpose, imposing bidirectional links between regions and obtaining a symmetric version, $W_{81-sym}^{net} = W_{81}^{net} + W_{81}^{net\prime}$. In de la Mata and Llano (2013), $W_{81_{born}}^{net}$ and $W_{81_{residence}}^{net}$ were used independently as two alternative W matrices, with very similar results. This matrix has also the virtue of capturing a stock of interregional relations with a 20-year lag with respect to the interregional bilateral flows used as endogenous variables in all of our models. This strategy overcomes the main criticism of endogeneity and circular causation.

Figure 15.4 helps determine whether the patterns described by the two baseline W matrices considered in this work (contiguity and social networks) are similar or very different. Cells with an “O” represent country-pairs that are contiguous but not considered demographic neighbors. Cells with an “X” are country-pairs that are

demographic neighbor of Andalucía, Baleares and Murcia and not of Madrid, because its relative magnitude is higher for the former group of regions than for the latter.

considered demographic neighbors but are non-contiguous. Finally, cells with a "⊗" represent country-pairs that are both contiguous and demographic neighbors. From Fig. 15.4, although 36 (of a total 289) country-pairs are neighbors in both matrices, 20 are contiguous but not demographic neighbors and 22 are demographic neighbors but non-contiguous. Thus a certain level of complementarity between both W matrices exists. Cataluña, for example, is simultaneously (1) contiguous with but not a demographic neighbor to the Comunidad Valenciana, (2) a demographic neighbor to non-contiguous regions like Andalucía and the Islas Baleares and (3) a demographic neighbor and contiguous region to Aragón. By working with two W matrices instead of just one, we expand our ability to capture complexities and complete relations.

15.4.2 Alternative Measures for Capturing the Pro-Trade Effect of Social Networks

As a robustness check, we define certain alternative social-network measures, which enter into the model by substituting for the interregional migration stocks captured by m_{ij} and m_{ji}, or $m\_net_{ij} = (m_{ji} + m_{ij})$ in the case of net effects.

For the sake of simplicity, since all these alternative variables are dyadic, and connect the trading regions i and j, we retain the same variable names (m_{ij}; m_{ji}; m_net_{ij}) as in Eq. (15.7). However, the model is re-estimated 18 times with these alternative proxies for the social links between each pair of Spanish regions. It is important to remark that we intend this robustness analysis to consider alternative channels through which information and taste effects might be enhancing interregional trips and, thereby, the corresponding interregional flows of services in euros.

A brief description of each of these variables is shown in Table 15.1. Here, as when the stock of migrants was considered, these variables are likely to have a bidirectional effect. That is, an individual will travel to visit the members of his social network in regions other than his region of residence, but the members of his social network will also travel to visit him.

The variables **soc-net-2** and **soc-net-10** are equivalent to the interregional stock of migrants from the 1981 Spanish census but draw from the 2001 and 1991 censuses respectively. The use of these two alternative variables will illustrate the stability of interregional links as well as the persistence of the effects in different periods. The **soc-net-8** variable restricts this concept to employed individuals over 16 years of age. Despite some differences, the pattern of interregional migrations is similar for all migrant stocks[9] and similar to the born-residence links of 1981.

[9]The main emigration stocks are found from Andalucía to Cataluña; from Castilla y León, Castilla–La Mancha, Andalucía and Extremadura to Madrid; from Castilla–La Mancha and Andalucía to the Comunidad Valenciana; from Castilla y León to the País Vasco and Cataluña; and from Extremadura to Cataluña.

Table 15.1 Alternative social-network matrices

Social-network variable	Definition	Source	Interpretation—social networks
Soc_net_2	Stock of individuals born in region i and residing in region j in 2001	Spanish census, 2001, INE	Effect of emigration
Soc_net_3	Stock of individuals owning a second home in region i and residing in region j in 2001	Spanish census, 2001, INE	Effect of second homes owned by non-residents
Soc_net_4	Stock of individuals residing in region j in 2001 and with mothers born in i	Spanish census, 2001, INE	Effect of second-generation emigration on region of mother's birth
Soc_net_5	Stock of individuals residing in region j in 2001 and with fathers born in i	Spanish census, 2001, INE	Effect of second-generation emigration on region of father's birth
Soc_net_6	Individuals whose previous residence was i and who resided in j in 2001	Spanish census, 2001, INE	Effect of previous residence
Soc_net_7	Stock of individuals who lived in i in 1991 and in j in 2001	Spanish census, 2001, INE	Effect of residence 10 years earlier
Soc_net_8	Stock of individuals born in region i and living in j in 2001 (employed and over 16)	Spanish census, 2001, INE	Effect of emigrations for employed individuals over 16
Soc_net_9	Stock of individuals who work in i and lived in j in 2001 (employed and over 16)	Spanish census, 2001, INE	Social networks generated by commuting
Soc_net_10	Stock of individuals who were born in region i and lived in region j in 1991	Spanish census, 1991, INE	Effect of emigration
Soc_net_11	Stock of individuals that lived in i in 1981 and live in j in 1991	Spanish census, 1991, INE	Effect of residence 10 years earlier
Soc_net_12	Stock of individuals that lived in i from 1981 to 1991 and moved to j in 1991. (Note: said individuals could have lived in multiple places over 10 years)	Spanish census, 1991, INE	Effect of previous residences
Soc_net_13	Stock of individuals living in region j in 1991 and with fathers born in i	Spanish census, 1991, INE	Effect of second-generation emigration on region of father's birth

(continued)

Table 15.1 (continued)

Social-network variable	Definition	Source	Interpretation—social networks
Soc_net_14	Stock of individuals living in region *j* in 1991 with mothers born in *i*	Spanish census, 1991, INE	Effect of second-generation emigration on region of mother's birth
Soc_net_15	Stock of individuals with fathers born in region *i* and mothers born in region *j*	Spanish census, 1991, INE	Effect of marriages
Soc_net_16	Average number of trips to *j* taken by individuals living in *i* in 2000–2004	Familitur 2000–2004, IET	Social networks generated during previous trips and inertia on destination
Soc_net_17	Average number of overnight stays in *j* in 2000–2004 by individuals living in *i* (all kinds of establishments)	Familitur 2000–2004, IET and Encuesta de Ocupación, INE	Social networks generated during previous trips and inertia on destination
Soc_net_18	Average number of overnight stays in j in 2000–2004 by individuals living in *i* (hotels, apartments, rural tourism, campsites)	Encuesta de Ocupación 2000–2004, INE	Social networks generated during previous trips and inertia on destination
Soc_net_19	Parcels received in *i* and sent by *j* in 1995–2000	Ministerio de Fomento	Proxy of interregional information flows or social networks

This new measure is meant to determine whether information and taste effects are equivalent for employed people and for the general population. The purpose of testing this is twofold: (1) on the one hand, part of our interregional flows of services can be caused by professional trips within Spain; (2) on the other, we should remember that information and taste effects can be transmitted between co-workers as well as between relatives and friends. Moreover, social connectivity can operate between different generations and social groups. An 'active' person's decision to travel, for example, can affect the travel decisions of other active or non-active people.

Soc-net-3 measures the impact of second-home ownership. This variable is drawn from the 2001 Spanish census and defined as the stock of people living in one region and owning a second home in any other. Although some of the main bilateral relations exist between region-pairs with strong migration relationships, others do not. For example, while immigrants from Andalucía living in Cataluña account for almost 11 % of the total stock of interregional migration, residents in Cataluña owning a second home in Andalucía account for just 2 % of total second homes in a region other than the region of residence. People living in Madrid and owning a second home in Castilla–La Mancha or Castilla y León represent the 11.7 % and 10.3 % respectively of total second homes in a region other than the region of residence, while emigrants from these regions living in Madrid each account for the 6.5 % of total interregional migration stocks, according to the 2001 Spanish census. It is also important to note the high share of second homes in the Comunidad Valenciana owned by residents in Madrid (10.4 % of the total), while emigrants from the Comunidad Valenciana in Madrid accounted for less than 1 % of total interregional migration stocks. An additional example of this unclear relationship between interregional migration stocks and interregional second-home ownership is found in the País Vasco. First, residents in the País Vasco that own a second home in Castilla y León account for 4.6 % of total second homes owned by residents of any other region. This can be explained by the share of emigrants from Castilla y León living in the País Vasco, but it is also notable that Basques own a large share of second homes in nearby regions, such as Cantabria, and represent 3.2 % of total second homes in Cantabria owned by residents in different regions, whereas first-generation Cantabrian emigrants in the País Vasco account for less than 0.5 % of total interregional migration stocks, according to the 2001 Spanish census. Although this variable is affected by certain interregional migration relationships, it also describes other patterns related to frequent trips by one region's residents to other regions, patterns that could promote the advantages of owning a second home in these regions. Because of the bidirectional effect of this variable, we should expect: (1) that the larger the share of second homes owned by non-residents, the larger the interregional export flows of services from the region of residence to the region where the second homes are located, and (2) that personal relationships created in the region where the second home is located will create incentives to travel to the region of residence of the individuals who own the second homes.

Soc-net-4, **soc-net-5**, **soc-net-13** and **soc-net-14** concern the social networks created between the region of residence and the birthplace of the residents' mothers or fathers as drawn from the 2001 (**soc-net-4**, **soc-net-5**) and 1991 Spanish censuses (**soc-net-13**, **soc-net-14**). These variables try to measure the impact of second-generation migration, although they can also capture the effect of families that move to other regions once their children are born; such children are considered first-generation or generation 1.5. In any case, in a country like Spain, part of the social network of individuals whose parents are migrants might pertain to the parents' family in the region of origin, independently of the individuals' region of residence. Despite some differences, the largest interregional stocks correspond to those of **soc-net-2** and **soc-net-10**. A fifth variable from the 1991 census (**soc-net-15**) relates the birth region of the father and mother. It shows the strongest links between contiguous regions or regions linked by migration stocks (birth vs. residence). All these variables are in relation to the previously mentioned 'mixed couples' concept, where the two partners are born in different regions of the country.

In addition, migrations that take into account the link between previous and current places of residence are relevant to determining the existence of social networks. We are drawing our links between current and previous region of residence (**soc-net-6**) from the 2001 census (and disregarding individuals' date of migration), our links between current region of residence and region of residence 10 years earlier from the 2001 and 1991 censuses (**soc-net-7, soc-net-11**) and our links with any of region of residence over the previous 10 years (**soc-net-12**) from the 1991 census. Of course, the previous region of residence sometimes coincides with an individual's birth region, but not always. For instance, an individual might migrate to a region and spend part of his life there before moving back to his home region for retirement. Such a displacement from host to home region is captured as an interregional movement by these variables, whereas in the matrix capturing the birth-vs.-residence relationship it is counted as an intraregional migration (birth and residence in the same region), although the person in question would still probably keep friends and part of his family in the region where he has been living part of his life. Thus the birth-vs.-residence variable is unable to capture this type of relation. On the other hand, we can capture an individual migration dating more than 10 years into the past as an intraregional movement by using the matrices describing past vs. actual residence. But in this case we cannot capture the migration as an effect of the social network in the migrant's homeland, whereas the birth-vs.-residence matrix would allow us to do so.

An additional cause of social-network creation is work relationships. To take this into account, we are including links between regions of residence and workplace regions (**soc-net-9**). Commuters may create an additional social network with co-workers, providing them with information about their regions of residence as well as feeding their home-region social networks with information about their workplace regions. The main commuting links exist between close and contiguous regions, like Madrid and Castilla–La Mancha (and vice versa), Castilla y León and Madrid, and the Comunidad Valenciana and Murcia. It is surprising to find relatively strong links between such distant regions as Extremadura and Madrid. It could be that certain people spend only a short part of the year working in other regions and thus do not change their region of residence. It could also be that at the time the census they were living in a region (region of residence) where they used to work.

Additionally, past interregional trips (**soc-net-16**) and overnight stays, whether in any kind of establishment (**soc-net-17**) or in a regulated establishment (**soc-net-18**), are included. Such trips correspond to the average reported in the official statistics for 2000–2004—that is, the period preceding the one captured by the endogenous variable (in euros). Past bilateral trips can help account for more recent flows in two ways. First, traveling individuals come into contact with residents in their destination regions and can create a network with them, thereby inspiring trips from these destination regions to the individuals' regions of origin. We can capture this kind of effect by including these variables. Moreover, their transpose versions capture the inertia of the series and how the trips of one region's residents to any other region can subsequently inspire fellow residents of the origin region to travel to the same destination. Finally, we include a matrix of parcel posts **soc-net-19** as a proxy for social and business networks. This last variable captures both tight social-network links (as between Andalucía and Madrid) and tight business-network links (as between Madrid and Cataluña). As we explain below, the nature of this variable has implications for the results generated with it. Although with this variable we try to capture all kinds of networks—and not just social networks driven by different types of migration—the truth is that high parcels links can be found between regions with strong social and business links as well as between distant regions, so post and parcel traffic might be a satisfactory alternative to face-to-face relations for the members of a social network to keep in contact.

Figure 15.5a, b show the pattern of the 18 alternative social-network measures described in Table 15.1. Although all the variables enter the model as column vectors, they are all obtained as the vectorialization of an equivalent set of origin–destination matrices. For comparison, the first graph in both Fig. 15.5a, b corresponds to the pattern for the migration variable used in the previous section, which represents the stock of people born in one region and residing in any other, as reported in the 1981 Spanish census. The other 18 graphs correspond to the origin–destination matrices of these alternative measures for social networks, where i and j are ranked in accord with the 1981 census stock of interregional migrants. To avoid scale problems, intraregional flows are not included in these graphs. However, both intra- and interregional connections are included when they are entered into the regressions. A glance at these graphs should make the differences and similarities between the flows clear.

15.4.3 Estimation Results

Here we compare results from the sequence of models estimated for the bilateral flows between 17 NUTS two Spanish regions ($N = 17 \times 17 = 289$ observations based on the average of the flows in 2005–2009), with Ceuta and Melilla excluded. In this case, since two of the alternative social network variables (**soc-net-17** and **soc-net-18**) that we want to test is the previous trips, we have decided to select the flows for the last 5 years available in the dataset in order to construct the dependent variable. All the variables (except dummy variables) are averaged and log-transformed, as is customary in the estimation of gravity models. We could have estimated the same specifications for each year, but, for the sake of simplicity, in this section we will comment on the results with averaged data, which reduces the effect of outliers.

Table 15.2 shows the results for three different specifications estimated by Ordinary Least Squares, all of them accounting for more than 84 % of the variation of the 289 bilateral flows. The first excludes both m_{ij} and m_{ji}, the second includes both, and the third substitutes m_net_{ij} for both. The estimated coefficients are significant and have the expected signs—positive for size variables and negative for distance—but the signed numerical value of the latter increases once the social-network variables are included. Similarly, the border-effect variable halves when social-network variables are introduced, suggesting, in agreement with Garmendia et al. (2012), that social networks reduce the magnitude of the border effect. However, we still have a positive and significant coefficient, which suggests that bilateral flows are more than 150 % larger than interregional ones, even when we

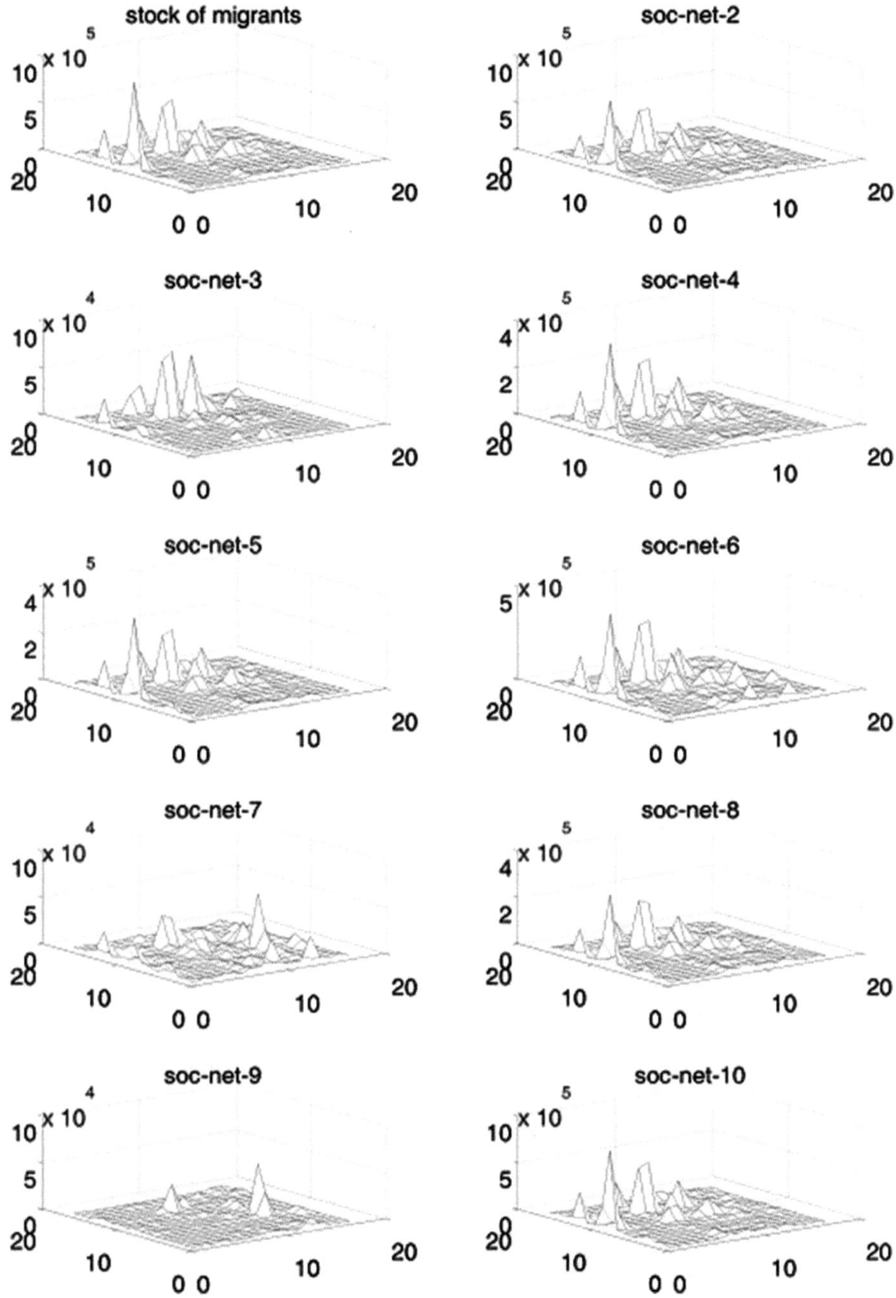

Fig. 15.5 (**a**, **b**) Geographical pattern of alternative social-network measures

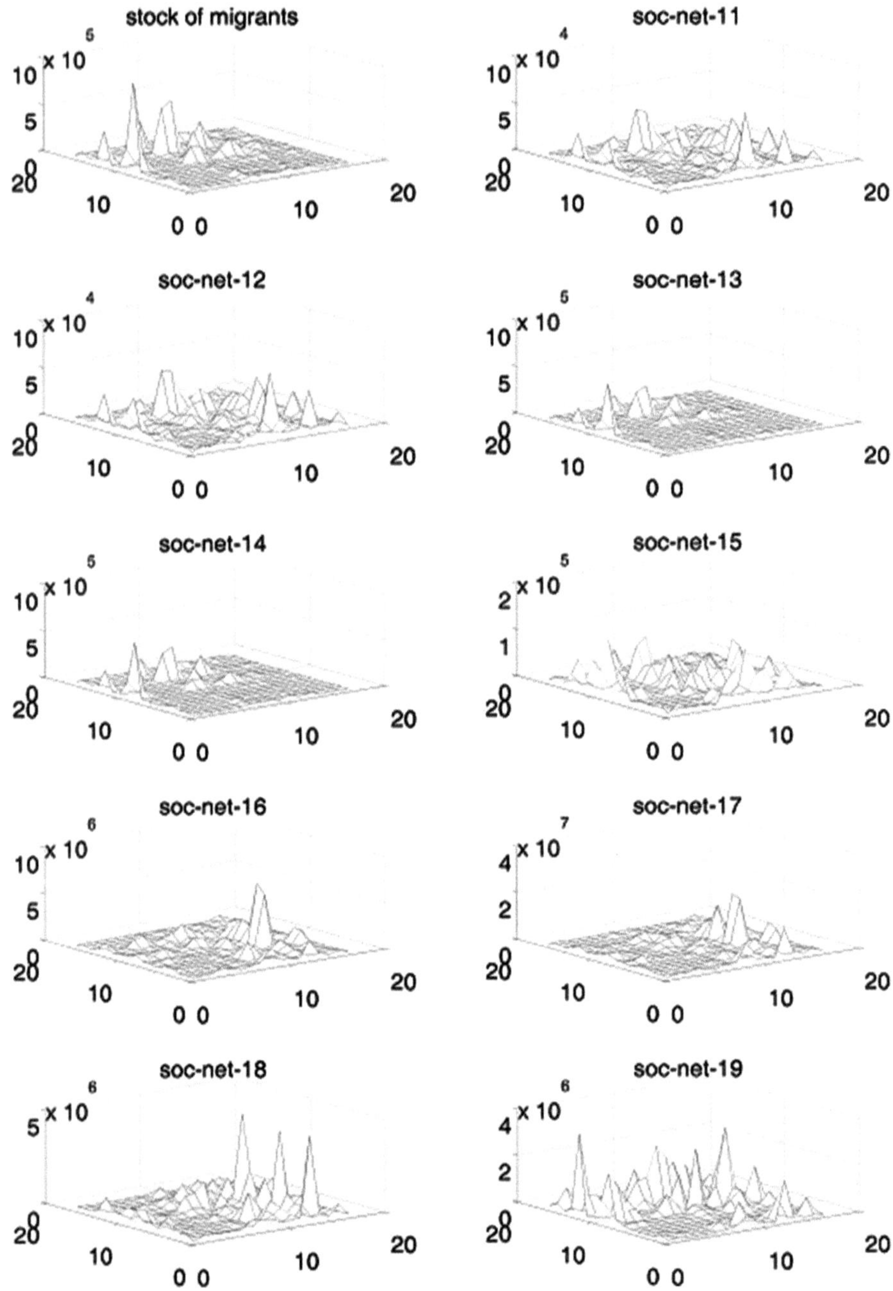

Fig. 15.5 (continued)

Table 15.2 Ordinary least squares

	(1)	(2)	(3)
R-squared	0.848	0.881	0.876
Rbar-squared	0.846	0.878	0.874
i_N	−26.365*** (−12.63)	−27.701*** (−13.187)	−24.51*** (−12.881)
gva_i	0.84*** (24.782)	0.57*** (12.747)	0.647*** (16.589)
pop_j	0.942*** (24.006)	0.683*** (14.22)	0.674*** (13.802)
inc_j	1.337*** (7.075)	1.76*** (8.776)	1.395*** (8.158)
d_{ij}	−0.454*** (−9.19)	−0.107* (−1.806)	−0.16*** (−2.764)
$ownreg_{ij}$	1.903*** (10.633)	0.957*** (4.896)	0.981*** (4.935)
m_{ij}		0.06** (1.994)	
m_{ji}		0.248*** (6.817)	
m_net_{ij}			0.142*** (7.985)

Source: Authors' calculations
T statistics in brackets
Dependent variable: interregional monetary flows of Accommodations and Restaurants generated by trips. (Average 2005–2009.)
Significance: *p < 0.1; **p < 0.05; ***p < 0.01

control for region size, interregional distance and interregional social networks. This result, obtained with trip-generated bilateral flows only, contrasts with the results in de la Mata and Llano (2013), where the inclusion of other types of intraregional flows, such as travel-agency services and non-trip-linked consumption in Restaurants and the Like, generated a more intense 'border effect'.

Finally, we also obtain a positive and significant impact for all social-network variables.

We now move on from these first estimates to consider several statistical tests, with the aim of motivating the inclusion of spatial lag and/or spatial error terms. This analysis is conducted by computing the I-Moran, and the classic and robust versions of the LM-lag and the LM-error statistics over the residuals obtained for the three models. In all of them we consider the spatial structure based on three different spatial weight matrices (each row-normalized): (1) W_i^{spa}, to capture the "spatial origin-based" autocorrelation; (2) W_j^{spa}, to capture the "spatial destination-based" autocorrelation; and (iii) $W^{spa} = W_i^{spa} + W_j^{spa}$, to capture the aggregate spatial autocorrelation (as previously stated, we omit the origin-to-destination-based element). The results for the three models, five tests and three spatial autocorrelation matrices are reported in the first three columns of Table 15.3. All cases show spatial autocorrelation in the residuals (Moran I analysis). This result is found for the 'origin-based' and 'destination-based' weight matrices, as well as when both are mixed in a single spatial matrix ($W^{spa} = W_i^{spa} + W_j^{spa}$). As for the LM tests, in all cases except when both 'emigrants' and 'immigrants' are introduced and $W = W_i + W_j$ is used (Model 2, LM error tests for spatial correlation in the dependent variable), the test confirms the suitability of a spatial lag model (SAR) as well as a spatial autoregressive error model (SEM). When the robust version of

Table 15.3 Spatial autocorrelation tests

	(1)	(2)	(3)	(4)	(5)	(6)
Origin-based autocorrelation with row-normalized 'Wo' (neighbors of exporting region *i*)						
Moran I-test for spatial correlation in residuals						
Moran I	0.201	0.147	0.152	0.168	0.112	0.076
Moran I-statistic	5.213	3.969	4.026	3.352	2.340	1.642
Marginal probability	0.000	0.000	0.000	0.001	0.019	0.101
Mean	−0.011	−0.014	−0.012	−0.012	−0.014	−0.013
Standard deviation	0.041	0.041	0.041	0.054	0.054	0.054
LM error tests for spatial correlation in residuals						
LM value	23.612	12.616	13.432	9.621	4.235	1.939
Marginal probability	0.000	0.000	0.000	0.002	0.040	0.164
chi(1) .01 value	6.635	6.635	6.635	6.635	6.635	6.635
LM error tests for spatial correlation in dependent variable						
LM value	14.567	66.299	73.063	55.612	40.231	39.542
Marginal Probability	0.000	0.000	0.000	0.000	0.000	0.000
chi(1) .01 value	6.640	6.640	6.640	6.640	6.640	6.640
Robust LM error test						
LM value	29.819	22.948	24.320	2.153	2.510	5.743
Marginal probability	0.000	0.000	0.000	0.142	0.113	0.017
chi(1) .01 value	6.640	6.640	6.640	6.640	6.640	6.640
Robust LM lag test						
LM value	20.774	76.632	83.951	48.145	38.506	43.346
Marginal probability	0.000	0.000	0.000	0.000	0.000	0.000
chi(1) .01 value	6.640	6.640	6.640	6.640	6.640	6.640

Destination-based autocorrelation with row-normalized 'Wd' (neighbors of exporting region *j*)						
Moran I-test for spatial autocorrelation in residuals						
Moran I	0.373	0.423	0.446	0.494	0.518	0.561
Moran I-statistic	9.329	10.700	11.196	9.314	9.849	10.601
Marginal probability	0.000	0.000	0.000	0.000	0.000	0.000
Mean	−0.009	−0.013	−0.011	−0.009	−0.012	−0.011
Standard deviation	0.041	0.041	0.041	0.054	0.054	0.054
LM error tests for spatial correlation in residuals						
LM value	80.817	103.986	115.851	82.788	91.045	106.766
Marginal probability	0.000	0.000	0.000	0.000	0.000	0.000
chi(1) .01 value	6.635	6.635	6.635	6.635	6.635	6.635
LM error tests for spatial correlation in dependent variable						
LM value	25.471	17.382	25.802	47.193	30.054	26.036
Marginal probability	0.000	0.000	0.000	0.000	0.000	0.000
chi(1) .01 value	6.640	6.640	6.640	6.640	6.640	6.640
Robust LM error test						
LM value	69.973	94.556	104.028	37.475	61.496	84.276
Marginal probability	0.000	0.000	0.000	0.000	0.000	0.000
chi(1) .01 value	6.640	6.640	6.640	6.640	6.640	6.640
Robust LM lag test						
LM value	14.626	7.952	13.979	1.879	0.505	3.546
Marginal probability	0.000	0.005	0.000	0.170	0.477	0.060
chi(1) .01 value	6.640	6.640	6.640	6.640	6.640	6.640

(continued)

Table 15.3 (continued)

	(1)	(2)	(3)	(4)	(5)	(6)
Autocorrelation using row-normalized first contiguity matrix 'W = Wo + Wd' (neighbors of *ij*)						
Moran I	0.312	0.353	0.401	0.326	0.315	0.339
Moran I-statistic	9.766	11.218	12.555	8.257	8.052	8.613
Marginal probability	0.000	0.000	0.000	0.000	0.000	0.000
Mean	−0.011	−0.015	−0.013	−0.010	−0.013	−0.012
Standard deviation	0.033	0.033	0.033	0.041	0.041	0.041
LM error tests for spatial correlation in residuals						
LM value	84.063	107.736	139.111	62.365	57.960	67.365
Marginal probability	0.000	0.000	0.000	0.000	0.000	0.000
chi(1) .01 value	6.635	6.635	6.635	6.635	6.635	6.635
LM error tests for spatial correlation in dependent variable						
LM value	8.238	2.324	3.868	63.589	44.886	44.123
Marginal probability	0.004	0.127	0.049	0.000	0.000	0.000
chi(1) .01 value	6.640	6.640	6.640	6.640	6.640	6.640
Robust LM error test						
LM value	76.030	106.396	136.111	15.986	22.056	29.357
Marginal probability	0.000	0.000	0.000	0.000	0.000	0.000
chi(1) .01 value	6.640	6.640	6.640	6.640	6.640	6.640
Robust LM lag test						
LM value	0.206	0.984	0.867	17.210	8.982	6.115
Marginal probability	0.650	0.321	0.352	0.000	0.003	0.013
chi(1) .01 value	6.640	6.640	6.640	6.640	6.640	6.640
W matrix based on . . .	**Contiguity**	**Contiguity**	**Contiguity**	**Social networks**	**Social networks**	**Social networks**

Source: Authors' calculations

Dependent variable: interregional monetary flows of Accommodations and Restaurants generated by trips. (Average 2005–2009.)

these two previous tests is used, non-significant results are obtained in the robust LM error tests for spatial autocorrelation in the dependent variable generate non-significant results when $W = W_i + W_j$, but the results are indeed significant when '*origin*'- and '*destination*'-based dependence are tested for separately.

We then conduct a similar exercise using the network (demographic) weight matrices to analyze the results for the same three models. These results are reported in the columns (4)–(6) of Table 15.3, and consider three alternative demography-based weight matrices: namely, the origin-based demographic-neighbor structure (W_i^{net}), the destination-based demographic-neighbor structure (W_j^{net}) and the aggregate origin + destination-based demographic-neighbor structure ($W^{net} = W_i^{net} + W_j^{net}$). Although most of the tests confirm the presence of network (demographic) autocorrelation effects when origin- and destination-based weight matrices are used, some tests are non-significant in some cases.[10]

In conclusion, although non-significant cases exist,[11] the significant results obtained in most cases, for both spatial and demographic weight matrices, support the wisdom of estimating a number of alternative specifications, which would preferably consider two potential sources of autocorrelation (spatial and demographic) affecting the dependent variable and/or the disturbance term. We therefore now proceed to analyze the results obtained using the Spatial Lag Model (SAR), the Spatial Error Model, the Spatial General Model (SAC) and the Spatial Durbin Model (SDM). These models have been estimated with maximum likelihood methods (cf. LeSage and Pace 2009, Chapter 3).

Next we analyze the results obtained for the augmented gravity models that consider the presence of spatial and/or network (in our case, demographic) effects. But first it is important to keep in mind, as pointed out in LeSage and Pace (2009), Chapter 8, that the coefficient estimates on the explanatory variables in these models are not interpretable in the same fashion as those in non-spatial models. However, the sign of the coefficient estimates reflects the correct direction of impact on flows that would arise from changes in the explanatory variables.[12]

Estimation results for the spatial autoregressive model (SAR) are shown in Table 15.4. Unlike non-spatial least-squares estimates, which treat all flows as independent, these models allow for the spatial dependence of flows for neighboring regions and for spatial dependence based on the influence of social networks. The

---

[10]Non-significant results are found when: (1) the W_i is considered in the model without migration variables and with m_{ij} and m_{ji} included separately (column 4 and 5) according to the Robust LM test in the residuals; and when the net migration variable is included (column 6) according to the Moran I test and to the LM error tests for spatial correlation in residuals; (2) the W_j is considered in the model without migration variables and with m_{ij} and m_{ji} included separately (column 4 and 5) according to the Robust LM lag test.

[11]For these non-significant results it is important to remark that the tests used here cannot combine the two alternative autocorrelation effects at the same time, while some of our models can.

[12]The correct approach to calculating partial derivatives, showing the impact of changes in the explanatory variables on the dependent variable in spatial gravity models, is studied in Lesage and Thomas-Agnan (2012).

two specifications that include any social-network measure ($m_{ij}, m_{ji}, m\_net_{ij}$) have each been estimated with the two different W matrices considered. The first and second columns in Table 15.4 consider the spatial dependence of flows as based on the contiguity matrix, while the third and fourth column consider the spatial dependence based on demographic links.

In all cases, the coefficients for size variables are significant and have positive signs; the coefficient controlling for intraregional flows is also significant, with a coefficient ranging from 1.051 (column 1) to 1.135 (column 4). For the distance variable, we obtain a low negative coefficient, significant in all the cases except where migration variables are included separately and spatial dependence is based on contiguity. In addition, the trade-creation effect of migration is confirmed in all cases, although the magnitude of the impact depends on the type of autocorrelation considered and on the social-network variable included (emigrants, immigrants or total migration linkage). When immigrants and emigrants are included separately, immigrants have a greater effect than emigrants. In fact, the effect of emigration is not significant when spatial lag based on demographic structure is considered. When the effect of migration is measured as the net effect of emigrants and immigrants, the effect is positive and significant but lower than that of immigrants when the emigrant and immigrant stocks are included separately. Finally, the estimated parameter ρ, which captures the dependence of flows, is positive in all cases although non-significant, unless at 5 % when the W matrix considered is the contiguity matrix. It is positive and highly significant when we control for the dependence of flows based on social-network links.

Judged by likelihood-function values, the higher pseudo R^2 and lower noise variance estimate ($\widehat{\sigma}^2$[13]) model in column 3, with dependence based on social networks and emigrants and immigrants included separately, has the best fit.

Once we have confirmed the presence of autocorrelation in the flows, it is interesting to test whether a similar autocorrelation exists also in the residuals of the models. Table 15.5 shows the results for the spatial error model. As before, we get positive and significant coefficients for the variables that capture the size of the regions. In this case, the distance and the 'intra' variables are non-significant when the spatial autocorrelation based on contiguity is controlled for (columns 1 and 2), while they are significant when the network autocorrelation of the flows is controlled for (columns 3 and 4). The effect of the migration variables is significant and positive in all cases, although the magnitude of their effect depends on the type of autocorrelation considered: when we consider contiguity, the effect of emigrants is greater than that of immigrants, while the opposite is true when we consider social-network autocorrelation. The parameter estimates of the spatial correlation of the residuals are positive and significant in all cases, with greater magnitudes generated by contiguity.

After confirming the presence of spatial and demographic autocorrelation in the flows and the residuals, we focus on the results for the general spatial model and

[13]The pseudo R^2 was calculated using $\widehat{T}'\widehat{T}/T'T$, where $\widehat{T} = (i_N - \rho_1 W^{spa} - \rho_2 W^{net})^{-1} X\widehat{\beta}$.

Table 15.4 Spatial autoregressive model

	(1)	(2)	(3)	(4)
R-squared	0.879	0.874	0.884	0.878
Rbar-squared	0.876	0.871	0.881	0.875
sigma^2	0.267	0.276	0.231	0.240
log-likelihood	−118.840	−123.750	−100.360	−106.229
i_N	−27.611*** (−13.379)	−24.641*** (−13.182)	−28.638*** (−14.911)	−25.633*** (−14.697)
gva_i	0.568*** (12.927)	0.639*** (16.613)	0.507*** (12.007)	0.578*** (15.485)
pop_j	0.673*** (14.146)	0.661*** (13.7)	0.644*** (14.472)	0.635*** (13.979)
inc_j	1.735*** (8.78)	1.391*** (8.283)	1.799*** (9.812)	1.454*** (9.279)
$ownreg_{ij}$	1.051*** (5.08)	1.101*** (5.243)	1.109*** (6.086)	1.135*** (6.114)
d_{ij}	−0.095 (−1.615)	−0.14** (−2.437)	−0.107** (−1.987)	−0.158*** (−2.975)
m_{ij}	0.061** (2.067)		0.032 (1.145)	
m_{ji}	0.238*** (6.532)		0.211*** (6.241)	
m_net_{ij}		0.137*** (7.688)		0.109*** (6.318)
rho	0.034 (1.402)	0.044* (1.792)	0.252*** (6.175)	0.257*** (6.226)
W matrix	Contiguity	Contiguity	Demography	Demography

Source: Authors' calculations
T statistics in brackets
Dependent variable: interregional monetary flows of Accommodations and Restaurants generated by trips. (Average 2005–2009.)
Significance: *$p<0.1$; **$p<0.05$; ***$p<0.01$

Table 15.5 Spatial error model

	(1)	(2)	(3)	(4)
R-squared	0.935	0.934	0.914	0.913
Rbar-squared	0.933	0.932	0.912	0.911
sigma^2	0.147	0.149	0.194	0.196
log-likelihood	−59.207	−60.239	−87.697	−89.973
i_N	−22.725*** (−7.86)	−24.637*** (−9.388)	−28.13*** (−12.306)	−25.722*** (−13.079)
gva_i	0.542*** (11.264)	0.514*** (11.593)	0.545*** (10.845)	0.601*** (14.307)
pop_j	0.54*** (9.327)	0.544*** (9.392)	0.693*** (12.511)	0.696*** (12.437)
inc_j	1.389*** (4.577)	1.609*** (6.013)	1.867*** (7.764)	1.564*** (8.241)
$ownreg_{ij}$	0.227 (1.368)	0.218 (1.311)	0.62*** (3.735)	0.649*** (3.904)
d_{ij}	−0.051 (−0.89)	−0.047 (−0.818)	−0.165*** (−2.813)	−0.185*** (−3.182)
m_{ij}	0.282*** (6.744)		0.091*** (2.811)	
m_{ji}	0.158*** (3.483)		0.215*** (5.517)	
m_net_{ij}		0.222*** (11.617)		0.145*** (7.786)
lambda	0.853*** (23.602)	0.844*** (22.342)	0.599*** (9.784)	0.609*** (10.069)
W matrix	Contiguity	Contiguity	Demography	Demography

Source: Authors' calculations
T statistics in brackets
Dependent variable: interregional monetary flows of Accommodations and Restaurants generated by trips. (Average 2005–2009.)
Significance: *$p<0.1$; **$p<0.05$; ***$p<0.01$

the four specifications described above: SAC-I: ($W_1 = W^{spa}$; $W_2 = W^{net}$); SAC-II: ($W_1 = W^{net}$; $W_2 = W^{spa}$), SAC-III: ($W_1 = W_2 = W^{spa}$); SAC-IV: ($W_1 = W_2 = W^{net}$). These results are shown in Table 15.6.

The first thing to note is the strong similarity between the two specifications in each of the four cases. The more remarkable difference across each of the four cases is that in SAC-II and SAC-III (when the spatial autocorrelation in the residuals is based on the contiguity matrix), neither the dummy controlling for intraregional flows nor the distance variable is significant. However, in SAC-I and SAC-IV, both of which use W^{net} on the error term, the negative coefficient of distance runs from −0.16 to −0.19 and the dummy coefficient for intraregional flows runs from 0.5 to 0.6; these are close to the values we obtain in the SEM model when using the W^{net}. In SAC-II and SAC-III, the effect of emigrants is greater than the effect of immigrants, while the opposite is the case in SAC-I and SAC-IV. In addition, with regard to the parameters of spatial and network dependence, it is important to highlight that the parameter measuring the dependence in the residuals is positive and significant in all cases, and is of lesser magnitude when the dependence is based on social networks rather than contiguity. On the other hand, the spatial lag of the flows is non-significant except with SAC-III, but in this case we get a negative sign.

Finally, the results reported in Table 15.7 for the SDM are complementary to those for the SAR, the SEM and the SAC estimates: the coefficients for the spatial and network (demographic) autocorrelation terms are positive and significant for the dependent variable, with high values for ρ in the six specifications reported. Moreover, the coefficients for the spatial and network (demographic) autocorrelation terms for the explanatory variables are not always significant and the signs vary with the variable. For example, variables such as $W\text{-}gva_i$ and $W\text{-}pop_j$ show negative and significant coefficients for all specifications, suggesting that, on average, flows between the trading regions decrease as their neighbors' population and hospitality-industry gross value added increase—whether we define a 'neighbor' geographically (shared border), by the intensity of demographic links or both. In another example, a negative sign in the lag of both the emigrant and the net migration variables suggests that trade flows between a given country-pair decrease as their neighbors' average emigration (or emigration + immigration) stocks increase. We might attribute these results to some kind of competition between regions. Finally, with regard to the effect of distance on bilateral trade flows when an SDM is estimated, it is remarkable that the coefficient is negative and significant when we include the W^{net} matrix in the pattern of the spatial autocorrelation considered (in Table 15.6, −0.186 and −0.2), but non-significant when we include the contiguity-based W^{spa} matrix.

Table 15.6 Spatial general model

	SAC-I $W_1 = W^{spa}$; $W_2 = W^{net}$		SAC-II $W_1 = W^{net}$; $W_2 = W^{spa}$		SAC-III $W_1 = W_2 = W^{spa}$		SAC-IV $W_1 = W_2 = W^{net}$	
	(1)	(2)	(3)	(4)	(5)	(6)	(7)	(8)
R-squared	0.914	0.913	0.934	0.934	0.937	0.936	0.917	0.919
Rbar-squared	0.912	0.912	0.932	0.933	0.936	0.935	0.915	0.917
sigma^2	0.193	0.195	0.150	0.149	0.142	0.144	0.186	0.183
log-likelihood	−87.803	−89.666	−60.442	−59.994	−53.564	−55.061	−87.237	−88.672
i_N	−28.153*** (−12.292)	−25.722*** (−13.064)	−23.058*** (−8.011)	−24.884*** (−9.322)	−22.781*** (−8.038)	−24.352*** (−9.527)	−26.995*** (−10.887)	−24.097*** (−11.137)
gva_i	0.545*** (10.823)	0.602*** (14.271)	0.545*** (11.372)	0.513*** (11.569)	0.526*** (11.112)	0.502*** (9.607)	0.541*** (10.504)	0.589*** (13.763)
pop_j	0.699*** (12.443)	0.7*** (12.327)	0.544*** (9.489)	0.544*** (9.373)	0.539*** (9.487)	0.544*** (9.607)	0.696*** (12.139)	0.704*** (11.962)
inc_j	1.874*** (7.756)	1.566*** (8.232)	1.407*** (4.741)	1.621*** (6.025)	1.472*** (4.93)	1.657*** (6.359)	1.836*** (7.281)	1.529*** (7.721)
$ownreg_{ij}$	0.593*** (3.446)	0.634*** (3.688)	0.267 (1.543)	0.233 (1.343)	0.104 (0.62)	0.091 (0.544)	0.496*** (2.745)	0.468*** (2.603)
d_{ij}	−0.168*** (−2.873)	−0.187*** (−3.213)	−0.05 (−0.88)	−0.046 (−0.809)	−0.067 (−1.209)	−0.066 (−1.179)	−0.177*** (−3.034)	−0.197*** (−3.408)
m_{ij}	0.091*** (2.802)		0.272*** (6.484)		0.279*** (6.8)		0.101*** (3.058)	

m_{ji}	0.216*** (5.524)		0.16*** (3.531)		0.172*** (3.838)		0.217*** (5.457)	
m_net_{ij}		0.145*** (7.75)		0.22*** (11.042)		0.227*** (12.072)		0.154*** (7.973)
rho	−0.013 (−0.592)	−0.007 (−0.305)	0.008 (0.186)	0.018 (0.428)	−0.075*** (−3.358)	−0.078*** (−3.57)	−0.082 (−1.379)	−0.123** (−2.065)
lambda	0.608*** (9.94)	0.617*** (10.199)	0.824*** (19.404)	0.849*** (22.422)	0.853*** (23.286)	0.836*** (21.047)	0.682*** (10.506)	0.74*** (12.736)

Source: Authors' calculations
T statistics in brackets
Dependent variable: interregional monetary flows of Accommodations and Restaurants generated by trips. (Average 2005–2009.)
Significance: *$p < 0.1$; **$p < 0.05$; ***$p < 0.01$

Table 15.7 Spatial Durbin model

	(1)	(2)	(3)	(4)	(5)	(6)
R-squared	0.915	0.898	0.897	0.892	0.906	0.900
Rbar-squared	0.911	0.893	0.8922	0.887	0.901	0.895
sigma^2	0.150	0.160	0.1867	0.190	0.164	0.152
Log-likelihood	−46.401	−58.182	−77.223155	−81.683	−58.242	−54.474
i_N	−15.823*** (−7.289)	−14.588*** (−7.516)	−11.364*** (−3.111)	−7.371** (−2.299)	−18.357*** (−8.206)	0.173 (0.052)
gva_i	0.56*** (10.045)	0.47*** (8.895)	0.527*** (8.364)	0.597*** (12.273)	0.589*** (9.535)	0.561*** (10.939)
pop_j	0.592*** (8.496)	0.579*** (8.081)	0.734*** (9.62)	0.791*** (10.606)	0.652*** (8.321)	0.677*** (9.319)
inc_j	0.626** (2.45)	0.649*** (2.843)	1.978*** (6.364)	1.531*** (6.818)	0.899*** (3.295)	2.09*** (7.142)
$ownreg_{ij}$	0.598** (2.401)	0.433* (1.701)	0.922*** (3.961)	1.029*** (4.523)	0.928*** (3.607)	0.901*** (3.719)
d_{ij}	−0.028 (−0.453)	−0.045 (−0.707)	−0.186*** (−3.008)	−0.2*** (−3.205)	−0.075 (−1.164)	−0.093 (−1.515)
m_{ij}	0.365*** (7.958)		0.073** (1.996)		0.258*** (6.361)	
m_{ji}	0.051 (0.986)		0.203*** (4.257)		0.065 (1.335)	
m_net_{ij}		0.224*** (9.619)		0.123*** (5.46)		0.162*** (7.022)
$W\text{-}gva_i$	−0.306*** (−3.202)	−0.143 (−1.64)	−0.225** (−2.289)	−0.255*** (−3.001)	−0.329*** (−3.173)	−0.311*** (−3.517)
$W\text{-}pop_j$	−0.242** (−2.242)	−0.219** (−2.01)	−0.432*** (−3.536)	−0.551*** (−4.744)	−0.237** (−1.99)	−0.524*** (−4.498)
$W\text{-}inc_j$	0.495*** (2.616)	0.265 (1.454)	−1.32*** (−2.983)	−1.212*** (−3.549)	0.376* (1.879)	−2.323*** (−4.979)
$W\text{-}ownreg_{ij}$	1.164*** (3.226)	1.244*** (3.374)	0.483 (1.483)	0.421 (1.28)	1.125*** (3.053)	1.046*** (2.972)
$W\text{-}d_{ij}$	−0.022 (−0.245)	−0.087 (−0.967)	0.18* (1.895)	0.137 (1.441)	0.031 (0.302)	−0.025 (−0.272)
$W\text{-}m_{ij}$	−0.449*** (−8.267)		−0.111* (−1.862)		−0.39*** (−6.577)	
$W\text{-}m_{ji}$	0.072 (1.036)		−0.035 (−0.494)		0.105 (1.446)	
$W\text{-}m\_net_{ij}$		−0.239*** (−7.551)		−0.081** (−2.42)		−0.186*** (−5.613)
rho	0.584*** (9.507)	0.657*** (11.492)	0.494*** (7.405)	0.54*** (8.42)	0.575*** (8.523)	0.741*** (12.551)
W matrix	Contiguity	Contiguity	Demography	Demography	Contiguity + Demography	Contiguity + Demography

Source: Authors' calculations
T statistics in brackets
Dependent variable: interregional monetary flows of Accommodations and Restaurants generated by trips. (Average 2005–2009.)
Significance: *p<0.1; **p<0.05; ***p<0.01

Another thing worthy of note is the difference in the significance of the coefficients of the migration variables depending on the model estimated. When a SAR model is estimated, the level of significance and the magnitude of the coefficient for emigrants is lower than for immigrants (0.21 in column 3 of Table 15.4), while both variables are significant and positive when an SEM or SAC model is estimated. Finally, when an SDM is estimated, the significant effect is found for the stock of emigrants and not for immigrants except when we consider W^{net} (column 3 in Table 15.7), where both emigrants and immigrants are significant and immigrants get a higher coefficient. The effect of migration on trade flows, regardless of its direction (emigrants or immigrants), does not disappear when the spatial autocorrelation of the flows is controlled for, although it changes with the type of model.

Next, Fig. 15.6a, b reports the Moran scatterplots for the residuals of the main specifications that use row-normalized spatial ($W^{spa} = W_i^{spa} + W_j^{spa}$) and network (demographic) ($W^{net} = W_i^{net} + W_j^{net}$) weight matrices to capture the aggregate spatial autocorrelation of both exporting and importing regions. As in LeSage and Pace (2009) and de la Mata and Llano (2013), each graph is divided into quadrants: Q-I (red points): *ij* flows where both the residuals and the average of neighboring *ij* flows (origin-based + destination-based) are above the mean; Q-II (green points): *ij* flows where the residuals are below the mean but the average of neighboring *ij* flows is above it; Q-III (blue points): *ij* flows where both the residuals and the average of the neighboring *ij* flows are below the mean; Q-IV (purple points): *ij* flows where the residuals are above the mean and the average of neighboring *ij* flows is below it.

By means of the Moran scatterplot we can verify a positive association between the residuals (horizontal axis) and the spatial lag (vertical axis). The magnitude of this positive association grows as the number of green and purple points decreases and the number of blue and red points increases. Here unlike in other papers using scatterplots, the residuals cannot be plotted in a map, because our dataset is referred to each region-pair. Such a graphical analysis would required specialized GIS systems for transport modeling (Berglund and Karström 1999a, b), which are beyond the scope of this paper. The results in Fig. 15.6a, b suggest a positive association between the residuals of the three main specifications obtained by simple OLS estimation and the two different cross-section autocorrelation structures—one purely spatial, the other purely demographic—under consideration. It is also worth mentioning the differences in the shapes of the dot clouds generated by each weight matrix, which indicate the complementary nature of both structures.

Then, Fig. 15.6a, b show the Moran scatterplots for the residuals obtained from the SAR, SEM, SDM and SAC-I-IV estimations, and a row-normalized weight matrix obtained as a sum over all the weight matrices described here

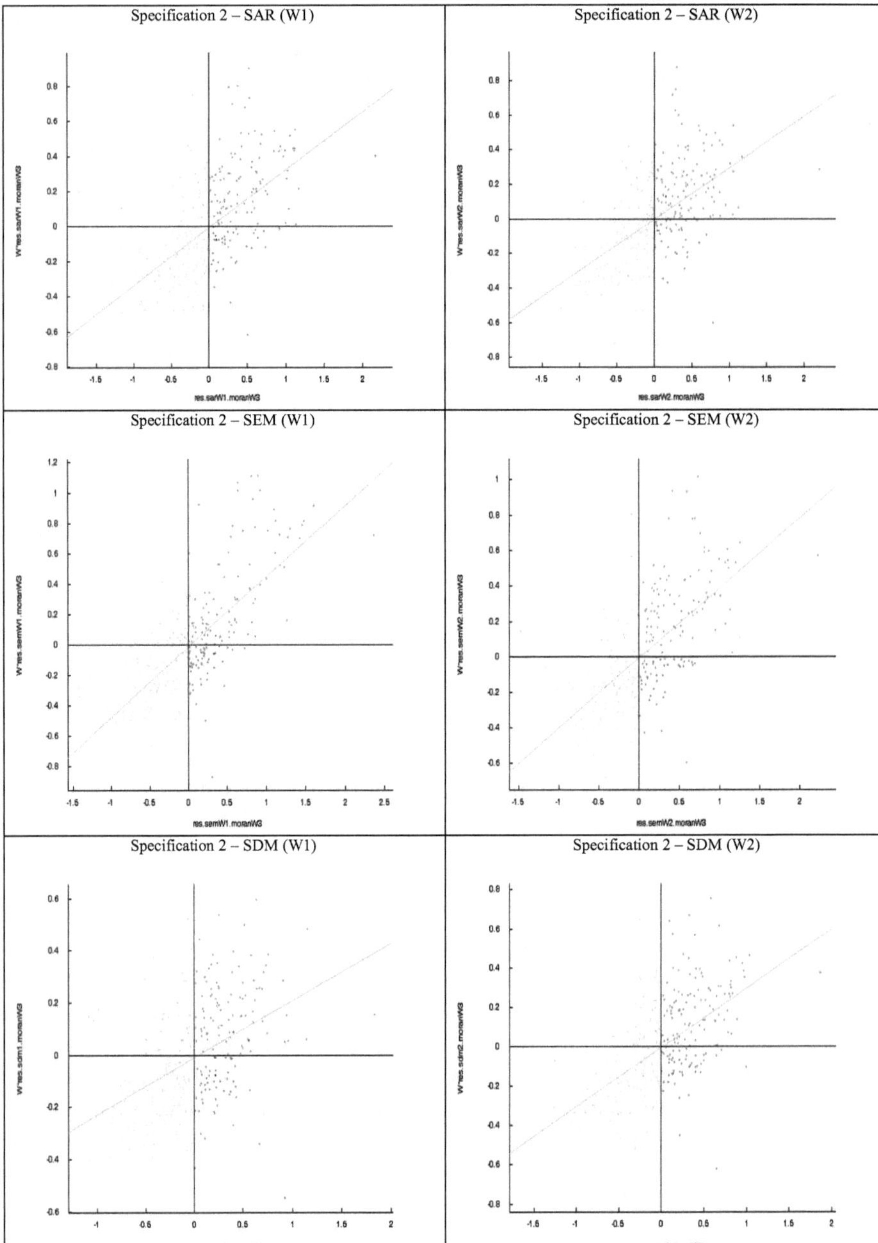

Fig. 15.6 (**a**) I-Moran scatterplot on residuals from SAR, SEM and SDM estimates. Y = Residuals with "average" flows and stocks for 2000–2009. Scatterplot uses $W_3 = W^{spa} + W^{net}$. (**b**) I-Moran scatterplot on residuals from SAC estimates. Y = Residuals with average flows and stocks 2000–2009. Scatterplot uses $W_3 = W^{spa} + W^{net}$

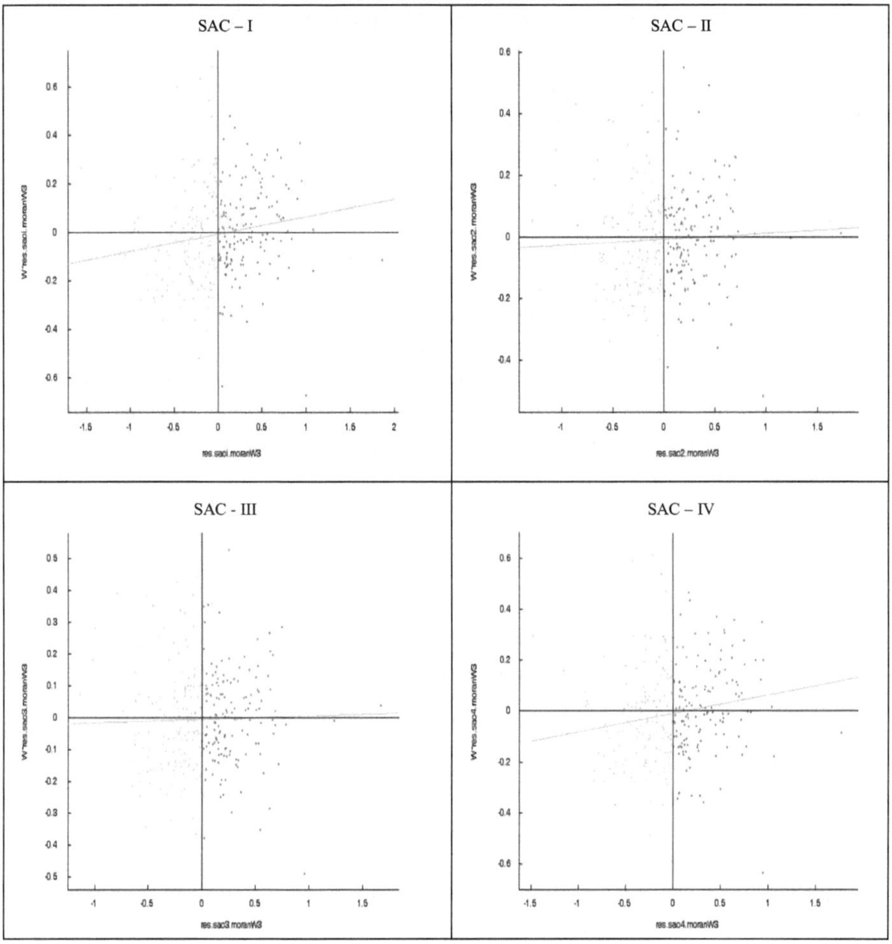

Fig. 15.6 (continued)

($W_3 = W^{spa} + W^{net}$).[14] This approach is an attempt to show in a single picture whether after the use of these spatial models the residuals still show a significant association with a lag based on spatial and demographic structure. As these graphs show, the SAR, SEM and SDM still have a clear positive relation, while the SAC model—especially SAC-II and SAC-III—seems to do a better job of eliminating the positive association between the residuals and the spatial and demographic lags.

[14]The Moran scatterplots for the residuals using each matrix W^{spa} and W^{net} instead of the sum of both and for the rest of the models are available upon request.

15.4.4 Results Using Alternative Measures for Social Networks

In this section we test the preferred model as determined by the residuals in Fig. 15.6a, b—that is, the SAC-III model[15] (column 5 of Table 15.6)—using the alternative social-network measures described in Table 15.1. Table 15.8 shows the corresponding results. It is important to remark that the alternative social-network measures enter into the model as substitutes for the 1981 interregional migration stocks through the vector variables (m_{ij}, m_{ji}, m_net_{ij}), while the $W_1 = W_2 = W^{spa}$ is just based on spatial contiguity as in the baseline model (SAC-III).

The results obtained with these alternative variables are, in general, robust with those obtained in the previous models, with expected signs and levels of significance. As for the size of the trading regions as measured by gross value added (for the exporting region), population and per-capita income (for the importing region), positive and significant signs are obtained in all cases, much as with the baseline model in Table 15.6. The only remarkable difference occurs when social networks created by previous trips with stays in regulated establishments are included (**soc_net_18**), where the coefficients decrease notably. Also, when the variables **soc_net_16**, **soc_net_17** and **soc_net_18** are included, the coefficient for per-capita income is lower than one—reducing its significance in the latter-, contrary to what happens in all other cases. These results can be attributed to gravity's effect on previous trips, so part of the effect of the gravity variables is captured in the coefficient for previous trips.

It is interesting to note that, while the intraregional dummy gets a positive and significant sign in some cases, certain social-network variables help overcome this home bias (**soc-net-2**; **soc-net-11**; **soc-net-15**; **soc-net-16**; **soc-net-17**; **soc-net-18 and soc-net-19**) or reduce its significance (**soc-net-3**; **soc-net-14**). When the variables **soc-net-7** and **soc-net-12** (which concern individuals' previous residences) are used, the intraregional dummy gets a negative sign, probably because of the disproportionate intraregional linkages (more than 95 %) in each of the two variables.

Another interesting result is that, as in column 3 of Table 15.6, the distance variable is in most cases non-significant when alternative social-network measures are considered—with the following exceptions: **soc-net-6**; **soc-net-16** and **soc-net-18** (significant at 5 %), **soc-net-11 and soc-net-12** (significant at 10 %) and **soc-net-19**. The last variable contains 'parcel flows' as a proxy for networks. That this variable gets the most significant coefficient for distance and the highest coefficient for the *intra* variable has to do with its nature, which allows it to capture other kinds of relations (e.g., business networks) as well. Parcel flows, moreover, can substitute for face-to-face contact when travel costs are high, as it over-weights the existence of networks at greater distances.

---

[15]The results using the alternative social network variables for the SAC-II model (column 3 of Table 15.6) are reported in the Appendix. This model was the one that perform better in de la Mata and Llano (2013).

Table 15.8 Alternative spatial general model (SAC-III: $W_1 = W_2 = W^{spa)}$)

Social-network measure used for elements m_{ij} and m_{ji}	R-squared	Rbar-squared	sigma^2	Log likelihood	i_N	gva_i	pop_j	$pcincome_j$	$ownreg_{ij}$	d_{ij}	m_{ij} = *Social networks*	m_{ji} = *Social networks'*	rho	lambda
Soc_net_2	0.9386	0.937	0.1385	−48.454998	−24.304***	0.471***	0.51***	1.707***	0.028	−0.064	0.228***	0.252***	−0.07***	0.836***
Soc_net_3	0.9518	0.9506	0.1088	−12.525703	−17.87***	0.529***	0.544***	1.063***	0.63***	−0.015	0.314***	0.114***	−0.062***	0.816***
Soc_net_4	0.9376	0.936	0.1408	−51.877311	−24.44***	0.499***	0.531***	1.711***	0.257*	−0.057	0.235***	0.221***	−0.076***	0.844***
Soc_net_5	0.9368	0.9352	0.1424	−53.131846	−24.701***	0.508***	0.536***	1.722***	0.204	−0.062	0.245***	0.216***	−0.073***	0.837***
Soc_net_6	0.9386	0.9371	0.1384	−48.555903	−22.713***	0.473***	0.515***	1.563***	−0.128	−0.107**	0.25***	0.231***	−0.069***	0.833***
Soc_net_7	0.9458	0.9444	0.1223	−25.723318	−18.626***	0.406***	0.372***	1.408***	−1.634***	−0.071	0.119**	0.492***	−0.06***	0.763***
Soc_net_8	0.9391	0.9376	0.1373	−47.640128	−22.986***	0.447***	0.488***	1.661***	−0.006	−0.06	0.221***	0.278***	−0.066***	0.84***
Soc_net_9	0.9361	0.9345	0.144	−49.762395	−22.51***	0.523***	0.6***	1.456***	0.09	0.038	0.201***	0.154***	−0.046**	0.772***
Soc_net_10	0.9375	0.9359	0.1409	−52.324179	−23.53***	0.502***	0.533***	1.585***	0.1	−0.066	0.248***	0.206***	−0.076***	0.844***
Soc_net_11	0.9403	0.9388	0.1346	−40.297177	−18.066***	0.421***	0.419***	1.307***	0.386***	−0.089*	0.044	0.502***	−0.06***	0.775***
Soc_net_12	0.9404	0.9389	0.1344	−41.140492	−18.702***	0.422***	0.424***	1.353***	−1.137***	−0.098*	0.061	0.493***	−0.062***	0.777***
Soc_net_13	0.939	0.9375	0.1375	−49.257076	−23.329***	0.512***	0.521***	1.585***	0.172	−0.054	0.274***	0.201***	−0.078***	0.857***
Soc_net_14	0.9384	0.9368	0.139	−50.961368	−23.105***	0.513***	0.526***	1.553***	0.279*	−0.042	0.264***	0.193***	−0.075***	0.846***
Soc_net_15	0.9268	0.925	0.165	−72.119997	−32.622***	0.622***	0.66***	2.225***	0.741***	−0.069	−0.127	0.493*	−0.066***	0.812***
Soc_net_16	0.9559	0.9548	0.0995	3.1876671	−16.369***	0.4***	0.503***	0.841***	0.618***	−0.112**	0.11***	0.414***	−0.043**	0.78***
Soc_net_17	0.9618	0.9608	0.0862	23.316959	−15.942***	0.417***	0.443***	0.721***	0.374***	−0.055	0.087***	0.48***	−0.056***	0.791***
Soc_net_18	0.9706	0.9699	0.0663	58.039691	−6.513***	0.158***	0.108**	0.304*	0.55***	−0.09**	0.138***	0.784***	−0.058***	0.826***
Soc_net_19	0.904	0.9016	0.2164	−109.23021	−26.75***	0.8***	0.948***	1.347***	1.564***	−0.276***	0.011	0.019*	−0.058**	0.781***

Source: Authors' calculations

Dependent variable: interregional monetary flows of Accommodations and Restaurants generated by trips. (Average 2005–2009.)

T statistics in brackets

Significance: *p<0.1; **p<0.05; ***p<0.01

The effect of social networks is confirmed in both directions in most cases, with coefficients similar to the one in the baseline regression. There are some exceptions. For example, with the variables **soc-net-11** and **soc-net-12** the social-network effect is confirmed in only one direction, and with **soc-net-15** and **soc-net-19** it seems to have almost no impact. As previously stated, the latter can serve as an alternative form of contact, other than trips, with the members of a social network. In **soc-net-16**, **soc-net-17** and **soc-net-18**, the effect is confirmed in both directions, although at different intensities, with stronger effects linked with a certain inertia in the flows.

In all cases, the positive autocorrelation in the residuals is confirmed and the spatial lag of the dependent variable is found to be significant, although with a negative impact. In the SAC-II model, when the spatial lag of the dependent variable is based on demography, it is significant and positive when the variable **soc-net-19** is included.

Table 15.9 in the Appendix shows a similar analysis for all the alternative matrices, but the social-network variable is included only in its unidirectional version ($m\_net_{ij} = \left(m_{ji} + m_{ij}\right)$). This produces similar results.

15.5 Conclusions

In this article we have analyzed the relation between interregional trade in services and social networks and how these social networks can explain part of the resulting border effect on such services. We have also considered whether interregional trade flows in tourism-related services exhibit spatial and/or social-network dependence. Conventional empirical gravity models assume that the magnitude of bilateral flows between regions are independent of flows to/from geographically proximate regions or to/from regions connected by social/cultural/ethnic networks.

We provide an extended empirical specification that relaxes the assumption of independence between bilateral flows inherent to any least-squares regression. Our argument is that bilateral flows between an exporting region i and an importing region j can exhibit dependence on: (1) flows to regions that are geographically near exporting and importing regions i and j (spatial dependence) and (2) flows to regions that are socially/demographically "related" to exporting and importing regions i and j. We have used a spatial weight matrix elaborated in the way suggested by LeSage and Pace (2008) to quantify the spatial structure of the connectivity between interregional bilateral flows. And we have constructed a social-network matrix with information on the bilateral stock of interregional migrants between 17 Spanish regions.

Estimates from a set of models have shown evidence of statistically significant spatial and network (demographic) dependence in the bilateral flows of the service trade considered. The analysis has been applied to data averages for the period

2005–2009, with alternative datasets for migration stocks and alternative definitions for network effects. It has produced robust results and shown the high inertia that exists in these social phenomena, where patterns from 1981 affect flows that exist 20 years later. We might interpret the significant network dependence thus brought to light as a general preference for destinations in or near one's home region or for destinations in or near regions where natives of one's birth region have settled heavily. Significant spatial dependence is an indication that bilateral flows between two regions are associated to those to/from neighboring regions.

One finding of interest is that the introduction of explanatory variables to control for emigrant and immigrant stocks and for spatial and network dependence (as well as conventional measures of the economic size of origin and destination regions) results in a low coefficient estimate for bilateral distance between origin and destination regions and a high coefficient for the internal border effect—such that distance and home bias are, in certain cases, no longer significant. This suggests that social networks might exert sufficient influence on the selection of destinations to overcome the traditional obstacle of distance, which typically diminishes the magnitude of bilateral flows. It also suggests that the distribution of social networks over short distances may partly explain the gravity effect on trip decisions, especially within the region of residence.

Further analysis for the interpretation of these parameters, in the spirit of Lesage and Thomas-Agnan (2012), is certainly in order. Although the effect of social networks has been widely tested in this work, it would be an important next step to take into consideration, for instance, the effect of business networks.

Acknowledgments The authors wish to express their gratitude to James LeSage for his help in improving previous versions of this paper. This paper has been developed over the course of various research projects: TransporTrade S2007/HUM/497 (www.uam.es/transportrade), funded by the Education Department of the Madrid Regional Government; the Project (ECO2010-21643/ECON), funded by the Spanish Ministry of Science and Innovation; and the DESTINO Project (Ministerio de Fomento).

Appendix

Tables 15.9, 15.10, and 15.11

Table 15.9 Alternative spatial general model (SAC-III: $W_1 = W_2 = W^{spa)}$)

$(m_{ji} + m_{ij})$ social-network measure	R-squared	Rbar-squared	sigma^2	Log likelihood	i_N	gva_i	pop_j	$pcincome_j$	$ownreg_{ij}$	d_{ij}	$m_{ij} + m_{ji} = Social\ net\text{-}works + Social\ networks'$	rho	lambda
Soc_net_2	0.9387	0.9374	0.1381	−49.048119	−24.067***	0.474***	0.51***	1.68***	0.026	−0.064	0.24***	−0.072***	0.842***
Soc_net_3	0.9487	0.9476	0.1157	−21.299598	−22.416***	0.491***	0.542***	1.572***	0.619***	−0.01	0.217***	−0.063***	0.813***
Soc_net_4	0.9371	0.9358	0.1417	−52.893313	−24.618***	0.498***	0.532***	1.726***	0.267*	−0.057	0.228***	−0.071***	0.833***
Soc_net_5	0.9368	0.9355	0.1424	−53.274376	−25.171***	0.502***	0.534***	1.781***	0.195	−0.061	0.232***	−0.074***	0.838***
Soc_net_6	0.9352	0.9338	0.1461	−54.70218	−23.107***	0.484***	0.515***	1.526***	0.013	−0.086	0.235***	0.004	0.81***
Soc_net_7	0.9454	0.9442	0.1231	−30.728987	−19.87***	0.376***	0.406***	1.528***	−1.638***	−0.07	0.306***	−0.064***	0.825***
Soc_net_8	0.939	0.9377	0.1375	−48.170558	−22.387***	0.455***	0.493***	1.586***	0.005	−0.062	0.247***	−0.066***	0.84***
Soc_net_9	0.936	0.9346	0.1444	−49.787451	−21.801***	0.53***	0.599***	1.377***	0.093	0.037	0.177***	−0.045**	0.771***
Soc_net_10	0.9371	0.9358	0.1417	−52.500915	−24.027***	0.494***	0.535***	1.645***	0.095	−0.066	0.228***	−0.078***	0.836***
Soc_net_11	0.9389	0.9376	0.1377	−46.622531	−19.566***	0.398***	0.433***	1.468***	0.377***	−0.084	0.274***	−0.063***	0.823***
Soc_net_12	0.9395	0.9382	0.1364	−45.094657	−19.931***	0.403***	0.439***	1.481***	−1.144***	−0.093*	0.278***	−0.064***	0.813***
Soc_net_13	0.9382	0.9369	0.1393	−50.176938	−24.795***	0.491***	0.523***	1.753***	0.169	−0.05	0.239***	−0.075***	0.842***
Soc_net_14	0.938	0.9367	0.1397	−50.642191	−24.427***	0.494***	0.527***	1.707***	0.271*	−0.039	0.23***	−0.074***	0.843***
Soc_net_15	0.9262	0.9247	0.1663	−73.29523	−31.876***	0.634***	0.658***	2.138***	0.751***	−0.073	0.181***	−0.064***	0.807***
Soc_net_16	0.9527	0.9517	0.1067	−10.272406	−18.867***	0.404***	0.491***	1.106***	0.616***	−0.112**	0.261***	−0.048***	0.824***
Soc_net_17	0.9561	0.9551	0.099	−0.79809748	−21.111***	0.38***	0.437***	1.295***	0.361***	−0.05	0.286***	−0.061***	0.842***
Soc_net_18	0.9611	0.9603	0.0877	1.2536318	−11.097***	0.099**	0.155***	0.795***	0.53***	−0.087**	0.458***	−0.089***	0.965***
Soc_net_19	0.904	0.9019	0.2164	−109.11979	−26.691***	0.8***	0.948***	1.34***	1.565***	−0.275***	0.015***	−0.058**	0.782***

Source: Authors' calculations
T statistics in brackets
Dependent variable: interregional monetary flows of Accommodations and Restaurants generated by trips. (Average 2005–2009.)
Significance: *p < 0.1; **p < 0.05; ***p < 0.01

Table 15.10 Alternative spatial general model (SAC-II: $W_1 = W^{net}$; $W_2 = W^{spa}$)

Social-network measure used for elements m_{ij} & m_{ji}	R-squared	Rbar-squared	sigma^2	Log likelihood	i_N	gva_i	pop_j	$pcincome_j$	$ownreg_{ij}$	d_{ij}	m_{ij} = *Social networks*	m_{ji} = *Social networks'*	rho	lambda
Soc_net_2	0.9361	0.9345	0.144	−53.799	−24.598***	0.483***	0.51***	1.653***	0.161	−0.044	0.24***	0.228***	0.013	0.832***
Soc_net_3	0.9497	0.9485	0.1133	−17.638	−18.863***	0.531***	0.535***	1.072***	0.75***	0.009	0.113***	0.304***	0.043	0.806***
Soc_net_4	0.936	0.9344	0.1443	−57.039	−24.32***	0.511***	0.53***	1.625***	0.36**	−0.039	0.205***	0.245***	0.005	0.869***
Soc_net_5	0.9349	0.9332	0.1469	−58.750	−24.434***	0.522***	0.536***	1.631***	0.303*	−0.045	0.203***	0.254***	−0.009	0.853***
Soc_net_6	0.9354	0.9338	0.1456	−54.168	−23.54***	0.485***	0.517***	1.537***	0.059	−0.084	0.222***	0.236***	0.038	0.803***
Soc_net_7	0.9431	0.9417	0.1283	−30.291	−19.136***	0.42***	0.372***	1.372***	−1.442***	−0.05	0.494***	0.099*	0.012	0.731***
Soc_net_8	0.9368	0.9352	0.1425	−52.733	−23.3***	0.458***	0.488***	1.614***	0.116	−0.042	0.268***	0.22***	0.012	0.836***
Soc_net_9	0.9342	0.9325	0.1484	−51.505	−23.302***	0.527***	0.593***	1.464***	0.207	0.056	0.148***	0.199***	0.029	0.732***
Soc_net_10	0.9353	0.9337	0.1458	−58.648	−23.645***	0.517***	0.534***	1.51***	0.23	−0.047	0.189***	0.253***	0.013	0.857***
Soc_net_11	0.9374	0.9358	0.1411	−44.377	−18.926***	0.436***	0.426***	1.282***	0.544***	−0.068	0.491***	0.029	0.032	0.738***
Soc_net_12	0.9382	0.9367	0.1393	−44.842	−19.448***	0.433***	0.424***	1.337***	−0.959***	−0.075	0.483***	0.054	0.02	0.769***
Soc_net_13	0.9365	0.9349	0.1431	−56.332	−22.801***	0.528***	0.522***	1.472***	0.269	−0.038	0.19***	0.282***	−0.021	0.862***
Soc_net_14	0.9365	0.935	0.1431	−55.804	−22.853***	0.528***	0.525***	1.453***	0.386**	−0.025	0.178***	0.272***	0.003	0.865***
Soc_net_15	0.9226	0.9206	0.1746	−76.889	−32.887***	0.633***	0.666***	2.14***	0.94***	−0.058	0.482*	−0.151	0.048	0.754***
Soc_net_16	0.9545	0.9534	0.1025	0.141	−16.392***	0.402***	0.495***	0.81***	0.678***	−0.097**	0.416***	0.11***	−0.005	0.764***
Soc_net_17	0.9596	0.9586	0.0912	16.755	−16.361***	0.423***	0.435***	0.699***	0.477***	−0.033	0.476***	0.084***	0.014	0.765***
Soc_net_18	0.9687	0.9679	0.0705	50.812	−7.654***	0.164***	0.103**	0.329*	0.661***	−0.064*	0.771***	0.135***	0.044	0.804***
Soc_net_19	0.9029	0.9005	0.2189	−103.665	−28.687***	0.75***	0.869***	1.461***	1.714***	−0.249***	0.017	0.006	0.197***	0.622***

Source: Authors' calculations
T statistics in brackets
Significance: *p<0.1; **p<0.05; ***p<0.01
Dependent variable: Interregional monetary flows of Accommodations and Restaurants generated by trips. (Average 2005–2009.)

Table 15.11 Alternative spatial general model (SAC-II: $W_1 = W^{net}$; $W_2 = W^{spa)}$)

$(m_{ji} + m_{ij})$ social-network measure	R-squared	Rbar-squared	sigma^2	Log likelihood	i_N	gva_i	pop_j	$pcincome_j$	$ownreg_{ij}$	d_{ij}	$m_{ij} + m_{ji} =$ *Social networks + Social networks'*	rho	lambda
Soc_net_2	0.9357	0.9344	0.1448	−54.440	−24.527***	0.487***	0.512***	1.635***	0.179	−0.044	0.232***	0.017	0.821***
Soc_net_3	0.9465	0.9453	0.1207	−24.947	−23.48***	0.492***	0.53***	1.563***	0.765***	0.019	0.208***	0.068*	0.783***
Soc_net_4	0.9348	0.9334	0.1469	−58.161	−24.545***	0.507***	0.53***	1.672***	0.35**	−0.038	0.228***	−0.023	0.843***
Soc_net_5	0.9341	0.9327	0.1485	−59.944	−25.076***	0.512***	0.533***	1.72***	0.288*	−0.043	0.231***	−0.025	0.839***
Soc_net_6	0.9354	0.934	0.1457	−53.950	−23.57***	0.484***	0.516***	1.545***	0.054	−0.084	0.23***	0.035	0.802***
Soc_net_7	0.9434	0.9422	0.1275	−36.195	−20.19***	0.384***	0.403***	1.496***	−1.522***	−0.05	0.303***	0.002	0.829***
Soc_net_8	0.9369	0.9356	0.1422	−53.356	−22.617***	0.463***	0.491***	1.547***	0.104	−0.044	0.245***	0.001	0.843***
Soc_net_9	0.9343	0.9329	0.1481	−51.806	−22.78***	0.532***	0.59***	1.391***	0.226	0.055	0.171***	0.049	0.74***
Soc_net_10	0.9344	0.933	0.1478	−58.535	−24.648***	0.507***	0.537***	1.608***	0.255	−0.045	0.219***	0.022	0.836***
Soc_net_11	0.9363	0.9349	0.1436	−51.330	−20.428***	0.412***	0.436***	1.449***	0.518***	−0.062	0.264***	0.032	0.804***
Soc_net_12	0.9364	0.935	0.1435	−50.302	−20.899***	0.419***	0.444***	1.46***	−0.911***	−0.071	0.264***	0.038	0.776***
Soc_net_13	0.9358	0.9344	0.1448	−56.460	−25.017***	0.502***	0.524***	1.703***	0.283*	−0.033	0.235***	0	0.853***
Soc_net_14	0.9362	0.9349	0.1437	−56.586	−24.663***	0.501***	0.525***	1.665***	0.37**	−0.022	0.228***	0.006	0.867***
Soc_net_15	0.9232	0.9216	0.173	−77.162	−32.175***	0.644***	0.66***	2.078***	0.904***	−0.058	0.17***	0.027	0.785***
Soc_net_16	0.9507	0.9496	0.1112	−13.550	−19.063***	0.406***	0.483***	1.079***	0.69***	−0.097**	0.259***	0.012	0.785***
Soc_net_17	0.9537	0.9527	0.1043	−5.7959	−21.833***	0.385***	0.429***	1.283***	0.48***	−0.026	0.28***	0.042	0.812***
Soc_net_18	0.9585	0.9576	0.0936	3.138	−12.67***	0.104**	0.144**	0.85***	0.647***	−0.064	0.45***	0.073**	0.888***
Soc_net_19	0.903	0.901	0.2186	−103.802	−28.58***	0.752***	0.87***	1.448***	1.712***	−0.248***	0.011**	0.195***	0.63***

Source: Authors' calculations

T statistics in brackets

Significance: *$p < 0.1$; **$p < 0.05$; ***$p < 0.01$

Dependent variable: interregional monetary flows of Accommodations and Restaurants generated by trips. (Average 2005–2009.)

References

Angulo AM, Mtimet N, Dhehibi B, Atwi M, Ben Youssef O, Gil JM, Sai MB (2011) A revisited gravity equation in trade flow analysis: an application to the case of Tunisian olive oil exports. Investigaciones Regionales 21:225–239

Anselin L (1988) Spatial econometrics: methods and models. Kluwer Academic Publishers, Dordrecht

Athanasopoulos G, Hyndman RJ (2008) Modelling and forecasting Australian domestic tourism. Tour Manage 29(1):19–31

Behrens K, Ertur C, Koch W (2012) 'Dual' gravity: using spatial econometrics to control for multilateral resistance. J Appl Econ 27:773–794

Belderbos R, Sleuwaegen L (1998) Tariff jumping FDI and export substitution: Japanese electronics firms in Europe. Int J Ind Organ 16(5):601–638

Berglund S, Karström A (1999a) Identifying local spatial association in flow data. J Geogr Syst 1(3):219–236

Berglund S, Karström A (1999b) Technical report: computing G_i and G_{ij}. Program documentation. Mimeo

Black WR (1992) Network autocorrelation in transport network and flow systems. Geogr Anal 24(3):207–222

Bolduc D, Laferriere R, Santarossa G (1992) Spatial autoregressive error-components in travel flow models. Reg Sci Urban Econ 22(3):371–385

Chen N (2004) Intra-national versus international trade in the European Union: why do national borders matter? J Int Econ 63(1):93–118

Combes PP, Lafourcade M, Mayer T (2005) The trade-creating effect of business and social networks: evidence from France. J Int Econ 66(1):1–29

Chun Y (2008) Modeling network autocorrelation within migration flows by eigenvector spatial filtering. J Geogr Syst 10(4):317–344

Chun Y, Griffith DA (2011) Modeling network autocorrelation in space-time migration flow data: an eigenvector spatial filtering approach. Ann Assoc Am Geogr 101(3):523–536

De la Mata T, Llano C (2012a) Spatial pattern and domestic tourism: an econometric analysis using inter-regional monetary flows by type of journey. Pap Reg Sci 91(2):437–470

De la Mata T, Llano C (2012b) How tradable are non-tradables? Measuring interregional flows of accommodation, restaurants and travel agencies in Spain. Mimeo

De la Mata T, Llano C (2013) Social networks and trade of services: modelling interregional flows with spatial and network autocorrelation effects. J Geogr Syst 15(3):319–367. doi:10.1007/s10109-013-0183-6

Dunlevy JA, Hutchinson WK (1999) The impact of immigration on American import trade in the late nineteenth and early twentieth centuries. J Econ Hist 59(4):1043–1062

Dunlevy JA., Hutchinson WK (2001) The pro-trade effect of immigration on American exports during the late nineteenth and early twentieth centuries. IZA Discussion Papers 375, Institute for the Study of Labor (IZA). http://ideas.repec.org/p/iza/izadps/dp375.html

Egger P, Larch M (2008) Interdependent preferential trade agreement memberships: an empirical analysis. J Int Econ 76(2):384–399

Eriksen L, Ahmt T (1999) Measuring and modelling the regional impact of tourism in Denmark. Int J Tour Res 1(5):313–327

Evans CL (2006) Border effects and the availability of domestic products abroad. Can J Econ-Revue Canadienne D Economique 39(1):211–246

Fischer MM, Griffith DA (2008) Modeling spatial autocorrelation in spatial interaction data: an application to patent citation data in the European Union. J Reg Sci 48(5):969–989

Garmendia A, Llano C, Minondo A, Requena F (2012) Networks and the disappearance of the intranational home bias. Econ Lett 116(2):178–182

Ghemawat P, Llano C, Requena F (2010) Competitiveness and interregional as well as international trade: the case of Catalonia. Int J Ind Organ 28(4):415–422

Girma S, Yu ZH (2002) The link between immigration and trade: evidence from the United Kingdom. Rev World Econ (Weltwirtschaftliches Archiv) 138(1):115–130
Gould DM (1994) Immigrant links to the home country—empirical implications for United-States bilateral trade-flows. Rev Econ Stat 76(2):302–316
Head K, Mayer T (2010) Illusory border effects: distance mismeasurement inflates estimates of home bias in trade. In: Brakman S, van Bergeijk P (eds) The gravity model in international trade: advances and applications. Cambridge University Press, Cambridge
Head K, Ries J (1998) Immigration and trade creation: econometric evidence from Canada. Can J Econ-Revue Canadienne D Economique 31(1):47–62
Helliwell JF (1996) Do national borders matter for Quebec's trade? Can J Econ-Revue Canadienne D Economique 29(3):507–522
Helliwell JF (1997) National borders, trade and migration. Pac Econ Rev 2(3):165–185
Ledyaeva S (2009) Spatial econometric analysis of foreign direct investment determinants in Russian regions. World Econ 32(4):643–666
Lesage JP, Fischer MM (2008) Spatial growth regressions: model specification, estimation and interpretation. Spat Econ Anal 3(3):275–304
LeSage JP, Pace RK (2008) Spatial econometric modeling of origin–destination flows. J Reg Sci 48(5):941–967
LeSage JP, Pace RK (2009) Introduction to spatial econometrics. Chapman & Hall/CRC Press, Boca Raton
Lesage JP, Thomas-Agnan C (2012) Interpreting spatial econometric origin–destination flow models. Working Paper, Mimeo presented in Southern Regional Science Association Conference hold in Charlotte, March, 2012
Llano C, de la Mata T (2009) El comercio interregional en España: Una estimación de los flujos bilaterales del sector turismo. Revista ICE 848:67–87
McCallum J (1995) National borders matter: Canada-U.S. regional trade patterns. Am Econ Rev 85:615–623
Millimet DL, Osang T (2007) Do state borders matter for U.S. intranational trade? The role of history and internal migration. Can J Econ, Canadian Economics Association 40(1):93–126
Okubo T (2004) The border effect in the Japanese market: a gravity model analysis. J Jpn Int Econ 18(1):1–11
Podolny JM, Page KL (1998) Network forms of organization. Annu Rev Sociol 24:57–76
Porojan A (2001) Trade flows and spatial effects: the gravity model revisited. Open Econ Rev 12(3):265–280
Portes R, Rey H (2005) The determinants of cross-border equity flows. J Int Econ 65(2):269–296
Rauch JE (2001) Business and social networks in international trade. J Econ Lit 39(4):1177–1203
Rauch JE, Casella A (2003) Overcoming informational barriers to international resource allocation: prices and ties. Econ J 113(484):21–42
Rauch JE, Trindade V (2002) Ethnic Chinese networks in international trade. Rev Econ Stat 84(1):116–130
Requena F, Llano C (2010) The border effects in Spain: an industry-level analysis. Empirica 37(4):455–476
Wagner D, Head K, Ries J (2002) Immigration and the trade of provinces. Scott J Polit Econ 49(5):507–525
White R, Tadesse B (2008) Cultural distance and the US immigrant-trade link. World Econ 31(8):1078–1096
Wolf HC (2000) Intranational home bias in trade. Rev Econ Stat 82(4):555–563

Chapter 16
On the Mutual Dynamics of Interregional Gross Migration Flows in Space and Time

Timo Mitze

Keywords Interregional migration • Dynamic spatial panel • Network autocorrelation • Multiplier analysis

JEL: R23, C21, C23

16.1 Introduction

Lately, new methods to estimate spatial dynamic panel data models and to meaningfully interpret their regression results have been proposed in the literature (see Elhorst 2012). Researchers are now able to consistently track the dynamic evolution of economic and social processes over space and time as well as provide answers with respect to short and long-run impacts of direct and space-related indirect variable changes in a multivariate context. This paper applies a spatial dynamic panel model to analyse the link between interregional out-migration flows and regional labor market signals.[1] The approach thus seek to extend recent empirical work, which has highlighted the importance of mutual dynamic features in models of migration flows when having space-time panel data at hand. For instance, Chun and Griffith (2011) have shown by means of an Eigenvector filtering approach in a generalized linear mixed model that—over time—the impact of network autocorrelation on U.S. interstate migration is strongly present.

[1] In the migration literature, typically the terms 'interregional' and 'internal' migration are used interchangeably to define pairwise migratory movements between different regions of a national territory. Throughout the remainder of this manuscript, I will use the former term.

T. Mitze (✉)
Department of Business and Economics, University of Southern Denmark, Alsion 2, DK-6400 Sønderborg, Denmark

Rheinisch-Westfälisches Institut für Wirtschaftsforschung, Essen, Germany
The Rimini Centre for Economic Analysis, Rimini, Italy
e-mail: tmitze@sam.sdu.dk

R. Patuelli, G. Arbia (eds.), *Spatial Econometric Interaction Modelling*, Advances in Spatial Science, DOI 10.1007/978-3-319-30196-9_16

For this particular analysis, I focus on the consistent estimation and interpretation of the different effects on migration stemming from regional labor market signals in the short and long-run as well as with regards to their direct effect and associated indirect spatial spillovers in such a regional migration network. Using data for pairwise migration flows among the 16 German states over the period 1993–2009, the estimation results indicate that, first of all, both temporal and spatial autocorrelation are strongly present. Moreover, compared to standard non-spatial estimations, the results show that spatially augmented network estimators significantly enrich the interpretation of the overall impact of different regional labor market signals.

With respect to the latter type of estimators, this study applies time-dynamic versions of the Spatial Autoregressive (SAR) and Spatial Durbin Model (SDM). Regarding the economic interpretation of the results, particularly regional differences in real income growth, the labor participation rate and real-estate prices are found to impact on interregional out-migration flows. The estimated coefficients signs of the obtained space-time summary measures thereby hint at the validity of the neoclassical migration model in predicting interregional flows. Robustness checks further show that some of the estimated labor market adjustment mechanisms are sensitive to the choice of the underlying network weighting matrix and thus the spatial dimension of the specified migration network.

The remainder of the paper is organized as follows: The next section starts with a brief description of the neoclassical migration model and reviews the recent empirical literature dealing with interregional migration flows in Germany. Observing that most contributions abstract from a simultaneous space-time dynamic specification, in what follows, different empirical extensions to the neoclassical migration model are discussed, where the focus rests upon including both type of effects in a network modelling context. Section 16.3 translates the model into an proper econometric specification, while Sect. 16.4 reports data properties, estimation results and associated impact summary measures. Multiplier analysis and robustness checks are performed as well. Section 16.5 concludes the paper.

16.2 Neoclassical Migration Model with a Spatial Dimension

In the neoclassical migration model, a representative agent decides to move between two regions if this improves his welfare position relative to the case of not moving. As elaborated by Harris and Todaro (1970) for a macro-theoretical perspective, the key determinant in the model is the expected income differential between regions net of 'transportation' costs.[2] Expected income is typically expressed as a function of the agent's (real) income and the probability of being employed, with the latter

[2]The micro-foundation of the neoclassical migration model was first introduced by Sjaastad (1962). For a recent overview of different migration theories see, for instance, Hagen-Zanker (2008).

being inversely related to the regional unemployment rate. The model thus predicts that a (relative) increase in the home region's real income *ceteris paribus* leads to lower migratory out-flows, while a (relative) real income increase in the alternative region j results in higher out-migration from the home region i to the destination region j. Opposite effects are noted for differences in regional unemployment rates.

There are many contributions to the empirical literature that test the validity of the neoclassical framework. In a literature survey for German interregional migration, Alecke et al. (2010) have recently shown that while microeconometric approaches tend to identify regional unemployment rates as the key driver of interregional migration processes (see e.g. Schwarze and Wagner 1992; Wagner 1992; Burda 1993; Büchel and Schwarze 1994; Brücker and Trübswetter 2004), macroeconomic studies assign a more prominent role to regional income differentials in predicting German interregional migration flows (see e.g. Burda and Hunt 2001; Parikh and Van Leuvensteijn 2003; Hunt 2006). Using a panel VAR approach, Alecke et al. (2010) find that both the wage/income and the unemployment rate channel are consistent with the theoretical expectations of the neoclassical migration model.

Increasingly, empirical research has also accounted for the role of temporal adjustment processes among migration flows and the existence of information lags in the transmission process from the explanatory to the endogenous variable. The inclusion of a time lagged endogenous variable has proven to be an important factor in the adjustment path of interregional migration flows (see e.g. Etzo 2011) and may reflect different channels through which past flows affect current migration (e.g. as migrants serve as communication links for friends and relatives left behind). These social linkages, in turn, are expected to have a potential impact on prospective migrants who want to live in an area where they share cultural and social backgrounds with other residents (see e.g. Chun 1996; Rainer and Siedler 2009).

The existence of such social networks not only hints at the presence of temporal adjustment processes, but may also affect the spatial orientation of migration flows. Nevertheless, in most empirical applications migration flows are still assumed to be independent of each other. Motivating the inclusion of spatial network effects, Chun (2008) points out that individual migration decisions should be seen as the result of choice processes in space, which are likely to be influenced by other migration flows at the macro level. Outflows from a particular origin may thus be correlated with other outflows that have the same origin and geographically proximate destination regions given unobservable characteristics of origins and destinations in the sample. This small example also highlights that the introduction of spatial autocorrelation increases the model's complexity compared to the case of purely temporal autocorrelation. While the latter is only one-dimensional and one-directional, resulting in correlation that arise from a single variable pair, spatial dependence is two-dimensional and multi-directional, resulting in correlation arising from a number of variable pairs.

For the case of (dyadic) flow data, the associated dependency structure has to be measured in terms of network autocorrelation. Starting from a standard spatial weighting matrix $\mathbf{W}$ as an n-by-n matrix of spatial connectivity among the set of n regions in the sample, a network matrix $\mathbf{W}^N$ can be constructed, which extends the two-dimensional space for $n \times n$ origin region (i), destination region (j) pairs $\{i,j|i \neq j; i,j = 1,\ldots,n\}$ to a four dimensional space with $n^2 \times n^2$ origin-destination linkages $\{i,j,r,s|i \neq j, r \neq s; ij = 1\ldots,n^2; rs = 1,\ldots,n^2\}$. Given that migration data typically abstracts from intraregional flows, the network matrix can defined as a non-negative symmetric matrix of the form $[(n^2-n)\times(n^2-n)]$ leaving intraregional flows aside.

Based on this information, a network weight matrix ($\mathbf{W}^N$) can be constructed as a combination of origin- ($\mathbf{W}_O^N$) and destination-related interactions ($\mathbf{W}_D^N$) with (Chun and Griffith 2011)

$$\mathbf{W}_O^N = \mathbf{W} \otimes \mathbf{I} \tag{16.1}$$

$$\mathbf{W}_D^N = \mathbf{I} \otimes \mathbf{W} \tag{16.2}$$

$$\mathbf{W}^N = \mathbf{W} \oplus \mathbf{W} = \mathbf{W} \otimes \mathbf{I} + \mathbf{I} \otimes \mathbf{W} = \mathbf{W}_O^N + \mathbf{W}_D^N, \tag{16.3}$$

where $\mathbf{I}$ is an n-by-n identity matrix, $\otimes$ and $\oplus$ denote the Kronecker product and Kronecker sum, respectively. For the binary case, elements w_O^N of the origin-based network weight matrix can be defined as

$$w_O^N(i,j;r,s) = \begin{cases} 1 \text{ if } j = s \text{ and } w(i,r) = 1, \\ 0 \text{ otherwise,} \end{cases} \tag{16.4}$$

where $w(i,r)$ are the elements of a $(n \times (n-1))$ spatial weight matrix (first-order contiguity) taking values of one, if i and r are linked to each other, and zero otherwise. In this framework, the network weight matrix $\mathbf{W}_O^N$ specifies an origin-based neighborhood for each origin-destination pair (i,j) by assigning a second pair (r,s) as its neighbor if the origin regions i and r are contiguous spatial units and $j = s$ (Fisher and Griffith 2008). The underlying spatial link between origins i and r may, for instance, be measured in terms of common boundaries or equivalently by defining a threshold distance between i and r. Similarly, elements of the destination based network weights matrix $\mathbf{W}_D^N$ consists of the following elements w_D^N

$$w_D^N(i,j;r,s) = \begin{cases} 1 \text{ if } i = r \text{ and } w(j,s) = 1, \\ 0 \text{ otherwise,} \end{cases} \tag{16.5}$$

where $w(j,s)$ is the binary indicator for spatial correlation between j and s in a first-order contiguity matrix as outlined above. As Chun and Griffith (2011) point out, a desirable feature of the above defined network scheme is that its design can be motivated by spatial search models, which allow an economic interpretation of the obtained spatially lagged regression coefficients. Thereby, $\mathbf{W}_O^N$ proxies the so-called 'intervening opportunities' effect, which models movements of people in space upon the idea that the number of migration flows between two regions is determined by the availability of different intervening opportunities (such as the number of available jobs) existing between the origin and the destination.

The specification of $\mathbf{W}_D^N$ can be motivated by the so-called 'competing destinations' effect (see e.g. Fotheringham 1983; Hu and Pooler 2002). The basic idea of the latter is to model human behavior as a spatial choice process based on the assumption that the actual choice occurs through hierarchical information processing since migrants are supposed to be only able to evaluate a limited number of alternatives at a time. Prospective migrants tend to simplify the alternatives by categorizing all alternatives into clusters, where the probability that one destination in a certain cluster will be chosen is related to the other regions in that cluster. This clustering process in turn requires that spatial proximity of destinations has an influence on the destination choice of migrants from one particular origin.

In the following, it is assumed that both effects operate simultaneously advocating the use of the combined matrix $\mathbf{W}^N$. Besides the above mentioned behavioral motivations for the existence of network effects, Zimmer (2008) argues that also herd behavior among migrants may lead to the occurrence of such patterns. In other words, under imperfect information the destination choice of other migrants may be interpreted as a positive signal regarding the quality of migration choice having a positive impact on the own migration decision. Such spatial herd behavior may thus entail positive space-time covariances in the dynamic adjustment processes taking place for the interregional migration network. This calls for a mutually dynamic empirical modelling strategy, which will be outlined in the next section.

16.3 Econometric Specification

To set up a model of interregional migration flows, this paper uses a fairly general modelling framework with both serial and spatial correlation being present in data generating process. In its triple-indexed form, the regression equation in log-log specification can be stated as

$$\begin{aligned} m_{i,j,t} &= \alpha \left(m_{i,j,t-1}\right) + \rho \left(\sum_{r,s \neq i,j} w_{(i,j;r,s),t} \times m_{r,s,t} \right) \\ &\quad + \beta \left(\mathbf{X}_{i,j,t-1}\right) + \gamma \left(\sum_{r,s \neq i,j} w_{(i,j;r,s),t} \times \mathbf{X}_{r,s,t-1} \right) + \iota_{i,j} + \epsilon_{i,j,t}, \quad (16.6) \end{aligned}$$

where $m_{i,j,t}$ is a measure of regional gross out-migration from state i to j (with $i,j = 1\ldots,n$) for time period t (with $t = 1,\ldots,T$) as a log-linearized function $\phi(\cdot)$ of its own time lag ($m_{i,j,t-1}$), a contemporaneous spatial lags of the dependent variable ($\sum_{r,s\neq i,j} w_{(i,j;r,s),t} \times m_{i,j,t}$) as well as a vector of labor market signals ($\mathbf{X}$) and their spatial lags, which both enter as one-period lagged values in order to account for information lags and reduce the reversed causality problem. $\iota_{i,j}$ is a vector of (fixed or random) individual effects to be specified by the researcher and $\epsilon_{i,j,t}$ is the model's error term. In the following, $\iota_{i,j}$ and $\epsilon_{i,j,t}$ are assumed to be independent over the cross-sectional dimension with $\epsilon_{i,j,t}$ being distributed as $N(0, \sigma_\epsilon^2)$, whereas $\iota_{i,j}$ is a vector of fixed effects to be estimated. The use of the fixed effects specification can motivated by the fact that empirical applications in spatial econometrics typically use space-time data of adjacent spatial units located in unbroken study areas. Thus, this study area typically takes the form of a fixed population of regions rather than a randomly drawn sample from a underlying regional population. In this setting, fixed effects estimation is the more appropriate choice (Elhorst 2012).

As demonstrated above, the elements $w_{(i,j;r,s),t}$ of the network weight matrix $\mathbf{W}^N$ are defined in a four dimensional space of origin-destination linkages varying by i, j, r and s, where i and r denote flow origins and j and s flow destinations for each time period t, respectively. α, ρ, β and γ are coefficients to be estimated. Since the model in Eq. (16.6) only includes a contemporaneous spatial lag of the dependent variable, it is also referred as space-time simultaneous model (see Anselin et al. 2007). The choice of this model puts certain restrictions on the functional form of the model and implies that all explicitly modelled spatial effects are assumed to take place within each time period of observation.[3] Although this modelling approach is clearly a simplification compared to a full space-time dynamic approach, which also accounts for time lags of the spatially lagged endogenous variable, Elhorst (2012) points out that the loss of this restriction due to the limited flexibility of the ratio between the indirect and direct effects is rather small compared to the pro of avoiding severe identification problems.[4]

The regression equation in Eq. (16.6) is also referred to as a spatial Durbin model (SDM), which provides a general basis for including different types of spatial interdependencies. LeSage and Pace (2009) put forward different arguments why the SDM provides a sufficiently general modelling basis: First, the model can be derived as a data generating process for an ordinary least-squares regression model in the presence of spatially omitted variables. The inclusion of spatial effects thus helps to control for the latter bias. Second, the regression coefficients of the spatial lags of the endogenous and explanatory variables can be interpreted as spatial (network) spillovers. For instance, one might be interested in assessing the strength of substitutive or complementary effects emanating from changes in the relative unemployment rate between r and s on migration flows between i and j given that i and r (or j and s) are neighboring regions.

Since the SDM nests the spatial autoregressive (SAR) model as a specific case, it is further possible to test for the validity of the SDM versus SAR based on the following coefficient restrictions $H_0 : \gamma = 0$ and $H_0 : \gamma + \rho\beta = 0$ (see Burridge 1981; LeSage and Pace 2008). Finally, given that Eq. (16.6) is a combination of a time and spatial autoregressive model, we need to ensure that the resulting process is

[3]For a general classification scheme of different combination including time-space lags in a regression framework, see Anselin et al. (2007).

[4]Additionally, it reduces the likely problem of multicollinearity among the regressors given that spatial dependence tends to arise from temporal dependence.

stationary. The stationarity restrictions in this model are stronger than the individual restrictions imposed on the coefficients of a pure spatial or time dynamic model (see Elhorst 2012). In this case, dynamic stability requires that the combination of the time autoregressive parameter α and the spatial lag coefficient ρ satisfies $|\alpha| + |\rho| < 1$. The spatially augmented specifications will be estimated by means of the bias corrected ML-approach proposed in Lee and Yu (2010).

16.4 Data and Regression Results

16.4.1 Variable Definition and Data Properties

For the empirical analysis, annual data for the 16 German federal states in the period 1993–2009 is used, which has been retrieved from the official migration statistics of the German statistical office.[5] Out-migration flows from *i* to *j* at time *t* ($m_{i,j,t}$) serve as the endogenous variable of the model. Among the set of explanatory variables in **X** adjusted real wages (wr^{adj}) and regional unemployment rates (ur) are used as key labor market variables. Further, labor productivity (ylr), the labor participation rate (q), a regional human capital composite indicator (hk), regional real estate prices proxied by the price for building land per sqm (p^l) and the sum of population in *i* and *j* ($spop$) are selected as additional controls. The latter variable seeks to control for the fact the populous regions tend to have higher in- and out-migration flows as such. All variables are used as logarithmic transformations.[6]

Since the correlation between wages and productivity is expected to be high according to the marginal revenue productivity theory of wages (see Zierahn 2012), the empirical analysis separates the effects of wages and productivity by estimating a proxy for the "excessive wage" (see Südekum and Blien 2004). The latter subtracts the productivity effect from wage rate changes by running an auxiliary regression (with all variables in logarithmic transformation) of the form

$$wr_{i,t} = \delta_1 wr_{i,t-1} + \delta_2 \Delta yrl_{i,t} + \delta_3 \Delta yrl_{i,t-1} + \iota_i + \lambda_t + v_{i,t} \qquad (16.7)$$

The real wage for region *i* at time *t* depends on its own time lag, current productivity growth (Δyrl), where Δ is the difference operator as $\Delta yrl_{i,t} = (yrl_{i,t} - yrl_{i,t-1})$, as well as time period (λ_t) and regional fixed effects (ι_i), respectively. Using the fitted values $\widehat{wr}_{i,t}$ of this regression, the adjusted wage ($wr^{adj}_{i,t}$) can then be calculated as $wr^{adj}_{i,t} = \widehat{wr}_{i,t} - \hat{\delta}_2(\Delta yrl_{i,t})$. It is defined as the wage, not ascribed to the evolution in productivity and is taken as explanatory variable in the migration

[5]The first two sample years after German re-unification are dropped due to missing data and structural breaks in the time series.

[6]A description of variable definitions and data sources is given in the appendix (see Table A.1).

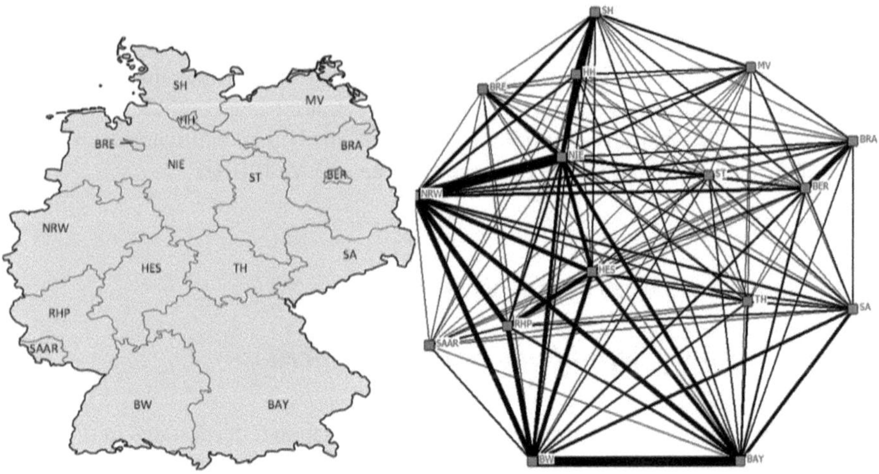

Fig. 16.1 Network graph of state-level migration flows in 2009. Note: *BW* = Baden-Württemberg, *BAY* = Bavaria, *BER* = Berlin, *BRA* = Brandenburg, *BRE* = Bremen, *HH* = Hamburg, *HES* = Hessia, *MV* = Mecklenburg-Vorpommern, *NIE* = Lower Saxony, *NRW* = North Rhine-Westphalia, *RHP* = Rhineland-Palatine, *SAAR* = Saarland, *SA* = Saxony, *ST* = Saxony-Anhalt, *SH* = Schleswig-Holstein, *TH* = Thuringia. The size of ties between state pairs measures the respective relative strength of interstate migratory linkages

equation.[7] Moreover, as the number of parameters to be estimated in the migration equation may become very large, all explanatory variables are restricted to enter as interregional differences, where $\tilde{x}_{i,j,t}$ for any variable $x_{i,j}$ at time t is defined as $\tilde{x}_{i,j,t} = (x_{i,t} - x_{j,t})$.

Figure 16.1 visualizes the network dimension of migration flows among the 16 states for the sample year 2009. The size of ties between state-pairs thereby measures the respective relative strength of two-sided interstate migratory flows. As Fig. 16.1 shows, most migration flows take place over short-distances between neighboring states. Moreover, populous states such as Bavaria, Baden-Württemberg and North Rhine-Westphalia also show to have relatively strong positions in the German migration network.

Throughout the empirical analysis, we will construct different empirical proxies for $\mathbf{W}^N$ to capture the spatial dimension of the German migration network. As default specification, we use information on geographical distances between states and define a 200 km threshold distance in order to assign spatial neighbors by means of a binary, row-standardized $\mathbf{W}^N$ matrix.[8] The choice for the latter cutoff value can be motivated by the fact that, on the one hand, the spatial weighting matrix should

[7]Regression details for the auxiliary wage equation can be obtained from the author upon request.

[8]Distance between two states is thereby calculated as the road distance in kilometers between a population weighted average of combination of pairs among the (up to three) major cities for each federal state.

be able to reflect the dominant trend of short-distance migration in Germany. On the other hand, the chosen weighting scheme should not be too tight in terms of producing isolated regions given that the average minimum distance between states in Germany is roughly 145 km. Thus, I have tried to trim the threshold value in such a way that it lies between the two extremes 1.) each federal state is an isolated island and 2.) each state is connected to everybody else. This approach is broadly in line with Zimmer (2008) as an earlier empirical application of spatial network estimation of German interregional migration flows and thus allows for a comparison with the former results. To check the sensitivity of the results with respect to alternative distance bands as well as a border-based contiguity specification for $\mathbf{W}^N$, I perform robustness tests in Sect. 16.4.3.

Prior to estimation, the data properties should also be carefully analysed in order to avoid any estimation bias. Basically, the following questions arise: (1) What is the correct functional form of the model given the empirical distribution of migration flows? (2) What are the time series properties of the data? and (3) Do global indicators of spatial (network) association ex-ante support the need for a spatially augmented regression design?

The first question has important implications for the functional form of the regression approach. In Eq. (16.6), a (log-)linear relationship among the variables is assumed to hold. However, such a model is only suitable when out-migration (or its logarithmic transformation) is, in fact, a continuous normally distributed variable. Alternatively, one could treat these observations as count data and use a (zero-inflated) Poisson regression. As Devillanova and Garcüa-Fontes (2004) point out, the latter approach is particularly useful if the number of locations considered is large and contains a high proportion of zero or very small values. This, however, is not the case for this data set, which is based on a rather high level of regional aggregation (NUTS1 level). Nevertheless, tests for the statistical distribution of log-transformed migration flows are provided. Figure 16.2 therefore plots univariate kernel density estimates for the logarithmic transformation of out-migration flows for different sample periods. Additionally, the outcome of Skewness and Kurtosis tests for normality are reported in Table 16.1. The results show that the (joint) null hypothesis of a normal distribution for the logarithm of migration flows cannot be rejected for reasonable confidence levels in most sample periods. The use of a log-linear specification for the estimation of Eq. (16.6) thus appears to be an appropriate modelling choice.

Given the moderate time dimension with $T = 19$, I also check for the time-series properties of the variables in order to avoid any spurious regression bias.[9] Table 16.2 reports the results of the Im et al. (2003) and Pesaran (2007) panel unit roots tests. The test results clearly reject the null hypothesis of non-stationarity for all variables based on reasonable confidence levels, however, one has to note that growth rates for labor productivity and prices for building land per sqm. (Δylr, Δp^l)

[9]For $T = 19$, the sample range includes all available time periods from 1991–2009. As outlined above, for estimation purposes, the first 2 years after German re-unification will be dropped later on.

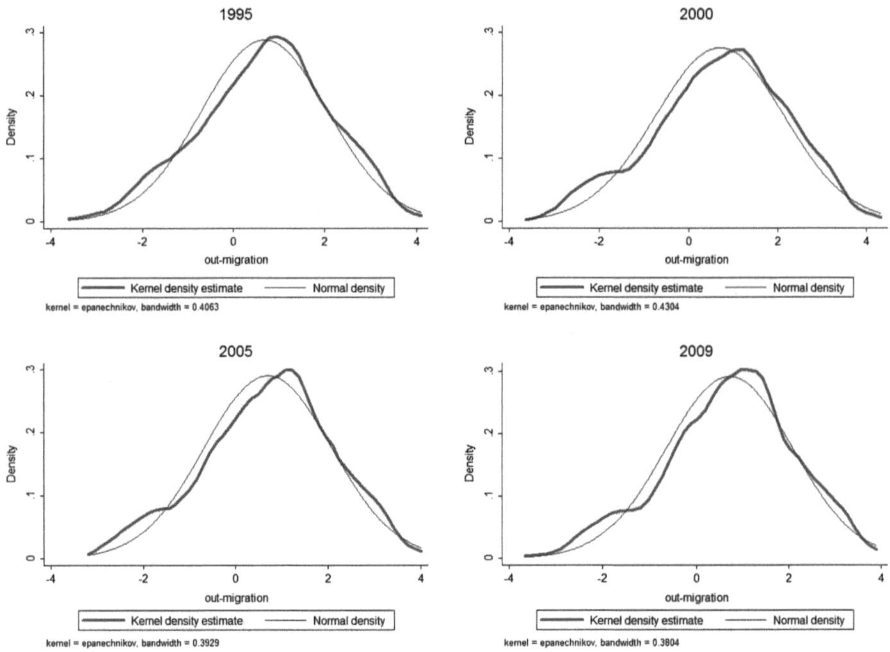

Fig. 16.2 Kernel density estimates for log-transformed out-migration flows. Note: The *solid line* shows the fitted values of univariate kernel density estimation. The *dotted line* shows a normal distribution

have been used since their levels turned out to be non-stationary. Finally a test to detect structural breaks in the time series is conducted, which-if a structural break is present-might bias the results of the unit root tests. Adapting a sequential testing procedure proposed by Tzavalis (2008), the results, however, indicate that all variables are stationary and that no structural break is present.[10]

Finally, the potential role played by spatial dependence in migration flows is investigated. For panel data settings, (Mutl and Pfaffermayr 2010) as well as Lopez et al. (2011) have recently proposed spatio-temporal extensions of Moran's I (*STMI*).[11] By means of Monte Carlo simulations, Lopez et al. (2011) have shown that the *STMI* has a satisfactory small sample behavior compared to other 'spatialized' test statistics for the cross-sectional independence of the residuals. To apply the *STMI* test, the above specified binary $\mathbf{W}^N$ matrix based on a 200 km distance band is used. For the dependent variable $m_{ij,t}$ the value for the extended Moran's I is $STMI = 0.481$, the corresponding test statistic is $Z_{STMI} = 23.51$. Hence, under the assumption of normality, this result strongly rejects the null hypothesis of independence among network flows. The upper part of Fig. 16.3 additionally plots the results of the *STMI* graphically based on the correlation of the

[10]Detailed test results can be obtained from the author upon request.

[11]Earlier concepts have already been proposed by (Cliff and Ord 1981) as well as Griffith (1981).

Table 16.1 Skewness/kurtosis tests for normality of out-migration flows

Year	Prob. (skewness)	Prob. (kurtosis)	Prob. (joint)
1993	(0.07)	(0.15)	(0.07)
1994	(0.08)	(0.23)	(0.11)
1995	(0.08)	(0.29)	(0.12)
1996	(0.08)	(0.35)	(0.14)
1997	(0.08)	(0.35)	(0.14)
1998	(0.03)	(0.66)	(0.08)
1999	(0.04)	(0.29)	(0.08)
2000	(0.04)	(0.24)	(0.06)
2001	(0.05)	(0.15)	(0.05)
2002	(0.03)	(0.33)	(0.06)
2003	(0.03)	(0.37)	(0.07)
2004	(0.08)	(0.21)	(0.10)
2005	(0.06)	(0.30)	(0.10)
2006	(0.06)	(0.42)	(0.12)
2007	(0.03)	(0.69)	(0.08)
2008	(0.05)	(0.42)	(0.11)
2009	(0.03)	(0.73)	(0.09)

Note: Reported results are p-values for normality tests based on skewness, kurtosis and a combined test statistic

Table 16.2 Im et al. (2003) IPS and Pesaran (2007) CIPS panel unit root test for variables

IPS and CIPS tests for $N \times (N-1), T = (240, 19)$

H_0: All cross-sections contain unit roots

Specification	$\overline{IPS}$	p-value	$\overline{CIPS}$	p-value
$m_{i,j,t}$	−16.09	(0.00)	−10.39	(0.00)
$\widetilde{ur}_{i,j,t}$	−14.65	(0.00)	−12.82	(0.00)
$\widetilde{wr}_{i,j,t}$	−86.87	(0.00)	−8.35	(0.00)
$\Delta\widetilde{ylr}_{i,j,t}$	−67.40	(0.00)	−28.70	(0.00)
$\tilde{q}_{i,j,t}$	−12.25	(0.00)	−7.57	(0.00)
$\widetilde{hc}_{i,j,t}$	−6.99	(0.00)	−2.06	(0.02)
$\Delta\widetilde{p^l}_{i,j,t}$	−48.01	(0.00)	−32.49	(0.00)
$spop_{i,j,t}$	−40.11	(0.00)	−27.25	(0.00)

Note: Including a constant term; optimal (average) lag length selection for the IPS test according to the AIC. The same lag length was then imposed for the CIPS test

standardized net-migration variable and its spatial lag. Finally, standard Moran's I statistics for each individual year have been computed in the lower part of Fig. 16.3, which show that network dependency is present in each sample year and even increase towards the end of the sample.

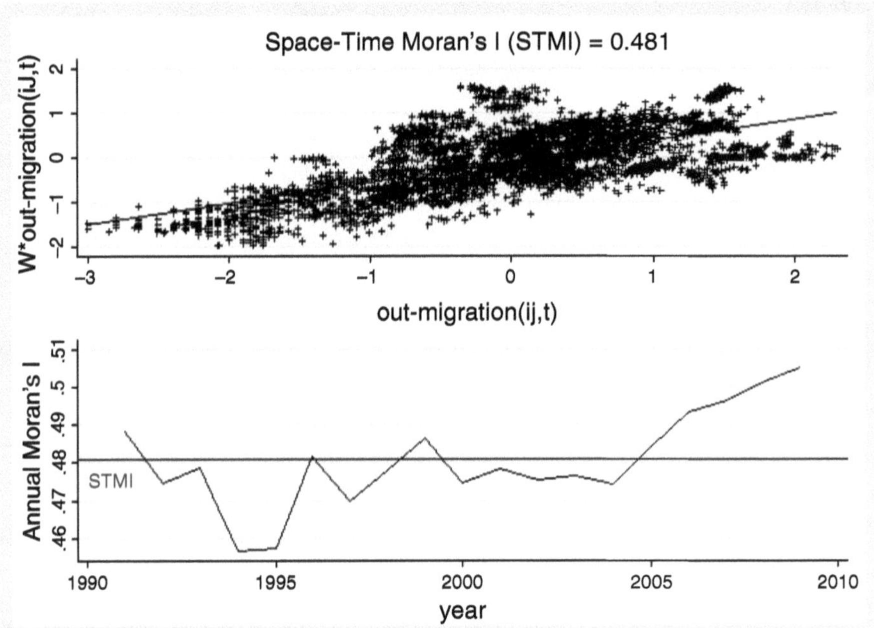

Fig. 16.3 Fitted scatter-plot for the spatio-temporal Moran's *I* (*STMI*). Note: The *upper part* of the figure displays the scatter-plot of out-migration and its spatial lag (calculated using the default 200 km distance band). The slope coefficient of the included regression line equals the computed STMI value. In the *lower part* of the figure, the *red line* highlights the overall STMI value for the whole sample, while the *blue line* shows the standard Moran's *I* values for the individual sample years

16.4.2 Regression Results, Summary Measures and Multiplier Analysis

First, a non-spatial dynamic Fixed-Effects model (DFE) is estimated to serve as benchmark specification. There is already a significant body of literature dealing with the proper estimation of such time-dynamic panel data models given that the lagged endogenous variable is correlated with the model's error term. In order to obtain consistent parameter estimates for the DFE model, an analytical bias correction as proposed in Kiviet (1995) will be used. The results for the DFE specification are shown in column I of Table 16.3. Extending this benchmark specification, consecutively spatial dynamics is introduced to the model by means of spatially lagged variables using the above defined network matrix with a threshold distance value of 200 km to define neighboring network flows. One has to note that in the regression equations, all further regressors enter as one-period lagged values in order to account for information lags and to minimize the risk of reversed causality.

Table 16.3 ML-estimation results for the dynamic spatial migration model

Model	DFE	DFE-SAR	DFE-SDM	DFE-SDM
$\widetilde{ur}_{i,j,t-1}$	0.070***	0.014	−0.024	0.011
	(0.0272)	(0.0248)	(0.0433)	(0.0259)
$\widetilde{wr}^{adj}_{i,j,t-1}$	−0.029	−0.054**	−0.033	−0.043*
	(0.0367)	(0.0266)	(0.0391)	(0.0265)
$\Delta\widetilde{ylr}_{i,j,t-1}$	−0.125***	−0.090***	−0.056	−0.063**
	(0.0419)	(0.0311)	(0.0422)	(0.0296)
$\tilde{q}_{i,j,t-1}$	0.361***	0.196	−0.117	0.093
	(0.1391)	(0.1306)	(0.2257)	(0.1374)
$\widetilde{hk}_{i,j,t-1}$	0.025	0.014	−0.039*	−0.033
	(0.0212)	(0.0181)	(0.0221)	(0.0224)
$\Delta\widetilde{p^l}_{i,j,t-1}$	0.031***	0.012*	0.016	0.014*
	(0.0085)	(0.0076)	(0.0101)	(0.0077)
$spop_{i,j,t-1}$	−0.053	−0.031	−0.009	−0.025
	(0.0334)	(0.0222)	(0.0277)	(0.0259)
$m_{i,j,t-1}$	0.824***	0.624***	0.623***	0.625***
	(0.0121)	(0.0236)	(0.0237)	(0.0236)
$\sum w_{(i,j;r,s),t} \times m_{r,s,t}$		0.306***	0.306***	0.310***
		(0.0174)	(0.0175)	(0.0175)
$\sum w_{(i,j;r,s),t} \times \widetilde{ur}_{r,s,t-1}$			0.057	
			(0.0467)	
$\sum w_{(i,j;r,s),t} \times \widetilde{wr}^{adj}_{r,s,t-1}$			−0.057	
			(0.0514)	
$\sum w_{(i,j;r,s),t} \times \Delta\widetilde{ylr}_{r,s,t-1}$			−0.089	−0.042**
			(0.0584)	(0.0169)
$\sum w_{(i,j;r,s),t} \times \tilde{q}_{r,s,t-1}$			0.437*	0.128**
			(0.2581)	(0.0581)
$\sum w_{(i,j;r,s),t} \times \widetilde{hk}_{r,s,t-1}$			0.083***	0.069***
			(0.0269)	(0.0264)
$\sum w_{(i,j;r,s),t} \times \Delta\widetilde{p^l}_{r,s,t-1}$			−0.006	
			(0.0144)	
$\sum w_{(i,j;r,s),t} \times spop_{r,s,t-1}$			−0.079	
			(0.0604)	

(continued)

Table 16.3 (continued)

Model	DFE	DFE-SAR	DFE-SDM	DFE-SDM
$N \times T$	3600	3600	3600	3600
LM_{SAR}	220.18 (0.00)			
LM_{SEM}	0.439 (0.51)			
$H_0 : \rho = 0$			307.19*** (0.00)	312.20*** (0.00)
$Coef : \alpha + \rho$		0.930*** (0.0238)	0.929*** (0.0245)	0.934*** (0.0243)
$H_0 : \lvert\alpha\rvert + \lvert\rho\rvert \geq 1$		8.61*** (0.00)	8.25*** (0.00)	7.33*** (0.00)

Note: ***, **, * denote significance at the 1, 5 and 10 %-level. Standard errors in brackets. In the case of post-estimation tests, the results of Wald F-tests and corresponding p-values are reported

To test for the importance of spatial network effects, LM_{SEM} and LM_{SAR} tests—as proposed in Elhorst (2010)—will be applied to the within-transformed residuals of the non-spatial DFE specification. The tests can be used in order to test the null hypothesis whether the coefficient of the spatial lag variables in the spatial error model (SEM) and spatial autoregressive (SAR) model turn out to be statistically insignificant, in which place the DFE would be the optimal choice. Although the LM_{SEM} test does not reject the null hypothesis of no spatial correlation in the error term, the LM_{SAR} test strongly hints at the presence of global spillovers induced by the spatial lag of the endogenous variable (see column I of Table 16.3).

Thus, switching to the DFE-SAR specification, the associated regression results are shown in column II of Table 16.3. As the results show, the spatial lag term of the dependent variable enters statistically significant into the model and indicates the presence of positive spatial autocorrelation among interregional migration flows. The coefficient size of $\rho = 0.306$ is thereby in line with earlier evidence on network effects among German interregional migration reported in Zimmer (2008).[12] Since the DFE-SAR comprises spatial and temporal dynamics, the validity of the restriction $H_0 : |\alpha| + |\rho| < 1$ has to be tested for the stationarity condition to hold. As Table 16.3 shows, however, the null hypothesis of dynamic stationarity cannot be rejected for reasonable confidence levels in the case of the DFE-SAR. Comparing the estimation results for the DFE and DFE-SAR, the table shows that the inclusion of joint space-time autocorrelations also affects the statistical significance of the included labor market signals. While regional unemployment rate differences have shown to be a statistically significant driver of out-migration flows in the DFE specification, they turn out to be statistically insignificant in the DFE-

[12]For static SARAR specifications, Zimmer (2008) reports values for ρ ranging from 0.23 to 0.48.

SAR extension. At the same time, in the latter model a stronger weight is given to the adjusted wage rate differential among German states. Although, regional differences in the growth rate of labor productivity turn out to be highly statistically significant in both specifications, though.

Extending the DFE-SAR specification to the DFE-SDM case, it is possible to test for the validity of the augmentation by means of common factor restrictions (Burridge 1981) as $H_0 : \rho = 0$ and $H_0 : \gamma + \rho\beta = 0$. Using a set of Wald F-tests, the second restriction will be explicitly tested for each exogenous regressor with the intention to capture the mutual spatial dynamics present in the data, on the one hand, while reducing the number of regressors to a minimum, on the other hand. Starting from a fully specified SDM in column III of Table 16.3, the post-estimation tests indicate that only for three variables, namely $\Delta\widetilde{ylr}_{i,j,t-1}$, $\tilde{q}_{i,j,t-1}$ and $\widetilde{hc}_{i,j,t-1}$, the null hypothesis of $H_0 : \gamma + \rho\beta = 0$ can be rejected at reasonable confidence levels.[13] Thus, column IV of Table 16.3 reports the final form of the DFE-SDM with spatial lags for $\Delta\widetilde{ylr}_{i,j,t-1}$, $\tilde{q}_{i,j,t-1}$ and $\widetilde{hc}_{i,j,t-1}$ besides the spatial lag of the endogenous variable. As for the DFE-SAR regression results, also for the DFE-SDM case the null hypothesis of dynamic stationarity cannot be rejected for reasonable confidence levels. Thus, given that our empirical identification strategy hints at the fact that the DFE-SDM with partial parameter restrictions on the set of exogenous regressors is the optimal choice, in the following, economic interpretation of the regression results will be based on this latter specification.

The "specific-to-general" modelling strategy has identified the dynamic DFE-SDM specification as most appropriate model presentation. Since this model is characterized by a high degree of simultaneity and complexity, the corresponding regression output cannot be interpreted as such. Instead meaningful summary measures for the short-term and long-term marginal effect of a change in an exogenous variable in **X** on out-migration will be reported. The measures allow tracking the evolution of the different spatial effects for each regressor over space and time and thus allow to test for the validity of the neoclassical migration theory. In the short-run, the direct and spatially indirect effects measure the instantaneous impact of regional labor market signals on migration flows. The direct effect thereby measures the impact of a unit change in the kth explanatory variable from **X** for each origin-destination pair (i,j) on migratory flows between i and j, while the spatially indirect effect measures the change in migration flows between i and j due to a percentage change in the kth explanatory variable in **X** for neighboring pairs (r, s). The sum of the direct and indirect effect is the total effect. Taken together, these measures allow for the analysis of the overall impact of regional labor market signals on interregional migration flows.[14]

---

[13] Detailed test results are given in Table A.2 the appendix.

[14] As Elhorst (2011) points out, although the calculation of the above effects is straightforward, no direct statistical inference on these measures can be performed. The reason is that they are composed of different coefficient estimates according to complex mathematical formulas and the dispersion of the effects depends on the dispersion of all coefficient estimates involved. This paper

In the long-run, direct, indirect and total effects for each explanatory variable additionally need to be corrected by the degree of temporal adjustment processes taking place, which are determined by the size of α. Formally, the latter long-run effect can be computed from the (systematic part of the) reduced form of Eq. (16.6) stacked over the (dyadic) cross-sectional dimension i, j as

$$m_t = [(1-\alpha)\mathbf{I} - \rho\mathbf{W}^N]^{-1}[\beta\mathbf{X}_t + \gamma\mathbf{W}^N\mathbf{X}_t]. \tag{16.8}$$

Then, for the kth regressor it is possible to decompose this reduced form equation into three long-run summary measures M^{lr} as

$$M^{lr}_{total}(k) = z'\left([(1-\alpha)\mathbf{I} - \rho\mathbf{W}^N]^{-1}[\mathbf{I}\beta_k + \gamma_k\mathbf{W}^N]\right) z\,(1/N) \tag{16.9}$$

$$M^{lr}_{direct}(k) = trace\left([(1-\alpha)\mathbf{I} - \rho\mathbf{W}^N]^{-1}[\mathbf{I}\beta_k + \gamma_k\mathbf{W}^N]\right)(1/N) \tag{16.10}$$

$$M^{lr}_{indirect}(k) = M^{lr}_{total}(k) - M^{lr}_{direct}(k) \tag{16.11}$$

with z as $N = n \times (n-1)$ vector of ones. For the computation of short-term effects, the term $(1-\alpha)^{-1}$ can be ignored (see LeSage and Pace 2009). Given the dynamic nature of our model, it is then also possible to track the temporal evolution from the short- to the long-term effects by means of multiplier analysis (see Debarsy et al. 2011; Lütkepohl 2005). For each period s, an interim multiplier D_s as $D_s = (\alpha)^s \times B^{-1}$ is calculated, where $B = (\mathbf{I} - \rho\mathbf{W}^N)$, which models the speed of adjustment of the migration response to a change in regional labor market signals. Based on these interim multipliers, cumulative effects up to time period s can be calculated as $\sum_{s=0}^{S} D_s$.

Table 16.4 reports the simulated short- and long-term direct, indirect and total effects for the preferred DFE-SDM specification from column IV in Table 16.3. Focusing on the long-run effect first, the table reports statistically insignificant results for the regional unemployment and adjusted wage rate differential. In contrast, out-migration flows are shown to be negatively affected by regional differences in the labor productivity growth rate. Here, we observe that both direct and spatially indirect network effects are at work. For regional differences in the labor participation rate, the simulated long-run summary measures hint at statistically significant positive total effects on out-migration flows, where the total effect is driven by indirect network spillovers. This indicates that not only direct changes between regional labor market signals affect migration flows between i and j, but also indirect changes between (neighboring) third party states may trigger pull effects on regional out-migration flows.

thus follows LeSage and Pace (2009), Elhorst (2011) and simulates the distribution of the effects using the estimated variance-covariance of the regression analysis.

Table 16.4 Direct, indirect and total effect for DFE-SDM migration equation

	Short-run			Long-run		
	Direct	Indirect	Total	Direct	Indirect	Total
$\widetilde{ur}_{i,j,t-1}$	0.005	0.002	0.007	0.013	0.005	0.019
	(0.0112)	(0.0043)	(0.0156)	(0.0298)	(0.0115)	(0.0414)
$\widetilde{wr}^{adj}_{i,j,t-1}$	−0.016	−0.006	−0.022	−0.042	−0.016	−0.058
	(0.0111)	(0.0043)	(0.0154)	(0.0295)	(0.0115)	(0.0409)
$\Delta\widetilde{ylr}_{i,j,t-1}$	−0.026**	−0.029***	−0.055***	−0.068**	−0.078***	−0.146***
	(0.0117)	(0.0099)	(0.0195)	(0.0309)	(0.0260)	(0.0509)
$\tilde{q}_{i,j,t-1}$	0.049	0.078***	0.127*	0.131	0.207***	0.339*
	(0.0587)	(0.0269)	(0.0755)	(0.1561)	(0.0706)	(0.2000)
$\widetilde{hk}_{i,j,t-1}$	−0.009	0.028**	0.020*	−0.023	0.076**	0.053*
	(0.0081)	(0.0113)	(0.0121)	(0.0215)	(0.0296)	(0.0319)
$\Delta\widetilde{p^l}_{i,j,t-1}$	0.006**	0.002**	0.008**	0.015**	0.006**	0.020**
	(0.0028)	(0.0011)	(0.0038)	(0.0073)	(0.0028)	(0.0101)
$spop_{i,j,t-1}$	−0.008	−0.003	−0.012	−0.022	−0.009	−0.031
	(0.0087)	(0.0033)	(0.0121)	(0.0231)	(0.0089)	(0.03208)

Note: ***, **, * denote significance at the 1, 5 and 10 %-level based on partial derivatives and parameter simulations as described in the text. For the SDM, the restricted parameter specification according to column IV in Table 16.3 is used

Both the negative correlation between regional out-migration and regional differences in labor productivity growth as well as the positive correlation between out-migration and changes in the labor participation rate are in line with the neoclassical migration model. The latter model predicts that a relative increase in the regional income level should diminish outward oriented migration flows, while an increase in the labor participation rate should be seen as an substitutive adjustment mechanisms to restore labor market disequilibria. Hence, it can be expected that relative changes in the labor participation rate co-move uni-directionally with the evolution of gross out-migration flows. In the case of labor productivity growth, this variable captures the migration effect stemming from relative changes in the expected income across regions as outlined in Sect. 16.2.

Moreover, the scalar summary measures show statistically significant and positive indirect network effects of regional differences in human capital endowments on out-migration, while real estate price differences show the theoretically expected positive relationship with out-migration flows. In other words, with increasing regional real estate prices in state i, the costs of living in this region rise, which thus induce a further pressure on out-migration flows from i to j. For the latter variable the results hint at positive direct as well as indirect effects. The statistically significant effect of the human capital variable underlines the importance to properly account for differences in the skill-level of the work force as an explicit factor in regional production (as e.g. outlined in the new growth theory) and an important driver of labor market dynamics through migratory behavior.

Finally, in order to take a closer look at the adjustment dynamics of the direct and indirect effects for each variable over time, cumulative multipliers for a time horizon of up to 10 years have been computed. The graphical presentation of these cumulative multipliers in Fig. 16.4 shows that the speed of adjustment towards the long-run impact is rather fast and mostly occurs within the first 3 years. Regarding the interplay of the direct and indirect effects per variable, in all cases uni-directed direct and indirect effects are observed although the model is not restricted to a common global multiplier process ex-ante as it is the case in the

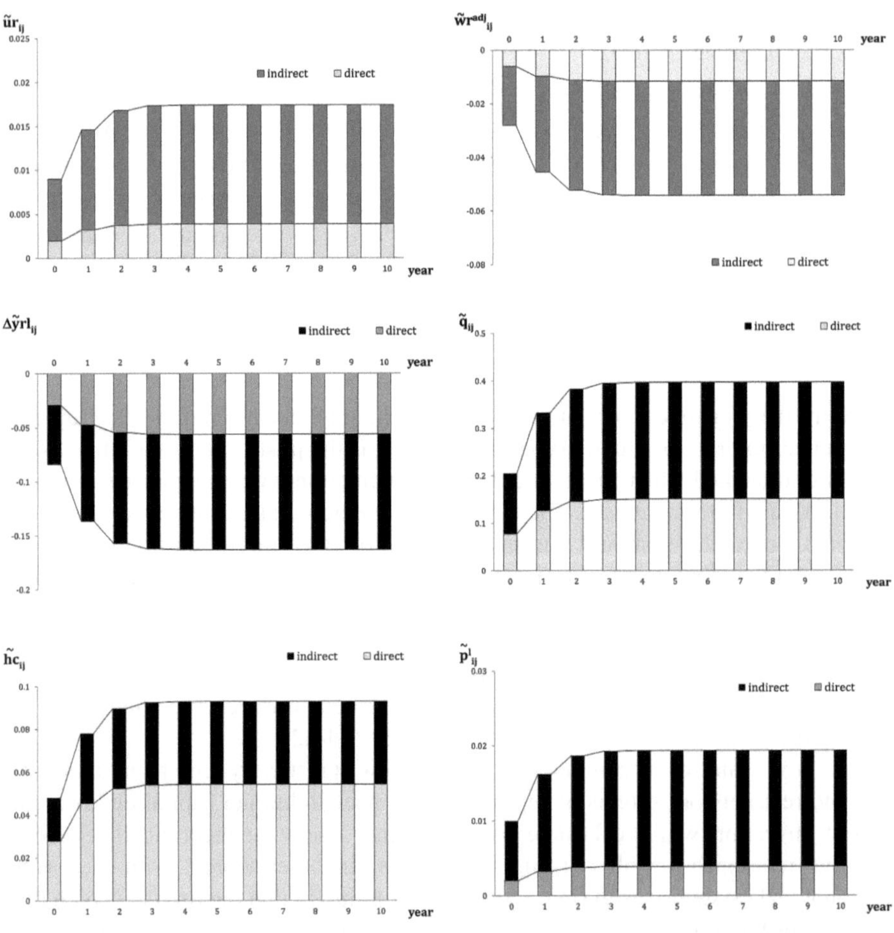

Fig. 16.4 Dynamic cumulative multipliers for direct and indirect effects. Source: Based on the simulated effects for the DFE-SDM according to Table 16.4. *Hatched bars* indicate statistically insignificant effects. Multiplier results for *spop* are omitted and can be obtained from the author upon request

DFE-SAR specification. The results shown in Fig. 16.4 finally highlight the fact, that for most variables the indirect spatial effect dominates the direct counterpart. In other words, spatial network effects play a key role in assessing the overall impact of regional labor marked differences on regional out-migration flows. All in all, these findings support earlier empirical evidence for German interregional migration provided by Zimmer (2008), who finds that besides an increase in expected income, network effects seem to have the strongest influence on the decision to migrate.

16.4.3 Robustness Checks

Before drawing conclusions, the robustness of the above findings with respect to the choice of the underlying imposed spatial structure to construct $\mathbf{W}^N$ has to be inspected. The latter aspect is a common point of critique in spatial econometric applications. Arbia and Fingleton (2008), for instance, call for more research on the robustness of outcomes to variations in assumptions about the weight matrix structure should be carried out in order to allay such criticism. Although LeSage and Pace (2010) have recently shown that the sensitivity of spatial econometric models is rather due to model misspecification and misinterpretation of regression coefficients as true partial derivatives (and not the form of $\mathbf{W}$). However, to be sure about this, five alternative network weight matrices both as a common border based first order (queen-type) contiguity matrix as well as different threshold distances with $d = (175, 250, 300)$ in kilometers will be computed.[15]

Looking at the key summary statistics for the different network weight matrices, Table 16.5 displays these characteristics of the different weighting schemes including the minimum, mean and maximum value of each matrix entry as well as the total and average number of linkages. The table shows that the benchmark matrix with a threshold value of $d = 200$ lies within (but at the lower bound of) the range of the chosen alternative specifications. Calculating a measure of similarity between two matrices, where the correlation coefficient for their spatial lags based on an independent identically distributed normal variable u as $\mathbf{W}^N u$ is used, the observed similarity is the highest for the combination $Corr(\mathbf{W}^N_{d200}, \mathbf{W}^N_{d175} = 0.85)$ and steadily decreases for larger distance bands. Nevertheless, in all cases the correlation is sufficiently high in order not to expect significant deviations in the economic interpretation of the obtained effects.

The results in Fig. 16.5 present the simulated long-term direct and indirect effects for the DFE-SDM based on alternative network weighting schemes. Hollow bars indicate statistically insignificant results. As the figure shows, despite some degree

[15]We restrict the computation of weight matrices to a minimum threshold distance of $d = 175$ km in order to avoid modelling network flows without neighbors in the network.

Table 16.5 Descriptive characteristics of the different network weight matrices

	d200	d175	d250	d300	Border
Dimension	240 × 240	240 × 240	240 × 240	240 × 240	240 × 240
Normalization	Row-sum	Row-sum	Row-sum	Row-sum	Row-sum
Min. value	0.143	0.200	0.125	0.077	0.083
Mean value	0.004	0.004	0.004	0.004	0.004
Max. value	1.000	1.000	1.000	0.333	0.500
Total links	784	560	1288	2072	1568
Mean no. of links	3.2663	2.333	5.366	8.633	6.53
Corr($\mathbf{W}^N_{d200}$, $\mathbf{W}^N_i$)	1.000	0.849	0.715	0.565	0.516

of heterogeneity among the simulated effects, in most cases, the result obtained from the benchmark network weight matrix with $d = 200$ km are qualitatively confirmed by the alternative network specifications. For regional unemployment rate differences all specifications report statistically insignificant direct and indirect effects. For labor productivity growth, the direct and indirect effects are persistently negative and statistically significant. However, while the estimated direct effect remains rather constant in size across the different specifications, the size of the indirect network increases for larger distance bands and the border-based weights. This result may indicate that productivity differences exhibit strong indirect migration signals for long-range flows. Similarly, negative effects stemming from wage rate differences (both direct as well as indirect) also turn significant only for larger distance threshold values and may be rooted in the distinct wage gap between West and East German federal states. The empirical findings support earlier empirical evidence for Germany provided by Zimmer (2008), who finds that besides an increase in expected income, network seem to have the strongest influence on the decision to migrate.

For the labor participation rate, I observe that there is no direct effect on regional out-migration flows, however, in most specification the indirect effect is estimated to be negative. Similar results are also found for interregional differences in human capital endowments. Finally, for differences in real estate prices, statistically significant effects on out-migration flows are observed only for tightly specified geographical threshold distances, while estimation results based on wider distance bands seem to dilute the real estate market pricing signal. Summing up, given that the observed heterogeneity in the empirical results is rather moderate, the general picture drawn in Fig. 16.5 supports the conclusion of LeSage and Pace (2010) that appropriately fitted models using different forms of $\mathbf{W}^N$ are not likely to produce estimates for the different effects that substantially differ from each other. However, especially for wage rate differences, on the one hand, and real estate prices, on the other hand, the results seem to be sensitive with respect to the chosen type of $\mathbf{W}^N$. The results thus call for a careful treatment of network weights in the light of migration flow analyses given that effects may be amplified or diluted by the former choice.

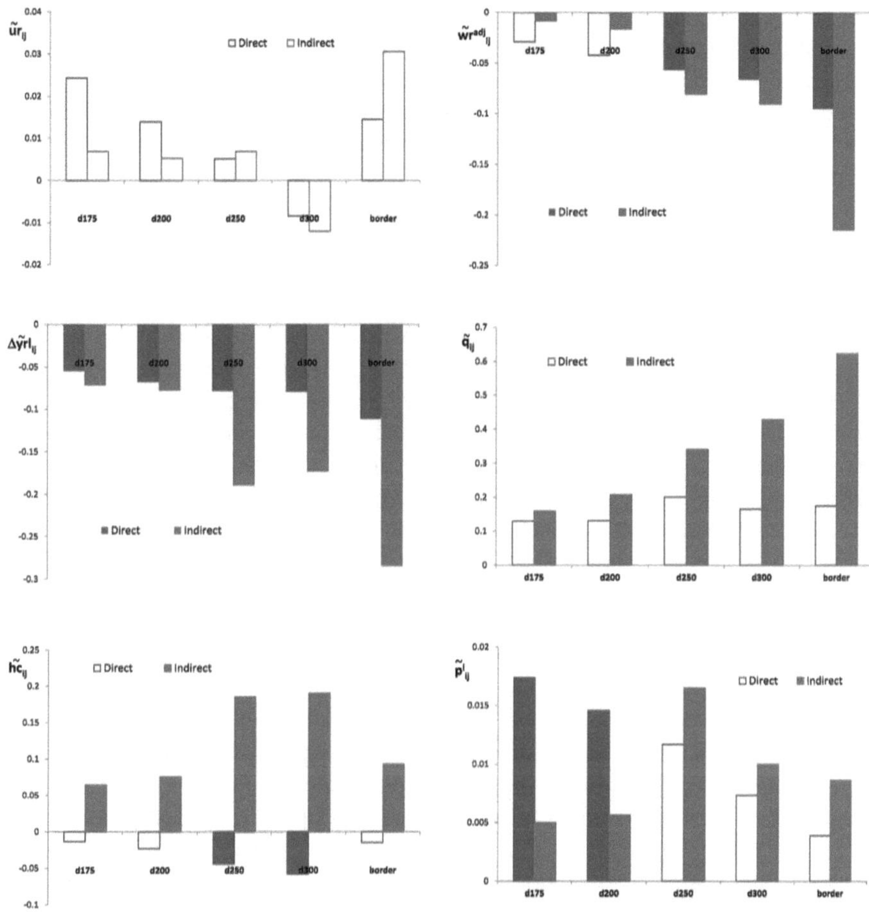

Fig. 16.5 Comparison of long-term effects for different network weight matrices. Source: *Hollow bars* indicate statistically insignificant results. Based on DFE-SDM specification. Results for *spop* are not reported and can be obtained from the author upon request

16.5 Conclusion

The aim of this paper was to consistently estimate and interpret dyadic econometric models of interregional population flows which are driven by spatial and temporal dynamics. Using panel data for interregional out-migration among the 16 German federal states throughout the period 1993–2009 and applying recent advances in panel econometric modelling as well as the computation of meaningful scalar summary measures for spatial dynamic models, the empirical results show that standard non-spatial migration specifications are likely to obtain biased parameter estimates due to the omission of relevant network factors. Based on the specification of a space-related network weight matrix, it was then possible to broaden the scope of the analysis and conduct a "specific-to-general" modelling strategy, which identified the dynamic spatial Durbin model (DFE-SDM) as preferential empirical specification. This model is driven by temporal and spatial dynamics in the dependent variable as well as by direct and indirect network effects stemming from the set of regressors. The latter are proxied by different regional labor market signals that are derived from neoclassical migration theory.

The long-run results show that state-level gross out-migration flows are negatively correlated with regional differences in labor productivity growth, capturing the effect of changes in expected income as predicted by the neoclassical migration theory. For network weighting matrices with larger threshold distances, changes in the relative regional (adjusted) wage rate differential are also found to have a negative impact on out-migration flows. Changes in the relative regional labor participation rate show the theoretically expected positive correlation with out-migration flows indicating that adaptions in the migration and labor participation behavior can be seen as an alternative adjustment mechanisms to restore labor market disequilibria. Similarly, differences in real estate prices across regions show the theoretically expected pricing signal on migration flows, namely that increasing relative prices in state i are a push factor for regional out-migration flows from i to j.

In order to take a closer look at the relative dynamic evolution the direct and indirect network effects for each variable over time, cumulative multipliers for a time horizon of up to 10 years have been computed. The results show that for all variables the speed of adjustment towards the long-run impact is rather fast and mostly occurs within the first 3 years. Regarding the interplay of the direct and indirect effects by variable, the estimation results uniformly hint at additive linkages. Overall, the obtained results underline the importance of a decomposition of the total effects of labor market signals on interregional migration flows by means of their spatial and temporal dynamics. A robustness analysis has finally shown that—although the obtained effects remain roughly stable for alternatively specified network weight matrices—the estimated impact for some variables such as adjusted wage and real estate price differences may be sensitive to the choice of the network weighting scheme. The proper specification and interpretation of network models for dyadic flow data should thus be subject to further research efforts in the field.

Acknowledgements I thank the editors of this book, Giuseppe Arbia and Roberto Patuelli, as well as an anonymous reviewer for helpful comments. Moreover, I acknowledge the help from Gordon Hughes by sharing his Stata code.

Variable Definitions

See Tables A.1 and A.2.

Table A.1 Data description and source

Variable	Description	Source
$m_{i,j,t}$	Total number of out-migration from i to j in 1000	Destatis (2012)
$yl_{i(j),t}$	Gross domestic product per Employee in 1000 Euro in $i(j)$	VGRdL (2012)
$py_{i(j),t}$	GDP deflator for state $i(j)$	VGRdL (2012)
$ylr_{i(j),t}$	Real labour productivity defined as $(yl_{i(j),t} - py_{i(j),t})$	VGRdL (2012)
$pop_{i(j),t}$	Population in 1000 in $i(j)$	VGRdL (2012)
$emp_{i(j),t}$	Total employment persons in 1000 in $i(j)$	VGRdL (2012)
$unemp_{i(j),t}$	Total unemployment in 1000 in $i(j)$	VGRdL (2012)
$ur_{i(j),t}$	Unemployment rate defined as $(unemp_{i(j),t} - emp_{i(j),t})$	VGRdL (2012)
$pcpi_{i(j),t}$	Consumer price index based on Roos (2006) and regional CPI inflation rates	Roos (2006), Destatis (2012)
$wr_{i(j),t}$	Real wage rate defined as wage compensation per employee deflated by $pcpi_{i(j)t}$	VGRdL (2012)
$q_{i(j),t}$	Labor market participation rate in region defined as $(emp_{i(j),t} - pop_{i(j),t})$	VGRdL (2012)
$hk_{i(j),t}$	Human capital index as weighted average of: (1) high school graduates with university qualification per total pop. between 18–20 years, (2) number of university degrees per population between 25–30 years, (3) share of employed persons with a university degree relative to total employment, (4) number of patents per total population	Destatis (2012)
$p^l_{i(j)t}$	Real estate prices as price for building land per qm in $i(j)$, in Euro	Destatis (2012)
$dist_{i,j}$	Geographical distance between state i and j calculated as the road distance in kilometers between a population weighted average of major city pairs for each pairwise combination of regions	Own computation based on www.map24.de

Note: All variables in logarithmic transformation. For Bremen, Hamburg, Schleswig-Holstein (Rhineland-Palatine and Saarland prior to 1995) no consumer price inflation rates are available. West German aggregate rates are used instead. In order to construct time series for the price of building land (p^l) no state level data before 1995 was available. Average growth rate between 1995 and 1999 have been used to construct values prior to 1995 for each state

Table A.2 Test for common factor restriction $H_0 : \gamma + \rho\beta = 0$ in DFE-SDM

Variable	Test statistic	p-value
$\widetilde{ur}_{i,j,t-1}$	1.82	(0.18)
$\widetilde{wr}^{adj}_{i,j,t-1}$	2.19	(0.14)
$\Delta\widetilde{ylr}_{i,j,t-1}$	4.18**	(0.04)
$\tilde{q}_{i,j,t-1}$	3.80**	(0.05)
$\widetilde{hk}_{i,j,t-1}$	9.18***	(0.00)
$\Delta\widetilde{p^l}_{i,j,t-1}$	0.01	(0.93)
$spop_{i,j,t-1}$	2.03	(0.15)

Note: ***, **, * denote significance at the 1, 5 and 10 %-level
The test statistic is distributed as $\chi^2(1)$

References

Alecke B, Mitze T, Untiedt G (2010) Internal migration, regional labour market dynamics and implications for German East-West disparities: results from a panel VAR. Jahrbuch für Regionalwissenschaft/Rev Reg Res 30(2):159–189

Anselin L, Le Gallo L, Jayet H (2007) Spatial panel econometrics. In: Matyas L, Sevestre P (eds) The econometrics of panel data fundamentals and recent developments in theory and practice. Springer, Berlin

Arbia G, Fingleton B (2008) New spatial econometric techniques and applications in regional science. Pap Reg Sci 87(3):311–317

Brücker H, Trübswetter P (2004) Do the best go West? An analysis of the self-selection of employed East-West migrants in Germany. IZA Discussion Papers No.986

Büchel F, Schwarze J (1994) Die Migration von Ost- nach Westdeutschland - Absicht und Realisierung. Mitteilungen aus der Arbeitsmarkt- und Berufsforschung 27(1):43–52

Burda MC (1993) The determinants of East-West German migration. Some first results. Eur Econ Rev 37:452–461

Burda MC, Hunt J (2001) From reunification to economic integration: productivity and the labour market in East Germany. Brook Pap Econ Act 2:1–92

Burridge P (1981) Testing for a common factor in a spatial autoregression model. Environ Plan A 13(7):795–800

Chun J (1996) Interregional migration and regional development. Avebury Press, Aldershot

Chun Y (2008) Modelling network autocorrelation within migration flows by eigenvector spatial filtering. J Geogr Syst 10(4):317–344

Chun Y, Griffith D (2011) Modelling network autocorrelation in space-time migration flow data: an eigenvector spatial filtering approach. Ann Assoc Am Geogr 101(3):523–536

Cliff A, Ord J (1981) Spatial and temporal analysis: autocorrelation in space and time. In: Wrigley N, Bennett R (eds) Quantitative geography: a British view, Chap. 10. Routledge, London, pp 104–110

Debarsy N, Ertur C, LeSage J (2011) Interpreting dynamic space-time panel data models. Stat Methodol, online first

Destatis (2012) Bevölkerung und Erwerbstätigkeit. Wanderungen. Fachserie 1, Reihe 1.2, various issues. Statistisches Bundesamt (Destatis), download from: https://www.destatis.de/DE/Publikationen/Thematisch/Bevoelkerung/Wanderungen/Wanderungen.html

Devillanova C, Garcüa-Fontes W (2004) Migration across Spanish provinces: evidence from the social security records (1978–1992). Investig Econ 28(3):461–487

Elhorst JP (2010) Spatial panel data models. In: Fischer M, Getis A (eds) Handbook of applied spatial analysis. Springer, Berlin, pp 377–407

Elhorst JP (2011) Matlab software for spatial panels. In: IVth world conference of the spatial econometrics association (SEA), Chicago, 9–12 June 2010. Revised version in Spring 2011, download from: http://www.regroningen.nl/elhorst/software.shtml

Elhorst JP (2012) Dynamic spatial panels: models, methods and inferences. J Geogr Syst 14:5–28

Etzo I (2011) The Determinants of recent interregional migration flows in Italy: a panel data analysis. J Reg Sci 51(5):948–966

Fisher M, Griffith DA (2008) Modelling spatial autocorrelation in spatial interaction data: an application to patent citation data in the European union. J Reg Sci 48(5):969–989

Fotheringham A (1983) A new set of spatial-interaction models: the theory of competing destinations. Environ Plan A 15:15–36

Griffith DA (1981) Interdependence in space and time: numerical and interpretative considerations. In: Griffith DA, MacKinnon R (eds) Dynamic spatial models. Plenum, New York, pp 258–287

Hagen-Zanker J (2008) Why do people migrate? A review of the theoretical literature. MPRA Paper 28197, University Library of Munich, Germany

Harris JR, Todaro MP (1970) Migration, unemployment and development: a two sector analysis. Am Econ Rev 60:126–142

Hu P, Pooler J (2002) An empirical test of the competing destinations model. J Geogr Syst 4:301–323

Hunt J (2006) Staunching emigration from East Germany: age and the determinants of migration. J Eur Econ Assoc 4(5):1014–1037

Im K, Pesaran M, Shin Y (2003) Testing for unit roots in heterogeneous panels. J Econ 115:53–74

Kiviet J (1995) On bias, inconsistency, and efficiency of various estimators in dynamic panel data models. J Econ 68:53–78

Lee L, Yu J (2010) A spatial dynamic panel data model with both time and individual fixed effects. Econ Theory 26(2):564–597

LeSage J, Pace RK (2008) Spatial econometric modeling of origin-destination flows. J Reg Sci 48(5):941–967

LeSage J, Pace RK (2009) Introduction to spatial econometrics. CRC Press, New York

LeSage J, Pace RK (2010) The biggest myth in spatial econometrics (December 1, 2010). Available at SSRN: http://ssrn.com/abstract=1725503 or http://dx.doi.org/10.2139/ssrn.1725503.

Lopez F, Matilla-Garcia M, Mur J, Ruiz M (2011) Testing for the hypothesis of independence in spatio-temporal data. Pap Reg Sci 90(3):663–685

Lütkepohl H (2005) New introduction to multiple time series analysis. Springer, Berlin

Mutl J, Pfaffermayr M (2010) A note on the Cliff and Ord test for spatial correlation in panel models. Econ Lett 108(2):225–228

Parikh A, Van Leuvensteijn M (2003) Interregional labour mobility, inequality and wage convergence. Appl Econ 35:931–941

Pesaran H (2007) A simple panel unit root test in the presence of cross section dependence. J Appl Econ 22:265–312

Rainer H, Siedler T (2009) Social networks in determining migration and labour market outcomes: evidence from the German Reunification. Econ Transit 17(4):739–767

Roos M (2006) Regional price levels in Germany. Appl Econ 38(13):1553–1566

Schwarze J, Wagner G (1992) Abwanderung von Arbeitskrüften und Einkommenspolitik. DIW Wochenbericht 59:58–61

Sjaastad L (1962) The costs and returns of human migration. J Polit Econ 70(5):80–93

Südekum J, Blien U (2004) Wages and employment growth: disaggregated evidence for West Germany. IZA Discussion Papers 1128, Institute for the Study of Labor (IZA)

Tzavalis E (2008) Structural breaks and unit root tests for short panels. In: 15th international conference on panel data, Bonn

VGRdL (2012) Volkswirtschaftliche Gesamtrechnungen der Bundesländer (Regional Accounts for German States), download from: http://www.vgrdl.de/VGRdL/

Wagner G (1992) Arbeitslosigkeit, Abwanderung und Pendeln von Arbeitskrüften der neuen Bundeslünder. In: Sozialer Fortschritt, pp 84–89

Zierahn U (2012) The importance of spatial autocorrelation for regional employment growth in Germany. Jahrbuch für Regionalwissenschaft/Rev Reg Res 31(1):19–43

Zimmer M (2008) Network effects on domestic migration flows across Germany – A spatial autoregressive perspective with spatially structured origin and destination effects and heteroskedastic innovations. In: Seventh workshop on spatial econometrics and statistics, Paris, 9–10 June 2008

Chapter 17
Residential Relocation in a Metropolitan Area: A Case Study of the Seoul Metropolitan Area, South Korea

Monghyeon Lee and Yongwan Chun

Keywords Network autocorrelation • Residential relocation • Seoul metropolitan area • Spatial interaction model

JEL Classifications: C14, O18, R21

17.1 Introduction

A quantitative modeling for population movement is often performed with gravity type spatial interaction models. These models, which are inspired by Newton's law of gravity, explain population movements with population sizes at origins and destinations plus the level of separation between an origin and a destination which is commonly measured with distance between them. Spatial interaction models have been further extended by incorporating variables to reflect the characteristics of origins and destinations. While entropy-maximization techniques are used to estimate spatial interaction models (Wilson 1974), regression type techniques have also been widely utilized, including linear regression (Greenwood 1985), Poisson regression (Flowerdew and Aitkin 1982), and negative binomial regression (Liu and Shen 2013). Recent research points out that empirical flow data are not likely to be independent, and shows how spatial interaction models can be improved by incorporating a dependence structure among the flows in their model specifications, also called network autocorrelation (e.g., Griffith 2007; Chun 2008; LeSage and Pace 2008). This framework to incorporate network autocorrelation has been applied to different types of flows including population migration (Chun and Griffith 2011), knowledge spill over (Fischer and Griffith 2008), commuting (Griffith 2009), commodity flows (Chun et al. 2012), and tourism flows (Patuelli et al. 2013).

M. Lee (✉) • Y. Chun
School of Economic, Political and Policy Science, The University of Texas at Dallas, Richardson, TX, USA
e-mail: mxl120631@utdallas.edu; ywchun@utdallas.edu

R. Patuelli, G. Arbia (eds.), *Spatial Econometric Interaction Modelling*, Advances in Spatial Science, DOI 10.1007/978-3-319-30196-9_17

As a prominent type of population movement in a geographical space, residential relocation is also frequently investigated utilizing a spatial interaction model framework. Residential relocation refers to movements within a small area such as city or metropolitan area, and has an influence on urban environments such as urban structure (Krizek 2003) and travel patterns (Buchanan and Barnett 2006). It is contrasted to interregional migration, which often involves long distance movements. While interregional migration is generally caused by a job status change, residential relocation does not necessarily have the same cause. Studies investigate residential relocation largely in the context of housing market, neighborhood changes, and accessibility (Clark 1982). However, many of these studies do not explicitly incorporate network autocorrelation in their model specifications and, hence, the statistical results of the studies might be unreliable.

This paper investigates residential relocation in the Seoul metropolitan area, South Korea. With an extreme concentration of population (about 50 % of the total population in South Korea), this metropolitan area has experienced a number of urban issues, such as high housing prices (Kim 1993; La Grange and Jung 2004) and urban sprawl (Cho 2006), thus gaining a lot of attention from researchers. This paper utilizes a spatial interaction modeling framework and further extends it to account for network autocorrelation among residential relocation flows using the eigenvector spatial filtering technique. The rest of this paper is organized as follows. Sect. 17.2 reviews relevant literature on residential relocation, and the study area is introduced in the following Sect. 17.3. Then Sect. 17.4 provides methods and Sect. 17.5 presents analysis results. Conclusions are given in the final section.

17.2 Literature Review

There is an established set of literature covering residential relocation and/or residential mobility (Rossi 1955; Clark and Onaka 1983; Gober 1992; Clark et al. 2000). This research focuses mainly on three factors in examining residential relocation: household characteristics as decision makers (behavioral perspective), housing market characteristics (supply–demand perspective), and neighborhood characteristics (geographical perspective). The behavioral perspective approach explains that residential relocation occurs as individual households are motivated to seek a new location to reside, while the supply–demand perspective approach places more emphasis on conditions that affect the housing market, including housing price, housing policy, and physical characteristics of building. From the geographical perspective, residential mobility can be mainly determined by the characteristics of neighborhoods such as land value, transportation accessibility, and distance of the movement.

From the behavioral perspective, researchers have investigated residential relocation with more of a focus on decision maker's circumstances and events such as family size, income, education levels, and life cycle. Studies (e.g., Rossi 1955; Clark and Onaka 1983) discuss the characteristics of migrants as an essential determinant for residential relocation. Specifically, life cycle is emphasized as an important factor (Rossi 1955; Clark and Onaka 1983; Mulder 1993; Clark et al. 2000). Life events such as marriage, birth, and retirement lead to a change in stage of life and, accordingly, generate different needs for housing. For example, people often need more space as their family grow with the birth of a child and may consider moving into an area with desirable schools. The impacts of life cycle on housing mobility are substantial also for aged people, as residential relocation often happens when they retire (Rogers and Castro 1981) and expect better health and social services (Longino 1980). The characteristics of individual decision makers are also considered as an important factor for residential relocation in the framework of a value-expectancy model (Golledge and Stimson 1997). This model argues that residential relocation occurs through a process in which each decision maker wants to achieve a personally valued goal, which includes wealth, comfort, status, and morality. In other words, each decision maker assesses a personalized trade-off between remaining at the previous location and moving to a later location and decides to move when the decision maker expects a better return with the relocation (Pacione 2001).

However, these behavioral perspective approaches have been criticized because the models emphasize only the demand side but not the supply side. Nijkamp et al. (1993) suggest that supply factors such as local and federal government policies can affect housing mobility. Smith (1996) also identifies public clearance or gentrification as substantial supply side factors. Other factors that are recognized in the literature include housing policy (Forrest and Murie 1990; Knox 1993), housing tenure (Sullivan and Murphy 1984), building structure (Ball 1986), housing prices (de Palma et al. 2005), and neighborhood conditions (Ludwig et al. 2000). Intra-urban migration is tightly related to housing opportunities and constraints on housing choices for certain groups of people (White 1985). Residential relocation processes cannot be explained only by their preferences and choices because a housing market significantly affects decisions; the decisions of migrants are based on the characteristics of available houses on the market (e.g., location, size, tenure, price, and government policies). In addition, because intra-urban relocation frequently happens within the same local housing market, a local housing market needs to be factored into explaining residential relocation (Dieleman 2001). Generally, residential relocation can be better explained by simultaneously reflecting the behavioral and the demand–supply perspectives in a model specification (Clark and Onaka 1983; Nijkamp et al. 1993).

Geographical characteristics have an influence on a choice for a new residential location. Well-recognized factors in the literature include traffic conditions, the homogeneity of cultural community, and distance to work place. The travel behavior of residents can dominate in decision of residential relocation over other preferences of household (Jonas et al. 2012). In an empirical study, Jonas et al. (2012) find that the mobility conditions of people keep them in their current residential locations. Access to private transportation or, alternatively, access to public transportation highly influences residential dissonance and relocation in both urban and rural areas. A social network and community tied by culture/language are substantially important in residential relocation (Teixeira and Murdie 1997). A co-ethnic or co-cultural relationship leads migrants to live closely together in a neighborhood and to construct a community. This phenomenon is often accelerated by people who own real estate business and share a common culture. The distance between home and workplace is one of the key reasons for residential relocation (Clark et al. 2003). A majority of people tend to stay within an area such as a city, the same housing market, or the same labor area rather than cross boundaries. Even though commuting distance is not the only reason for residential relocation, there is a marked tendency for households to move nearer to their workplace (Dieleman 2001).

The impact of political and government system has been investigated. A transitional economy also has been recognized as a unique factor for residential relocation in cities that were formerly governed by the economics of socialism. Under the socialist system, residential relocation was limited by a residence permit system and allocations of housing units (Daniell and Struyk 1997). For example, Daniell and Struyk (1997) found that residential relocation in Moscow, Russia occurs selectively among householders in a high social status. However, a residential relocation rate increased regardless of social status when the restrictions were mitigated with the change of regime. Restrictions from local or federal governments previously had enormous effects on residential relocation, but the income level of households became a major factor. A similar pattern occurs after the Chinese government announced their new land-lease system (Wu 2004; Gu and Liu 1997). Consequently, the movement of laborers became one of the main factors for residential relocation in China (Wu 2004). The impact of political or government systems has been also investigated in western countries. Ladd and Ludwig (1997) investigated the impact of the federal housing assistance in Baltimore, Maryland. Strassmann (2001) found that European governments tend to have more complex interventions in land use, finance, construction, and housing price than governments in other countries.

17.3 Study Area: The Seoul Metropolitan Area

This study investigates residential relocation within the Seoul metropolitan area (SMA) in South Korea, which includes the city of Seoul, the city of Incheon, and Gyeonggi province. Province is the highest ranked administrative units in South Korea. Seoul and Incheon are special cities, which have an equivalent status to provinces. The city of Seoul, which is located at the center of the SMA, is the capital of South Korea and has been a center for economic, political, and cultural activities in the county. Figure 17.1a displays the location of the SMA, highlighted in a darker color, along with other provinces and the special cities in total 9 provinces and 7 cities. The population of Seoul is approximately 10.3 million in December 2010

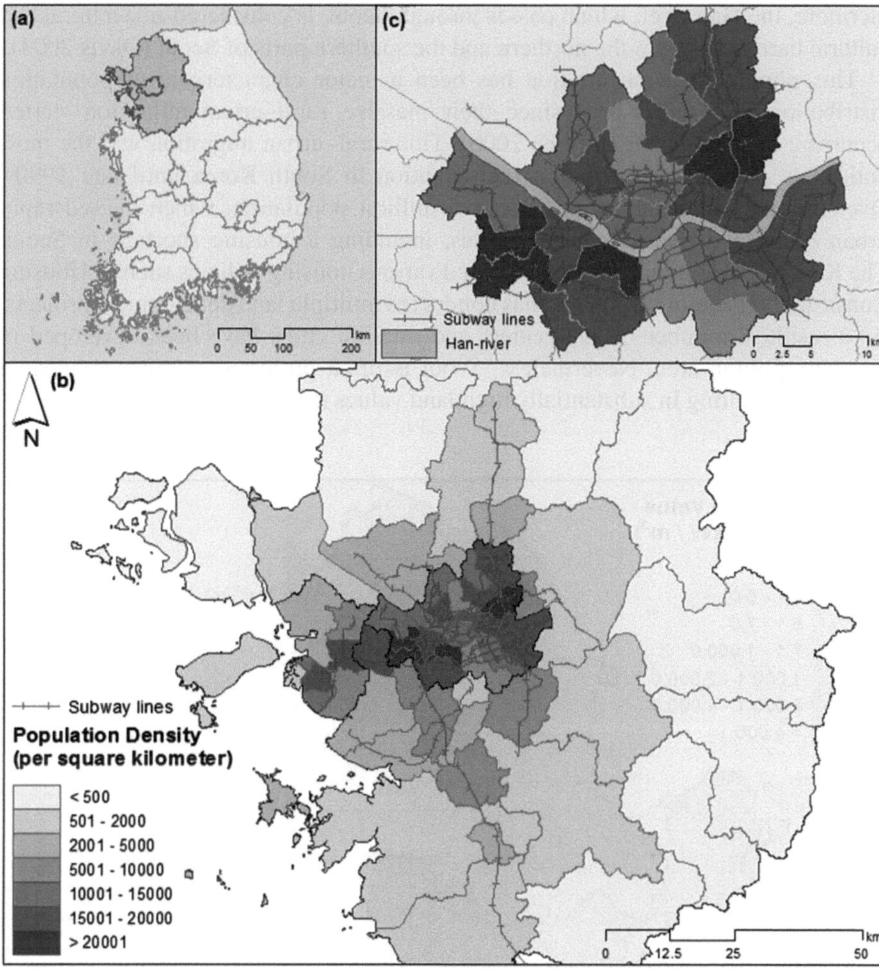

Fig. 17.1 The Seoul metropolitan area with its population densities and the metro subway lines in 2010

according to the national resident registration reported by the government (http://rcps.egov.go.kr/). Incheon is the third most populous city with 2.76 million population, and Gyeonggi has 11.79 million population. That is, almost the half of total population in South Korea is concentrated within the SMA. Figure 17.1b shows the distribution of population at the *Si-Gun-Gu* level that is compatible with the county level in the United States. This figure also displays subway lines encompassing the SMA. Since this subway system furnishes an important method of public transportation, easy access to the subway lines has been an attractive living condition. Figure 17.1c displays population densities and the subway lines only within the boundaries of Seoul. This shows a highly concentrated population in Seoul, especially compared with the outskirts of the SMA, which are mostly rural areas. Furthermore, the Han river, which passes through Seoul, is considered as a natural and cultural barrier between the northern and the southern parts of Seoul (Davis 2004).

This population concentration has been a major characteristic of population distribution in South Korea since their massive rural–urban migration started occurring in 1960s (Lee and Lee 2008). This rural–urban migration was the most noticeable pattern of population redistribution in South Korea until late 1990s. Over this period, Seoul gained about 5 million population, which caused rapid urbanization and related housing issues, including a housing shortage in Seoul. The Korean government has implemented various housing policies such as Housing Construction Promotion Act and has conducted multiple land development projects. As a result, a number of sub-centers and satellite cities have been developed in the metropolitan area. Nevertheless, Seoul is often preferred to other residential locations, resulting in substantially high land values (see Fig. 17.2).

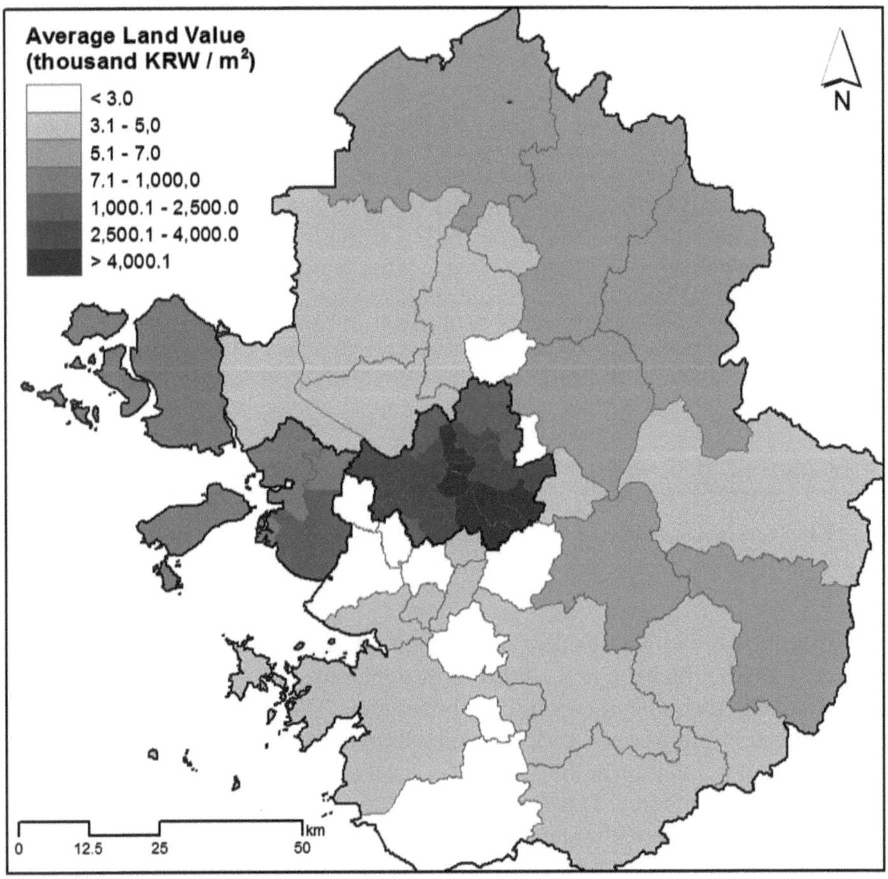

Fig. 17.2 Land values of the Seoul metropolitan area in 2010

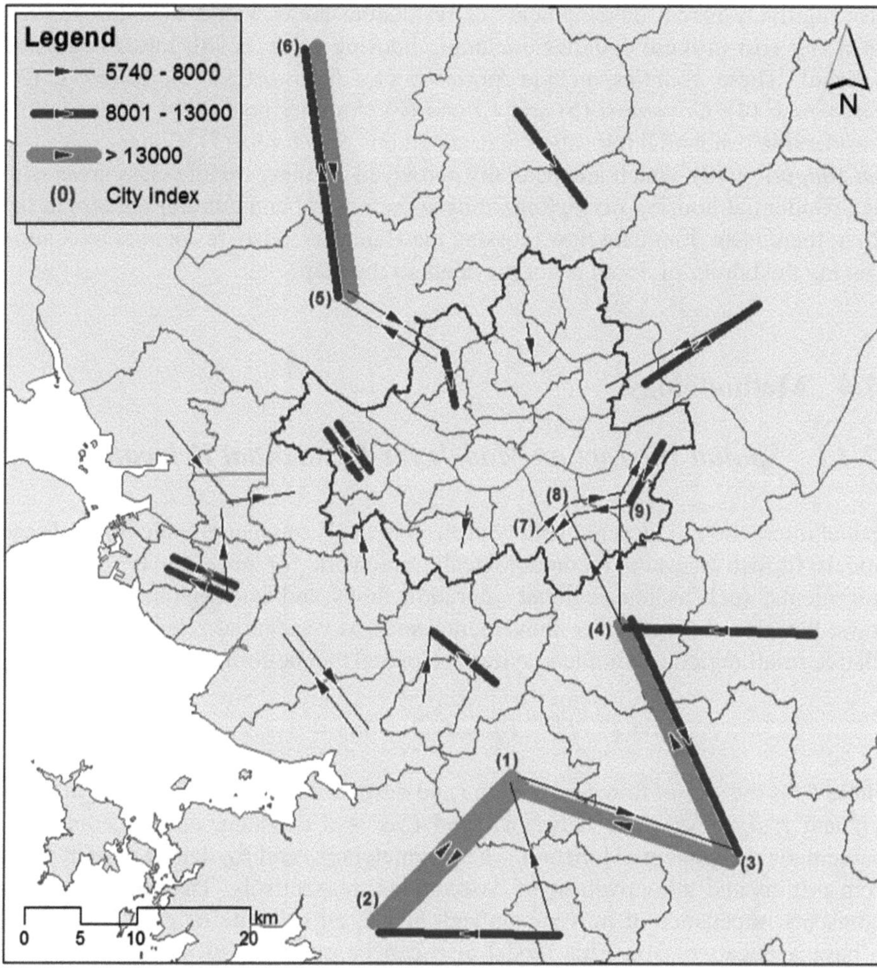

Fig. 17.3 Major residential relocation flows in 2010 (top 1 % of flows)

Although the population growth caused by the rural–urban migration has been currently weakened, residential relocation within the SMA is still dynamic. More than 70 % of residential relocation in Seoul occurs within the boundaries of the city (Choi and Cho 2005a), and about 50 % of residential relocation in the SMA are internal movements (Lee and Lee 2008). Recent studies (e.g., Kwon and Lee 1995; Choi 2004; Choi and Cho 2005b) suggest that residential relocation in the area is mostly affected by industrial structure change, housing supply–demand, government policy, housing value, and housing ownership.

Figure 17.3 shows some dominant residential relocation flows (top 1 %) in the SMA in 2010. The major flows appear between counties (*Si-Gun-Gu*) that are located outside of Seoul but close to the boundaries of Seoul. These counties have relatively recent developments of residential areas within their boundaries, but living cost in these counties, including housing price, is still lower compared to Seoul. These counties include *Suwon-si* (1), *Hwasung-si* (2), *Yongin-si* (3), *Sungnam-si* (4), *Goyang-si* (5) and *Paju-si* (6). Another noticeable pattern is that considerable residential relocation appears among *Seocho-gu* (7), *Gangnam-gu* (8), *and Songpa-gu* (9), which are generally perceived as upper middle class areas with high residential housing price. Regarding some natural and cultural borders in the SMA, there is no dominant flow crossing the Han river. Also, residential relocation crossing the border of Seoul is not prevalent in the map.

17.4 Methodology

17.4.1 Spatial Interaction Models for Residential Relocation

Spatial interaction models are widely utilized in analyzing geographic flows. These models furnish a useful methodological framework for not only long distance movements, such as interregional migration flows and interregional commodity flows, but also short distance movements, such as residential relocation within a relative small region. A simple gravity type model can be formulated as follows:

$$F_{ij} = e^{\alpha} \cdot P_i^{\beta_O} \cdot P_j^{\beta_D} \cdot d_{ij}^{\beta_{dist}}, \quad i,j = 1, \ldots, n \tag{17.1}$$

where F_{ij} is the size of flow from origin i and destination j, P_i and P_j are populations at i and j, d_{ij} is distance between i and j, α is a constant, and e denotes the mathematical exponential function. The parameters β_O and β_D denote emissiveness from origins and attractiveness of destinations, respectively. The parameter β_{dist} represents impedance of movements and, hence, an estimate of β_{dist} is expected to have a negative sign. This model also can be extended to include additional covariates to reflect the characteristics of origins and destinations such as a socio-economic conditions which potentially have an impact on the size of movements. Greenwood and Hunt (2003) provide an extensive review of spatial interaction modeling.

This spatial interaction model is often estimated with regression type estimators. Linear regression is commonly used with log-transformation on both sides of Eq. (17.1), which is under a log-normal approximation assumption. When a dependent variable is count type such as the number of migrants, Poisson regression is preferred over linear regression (Flowerdew and Aitkin 1982). A Poisson distribution is commonly utilized to model count values. Further, Poisson regression can effectively deal with unequal variance for individual counts, while linear regression assumes an equal variance. Alternatively, negative binomial regression is employed especially when a Poisson model suffers from overdispersion (e.g., Burger et al. 2009; Chun 2014). A Poisson regression model specification can be rewritten from

Eq. (17.1) as follows:

$$F_{ij} = g^{-1}\left[\alpha + \beta_O \cdot \ln(P_i) + \beta_D \cdot \ln\left(P_j\right) + \beta_{dist} \cdot \ln\left(d_{ij}\right)\right], \quad i,j = 1,\ldots,n \quad (17.2)$$

where F_{ij} is assumed to follow a Poisson distribution, $g(\cdot)$ is a link function between the dependent variable and the linear combination of independent variables. For the link function, $g(\cdot)$, the natural logarithm is commonly used for Poisson regression. So $g^{-1}(\cdot)$ is the mathematical exponential function here. When additional covariates are involved to reflect the characteristics of origins and destinations, Eq. (17.2) can be expressed by replacing the population terms with matrix notions for origin and destination covariates, $\ln(\boldsymbol{x}_i) \cdot \boldsymbol{\beta}_O$ and $\ln(\boldsymbol{x}_j) \cdot \boldsymbol{\beta}_D$. A negative binomial regression model can be expressed also with Eq. (17.2) replacing the distribution of F_{ij} with a negative binomial distribution.

However, the estimates by these regression methods are likely to be statistically unreliable when the independence assumption is violated. Hence, when spatial autocorrelation in network flows, also called network autocorrelation, is present, an appropriate method is required to accommodate it in a model specification (Black 1992; Griffith and Jones 1980; Fischer and Griffith 2008; Griffith 2009). The spatial autoregressive model specification, including simultaneously autoregressive (SAR) model, is often utilized to account for network autocorrelation (e.g., Bolduc et al. 1989; Chun et al. 2012). LeSage and Pace (2008) provide details about how this model specification can be implemented. Alternatively, eigenvector spatial filtering (ESF) has been utilized. Studies (e.g., Griffith 2007; Chun 2008; Patuelli et al. 2011) show that the ESF method successfully explains network autocorrelation in spatial interaction models. Furthermore the ESF method provides a way to effectively visualize network autocorrelation components (Griffith 2011a) and can be extended to space-time flow modeling (Chun and Griffith 2011).

The ESF method utilizes the spectral decomposition of a transformed spatial weights matrix, $\left(\mathbf{I} - \mathbf{1}\mathbf{1}^{\mathrm{T}}/n\right)\mathbf{B}\left(\mathbf{I} - \mathbf{1}\mathbf{1}^{\mathrm{T}}/n\right)$ where $\mathbf{B}$ is an n-by-n spatial weights matrix, $\mathbf{1}$ is a vector of ones with an n-by-1 dimension, and $\mathbf{I}$ is an n dimensional identity matrix. The n eigenvectors of this matrix, which are orthogonal and uncorrelated with each other, represent underlying spatial autocorrelation patterns. The ESF method introduces a set of the eigenvectors in a regression model as proxy variables to isolate spatial autocorrelation (Griffith 2003). As a result, ESF allows to estimate regression parameters with standard estimation methods such as maximum likelihood. A proper set of eigenvectors needs to be identified based on the principal of parsimony. A stepwise process to maximize model fit or to minimize spatial autocorrelation at each step can be utilized (Tiefelsdorf and Griffith 2007). Detail discussions about the ESF method can be found in Griffith (2003).

Modeling network autocorrelation with the ESF method requires defining a network weights (or link) structure which can be organized in a matrix. Extending a spatial autocorrelation structure embedded among regions where flows are observed, a network weights matrix can be easily defined. Because a flow occurs from an origin to a destination, a spatial autocorrelation structure can be embedded around origins and/or destinations. With a spatial weights matrix, $\mathbf{B}$, an n^2-by-n^2 network weights matrix, $\mathbf{B}^N$, can be generated with Kronecker product and Kronecker sum operations (Chun 2008; LeSage and Pace 2008). A network weights matrix to reflect a spatial autocorrelation structure around an origin given a same destination can be generated with $\mathbf{I} \otimes \mathbf{B}$ where $\mathbf{I}$ is an identity matrix with dimension n and $\otimes$ denotes the Kronecker product. Similarly, a network weights matrix to reflect a spatial autocorrelation structure around a destination given a same origin can be generated with $\mathbf{B} \otimes \mathbf{I}$. Additionally, a network weights matrix can be generated by $\mathbf{B} \otimes \mathbf{B}$, which reflects the spatial autocorrelation structure of a given flow with flows occurring from its origin spatial neighbors to its destination neighbors. These three effects can be modeled by three separate weights matrices in a model specification (LeSage and Pace 2008). A further specification can be defined by the combination of these three matrices; for example, $\mathbf{B}^N = \mathbf{I} \otimes \mathbf{B} + \mathbf{B} \otimes \mathbf{I}$ which reflects the origin and destination based on spatial structures (Chun 2008) and $\mathbf{B}^N = \mathbf{I} \otimes \mathbf{B} + \mathbf{B} \otimes \mathbf{I} + \mathbf{B} \otimes \mathbf{B}$ in which these three types of matrices are combined (Chun 2013). Once a network weights matrix is decided, well known spatial autocorrelation indices, including Moran's I, can be utilized to measure a level of network autocorrelation.

Extending Eq. (17.2), an ESF model specification for a spatial interaction model can be written as follows:

$$F_{ij} = g^{-1}\left[\alpha + \beta_O \cdot \ln(P_i) + \beta_D \cdot \ln\left(P_j\right) + \beta_{dist} \cdot \ln\left(d_{ij}\right) + \mathbf{E}_{ij} \cdot \boldsymbol{\gamma}\right],\; i,j = 1, \ldots, n \tag{17.3}$$

Here, $\mathbf{E}_{ij}$ is a row vector corresponding to F_{ij} in a set of selected eigenvectors from a whole eigenvector set, which is generated from $\left(\mathbf{I}_N - \mathbf{1}_N \mathbf{1}_N^{\mathrm{T}}/\mathrm{N}\right) \mathbf{B}^N \left(\mathbf{I}_N - \mathbf{1}_N \mathbf{1}_N^{\mathrm{T}}/\mathrm{N}\right)$, where $\mathrm{N} = n^2$, $\mathbf{I}_N$ is an n^2 dimensional identity matrix, $\mathbf{1}_N$ is a vector of ones with an n^2-by-1 dimension. And $\boldsymbol{\gamma}$ is a vector of parameters. As described above, a set of selected eigenvectors can be identified with a stepwise regression technique.

17.4.2 Model Specification

In this paper, residential relocation in the SMA is modeled with 11 covariates. Five variables to reflect the characteristics of origins are subway station density, land value, residential land value change rates, home ownership rates, and college graduation rates. These five characteristics for destinations are also included. Finally, distance is included for distance decay. *Subway densities* are expected to an attractive factor for residential relocation because the subway system provides the major public transportation model in the SMA (Goh et al. 2012). It is generally expected that *land value* and *residential land value change rates* are associated to economic behavior in residential relocation decisions. Therefore, a high land value and an increase of high residential land value change rate (i.e., positive values) are expected to be positively related to the size of outflows from origins and negatively associated to inflows to destinations. Since *home ownership* is commonly considered as an impeding factor for residential relocation, a negative association to residential relocation is anticipated. *College graduation rates* can directly reflect an education level of population at origins and destinations, but this may indirectly reflect the composition of population because young generation tends to have a high rate of college graduation.

Because *distance* plays an impeding role for residential relocation, a strong negative association is expected. Inter-county distance is measured between the centroids of origins and destinations. Intra-county distance is calculated as $d_{ii} = \sqrt{R_i/\pi}$ where R_i is the areal size of spatial unit i and π is the mathematical constant pi. Following Kim et al. (2012), when this intra-county distance is longer than any inter-county distance from county i, this intra-county distance is further adjusted; that is, $d_{ii}^* = \left(d_{i\cdot}^{min}/d_{ii}\right) \cdot d_{i\cdot}^{min}$, if $d_{ii} > d_{i\cdot}^{min}$ where $d_{i\cdot}^{min}$ is the minimum inter-county distance from county i. This distance calculation avoids unrealistic zero distance for intra movements and ensures that intra-county distance is shorter than inter-county distance.

A spatial interaction model for residential relocation in the SMA is similarly specified as Eq. (17.2). These models are estimated using generalized linear models, specifically, Poisson regression and negative binomial (NB) regression. Unlike Eq. (17.2), the models contain an offset variable which reflects the number of expected flows between each dyad of origin and destination. An offset model specification allows to model variations in a response variable around an expectation based on a global rate rather than variations in raw counts.[1] With a global movement rate that can be calculated as a ratio between the number of migrants and total population across an entire study area, an expected number of migrants for a spatial unit can be calculated by multiplying the global movement rate and its population size. With expected values based on a global movement rate as an offset on the right side, a Poisson or NB regression model with log-link is specified as

$$\ln(observed) = \ln(expected) + x\beta. \tag{17.4}$$

Here, ln(*expected*) is an offset term. A simple arrangement shows that this specification compatibly models with ln(*observed/expected*), which is a ratio between observed and expected values.

A remaining issue is to calculate expected flows between origin i and destination j, $\mathrm{E}[F_{ij}]$. As a flow is observed with an origin and a destination, an expected number of a flow can be defined as:

$$\mathrm{E}\left(F_{ij}\right) = \frac{1}{2}\left[\mathrm{E}\left(F_i^O\right) + \mathrm{E}\left(F_j^D\right)\right] = \frac{1}{2}\left[\frac{\sum F_{i\cdot}}{\sum P_i}P_i + \frac{\sum F_{\cdot j}}{\sum P_j}P_j\right] = \frac{1}{2}\left[\lambda^O P_i + \lambda^D P_j\right] \tag{17.5}$$

[1] An offset model specification is commonly utilized in modeling disease rates (e.g. Lawson et al. 2003).

where $E(F_i^O)$ denotes expected outflows from origin i, $E(F_j^D)$ denotes expected inflows to destination j, $F_{i\cdot}$ denotes the sum of outflows from origin i, $F_{\cdot j}$ denotes the sum of inflows to destination j, and P_i and P_j respectively denote population at i and j. That is, the expected flows for F_{ij} is calculated as an average of expected outflows from i and expected inflows to destination j. Here, a gross outflow rate, λ^O, is defined as a ratio between the sum of all outflows and the sum of population across all spatial units. Similarly, a gross outflow rate, λ^D, is defined as a ratio between the sum of all inflows and the sum of population across all spatial units. Because flows are observed among a given set of spatial units, the sum of outflows is the same as the sum of inflows: that is, $\sum_i F_{i\cdot} = \sum_i \sum_j F_{ij} = \sum_j \sum_i F_{ij} = \sum_j F_{\cdot j}$. Also $\sum P_i$ is same as $\sum P_j$ for the same reason. Hence, $\lambda^O = \lambda^D$ and the Eq. (17.5) can be simplified as:

$$E(F_{ij}) = \frac{1}{2}\left[\lambda^O P_i + \lambda^D P_j\right] = \frac{1}{2}\left[\lambda\left(P_i + P_j\right)\right] \quad (17.6)$$

where $\lambda^O = \lambda^D = \lambda$. The expected flows indicate that the number of flows from origin i and destination j based on the global movement rate (λ) and their population sizes. With the logarithm of these expected values as offset, a spatial interaction model fits to the variations of flows around expected flows in which population sizes are already adjusted. Hence, population sizes at origins and destinations are not included as a control variable in this model specification.

Model I is specified with the 11 covariates and an offset term. It can be expressed as:

$$F_{ij} = g^{-1}\left[\ln\left(E\left(F_{ij}\right)\right) + \alpha + \ln\left(\boldsymbol{x}_i\right)\cdot\boldsymbol{\beta}_O + \ln\left(\boldsymbol{x}_j\right)\cdot\boldsymbol{\beta}_D + \ln\left(d_{ij}\right)\cdot\beta_{dist}\right] \quad (17.7)$$

where $\boldsymbol{x}_i$ denotes origin covariates, $\boldsymbol{x}_j$ denotes destination covariates, and d_{ij} denotes distance between i and j. (α, $\boldsymbol{\beta}_O, \boldsymbol{\beta}_D, \beta_{dist}$) are parameters to be estimated. Here, $g^{-1}(\cdot)$ is the mathematical exponential function.

Model II is specified to investigate the impact of borders among three sub-regions on residential relocation in the SMA. The three sub-regions are the River North in Seoul (also called *Gangbuk*), the River South in Seoul (also called *Gangnam*), and the outside of Seoul (see Fig. 17.1). Since, the Han river, which passes through Seoul east to west, is widely accepted as the boundary of economic and cultural disparities between the northern and southern parts of Seoul (Davis 2004; Kim 2009), it would be interesting to examine whether or not residential relocation is influenced by the border of Seoul in the SMA as well as the disparities in the city. Specifically, the behavior of distance decay is further investigated with statistical interaction terms between the distance variable and a categorical variable for the nine flow types among the three sub regions. The notations of N (denoting the River North in Seoul), S (denoting the River South in Seoul), and O (denoting the outside of Seoul), are used as the categorical variable code for residential relocation NN, NO, NS, ON, OO, OS, SN, SO, and SS, in which the first character indicates an origin region and the second indicates a destination region. Model II can be written as:

$$F_{ij} = g^{-1}\left[\ln\left(\mathrm{E}\left(F_{ij}\right)\right) + \alpha + \ln\left(\boldsymbol{x}_i\right)\cdot\boldsymbol{\beta}_O + \ln\left(\boldsymbol{x}_j\right)\cdot\boldsymbol{\beta}_D + \ln\left(d_{ij}\right)\cdot\beta_{dist} + \ln\left(d_{ij}\right) : x_c\cdot\beta_c\right] \quad (17.8)$$

where x_c is a categorical variable for the nine flow types and β_c is a corresponding parameter. This categorical variable is prepared with a centered coding scheme[2] so that its parameter β_c for the interaction term indicates a deviation from the global distance parameter, β_{dist}. These models are estimated with standard Poisson and NB regression, and further ESF Poisson and ESF NB regression.

17.5 Results

Table 17.1 reports these four estimation results. The ESF models contain 236 eigenvectors for the Poisson model and 91 eigenvectors for the NB model. These results confirm that accounting for network autocorrelation with the ESF method significantly improves the spatial interaction model in both Poisson and NB regression: the p-value of 0.0000 for the likelihood ratio test for the Poisson models and the p-value 0.0000 for the NB models.[3] Their AIC values also indicate that the ESF models are improved from their counterpart models. In fact, the decrease of the AIC value is very noticeable in the Poisson models. Among the four models, the ESF NB model can be preferred over the other models with the smallest AIC value.

The estimate for the overdispersion parameter also dramatically decreased from 2490.19 in the standard Poisson model to 559.31 in the ESF Poisson model. This decrease aligns with findings in the literature that overdispersion decreases when network autocorrelation is accounted for (e.g., Chun and Griffith 2011). However, the large value for overdispersion, which is supposed to be 1 for a Poisson distribution, still indicates a potential issue in the Poisson model specification and may suggest that a NB model is more appropriate. The decrease of dispersion parameter estimate by accounting for network autocorrelation is also observed from the NB models. While the dispersion parameter for the standard NB model is 0.5734, one for the ESF NB model is 0.2968. This may indicate that a portion of the dispersion is contributed by network autocorrelation, and that accounting for network autocorrelation by the eigenvectors leads to the decrease of dispersion (Griffith 2011b).

---

[2]Using contr.sum() function in R.

[3]The test statistics of the likelihood ratio test for the Poisson models is 4,099,762 with 236 degrees of freedom. For the NB models, the test statistic is 3082.44 with 91 degrees of freedom.

Table 17.1 The estimation results of Model I using Poisson and NB regression in the standard and the ESF specifications

	Poisson						Negative binomial					
	Standard			Spatial filtering			Standard			Spatial filtering		
Variables	Estimate	Std. err.		Estimate	Std. err.		Estimate	Std. err.		Estimate	Std. err.	
Intercept	25.5850	0.4330	***	23.6601	0.4199	***	23.3207	0.3076	***	20.4352	0.2845	***
O_subway density	−0.7261	0.1011	***	−0.3449	0.0752	***	−0.3289	0.0413	***	−0.2326	0.0369	***
O_land value	−0.0835	0.0100	***	−0.0355	0.0087	***	−0.1029	0.0052	***	−0.0143	0.0049	**
O_land value change rate	−0.7796	0.3853	*	−2.4433	0.2946	***	−1.6915	0.1978	***	−1.9650	0.1670	***
O_home ownership rate	0.8100	0.1869	***	0.9438	0.1443	***	1.0306	0.0913	***	0.3849	0.0779	***
O_college graduation rate	0.0917	0.0866		−0.1032	0.0652		0.2296	0.0409	***	0.1617	0.0382	***
D_subway density	−0.5201	0.0947	***	−0.3132	0.0724	***	−0.2468	0.0412	***	−0.2448	0.0368	***
D_land value	−0.0800	0.0099	***	−0.0298	0.0087	***	−0.0706	0.0052	***	0.0032	0.0049	
D_land value change rate	−0.7404	0.3888		−2.3398	0.297	***	−1.5090	0.1978	***	−1.9770	0.1669	***
D_home ownership rate	0.4732	0.1853	*	0.7162	0.143	***	0.7365	0.0913	***	0.3064	0.0778	***
D_ college graduation rate	0.1371	0.0861		−0.1301	0.065	*	0.1342	0.0409	**	0.0600	0.0382	
Distance	−2.1721	0.0276	***	−2.1892	0.0278	***	−1.8708	0.0201	***	−1.8934	0.0207	***
Number of selected EVs	–			236			–			91		
AIC	6,044,150			1,944,860			56,867.79			53,967.34		
Log-likelihood	−3,022,063			−972,182.90			−28,420.89			−26,879.67		
(Over) dispersion	2490.19			559.31			0.5734			0.2968		

(1) The overdispersion was considered in calculating standard errors of the Poisson models
(2) Significance codes: 0 '***' 0.001 '**' 0.01 '*' 0.05

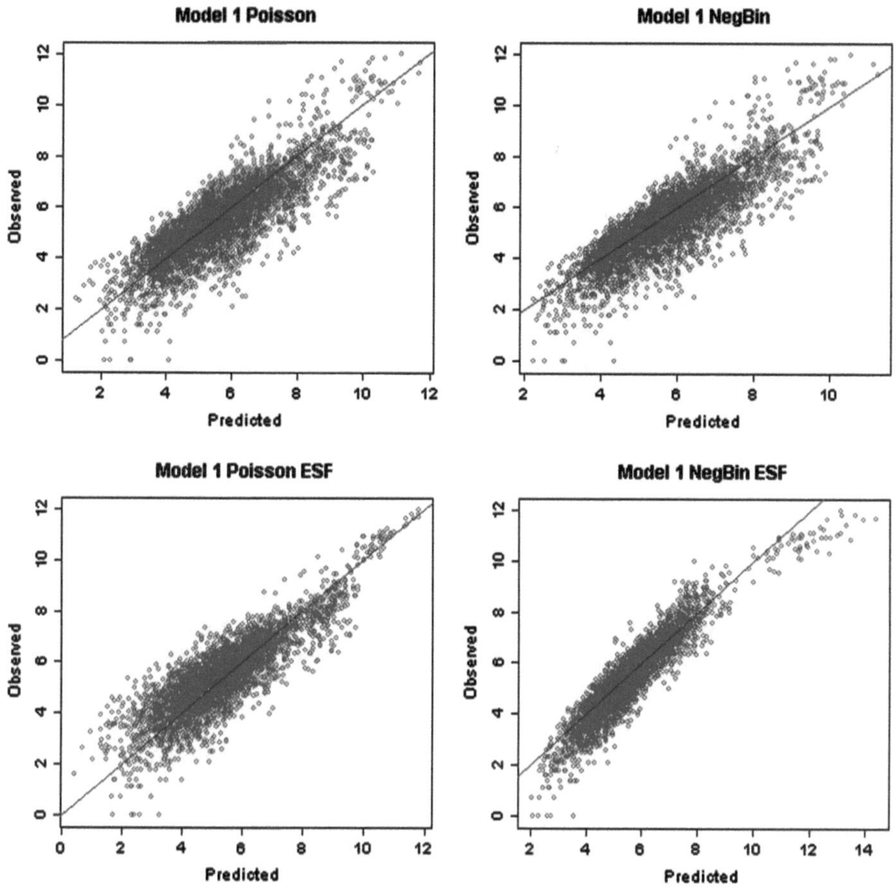

Fig. 17.4 The scatterplots of observed versus predicted values for Model I

Figure 17.4 displays scatterplots of observed versus predicted values from these four specifications in the natural log scale. These scatterplots generally show that the spatial interaction models produce a good fit to the empirical dataset. However, the better model fits of the ESF models than their counterpart standard models are observed can be observed, as the points in the ESF models are more closely located to the perfect fit line. One interesting finding is that the ESF Poisson model has a better prediction for the flows with large values (larger than approximately 10) than the ESF NB model. These large values are observed from internal flows within a spatial unit. The ESF NB model tends to over-predict for the internal flows.

The ESF models lead to changes of statistical significance for some covariates in both Poisson and NB models. Regarding to the Poisson models, *land value change rate at origins* is not significant in the standard model at the 1 % level but becomes significant in the ESF model at the same level. Similarly, *land value change rate at origins* also becomes statistically significant in the ESF model at the 1 % level.

The statistical significance at the 1 % level for the other variables remains the same. Between the standard and ESF NB models, only two variables experience the change of statistical decision at the 1 % level. *Land value at destinations* and *college graduation rate* are significant in the standard NB model but not in the ESF NB model. The other variables are significant in both of the standard and the ESF NB models at the same level.

Table 17.2 reports the estimation results by the standard Poisson, the standard NB, the ESF Poisson, and the ESF NB regression for Model II. These results also show that the ESF model specification improves the spatial interaction models in both Poisson and NB specifications by accounting for network autocorrelation. The ESF Poisson and ESF NB models have smaller AIC values (56,804.49 and 53,946.5, respectively) than their counterpart standard specifications (5,641,626 and 1,922,540 correspondingly). Also the decrease of estimate for the overdispersion parameter in the Poisson model (from 2,236.71 to 554.68) and the dispersion parameter in the NB models (from 0.5641 to 0.2948) is observed when network autocorrelation is accounted for. Because of the large estimates for overdispersion in the standard and the ESF Poisson models, the NB models are also preferred in Model II. The scatterplots of observed versus predicted values from the four specifications in Fig. 17.5 illustrate the improved model fits of the ESF models. The points are closely located to the perfect fit line for the ESF models. On the other hand, the over-prediction tendency for the internal flows by the ESF NB model is also observed.

In Model II, the changes of statistical inference between the standard and ESF models are also observed. For the Poisson case, the variable *land value at origins* is significant in the standard model but not in the ESF model at the 1 % level. In contrast, *home ownership rates* is not significant in the standard model but becomes significant in the ESF model at the 1 % level. For the NB cases, *land value at origins* and *land value at destinations* are significant in the standard model, but they become insignificant in the ESF model at the 1 % level. The statistical interaction between the categorical variable and the distance variable experience a change of statistical decision at the 1 % level for three cases: OO and SS for the Poisson and OO for the NB cases.

Among the eight models, the ESF NB for Model II with the smallest AIC value is possibly preferred. Overall, the Model II specifications have a better fit than their counterpart specifications in Model I. Based on the ESF NB in Model II, residential relocation in the SMA is negatively associated to *subway station density* and *residential land value change rate* at both origins and destinations. The negative association to *subway station density at origins and destinations* may indicate that residential relocation occurs less than the overall rate in areas with a better access to the subway system. In other words, better public transportation access is an attractive factor, so people tend not to move out from those areas. Subsequently, in-migration to those areas can be limited because of the lower availability of housing units for relocation. The negative association to *residential land value change rate at destinations* may imply that an increase of land value at destinations is less attractive economically for residential relocation. However, the negative association

Table 17.2 The estimation results of Model II using Poisson and NB regression in the standard and the ESF specifications

	Poisson						Negative binomial					
	Standard			Spatial filtering			Standard			Spatial filtering		
Variables	Estimate	Std. err.		Estimate	Std. err.		Estimate	Std. err.		Estimate	Std. err.	
Intercept	23.9897	0.4373	***	23.4321	0.4465	***	23.4014	0.3266	***	20.5633	0.3134	***
O_subway density	−0.5974	0.0979	***	−0.3498	0.0764	***	−0.3176	0.0428	***	−0.2104	0.0364	***
O_land value	−0.0643	0.0131	***	−0.0184	0.0152		−0.1030	0.0067	***	−0.0170	0.0074	*
O_land value change rate	−1.1824	0.3751	***	−2.4857	0.2985	***	−1.5274	0.2017	***	−1.9314	0.1648	***
O_home ownership rate	0.5719	0.1956	**	0.9161	0.1534	***	1.0278	0.0959	***	0.3468	0.0804	***
O_college graduation rate	0.0700	0.0842		−0.0906	0.0684		0.1838	0.0418	***	0.1421	0.0381	***
D_subway density	−0.4324	0.0922	***	−0.3148	0.0737	***	−0.2752	0.0427	***	−0.2277	0.0363	***
D_land value	−0.0711	0.0133	***	−0.0575	0.0156	***	−0.0862	0.0067	***	−0.0140	0.0074	
D_land value change rate	−1.1014	0.3803	***	−2.275	0.3018	***	−1.0886	0.2017	***	−1.7409	0.1648	***
D_home ownership rate	0.3152	0.1931		0.7892	0.1527	***	0.8420	0.0959	***	0.3424	0.0804	***
D_college graduation rate	0.1038	0.0838		−0.1484	0.0685	*	0.0572	0.0418		0.0171	0.0381	
Distance	−2.1101	0.0286	***	−2.1499	0.0298	***	−1.8792	0.0222	***	−1.8972	0.0219	***
Border.NN: Distance	0.0005	0.0084		0.0197	0.0092	*	−0.0240	0.0067	***	−0.0241	0.0067	***
Border.NO: Distance	−0.0282	0.0156		−0.0256	0.0139		−0.0166	0.0050	***	−0.0194	0.0042	***
Border.NS: Distance	−0.0128	0.0149		0.0131	0.0111		0.0037	0.0063		0.0123	0.0059	*
Border.ON: Distance	−0.0041	0.0143		0.0085	0.0132		0.0013	0.0050		−0.0049	0.0042	
Border.OO: Distance	0.0605	0.0096	***	0.0030	0.0101		−0.0174	0.0053	**	−0.0067	0.0065	
Border.OS: Distance	−0.0140	0.0136		0.0051	0.0122		0.0144	0.0052	**	0.0128	0.0044	**
Border.SN: Distance	−0.0106	0.0149		0.0018	0.0110		0.0003	0.0063		0.0061	0.0058	
Border.SO: Distance	−0.0432	0.0147	**	−0.0477	0.0126	***	−0.0083	0.0052		−0.0073	0.0044	
Border.SS: Distance	0.0520	0.0091	***	0.0220	0.0093	*	0.0467	0.0070	***	0.0311	0.0065	***
NO. selected EVs	–			234			–			87		
AIC	5,641,626			1,922,540			56,804.49			53,946.5		
Log-likelihood	−2,820,793			−961,016.2			−28,381.25			−26,865.25		
(Over) dispersion	2236.17			554.68			0.5641			0.2948		

(1) The overdispersion was considered in calculating standard errors of the Poisson models; (2) Significance codes: 0 '***' 0.001 '**' 0.01 '*' 0.05

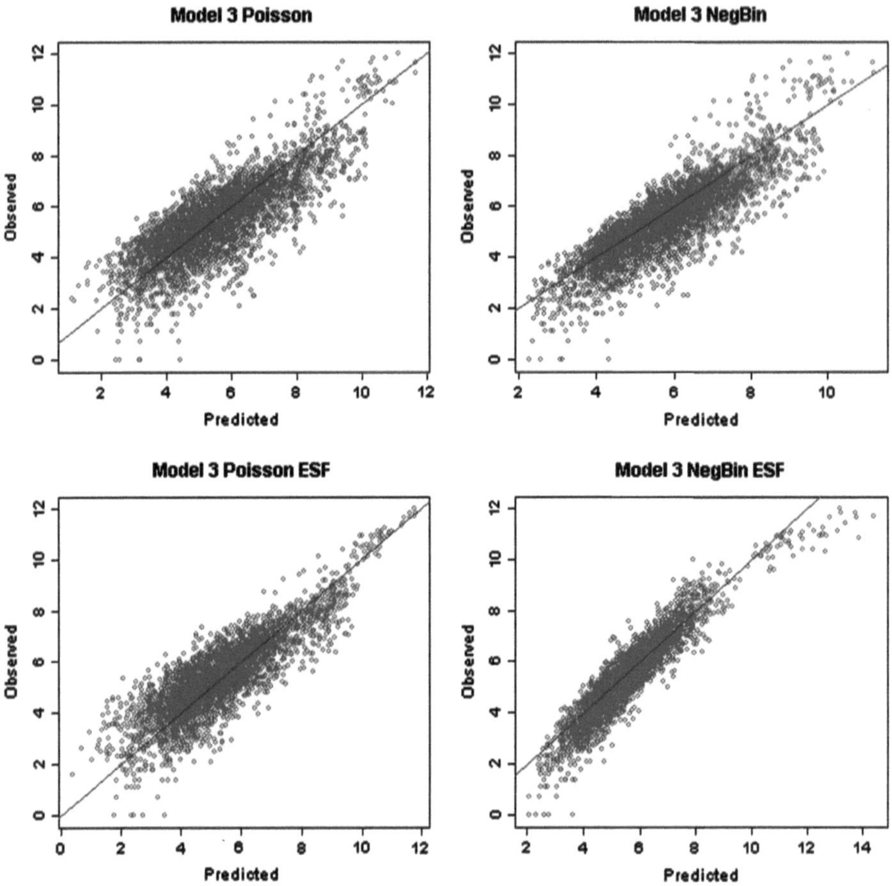

Fig. 17.5 The scatterplots of observed versus predicted values for Model II

to *residential land value change rate at origins* is counter intuitive because an increase of land value at origins may be expected as a push factor. Also, it is positively associated to *college graduation rate at origins* and *home ownership rates, both at origins and destinations.* The positive sign of *college graduation rate at origins* could suggest that counties (*Si-Gun-Gu*) with a higher college graduation rate tend to experience a higher out-migration than the global movement pattern. This can be explained by a high movement tendency by young adults, who generally have a high level of education and reside in urban areas. The significant positive associations of *home ownership rates both at origins and destinations* are counter intuitive because home ownership is a well-known impeding factor. However, Helderman et al. (2006) identify three factors that can counterbalance the impeding effects of home ownership on residential relocation. These factors are an increase of young population in the composite of home owners, an increase of dynamics within owner-occupied segments as home ownership becomes more common, and macro factors such as economic growth. Although a further investigation is required to identify factors, continuous developments of large scale residential areas around the outskirts of Seoul may provide an explanation of the residential location pattern (e.g. Jun 2012).

These results show that distance decay effect is highly significant. The global distance decay parameter for the ESF NB is -1.8972. The estimates for the interactions between the distance and the dummy variables show that four types of flows have a significantly different distance decay effect from the global distance decay at the 1 % level. The negative significant estimate for the interaction between distance and NN (-0.0241) means that the distance decay effect within the River North region in Seoul is -1.9213 ($= -1.8972 - 0.0241$). This indicates that residential relocation within the River North region in Seoul tends to occur in a shorter distance than the overall residential relocation in the SMA. Also, residential relocation from the River North region to outside of Seoul tends to move a short distance (the estimate for the interaction between distance and NO is -0.0194). In contrast, the estimates for the interactions of OS and SS with distance are positively significant. Their estimated distance decay effects are -1.8844 ($= -1.8972 + 0.0128$) and -1.8661 ($= -1.8972 + 0.0311$), respectively. These demonstrate that residential relocation from outside of Seoul to the River South region and within the River South regions tends to occur over a longer distance than the overall pattern in the SMA. Also the interaction between distance and NS is significant at the 5 % level. These significant parameter estimates suggest that people tend to move a longer distance when they move to and within the River South region.

17.6 Conclusions

This paper examines residential relocation in the SMA in 2010 using gravity type spatial interaction models. Since the dependent variable has the counts of population movements, or non-negative integer values, Poisson and NB regression are used to estimate the spatial interaction models. The results show that the residential relocation is effectively modeled with spatial interaction models. Among the different model specifications, the ESF NB model specification is preferred to the other models. The results of the ESF NB Model II may indicate that residential relocation in the SMA is significantly associated to *subway stations density* which is a major public transportation method in the SMA, and *residential land value change rates* which can be interpreted an economic factor. It shows a positive association to *college graduation rate at origins*. Since a high college graduate rate is observed in the population group with a large portion of young adults, this might represent a high movement tendency of young adults. The model shows a significant distance-decay effect. Interestingly, the results show that the distance-decay effects vary among the three regions: the River South in Seoul, the River North in Seoul, and outside of Seoul.

There are two notable methodological features in the paper. First, the eigenvector spatial filtering method is utilized in order to account network autocorrelation in residential relocation flows. This paper empirically shows that network autocorrelation exists among residential relocation flows and, subsequently that residential relocation needs to be specified to appropriately account for network autocorrelation. The eigenvector spatial filtering method improved the spatial interaction models with a set of selected eigenvectors that successfully explained network autocorrelation in the empirical dataset. This improvement is observed from both Poisson and NB specifications. Further, the decrease of the estimated (over-) dispersion parameter values in the ESF model specification by accounting for network autocorrelation confirms findings in existing studies (e.g., Curry 1972; Chun and Griffith 2011). Nevertheless, the ESF Poisson models suffer from an excessive overdispersion that can suggest that the ESF NB models are preferable.

Second, these spatial interaction models employed an offset term in their model specification to control population sizes at origins and destinations. With these offset specifications, this paper shows how to model the variations of flow volumes around expected values rather than raw counts. Conventionally, spatial interaction models have not been specified with an offset term in Poisson and/or NB regression. This offset specification provides a good alternative way to control the effects of population sizes. Because population sizes have an obvious positive association to the magnitude of flows in most empirical flow modeling, the sizes of population should stay in a model specification although they are not very interesting and are often treated as nuisance variables. An offset specification does not need to include population sizes as independent variables and, thus, other potentially interesting variables that might have a high correlation could still remain in a model specification. The empirical analysis illustrates that this specification is potentially useful, but this needs to be further investigated in future research.

References

Ball M (1986) The built environment and the urban question. Environ Plan D 4:447–464

Black WR (1992) Network autocorrelation in transport network and flow systems. Geogr Anal 24(3):207–222

Bolduc D, Dagenais MG, Gaudry MJI (1989) Spatially autocorrelated errors in origin–destination models: a new specification applied to aggregate mode choice. Transp Res B 23(5):361–372

Buchanan N, Barnett R (2006) Peripheral residential relocation and travel pattern change. Urban Policy Res 24(2):217–236

Burger M, van Oort F, Linders GJ (2009) On the specification of the gravity model of trade: zeros, excess zeros and zero-inflated estimation. Spat Econ Anal 4(2):167–190

Castro LJ, Rogers A (1981) Model migration schedules. International Institute for Applied Systems Analysis, Laxenburg

Cho J (2006) Urban planning and urban sprawl in Korea. Urban Policy Res 23(2):203–218

Choi E (2004) The analysis of spatial characteristics on inter-regional migration. J Seoul Inst 5(3):49–66

Choi E, Cho D (2005a) The characteristics of intra-urban migration in Seoul. J Korean Assoc Reg Geogr 11(2):169–186
Choi E, Cho D (2005b) The economic barrier and characteristics of intra-urban migration in Seoul. J Seoul Inst 6(4):1–20
Chun Y (2008) Modeling network autocorrelation within migration flows by eigenvector spatial filtering. J Geogr Syst 10:317–344
Chun Y (2013) Network autocorrelation and spatial filtering. In: Scherngell T (ed) The geography of networks and R&D collaborations. Springer, Berlin, pp 99–113
Chun Y (2014) Analyzing space-time crime incidents using eigenvector spatial filtering: an application to vehicle burglary. Geogr Anal 46(2):165–184
Chun Y, Griffith DA (2011) Modeling network autocorrelation in space-time migration flow data: an eigenvector spatial filtering approach. Ann Assoc Am Geogr 101(3):523–536
Chun Y, Kim H, Kim C (2012) Modeling interregional commodity flows with incorporating network autocorrelation in spatial interaction models: an application of the U.S. interstate commodity flows. Comput Environ Urban Syst 36(6):583–591
Clark WAV (1982) Recent research on migration and mobility: a review and interpretation. Prog Plan 18:1–56
Clark WAV, Onaka J (1983) Life cycle and housing adjustment as explanations of residential mobility. Urban Stud 20:47–57
Clark WAV, Deurloo MC, Dieleman FM (2000) Housing consumption and residential crowding in US housing markets. J Urban Aff 22(1):49–63
Clark WAV, Huanh Y, Withers S (2003) Does commuting distance matter? Commuting tolerance and residential change. Reg Sci Urban Econ 33:199–221
Curry L (1972) A spatial analysis of gravity flows. Reg Stud 6:131–47
Daniell J, Struyk R (1997) The evolving housing market in Moscow: indicators of housing reform. Urban Stud 34:235–254
Davis LK (2004) Reshaping Seoul: redevelopment, women and insurgent citizenship. Doctoral dissertation, Johns Hopkins University
de Palma A, Motamedi K, Picard N, Waddell P (2005) A model of residential location choice with endogenous housing prices and traffic for the Paris region. Eur Transp 31:67–82
Dieleman F (2001) Modeling residential mobility; a review of recent trends in research. J Hous Built Environ 16:249–265
Fischer MM, Griffith DA (2008) Modeling spatial autocorrelation in spatial interaction data: an application to patent citation data in the European Union. J Reg Sci 48:969–989
Flowerdew R, Aitkin M (1982) A method of fitting the gravity model based on the Poisson distribution. J Reg Sci 22(2):191–202
Forrest R, Murie A (1990) A dissatisfied state? Consumer preferences and council housing in Britain. Urban Stud 27:617–635
Gober P (1992) Urban housing demography. Prog Hum Geogr 16:171–189
Goh S, Lee K, Park JS, Choi MY (2012) Modification of the gravity model and application to the metropolitan Seoul subway system. Phys Rev E 86(2):026102
Golledge RG, Stimson RJ (1997) Spatial behaviour: a geographical perspective. Guilford Press, New York
Greene RP, Pick JB (2006) Exploring the urban community. Pearson Prentice Hall, Upper Saddle River
Greenwood M (1985) Human migration: theory, models and empirical studies. J Reg Sci 25(4):521–544
Greenwood MJ, Hunt GL (2003) The early history of migration research. Int Reg Sci Rev 26(1): 3–37
Griffith DA (2003) Spatial autocorrelation and spatial filtering: gaining understanding through theory and scientific visualization. Springer, Berlin
Griffith DA (2007) Spatial structure and spatial interaction: 25 years later. Rev Reg Stud 37(1): 28–38

Griffith DA (2009) Modeling spatial autocorrelation in spatial interaction data: empirical evidence from 2002 Germany journey-to-work flows. J Geogr Syst 11:117–140
Griffith DA (2011a) Visualizing analytical spatial autocorrelation components latent in spatial interaction data: an eigenvector spatial filter approach. J Geogr Syst 35(2):140–149
Griffith DA (2011b) Positive spatial autocorrelation impacts on attribute variable frequency distributions. Chil J Stat 2(2):3–28
Griffith DA, Jones KG (1980) Explorations into the relationship between spatial structure and spatial interaction. Environ Plan A 12:187–201
Gu J, Liu F (1997) The problem of residential relocation, Shanghai in the next century: thinking on social development problems Shanghai 'Nine-Fifth' social development research group. Shanghai Social Science Academy, Shanghai, pp 396–402
Helderman AC, Ham M, Mulder CH (2006) Migration and home ownership. Tijdschr Econ Soc Geogr 97(2):111–125
Jonas DV, Ben D, Veroniqu VA, Frank W (2012) Reducing car use: changing attitudes or relocating? The influence of residential dissonance on travel behavior. J Transp Geogr 22:1–9
Jun MJ (2012) The effects of Seoul's new-town development on suburbanization and mobility: a counterfactual approach. Environ Plan A 44(9):2171–2190
Kim K (1993) Housing prices, affordability, and government policy in Korea. J Real Estate Financ Econ 6:55–71
Kim S (2009) Re-locating the national: spatialization of the nation past in Seoul. Policy Futures Educ 7(2):256–265
Kim C, Sang S, Chun Y, Lee W (2012) Exploring urban commuting imbalance by jobs and gender. Appl Geogr 32(2):532–545
Knox C (1993) Compulsory competitive tendering in Northern Ireland local government. Local Govern Stud 19(2):208–225
Krizek KJ (2003) Residential relocation and changes in urban travel: does neighborhood-scale urban form matter? J Am Plann Assoc 69(3):265–281
Kwon Y, Lee J (1995) Spatial pattern of migration in the Seoul metropolitan area. J Korea Plann Assoc 30(4):21–39
La Grange A, Jung H (2004) The commodification of land and housing: the case of South Korea. Hous Stud 19(4):557–580
Ladd H, Ludwig J (1997) Federal housing assistance, residential relocation, and educational opportunities: evidence from Baltimore. Am Econ Rev 87(2):272–277
Lawson AB, Browne WJ, Vidal Rodeiro CL (2003) Disease Mapping with WinBUGS and MLwiN. Wiley, Chichester
Lee H, Lee S (2008) The Influence of new town development on the changes of the migration and commuting patterns in the capital region. J Korean Geogr Assoc 43(4):561–579
LeSage J, Pace R (2008) Spatial econometric modeling of origin–destination flows. J Reg Sci 48(5):941–967
Liu Y, Shen J (2013) Spatial patterns and determinants of skilled internal migration in China, 2000–2005. Pap Reg Sci. doi:10.1111/pirs.12014
Longino CF (1980) Residential relocation of older people metropolitan and nonmetropolitan. Res Aging 2(2):205–216
Ludwig J, Duncan G, Pinkston J (2000) Neighborhood effects on economic self-sufficiency: evidence from a randomized housing-mobility experiment. Georgetown University, unpublished paper
Mulder CH (1993) Migration dynamics: a life course approach. Thesis Publishers, Amsterdam
Nijkamp P, Van Wissen L, Rima A (1993) A household life cycle model for residential relocation behaviour. Socioecon Plann Sci 27(1):35–53
Pacione M (2001) Urban geography: a global perspective. Routledge, London
Patuelli R, Griffith DA, Tiefelsdorf M, Nijkamp P (2011) Spatial filtering and eigenvector stability: space-time models for German unemployment data. Int Reg Sci Rev 34(2):253–80
Patuelli R, Mussoni M, Candela G (2013) The effects of World Heritage Sites on domestic tourism: a spatial interaction model for Italy. J Geogr Syst 15(3):369–402

Rogers A, Castro LJ (1981) Model migration schedule. International Institute for Applied Systems Analysis, Laxenburg

Rossi PH (1955) Why families move: A study in the social psychology of urban residential mobility. Free Press, Glencoe

Smith N (1996) The new urban frontier: gentrification and the revanchist city. Routledge, London

Strassmann WP (2001) Residential mobility: contrasting approaches in Europe and the United States. Hous Stud 16(1):7–20

Sullivan O, Murphy MJ (1984) Housing pathways and stratification: some evidence from a British national survey. J Soc Policy 13(02):147–165

Teixeira C, Murdie RA (1997) The role of ethnic real estate agents in the residential relocation process: a case study of Portuguese homebuyers in suburban Toronto. Urban Geogr 18(6):497–520

Tiefelsdorf M, Griffith DA (2007) Semiparametric filtering of spatial autocorrelation: the eigenvector approach. Environ Plan A 39(5):1193–1221

White P (1985) Levels of intra-urban migration in Western European cities. Espace, populations, sociétés 3(1):161–169

Wilson AG (1974) Urban and regional models in geography and planning. Wiley, London

Wu F (2004) Intraurban residential relocation in Shanghai: modes and stratification. Environ Plan A 36(1):7–26

Chapter 18
Conclusions: The Future of Spatial Interaction Modelling

Giuseppe Arbia and Roberto Patuelli

Keywords Gravity • Spatial econometrics • Spatial interaction

JEL Classifications: C18, C51, R11

18.1 A Reappraisal of the Presented Contributions

The present volume showcased a series of papers related to some of the most recent developments in the field of spatial econometric methods applied to spatial interaction modelling. In particular, this book was motivated by the need to testify, through a collection of methodological and empirical studies, how the various approaches that have been present in this field in the last decades have recently developed, by including tools that are typical of spatial statistics and spatial econometrics, giving birth to a somewhat novel discipline characterized by a body of methods and techniques known under the heading of *spatial econometric interaction models* (LeSage and Pace 2009).

Looking at the contributions reported here, the reader can have a good snapshot of the current state-of-the-art in the field. In particular, from a theoretical point of view, the papers contained in this volume witness the various methodological progress made recently in the analysis of gravity-type modelling (e.g., in the chapters by Griffith and Fischer, Tamesue and Tsutsumi, and Patuellli, Linders, Metulini and Griffith), in the definition of exogenous and endogenous spatial interaction (LeSage and Fischer), in the analysis of the effects of spatial dependence on flow data (Bavaud, as well as Beenstock and Felsenstein), in the Bayesian

G. Arbia (✉)
Department of Statistics, Università Cattolica del Sacro Cuore, Rome, Italy
e-mail: giuseppe.arbia@rm.unicatt.it

R. Patuelli
Department of Economics, University of Bologna, Bologna, Italy

The Rimini Centre for Economic Analysis (RCEA), Rimini, Italy
e-mail: roberto.patuelli@unibo.it

R. Patuelli, G. Arbia (eds.), *Spatial Econometric Interaction Modelling*, Advances in Spatial Science, DOI 10.1007/978-3-319-30196-9_18

approach to spatial interaction modelling (the chapters by LeSage and Satici, Deng, and LeSage and Llano), and in assessing the effect of scale on spatial interaction model parameters (Arbia and Petrarca). Under the applied point of view this book also provides a good overview of the typical areas of application of spatial econometric interaction models, such as tourism (Patuelli, Mussoni and Candela), transportation (Diaz-Lanchas, Gallego, Llano and de la Mata), social networks (Llano and de la Mata), migration (Mitze), urban development (Lee and Chun) and trade (Mastromarco, Serlenga and Shin).

18.2 Future Roads of Spatial Interaction

If it is certainly true that the progress in the field has been tremendous in the last 50 years or so, starting from the publication of the first prototype gravity-type models (Isard 1960; Tinbergen 1962; Wilson 1970), it is equally fair to recognize that a lot still remains to be done in different directions in order to answer the current and future challenges of the discipline. In particular, the measurement of spatial and network autocorrelation in flow data is still nowadays for the most part based on the typical spatial autocorrelation indices that assume normally distributed random variables. However, flow data are, by definition, non-negative and discrete, which raises the important question of whether the classical spatial correlation measures, like Moran's *I* or Geary's G indices, are the most appropriate ones to characterize the phenomenon. A step forward in this direction could be represented by the use of alternative indices that explicitly account for non-normality in flow data like those reported in Jacqmin-Gadda et al. (1997); Arbia and Lafratta (2005); Lin and Zhang (2007) or Griffith (2010). A further problem of spatial interaction modelling that is often overlooked and needs to be properly considered is represented by the possible presence of heteroskedasticity in the regression disturbances. As it is well known, heteroskedastic disturbances destroy the properties of the estimators and may lead to wrong hypothesis testing decisions. However, spatial units are often characterized by heterogeneity in many important characteristics (e.g., in their size) and hence in most empirical situations the homoscedasticity assumption may not be sustainable. An example of a heteroskedastic spatial interaction modeling of commodity flows can be found in Trang et al. (2016), based on the advances introduced in the literature by Kelejian and Prucha (see Kelejian and Prucha 2007, 2010; and Arbia 2014b, for a review). A typical application of spatial interaction models that could be greatly influenced by the presence of spatial dependence in flow data is the process of interpolation. In this field it is necessary to develop appropriate methods that could help in filling gaps in data while considering autocorrelation issues (as a starting point, see, e.g., Polasek et al. 2012). Furthermore, the spatial econometric interaction modelling literature still appears to be scarcely considering special cases in which the distribution of flow data does not conform to the expected one for Poisson models. A typical example is the case of zero-inflation (Burger et al. 2009), which is indeed very frequent in empirical cases. Regression models that explicitly and separately consider spatial effects in the zero-inflation and count parts (Metulini et al. 2015) should be developed in order to enrich the set of tools available to researchers and practitioners facing challenging data sets. Finally, another field where the introduction of innovation is needed is in the area of efficient visualization especially in the presence of a very large number of origins and destinations.

So far the interest in spatial interaction models have been motivated by the need to explain the aggregated flows of individual agents, goods, or information occurring between discrete partitions of space. In this book, as an example, all papers refer to flows as they are observed between, cities, metropolitan areas, provinces, regions or states. However, the big data revolution that we are currently experiencing has the potential to revolutionize our current approach to the analysis of flows providing detailed datasets describing the movements of individuals over space and their interacting behavior. New and alternative methods of data collection (such as crowd sourcing, GPS positioning devices, cell phones data, drones, satellite images and many others) will more and more be able to provide detailed information about the movements of economic agents, of goods and information over geographical space. For example, in many instances data are already available sourced from sample information obtained through cell phone movements; furthermore, satellite images provide data on flows proxied by the remotely sensed quantity of lighting on the earth; drones can acquire information about the movement of people; sensors located on individuals can perfectly describe their daily commuting trip. These are only a few examples of how the process of data acquisition is changing dramatically in these days. This huge amount of information about individual flows made available to researcher and practitioners, while solving at its very root the modifiable areal unit problem (MAUP; see the chapter by Arbia and Petrarca), also raises entirely new problems of method and interpretation under many different points of view. Some of them are not of direct interest to spatial econometrics (such as the confidentiality and ethical issues connected with the process of automatic data acquisition), some are potentially very relevant (such as the computational issues raised by analyzing with the current techniques very large sample sizes; see, e.g., LeSage and Pace 2007; Arbia 2014a; Arbia et al. 2015), but some of them will definitely constitute the big challenge faced by all researchers involved in this field in the next few years. The big data revolution is already manifesting itself in many scientific fields, and the ability of the scientific community to answer to these questions will determine the future of the spatial econometrics of spatial interaction.

References

Arbia G (2014a) Pairwise likelihood inference for spatial regressions estimated on very large datasets. Spat Stat 7:21–39

Arbia G (2014b) A primer for spatial econometrics: with applications in R. Palgrave Macmillan, New York

Arbia G, Lafratta G (2005) Exploring nonlinear spatial dependence in the tails. Geogr Anal 37(4):423–437
Arbia G, Bee M, Espa G, Santi F (2015) Fitting spatial econometric models through the unilateral approximation. DEM Discussion Papers 2014/08, University of Trento, Trento
Burger M, van Oort F, Linders GJ (2009) On the specification of the gravity model of trade: zeros, excess zeros and zero-inflated estimation. Spat Econ Anal 4(2):167–190
Griffith DA (2010) The Moran coefficient for non-normal data. J Stat Plann Inference 140(11):2980–2990
Isard W (1960) Methods of regional analysis. MIT Press, Cambridge
Jacqmin-Gadda H, Commenges D, Nejjari C, Dartigues JF (1997) Tests of geographical correlation with adjustment for explanatory variables: an application to dyspnoea in the elderly. Stat Med 16(11):1283–1297
Kelejian HH, Prucha IR (2007) HAC estimation in a spatial framework. J Econom 140(1):131–154
Kelejian HH, Prucha IR (2010) Specification and estimation of spatial autoregressive models with autoregressive and heteroskedastic disturbances. J Econom 157(1):53–67
LeSage JP, Kelley Pace R (2007) A matrix exponential spatial specification. J Econom 140(1):190–214
LeSage JP, Pace RK (2009) Introduction to spatial econometrics. CRC Press, Boca Raton
Lin G, Zhang T (2007) Loglinear residual tests of Moran's *I* autocorrelation and their applications to Kentucky breast cancer data. Geogr Anal 39(3):293–310
Metulini R, Patuelli R, Griffith DA (2015) Estimating a spatial filtering gravity model for bilateral trade: functional specifications and estimation challenges. Paper presented at the European Trade Study Group 2015, Paris
Polasek W, Llano C, Sellner R (2012) Bayesian methods for completing data in spatial models. Rev Econ Anal 2(2):192–214
Tinbergen J (1962) Shaping the world economy: suggestions for an international economic policy. Twentieth Century Fund, New York
Trang HTT, Arbia G, Miyata Y (2016) The analysis of commodity flows in San-En-Nanshin region (Japan) with heteroskedastic spatial interaction models. Mimeo
Wilson AG (1970) Entropy in urban and regional modelling. Pion, London

MIX
Papier aus verantwortungsvollen Quellen
Paper from responsible sources
FSC® C105338

If you have any concerns about our products,
you can contact us on
ProductSafety@springernature.com

In case Publisher is established outside the EU,
the EU authorized representative is:
Springer Nature Customer Service Center GmbH
Europaplatz 3, 69115 Heidelberg, Germany

Printed by Libri Plureos GmbH
in Hamburg, Germany